D1446528

The Upaniṣads

The Upaniṣads are among the most sacred foundational scriptures in the Hindu religion. Composed from 800 BCE onwards and making up part of the larger Vedic corpus, they offer the reader "knowledge lessons" on life, death, and immortality. While they are essential to understanding Hinduism and Asian religions more generally, their complexities make them almost impenetrable to anyone but serious scholars of Sanskrit and ancient Indian culture.

This book is divided into five parts:

- Composition, authorship, and transmission of the Upaniṣads;
- The historical, cultural, and religious background of the Upaniṣads;
- Religion and philosophy in the Upaniṣads;
- The classical Upaniṣads;
- The later Upaniṣads.

The chapters cover critical issues such as the origins of the Upaniṣads, authorship, and redaction, as well as exploring the broad religious and philosophical themes within the texts. The guide analyzes each of the Upaniṣads separately, unpacking their contextual relevance and explaining difficult terms and concepts. *The Upaniṣads: A Complete Guide* is a unique and valuable reference source for undergraduate religious studies, history, and philosophy students and researchers who want to learn more about these foundational sacred texts and the religious lessons in the Hindu tradition.

Signe Cohen is Associate Professor of South Asian Religions at the University of Missouri, USA.

The Upaniṣads

A Complete Guide

Edited by Signe Cohen

Library
Quest University Canada
3200 University Boulevard
Squamish, BC V8B 0N8

Routledge
Taylor & Francis Group
LONDON AND NEW YORK

First published 2018
by Routledge

2 Park Square, Milton Park, Abingdon, Oxfordshire OX14 4RN
52 Vanderbilt Avenue, New York, NY 10017

Routledge is an imprint of the Taylor & Francis Group, an informa business

First issued in paperback 2019

Copyright © 2018 selection and editorial matter, Signe Cohen; individual chapters, the contributors.

The right of Signe Cohen to be identified as the author of the editorial material, and of the authors for their individual chapters, has been asserted in accordance with sections 77 and 78 of the Copyright, Designs and Patents Act 1988.

All rights reserved. No part of this book may be reprinted or reproduced or utilised in any form or by any electronic, mechanical, or other means, now known or hereafter invented, including photocopying and recording, or in any information storage or retrieval system, without permission in writing from the publishers.

Notice:
Product or corporate names may be trademarks or registered trademarks, and are only for identification and explanation without intent to infringe.

British Library Cataloguing-in-Publication Data
A catalogue record for this book is available from the British Library

Library of Congress Cataloging-in-Publication Data
A catalog record for this book has been requested

ISBN: 978-1-138-79505-1 (hbk)
ISBN: 978-0-367-26199-3 (pbk)

Typeset in Times New Roman
By Out of House Publishing

Yājñavalkya

for Valerie Roebuck

"A man of simple solutions and somewhat coarse words"
– Jan Gonda, *Vedic Literature* p. 353

Of course I wanted cows. Not for their own sake, though,
    But for myself. BU 3.1.2; 4.1.1; 2.4.5
 Kātyāyanī shall have them when I go.
  Cattle and gold – these are human wealth.
 (I eat their flesh, too, if it's succulent.) ŚB 3.1.2.21
   But I prize something else:
 Knowledge, and victory in argument.
  Brahmins from Kurukṣetra I defeat,
  But not you, dear. With you I don't compete.

Listen, my dear Maitreyī. It isn't for my sake BU 2.4.5; 4.5.6
    That I am dear
 To you, or to Kātyāyanī. What makes
  Me dear is yourself. What if you weren't here,
 Or if you weren't you, but something without
   A self? Now is it clear?
 Or look at it the other way about:
  Before you, even you, are dear to me,
  I first must be aware. I first must be.

Now, as a man delighting in his love's embrace BU 4.3.21
(Kātyāyanī
Would say "Indeed! Which one?") knows neither this
Nor that, nor which is he and which is she,
So the self, when it neither wakes nor dreams,
Can only know, and be.
And what the ocean is to all the streams, BU 2.4.11; 4.5.12
The tongue to flavors, and the eye to sights –
And yes, the private parts to all delights –

Such is the self to all sensations, thoughts and actions.
But when you die BU 2.4.12–14; 4.4.12; 4.5.13–15
You'll be a unity, with no perceptions.
Don't be so worried. Let me tell you why:
Perception only happens if there's two –
Something that isn't I.
That's my immortal legacy to you. BU 2.4.3; 4.5.4; 4.5.15
I'll see Kātyāyanī before I go.
Give her her due: she knows what women know. BU 4.5.1

Dermot Killingley
December 30, 2016

Contents

Contributors

Brian Black is in the Department of Politics, Philosophy, and Religion at Lancaster University, in the United Kingdom. He has been inspired and fascinated by the Upaniṣads for more than twenty years. His research interests include Indian religions, comparative philosophy, the use of dialogue in Indian religious and philosophical texts, and Hindu and Buddhist ethics. He is author of the book *The Character of the Self in Ancient India: Priests, Kings, and Women in the Early Upaniṣads* (State University of New York 2007); he is co-editor (with Simon Brodbeck) of the book *Gender and Narrative in the Mahābhārata* (Routledge 2007); and he is co-editor (with Laurie Patton) of the book series *Dialogues in South Asian Traditions: Religion, Philosophy, Literature and History* (Routledge). He is currently writing a book on dialogue in the *Mahābhārata*.

Simon Brodbeck is Reader in Religious Studies at Cardiff University, Wales. He is co-editor of *Gender and Narrative in the Mahābhārata* (Routledge 2007) and the Equinox journal *Religions of South Asia*, and author of *The Mahābhārata Patriline: Gender, Culture, and the Royal Hereditary* (Ashgate 2009) and some two dozen articles on aspects of the Mahābhārata and Rāmāyaṇa. His work in progress is an accessible English translation of the critically reconstituted Harivaṃśa.

Signe Cohen (PhD University of Pennsylvania) is Associate Professor of South Asian Religions at the University of Missouri. She is the author of *Text and Authority in the Older Upanisads* (Brill 2008) as well as articles on Sanskrit texts, ancient automata, and postmodernism in the Harry Potter series. Her current book project involves ancient Hindu and Buddhist robot tales. In her work, she explores how these ancient texts about mechanically constructed beings express fundamental religious ideas about the soul and soullessness.

Jonardon Ganeri is a philosopher who draws on a variety of philosophical traditions to construct new positions in the philosophy of mind, metaphysics, and epistemology, writing chiefly about the philosophies of South Asia in dialogue with other ancient and contemporary philosophical cultures. He is the author of *The Self*, *The Concealed Art of the Soul*, and *The Lost*

Age of Reason, all published by Oxford University Press. He joined the Fellowship of the British Academy in 2015, and won the Infosys Prize in the Humanities the same year, the first philosopher to do so. Open Minds magazine named him of its fifty global "open minds" for 2016.

Dermot Killingley graduated in Sanskrit in Oxford University in 1959, and gained a PhD in Indian philosophy in SOAS, University of London. He taught in the Department of Indian Studies, University of Malaya, from 1961 to 1968, and in the Department of Religious Studies, Newcastle University, from 1970 to 2000, when he retired as Reader in Hindu Studies. In 2008 he was a Visiting Professor in the University of Vienna. He is joint editor (with Simon Brodbeck and Anna King) of *Religions of South Asia* (RoSA). He has published research on ancient Indian thought, and on its modern interpreters, particularly Rammohun Roy, Vivekananda, and Radhakrishnan. His books include *Rammohun Roy in Hindu and Christian Tradition*, and a three-volume course, *Beginning Sanskrit*, completed in collaboration with the late Dr Siew-Yue Killingley.

Steven E. Lindquist is Associate Professor of Religious Studies and Director of Asian Studies at Southern Methodist University in Dallas, TX. He has published on topics such as late-Vedic narrative, riddle-poems, genealogy, and numismatics. He edited a festschrift in honor of his mentor entitled *Religion and Identity in South Asia and Beyond: Essays in Honor of Patrick Olivelle* (Anthem Press) and his monograph on the literary life of Yājñavalkya is forthcoming with State University of New York. His research interests include the Brāhmaṇas and Upaniṣads, ancient Indian religious history, comparative asceticism, narrative, and literary theory.

Elizabeth Schiltz received her BA from Ohio Wesleyan University, and her PhD from Duke University. She has the good fortune to hold the Purna, Rao, Raju Chair of East–West Philosophy in the Department of Philosophy at the College of Wooster. Her publications include "Two Chariots: Moral Psychology in Plato's Phaedrus and the Kaṭha Upanishad," in the July 2006 issue of *Philosophy East and West*, and "How to Teach Comparative Philosophy," in the April 2014 issue of *Teaching Philosophy*.

Jacqueline Suthren Hirst is Senior Lecturer in South Asian Studies at the University of Manchester. Her main research interest is in Vedānta traditions, whose triple foundation of authoritative texts includes the principal Upaniṣads. Her book on *Śaṃkara's Advaita Vedānta: A Way of Teaching* (Routledge 2005) demonstrates the multiple ways in which Śaṃkara finds pedagogical resources as well as Advaitin content in the Upaniṣadic texts. Her other books include *Sita's Story* (RMEP 1997) and *Religious Traditions in Modern South Asia* (Routledge 2011), co-authored with John Zavos. She runs the annual Sanskrit Tradition in the Modern World symposium and has contributed to TAROSA, a website with resources for teaching across the religious traditions of South Asia.

Abbreviations

AA	Aitareya Āraṇyaka
AB	Aitareya Brāhmaṇa
AU	Aitareya Upaniṣad
AV	Atharvaveda
BhG	Bhagavadītā
BU	Bṛhadāraṇyaka Upaniṣad
CU	Chāndogya Upaniṣad
IU	Īśā Upaniṣad
JBU	Jaiminīya Brāhmaṇa Upaniṣad
KU	Kaṭha Upaniṣad
KeU	Kena Upaniṣad
KsU	Kauṣītaki Upaniṣad
MaU	Māṇḍūkya Upaniṣad
Mbh	Mahābhārata
MtU	Maitrī Upaniṣad
MU	Muṇḍaka Upaniṣad
PU	Praśna Upaniṣad
RV	Ṛgveda
SB	Śatapatha Brāhmaṇa
SU	Śvetāśvatara Upaniṣad
SV	Sāmaveda
TA	Taittirīya Āraṇyaka
TB	Taittirīya Brāhmaṇa
TU	Taittirīya Upaniṣad
YV	Yajurveda

1 Introduction

What is an Upaniṣad?

Signe Cohen

The Upaniṣads are among the most important religious and philosophical Hindu texts. Significant ideas that are still embraced by millions of Hindus today, such as *ātman* (the eternal self), *brahman* (the cosmic divine force), *karma*, reincarnation, and the idea that salvation can be defined as freedom from an endless cycle of death and rebirth are first formulated in these ancient Sanskrit texts.

The Upaniṣads are a genre of philosophical and religious texts that flourished in India from about 700 BCE onwards. The texts are composed in Sanskrit, an ancient Indo-European tongue that is the distant ancestor of modern Indian languages such as Hindi, Bengali, Panjabi, Marathi, and Gujarati. Some of the oldest Upaniṣads are prose texts, while many later ones are composed in verse. The Upaniṣadic texts range in length from the *Bṛhadāraṇyaka Upaniṣad*, which fills 60–70 pages of printed Sanskrit text, to the brief *Īśā Upaniṣad* in just eighteen verses and the *Māṇḍūkya Upaniṣad* in twelve short prose sections. There are hundreds of texts called Upaniṣads, all dealing with the same central theme – the mystical identity between the cosmic force *brahman* and the immortal inner self of a living being, *ātman*. Texts titled *Upaniṣad* have been composed in Sanskrit throughout the middle ages and into the early modern era. As a genre, the Upaniṣads can be defined as philosophical texts exploring the relationship between *brahman* and *ātman* for the purposes of spiritual liberation.

Central to all Upaniṣads is the idea that all humans are bound to an unsatisfying existence by our ignorance, and that true knowledge is the path to liberation. *Jñāna*, or knowledge, is a profound understanding of the reality underlying all appearance. The Upaniṣads differentiate between two forms of knowledge. The lower (*aparā*) knowledge is merely knowledge for its own sake, such as traditional learning and familiarity with sacred scriptures. The higher (*parā*) knowledge, on the other hand, is the intuitive knowledge "by which one grasps the imperishable."[1] This soteriological knowledge of *brahman* is often imparted by a teacher, although one theistic Upaniṣad suggests that one can also gain knowledge "through the grace of God."[2] Ignorance (*avidyā*), on the other hand, is that which holds a person back from enlightenment and must be avoided at all costs. Ignorance is often compared to a tangled knot,[3] or to fetters that bind a person to an unsatisfying existence.[4] Upaniṣadic characters who realize their own ignorance often immediately set out on a quest for a knowledgeable teacher. Knowledge leads to liberation (*mokṣa*) from death and rebirth, which is often compared to being released from chains or fetters.

What does "Upaniṣad" mean?

The etymology of the term *upaniṣad* is still the subject of some debate. The word is derived from the Sanskrit verb *sad*, preceded by the preverbs *upa-* and *ni-*. The most common meaning of *sad* is "to sit." The preverb *upa-* may express proximity ("near"), and the preverb *ni-* a downward motion. *Upaniṣad* may therefore be translated as "sitting down near" someone. The term is traditionally interpreted as a reference to the student sitting down at the teacher's feet to receive the secret teachings about *ātman* and *brahman*. The Upaniṣads themselves often refer to teachers and students and the process of learning; in fact, the student–teacher relationship is the primary social relationship in the Upaniṣadic texts, far more significant than the relationships between parents and children or between husband and wife. Finding the right teacher is crucial, as the wisdom seekers in the Upaniṣads discover. The seekers in the Upaniṣadic texts end up finding the knowledge they need both in learned Brahman priests and in more unlikely preceptors such as kings, or even talking animals. The teacher's background matters far less than the knowledge he (or she or it) possesses. It is perhaps reasonable, then, that the texts themselves are named after the act of sitting down at the feet of a teacher to absorb the essential ideas about *ātman* and *brahman*.

Other etymologies of the term *upaniṣad* have also been proposed. The Sanskrit scholar Oldenberg suggests a connection between *upaniṣad* and the Sanskrit noun *upāsana*, "worship."[5] Deussen proposes the meaning "secret doctrine,"[6] and Schayer "the equivalence between two magical substances."[7] Gren-Eklund argues that the word *upaniṣad* may originally have denoted "the fact of two things being placed in a relation to each other."[8] Falk suggests, based on usage of the verb *sad* with the prefixes *upa-* and *ni-* in the older Vedic language, that the term *upaniṣad* should be rendered "effective power" ("bewirkende Macht").[9] Olivelle, in his standard edition and translation of the Upaniṣads, translates the term *upaniṣad* "hidden connection," "hidden name," or "hidden teachings."[10] Witzel, in his edition of the *Kaṭha Āraṇyaka*, translates *upaniṣad* as "formula of magical equivalence."[11]

Another possible translation of *upaniṣad* is "that which lies (*sad*) beneath," or "underlying reality."[12] This meaning is not too far removed from Olivelle's "hidden connection." The Upaniṣads are intensely occupied with the process of enlightenment as a gradual progression toward the ultimate, underlying reality. It is possible that this central Upaniṣadic idea of a quest for another level of reality beneath the visible world inspired the name of these texts. This interpretation is supported by several Upaniṣadic passages:

> As a spider sends out its thread, and as sparks spring from the fire, so do all the breaths, all worlds, all gods, and all beings spring from the *ātman*. Its *upaniṣad* is the real behind the real …[13]
>
> I ask you about that person who is the *upaniṣad*, who carries the other persons away, who brings them back, and who rises above them.[14]
>
> When someone knows the *upaniṣad* that is *brahman* in this way, the sun does not rise or set for him; it is always day for him.[15]
>
> This is the teaching. This is the *upaniṣad* of the Veda.[16]
>
> That is *brahman*, the highest *upaniṣad*, which is rooted in asceticism and knowledge of the self.[17]
>
> It is hidden in the secret *upaniṣads* of the Veda. Know it, you Brahmans [priests], as the womb of *brahman*.[18]

The *Chāndogya Upaniṣad* contains a story of a god and a demon, Indra and Virocana, who both approach the divine teacher Prajāpati and ask him to teach them about the *ātman* (the inner self). The demon Virocana becomes convinced that the *ātman* is nothing but the physical body, and he shares this idea of a "secret underlying reality" with the other demons:

> This is indeed the *upaniṣad* that demons believe in: They perform the last rites for the dead person with gifts of food and clothing and jewelry, for they believe that they will win the next world in this way.[19]

Even though Virocana completely misunderstands what the *ātman* is, the usage of the term *upaniṣad* here is telling. It is possible that the genre name *Upaniṣad* originated precisely in the texts' preoccupation with the ultimate, underlying reality. This usage of the term *upaniṣad* can be traced back to the earlier ritual literature of the Brāhmaṇas. As Falk has demonstrated, the commonly occurring phrase "A is the *upaniṣad* of B" usually indicates that A is that which causes B to come into existence.[20] Renou compares *upaniṣad* to the Pali term *upanisā* ("cause").[21] Since the main theme of the Upaniṣads is the quest for the ultimate reality and the first cause, it is not surprising that this concept is reflected in the names of the texts themselves. Additionally, seeing *upaniṣad* as a reference to the esoteric underlying reality fits quite well with the Indian commentarial tradition's explanation of *upaniṣad* as *rahasya* ("secret").

How many Upaniṣads are there?

The medieval *Muktikā Upaniṣad* lists 108 Upaniṣads, broken down into:

1) "Principal" (*mukhya*) Upaniṣads: *Īśā*, *Bṛhadāraṇyaka*, *Kaṭha*, *Taittirīya*, *Śvetāśvatara*, *Praśna*, *Muṇḍaka*, *Māṇḍūkya*, *Kena*, *Chāndogya*, *Maitrāyaṇī (=Maitrī)*, *Kauṣītaki*, and *Aitareya*.

2) "General" (*sāmānya*) Upaniṣads: *Subāla, Māntrika, Nirālamba, Paiṅgala, Adhyātmā, Muktikā, Sarvasāra, Śukarahasya, Skanda, Śārīraka, Garbha, Ekākṣara, Akṣi, Prāṇāgnihotra, Sūrya, Ātmā, Vajrasūcī, Mahā, Sāvitrī, Ātmabodha,* and *Mudgala.*
3) "Ascetic" (*saṃnyāsa*) Upaniṣads: *Jābāla, Paramahaṃsa, Advayatāraka, Bhikṣuka, Turīyātīta, Yājñavalkya, Śāṭyāyanīya, Brahma, Tejobindu, Avadhūta, Kaṭharudra, Nāradaparivrājaka, Paramahaṃsa, Parivrājaka, Parabrahma, Āruṇeya, Maitreya, Saṃnyāsa, Kuṇḍikā,* and *Nirvāṇa.*
4) Yoga Upaniṣads: *Haṃsa, Triśikhi, Maṇḍalabrāhmaṇa, Amṛtabindu, Amṛtanāda, Kṣurikā, Dhyānabindu, Brahmavidyā, Yogatattva, Yogaśikhā, Yogakuṇḍalinī, Varāha, Śāṇḍilya, Pāśupata, Mahāvākya, Yogacūḍāmaṇi, Darśana,* and *Nādabindu.*
5) Upaniṣads devoted to the goddess (*Śākta* Upaniṣads): *Sarasvatīrahasya, Sītā, Annapūrṇā, Devī, Tripuratāpinī, Bhāvana, Tripurā, Saubhāgyalakṣmī,* and *Bahvṛca.*
6) Viṣṇu Upaniṣads (*Vaiṣṇava* Upaniṣads): *Tārasāra, Nārāyaṇa, Kalisantaraṇa, Nṛsiṃhatāpanī, Mahānārāyaṇa, Rāmarahasya, Rāmatāpanīya, Gopālatāpanīya, Kṛṣṇa, Hayagrīva, Dattātreya, Gāruḍa, Vāsudeva,* and *Avyakta.*
7) Śiva Upaniṣads (*Śaiva* Upaniṣads): *Kaivalya, Kālāgnirudra, Dakṣiṇāmūrti, Rudrahṛdaya, Pañcabrahma, Atharvaśikha, Bṛhajjābāla, Śarabha, Bhasma, Gaṇapati, Rudrākṣa, Jābāli,* and *Atharvaśikhā.*

The "principal" Upaniṣads in the *Muktikā Upaniṣad* are, with two exceptions (*Maitrāyaṇī* and *Kauṣītaki*), texts to which the famous eighth-century commentator Śaṅkara composed commentaries. These "principal" Upaniṣads are often regarded as the oldest ones, and for many Hindus, these are the Upaniṣads that define the genre. There are many more texts called "Upaniṣad" than the 108 named in the *Muktikā Upaniṣad,* but it is likely that precisely 108 texts were listed because the number is sacred in Hinduism.[22] Altogether, there are over 200 texts called "Upaniṣad," ranging from the old eighth-century BCE Upaniṣads to the sixteenth-century CE Allah Upaniṣad, which identifies the God of Islam with the inner self (*ātman*). What all of these texts have in common is a preoccupation with the mystical identity between *ātman* and *brahman.* In 1965, the Indian Christian theologian Dhanjibhai Fakirbhai even published his own text under the name *Kristopanishad* ("The Upaniṣad of Christ"). While this is hardly an Upaniṣad in the traditional sense, it blends Upaniṣadic ideas with Christian theology. Fakirbhai describes the Christian God in the same way as the classical Upaniṣads characterize *ātman/brahman,* as *saccidānanda,* "being," "consciousness," and "bliss."[23] The invocation of the Hindu genre name Upaniṣad in the title of the *Kristopanishad* and the use of Upaniṣadic rhetoric become an assertion of ancient authority.

The importance of the Upaniṣads

For devout Hindus, the Upaniṣads are considered *śruti*, or authoritative sacred text. There are two distinct terms used for sacred texts in Hinduim, *śruti* and *smṛti*. *Śruti*, which can be translated as "that which is heard," is a category than encompasses the oldest Sanskrit texts: the four Vedas, the ritual Brāhmaṇa and Āraṇyaka texts, and the principal Upaniṣads. *Smṛti* ("that which is remembered") includes works on the six *Vedāṅgas* (auxiliary Vedic sciences: phonetics, prosody, grammar, etymology, rituals, and astrology), the epic poems of the *Mahābhārata* and the *Rāmāyaṇa*, legal literature, and the mythological texts of the Purāṇas. Although both groups of texts are considered holy, the texts classified as *śruti* are more authoritative.

The holiness of the *śruti* texts are underscored by the reluctance to write them down; they are meant to be heard (hence the term *śruti*) as they are passed down orally from teachers to students, from generation to generation. While manuscripts of the *Rāmāyaṇa* and the *Mahābhārata* and later Purāṇas are plentiful in India, written forms of the Vedas and the Upaniṣads are both rare and chronologically quite late. The oldest extant manuscript of the *Ṛgveda* is from the fourteenth century.[24] Manuscripts of the Upaniṣads can be dated to the sixteenth[25] and eighteenth centuries,[26] almost two millennia after the texts' probable date of composition.

As *śruti*, the Upaniṣads are sources of religious authority. While the Vedas, the ultimately holy texts for Hindus, are often more revered than read,[27] many of the teachings of the Upaniṣads are essential for later Hinduism. The Upaniṣadic ideas of *ātman*, *brahman*, salvation through knowledge, reincarnation, and *karma* are foundational ideas for most forms of later Hindu theology.

There are six recognized schools of classical Hindu philosophy: Sāṃkhya, Yoga, Nyāya, Vaiśeṣika, Mīmāṃsā, and Vedānta. Two of these schools, Sāṃkhya and Yoga, can trace many of their teachings back to the Upaniṣads. The Sāṃkhya concepts of *puruṣa* (the eternal spirit), *prakṛti* ("nature," the cosmic primordial matter), and the three *guṇas* ("qualities") that make up the primordial nature can be traced back to the Upaniṣads, as can early forms of Yogic meditation, breathing techniques and postures. The Vedānta philosophy is in its entirety based on the Upaniṣads (*Vedānta*, "the end/fulfillment of the Vedas" is also another name for the Upaniṣads themselves) and the different later commentaries to these texts. The eighth-century commentator Śaṅkara argued in his commentaries to the Upaniṣads that there is absolutely no difference between *ātman* and *brahman*; this interpretation of the Upaniṣads gave rise to the sub-school of Vedānta known as *Advaita Vedānta* (monistic or non-dualistic Vedānta). *Advaita Vedānta* may be the most influential school of Indian philosophy today. The eleventh–twelfth century philosopher Rāmānuja argued in his *Brahmasūtrabhāṣya* that *brahman* must be understood as a personal god, rather than an impersonal principle, and that this god contained all *ātmans* within himself, but still remained greater than the sum of all *ātmans*. Rāmānuja became the founder of the sub-school of Vedānta known as Viśiṣṭha *Advaita* (modified non-dualistic Vedānta). The thirteenth-century philosopher Madhva also wrote commentaries on the thirteen "principal" Upaniṣads. In his work, he argued that *ātman* and God/ *brahman* are entirely different, and this became the foundation for the *Dvaita* (dualist) school of Vedānta.

Translations and influence on Western culture

The first translation of the Upaniṣads was Dara Shikoh's rendition into Persian in 1656 (see Chapter 21), which included fifty Upaniṣads. This Persian text was then re-translated into Latin in 1801 by a Frenchman, Anquetil Duperron. Anquetil Duperron's Latin Upaniṣad translation made a deep impression on the German philosopher Arthur Schopenhauer (1788–1860), who again influenced many European thinkers such as Friedrich Nietzsche, Carl Gustav Jung and Joseph Campbell. Chapter 22 examines the influence on the Upaniṣads on Schopenhauer's work.

The first translation of an Upaniṣad into English was Colebrooke's 1805 translation of the *Aitareya Upaniṣad.* Numerous other Upaniṣad translations soon followed. Among the best known ones today are Max Müller's translation of twelve of the principal Upaniṣads (*Chāndogya*, *Talavakāra (=Kena)*, *Aitareya*, *Kauṣītaki*, *Vājasaneyī (=Īśā)*, *Kaṭha*, *Muṇḍaka*, *Taittirīya*, *Bṛhadāraṇyaka*, *Śvetāśvatara*, *Praśna*, and *Maitrī*) in the *Sacred Books of the East* series in 1879 and 1884, Paul Deussen's 1897 translation of sixty Upaniṣads,[28] Robert E. Hume's 1921 translation of thirteen Upaniṣads (the twelve translated by Müller plus the *Māṇḍūkya Upaniṣad*), Sarvepalli Radhakrishnan's 1953 translation of eighteen Upaniṣads (the thirteen translated by Müller plus *Subāla*, *Jābala*, *Paiṅgala*, *Kaivalya*, and *Vajrasūcikā*), Patrick Olivelle's 1998 translation of twelve principal Upaniṣads (the *Maitrī Upaniṣad* not included) and Valerie Roebuck's 2000 translation of the thirteen principal Upaniṣads.

Mention must also be made of the 1937 translation of ten Upaniṣads by Shree Purohit Swami and the Irish poet W. B. Yeats (1865–1939). The translation itself is more lyrical than accurate, but it represents an interesting stage in Yeats' career as a writer and reflects his deep interest in India and Indian thought.

Another Western poet who found inspiration in the Upaniṣads was T. S. Eliot (1888–1965), who studied Sanskrit as a young man at Harvard under renowned Sanskrit professors C. R. Lanman and James H. Woods.[29] In his 1922 poem *The Waste Land*, Eliot retells an episode from *Bṛhadāraṇyaka Upaniṣad* 5.2. The Upaniṣad tells us that the creator god Prajāpati had three kinds of children – gods, humans, and demons. He spoke the same syllable to each of his groups of children: *Da*. The gods interpreted the syllable to mean *dāmyata* ("show restraint"). The humans understood it to mean *datta* ("give!"). The demons decided that *da* must stand for *dayadhvam* ("show compassion"). This Upaniṣadic tale is evoked in the section called "What the Thunder Said" of Eliot's poem, and has inspired numerous Western readers to seek the origin of the mystical *Datta, Dayadhvam, Damyata* in the Upaniṣads.

The Upaniṣads also influenced the American transcendentalist Ralph Waldo Emerson (1803–1882), the poet Walt Whitman (1819–1892), and the Russian novelist Leo Tolstoy (1828–1910). And perhaps most significantly, these ancient texts continue to impress and inspire new generations of readers, whether they rely on a translation or are fortunate enough to be able to read the texts in the original Sanskrit.

Notes

1 *Muṇḍaka Upaniṣad* 1.1.5.
2 *Śvetāśvatara Upaniṣad* 6.21.
3 *Chāndogya Upaniṣad* 7. 26. 2, *Kaṭha Upaniṣad* 6.15, *Muṇḍaka Upaniṣad* 2.1.10, 2.2.8, and 3.2.9.
4 *Śvetāśvatara Upaniṣad* 1.8, 2.15, 4.15–16, 5.13, 6.13.
5 H. Oldenberg, "Vedische Untersuchungen 6: Upaniṣad" *Zeitschrift der deutschen morgenländischen Gesellschaft* 59 (1896): 457–462.
6 P. Deussen, *Allgemeine Geschichte der Philosophie.* Band 1, Teil 2: *Die Philosophie der Upanishaden.* Leipzig: Brockhaus, 1899: 13.
7 Quoted from J. Charpentier, "*Kāṭhaka Upaniṣad.* Translated with an Introduction and Notes" *Indian Antiquary* 57 (1928): 203.
8 G. Gren-Eklund, "Causality and the Method of Connecting Concepts in the Upaniṣads" *Indologica Taurinensia* 12 (1984): 117.
9 H. Falk, "Vedisch *upaniṣád*" *Zeitschrift der deutschen morganändischen Gesellschaft* 136 (1986): 80–97.
10 Olivelle 1998.
11 M. Witzel, *Kaṭha Āraṇyaka: Critical Edition with a Translation into German and an Introduction.* Cambridge, MA: The Department of Sanskrit and Indian Studies, Harvard University, 2004: xliii.
12 S. Cohen, *Text and Authority in the Older Upaniṣads.* Leiden: Brill, 1998.
13 *Bṛhadāraṇyaka Upaniṣad* 2.1.20.
14 *Bṛhadāraṇyaka Upaniṣad* 3.9.26.
15 *Chāndogya Upaniṣad* 3.11.3.
16 *Taittirīya Upaniṣad* 1.11.4.
17 *Śvetāśvatara Upaniṣad* 1.16.
18 *Śvetāśvatara Upaniṣad* 5.6.
19 *Chāndogya Upaniṣad* 8.8.5.
20 Falk 1986: 80–97.
21 Renou 1945: 56, quoted from Falk 1986.
22 108 is 1 to the first power times 2 to the second power times 3 to the third power.
23 Dhanjibhai Fakirbhai, *Kristopanishad (Christ-Upanishad).* Bangalore: The Christian Institute for the Study of Religion and Society, 1965.
24 Stephanie Jamison and Joel Brereton, *The Rigveda: The Earliest Religious Poetry of India.* Oxford: Oxford University Press, 2014.
25 See Carlos Alberto Pérez Coffie: *Bṛhadāraṇyakopaniṣad II: Critical Edition of the Second Chapter of the Kāṇva Recension According to Accented Manuscripts with a Critical-Exegetical Commentary.* PhD dissertation, Harvard University 1994: 17.

26 See Pérez Coffie: 18.
27 See Louis Renou, The Destiny of the Veda in India. Delhi: Motilal Banarsidass, 1965 and Wilhelm Halbfass, "The Idea of the Veda and the Identity of Hinduism" in *Tradition and Reflection: Explorations in Indian Thought*. Albany, NY: SUNY, 1991: 1–22.
28 Originally in German, but later translated into English.
29 See Jeffry M. Perl and Andrew P. Tuck, "The Hidden Advantage of Tradition: On the Significance of T. S. Eliot's Indic Studies" *Philosophy East and West* 35 (1985): 116–131.

Further reading

Deussen, P. 1897. *Sechzig Upanishads des Veda*. Leipzig: F. A. Brockhaus. Translated by V. M. Bedekaar and G. B. Palsule as *Sixty Upaniṣads of the Veda*. 2 vols. Delhi: Motilal Banarsidass, 1980.

Deussen, P. 1919. *The Philosophy of the Upanishads*. Translated by A. S. Geden. Edinburgh: T&T Clark.

Hume, R. E. 1921. *The Thirteen Principal Upanishads*. Oxford: Oxford University Press.

Müller, F. Max. 1879–1884. *The Upaniṣads*. Oxford: Clarendon Press.

Olivelle, P. 1998. *The Early Upaniṣads: Annotated Text and Translation*. New York/Oxford: Oxford University Press.

Purohit, S., and W. B. Yeats. 1937. *The Ten Principal Upanishads*. New York: Macmillan.

Radhakrishnan, S. 1953. *The Principal Upanishads*. New York: Harper.

Ranade, R. D. 1926. *A Constructive Survey of Upanishadic Philosophy, Being an Introduction to the Thought of the Upanishads*. (Reprint Bombay: Bharatiya Vidya Bhavan, 1986.)

Roebuck, V. 2000. *The Upanishads*. London: Penguin.

Part I

Composition, authorship, and transmission of the Upaniṣads

2 The date of the Upaniṣads

Signe Cohen

When were the Upaniṣads composed? It is almost impossible to arrive at a conclusive answer to this question based on the evidence available to us today. Most ancient Sanskrit texts, including the Vedas and the oldest Upaniṣads, were transmitted orally from generation to generation for many centuries before they were committed to writing. In textual traditions that involve writing (on paper, parchment, papyrus, birch bark, vellum, or some other material), the manuscript itself can be dated through carbon-14 dating or other scientific methods. Even in cases when early written material exists, it is of course still possible that the text itself is older than the earliest known manuscript; the text may have been transmitted orally before it was written down, or earlier manuscripts may have been lost. But in the case of the older Upaniṣads and the Vedas, there is nothing to carbon date. All extant manuscripts are so late (maybe two millennia later than a reasonable date of composition for the texts) that they provide no insight into when the texts first came into being.

How do we even begin to date an orally transmitted text? Scholars rely on five main methods that are used to date ancient Sanskrit texts:

1) The relationship of the text to other known texts from ancient India
2) References in the text to things that can be dated through archaeological methods, such as the use of iron or rice cultivation, or to historical figures or events
3) Linguistic evidence
4) Metrical evidence
5) The development of religious or philosophical ideas in the text.

In the following, we will discuss each of these methods in more detail.

The relationship to other texts

The Hindu tradition itself recognizes a firm chronology of ancient sacred texts: First come the four Vedas (the *Ṛgveda, Sāmaveda*, *Yajurveda*, and *Atharvaveda*), then the ritual texts call the Brāhmaṇas, then the more arcane ritual texts of the Āraṇyakas, and then the Upaniṣads. Later, after the Upaniṣads, follow the great epic poems of the *Mahābhārata* (which includes the well-known *Bhagavadgītā*) and the *Rāmāyaṇa*, and the mythological texts called the Purāṇas. There is no reason to doubt this relative chronology, which is further supported by linguistic and metrical evidence. The language of the Vedas is, for example, far more archaic than the language of the older Upaniṣads, which is in turn more ancient than the language of the epics. Based on the development of language, meter, and ideas, it is reasonable to assume that the oldest Upaniṣads were composed around 500–700 years after the oldest of the Vedas, the *Ṛgveda*. But when was the *Ṛgveda* composed?

Many different dates have been proposed for the *Ṛgveda*, ranging from 4000 BCE to 1000 BCE. Those who date the *Ṛgveda* very early often rely on astronomical symbolism in the Vedic texts,[1] or on identification between Vedic culture and the archaeological remnants of the Indus Civilization, which flourished in an area that corresponds to current-day northwest India and Pakistan from around 3500 BCE to 1800 BCE.[2] Many scholars find a date of around 1500–1200 BCE for the *Ṛgveda* to be reasonable, based in part on the similarities between the language of the *Ṛgveda* and that of the ancient Iranian text called the *Avesta*. The language of the *Ṛgveda*, the earliest known form of Sanskrit, is often simple referred to as "Vedic." Sanskrit is an Indo-European language, and as such it is distantly related to languages like Latin, Greek, and even English. Sanskrit belongs to the Indo-Iranian branch of the Indo-European languages, and one of its closest relatives is the ancient Iranian language Avestan (the language of the sacred text of the Zoroastrians, the *Avesta*). Vedic Sanskrit and Avestan are quite close to one another and almost mutually intelligible. In addition to numerous similarities of grammar and vocabulary, the *Ṛgveda* and the *Avesta* also share some stock phrases and poetic metaphors, and even the names of some gods, demons, and men. It is likely that the Avestan and the Vedic language both evolved from a common ancestor language some 500 years or so prior to the composition of the two texts. The dating of the *Avesta* can therefore help us find an approximate date for the composition of the *Ṛgveda*. Unfortunately, the dating of the *Avesta* is itself contested, although more evidence exists in this case in the form of early Iranian manuscripts. Scholarly estimates of the date of the *Avesta* range from 1400 to 600 BCE, although more scholars lean toward an earlier date. It seems likely, based on the linguistic similarities between the *Avesta* and the *Ṛgveda*, that the *Ṛgveda* was composed within a few centuries of the Zoroastrian text.

Another more tangible piece of external evidence for the date of the *Ṛgveda* is the so-called "Mitanni Treaty," an ancient military agreement between the Hittite and Mitanni people of Anatolia (today's Turkey and Syria). Their treaty, conveniently carved into stone, can be reliably dated to around 1400 BCE. For reasons that are not well understood, parts of this inscription are in a very early form of Sanskrit. Vedic gods, such as Mitra, Varuṇa, and Indra, are invoked in the treaty. The linguistic forms of the Mitanni treaty indicate that the text is probably a few centuries older the *Ṛgveda*. Since this treaty was composed so very far from Vedic-speaking India, it is of course possible that the Mitanni language reflects the Vedic Sanskrit spoken by people who had left India generations earlier. The language spoken by expatriates isolated from their homeland often preserves more archaic features than the language currently spoken in the place they emigrated from, so we cannot say for certain that the *Ṛgveda* must be later than 1400 BCE.

It is generally accepted in the Indian tradition that the *Ṛgveda* is the oldest of the four Vedas, that the *Atharvaveda* is the youngest, and that the other two Vedas (the *Sāmaveda* and the *Yajurveda*) fall somewhere in between. One argument that is frequently used in the dating of the Vedas is the references to metal in the Vedic texts. Bronze, gold, and copper are mentioned in all the Vedas, but references to iron are only found in the *Atharvaveda*. Since iron is attested in the archaeological record in India from around 1000 BCE, many scholars have consequently dated the *Atharvaveda* to around 1000–900 BCE. Others have pointed out that silver is not mentioned in the *Ṛgveda* either, and have consequently dated the *Ṛgveda* to before 4000 BCE. It is, of course, quite possible that the authors of the poems of the *Ṛgveda* were well acquainted with silver or iron without mentioning it in their hymns to the gods.

Archaeologists have identified a late Iron Age culture in north India known as the Painted Grey Ware Culture that lasted from about 1200 BCE to 600 BCE. The culture is named after its characteristic grey pottery painted with black patterns. The Painted Grey Ware culture is associated with permanent village settlements, domesticated horses, and metallurgy, and many scholars agree that it likely corresponds to middle to late Vedic culture (i.e. the time of the *Atharvaveda* and *Brāhmaṇas*). This may place the *Ṛgveda* around 1500–1200 BCE.

It should be evident from the above discussion that the date of the *Ṛgveda* cannot be determined with any great accuracy. Consequently, the dates of the Upaniṣads that followed, centuries later, must also remain subject to speculation. Many scholars accept a date of ca. 1500–1200 BCE for the *Ṛgveda*, and thus possibly a date of ca. 1000–500 BCE for the earliest Upaniṣads, but there is still a great deal of uncertainty surrounding these dates.

Another possible factor in dating the Upaniṣad is the relationship of the Upaniṣadic texts to those of early Buddhism. Some scholars have argued that the oldest Upaniṣads, such as the *Bṛhadāraṇyaka* and the *Chāndogya,* were composed prior to the rise of Buddhism, whereas some of the later Upaniṣadic texts (the *Maitrī Upaniṣad* in particular) may display some familiarity with Buddhist ideas. There are, however, others who have argued that the authors of the Upaniṣads knew nothing at all about Buddhism.[3] *If* the "middle Upaniṣads," such as the *Kaṭha, Śvetāśvatara,* and *Maitrī* were composed around the time when Buddhism arose or some centuries after, this may place these texts around the fourth–second century BCE. The precise dating of the historical Buddha and the earliest Buddhist texts is unfortunately also a complicated issue on which there are several scholarly opinions.[4]

Historical and archaeological evidence

As we will see in Chapter 5, there are significant gaps in our knowledge of the history of ancient India. The names of a few kings and dynasties are known, but none of these kings are mentioned in the Upaniṣads, nor are other historical figures such as the Buddha or Mahāvīra, the founder of Jainism. The Upaniṣads do not refer to any external events that can be dated, such as famous battles or the appearance of comets in the sky.

Since the Upaniṣads are primarily religious and philosophical texts, they are not concerned with painting a detailed picture of the society in which they were composed. We can nevertheless get some information from the texts that can give indirect evidence for the date of composition. The Upaniṣadic texts mention rice, barley, millet, lentils, wheat, and sesame, but all these crops are found in the Indian archaeological record from around 2500 BCE, so this does not help with the dating of the texts. Domesticated animals, especially cows, horses, goats, and sheep, are also mentioned, but they were all domesticated quite early in India, and references to them in the Upaniṣads also do not contribute to the dating. The Upaniṣads do, however, refer to kings and their courts, as well as to fixed, possibly urban, dwelling places. This evidence is quite helpful, as urbanization and state formation can be traced in the archaeological record.

The kingdoms of Kuru and Pañcāla are mentioned frequently in the Upaniṣads, and as we will see in Chapter 5, the oldest Upaniṣads are familiar with a geographical area located in northeast India. Many of the geographical locations referenced in the Upaniṣads overlap with the sites of the archaeological Northern Black Polished Ware Culture, which flourished from around 700 to 500 BCE. The Painted Grey Ware sites (1200–600 BCE) mentioned above are a little to the west of the geographical locations associated with the early Upaniṣads, but Kāśī (modern day Varanasi) and the kingdoms of Kuru and Pañcāla are both important in the Upaniṣads and significant Northern Black Polished Ware culture sites. This culture is characterized by growing urbanization, social stratification, and trade, all of which are consistent with the society described in the Upaniṣads.

Linguistic evidence

The Sanskrit language has a long history, and like all living languages, it changed and developed over the centuries. The archaic Sanskrit of the Vedas differs, both in grammatical features, vocabulary, and rules for sound combinations (*sandhi*) from classical Sanskrit as it is found in the epic poems *Mahābhārata* and *Rāmāyaṇa* and later texts. The language of the Upaniṣads ranges from late Vedic Sanskrit in Upaniṣads like the *Bṛhadāraṇyaka* to classical Sanskrit in many of the Vaiṣṇava and Śaiva Upaniṣads. While the linguistic evidence cannot help us arrive at a precise date for a particular Upaniṣad, it is immensely useful for dating Upaniṣads relative to one another. In general, the more Vedic grammatical forms and words we find in an Upaniṣadic text, the older it is. There are exceptions to this, however; some later Upaniṣads such as the *Bāṣkalamantra Upaniṣad* deliberately use archaic language, probably to lend the text an air of authority. This artificially archaizing language is, however, quite easy to recognize; the authors of the *Bāṣkalamantra Upaniṣad* sprinkle the "typical" Vedic particle *u* throughout the text, but the grammatical endings and metrical forms used in the Upaniṣad are otherwise characteristic of later classical Sanskrit.

It is also important to note that each of the older Upaniṣads is affiliated with a particular school of Vedic transmission (*śākhā*), which will be described in more detail in Chapters 3 and 4. Some of these schools are more conservative in their textual transmission than others. Each *śākhā* has also preserved some linguistic peculiarities. A linguistic analysis of an Upaniṣadic text must take these issues into consideration, since it is crucial to distinguish between genuine linguistic archaic form indicating an early date of composition for a particular text, and preserved archaisms common to an entire Vedic school.

To complicate matters further, certain linguistic phenomena[5] were innovations that arose in one geographic area[6] and later spread to surrounding areas over the next centuries. When we find such a form in a textual passage, this may indicate an earlier date if the text was composed in the area where the innovation originated, and a later date if the text can be shown to have been composed in a different area. In determining the age of a textual passage based on linguistic criteria it is necessary to bear in mind the distinction between chronology and geography. For example, the *Chāndogya Upaniṣad* uses the past form *perfect* far more often than the *imperfect* in narratives. This linguistic fact may be interpreted in two different ways. It is either a sign of very late composition for an Upaniṣad, or a sign that the text was composed in the Central Eastern area.[7] When other linguistic factors are taken into consideration, it becomes apparent that the latter explanation is the more likely one.

Metrical evidence

Although some of the older Upaniṣads, such as the *Bṛhadāraṇyaka*, *Chāndogya*, and *Aitareya*, are composed in prose, many of the Upaniṣads are in verse. The metrical forms of these texts provide additional evidence for the relative age of the Upaniṣad.

The two main meters (verse forms) used in the Upaniṣads are *triṣṭubh-jagatī*, a meter that consists of four lines of eleven or twelve syllables each, and *anuṣṭubh-śloka*, a meter with four verse lines of eight syllables each. The rhythms of Sanskrit meters are not determined by stressed and unstressed syllables, as in English, but by the patterns of long and short syllables, as in Latin. There are several variations of each of the Sanskrit meters, and it is possible to trace the historical development of each meter. Metrical analysis of Upaniṣadic texts can therefore be helpful both in dating Upaniṣadic relative to one another and in identifying later interpolations with one text.

The development of religious and philosophical ideas in a text

Although this is a method frequently used by scholars attempting to create a chronological list of the Upaniṣads, it is perhaps the least reliable tool for dating a text. Certain ideas emerge earlier in some *śākhās* (schools of transmission) of Upaniṣads than in others. For example, theism (the belief in a personal god) can be found very early (based on linguistic criteria) in the Upaniṣads affiliated with the *Ṛgveda*, while theism is a much later development in the Upaniṣads affiliated with other Vedas. If we were to date the Upaniṣads solely on the basis of the stage of development of theistic ideas, the result would be completely at odds with the metrical and linguistic evidence. It is sometimes possible to trace the historical development of ideas in the Upaniṣads, but this is not a reliable dating method in itself.

Conclusions: Dating the Upaniṣads

As will be evident form the observations above, it is not possible to arrive at an absolutely certain date of composition for the Upaniṣads. The oldest of the Upaniṣadic texts, the *Bṛhadāraṇyaka* and the *Chāndogya*, may date to around 800–500 BCE, but it is also possible that these dates are off by centuries. David Knipe dates the oldest Upaniṣads to the eighth century BCE.[8] Patrick Olivelle dates the *Bṛhadāraṇyaka Upaniṣad* and the *Chāndogya Upaniṣad*, which are almost unanimously recognized as the most ancient extant Upaniṣads, to the seventh–sixth centuries BCE "give or take a century or so."[9]

Although it is difficult to date the Upaniṣads with any greater precision, it is possible to arrive at an internal chronology of the classical Upaniṣads. The list below, arranging the Upaniṣads in roughly chronological order, is based on linguistic and metrical evidence. The relative dating of some of the texts may be wrong, but it should be a reasonable approximation based on the available evidence.[10]

1) The *Mādhyaṃdina* recension of the *Bṛhadāraṇyaka Upaniṣad*
2) *Chāndogya Upaniṣad*
3) *Aitareya Upaniṣad*
4) *Kauṣītaki Upaniṣad*
5) The *Kāṇva* recension of the *Bṛhadāraṇyaka Upaniṣad*
6) *Taittirīya Upaniṣad*
7) *Īśā Upaniṣad*
8) *Praśna Upaniṣad*
9) *Muṇḍaka Upaniṣad*

10) *Kaṭha Upaniṣad*
11) *Śvetāśvatara Upaniṣad*
12) *Kena Upaniṣad*
13) *Maitrī Upaniṣad*
14) *Māṇḍūkya Upaniṣad*
15) *Mahānārāyaṇa Upaniṣad*
16) *Kaivalya Upaniṣad*
17) *Bāṣkalamantra Upaniṣad*
18) The later Vaiṣṇava, Śaiva, Śākta, Saṃnyāsa and Yoga Upaniṣads.

The Upaniṣads in the last category on this list no longer contain any traces of Vedic grammar or metrical forms and were likely composed long after the others mentioned above. These Upaniṣads contain references to deities, religious movements, and ideas that flourished in India from the Middle Ages onwards, and are likely composed after the eleventh century.

Notes

1 See for example Subhash Kak: "Vedic Astronomy and Early Indian Chronology" in Bryant and Patton 2005: 309–331.
2 For a full and balanced discussion of this argument, see E. Bryant, *The Quest for the Origins of Vedic Culture: The Indo-Aryan Migration Debate*. Oxford: Oxford University Press, 2001.
3 For more discussion on this topic, see Chapter 8 on Buddhism and the Upaniṣads.
4 For an excellent exploration of these issues, see H. Bechert (ed.), *When Did the Buddha Live? The Controversy on the Dating of the Historical Buddha.* Delhi: Sri Satguru Publications, 1995.
5 For example genitive/ablative singular forms in *-ai* of feminine nouns ending in *-ā* or *-ī* (instead of the older forms in *-ā'*), or genitive/ablative in *-ai* of feminine nouns ending in *-i* (instead of in *-e'*).
6 In this case, that of the *Taittirīya* school, see M. Witzel, "Tracing the Vedic Dialects" in C. Caillat (ed.) *Dialectes dans les littératures indo-aryennes*. Paris: Collège de France/Institut de Civilisation Indienne, 1989: 136.
7 Compare Witzel 1989: 146.
8 D. Knipe, *Hinduism: Experiments in the Sacred.* Prospect Heights: Waveland Press, 1991.
9 P. Olivelle, *The Early Upaniṣads*. Oxford: Oxford University Press, 1998.
10 Cohen 2008.

Further reading

Bryant, E. and L. Patton. 2005. *The Indo-Aryan Controversy: Evidence and Inference in Indian History*. London/New York: Routledge.

Cohen, S. 2008. *Text and Authority in the Older Upaniṣads*. Leiden: Brill.

3 The authorship of the Upaniṣads

Signe Cohen

Individual vs. collective authorship

Very few of the existing Upaniṣads can be attributed to a single individual author. One of the few exceptions to this is the *Śvetāśvatara Upaniṣad*, ascribed in the text itself to a man by the name of Śvetāśvatara (whose name means "the one who owns a white mule"):

> By the power of his austerities and by the grace of God, the wise Śvetāśvatara first came to know *brahman* and then proclaimed it ...[1]

On the face of it, this stanza seems to say that an individual by the name of Śvetāśvatara is the author of the Upaniṣad, and that his composition of the text was inspired both by his ascetic lifestyle and his devotion to a personal god. This does not necessarily, however, mean that Śvetāśvatara was a historical person. Many ancient Indian texts, even those that are so vast and contain such metrically and linguistically diverse material that they can hardly be attributed to a single author, are ascribed to mythical sages and poets: Vālmiki is traditionally held to be the author of the *Rāmāyaṇa* epic, Vyāsa of the enormous *Mahābhārata* epic, and the legendary Atharvan of the *Atharvaveda*.

The *Śvetāśvatara Upaniṣad* is also called the *Śvetāśvatārāṇam Mantropaniṣad*, or "The *Mantra* Upaniṣad of the Svetāśvataras." This alternative title, with the name Śvetāśvatara in the plural, suggests that Śvetāśvatara may not have been a single individual, but rather the name of a scholastic tradition. As Witzel points out, the *Caraṇavyūha* mentions a *Śvetāśvatara śākhā*, or scholastic branch of transmission.[2] Hauer, however, regards the existence of such a *śākhā* unattested elsewhere, as a "spätindische Fiktion" ("a late Indian fiction").[3]

The Śvetāśvatara mentioned in one of the last stanzas of the Upaniṣad may simply be a mythical figure, the legendary founder of a scholastic tradition, rather than an individual Upaniṣadic author. On the other hand, the individuality expressed in this stanza is also reflected in the text itself. The *Śvetāśvatara Upaniṣad* contains several unique and innovative teachings, such as the idea of a tri-partite *Brahman*, two levels of the *ātman*, and the existence of an eternal female principle. Is this text the work of a unique individualist among the Upaniṣadic authors, or is it, like most of the Upaniṣadic texts, the product of a particular scholarly circle?

Individual authorship is a comparatively late phenomenon in the long and rich history of Sanskrit literature. While some of the ancient hymns of the *Ṛgveda* are ascribed to individual named seers (*ṛṣi*), many are anonymous. But the later Hindu tradition has largely disregarded the claims to authorship of individual *Ṛgvedic* hymns and declared the Vedas *apauruṣeya* (of non-human origin), eternal and authorless. The other Vedas, the Brāhmaṇas, Āraṇyakas and Upaniṣads, are likewise for the most part either anonymous or ascribed to figures from the legendary past.

Even when later Sanskrit texts are ascribed to individuals, the authors are often difficult to date with any precision, and the authenticity of the works ascribed to them has regularly been the subject of scholarly debate. The Buddhist philosopher and poet Aśvaghoṣa may have composed Sanskrit plays and epic poems in the first or second century of the common era, but scholars still debate which ones of the texts ascribed to him are really his. Some of the most beautiful and intricate poems and plays of the Sanskrit language are ascribed to the Hindu author Kālidāsa, but it is unclear whether he lived in the first century BCE or the fifth century CE. Some scholars argue that some of the works published under his name are not his, while others have proposed that there may have been multiple Kālidāsas. The names of famous Sanskrit authors, such as Kālidāsa, Vyāsa, Nagārjuna, Vasubandhu and Bhartṛhari, were associated with numerous works of differing quality that could not possibly stem from the same person.

The phenomenon of plagiarism, or presenting someone else's work as one's own in order to gain wealth or prestige, is entirely unknown in ancient India. In fact, many Sanskrit authors appear to have done precisely the opposite of what a plagiarist would do; instead of claiming credit for another's work, they claimed that their own work was composed by someone else, preferably a famous literary figure. Sometimes later authors might add to the texts of their predecessors, as was likely the case with Kālidāsa's well-known poem *Meghadūta* ("The Cloud Messenger").[4]

The authors of the Upaniṣads

Who composed the Upaniṣads? The texts are in all likelihood the literary products of scholarly collectives, rather than individual authors. The oldest Upaniṣads, like the Vedas before them, were transmitted orally within closed groups of Brahman priests who were trained religious specialists. These schools of transmission are called *śākhās*, "branches" or "schools." The *Caraṇavyūha* by Śaunaka lists all the known *śākhās* at the time. This list includes five schools of the *Ṛgveda*, forty-four schools of the *Yajurveda*, twelve of the *Sāmaveda*, and nine of the *Atharvaveda*. Many of these schools are now only known by name, while others have become extinct. A few still exist today; the *Mādhyaṃdina* school of the *White Yajurveda* is still popular in north India, the *Kāṇva* school of the *White Yajurveda* is kept alive by Kannada-speaking Brahmans in Karnataka in southwestern India, the *Taittirīya* school of the *Black Yajurveda* is present in south India, the *Jaiminīya* school of the *Sāmaveda* is recited among Nambudiri Brahmans in Tamilnadu in south India, etc.

Each *śākhā* is responsible for the accurate oral transmission of one of the Vedas (originally only the *Ṛgveda*, *Yajurveda*, and the *Sāmaveda*; later *Atharvaveda śākhās* also sprung up). Over time, each *śākhā* began adding different texts to the core Vedic text (*saṃhitā*) that they transmitted: Ritual texts called Brāhmaṇas, Āraṇyakas devoted to particularly dangerous or esoteric rites, and eventually Upaniṣads that explained the connection between a person's inner self (*ātman*) and the cosmic force (*brahman*). Many Upaniṣads are formally affiliated with a particular Veda, such as the *Ṛgveda* or the *Black Yajurveda*. This is not merely an arbitrary classification, but a statement of origin: The Upaniṣad originated within the scholarly and priestly communities that were responsible for transmitting that particular Veda. The Upaniṣads emerged as the intellectual products, not of individuals, but of schools of intellectuals who had specialized in one particular ancient Vedic text. Thus, the *Aitareya* and *Kauṣītaki Upaniṣad* were composed by priests who specialized in the transmission of the *Ṛgveda*, the *Taittirīya*, *Kaṭha*, and *Śvetāśvatara Upaniṣad* by specialists in the *Black Yajurveda* (a version of the text that includes commentary), the *Bṛhadāraṇyaka* and *Īśā Upaniṣad* by specialists in the *White Yajurveda* (the version without embedded commentary), the *Chāndogya* and *Kena Upaniṣad* by specialists in the *Sāmaveda*, and the *Muṇḍaka*, *Praśna*, and *Māṇḍūkya Upaniṣad* by priests trained in the tradition of the *Atharvaveda*.

Each *śākhā* must have regarded the texts they transmitted and composed as their own collective property, as indicated by the frequent warnings in the Upaniṣads against teaching the text to someone who is not one's son or student:

> So a father should teach this formulation of truth only to his oldest son or to a worthy student, and never to anybody else, even if he were to offer him this whole earth surrounded by waters and full of wealth, for this formulation is greater than all those things![5]
>
> This highest secret was proclaimed in a former age in the Vedānta. One would not reveal it to someone who does not have a calm disposition, or to one who is not one's son or student.[6]

Over time, however, Upaniṣads were gradually detached from their Vedic *śākhās* and began to assume a life of their own. By the time Śaṅkara composed his commentaries to ten (or eleven, if we accept his commentary on the *Śvetāśvatara* as genuine) of the oldest Upaniṣads in the eighth century, the *śākhā* affiliation of an Upaniṣad had become a mere formality, an archaic remnant from a former age.

Later Upaniṣads, like the medieval Upaniṣads devoted to gods such as Śiva, Viṣṇu or the Goddess or to the practice of Yoga or the renunciation of all worldly goods, still claim *śākhā* affiliations, but at this point, these associations with particular Vedas no longer tell us anything about the texts' authorship. Instead, these later Upaniṣads were composed by people who felt a strong affection for a particular deity, or by groups who embraced a specific lifestyle. Interestingly enough, even the later Upaniṣads are still anonymous. The ideas they promote are far more important than their authorship.

In the oldest Upaniṣads, the concerns of the *śākhā* that composed it still resonate throughout the texts. The *Ṛgveda* consists of hymns to the various Vedic deities, the *Sāmaveda* of chants to be sung during the Vedic rituals, the *Yajurveda* of sacrificial formulas and specific instructions for how to perform the elaborate Vedic rites. The *hotṛ*, or *Ṛgveda* priest, was in charge of invoking the gods during the Vedic ritual, the *udgātr*, or *Sāmaveda* priest would chant, the *adhvaryu* or *Yajurveda* priest was responsible for any ritual actions – and later a fourth priest, the *brahman*, associated with the *Atharvaveda*, was in charge of supervising the ritual as a whole. This ritual specialization is reflected in the texts each type of priest transmitted in his *śākhā*, including the Upaniṣads composed within that school. The Upaniṣads of the *Ṛgveda* include more references to Vedic gods and to the creation of the world than the Upaniṣads of other *śākhās*, while the Upaniṣads of the *Sāmaveda* are preoccupied with songs and chants and sacred sounds, the Upaniṣads of the *Yajurveda* with actions (*karma*) and their results, and the Upaniṣads of the *Atharveveda* dwell on understanding the mysterious *brahman*. These *śākhā*-specific concerns can be seen in all the oldest Upaniṣads, but are largely absent from the later Vaiṣṇava, Śaiva, Śākta, Yoga, or Saṃnyāsa Upaniṣads. These later Upaniṣads are still formally affiliated with particular *śākhās*, but the Vedic associations are no longer any indications of the text's themes; they seem to be more claims to ancient Vedic authority than anything else.

But if the oldest Upaniṣads were composed by Vedic *śākhās*, rather than by individual authors, how do we explain the strong individual voices that emerge from many of the Upaniṣadic texts? Charismatic teachers, proposing radical new ideas, are often described in the Upaniṣads: Yājñavalkya and King Janaka in the *Bṛhadāraṇyaka Upaniṣad*, Uddālaka Āruṇī, Sanatkumāra and Satyakāma Jābāla in the *Chāndogya Upaniṣad*, and Pippalāda in the *Praśna Upaniṣad*. Are these historical figures whose words and ideas have contributed to the Upaniṣads, or mere literary personifications of new and intriguing teachings flourishing during the time of the Upaniṣads? The Sanskrit scholar W. Ruben attempted to draw a portrait of each of the "philosophers of the Upaniṣads" and their teachings, and treated each Upaniṣadic teacher as a historical figure whose ideas were captured in the Upaniṣadic texts.[7] Since many of these teachers are legendary figures also mentioned in texts that are much older than the Upaniṣads, this seems unlikely. Yājñavalkya, the charismatic philosopher of the *Bṛhadāraṇyaka Upaniṣad*, is also featured in an older text from the same *śākhā*, the *Śatapathabrāhmaṇa* (ca. eighth century BCE). In the Brāhmaṇa text, as in the Upaniṣad, Yājñavalkya is demonstrating his great knowledge in front of king Janaka of Videha. Instead of explaining the ultimate truth about *ātman*, however, the Brāhmaṇa's Yājñavalkya tells the king how to perform the *Agnihotra* sacrifice, focusing on appropriate substitutions if one is missing one of the usual items needed for the sacrifice, such as rice, barley, or herbs.[8] Yājñavalkya's philosophy of salvation in the Upaniṣad is far removed from his ritual expertise in the Brāhmaṇa. The *character* of Yājñavalkya remains constant, however; he is just as knowledgeable and confident in both texts. Śvetaketu, a character from the *Bṛhadāraṇyaka* and *Chāndogya Upaniṣad*, also makes an appearance as a ritual expert in the earlier *Śatapathabrāhmaṇa*.[9] His character in the Upaniṣad is also very different from that in the Brāhmaṇa text. It does not seem likely, therefore, that either Yājñavalkya or Śvetaketu were modeled on actual historical figures preserved in the memories of the Upaniṣadic authors. Rather, they seem to be characters that function in a particular way within the texts of particular *śākhā*, in order to demonstrate specific forms of knowledge. The vividness of many of the Upaniṣadic characters likely owe more to the literary skills of the authors than to any inspiration they may have drawn from actual historical figures. As Patrick Olivelle has demonstrated in his study of Śvetaketu in the *Bṛhadāraṇyaka*, *Chāndogya*, and *Kauṣītaki Upaniṣad*,[10] Upaniṣadic authors may have particular theological and literary reasons for developing a character in a certain way.

Text as property

At the root of Western textual scholarship lies the notion of text as personal property. A text is often seen as the work and intellectual possession of one person, and any changes occurring to the text after its original creation are regarded in a negative light. To change a text composed by another is an infringement on the author's right of ownership over his or her text. Interpolations are seen, in some sense, as "copyright violations," and they are best removed in order that the author's *Urtext* (original text) can be restored.

Western textual scholars are notorious for imposing their own cultural ideas about authorship and individuality on ancient Sanskrit texts. The very learned Sanskrit scholar Hertel, for example, argued that the *Muṇḍaka Upaniṣad* must have been composed by at least three different authors or editors, based on whether or not particular verses had a breathing pause (caesura) in the middle.[11] As chronological study of Sanskrit meter shows, however, the caesura in this particular meter was weakening around the time when the *Muṇḍaka Upaniṣad* was likely composed; some verse lines had breathing pauses, and some did not. To assume that individual authors composed different parts of the text while making deliberate decisions about whether to include a caesura is to make things unnecessarily complicated.

Many Western scholars have ventured on quests for Upaniṣadic *Urtexts*, pruning away later verses or parts that did not strike them as original on other grounds, sometimes with questionable results. Otto Böhtlingk's reconstructed Upaniṣadic texts have been "emended" to the point where they have very little to do with the texts as they have traditionally been transmitted.[12] It is certainly legitimate to examine an ancient Sanskrit text with modern linguistic and textual tools and identify different chronological layers of a text. But to discard any portion of the text that may be a later interpolation is to ignore vital parts of the Upaniṣads' long and rich history of transmission.

When a text is composed by a collective, rather than by an individual, it will inevitably contain material from different sources, and perhaps also contradictory ideas. *All* of this material, is, however, a part of the Upaniṣadic text. Even material that seems so intellectually and stylistically unified that it could be the work of a single author could simply represent a form of the text that was edited by a particular person or group at one point in time.

As a case in point, we may turn to the oldest extant Upaniṣadic text, the *Bṛhadāraṇyaka Upaniṣad.* Through an accident of preservation, the *Bṛhadāraṇyaka Upaniṣad* has been transmitted in two distinct versions, the *Kāṇva* recension and the *Mādhyaṃdina* recension. These two versions of the same text differ considerably in linguistic form, and probably also in age. The fact that two distinct versions of this Upaniṣad exist serves as a reminder that each Upaniṣad must have flourished in multiple recensions at some point in time. We cannot, however, identify one of these recensions as the "original" one from which the other one was derived. The two recensions at our disposal are simply two distinct manifestations of the textual complex we call the *Bṛhadāraṇyaka Upaniṣad.* Which one is the real Upaniṣad? Clearly, they both are.

A sense of textual ownership is rarely encountered in ancient India. The Upaniṣads and other orally transmitted texts were not regarded as the intellectual property of individual authors. The Indian literary tradition has always placed a greater emphasis on authority than on authorship. The authority of an Upaniṣad is demonstrated through its affiliation with a Vedic school, through Vedic quotations and references to other well-known texts, through the appearance of trustworthy characters in the text, and finally and most importantly, through the soteriological message contained in the text itself.

If an Upaniṣad belongs to anyone, it belongs to the *śākhā* that transmitted it. It is within the *śākhā* that older texts were transmitted and new texts composed as the intellectual climate of the times changed. In the overall context of Hinduism, the Upaniṣads are relevant because they explain truths leading to liberation from *saṃsāra*, not because of who the composers of these texts were. The emphasis in Indian religious literature is always on the message, rather than the messenger.

The Upaniṣads were not regarded as the property of individual authors, but rather as the property of the transmitters of the *śākhā* who passed the text on to initiated students. For this reason, several Upaniṣadic texts are named after the schools that transmitted them: the *Aitareya Upaniṣad*, the *Taittirīya Upaniṣad*, the *Kaṭha Upaniṣad.*

Because the transmitters were, in some sense, the owners of the texts, they had the right to add, to explain, and to improve. Their voices are often woven into the transmitted text in the form of stanzas of commentary and interpolated passages. These interpolations do not, in the Indian cultural context, constitute a violation of the text, an infringement of unstated cultural "copyright rules." The "copyright" in ancient India belongs, not to the individual authors, but to the tradition of transmission itself.

Notes

1 *Śvetāśvatara Upaniṣad* 6.21.
2 M. Witzel, "Materialien zu den vedischen Schulen. I. Über die *Caraka-Śākhā* (Fortsetzung)" *Studien zur Indologie und Iranistik* 8–9 (1982–83): 183.
3 J. Hauer, *Der Yoga – Ein Indischer Weg zum Selbst*. Stuttgart: W. Kohlhammer, 1958: 118.
4 The first, more elegant, half of the poem is clearly the work of the author of the *Raghuvaṃśa* and *Śakuntalā*, whereas the second half appears to be composed by a much less proficient poet.
5 *Chāndogya Upaniṣad* 3.11.5.
6 *Śvetāśvatara Upaniṣad* 6.22.
7 W. Ruben, *Die Philosophen der Upaniṣaden*. Bern: A. Francke, 1947.
8 *Śatapathabrāhmaṇa* 11.3 ff.
9 *Śatapathabrāhmaṇa* 5.2.1.
10 Patrick Olivelle, "Yong Śvetaketu: A Literary Study of an Upaniṣadic Story" *Journal of the American Oriental Society* 119 (1999): 46–70.
11 J. Hertel, *Muṇḍaka Upaniṣad: Kritische Ausgabe mit Rodardruck der Erstausgabe. Indo-Iranische Quellen und Forschungen*, Heft III. Leipzig: H. Haessel Verlag, 1924.
12 See Patrick Olivelle, "Unfaithful Transmitters: Philological Criticism and Critical Editions of the Upaniṣads" *Journal of Indian Philosophy* 26 (1998): 173–187.

Further reading

Jha, V. N. (ed.) 1993. *Problems of Editing Ancient Texts*. Pune: Chaukhamba Sanskrit Pratisthan.

O'Flaherty, W. D. (ed.) 1979. *The Critical Study of Sacred Texts*. Berkeley, CA: Graduate Theological Union.

4 The redaction and transmission of the Upaniṣads

Signe Cohen

> This highest secret was proclaimed
> In the Vedānta in a former age.
> It should not be transmitted to one who is not tranquil,
> Or to one who is not a son or a student.[1]

This stanza from the *Śvetāśvatara Upaniṣad* tells us several essential things about the transmission of the Upaniṣads. First of all, the Upaniṣads are meant to be passed on within a particular scholastic lineage or within a family. Scholastic lineages have existed in India since Vedic times, and each Vedic text was passed to the next generation within a particular "school" (*śākhā*) of Vedic recitation. Each *śākhā* was responsible for the transmission of one of the Vedas, and each school added other texts to that of the original text or *saṃhitā* of the *Ṛgveda*, *Yajurveda*, *Sāmaveda*, and eventually also the *Atharvaveda*. Each *śākhā* composed Brāhmaṇa texts that explored the rituals in great detail, Āraṇyaka texts that described particularly dangerous and esoteric rites, and, eventually, Upaniṣads that explained the mystical unity between *ātman* and *brahman*. When we say, for example, that the *Bṛhadāraṇyaka Upaniṣad* is formally affiliated with the *White Yajurveda*, this means that this Upaniṣad was composed by the same lineage of scholars that was responsible for memorizing and transmitting the version of the *Yajurveda* known as the White recension. In the case of the older Upaniṣads, this affiliation with a particular school of Vedic transmission is usually genuine, and we can often see many of the ideas and concerns characteristic of that particular *śākhā* reflected in the Upaniṣad as well. Some of the latest Upaniṣads, however, such as the medieval Yoga or Saṃnyāsa ("renunciation") Upaniṣads, composed perhaps a millennium after the oldest Upaniṣadic texts, claim association with a particular Veda simply as a way to establish their textual authority. These texts were likely no longer composed by members of that particular school, and they were simply affiliated *post facto* with a Vedic *śākhā* because the older Upaniṣads claimed such affiliations.

Second, we should note that the stanza from the *Śvetāśvatara Upaniṣad* claims that the contents of the Upaniṣad are secret. The Upaniṣads often express the importance of confidential transmission of teachings, restricted to those who are granted privileged access to the sacred knowledge:

> "Yājñavalkya," said Ārtabhāga, "when a man dies, and his speech goes into the fire, and his breath into the wind, and his sight into the sun, his mind into the moon, his hearing into the directions of the sky, his body into the earth, his *ātman* into space, his body hair into the plants, the hair on his head into the trees, and his blood and semen into water – then what becomes of that man?"
>
> Yājñavalkya said: "My dear, we can't talk about this in public. Take my hand, Ārtabhāga, and let's go and discuss this privately."[2]
>
> So a father should teach this formulation of truth only to his oldest son or to a worthy student, and never to anybody else, even if he were to offer him this whole earth surrounded by waters and full of wealth, for this formulation is greater than all those things![3]
>
> "Come, I will tell you this secret and eternal *brahman*, and what happens to the *ātman* when it reaches death, Gautama."[4]

Passages like these suggest that the Upaniṣadic texts and their ideas were regarded as the property of the *śākhās* that transmitted them, and that the texts should not be made accessible to outsiders. In spite of these references to the Upaniṣadic doctrines as secret, there is some evidence, such as quotations that wander across *śākhā* boundaries, that the Upaniṣads were known outside the traditions of recitation that transmitted the texts from teachers to students.

What is the reason for the air of privacy and secrecy surrounding the Upaniṣadic doctrines? Access to the texts of a certain *śākhā* was traditionally limited to men trained in that specific tradition, or men belonging to other related schools of textual recitation. The insistence on secrecy in the Upaniṣads may, in part, be seen as a natural articulation of a closed system of textual transmission.

But additionally, the air of secrecy creates boundaries; knowledge is only accessible to those within the group. Secrecy is therefore an important factor in the creation of social identity and maintaining a text's prestige vis-à-vis rival textual traditions. As we know from the study of religious groups that invoke secrecy, such as Greek mystery religions and the Freemasons, the function of a code of secrecy is not merely to keep certain ideas away from the public eye, but also to create a sense of *communitas* between the initiates. Through secrecy a sense of community is imparted to the members of the *śākhā*, and the authority of the tradition is communicated to those who are not members.

And finally, the stanza from the *Śvetāśvatara Upaniṣad* quoted at the beginning of the chapter suggests that the teachings the Upaniṣad professes are not entirely new; they were already "taught in a former age." Although many of the teachings of the Upaniṣads are radically new, such as the idea of the mystical identity of *ātman* and *brahman*, *karma*, reincarnation, and the idea of a final liberation, the Upaniṣads do not discard their Vedic heritage easily. Even if Vedic ritualism is rejected in favor of knowledge as a path to salvation, there is still a desire to trace that highest knowledge back to the earlier tradition. Simply put, there is still a reverence for scholastic lineage in the Upaniṣads, probably because the oldest Upaniṣads themselves were produced precisely by scholars who transmitted the Vedas from generation to generation.

*Śākhā*s and quotations

The Upaniṣadic texts abound in references to other Upaniṣads, but this intricate net of cross-references is not completely arbitrarily structured. An Upaniṣadic text is far more likely to contain quotations from and references to another Upaniṣad from the same *śākhā* than a text completely unrelated to it. We see, for example, that the *Īśā Upaniṣad* quotes from the *Bṛhadāraṇyaka*, another text affiliated with the *White Yajurveda*, while the *Maitrī Upaniṣad* cites the *Śvetāśvatara* and the *Kaṭha*, two other texts of the *Black Yajurveda*.

We may assume that there was significant communication between related branches of textual transmission, whereas the texts of one branch would be less well known by scholars and students from rival branches. Since individual Upaniṣads sometimes refute the ideas of texts belonging to rival schools of transmission, however, we must assume that the Upaniṣadic authors also had some familiarity with the teachings of other schools. The Upaniṣadic teachings, although not accessible to all, were probably kept less secret than some of the passages quoted above would suggest. The admonitions to secrecy are perhaps better seen, not as historical fact, but rather as claims to ownership: This text belongs to our *śākhā*, and others should not have access to it.

The Upaniṣads and their "parent" texts

Some of the very oldest Upaniṣads are simply portions of larger late Vedic texts, later identified as "Upaniṣads" because they deal with themes common to other Upaniṣadic texts, such as the identification of *brahman* and *ātman*. The *Bṛhadāraṇyaka Upaniṣad*, for example, forms the conclusion to the *Śatapathabrāhmaṇa*, a ritual text affiliated with the *White Yajurveda*. Similarly, the *Chāndogya Upaniṣad* comprises the last eight of the ten chapters of the *Chāndogya Brāhmaṇa*, the *Aitareya Upaniṣad* constitutes chapter 2, sections 4–6 of the *Aitareya Āraṇyaka*, the *Īśā Upaniṣad* is chapter 40 of the *Vājasaneyi Saṃhitā*, the *Kena Upaniṣad* is found in *Jaiminīya Upaniṣad Brāhmaṇa* 4.18.1–4.21.1, the *Taittirīya Upaniṣad* comprises chapters 7, 8, and 9 of the *Taittirīya Āraṇyaka*, and the *Mahānārāyaṇa Upaniṣad* is sometimes, but not always, included as the tenth book of the *Taittirīya Āraṇyaka*. In these Upaniṣads, which are usually deeply embedded into their "parent" texts, themes from the "parent" text often reverberate.[5]

Even the Upaniṣads that are independent texts are ascribed to a school of Vedic textual transmission, a *śākhā*. The Vedic affiliation of the older Upaniṣadic texts is usually more than a mere formality; the *śākhā* affiliation is reflected on all textual levels, from grammatical and linguistic minutiae to philosophical themes. Texts ascribed to the *Atharvaveda*, for example, tend to describe *brahman* as the mysterious unknown that one must strive to understand, whereas texts affiliated with other schools describe *brahman* as the known, and *ātman* as the unknown. Upaniṣads affiliated with the *Sāmaveda*, the Veda of Chants, are especially concerned with sacred sounds, chants, and *mantras*. The *Ṛgveda*, the most ancient Sanskrit text of them all, contains numerous hymns to the various gods, and in particular Indra, the god of thunder and war. It is interesting to note, therefore, that Indra is treated far more favorably in the Upaniṣads affiliated with the *Ṛgveda* than in any others. Theism, or the worship of personal gods, is largely absent in the oldest Upaniṣads, except for those ascribed to the *Ṛgveda*, perhaps because gods play such a central role in the Veda the Upaniṣadic authors are tasked with transmitting. The *Yajurveda*, or the Veda of Sacrificial Formulas, was transmitted by those priests who were responsible for the practical actions (*karma*) during the Vedic sacrifice. It is no surprise, then, that the new Upaniṣadic ideas of *karma* as a universal principle of just retribution for one's actions emerges precisely in the Upaniṣads affiliated with the *Yajurveda*.

The transmission of mnemonic texts

How were the Upaniṣads transmitted? Like the Vedas, Brāhmaṇas and Āraṇyakas before them, the Upaniṣads were passed on orally from teachers to students. Writing was never highly valued in ancient India, perhaps because the spoken language itself was considered sacred from Vedic times onwards, personified as the goddess Vāc ("Speech"). Traditionally, only men of the three highest castes were permitted to study the Vedas. Keeping sacred texts inaccessible to certain groups of people (women, servants, and outcastes) was a great deal easier when the texts were not committed to writing, which can easily fall into the "wrong" hands. The Upaniṣads themselves provide several examples of esoteric teachings being transmitted both to women and to men of uncertain caste, but the admonitions to secrecy are still found throughout the Upaniṣads. It is likely that the Upaniṣads were transmitted, as the Vedas were, orally from teachers to students over the generations.

How reliable is the transmission of orally transmitted texts? As Patrick Olivelle has demonstrated in his essay "Unfaithful Transmitters," the received texts of the Upaniṣads are generally at least as reliable as the ones reconstituted by modern critical editions of the texts, if not more.[6] Since traditional Indian transmitters and commentators on the Upaniṣadic texts are generally reluctant to emend the text as it has been transmitted to them, whether the received text makes immediate sense or not, the Indian tradition is likely to keep examples of archaic or dialect usage, even if they do not represent "correct" Sanskrit. Many modern (especially Western) editors of the texts, however, are quick to "emend" the text to what they feel is more grammatical Sanskrit. "When European scholars change an unusual form to its 'correct' grammatical form, we lose much of the dialectical variations evident in old Sanskrit," writes Olivelle.[7]

While it makes perfect sense to leave the Sanskrit text of the Upaniṣads as it is, it is nevertheless possible to identify later additions to some of the Upaniṣads. Very often, these later additions, characterized by later grammatical forms and relatively modern metrical variants, are likely part of a teacher's explanation of the text, which somehow ended up embedded in the Upaniṣadic text itself. It makes little sense to prune off these later parts of the texts and leave them out altogether, as some Western editors of the Upaniṣads have done. Any later additions are, after all, a significant part of the text's history of transmission and tell us a great deal about how the text may have been viewed centuries after its initial composition.

Many scholars have wanted to restore the Upaniṣads to their "original forms," but the concept of an original text does not necessarily make sense when applied to an orally transmitted text. Textual criticism, the occupation of many Western scholars of ancient texts, has been defined as "the systematic and critical examination of textual material, which most often exists in the form of handwritten manuscripts ... in order to establish the form of the text which is as close as possible to the original."[8]

This definition of textual criticism is based on the assumption that texts are written, and, further, that an "original" text was composed at one specific point in time. Ancient Indian texts were not, however, originally written documents. Nevertheless, many Indologists have turned to the text-critical models developed by scholars of Greek and Latin when studying Sanskrit texts.

The critical study of ancient written texts often invokes a genealogical model: There must have existed an original text, from which all extant manuscripts are thought to be derived, often through a series of other manuscripts that may or may not have been preserved. A scholar will gather all available manuscripts, and the manuscripts are then compared to each other in order to establish the genealogical relationship between them. This relationship can be illustrated in the form of a *stemma*, a genealogical tree. The scholar will then attempt to reconstruct an *archetype*, a theoretical state of text from which all the extant manuscripts could have been derived. The archetype may not be identical to the original text, but represents the best text one can arrive at by means of the available manuscripts. The text-critical scholar will then use his or her analytical skills to determine if any parts of the text are later interpolations or additions.

An oral text, on the other hand, cannot be said to have an "original" form. Oral texts are often built up around a central story line and a set of formulaic phrases, and are in some sense created anew every time they are recited. As scholars of oral epics from various cultures have demonstrated, oral texts like the Sanskrit *Mahābhārata* or the Homeric epics from ancient Greece are not the products of a single author's imagination. Rather, these texts are more akin to folk tales and folk songs, in that they are the product of a collective creative imagination and have evolved over centuries. Each person reciting the text may present a different version, and each is what John Miles Foley has called "only one possible recension of a multiform."[9] It is meaningless to search for the "original" *Mahābhārata*, the original *Odyssey*, or the original fairy tale of Cinderella. An oral text may over time assume a fixed form and eventually be transmitted in writing. A text-critical scholar analyzing a text with a long oral history must, however, always bear in mind that it is essentially different from a written text, even if it currently exists in a written form.

The earliest Sanskrit literature cannot, however, be accurately described as oral literature in precisely the same sense as the *Mahābhārata* or the Homeric poems. The Vedas and the Upaniṣads were transmitted orally, but unlike the oral epics, the texts were transmitted in a fairly fixed form. A highly developed mnemonic culture existed in ancient India, and students were expected to memorize the texts recited by their teachers very precisely. Sophisticated mnemonic techniques were developed to ensure that the transmission was flawless. Like the earliest Vedic texts, the Upaniṣads were committed to memory and recited from memory. Although the transmission of the Upaniṣads was not as strictly codified as that of the Vedas, it would still be misleading to classify the Upaniṣads as "oral literature" in the sense this term is most often used to refer to oral epics or folktales. A better designation for the earliest Indian texts, such as the Upaniṣads and the Vedas, would be *mnemonic literature*. Mnemonic literature is transmitted orally, like oral texts, but in a fixed form somewhat akin to written literature.

The distinction proposed here between oral and mnemonic texts corresponds in many ways to the indigenous Indian distinction between *śruti* and *smṛti*, texts that are "heard" and texts that are "remembered." The category of *śruti* encompasses mnemonic texts like the Vedas and the Upaniṣads, whereas *smṛti* is a category that contains the oral epics *Mahābhārata* and *Rāmāyaṇa*. *Śruti* implies a direct recitation of the text as heard, whereas *smṛti* implies, perhaps, a re-creation of the text from memory.

Śaṅkara and the transmission of the Upaniṣads

Often, the Upaniṣads are deeply embedded in commentarial works that explain the doctrines of the texts. The most famous commentaries to the Upaniṣads are those of Śaṅkara (eighth century CE), although numerous other commentaries may have existed before his. The only other pre-Śaṅkara commentary that has been preserved is Gauḍapāda's commentary on the *Māṇḍūkya Upaniṣad*.

Śaṅkara composed commentaries to ten (possibly eleven) of the oldest Upaniṣads: *Bṛhadāraṇyaka Upaniṣad*, *Chāndogya Upaniṣad*, *Aitareya Upaniṣad*, *Taittirīya Upaniṣad*, *Kena Upaniṣad*, *Īśā Upaniṣad*, *Kaṭha Upaniṣad*, *Muṇḍaka Upaniṣad*, *Praṣṇa Upaniṣad*, and *Māṇḍūkya Upaniṣad*. Śaṅkara may also be the author of a commentary on the *Śvetāśvatara Upaniṣad*. It is interesting to note that there are more textual variations in those of the oldest Upaniṣads that Śaṅkara ignored: the *Kauṣītaki Upaniṣad* and the *Maitrī Upaniṣad*. Both of these texts exist in several recensions that are quite different from one another. It is likely that Śaṅkara's popular and authoritative commentaries, which contained the texts of the Upaniṣads he was discussing, helped to establish authoritative versions of the Upaniṣadic texts themselves. Śaṅkara is not known to have been affiliated with any particular Vedic *śākhā*, but in many ways, his work on the Upaniṣads became the new standard for the generations after him, both for the interpretation of the texts and for establishing authoritative versions of the Upaniṣads.

Notes

1 *Śvetāśvatara Upaniṣad* 6.22.
2 *Bṛhadāraṇyaka Upaniṣad* 3.2.13.
3 *Chāndogya Upaniṣad* 3.11.5.
4 *Kena Upaniṣad* 5.6.
5 See Steven E. Lindquist's unpublished conference paper "Food, Sacrifice, and 'Deities' in *Aitareya Upanishad:* A Study in Vedic Intertextuality."
6 Olivelle 1998.
7 Olivelle 1998: 181.
8 Haugen and Thomassen 1990: 128.
9 Foley 1984: 81.

Further reading

Coburn, T. 1984. "'Scripture' in India: Toward a Typology of the Word in Hindu Life" *Journal of the American Academy of Religion* 52: 435–459.

Foley, J. M. 1984. "Editing Oral Epic Texts: Theory and Practice" in D. C. Greetham and W. Speed Hill (eds) *TEXT. Transactions of the Society for Textual Scholarship*, 1. New York: AMS Press.

Haugen, O. E., and Thomassen, E. 1990. *Den filologiske vitenskap*. Oslo: Solum.

Olivelle, P. 1998. "Unfaithful Transmitters: Philological Criticism and Critical Editions of the Upaniṣads" *Journal of Indian Philosophy* 26: 173–187.

Part II

The historical, cultural, and religious background of the Upaniṣads

5 Ancient India

Geographical, historical, and cultural background

Signe Cohen

Sanskrit, the ancient sacred language of Hinduism, was once spoken over large parts of what is today north India. The oldest surviving Sanskrit texts, the Vedas (composed ca. 1500–1000 BCE), are the holiest texts of Hinduism. Towards the end of the Vedic period, the Upaniṣads emerge as a separate genre of religious and philosophical literature. What do we know about the geographical, historical, and cultural background from which these significant texts emerged?

The Upaniṣads were composed during one of the most fascinating time periods in ancient Indian history. Around the time when the melodious Sanskrit of the Upaniṣads was first recited, two other religious traditions arose in India: Jainism and Buddhism, religions which challenged both the old pantheon of Hindu gods and established ideas about social hierarchy. In the Upaniṣads themselves, we can see religious and social ideas changing. Old ideas about a vaguely imagined heaven are replaced with new notions of reincarnation and liberation; the idea of individual *karma* replaces earlier speculations about the benefits to be gained from performing intricate sacrifices correctly. The worship of gods and goddesses of nature is gradually supplanted by meditations on the abstract cosmic force *brahman*. In this intellectually fertile climate, ideas traveled freely between the Hindu Upaniṣads and the texts of the emerging new religions of Jainism and Buddhism.

Geographical background

Based on place names mentioned in the texts, we know that the Upaniṣads were composed in areas of today's north India, from the Indus Valley in the northwest to the mouth of the Ganges river in the Bay of Bengal in the east, from the Himalaya mountains in the north to the Vindhya mountains in the south.

There have been attempts (notably Witzel 1987) at placing each individual Upaniṣad within a particular geographical area. The Videha region in eastern India (corresponding roughly to the modern state of Bihar) plays a significant part in the *Bṛhadāraṇyaka Upaniṣad*, while the Pañcāla region a little further to the west (roughly modern Uttar Pradesh) plays a larger role in the *Chāndogya Upaniṣad.*

The *Kauṣītaki Upaniṣad* lists the places one well-traveled man has visited, which gives us a good indication of the geography known to the Upaniṣadic authors: Uśinara (in present-day Panjab in the northwest), the land of Satvan (location unknown) and Matsya (present-day Rajasthan), Kuru and Pañcāla, Kāśī (Varanasi), and Videha (present-day Mithila/Bihar).

Many ancient Indian texts mention sixteen "Great Realms" (*mahājanapada*) in north India. Several of these are mentioned in the Upaniṣads: Kāśī (modern day Varanasi), Gandhāra (parts of modern-day Pakistan and Afghanistan), Kosala (modern-day Uttar Pradesh), Kuru (from around Delhi to western Uttar Pradesh), Matsya (around Jaipur), and Pañcāla (just east of Kuru). The Pañcāla-Kosala-Videha region is mentioned more often than any other in the older Upaniṣads. The "Great Realms" furthest from the Pañcāla-Kosala-Videha center, Aṅga further east, Assaka in the south, and Kamboji in the far north get no mention in the Upaniṣads at all. Gandhāra is mentioned in the *Chāndogya Upaniṣad,*[1] but only as an example of a far-away land.

Historical background

Whereas ancient Egyptian or Chinese scholars kept meticulous records of historical facts such as names and dates of kings and dynasties, the intellectuals of ancient India did not find such details of mundane life particularly interesting. Instead of writing history books, ancient Indian authors composed literary works, philosophical treatises, and works on mathematics, astronomy, and grammar. There are occasional glimpses of a king or a battle in texts devoted to other subjects, but overall, it is extremely difficult to reconstruct a reliable history of ancient India based on the textual sources available today. Even when texts are supplemented by archaeological and numismatic material, art and material culture, and travelers' accounts, there remain significant gaps in the modern knowledge of ancient Indian history. It is nevertheless possible to get a glimpse of ancient north Indian society from the texts of the Upaniṣads and compare this with information from other sources.

Significantly, the time period during which the oldest Upaniṣads are likely to have been composed is also an era of growing urbanization in northern India. From around 500 BCE onward, cities like Varanasi, Campā, Rājagṛha, and Ujjain began to flourish.[2] Trade becomes increasingly important, and silver and copper punch-mark coins are issued in this time period.

Agriculture was the main livelihood, and rice was a main crop. Ploughs were widely used. Agricultural pests were also known; the *Chāndogya Upaniṣad* states that the land of Kuru was once devastated by locusts.[3] Cows, which had been highly valued during the previous Vedic period as well, were still vitally important in the Upaniṣadic period, and a man's wealth was often measured by the number of cows he owned. When king Janaka of Videha offers a prize of a thousand cows to the most learned priest in the third chapter of the

Bṛhadāraṇyaka Upaniṣad, this is clearly a dazzling reward which everyone would want to win. Horses were domesticated, as were goats and sheep. There is frequent reference to milk, butter, and yoghurt in the Upaniṣads, as well as to sesame oil. The *Bṛhadāraṇyaka Upaniṣad* mentions cooked rice mixed with yoghurt and butter, cooked rice with sesame seeds and butter, and cooked rice with meat and butter,[4] which suggests that people may have eaten both vegetarian and non-vegetarian meals at the time of this Upaniṣad.

Horse-drawn chariots are frequently mentioned, while riding directly on a horse seems to be less common. Both sacred and secular music played an important part in people's lives. "The world of singing and music" is cited as one example of something that people might want in the *Chāndogya Upaniṣad*.[5]

Monarchy was the prevailing form of government. The ritual of anointing a king is mentioned in passing in the *Bṛhadāraṇyaka Upaniṣad*,[6] as is the possibility of appealing one's case to the king.[7] Kings appoint administrators to help with the day-to-day tasks of local rule, as suggested by the *Praśna Upaniṣad*: "As a king appoints administrators, telling them: You rule over these villages, and you rule over these other villages," in the same way the life-breath assigns the other breaths to their places.[8]

Several kings are mentioned by name in the Upaniṣads: King Janaka of Videha in the *Bṛhadāraṇyaka Upaniṣad*, King Ajātaśatru of Kāśī in the *Bṛhadāraṇyaka Upaniṣad* and the *Kauṣītakii Upaniṣad*, King Jaivali Pravāhaṇa of Pañcāla in the *Bṛhadāraṇyaka Upaniṣad* and *Chāndogya Upaniṣad*, and a King Bṛhadratha in the *Maitrī Upaniṣad*. None of these kings are known from other historical sources. A king Ajātaśatru ruled over Māgadha around 492–460 BCE, but it is very unlikely that the *Bṛhadāraṇyaka Upaniṣad*, which refers to king Ajātaśatru, could have been composed that late. There was a historical king by the name of Bṛhadratha (Bṛhadratha Maurya, who ruled over the Maurya Empire from about 187–180 BCE), but there is no evidence to tie him to the king of the same name mentioned in the *Maitrī Upaniṣad*. It is worth noting that while the Upaniṣads contain several lineages of students and teachers, there are no royal lineages. The Upaniṣads are simply not concerned with the history of politically powerful men; their goal is salvation, and only those kings searching for the knowledge that can lead to the ultimate understanding of *ātman* and *brahman* are of interest to the Upaniṣadic authors.

Cultural background

The society of the Sanskrit-speakers who called themselves Aryans was hierarchical in nature. People were divided into four castes (*varṇa*), or social classes: 1) *Brahmans*, priests, 2) *Kṣatriyas*, warriors, 3) *Vaiśyas*, farmers and merchants, and 4) *śūdras*, servants. This social stratification can still be observed in present-day India, although the caste system is no longer legal.

There is some evidence in the Vedas and Upaniṣads, however, that the caste system was not as rigid in the earliest times. While caste later became strictly hereditary and marriage between people from different caste backgrounds strongly discouraged, there are several examples in earlier texts of a more flexible caste system. It is quite possible, therefore, that caste was originally an occupational category rather than a fixed status based on one's parentage.

In the Upaniṣads, Brahman priests are still important, and Brahmans such as Yājñavalkya play a central part in the texts. But while Brahmans were integral to the earlier Vedic religion because only they could perform the intricate sacrificial rituals, the Upaniṣads show that it is not necessary to be a Brahman to understand the truth about *ātman* ("the self") and *brahman* ("the cosmic force"). When the priest Dṛpta Bālāki tries to teach king Ajātaśatru the truth about *brahman*, he discovers that the king actually understands *brahman* far better than he does, and he ends up asking the king to be his teacher instead.[9] Traditionally, Brahmans are the religious teachers, and for a priest to become the disciple of a king, who is a Kṣatriya by caste, is a "reversal of the norm."[10]

The Upaniṣads do suggest, however, that true knowledge can be found outside the closed group of specialized Brahmans. A worthy wisdom teacher can, in the Upaniṣads, be a king, a man of unknown caste,[11] or even an animal.[12] The previous role of Brahmans as sole proprietors of sacred knowledge is considerably weakened in the Upaniṣads. Brahmans can still be wise, like Yājñavalkya and Naciketas, but they attain prestige through the depth of their knowledge and their passion for further learning, not through the position into which they were born. A hierarchy of caste is still quite visible in the Upaniṣads, however, and it is an insult to call someone a Śūdra.[13]

The relative prominence of Kṣatriyas in the Upaniṣads have inspired speculations that the Upaniṣadic texts themselves may have originated in Kṣatriya, rather than Brahman, circles. As Brian Black and others have demonstrated, however, Kṣatriya authorship of the Upaniṣads is quite unlikely,[14] and most of the ideas voiced by Kṣatriyas in the Upaniṣads can be traced back to older Brahmanical texts. It is far more likely that the Upaniṣadic scenes where kings become the teachers of Brahmans are meant to demonstrate in a striking way that knowledge of *ātman* and *brahman* is far more important than ritual training.

The primary social relationship described in the Upaniṣads is that between a teacher and his students. It is the role of the teacher to impart knowledge to those who earnestly seek it, and it is the role of the student to seek knowledge of the ultimate reality. As Brian Black has noted, the Upaniṣadic teachers use different pedagogical tecniques; Uddālaka Āruṇi teaches Śvetaketu through practical hands-on experiments, Prajāpati teaches Indra by giving him initial false and incomplete information and waiting for his student to challenge him, and Yama teaches Naciketas through a difficult initiation.[15]

Gender in the Upaniṣads

The earliest Hindu tradition generally privileges the male over the female. While a few goddesses are mentioned in the Vedas, such as Uṣas, the goddess of dawn, and Vāc, the personification of sacred speech, the goddesses are vastly outnumbered by the male gods. Most named characters in the Vedas are male, and Vedic rituals are mostly performed by men and for men. Women did play a small, but significant part in the Vedic ritual, but mostly in their prescribed minor role as "the sacrificer's wife."[16]

There are, however, some indications of slightly more complex gender roles in the Upaniṣads. Two significant female characters, Gārgī Vācaknavī and Maitreyī, participate in religious and philosophical discussions with men.

According to *Bṛhadāraṇyaka Upaniṣad* 5.2–, the famous wisdom teacher Yājñavalkya has two wives, Maitreyī and Kātyāyanī. He decides to leave them both and devote himself fully to his search for religious meaning:

> "Maitreyī," said Yājñavalkya. "I am about to leave this place. So come and let me settle things between you and Katyāyanī."
>
> Maitreyī said: "If I were to own the whole earth full of wealth, sir, would I become immortal by that?" "No," said Yājñavalkya, "it will only let you live like a rich person. One cannot hope for immortality through wealth."
>
> Maitreyī said: "What use do I have for something that will not make me immortal? Tell me, sir, everything you know instead."
>
> Yājñavalkya said: "You have always been dear to me, and the way you speak now is dear to me. Come and sit, and I will explain it to you. Pay attention while I am explaining."

Maitreyī wisely chooses the gift of insight over material wealth. Kātyāyanī, her co-wife, has no speaking part in this Upaniṣad, but we are left to assume that she accepted the wealth without expressing an interest in religious or philosophical ideas. The Yājñavalkya-Maitreyī dialogue has frequently been read as a text indicating that the philosophy of the Upaniṣads is accessible to both men and women. Maitreyī is not her husband's equal, but he does treat her with love and respect and invites her to share in the metaphysical truths he has discovered.

While Maitreyī simply listens and learns while her husband Yājñavalkya speaks, another female character challenges some of Yājñavalkya's ideas. In the third chapter of the *Bṛhadāraṇyaka Upaniṣad*, Yājñavalkya encounters several wisdom teachers at the royal court of King Janaka and defeats them all in debate. The most intriguing among his intellectual challengers in the woman Gārgī Vācaknavī. She asks Yājñavalkya what lies beyond the visible world, and she uses the metaphor of weaving, drawing on a real-world skill with which many women in ancient India would have been familiar: "Tell me, since this whole world is woven back and forth on water, on what is water woven back and forth?"

As Yājñavalkya answers her questions, she keeps asking for something beyond the element Yājñavalkya identifies:

> "On air, Gārgī."
> "On what is air woven back and forth?"
> "On the worlds of the intermediate space, Gārgī."
> "On what are the worlds of the intermediate space woven back and forth?"
> "On the worlds of the Gandharvas, Gārgī."
> "On what are the worlds of the Gandharvas woven back and forth?"
> "On the worlds of the sun, Gārgī."
> "On what are the worlds of the sun woven back and forth?"
> "On the worlds of the moon, Gārgī."
> "On what are the worlds of the moon woven back and forth?"
> "On the worlds of the stars, Gārgī."
> "On what are the worlds of the stars woven back and forth?"
> "On the worlds of the gods, Gārgī."
> "On what are the worlds of the gods woven back and forth?"
> "On the worlds of Indra, Gārgī."
> "On what are the worlds of Indra woven back and forth?"
> "On the worlds of Prajāpati, Gārgī."
> "On what are the worlds of Prajāpati woven back and forth?"
> "On the worlds of *brahman*, Gārgī."
> "On what are the worlds of *brahman* woven back and forth?"
>
> Then Yājñavalkya said to her: "Do not ask beyond, Gārgī, or your head will split apart. You are asking beyond a deity one should not ask beyond. So Gārgī, do not ask beyond!" Then Gārgī Vācaknavī was silent.

The silencing of Gārgī can be interpreted in several different ways. It is possible that there is a gendered aspect to the discussion between Gārgī and Yājñavalkya, and that Yājñavalkya's final threat that leads to Gārgī's silence should be read as male authority resorting to threats of violence in order to silence a woman's voice. In the context of the Upaniṣads, Yājñavalkya's threat is not an idle one, however; another one of Yājñavalkya's opponents fails to heed a similar warning, and his head does indeed split apart.

But Gārgī Vācaknavī's name suggests that she is no novice when it comes to religious debate; the name "Gārgī" indicates that may be a descendant of the well-known Vedic sage Garga, and "Vācaknavī" means "eloquent." Her very name evokes a prestigious lineage of scholars and great learning. She alone among Yājñavalkya's debate opponents gets to challenge him twice, which elevates her above the other debaters, whose arguments are more easily dismissed. Since Gārgī's final question relates to the ineffable *brahman*, it is possible that Yājñavalkya's admonition to silence is not a mere patronizing dismissal of her question, but rather an indication that the debate has reached the point where nothing more can possibly be said: *brahman* is the ultimate cause, and there is nothing beyond.

Lindquist, in his study of women in the *Bṛhadāraṇyaka Upaniṣad*, warns against reading the Gārgī and Maitreyī episodes as evidence for the actual position of women in ancient Indian society, and suggests that scholars should instead focus on how these female characters function within the narrative of the text.[17]

The ritual to get "a learned daughter" mentioned in *Bṛhadāraṇyaka Upaniṣad* 6.4.17 suggests that Gārgī and Maitreyī may not have been anomalies among ancient Indian women in embracing scholarship and religious wisdom. The goddess Umā makes a brief appearance in *Kena Upaniṣad* 3–4, where she explains the highest *brahman* to the bewildered god Indra, further reinforcing the idea that the wisdom of the Upaniṣads was regarded as accessible to both males and females.

It is nevertheless the case, as Black has demonstrated, that the Upaniṣadic teachings about *ātman* are aimed at a predominantly male audience, and that *ātman* itself is described in terms relating to the male body.[18] *Puruṣa*, the cosmic person that is often identified with the *ātman*, is invariably gendered as male. The world of the Upaniṣads was, without doubt, still a patriarchal one, albeit one where women's voices were occasionally heard.

Notes

1 *Chāndogya Upaniṣad* 6.14.1.
2 Bronkhorst 2007: 4.
3 *Chāndogya Upaniṣad* 1.10.1.
4 *Bṛhadāraṇyaka Upaniṣad* 6.4.15–18.
5 *Chāndogya Upaniṣad* 8.2.8.
6 *Bṛhadāraṇyaka Upaniṣad* 1.4.11.
7 *Bṛhadāraṇyaka Upaniṣad* 1.4.14.
8 *Praśna Upaniṣad* 3.4.
9 *Bṛhadāraṇyaka Upaniṣad* 2.1.14.
10 *Bṛhadāraṇyaka Upaniṣad* 2.1.15.
11 Satyakāma Jābāla in *Chāndogya Upaniṣad* 4.4.
12 *Chāndogya Upaniṣad* 4.5.
13 *Chāndogya Upaniṣad* 4.2.
14 Black 2007: 103–105.
15 Black 2007: 57.
16 For a discussion of the role of women in Vedic rituals, see Stephanie Jamison, *Sacrificed Wife, Sacrificer's Wife: Women, Ritual, and Hospitality in Ancient India*. Oxford: Oxford University Press, 1996.
17 Linquist 2008.
18 Black 2007: 133ff.

Further reading

Black, B. 2007. *The Character of the Self in Ancient India. Priests, Kings, and Women in the Early Upaniṣads*. Albany, NY: State University of New York Press.

Bronkhorst, J. 2007. *Greater Magadha: Studies in the Culture of Early India*. Leiden: Brill.

Findly, E. B. 1985. "Gārgī at the King's court: Women and Philosophic Innovation in Ancient India" in Y. Y. Haddad and E. B. Findly (eds.) *Women, Religion, and Social Change*. New York: State University of New York, 37–58.

Jamison, S. 1996. *Sacrificed Wife, Sacrificer's Wife: Women, Ritual, and Hospitality in Ancient India*. New York/Oxford: Oxford University Press.

Lindquist, S. 2008. "Gender at Janaka's Court: Women in the *Bṛhadāraṇyaka Upaniṣad* Reconsidered" *Journal of Indian Philosophy* 36 (3): 405–426.

Thapar, R. 1978. *Ancient Indian Social History: Some Interpretations*. New Delhi: Orient Longman.

Witzel, M. 1987. "On the Localisation of Vedic Texts and Schools (Materials on Vedic Śākhas, 7)" in Gilbert Pollet (ed.) *India and the Ancient World: History, Trade and Culture before A. D. 650*. Leuwen: Department Orientalistik, 173–213.

6 The older Vedas and the Upaniṣads

Dermot Killingley

Veda

The word *veda* literally means "knowledge"; it is related to the verb *vetti* "knows." But whereas this verb can be used in a variety of contexts, the noun *veda* is restricted to a particular kind of knowledge, which is not easy to define. It includes ritual matters, and knowledge of the gods and the world beyond. But it can also refer to subjects as diverse as medicine and archery, as is shown by the name of the ancient Indian medical tradition, *Āyur-veda* "knowledge of long life," or the less well-known *dhanur-veda* "knowledge of the bow." Generally, *veda* is knowledge that is not altered by day-to-day circumstances, but is handed down unchanged for ever, usually in the form of texts. Although in the modern world a subject like medicine or weaponry changes so frequently that knowledge of it quickly becomes obsolete, and older practitioners often need to learn from their juniors, the ancient Indian view is that we learn from our elders, receiving knowledge handed down from earlier times. Ideas and practices did in fact change, as we shall see when discussing the history of Vedic thought and ritual, but change was usually expressed through reinterpretation of ancient texts, and by using old words and phrases in new senses. The idea that knowledge has been received and handed down through the generations from the ancients, and should be revered because it is ancient, is an essential part of the Vedic world-view. A similar view of knowledge prevailed in Europe until the Renaissance.

Veda in its usual sense means not just any kind of knowledge, but knowledge in the form of a text, and concerned with ritual. Traditions of knowledge such as Āyurveda and Dhanurveda are referred to – in post-Vedic texts – as *upaveda*s, "additional knowledges." The rituals will be discussed further in Chapter 7, but we cannot describe the Vedas without referring to ritual, because it underlies their structure; the Vedas represent the knowledge required to perform particular ritual functions, and each Veda provides a particular kind of ritual functionary with the knowledge he requires. ("He" because, although women have roles in the ritual, and named women are recorded as having contributed to the Vedas, the specialists who received and handed on the texts were required to be male.) These specialists are conventionally called priests, though as with all translated terms we should avoid letting it evoke irrelevant connotations.

The texts were not written down; they were transmitted orally, from teacher to student. (In the context of mobile phones, the word *text* is opposed to *voice*; but in the present context any sequence of words can be called a text, whether spoken or written.) This is reflected in another word for the Vedas, *śruti*, which means "hearing, what is heard." The Vedas consist essentially of sound; the Vedic texts do not mention writing, and even when writing became known, it was considered sinful to use it for the Vedas. As a verse in the *Mahābhārata* puts it, "Those who sell the Vedas, those who disparage the Vedas, and those who write the Vedas go to hell" (Mbh 13.24.70). Passing them on orally was itself a ritual act, in which the student repeated the words, and in the case of sung texts the melody, exactly as he heard them performed by the teacher. Rules for the conduct of both student and teacher during this process may be found in the second chapter of the law-book attributed to Manu (Olivelle 2005: 104–107); they are based on similar rules in older texts. In time, reciting the texts outside their ritual context became a ritual of its own (Killingley 2014).

It is often assumed by scholars who are not specialists in Indian studies that only written texts can be stable, and that oral texts are necessarily fluid. It has even been argued that the idea of a fixed text could not have arisen in a culture where writing was unknown (Goody 1987: 189). There is no doubt that many oral traditions do allow each reciter to introduce variants into what he or she has heard, whether by mistake or to exercise original artistry; this happens with ballads and folk songs, and in many epic traditions (Chadwick and Chadwick 1932–40; Lord 1960; Ong 1982). There is also no doubt that writing and printing have standardized such texts and given them a fixed form which they did not have before. But this is not an invariable rule (Killingley 2014: 124–126). It certainly does not apply in the history of India, where the *Mahābhārata*, which exists in hundreds of manuscripts, has variants in nearly every verse, and whole passages which exist in some versions but not others; whereas the Veda, which is transmitted orally, is remarkably stable. There are manuscripts of the Veda, but they are not as authoritative as the oral tradition. Writing is a useful technique for fixing a text, but it does not always do so, and other techniques for this purpose exist. Sound recording is one; another, analogous to it (Witzel 2003: 68), is strictly regulated oral transmission.

Reciting the Veda, unlike singing ballads or reciting oral epics, left no room for individual error or creativity. Transmitting the text from teacher to student required a great deal of time and effort, made possible by the existence of a class of people who were valued for their ability to perform rituals, including the speaking and singing of ritual texts, and who owed their personal status and family prestige to this ability. This class was called *brāhmaṇa*, meaning people of *brahman*, a word which, among many meanings, means the Vedic ritual and the Vedic texts. The word *brāhmaṇa* in this sense (it can also mean a class of texts, but we will come to that meaning later in this chapter) is commonly anglicized as *brahmin*, and we will use this form for convenience. We can get an idea of how brahmins' prestige depended on knowledge of texts from a story in the Upaniṣads of a father sending his son to study the Veda. He tells him:

> There is nobody in our family who has not studied and is only brahmin-related.
>
> (CU 6.1.1)

To be only brahmin-related (*brahma-bandhu*) is to be a brahmin by birth, without having the knowledge of the Veda which makes a true brahmin. Accordingly, the son goes away at the age of twelve, and comes back aged twenty-four having studied all the Vedas. A twelve-year period of study is often mentioned.

People unfamiliar with the subject often ask when the Vedas were written, but writing plays only a secondary part in their history; what they mean to ask is when the Vedas were composed. There are several answers to this question, from different points of view; some of them are discussed in Chapter 2. But the answer expressed by Sanskrit commentators on Vedic and other texts is that they were never composed, because they are eternal. Even if this answer is inconsistent with our view of the world, we should be aware of it if we are to understand Hindu texts, including the Upaniṣads themselves.

One Veda, three Vedas, four Vedas

Upaniṣads and other Vedic texts, and later Sanskrit texts, sometimes speak of "the Veda" in the singular, but they also call it the "three Vedas," or the "triple knowledge" (*trayī vidyā*). This refers to three collections of orally transmitted texts – the *Ṛgveda*, the *Yajurveda*, and the *Sāmaveda* – which contain the utterances spoken or sung in the Vedic ritual. These collections consist of three types of text: *ṛc*, *yajuṣ*, and *sāman*. (The difference between the individual words *ṛc* and *yajuṣ* and the forms *ṛg-* and *yajur-* which appear in the titles *Ṛgveda* and *Yajurveda* is a matter of sandhi, something which anyone studying Sanskrit learns about very soon, but which is outside the scope of this book. The difference between *sāman* and *sāma-* is a matter of grammar, which again does not concern us here.) Each of these collections is called a *saṃhitā*, meaning "collection," so their full names are *Ṛgveda Saṃhitā, Yajurveda Saṃhitā*, and *Sāmaveda Saṃhitā*. Together they constitute the Veda.

A *ṛc* is a stanza of three or four lines, metrical but unrhymed, which forms part of a hymn (*sūkta*), typically of around ten stanzas, praising or praying to a particular god. ("Lines" is an anachronism, since it refers to the way a stanza is laid out on a page; the Sanskrit word is *pāda*, meaning literally "foot.") The conventional term "hymn" is misleading if you associate it with congregational singing; it was chosen by European scholars, many of whom had studied Latin and ancient Greek before they studied Sanskrit, because the ancient Greek word *húmnos* meant a poem in praise of a god or hero. A *yajuṣ* is a phrase or sentence, usually in prose, which is pronounced while performing a particular action in the course of the ritual. These are often very simple phrases such as "O Viṣṇu, guard the offering" (*Taittirīya Saṃhitā* 1.1.3); they are not spoken aloud but muttered. A *sāman* is a tune to which a stanza is sung. The Sāmaveda includes words, most of them stanzas selected from the *Ṛgveda*. But these words are included only because the tunes would not be complete without them; the purpose of the Sāmaveda is to transmit the tunes (Gonda 1975: 314). The tunes, like the texts, are transmitted orally, without musical notation.

The general word for all these kinds of utterance – the spoken *ṛc*, the muttered *yajuṣ*, and the sung *sāman* – is *mantra*. Later, this word was applied to many other kinds of ritual utterance, such as *namaḥ śivāya* "Homage to Śiva," or *oṃ namo nārāyaṇāya* "Homage to Nārāyaṇa [a name of Viṣṇu]" (Gonda 1977: 247; 285); the syllables spoken and written in Tantric rites (Padoux 2003: 484–491); or the spells used by magicians, who are known as *mantravādī*s "mantra-speakers" (Fuller 1992: 237). What all these kinds of *mantra* have in common is that the form of words itself has power; a paraphrase or a translation would not have the same effect. There was even controversy among philosophers as to whether *mantra*s have meaning (Renou 1965: 46–50); certainly they are not part of ordinary language, and they are considered to be of superhuman origin.

Each of these three Vedas is learnt by a particular class of liturgical specialists, and used by them in performing their particular role in the ritual. The *Ṛgveda* is used by the *hotṛ*, the priest who invokes the gods and pours offerings (etymologically, the word can mean either). The *adhvaryu*, who with his team of assistants performs the manual operations of the ritual, mutters *yajuṣ*es to accompany actions such as laying out the consecrated ground, or placing an offering in the fire. The *sāman*s are sung by the *udgātṛ* and his team, especially in the rituals involving Soma, the sacred drink which is also a god. (We use the present tense here, but we are really describing the practice of the past; Vedic rituals are still occasionally performed, but these performances are reconstructions of past rituals, divorced from the social, political, and economic context, as well as much of the belief system, which supported Vedic ritual in ancient times.) The whole laborious process of transmitting the texts – including the music – was for the purpose of ritual performance, and the development of three Vedas, from what once was a single body of tradition, reflects the development of specialized ritual functions.

The hotṛ and the adhvaryu, and in some cases the udgātṛ, took part in a set of rituals called *śrauta*, which means "belonging to the *śruti* or Veda." These are sometimes conventionally called the "solemn" rituals, to distinguish them from the "household" (*gṛhya*) rituals or from earlier rituals – not that these other rituals were frivolous. The śrauta rituals were more elaborate than those for which the hymns were originally composed; they were initiated by kings and other wealthy men, who could afford to engage the team of priests and provide the offerings. The household rituals, some of which are referred to in *Ṛgveda* hymns, included life-cycle rituals for marriage, birth, and death. Besides these, there were rituals for personal purposes: cures, curses, rituals to gain success in agriculture, war, love or other spheres, and so on. These involved the recitation of hymns, of similar form to those of the *Ṛgveda*; about a fifth of them are actually taken or adapted from the *Ṛgveda*. These hymns are contained in a fourth collection, the *Atharvaveda*.

While the names of the other three Vedas indicate the type of utterance they contain – *ṛc*, *yajuṣ*, and *sāman* – the fourth Veda is named after a class of priests, the *Atharvan*s. It is also referred to, especially in early texts, including some Upaniṣads, by a pair of names: *Atharvan*s and *Aṅgiras*es. These are two legendary families of priests, said to be responsible for benevolent and malevolent practices respectively. This pair appears, for instance, in a passage about the divine origin of the Vedas and other texts:

> As smoke goes out in different directions from a fire laid with damp fuel, so all this – the Ṛgveda, Yajurveda, Sāmaveda, Atharva-Aṅgirasa, history (*itihāsa*), science (*vidyā*), upaniṣads, verses, rules, subcommentaries and commentaries – has been breathed out from that great being.
>
> (BU 2.4.10)

Here, the repertory of the Atharvans and Aṅgirases is not counted as a Veda, but is grouped with other bodies of learning (including upaniṣads, which in this early source could not mean all the texts we call Upaniṣads today; see above, pp. 2–3). But we do find it called a Veda in a later list of bodies of learning:

> The *Ṛgveda*, the *Yajurveda*, the *Sāmaveda*, the *Atharvaveda*, phonetics, ritual, grammar, etymology, meter, and astrology.
>
> (MU 1.1.5)

So instead of three Vedas we have four.

In Vedic thought, adding one to three may be more than arithmetic. We can see this by looking at other groups of three to which a fourth is added. Society comprises three functional classes: military and kingly power (*kṣatra*), priestly power (*brahman*), and the people (*viś*). The universe has three layers: earth, atmosphere, and sky. Time consists of past, present, and future. We pass our lives in waking, dreaming, and dreamless sleep; these three states of the self are discussed in several Upaniṣads (below, pp. 112, 117, 127–128, 353–354). But these triads are often turned into tetrads by adding a fourth member which is in some way different from the others. A late hymn of the Ṛgveda mentions a fourth social class, the *śūdra* (RV 10.90.12), whose function is later defined as serving the three others (*Manu* 1.91; Olivelle 2005: 91). Besides the three lines of verse that form the Gāyatrī *mantra*, there is a fourth which is beyond the sky (BU 5.14.1–7). Besides past, present, and future there is "whatever else is beyond the three times" (MaU 1).

Beyond the three states of waking, dreaming, and dreamless sleep is a fourth, which is not called a state but the self itself (MU 7). (Both BU 5.14 and the *Māṇḍūkya Upaniṣad* use the archaic word *turīya* "fourth," not the usual *caturtha*.) In the first of these examples, the śūdra is inferior to the other three; this is the pattern in other early tetrads, but in later Vedic texts the pattern is reversed, making the fourth superior (Bhattacharya 1978). A complex upaniṣadic passage on triads and tetrads takes *ṛc, sāman*, and *yajuṣ* – the three types of Vedic utterance – and adds a fourth: *brahman* (TU 1.5). This word has many overlapping meanings; it could mean the entirety of ritual utterance (Olivelle 1996: 181), or it could mean the sacred syllable *oṃ* which embodies all such utterance. But an Atharvanic priest might well have understood it as meaning the Atharvaveda.

When the Atharvaveda is added to the triad of Vedas, is it inferior or superior? Since texts continue to speak sometimes of three Vedas and sometimes of four, long after the time of the Upaniṣads, the Atharvaveda seems to be an outsider; and some brahmins deny its authority (Gonda 1975: 268). On the other hand the *Gopatha Brāhmaṇa*, a text expounding the rituals of the Atharvaveda, claims that it is superior to the other Vedas, and calls it the *brahmaveda*. This title connects the Atharvaveda with a fourth class of priests engaged in śrauta ritual, besides the *hotṛ*, *udgātṛ*, and *adhvaryu* who specialized in the Ṛgveda, Sāmaveda, and Yajurveda respectively. This fourth priest was called the *brahmán* (the accent distinguishes this word from *bráhman* which means "ritual utterance" and also, as upaniṣadic ideas developed, "the highest being"); his function is to direct the others, and to perform remedial rituals whenever any mistakes have been made (Bodewitz 1983; Bodewitz 1990: 17–18). He is the healer of the ritual (SB 1.7.4.19); he protects it (CU 4.17.10). While "the hotṛ's function is performed with the Ṛgveda, the adhvaryu's with the Yajurveda, and the chant with the Sāmaveda," the brahmán's function is performed "with this triple Veda" (SB 11.5.8.7); and while they work with speech, he works with mind (CU 4.16.2). Each of the three classes of priest claimed authority to perform this supervisory and all-embracing function (*Kauṣītaki Brāhmaṇa* 6.11; Keith 1920: 379–380). But it was also claimed by the brahmins of the Atharvaveda (Gonda 1975: 269–271); from their point of view, the Atharvaveda was the supreme Veda, the Veda of the *brahmán*.

Mantra, brāhmaṇa, āraṇyaka, and upaniṣad

Within each of the three, or four, classes of specialist priest (hotṛ, udgātṛ, adhvaryu, atharvan) there were several "branches" (*śākhā*, also called "schools" by modern scholars). These were lines of succession of teachers and pupils, in some cases flourishing in different geographical areas (Witzel 1987; Olivelle 1996: xxxvii–xl). Each branch had its own collection or recension (*saṃhitā*) of the text; so before the texts reached the fixed form described above, the oral transmission must have allowed authoritative teachers to introduce variations. We need not concern ourselves with these variations, but what does concern us is that different Vedic branches, as part of their development, added their own Upaniṣads to the recension they transmitted. Ancient sources name many such branches, but only one recension of the Ṛgveda survives, two of the Sāmaveda, and two of the Atharvaveda (Gonda 1975: 16, 313, 272). The Yajurveda was transmitted in two forms: the Black Yajurveda, in three recensions, and the White Yajurveda, in two. The difference between the Black and White Yajurveda will be explained below.

The most ancient texts transmitted by each branch are the *mantras* – the words spoken, muttered or sung in the course of the ritual. In the Ṛgveda, Sāmaveda and most of the Atharvaveda they are in verse, in stanzas of various meters; but in the Yajurveda they are mainly short sentences or phrases of prose, though they include some verses taken, with variations, from the *Ṛgveda Saṃhitā*. Later, prose texts called Brāhmaṇas were added which are not uttered in the ritual, but discuss the purpose and meaning of particular actions, utterances, and pieces of equipment used in the śrauta rituals. These discussions involve ideas about the gods and the world which can be partially traced in the *mantras*. They also presuppose familiarity with the ritual routines; these routines are prescribed in rules called *sūtra*s, of which each branch had its collection. The word *brāhmaṇa* which denotes these discursive texts means "belonging to *bráhman*": this means that they are related to the ritual utterances (*bráhman*), but distinct from them.

The practice of including brāhmaṇas as well as *mantras* originated in the Yajurveda. The *Taittirīya Saṃhitā*, a recension of the Yajurveda, has passages of this kind interspersed among the *mantras*, forming a kind of descriptive and explanatory commentary on the ritual (Keith 1914). Two other *Saṃhitā*s (the *Kāṭhaka* and the *Maitrāyaṇī*) are arranged similarly. These three saṃhitās are known collectively as the Black Yajurveda, in contradistinction to the White Yajurveda, which is differently arranged. The White Yajurveda, also known as the *Vājasaneyi Saṃhitā*, exists in two recensions: Kāṇva and Mādhyaṃdina; this point will become relevant in connection with the *Bṛhadāraṇyaka Upaniṣad* (Chapter 23) and the *Īśā Upaniṣad* (Chapter 28). Each of these recensions is named after the lineage of priests who first handed it down.

In the *Vājasaneyi Saṃhitā* or White Yajurveda, the brāhmaṇa material is not interspersed with the *mantras*. Instead, it is all in one collection, the *Śatapatha Brāhmaṇa*, "Brāhmaṇa of a hundred paths." This is the longest of all Vedic texts, and the best known of the brāhmaṇas; unlike many such texts, it has a widely available English translation (Eggeling 1882–1900). In time, the Black Yajurveda developed its own brāhmaṇa, the *Taittirīya Brāhmaṇa*, in addition to the brāhmaṇa material in the *Taittirīya Saṃhitā*.

The *Śatapatha Brāhmaṇa* includes discussions of questions about how the ritual should be performed, somewhat similar to those of the Talmud; these discussions involve consideration of the purpose and meaning of the rituals.

In most of the *Śatapatha Brāhmaṇa*, the authority who settles the questions is Yājñavalkya, who is also a prominent figure in the *Bṛhadāraṇyaka Upaniṣad.* (In books 6–9 of the Brāhmaṇa, however, the authority is not Yājñavalkya but Śāṇḍilya.) A sample of the style of discussion found in the *Śatapatha Brāhmaṇa*, and of Yājñavalkya's independent views, is provided by a discussion in the context of a ritual of initiation.

> He should not eat of the cow or the ox; for the cow and the ox support the whole world. The gods said: "The cow and the ox support the whole world. Let us put the vigor of the other animals into the cow and the ox." They put the vigor that had been in the other animals into the cow and the ox. That is why the cow and the ox eat the most. So if he ate of the cow or the ox, it would be like eating everything, or going to the end. He would be fit to be born as a monster; it would be ill fame: "He has aborted a woman's foetus!"; "He has done evil!" Therefore he should not eat of the cow or the ox. On this matter, Yājñavalkya said: "I eat it myself, if it is succulent."
>
> (SB 3.1.2.21)

It is not clear whether the prohibition discussed here is for the period of initiation or for all times, but certainly meat-eating was more general in the Vedic period than later. The passage exemplifies several features of the Brāhmaṇas. It starts with a rule, then gives a reason for it. It supports this with a narrative about the gods, a little myth of origin. It then discusses the rule, and gives the view of a ritual authority. These features do not all appear every time a ritual point is discussed, but the narrative element in particular is sometimes much longer than in this example. Narratives, including those about the origin of the world, are important in the Upaniṣads as well as the Brāhmaṇas; so too are the views of named authorities, including Yājñavalkya (Chapter 10).

Unlike many Vedic authorities, of whom we have only the names, we can gain some idea of Yājñavalkya's biography from the texts. He was "a man of simple solutions and somewhat coarse words" (Gonda 1975: 353), who used humor as a debating tactic (Black 2007: 77–78). He had a royal patron, Janaka, King of Videha. Videha lay in what is now northern Bihar and part of Nepal; so by the time of the *Śatapatha Brāhmaṇa*, Vedic culture had spread from the Punjab eastwards over much of northern India (above, pp. 35–37). He had the family name Vājasaneya, the family after which the *Vājasaneyi Saṃhitā* or White Yajurveda is named. There will be more about Yājñavalkya in Chapters 10, 11, 12, 13, 18, and 23.

Some branches of the Veda possess texts called *āraṇyaka*, which are similar in character to the Brāhmaṇas. This title indicates that they belong to the "wilderness" (*araṇya*), or, as it is more often translated, "forest": not necessarily a place full of trees, but a place remote from the village – that is, from habitation and agriculture. They deal with particularly powerful, and therefore dangerous, rituals. In language and style, and also in their ideas and ways of thinking, they represent a transitional stage between the Brāhmaṇas and the Upaniṣads (Gonda 1975: 424), though usually they remain ritual texts, which most parts of the Upaniṣads are not.

Finally – leaving aside the *sūtra*s, ritual rule-books which do not concern us – we come to the Upaniṣads: some in prose, some in verse. Each of these belongs to a particular branch of the Veda, and some of them are named after that branch, such as *Aitareya Upaniṣad* or *Taittirīya Upaniṣad*. There are no firm boundaries between Brāhmaṇa, Āraṇyaka, and Upaniṣad; this is apparent from the titles of some texts: *Bṛhadāraṇyaka Upaniṣad*, *Jaiminīya Upaniṣad Brāhmaṇa*. It is also apparent from the way in which some Upaniṣads have been transmitted: The *Bṛhadāraṇyaka Upaniṣad* is part of an Āraṇyaka, which itself is part of the *Śatapatha Brāhmaṇa*; the *Aitareya Upaniṣad* and the *Kauṣītaki Upaniṣad* are parts of the *Aitareya Āraṇyaka* and *Kauṣītaki Āraṇyaka* of the Ṛgveda; the *Taittirīya Upaniṣad* and the *Mahānārayaṇa Upaniṣad* are included in the *Taittirīya Āraṇyaka* of the Black Yajurveda; the *Īśā Upaniṣad* is part of the last chapter of the *Vājasaneyi Saṃhitā* or White Yajurveda; the *Kena Upaniṣad* is part of the *Jaiminīya Upaniṣad Brāhmaṇa* of the Sāmaveda. Further, some passages in the Brāhmaṇas are introduced with phrases such as "Now an instruction in upaniṣads" (SB 10.4.5.1); here, the word *upaniṣad* refers to the type of meditation by identification discussed in Chapter 13.

In the early Upaniṣads, their relation to particular Vedas is sometimes apparent in their content. The *Chāndogya Upaniṣad*, which belongs to the Sāmaveda, begins by discussing Vedic chant, with reference to the particular duties and skills of the *udgātṛ*. The *Bṛhadāraṇyaka Upaniṣad* begins with a passage on the horse sacrifice, the most extravagant of the Vedic rituals (surpassed only by the human sacrifice (*puruṣa-medha*), which perhaps is only mentioned in the texts as a theoretical culmination of the hierarchy of sacrifices). Others, such as the *Īśā Upaniṣad* of the White Yajurveda, may have been composed within the Vedic branch to which they belong, but do not show its ritual concerns. Eventually, Upaniṣads which had no particular Vedic affiliation came to be attached to the Atharvaveda by default: a consequence of the idea explained above, that the Atharvaveda is the *brahmaveda*. The number of Upaniṣads is indefinite: 108 is a traditional number, but is not exact. They include texts teaching the worship of Śiva as supreme God, and others doing the same for Viṣṇu or for the Goddess; some teaching yoga, and others *saṃnyāsa* (renunciation, the life of a homeless ascetic) (Olivelle 1992: 4–5). Though these upaniṣads have their place in the study of Indian religion, and are described in this book (Chapters 37–41), it is useful to separate them from the ones which are here called the classical Upaniṣads.

The structure of the Veda can be represented as a two-dimensional chart (see Figure 6.1). The vertical dimension represents the relation of later texts to earlier ones, and therefore an approximate dateless chronology with the earliest texts at the top, while the horizontal dimension represents the division of the tradition first into the three – or four – Vedas, and then into the branches

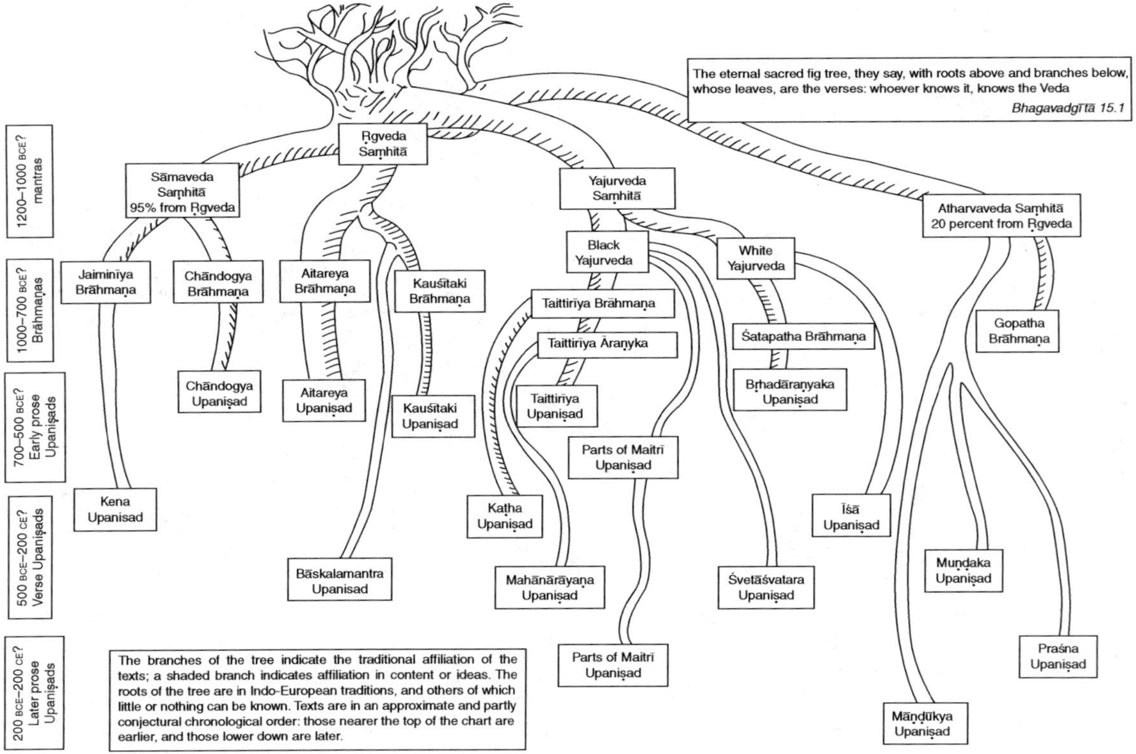
The eternal sacred fig tree, they say, with roots above and branches below, whose leaves, are the verses: whoever knows it, knows the Veda
Bhagavadgītā 15.1
1200–1000 BCE? mantras
1000–700 BCE? Brāhmaṇas
700–500 BCE? Early prose Upaniṣads
500 BCE–200 CE? Verse Upaniṣads
200 BCE–200 CE? Later prose Upaniṣads
Ṛgveda Saṃhitā
Sāmaveda Saṃhitā 95% from Ṛgveda
Yajurveda Saṃhitā
Atharvaveda Saṃhitā 20 percent from Ṛgveda
Black Yajurveda
White Yajurveda
Jaiminīya Brāhmaṇa
Chāndogya Brāhmaṇa
Aitareya Brāhmaṇa
Kauśītaki Brāhmaṇa
Taittirīya Brāhmaṇa
Taittirīya Āraṇyka
Śatapatha Brāhmaṇa
Gopatha Brāhmaṇa
Chāndogya Upaniṣad
Aitareya Upaniṣad
Kauśītaki Upaniṣad
Taittirīya Upaniṣad
Bṛhadāraṇyaka Upaniṣad
Parts of Maitrī Upaniṣad
Kena Upanisad
Kaṭha Upaniṣad
Īśā Upaniṣad
Bāskalamantra Upanisad
Mahānārāyaṇa Upaniṣad
Śvetāśvatara Upaniṣad
Muṇḍaka Upaniṣad
Praśna Upaniṣad
Parts of Maitrī Upaniṣad
Māṇḍūkya Upaniṣad
The branches of the tree indicate the traditional affiliation of the texts; a shaded branch indicates affiliation in content or ideas. The roots of the tree are in Indo-European traditions, and others of which little or nothing can be known. Texts are in an approximate and partly conjectural chronological order: those nearer the top of the chart are earlier, and those lower down are later.

Figure 6.1 The Upaniṣads in the Vedic tree.

with their various Upaniṣads. The whole recalls the recurrent Vedic image of an upside-down tree:

> He who now knows the tree with roots above and branches downward
> Would never believe that death would kill him.
>
> (TA 1.11.5; compare KU 6.1; MtU 6.4; BhG 15.1)

The oldest Vedic texts

The oldest part of the Veda, so far as the history of the texts can be reconstructed, is the *Ṛgveda Saṃhitā*. In spite of its importance, but partly because of its many problems of interpretation, it has only recently been reliably translated into English (Jamison and Brereton 2014). This is a collection of 1,028 hymns, each attributed to an author. The hymns are arranged in ten books (another conventional but anachronistic term; the Sanskrit term is *maṇḍala* "circle"); many of hymns in the first and the last book were composed later than the others. A typical hymn is about ten stanzas long, addressed to a particular god; the texts say there are thirty-three gods, though this number is not exact (Macdonell 1897: 19). Most of them are male. The hymns are rich in mythological material, but the stories are not so much narrated as alluded to, so that we often have to trawl through many hymns to reconstruct a myth. The authors are revered as sages (*ṛṣi*), and the poetic insight embodied in their hymns is valued as an offering to the gods (Gonda 1963). Some hymns, especially in the tenth book, set aside the traditional body of mythology and construct their own myths, often about the origin and nature of the world. It is these hymns, referred to by modern scholars as the speculative hymns, which most foreshadow the ideas found in the Upaniṣads; in particular, they link the world and its origin to the human being and to the ritual, as we shall see in the next chapter. Perhaps the most radical of the speculative hymns is RV 10.129, which tries to think of a time before the universe began. It begins "There was neither not-being nor beginning then," which is echoed in SB 10.5.3.1. After many unanswered questions and cryptic statements, it concludes: "Whence this creation came into being, whether he founded it or not – only he who is its supervisor in the highest heaven knows; or else he does not" (RV 10.129.7).

Modern perspectives on the Vedas

The meaning of Vedic literature varies with the different perspectives in which we can view it. Of the various Hindu traditions, some revere the Veda while others expressly reject it, without in either case discussing it in detail (Renou 1965). The tradition known as Pūrva Mīmāṃsā ("earlier exegesis") is mainly concerned with the Brāhmaṇas; in Vedānta, also called Uttara Mīmāṃsā ("later exegesis"), the part of the Veda that matters is the

Upaniṣads. When the pioneer modern Hindu thinker Rammohun Roy (1772–1833) mentions the Veda as his authority, he invariably means the Upaniṣads (pp. 220–221). The first Hindu thinker of modern times, perhaps the first of many centuries, to use the *mantras* extensively as a source of authority was Dayānanda Sarasvatī (1825–1883); his methods of exegesis were highly original (p. 224).

Scholars in the modern "Western" tradition (which includes many though not all Indian scholars) have inherited a perspective which sees the *Ṛgveda Saṃhitā* as the most ancient set of Vedic texts, and therefore, in the view of many, the most important; consequently, it is the most studied. This contrasts with the perspectives found within the Hindu tradition. In the *Bhagavadgītā*, for instance, it is the Sāmaveda, not the Ṛgveda, which is singled out as the chief of Vedas (BhG 10.22). According to the Yajurveda, the Yajurveda is the most precious: The *ṛc*es are honey, the *sāman*s are ghi – two commonly mentioned examples of rich food – but the *yajuṣ*es are *amṛta*, the drink of immortality (SB 11.5.7.5). This judgment shows the loyalty to one's own branch of the Veda, and rivalry between the branches, which are apparent in some Upaniṣads (Cohen 2008).

The motive to look for the earliest texts comes partly from the comparative method which was developed in nineteenth-century Europe for investigating the history of languages, and was later applied to the history of ideas; this method relies on the oldest available evidence for reconstructing a lost original. Another motive comes from the European Reformation: To go to the oldest texts is to find the authentic tradition, uncorrupted by priestcraft and scholasticism. Yet another comes from Romanticism: Friedrich Max Müller, who edited the *Ṛg-Veda Saṃhitā*, believed that he was uncovering humankind's primeval response to the wonders of nature, which he believed was also a part of the German and European heritage. His enthusiasm for the earliest texts, and his identification of their culture with his own, is apparent in his own words:

> One thing is certain: there is nothing more ancient and primitive, not only in India, but in the whole Aryan world, than the hymns of the Rig-Veda. So far as we are Aryans in language, that is in thought, so far the Rig-Veda is our own most ancient book.
>
> (Müller 1880:152–153).

The Upaniṣads, as well as the hymns, produced an enthusiastic response from some Europeans, including the philosopher Arnold Schopenhauer (Chapter 22), the philosopher and Sanskritist Paul Deussen, and the poet W. B. Yeats. They have also been taken up by modern Hindu thinkers (Chapter 20). The Brāhmaṇas, on the other hand, have generally remained a rare specialism even among professional scholars, whose works on the subject were not intended to attract general readers. Their world-view has been presented as "prescientific science" (Oldenberg 1919), and thus of historical interest; they are also of linguistic interest, as the earliest examples of continuous prose in any Indo-European language. To Indian scholars they have represented a low period between the hymns and the Upaniṣads, when "cold and dead formalities took the place of warm and living devotion" (Bhandarkar 1928 [1883]: 611), and the "freshness and simplicity" of the Ṛgvedic hymns "give place to the coldness and artificiality" of the Yajurveda, Sāmaveda, and Brāhmaṇas (Radhakrishnan 1929: 123). An exception to this low estimate of the Brāhmaṇas is a French study, arising from the school of sociology of religion led by Émil Durkheim (Hubert and Mauss 1929, first published 1898). It uses the Brāhmaṇas and related texts, together with biblical texts and some other sources, as the basis for a theory of ritual which has been influential in the study of religion.

While scholars have been enthusiastic about the poetry of the hymns or the philosophy of the Upaniṣads, many have been scathing about the ritualistic and symbolic thought of the Brāhmaṇas, with the unfortunate result that relatively few have studied them in depth, and even some of those have confessed to a sense of tedium (e.g. Eggeling 1882–1900: vol. 1, p. ix; vol. 5, pp. l–li). Admittedly the Brāhmaṇas are much less attractive as literature, as well as much longer, than either the hymns or the Upaniṣads, and they assume a familiarity with the ritual which is hard to obtain; but they show us the development of thought between the period of the hymns and that of the Upaniṣads, and neglect of them has made the latter appear more revolutionary than they are, leading to fruitless speculation about the sources of their ideas. Some acquaintance with the ideas of the Brāhmaṇas helps us to understand Upaniṣadic thought in historical depth, and to appreciate the real contribution made by their legendary thinkers to the development of Hindu theology and philosophy. We shall look at the development of ideas from the hymns through the Brāhmaṇas to the Upaniṣads in Chapter 7.

References

Bhandarkar, R. G. 1928. "Basis of Theism, and its Relation to the So-called Revealed Religions" in *Collected Works of Sir R. G. Bhandarkar*, vol. II. Poona [Pune]: Bhandarkar Oriental Research Institute. First published 1883, 603–616.

Bhattacharya, Dipak. 1978. "The Doctrine of Four in The Early Upaniṣads and Some Connected Problems" *Journal of Indian Philosophy* 6: 1–34.

Black, Brian. 2007. *The Character of the Self in Ancient India: Priest, Kings, and Women in the early Upaniṣads*. Albany, NY: State University of New York Press.

Bodewitz, H. W. 1983. "The Fourth Priest (the Brahmán) in Vedic ritual" in Ria Kloppenborg (ed.) *Selected Studies on Ritual in the Indian Religions. Essays to D. J. Hoens*. Leiden: Brill, 33–68.

Bodewitz, H. W. 1990. *The Jyotiṣṭoma Ritual: Jaiminīya Brāhmaṇa I, 66–364*. Leiden: Brill.

Chadwick, H. M., and Chadwick, N. K. 1932–40. *The Growth of Literature*. 3. vols. Cambridge: Cambridge University Press.

Cohen, Signe. 2008. *Text and Authority in the Older Upaniṣads*. Leiden: Brill.

Eggeling, Julius. 1882–1900. *The Satapathabrâhmana: According to the Text of the Mâdhyandina School.* 5 volumes (Sacred Books of the East series, vols. 12, 26, 41, 43, 44). Oxford: Clarendon Press.

Fuller, C. J. 1992. *The Camphor Flame: Popular Hinduism and Society in India.* Princeton, NJ: Princeton University Press.

Gonda, Jan. 1963. *The Vision of the Vedic Poets.* The Hague: Mouton.

Gonda, Jan. 1975. *Vedic Literature* (A History of Indian Literature Vol. 1, Fasc. 1). Wiesbaden: Harrassowitz.

Gonda, Jan. 1977. *Medieval Religious Literature in Sanskrit.* Wiesbaden: Harrassowitz.

Goody, Jack. 1987. *The Interface between the Written and the Oral.* Cambridge: Cambridge University Press.

Hubert, Henri, and Marcel Mauss. 1929. *Essai sur la nature et la fonction du sacrifice.* Paris: Alcan (first published in *L'année sociologique*, 1898, 29–138). English translation by W. D. Hall, *Sacrifice: Its Nature and Function.* London: Cohen and West, 1964.

Jamison, Stephanie W., and Joel P. Brereton (translators). 2014. *The Rigveda: the Earliest Religious Poetry of India.* New York: Oxford University Press.

Keith, A. B. 1914. *The Veda of the Black Yajuṣ School Entitled Taittirīya Saṃhitā: Translated from the Original Sanskrit Prose and Verse.* 2 vols. Cambridge, MA: Harvard University Press. (Reprint Delhi: Motilal Banarsidass, 1967.)

Keith, A. B. 1920. *Rigveda Brahmanas: The Aitareya and Kauṣītaki Brāhmaṇas of the Rigveda Translated from the Original Sanskrit.* Cambridge, MA: Harvard University Press. (Reprint Delhi: Motilal Banarsidass, 1971.)

Killingley, Dermot. 2014. "*Svādhyāya:* An Ancient Way of Using the Veda" *Religions of South Asia* 8: 109–130.

Lord, Albert B. 1960. *The Singer of Tales.* Cambridge, MA: Harvard University Press.

Macdonell, A. A. 1897. *Vedic Mythology.* Strassburg: Trübner. (Reprint Varanasi: Indological Book House, 1971).

Müller, F. Max. 1880. *Lectures on the Origin and Growth of Religion as Illustrated by the Religions of India.* London: Longmans Green.

Oldenberg, Hermann. 1919. *Vorwissenschaftliche Wissenschaft: die Weltanschauung der Brāhmana-Texte.* Göttingen: Vandenhoeck & Ruprecht.

Olivelle, Patrick. 1992. *Saṃnyāsa Upaniṣads: Hindu Scriptures on Asceticism and Renunciation.* New York: Oxford University Press.

Olivelle, Patrick. 1996. *Upaniṣads: Translated from the Original Sanskrit* (World's Classics series). Oxford: Oxford University Press.

Olivelle, Patrick. 2005. *Manu's Code of Law: A Critical Edition and Translation of the Mānava-Dharmaśāstra.* New York: Oxford University Press.

Ong, Walter J. 1982. *Orality and Literacy: The Technologizing of the Word.* London and New York: Methuen.

Padoux, André. 2003. "Mantra" in Gavin Flood (ed.) *The Blackwell Companion to Hinduism.* Oxford: Blackwell, 478–492.

Radhakrishnan, S. 1929. *Indian Philosophy*, vol. 1. 2nd edn. London: George Allen and Unwin.

Renou, Louis. 1956. *Hymnes spéculatifs du Véda.* Paris: Gallimard.

Renou, Louis. 1965. The Destiny of the Veda in India. Translated by Dev Raj Chandra. Delhi: Motilal Banarsidass. (Originally *Le destin du Veda dans l'Inde.* 1960. Paris: Boccard. This is volume 6 in a series of 17 by Louis Renou, *Études védiques et pāṇinéennes*, published by Boccard 1955–1969.)

Witzel, Michael. 1987. "On the Localisation of Vedic Texts and Schools" in G. Pollet (ed.) *India and the Ancient World: History, Trade and Culture before AD 650* (Orientalia Lovaniensia Analecta, 25). Leuven: Department Orientalistik, 174–213.

Witzel, Michael. 2003. "Vedas and Upaniṣads" in Gavin Flood (ed.) *The Blackwell Companion to Hinduism*. Oxford: Blackwell, 68–101.

Further reading

Cohen, Signe. 2008. *Text and Authority in the Older Upaniṣads*. Leiden: Brill.

Gonda, Jan. 1975. *Vedic Literature* (A History of Indian Literature Vol. 1, Fasc. 1). Wiesbaden: Harrassowitz.

Jamison, Stephanie W., and Joel P. Brereton (translators). 2014. *The Rigveda: the Earliest Religious Poetry of India*. New York: Oxford University Press.

Olivelle, Patrick. 1996. *Upaniṣads: Translated from the Original Sanskrit* (World's Classics series). Oxford: Oxford University Press, xxiii–lvi.

Patton, Laurie L. "Veda and Upaniṣad" in Sushil Mittal and Gene Thursby (eds) *The Hindu World*. New York: Routledge, 37–51.

Witzel, Michael. 2003. "Vedas and Upaniṣads" in Gavin Flood (ed.)*The Blackwell Companion to Hinduism*. Oxford: Blackwell, 68–101.

7 The religious and ritual background

Dermot Killingley

Changes over time

The body of literature described in Chapter 6 was accumulated over a period of centuries. We cannot be certain when that was, but the passage of time is evident from changes in language between earlier and later texts, and changes in the geographical places mentioned, as Vedic culture spread eastward and southward from the Punjab. During this period, ideas and practices also changed. Though most of the hymns of the Ṛgveda presuppose a ritual situation, and refer to ritual objects, actions, and practitioners as well as the gods to whom the rituals are addressed, these rituals were not the same as the ones referred to in the Brāhmaṇas, Āraṇyakas, and Upaniṣads, and codified in the sūtras (Gonda 1975: 84). These later rituals are the ones known as *śrauta* (above, p. 46); they take more time, space, and material than the ones referred to in the hymns, and require more participants, including the specialists who know the Ṛgveda and Yajurveda, and for some rituals the Sāmaveda. About 160 of the 1,028 Ṛgvedic hymns are not used in the śrauta rituals, showing that these rituals developed later than the compilation of the *Ṛgveda Saṃhitā* (Gonda 1978). Whereas we can only form a rough idea of the older rituals from what the hymns say, the śrauta rituals are described in detail in the sūtras and Brāhmaṇas.

The Vedic world-view

To understand the purpose of Vedic ritual, we have to understand how those who practiced it viewed the world. Indeed, when questions of how to perform ritual are raised in the Brāhmaṇas, the discussion often turns on questions about the nature of the world – about what has been called "prescientific science" (Oldenberg 1919). The answers to such questions are not always the same, and ideas developed over time.

The word which is usually translated "world" is *loka*. It can refer to two worlds: "this world" (*ayaṃ lokaḥ*) and "the other world," more literally "that world, yonder world, the world beyond" (*asau lokaḥ*) – either the world of the gods, or that of the dead (Gonda 1966: 84). The idea of two worlds is expressed in CU 8.6.2: "Just as the long main road goes to both villages, this one and the one beyond, so these rays of the sun go to both worlds, this one and the one beyond." But often we hear of more than two worlds (Gonda 1966: 53–66). The Ṛgvedic hymns, and many later texts, speak of three worlds: earth and sky, sometimes called a pair of bowls, and the atmosphere between them. But there can be more than three: CU 2.2 speaks of five worlds – earth, fire, atmosphere, sun, sky – corresponding to the five sections of the Sāmavedic chant (below, p. 259); while MU 1.2.3 speaks of seven worlds, which can be lost by failure to perform sacrifice properly. BU 4.3.33, discussed below (p. 128), also mentions seven: the world won by the ancestors, the world of the Gandharvas, the world of the creator Prajāpati, the world of Brahman, and, by implication, the worlds of humankind and of two grades of gods. Sometimes each god is said to have a world; but these worlds are united by Prajāpati into one heavenly world (Gonda 1966: 56). Less often mentioned (Gonda 1966: 53) is the world or worlds of the demons (IU 3) – the *asura*s, who appear as enemies of the gods in the Brāhmaṇas and Upaniṣads.

The Vedic texts in all stages say much about worlds, often about gaining or winning worlds through ritual performance – or, as we shall see below, through knowledge. Worlds may also be entered in dream:

> Wherever he wanders in dream, those are his worlds. So he may be a great king, or a great brahmin, or he may go the heights or the depths.
>
> (BU 2.1.18)

KU 6.5 likens the world of dream to the world of the ancestors, and KsU 4.2 and 4.15 link dream to Yama, the king of the ancestors. This suggests a belief that dreams enable us to communicate with the world of the dead. Whereas Vedic ritual as recorded in the hymns was often performed to secure success in this world, the Brāhmaṇas and Upaniṣads show an increased concern for security in the world of the dead.

Vedic ideas of existence after death

Existence after death is regarded in the Veda, including the Upaniṣads, as something to be achieved, by ritual or by knowledge, or the two together. Vedic thought thus contrasts with the Hindu thought of later periods, where liberation is seen as escape from repeated existence. The rituals for the dead are intended to secure a place for the deceased in the world of the ancestors, the *pitṛloka* ("world of the fathers"), beyond death. There, the dead are ruled over by Yama, the first man to die, who found the path to the world of the dead (RV 10.14.2; AV 18.3.13). Their position in that world depends on the merit they have won by their sacrifices. In a discussion of the gifts given to the priests by the patron of the sacrifice, we are told: "He who sacrifices, sacrifices thinking 'May I too have it in Yama's world'" (SB 4.3.4.27); and again: "Whatever else he gives, he gives with the desire 'May I too have it in the beyond'" (SB 4.3.4.32). Security in the world beyond depends also on the ancestral offerings made by the person's male descendants. This is one reason why sons are desirable in Vedic culture, which adheres to a patrilinear system of kinship and a patriarchal set of values.

The *Ṛg-Veda* includes some funeral hymns, which give us a glimpse of early Vedic death rituals and ideas about death. The dead enter the world of Yama, who, as the first man to die, is king of the dead:

> Go forth, go forth by the ancient paths by which our former ancestors departed.
>
> You shall see the two kings, exhilarated by *svadhā* [the ritual call announcing offerings to the dead]: Yama and the god Varuṇa.
>
> (RV 10.14.7)

The next stanza refers to good actions as a personal treasury laid up in the world of the dead, to be enjoyed after death:

> Join with the ancestors, with Yama, with your sacrifices and gifts in the highest heaven.
>
> Leaving faults behind, come home again. Join with your body, glorious.
>
> (RV 10.14.8)

The idea that actions determine one's destiny after death developed further, as we shall see in Chapter 12, and came to be applied to all kinds of action. But this verse refers only to ritual actions. The phrase "sacrifices and gifts" translates *iṣṭāpūrta*, a frequent expression from the *Ṛgveda* onwards. It was understood in later times as meaning ritual acts and works of public utility such as digging wells; but in the Veda *pūrta* means gifts to officiating brahmins as part of the ritual.

Many Vedic texts mention *amṛta* – "non-death; immortality" – but this may not mean eternal life. They also often speak of living for a hundred years; and this is equated with immortality (SB 10.1.5.4). "Immortality" thus means a full span of life in this world, free from premature death. Sometimes, however, it is a state beyond death; in this as in other matters, Vedic thought not only changed through time, but allowed diversity of opinion. Opinions were often expressed in the form of myths. In one of these, Prajāpati, the father of the gods, taught them the ritual of the great fireplace (described below), which made them immortal. But the god of Death objected:

> Death said to the gods: "Surely in this way all people will become immortal; then what share will there be for me?" They said: "From now on, no one shall be immortal with the body; only when you have taken that as your share, will someone who is to become immortal, either through

> knowledge or through ritual, be immortal, after separating from the body." … And those who know it in this way, or who do this ritual, come into being again when they have died, and when they come into being, they come into immortal life. And those who do not know this, or do not do this ritual, come into being again when they die, and become his [Death's] food again and again.
>
> (SB 10.4.3.9–10)

Here, immortality is a state reached after death, in which one is immune from further death. It is to be reached by performing the ritual referred to, or by knowing its meaning. Another proposal for escaping redeath is to make offerings to various forms of death:

> In all the worlds deaths are attached. If he did not make offerings to them, Death would find him in every world. By making offerings to the Deaths, he overcomes Death in every world.
>
> (SB 13.3.5.1)

The idea of redeath is older than that of rebirth. It is connected with a view that merit won by ritual is finite, and therefore exhaustible. In the Upaniṣads, the problem is solved by saying that whereas action is limited (KsU 2.5), knowledge can gain an infinite reward; but in the Brāhmaṇas the aim is to use both knowledge and ritual to make the results of ritual action secure. In a Brāhmaṇa myth which is better known in its Upaniṣad version, a young brahmin Naciketas confronts Death, who offers him three boons. As the first boon, Naciketas chooses to return to his father alive. As the second, he asks: "Tell me how to make my sacrifices and gifts imperishable." Death teaches him a ritual, and the narrator adds that a man's sacrifices and gifts do not perish if he performs and knows this ritual. As his third boon, Naciketas asks: "Tell me how to conquer re-death." Death teaches him the same ritual; the second and third boons are in effect the same. The story is re-told in KU 1–2; but there, in a typically Upaniṣadic twist to the story, Naciketas insists on knowledge, not a ritual, as his third boon (below, pp. 96, 103, 135–136, 317–318).

Overcoming death may take other forms than individual survival: A person may survive in their offspring: "O Agni, may I reach immortality with offspring" (RV 5.4.10). A verse passage in an early prose Upaniṣad considers this, but denies that it means survival after death (BU 3.9.28). Or one may survive by being dispersed into the environment:

> May your eyesight go to the sun, your breath to the wind; go to the sky and to the earth in due order. Or go to the waters, if that has been ordained for you; take your stand in plants, with your body.
>
> (RV 10.16.3)

This is one of many Vedic passages in which parts of the person, seen as a microcosm, are linked to parts of the macrocosm; the connections between eyesight and sun, and between breath and wind, are obvious. Dispersal in this manner is promised in the *Śatapatha Brāhmaṇa*, as the reward for knowledge of such connections.

> And when he who knows this passes away from this world, he passes into fire with his speech, into the sun with his eyesight, into the moon with his mind, into the directions with his hearing, and into the wind with his breath. Being made of them, he becomes whichever of these deities he chooses, and is at rest.
>
> (SB 10.3.3.8)

Here, besides eyesight and sun, breath and wind, we have other connections which are less clear. The sense of hearing corresponds to the directions (in modern terms, the points of the compass) because it can sense the direction from which a sound comes (as explained in BU 4.3.5). The connection between speech and fire is less clear, but it is often mentioned. Besides both being audible, both are essential elements of Vedic ritual (van Buitenen 1959: 178). They also both proceed from the mouth, since when fire is made by rubbing a piece of wood against another, the resulting spark has to be coaxed into flame by blowing – a process referred to in BU 1.4.6. The connection of the mind with the moon is even less clear; but it is frequently mentioned in Vedic texts (Gonda 1986). These connections are not flights of fancy; the consistency between them in different texts shows that they are part of a body of traditional knowledge.

Liberation

Existence after death, in whatever form, is liberation from the limitations of life as we find it. In the *Ṛgveda*, the desire for liberation is expressed especially in the hymns to Varuṇa, the god who is guardian of order (*ṛta* – a similar idea to what is later called *dharma*). These hymns include prayers for release from a noose (*pāśa*) (Rodhe 1946: 26). For instance:

> Release for us the upper noose, the middle one, and those below, that we may live!
>
> (RV 1.25.21)

The last phrase implies that the condition of those who are not released is not truly life; later, we will find it called death, contrasted with deathlessness or immortality. Does this mean physical death, or the absence of any sort of life after physical death, or a state in which one is physically alive but not participating in the divine order? Different passages of the Brāhmaṇas suggest different answers.

The nooses from which Varuṇa is asked to release his worshipers are associated with sin; as Varuṇa is the guardian of order, sin is an offense against him, and his hymns pray for release from it:

> Loosen sin from me, like a belt! ...
> Untie anguish from me, as a tether from a calf!
>
> (RV 2.28.5–6)

The offenses which evoke Varuṇa's anger need not be deliberate, or even conscious:

> That failure was not my own will; it was drink, anger, dice, thoughtlessness.
> The elder is involved in the offense of the younger; even sleep is no averter of evil.
>
> (RV 7.86.6)

"Dice," mentioned here among the causes of sin, is a conventional translation for a game of chance played with a large number of nuts of a particular species – not the cubes which we call dice (Macdonell and Keith 1912: vol. 1, pp. 2–5; O'Flaherty 1981: 239–243). Gambling is a prominent feature of Vedic culture; it had a place in certain rituals, especially the royal consecration (*rājasūya*). In this verse, however, it is a cause of sin. These dice or nuts are also the subject of an unusual hymn which reads more like a blues lyric than a devotional poem. In it, a failed gambler describes his misery. Having lost everything he has, and alienated his wife and family, he ends by calling the dice a net in which he wishes to be caught no longer (RV 10.34.14). In later literature, gambling reappears as a cause of compulsive, irrational, and even disastrous behavior; it triggers a series of disasters in the main story of the *Mahābhārata* (Mbh 2.44–2.72) and also in the subsidiary story of King Nala (Mbh 3.50–3.78). Dice, like drink and anger, are culturally approved in certain circumstances, but dangerous.

The metaphor of the noose continues in the Upaniṣads: The *Kaṭha Upaniṣad* speaks of the noose of widespread death which catches the fools who follow desires (KU 4.2). The *Maitrī Upaniṣad* (MU 4.2) describes a person facing death as tied with nooses made of the fruits of good and evil deeds; here, the fear of the bondage of sin which is found in the hymns to Varuṇa is overtaken by the idea that all action is binding, whether good or bad. The word *pāśa* "noose" is most frequent in the *Śvetāśvatara Upaniṣad*, which says repeatedly that on knowing God one is released from all nooses (below, p. 170).

Not all gods are guardians of order like Varuṇa, and some have particular sinful acts attributed to them. The warrior god Indra, who is the subject of more Ṛgvedic hymns than any other god, is celebrated for his killing of Vṛtra. Vṛtra, whose name means "enclosure" or "stoppage," appears in mythology as a demon who holds back the life-giving waters – either the rivers or rain – until

Indra releases them by killing him, thus making life possible; here the theme of bondage and release appears again, but in cosmic terms. Though Indra's deed is often praised as heroic, it is sometimes seen in Vedic texts as murder, making him a paradigmatic sinner who needs ritual acts to expiate his sin. He is also guilty of killing his father Tvaṣṭṛ. In one version of this myth, when the fire-god Agni performed an act of expiation for Indra,

> he suddenly burnt away all his sin. As a snake might be released from its slough, as one might pull the stalk out of a rush, just like that he was released from all sin.
>
> (*Jaiminīya Brāhmaṇa* 2.134)

Indra's sinfulness is recalled in an Upaniṣadic passage (KsU 3.1–2) which will be examined below (pp. 138–139).

The snake's sloughing of its skin, a powerful image of renewal, appears in another Brāhmaṇa passage, which illustrates the part played in the sacrifice by the mental attitude of the man who offers it (the *yajamāna* – see below, p. 66). This passage makes the bold claim that a man who sacrifices for himself is superior to one who sacrifices to the gods. The one who sacrifices to the gods is like an inferior bringing tribute to a king, while the one who sacrifices for himself knows that he is making himself a new body.

> As a snake might free itself from its skin, even so is he freed from this mortal body, from sin.
>
> (SB 11.2.6.13)

Here, the bondage of sin is seen as a necessary condition of human life, unless it is thrown off through ritual action performed with the right knowledge.

The image of the snake's slough appears again, in the Upaniṣads (BU 4.4.7; below, p. 137). Throughout the Veda, images and phrases recur in different contexts, with variations in wording and sometimes with profound differences of meaning.

While the way to release is described differently in different texts, sin and bondage, together with mortality, are the condition in which the Vedic poets and ritualists find themselves; the goal to which they aspire is liberation, deathlessness or immortality. This aspiration is often expressed in terms of a contrast between this world, subject to limitations of space and time – including the limitation of our life by death – and the world beyond. This contrast, and the aspiration to transcend the limitations of this world, may be found in many religious traditions, or even, it has been claimed, in all of them:

> Religion is always directed towards salvation, never towards life itself as it is given; and in this respect all religion, with no exception, is the religion of deliverance.
>
> (Van der Leeuw 1967: vol. 2, pp. 681–682)

This does not give us a license to read into the Upaniṣads and other Vedic texts whatever ideas we may have about salvation or sin; on the contrary, we need to be open to what they say about the limitations of this world and the freedom of the other world, if we are to understand what they mean by liberation.

One point to note is that release or liberation in the Vedic hymns often refers to a condition in this world, rather than beyond death. Sometimes, however, they ask for prosperity or security in the world of the dead. A place in that world is secured by ritual acts in this world (RV 10.14.8, quoted above, p. 60).

Vedic ritual

The general term for Vedic ritual is *yajña*. This is conventionally translated "sacrifice," but etymologically it has the more general meaning of an act of worship. It does not necessarily involve killing animals; many *yajña*s only involve offerings of plant or dairy products, and some are performed mentally, without material offerings. But the Brāhmaṇas give much of their attention to the more elaborate sacrifices, which do include the killing and cutting up of animals. The Vedas tend to deny the violence inherent in this process: The animals are killed by suffocation, not by a blow or cut, and they are not said to be killed but "quietened" or "pacified." The commonest victim is a goat, followed by sheep and cattle; for special purposes other victims are prescribed. The horse sacrifice, associated with kingship and conquest, is one of the rarer and more elaborate rituals; accordingly, it is dealt with extensively in the texts (e.g. SB 13.1–5). The list of animal sacrifices in the Brāhmaṇas culminates with the human sacrifice (*puruṣa-medha*); but this may have been included for the sake of completeness, without intending it to be performed. The Vedic accounts of it refer frequently to the hymn which describes the evolution of the world from a primal man (RV 10.90). One such account describes a primordial *puruṣa-medha*, initiated by the primal man (*puruṣa*) himself in order to "be the whole world" (SB 13.6.1.1); the sacrifice is interrupted by a voice telling him not to proceed (SB 13.6.2.13).

The most elaborate sacrifices are those involving the ritual drink Soma; it is these that require *sāman*s to be chanted by the *udgātṛ*, and they also involve animal offerings. What plant Soma was extracted from, and what psychotropic effects it may have had, are questions that have had many answers, none of them definitive, and that are beyond the scope of this book. Even if we knew what it was, and sampled it, that would not enable us to replicate the experience of the Vedic people, because it would not have the same associations for us as it had for them; it would be like trying to understand Proust by eating madeleines. What matters to us is the ritual and cosmological significance ascribed to Soma in the texts. The word *soma*, meaning something pressed out, refers primarily to the drink, not the plant; it is also the name of a god, who is embodied in the drink. Soma is the drink of immortality (*amṛta*, cognate with ancient Greek *ambrosía*, the food of the gods), and the life-giving fluid that nourishes and fertilizes the universe. Hence the texts can identify it, or him, with rain, milk or semen (Gonda 1965: 47–48). In the thought of the Brāhmaṇas, this cosmic function of Soma brings it into close association with the moon, whose waxing and waning makes it an embodiment of both the world of the dead and the renewal of life, and which, as in many cultures, is associated with rain and vegetation (Gonda 1965: 42–44). We will see in Chapter 12 how some of the Upaniṣads develop ideas about Soma, the moon and the renewal of life which they inherited from the Brāhmaṇas.

Each sacrifice takes place on a piece of ground consecrated for the purpose, not in a temple or other permanent sacred place. The most important part of the site is the *vedi*, conventionally but misleadingly called an altar; it is not built but dug. The marking out of the ground, building of shelters, digging of pits and so on are directed by the *adhvaryu*. Another important figure in Vedic ritual is the *yajamāna*: the word means one who has a sacrifice performed. The *yajamāna* is the one who receives the merit resulting from the sacrifice; he also provides the ground and the offerings, and makes gifts to the various members of the team of priests. To do this he has to be wealthy, and the typical *yajamāna* is a king. The Brāhmaṇas and Upaniṣads contain stories of discerning and generous kings who know how to engage the best priests, and brahmins who know how to attract the patronage of the best kings (Black 2007: 102, 106–112; CU 1.10–11; SB 11.6.2; SB 11.6.3; this story is elaborated in BU 3). The motive for the *yajamāna* to do all this is to provide a secure existence for himself. This may take the form of long life in this world, or the birth of sons who will carry on his lineage, and also maintain him in the world of the dead through ancestral offerings. Other ways of understanding security include entering a timeless world beyond the sun – since it is the sun that measures time by dividing it into days and years – and forming a body which is not subject to death. The aim of forming such a body is prominent in a particularly elaborate ritual, the *agnicayana* "piling of the fire," in which a great fireplace is built. Before discussing it, we must look closer at the key figure of Prajāpati.

Prajāpati

Each sacrifice replicates a primordial sacrifice: "What is done here is what the gods did" (SB 7.2.1.4; 7.3.2.6). The Brāhmaṇas switch frequently between the present time for which they lay down instructions, and the mythic time in which the actions were first performed. The mythic prototype of the *yajamāna* is Prajāpati, whose name means "lord of offspring," or "lord of the people" Prajāpati is also the prototype of the king (Black 2007: 102). He is named only six times in the *Ṛgveda Saṃhitā*; but one important occurrence is at the end of RV 10.121. The first nine stanzas of this hymn extol the cosmic powers of an unnamed god, each ending with the refrain "Who is the god that we should worship with sacrifice?" The final stanza answers the question by naming Prajāpati. He appears also in a marriage hymn, where he is asked to ensure the fertility of the marriage (RV 10.85.43) – fulfilling his function as lord of offspring.

Another hymn which is significant for understanding Prajāpati, though it does not mention his name, is RV 10.90, mentioned above, in which the world is derived, by a ritual process, from the primal man. The moon was born from his mind, the sun from his eyesight, the wind from his breath, the atmosphere from his navel, the sky from his head, the earth from his feet, and the directions from his hearing (RV 10.90.13–14). In this way, each part of the microcosm has its counterpart in the macrocosm. The first three correspondences and the last have been explained above; "the sky from his head" and "the earth from his feet" are easy to understand, while the atmosphere corresponds to the navel because it is between the two, and hollow. Though the production of the universe is described as a sacrifice (*yajña*) in which Man is the offering (RV 10.90.6), tethered (RV 10.90.15), and divided (RV 10.90.11), this does not mean that he is now a dismembered carcass; the hymn says he lives on, as "the universe, what is and what is to be, and lord of immortality" (RV 10.90.2).

Prajāpati is mentioned more frequently in the Atharvaveda than in the Ṛgveda, and he is prominent in the Brāhmaṇas. There, he is both the creator god and the lord of sacrifice; these two functions are inseparable, since creation is viewed as a cosmic sacrifice. In a myth which appears in many variants, the creative process starts with Prajāpati's desire or wish:

> This world in the beginning was Prajāpati – only one. He desired: "May I be; may I be procreated."
>
> (SB 11.5.8.1)

The idea that creation is initiated by desire recalls RV 10.129.4: "Desire came upon it in the beginning" (Killingley 2004: 270). "May I be procreated" (*prajāyeya*) recalls Prajāpati's name, "Lord of offspring"; it is only by procreation that he can be true to his name, and so be really himself. That is what he means by "May I be"; in other cosmogonies he says "May I be more; may I be procreated" (SB 6.1.1.8) or "May I be many; may I be procreated" (TU 2.6). He fulfils his desire by producing the universe; the many variants of this myth evoke copulation, or the hatching of an egg, or the heat (*tapas*) generated by ascetic practices. The same scenario is repeated in various forms in the Upaniṣads. There, the original being is variously called Prajāpati (PU 1.4), "a self in the form of a man" (BU 1.4.1), "Brahman" (BU 1.4.10), or "Being" (CU 6.2.1). Already in the Brāhmaṇas the original being has other names besides Prajāpati: it can be "Not-being" (*asat*, SB 6.1.1.1). This primordial Not-being becomes a "man" (*puruṣa*, SB 6.1.1.3), who then becomes Prajāpati (SB 6.1.1.5). The idea of a primordial Not-being is a departure from the "neither not-being nor being" which opens RV 10.129; it is expressly rejected in CU 6.2.1–2. Already in the Vedic hymns, mythology is not static; in the Brāhmaṇas and Upaniṣads, it is a field in which thinkers can be innovative, and sometimes combative.

In creating or becoming the world, Prajāpati becomes many, as he wished; but this is a loss as well as a gain. In Vedic thought, unity is perfection; it is both the source of existence and its goal. Thus creation itself is a fall, from which Prajāpati, or the *yajamāna*, needs to be restored by the ritual. This is expressed in various ways: Prajāpati feels empty, and needs to be fed with sacrificial victims (*Kauṣītaki Brāhmaṇa* 12,8, Keith 1920: 417; SB 3.9.4.1–4); his joints become loose (SB 1.6.3.35; 4.6.4.1); he is shattered (SB 6.1.2.12). The purpose of the *agnicayana*, the building of the great fireplace, is to restore Prajāpati, and in so doing to provide the *yajamāna* with an imperishable body. In a discussion of another ritual, performed at the new moon and full moon, it is explained that Prajāpati gave himself to the gods, and so he became the sacrifice. He redeemed himself from the gods by performing the new and full moon sacrifice; and the *yajamāna* does the same:

> When he performs the sacrifice, he redeems himself from the gods by the sacrifice itself, even as Prajāpati redeemed himself by it … Thus his whole sacrifice is redeemed, and it, the sacrifice, becomes the *yajamāna*'s body in the other world. The *yajamāna* who performs that redemption knowing this, has a complete body in the other world.
>
> (SB 11.1.8.5–6)

The mental component of ritual

The last sentence in the above quotation shows the importance of knowledge for successful performance of Vedic ritual. This is one of many passages in the Brāhmaṇas which explain the meaning of a ritual, and then promise rewards to those who not only perform it but know its meaning as it has been explained; we have quoted one already, on the gods' bargain with Death (SB 10.4.3.9–10; above, pp. 60–61). Similar promises occur in the Upaniṣads (BU 1.2.3; 1.2.5; CU 1.1.8). Conversely, there are warnings not to perform a ritual without knowing its hidden meaning (CU 2.24.2); or that if one does, his head will shatter (CU 1.10.8; see also pp. 40, 100, 199, 255). Another essential component of ritual is *śraddhā* "faith," meaning both belief in its efficacy and determination to perform it properly (the word is cognate with Latin *credo* "I believe," and means etymologically "placing of the heart"). Even if no material offering is available for the daily offering of milk in the fire (*agnihotra*), it is still possible to perform it "with truth in faith" (SB 11.3.1.4); that is, with truth as the offering and faith as the fire (SB 11.3.1.1). The same daily offering is replaced by an offering of food to one's own vital powers (CU 5.18–24). Even breathing can be made an "internal fire-offering" (KsU 2.5). This internalization of ritual is typical of the Upaniṣads; but such non-material performance of the *agnihotra* is prescribed in the Brāhmaṇas also (Bodewitz 1976: 136–144).

The Brāhmaṇas thus present not only a system of ritual, but a system of knowledge. The knowledge concerns the ritual itself, but also the natural world, and the nature of the human being; and it often involves connections or homologies between them. We have already seen such connections between parts of the man and parts of the universe in RV 10.90, and in RV 10.16.3, the funeral hymn which sends the dead man's eyesight to the sun, his breath to the wind; they occur again in a longer account of the dispersal of a person at death (BU 3.2.13).

The correspondences are counterfactual; if they were not, they would not be interesting, either to the Vedic thinkers or to us. They are not about cosmology or anatomy, but about a distinctive way of understanding the cosmos, the human person, and Vedic ritual. It is in this way that we should understand statements such as the ones which have floored many readers opening the Upaniṣads for the first time:

> The head of the sacrificial horse is the dawn. His eyesight is the sun, his breath is the wind … his limbs are the seasons … his joints are the months and half-months … His shaking is thunder. His urinating is rain. His speech is Speech.
>
> (BU 1.1.1)

We may be tempted to skip this passage and move on, perhaps to a creation myth in which Death is the origin of all beings (BU 1.2), or to a more attractive one which starts with a self alone in the form of a man (BU 1.4.1), and goes on to the well-known identification of the Self with *brahman* (BU 1.4.6; 1.4.10). But the opening passage about the horse reminds us that this Upaniṣad is part of the SB, which is part of the Yajurveda, the knowledge which equips the *adhvaryu* for his role as director of the physical operations of the ritual. (In the Mādhyaṃdina recension of the White Yajurveda, this passage appears also as SB 10.6.4; and a very similar passage appears in the Black Yajurveda's TS 7.5.25 (Keith 1914: 636–637) – a reminder that the boundary between Brāhmaṇas and Upaniṣads is fluid.) The *Chāndogya Upaniṣad*, which belongs to the Sāmaveda, begins similarly with a set of correspondences, linking the Sāmavedic chant to the macrocosm.

Sometimes the correspondence is based on a number. For instance, a gold plate used in the royal consecration has either a hundred holes, because man lives up to a hundred years, or nine holes, because there are nine orifices in the human body (SB 5.4.1.13); a vessel used in another ritual has a hundred holes or nine holes for the same reason (SB 5.5.4.27). In both cases, a correspondence is established between an object and an aspect of the *yajamāna*, ensuring that he is embodied in the ritual. Another significant number is 360, which in Vedic reckoning is the number of days in a year, counting twelve months of thirty days each (Macdonell and Keith 1912: vol. 2, pp. 411–413), and also the number of bones in the human body (an overestimate). The great fireplace, which is also the body of Prajāpati and of the *yajamāna*, is built with 360 bricks and 360 stones; it is thus equated with the year (SB 10.5.4.10) and with the body (SB 10.5.4.12). The fireplace is built in five layers – another number significant in the microcosm and in the macrocosm. The five layers are equated with five layers of Prajāpati's body (hairs, skin, flesh, bone, marrow), the five seasons, and the five directions (SB 6.1.2.17–19). The seasons are spring, summer, rains, autumn, and winter (Macdonell and Keith 1912: vol. 1, pp. 110–111), and the five directions are east, west, north, south, and upwards. A passage on animal sacrifice says: "The sacrifice is fivefold; the sacrificial animal is fivefold; there are five seasons in the year" (SB 11.7.4.4), the five sacrificial animals being goat, sheep, ox, horse and (at least theoretically) man (above, p. 51). The same pattern of pentads continues in the Upaniṣads:

> This same sacrifice is fivefold. The sacrificial animal is fivefold. Man is fivefold. The whole world, whatever there is, is fivefold. So he who knows this gains the whole world.
>
> (BU 1.4.17)

A more elaborate account lists the pentads in the macrocosm and the microcosm:

> Earth, atmosphere, sky, directions, intermediate directions; fire, wind, sun, moon, stars; water, plants, trees, space, self – that is with reference to beings. Now with reference to oneself: Breath, apart-breath, lower breath, up-breath, together-breath; sight, hearing, mind, speech, touch; skin, flesh, sinew, bone, marrow. After analysing in this way, the sage said: "The whole world is fivefold. By the fivefold one secures the fivefold."
>
> (TU 1.7)

The microcosmic pentads listed here are the five "breaths" (*prāṇa*) which are important in Upaniṣadic thought (though it is hard to match them with modern physiology); a variant of the common Vedic list of five faculties; and the five layers of the human body. The idea that man is fivefold, apparent already in the Brāhmaṇas, was developed further in the Upaniṣads, and further again in Sāṃkhya and Yoga philosophy (below, pp. 179–182). The list of faculties is not always the same, but it usually includes sight, hearing, and speech; the list of layers of the body is not quite the same five as in SB 6.1.2.17 above. The pentadic principle persists, though the membership of each pentad may vary.

How revolutionary are the Upaniṣads?

The theory of ritual developed in the Brāhmaṇas depended on ideas about the gods inherited from the *mantras*, but also developed and elaborated. It involved ideas about the world, including the role of the sun and moon in regulating seasons and the calendar; the human and animal body; and the role of plants and rain in supplying them with food. These ideas do not always match modern astronomy, biology, or anatomy, but they do show curiosity and a desire to systematize knowledge, and they sometimes show accurate observation. Because of the prominence of speech in the ritual, the theorists were particularly interested in words, leading eventually to remarkable developments in linguistic sciences, in which ancient India excelled over other ancient cultures. The Vedic schools produced texts on phonetics to ensure correct pronunciation of the *mantras*; and the grammarians whose work culminated in Pāṇini's set of rules, the *Aṣṭādhyāyī*, in the fourth century BCE, used methods of organizing rules which had been developed in the ritual sūtras (Staal 2003).

The Upaniṣads often, though not invariably, reject the ritual concerns of the Saṃhitās and Brāhmaṇas, teaching a knowledge which makes ritual unnecessary. But the concerns of the Brāhmaṇas continue to appear. Security from death is sought, but through knowledge rather than through ritual action. Much of the knowledge which the Upaniṣads teach is developed from ideas that are present in the Brāhmaṇas: the analysis of personality, and the correspondence of components of personality with components of the macrocosm. The continuity of Vedic thought is clear, particularly when we look at the *Bṛhadāraṇyaka* and the *Chāndogya*, the oldest, longest and most Brāhmaṇa-like of the Upaniṣads.

References

Black, Brian. 2007. *The Character of the Self in Ancient India: Priests, Kings, And Women In The Early Upaniṣads*. Albany, NY: State University of New York Press.

Bodewitz, H. W. 1976. *The Daily Evening and Morning Offering (Agnihotra) According to the Brāhmaṇas*. Leiden: Brill.

Gonda, Jan. 1965. *Change and Continuity in Indian Religion*. The Hague: Mouton.

Gonda, Jan. 1966. *Loka: World and Heaven in the Veda*. Amsterdam: Noord-Hollandsche Uitgevers Maatschappij (North Holland Publishing Company).

Gonda, Jan. 1975. *Vedic Literature* (A History of Indian Literature Vol. 1, Fasc. 1). Wiesbaden: Harrassowitz.

Gonda, Jan. 1978. *Hymns of the Ṛgveda Not Employed in the Solemn Ritual*. Amsterdam: North Holland.

Gonda, Jan. 1986. "Mind and Moon" in G. Bhattacharya (ed.) *Deyadharma: Studies in Memory of D. C. Sircar*. Delhi: Sri Satguru, 147–160.

Keith, A. B. 1914. *The Veda of the Black Yajuṣ School Entitled Taittirīya Saṃhitā: Translated from the Original Sanskrit Prose and Verse*. 2 vols. Cambridge, MA: Harvard University Press. (Reprint Delhi: Motilal Banarsidass, 1967.)

Keith, A. B. 1920. *Rigveda Brahmanas: The Aitareya and Kauṣītaki Brāhmaṇas of the Rigveda Translated from the Original Sanskrit*. Cambridge, MA: Harvard University Press. (Reprint Delhi: Motilal Banarsidass, 1971.)

Killingley, Dermot. 2004. "Kāma" in Sushil Mittal and Gene Thursby (eds)*The Hindu World*. New York: Routledge, 264–287.

Macdonell, A. A., and A. B. Keith, 1912. *Vedic Index of Names and Subjects*. 2 vols. London: John Murray. (Reprint Delhi: Motilal Banarsidass, 1958.)

O'Flaherty, Wendy Doniger. 1981. *The Rig Veda: An Anthology*. Harmondsworth: Penguin.

Oldenberg, Hermann. 1919. *Vorwissenschaftliche Wissenschaft: die Weltanschauung der Brāhmana-Texte*. Göttingen: Vandenhoeck & Ruprecht.

Rodhe, Sten Olof. 1946. *Deliver us from Evil: Studies on the Vedic Ideas of Salvation*. Lund: C. W. K. Gleerup.

Roebuck, Valerie. 2003. *The Upaniṣads. Translated and Edited* (Penguin Classics series). London: Penguin.

Staal, Frits. 2003. "The Science of Language" in Gavin Flood (ed.) *The Blackwell Companion to Hinduism*. Oxford: Blackwell, 348–359.

Van Buitenen, J. A. B. 1959. "Akṣara" *Journal of the American Oriental Society* 79: 186–187.

Van der Leeuw, Gerardus. 1967. *Religion in Essence and Manifestation*, translated by J. E. Turner. 2 vols. Gloucester, MA: Peter Smith.

Further reading

Black, Brian. 2007. *The Character of the Self in Ancient India: Priests, Kings, and Women in the early Upaniṣads*. Albany, NY: State University of New York Press.

Brockington, John. 1981. *The Sacred Thread: Hinduism in its Continuity and Diversity*. Edinburgh: Edinburgh University Press, 29–50.

Patton, Laurie L. "Veda and Upaniṣad" in Sushil Mittal and Gene Thursby (eds) *The Hindu World*. New York: Routledge, 37–51.

Witzel, Michael. 2003. "Vedas and Upaniṣads" in Gavin Flood (ed.) *The Blackwell Companion to Hinduism*. Oxford: Blackwell, 68–101.

8 The Upaniṣads and early Buddhism

Signe Cohen

The relationship between the Upaniṣads and early Buddhism is a complex one, and a great deal has been written on this topic. It is generally assumed that the earliest Upaniṣads, such as the *Bṛhadāraṇyaka*, the *Chāndogya Upaniṣad*, and the *Aitareya Upaniṣad*, are pre-Buddhist, and that some of the later Upaniṣads, such as the *Maitrī Upaniṣad*, are composed after the rise of Buddhism.

The precise nature of the relationship between the early Upaniṣads and Buddhism is not, however, at all well understood. Scholars are deeply divided on the topic of the possible influence of the Upaniṣads on early Buddhism. Some claim that Upaniṣadic ideas have influenced Buddhism in significant ways, while others maintain that there is no evidence that the authors of the early Buddhist texts were familiar with the Upaniṣads at all.

There can be no doubt that the older Upaniṣads and early Buddhism share ideas about the unsatisfying nature of earthly existence, of rebirth, *karma*, and final liberation, and of the role of knowledge in the process of salvation. The idea of *karma*, tentatively introduced in the *Bṛhadāraṇyaka Upaniṣad* as an esoteric doctrine a wisdom teacher can only share with his trusted student in secret, is fully accepted in the earliest Buddhism. Likewise, the idea of rebirth, mentioned in several of the older Upaniṣads, is a central tenet of early Buddhism. Like the Upaniṣads, Buddhism teaches that humans (and other living beings) are trapped in a cycle of death and rebirth, and that our next birth will be determined by our karma. And like the Upaniṣads, Buddhism proposes that our highest goal is to escape this cycle and reach liberation, and that the correct knowledge will make this possible. But were these ideas borrowed from the Upaniṣads into early Buddhism, or were they simply part of a "common property" of thoughts and ideas that many people shared during this time period?

In the following, I will outline the two main positions scholars have taken regarding the relationship between the Upaniṣads and early Buddhism.

1: There is no direct relationship between the Upaniṣads and early Buddhism

The main argument for this position is a simple one: There are no direct references to the Upaniṣads in the canonical texts of early Buddhism. While the Buddhist texts mention (and reject) one of the central ideas of the Upaniṣads, *ātman* (the self, *attā* in Pāli, the language of early Buddhism), no mention at all is made in Buddhist texts of the equally significant Upaniṣadic concept of *brahman*. The word *Brahmā* occurs in Buddhist texts, but always as a masculine noun meaning a Hindu god, rather than a neuter noun meaning "cosmic force." The important Upaniṣadic wisdom teachers, like Yājñavalkya and Pippalāda, are not mentioned in Buddhist texts, even though the teachers of other rival movements are.

It is possible, as Pratap Chandra argues,[1] that the authors of the early Buddhist texts were simply not familiar with the Upaniṣads at all. There are some shared ideas between Buddhism and the Upaniṣads, such as *karma*, reincarnation, and final liberation, but these ideas may not be direct borrowings, but rather thoughts originating in a cultural *milieu* from which both the Upaniṣads and early Buddhism found inspiration. Bronkhorst, in his in-depth study of ancient culture of the Greater Magadha region where Buddhism originated, suggests that ideas of *karma* and reincarnation originated in the local spiritual traditions of Greater Magadha and then entered both the Upaniṣadic tradition and Buddhism.[2]

Horsch[3] and Chandra[4] both argue that there is no evidence that the Buddha knew anything about the Upaniṣads. Horsch suggests that the reason why the Buddha was not acquainted with the Upaniṣads was that most of the Upaniṣads arose in a rural environment, as opposed to the urban setting of Buddhism, and that the Upaniṣads were transmitted in esoteric and priestly circles, to which the Buddha likely did not have access.[5]

2: The Upaniṣads influenced early Buddhism

The idea of an eternal self, *ātman*, is of central importance in the Upaniṣads. When Buddhism from the very beginning declares that there is no self (*attā* in Pāli, the language of the early Buddhist texts), could this be seen as an explicit response to and rejection of Upaniṣadic ideas? Could the language of awakening, which permeates Buddhism (*bodhi* = awakening, *Buddha* = the awakened one), be a biting response to the *Māṇḍūkya Upaniṣad's* notion of the four states of the self (awake, dreaming, dreamless sleep, and the mystical fourth state, deeper than dreamless sleep)? Enough sleeping – time to wake up?

Many scholars have proposed that the Upaniṣads influenced Buddhism in significant ways, even if some of the core teachings differ. Monier Williams suggested that the Buddha "had great sympathy with the philosophy of the Upaniṣads."[6] Ranade goes even further in suggesting that "all the main rudiments of Buddhism are present in embryo in the Upaniṣads."[7] Radhakrishnan even claims that the "Buddha did not look upon himself as an innovator, but only as the restorer of the ancient way, i.e. the way of the Upanishads."[8] A. K. Sharma writes that the "Buddha fully entered into the spirit of the Upanishads in his attitude towards the popular religion" (i.e. that of the *Brāhmaṇas*).[9]

While few other scholars have gone as far as Radhakrishnan in regarding Buddhism as a continuation of the Upaniṣads, many have pointed to parallels between the Upaniṣads and Buddhism. Although there are no direct quotes from the Upaniṣads in early Buddhism, there is some evidence of familiarity with the Upaniṣads, and particularly those affiliated with the *Black Yajurveda*, in early Buddhist texts. For example the Buddha's rejection of different forms of the self in *Dīgha Nikāya* 1, 86–87 may imply that he is familiar with the *Taittirīya Upaniṣad*.[10] The erroneous view the Buddha ascribes to "a recluse or a brahman" is certainly familiar from the Upaniṣads:

> O monks, a certain recluse or a brahman asserts the following doctrine and view: "The self, sir, has material form; it is composed of the four basic elements and originates from a father and mother. Since this self, sir, is annihilated and destroyed with the breakup of the body and does not exist after death, at this point the self is completely annihilated." In this way some proclaim the annihilation, destruction, and extermination of an existent being. Another says to him: "There is, sir, such a self as you claim. I do not deny that. But it is not at that point that the self is completely annihilated. For there is, sir, another self: divine, with material form, pertaining to the sense sphere, and feeding on edible nutriment. That you neither know nor see, but I know it and see it. Since *this* self, sir, is annihilated and destroyed with the breakup of the body and does not exist after death, at this point the self is completely annihilated." In this way others proclaim the annihilation, destruction, and extermination of an existent being. Another says to him: "There is, sir, such a self as you assert. That I do not deny. But it is not at that point that the self is completely annihilated. For there is, sir, another self: divine, of material form, mind-made, complete in all its limbs and organs, not destitute of any faculties. That you neither know nor see, but I know it and see it. Since *this* self, sir, is annihilated and destroyed with the breakup of the body and does not exist after death, at this point the self is completely annihilated." In this way others proclaim the annihilation, destruction, and extermination of an existent being. … Another one says to him: "There is, sir, such a self as you claim. I do not deny that. But it is not at that point that the self is completely annihilated. For there is, sir, another self belonging to the base of infinite consciousness, (reached by) completely surmounting the base of infinite space (by contemplating): 'Consciousness is infinite.' That you neither know nor see. But I know it and see it. Since *this* self, good sir, is annihilated and destroyed with the breakup of the body and

> does not exist after death – at this point the self is completely annihilated." In this way some proclaim the annihilation, destruction, and extermination of an existent being.

Three of the forms of self mentioned in the *Dīgha Nikāya* – the self made of food, the self made of mind, and the self made of understanding – correspond exactly to three of the five forms of *ātman* described in the *Taittirīya Upaniṣad*: The self made of food, the self made of breath, the self made of mind, the self made of understanding, and the self made of bliss. Although this passage from the *Dīgha Nikāya* also shows a familiarity with other brahmanical notions of self, such as a purely material one made up of the physical elements, the parallels with the *Taittirīya Upaniṣad* are nevertheless intriguing.

It is possible, in spite of the Buddha's rejection of the doctrine of *ātman*, that the notion of the five-fold self in the *Taittirīya Upaniṣad* influenced the Buddhist notion of the five aggregates (*skandha/khandha*) that make up a human being: Form, sensation, sensory perception, mental formations, and consciousness. Although these five *khandhas* do not make up a self according to Buddhist doctrine, they do function together as a pseudo-*ātman* in that they make up a living being, albeit temporarily.

Goto has noted a "striking resemblance" between the conversation between Yājñavalkya and king Janaka in *Bṛhadāraṇyaka Upaniṣad* 4 and the dialogue between the Buddha and king Ajātasattu in the *Sāmaññaphalasutta* of the *Dīghanikāya*,[11] a similarity pointed out already by Deussen.[12] Both dialogues involve a wisdom teacher and a king, summarize the necessary steps to take to reach spiritual liberation, and end with the king's enlightenment.

Another striking parallel between the Upaniṣads and early Buddhism may be found in the famous parable of the chariot of the *Kaṭha Upaniṣad* 3.3–4 (also referenced briefly in the *Śvetāśvatara Upaniṣad* and the *Maitrī Upaniṣad*, see ch. 31):

> Know the Self as the rider in a chariot
> And the body as the chariot
> Know the intellect as the charioteer
> And the mind as the reins.
>
> The senses are the horses,
> And the sense objects are the paths

The following passage from the Buddhist text *Mahānāradakassapa Jātaka* is intriguingly similar:

> Thy body is called a chariot, swift and provided with the mind as a charioteer … Mind pursues the path of self-control with its steeds all equally trained, desire and lust are an evil path, but self-control is the straight road. As the steed rushes along after forms and sounds and smells, intellect uses the scourge and the self is the charioteer.[13]

The parable of the chariot is also invoked again in the well-known Buddhist text *Dhammapada*: "He who restrains anger like a run-away chariot, he is a real driver; the others just hold the reins."[14]

Since this chariot parable is found primarily in the Upaniṣads of the *Black Yajurveda*, and in Buddhism, it is perhaps not unreasonable to assume that early Buddhism had some acquaintance with the Upaniṣads of the *Black Yajurveda*. That the Buddha himself had some knowledge of the *Black Yajurveda* may perhaps be implied in the clan name given to his wife in the *Apadāna* and the *Lalitavistara*: Kaccānā, i.e. Kātyāyanī.[15] This would seem to associate the Buddha's wife with the Kātyāyana school of the *Black Yajurveda*. A slight problem arises in assuming that the Buddha's wife belonged to a Brahman *gotra* or clan: As the wife of a prince, wouldn't she be a Kṣatriya (princely caste), rather than a Brahman (priestly caste)? Since the Buddha himself, Siddhattha Gotama, is also carrying the name of a brahman *gotra* (Gotama), we can only say that traditional Brahman names are encountered in the legend of the Buddha's life, no matter what the historical veracity of these legends are. To confuse matters further, the Buddha's foster-mother, Mahāprajāpatī, is referred to as *Gotamī*, a name associated with his father's family, even though she is supposedly related to the Buddha on his mother's side, rather than his father's. Rather than attempting to untangle the Buddha's family relations, we may simply conclude that the legends of his life contain some Brahman names, some of them associated with the *Black Yajurveda* tradition.

The assumption that there was some connection between the *Black Yajurveda* and early Buddhism is further confirmed by Upaniṣadic parallels in the Buddhist *Abhidharmamahāvibhāṣāśāstra*. As Hajime has pointed out,[16] this Sarvāstivāda text appears to quote a passage common to the *Kaṭha* and the *Śvetāśvatara Upaniṣad*: "Or the inner *ātman* exists in the heart of creatures, and is the size of a thumb. It is full of splendor." This quote corresponds to *Kaṭha Upaniṣad* 6.17 or *Śvetāśvatara Upaniṣad* 3.13: "A person the size of a thumb within the body always exists in the heart of creatures …" The same Sārvāstivāda text also appears to be familiar with *Śvetāśvatara Upaniṣad* 3.8: "We must know this person, and then we can pass beyond birth, decay, sickness, and death. There is no other path for going there."

One might also note that some of the main characters of the Upaniṣads reappear in the Buddhist *Jātaka* stories, legends of the Buddha's previous lives. The learned Uddālaka of the Buddhist *Uddālaka Jātaka*,[17] who attracts huge crowds of people due to his erudition, but who ultimately has to learn from the Buddha himself in a previous incarnation, is reminiscent of Uddālaka Āruṇi so frequently mentioned in the older Upaniṣads. Uddālaka Āruṇi's son, the proud Śvetaketu, is a main character in the *Bṛhadāraṇyaka Upaniṣad*, the *Chāndogya Upaniṣad*, and the *Kauṣītaki Upaniṣad*. A young man bearing the Pāli version of his name is the main character of the Buddhist *Setaketu Jātaka*.[18] In a rather humorous passage, Setaketu, who is the leader of a group of ascetics, hears that the king is coming to see them, and immediately instructs his ascetics to put on a good ascetic show by lying on thorn beds, doing the "swinging penance" or the "five fire penance" or reciting texts. Setaketu himself sits down more comfortably on a chair with a headrest and explains a book to a group of students. This reference to Setaketu may be seen as a gentle ridicule of Hindu ascetics, represented by a figure prominent in the Upaniṣads. But curiously, Setaketu is also in Buddhism the name of an enlightened bodhisattva, sometimes even the Buddha himself dwelling in the Tuṣita heaven waiting to become the future prince Siddhattha. This identification of Śvetaketu with the Buddha seems to indicate both a familiarity with the figure of Śvetaketu and respect for this Upaniṣadic character. There seems to be some evidence, in short, that the early Buddhist community was familiar with the world-view of the Upaniṣads, and that of the *Black Yajurveda* Upaniṣads in particular.

Conversely, it is also possible to see some influence from Buddhism in some of the later of the classical Upaniṣads. In a curious passage of the *Maitrī Upaniṣad*, the highest being is referred to as *nirātman* ("without an *ātman*"), a most unusual characteristic of the highest principle in the Upaniṣads,[19] where *ātman* itself is usually seen as the highest. It is possible to see strange phrase as a reference to Buddhism with its central idea of *anattā* ("no-self"), although the rest of the *Maitrī Upaniṣad*, with its elaborations on the nature of *ātman*, is clearly not Buddhist. The term is perhaps best translated as "without individuality" rather than "without self" in the *Maitrī Upaniṣad*, but the occurrence of this curious word hints at some familiarity with Buddhism, even if there is no acceptance of Buddhist doctrines. Similarly, the word *śūnya* ("empty") in the same passage in the *Maitrī Upaniṣad* is a term that resonates with Buddhist implications; in Buddhism, everything in the world is empty because everything is devoid of self, or eternal essence. The use of a few pieces of quasi-Buddhist vocabulary hardly makes the *Mautrī Upaniṣad* a Buddhist text, but it does hint at the possibility of historical connections between Buddhism and the Upaniṣads, especially those formally affiliated with the *Yajurveda*.

Notes

1 Chandra 1971.
2 Bronkhorst 2007.
3 Horsch 1968: 463.
4 Chandra 1971: 321.
5 Horsch 1968: 464.
6 Monier Williams 1888 (1964): 105.
7 Ranade 1926 (1968): 133.
8 Radhakrishnan 1923: 470.
9 Sharma 1928: 444.
10 Potter 1966: 569, note 1.
11 Goto 2005.
12 Deussen 1897: 456.
13 Quoted from Cowell 1895, Vol. VI: 125.
14 *Dhammapada* 17.2.
15 Kosambi 1953: 205.

16 Hajime 1955: 81.
17 Cowell 1895, Vol. IV: 188ff.
18 Cowell 1895, Vol. IV: 152ff.
19 *Maitrī Upaniṣad* 2.4.

References

Bronkhorst, J. 2007. *Greater Magadha: Studies in the Culture of Early India*. Leiden: Brill.

Chandra, P. 1971. "Was Early Buddhism Influenced by the Upaniṣads?" *Philosophy East and West* 21: 317–324.

Cowell, E. B. 1895. *Jātaka Stories*. Vols. I–VI. Cambridge: Cambridge University Press. (Reprint Delhi: Motilal Banarsidass, 1990).

Deussen, P. 1897. *Sechzig Upaniṣads des Veda, aus dem Sanskrit übersetzt und mit Einleitungen und Anmerkungen versehen*. Leipzig: F. A. Brockhaus.

Goto, T. 2005. "Yājñavalkya's Characterization of the Ātman and the Four Kinds of Suffering in Early Buddhism" *Electronic Journal of Vedic Studies* 12 (2): 70–84.

Hajime, N. 1955. "Upaniṣadic Tradition and the Early School of Vedānta as Noticed in Buddhist Scripture" *Harvard Journal of Asiatic Studies* 18: 74–104.

Horsch, P. 1968. "Buddhismus und Upaniṣaden" in J. C. Heesterman G. H. Schokker and V. I. Subramoniam (eds) *Pratidānam: Indian, Iranian, and Indo-European Studies Presented to Fransiscus Bernardus Jacobus Kuiper on his Sixtieth Birthday*, Hague/Paris: Mouton, 462–477.

Kosambi, D. D. 1953. "Brahmin Clans" *Journal of the American Oriental Society* 73: 202–208.

Monier Williams, M. 1888. Buddhism in Its Connexion with Brāhmanism and Hinduism, and Its Contrast with Christianity. (Reprint Varanasi: Chowkamba Sanskerit Series Office, 1964.)

Oldenberg, H. 1915. *Die Lehre der Upanishaden und die Anfänge des Buddhismus*. Göttingen: Vandenhoeck and Ruprecht.

Potter, K. 1966 *Encyclopedia of Indian Philosophies, Vol. VII: Abhidharma Buddhism to 150 A.D.* Delhi: Motilal Banarsidass.

Radhakrishnan, S. 1923. *Indian Philosophy*. 2 vols. London: George Allen & Unwin.

Ranade, R. D. 1926. A Constructive Survey of Upaniṣadic Philosophy, Being an Introduction to the Thought of the Upaniṣads. (Reprint Bombay: Bharatiya Vidya Bhavan, 1968.)

Sharma, A. K. 1928. "The Relation Between Buddhism and the Upanishads" *The Monist* 38: 443–477.

Further reading

Bronkhorst, J. 2007. *Greater Magadha: Studies in the Culture of Early India*. Leiden: Brill.

Chandra, P. 1971. "Was Early Buddhism Influenced by the Upaniṣads?" *Philosophy East and West* 21: 317–324.

Goto, T. 2005. "Yājñavalkya's Characterization of the Ātman and the Four Kinds of Suffering in Early Buddhism" *Electronic Journal of Vedic Studies* 12 (2), 70–84.

Horsch, P. 1968. "Buddhismus und Upaniṣaden" in J. C. Heesterman, G. H. Schokker, and V. I. Subramoniam (eds) *Pratidānam: Indian, Iranian, and Indo-European*

Studies Presented to Fransiscus Bernardus Jacobus Kuiper on his Sixtieth Birthday. Hague/Paris: Mouton: 462–477.

Monier Williams, M. 1888. *Buddhism in its Connexion with Brāhmanism and Hinduism, and its Contrast with Christianity*. (Reprint Varanasi: Chowkamba Sanskrit Series Office, 1964.)

Oldenberg, H. 1915. *Die Lehre der Upanishaden und die Anfänge des Buddhismus*. Göttingen: Vandenhoeck and Ruprecht.

Sharma, A. K. 1928. "The Relation Between Buddhism and the Upanishads" *The Monist* 38: 443–477.

9 The social background

Caste and gender in the Upaniṣads

Steven E. Lindquist

Introduction

Trying to understand the social world that ancient Indian texts present in their contents – and, in turn, the social world in which these texts were produced – is a complicated, even circular, endeavor. The earliest Indian material, the Vedas, consists of recitations meant for specific sacrificial purposes by narrow groups of technical specialists. For example, the Ṛgveda is the poetic liturgy recited during the course of a sacrifice by one type of priest, while the Yajurveda consists of recitations of the Adhvaryu, the priest who performs most of the ritual actions. As *śruti* (lit. "that which is heard" or "revealed texts"), references to the world outside of the religious imagination are usually incidental or secondary. This is also the case with the Upaniṣads, texts likewise composed by sacrificial specialists, albeit ones with goals different from the practical performance of rites. Their purpose was not the sacrifice itself, but rather an understanding of its abstract associations as well as the deeper role of the human being within the cosmos. In this vein, looking to the Upaniṣads to understand social constructs such as caste or the cultural perceptions of gender requires a significant degree of interpretative caution. It is one thing to discuss how the texts *imagine* a social world – particularly when such constructs are projected onto ancient sages and gods or onto hierarchies of flora, fauna, cosmological objects, and substances – and to talk about them within a confined literary sphere. It is something quite different to extrapolate that analysis onto actual individuals at particular times. Both are complicated, but the latter is far more speculative and subjective. In the past, a significant amount of scholarship has leaned towards interpretative extremes regarding "the position of women in ancient India" or whether caste is immutable and all-pervasive in the ancient world or fundamentally irrelevant to liberation in the Upaniṣads. These types of interpretations invariably privilege certain passages while massaging or bypassing others (for critiques of such approaches in regards to gender, see Jamison 1996; Vanita 2003; Lindquist 2008). Such interpretive strategies are, as far as I am concerned, untenable: The Upaniṣads do not speak with a singular voice on any issue and certainly not on complex social norms or realities. This chapter will largely confine itself to some aspects of caste and gender as reflected in the texts themselves.

Caste

Caste as a religious and social phenomenon is perhaps one of the most studied, and most fiercely debated, aspects of Indian studies *writ large*. For the classical material, the reader would be best to begin with the works of Kane (1962–1975), Dumont (1970), and Smith (1994) along with the related *dharmaśāstra* material (such as Rocher in Davis 2012; Olivelle 1999; Davis 2010; Lubin, Davis, and Krishnan 2010). Sathaye (2015) offers an insightful literary analysis of Viśvāmitra, a caste-crossing sage in ancient literary and modern performance genres. Marriott offers a brief, but useful, introduction to the basic terms (2004) as does Smith (2005).

The term caste in English-language scholarship often collapses two related Indian phenomena: *varṇa* (lit. "hue" or "color") and *jāti* ("birth group"). *Varṇa* is found as early as R̥gveda 10.90, the famed *puruṣasūkta* hymn where a cosmic person divides his own body into four discrete human social groups based on idealized social function: Brahmin ("priest") from the mouth, Kṣatriya ("warrior") from the arms, Vaiśya ("merchant") from the thighs, and Śūdra ("servant" or "serf") from the feet. The parallel of the body part to the social function is relatively obvious in these cases: Brahmins are associated with sacrificial recitation, Kṣatriyas with strength and protection, Vaiśyas with wealth and fertility, and the Śūdra with menial labor. Their creation, however, is inextricably tied to an extended creation of the whole cosmos: From this cosmic man (*puruṣa*) the sun is created from the eye, the mind from the moon, the midspace from the navel, and so on. Thus the entirety of existence is hierarchically mapped onto a human body and each is part of a mutually reinforcing ranked schema.

Jāti, endogamous birth groups that are especially associated with specific occupations (e.g. tanner or bard) and often viewed within the tradition as ranked subdivisions of *varṇa*, however, are not elaborated until the expert traditions on *dharma* (the *dharmasūtras* and *dharmaśāstras*, ca. third century BCE onwards). Occupational groupings associated with birth are known in the Upaniṣads, as are terms suggesting "low caste" (*vr̥ṣala*, BU 6.4.13) or "outcaste" (*caṇḍāla*/*cāṇḍāla* and *paulkasa*, BU 4.3.22, CU 5.10.7, CU 5.24.4), but detailed discussion is lacking.

Categorizing existence

The *varṇa* classification system is well-known in the Upaniṣads; indeed, as Smith (1994) has shown in great detail, the *varṇa* system is pervasive in taxonomies of all sorts from the Vedas onwards – whether of fauna, flora, celestial bodies, divinities, meters, or hymns. *Varṇa* becomes a principal ordering strategy and its reduplicative logic permits drawing hierarchical connections to innumerable phenomena. Since a leitmotif of the Upaniṣads is drawing connections from one set of phenomena to another – usually from the concrete to the abstract – utilizing the ordering and ranking strategy of the *varṇas* is common, if often assumed and subtle.

When *varṇa* is explicitly referenced in the Upaniṣads, Brahmin and Kṣatriya are the most commonly utilized classifications, both as a means to rank various properties or objects highly and in discussing the role and value of these social groups in isolation or in relation to each other. In this way, Upaniṣadic discussions usually privilege Brahmins first and foremost, but also the power-nexus of Brahmins and Kṣatriyas; that is, those who (at least, in theory) wield the most religious and social power respectively.

Brahmin self-criticism

Though the Brahmin class – and the various phenomena that are homologized to it – is almost universally considered the pinnacle of hierarchies within the Upaniṣads, the composers of the texts were also self-reflective of the fact that a purported ideal and lived reality were not one and the same. Indeed, while the composers were concerned with asserting their own privileged and idealized sacerdotal role, they were also concerned with criticizing those that they saw as falling short of that ideal, even if that critique is implicit or mild. Elsewhere, I have described this community-internal policing as a thematic juxtaposition of "Brahmin by birth" vs. "Brahmins by knowledge and practice," where the former generally (though not universally) is seen as necessary, but not sufficient (Lindquist 2008, 2011).

An explicit example of this is CU 6.1.1 in the story of Śvetaketu, a boy who is sent for Vedic study by his father.

> There was one Śvetaketu, the son of Āruṇi. One day his father told him: "Śvetaketu, take up the celibate life of a student, for there is no one in our family, my son, who has not studied and is the kind of Brahmin who is so only because of birth."
>
> (trans. Olivelle 1998)

The phrase translated here as "the kind of Brahmin who is so only because of birth" is *brahmabandhu*, a "nominal Brahmin." The negative critique in this passage is clear: the first and primary religious obligation of a Brahmin is initiation into Vedic study as a youth, known as *upanayana*, so as to be able to properly fulfill sacerdotal duties. A Brahmin who does not undertake initiation and subsequent study fails his religious and social duty, though he retains the formality of his status by birth. The suggestion that Uddālaka Āruṇi does not want his son to follow this lesser path indicates that at least some Brahmins must have done so.

The story continues that Śvetaketu returned to his father after twelve years of study, haughty in his learning, but his father explained to him that his learning was incomplete since he did not know the abstract Upaniṣadic teaching of the "rule of substitution" (*ādeśa*) which the father then proceeds to teach him. In this passage we get a two-fold hierarchy: A proper Brahmin fulfills his initial obligation of learning the Veda, but a truly educated one also learns the more abstract knowledge that the Upaniṣads themselves teach. The hierarchy of Brahmin-ness is: First, by birth; second, by primary Vedic learning; and third, by advanced Vedic learning, clearly lauding the content of the Upaniṣad of which this story is a part and thus the audience privy to its contents.

A similar criticism occurs with the parallel phrase, *rājanyabandhu*, in another version of the Śvetaketu story. Rājanya here is synonymous with Kṣatriya, though the emphasis may be more on royalty proper. In BU 6.2.3, Śvetaketu is shown to be ignorant, not by his father, but by a king who questions him. Śvetaketu calls the king a *rājanyabandhu*, perhaps a more general insult such as "an excuse of a prince" following Olivelle. The phrase, though, attains a double meaning in the narrative because the king's questions are related to what happens after death, questions appropriate of a Brahmin questioning another Brahmin in the Upaniṣads. This is reinforced in that Śvetaketu's father subsequently goes to learn from him, explicitly as the king's pupil. As such, the king is a "king in name only," because he has knowledge appropriate to, and is acting like, a Brahmin. Thus, the "insult" of not being a proper representative of one's *varṇa* is narratively turned into a positive statement.

This is the sense also found in an earlier story (SBM 11.6.2.1–10; cf. JB 1.22–25) where King Janaka is called a *rājanyabandhu* for knowing more about the esoteric meaning of the *agnihotra* sacrifice than a group of Brahmins. This particular story ends with Janaka receiving a boon permitting him to question the priest Yājñavalkya at will (*kāmapraśna*). The concluding line to the story is, "Thereafter, Janaka was a Brahmin" (*táto brahmā́ janaká āsa*).

There is no indication that Janaka's birth status of *rājanya* was seen as actually altered, but it appears that his social status shifts to allow him to inquire about religious topics that would otherwise have been restricted (as shown in a different story in BU 4, where this boon and Janaka's questioning reappears). His acquiring a social status of "Brahmin" is as much a direct critique of those he outwitted in his questioning as an affirmation of his pursuit of knowledge over entitlement.

Pursuit of knowledge over entitlement is also the theme of the story of Satyakāma in CU 4.4–9, though resolved differently. If the first story presumes a Brahmin birth, but creates a hierarchy based on religious learning following birth, the second story suggests that the social role normally associated with birth – at least in a very limited circumstance – can be bypassed by knowledge. Both of these stories emphasize how knowledge affirms or sidesteps a known birth status. It is in a third story, however, that an unknown birth status comes to be known, this time by moral disposition and action.

Satyakāma is a boy who desires to study the Veda, but he does not know who his father is and thus does not know his *varṇa*.

> One day Satyakāma Jābāla said to his mother Jabālā: "Mother, I want to become a vedic student. So tell me what my lineage is." She replied: "Son, I don't know what your lineage is. I was young when I had you. I was a maid then and had a lot of relationships. As such, it is impossible for me to say what your lineage is. But my name is Jabālā, and your name is Satyakāma. So you should simply say that you are Satyakāma Jābāla."
> (CU 4.1–2, trans. Olivelle 1998)

Satyakāma proceeds to approach a teacher, Hāridrumata Gautama, and repeats his mother's statement verbatim, including the details about her having several relationships! The Brahmin teacher is taken aback and says, "Who but a Brahmin could speak like that! Fetch some firewood, son. I will perform your initiation. You have not strayed from the truth" (CU 4.4.5 trans. Olivelle 1998). Satyakāma, then, is affirmed as a Brahmin, not because he knows his birthright, but because his own disposition to tell the truth in embarrassing detail fits the model of an idealized Brahmin and thus an actual birth status.

The true status of a Brahmin individual, in contrast to his context, is also the theme of the story of Raikva (CU 4.1–3). Jānaśruti Pautrāyaṇa, apparently a king, is trying to find an enigmatic figure named "Raikva, the gatherer" (*sayugvā raikva*), an individual eventually found in the non-Brahminical context of living under a cart and scratching his sores. Jānaśruti tries to entice Raikva twice with riches, the second time by also offering his daughter as a wife. Only after the daughter is included does Raikva agree to teach Jānaśruti, but not without calling Jānaśruti a *śūdra* in both instances.

This particular story is structured on a series of contrasts such as: A king called a *śūdra* vs. a Brahmin who does not live like one; the beautiful daughter to be given in marriage vs. the diseased-skinned bachelor; a palace and wealth vs. homelessness and poverty. He is "Raikva, the gatherer" because he knows the abstract principles that "gather" the lower principles, like in an ancient game of dice where the highest throw collects all the others and like Jānaśruti's gathering of wealth and fame in the story's frame. Raikva may also be seen as a "gatherer" in that wealth (and a wife) come to him eventually because of his knowledge. Unlike Satyakāma, Brahmin-ness is not portrayed in humbleness or truthfulness, but in the knowledge that one possesses.

Each of the examples given above suggest an ideal Brahmin and a critique of what does not attain that ideal. While the Upaniṣads are replete with explicit critiques of others' ritual and philosophical understandings, often of important representatives of particular schools of thought (see BU 3, for example), here the criticisms are of the larger institution of Brahminhood, particularly a Brahminhood solely defined by birth.

Given the preponderance of positive portrayals of Brahmin dominance in the Upaniṣads, however, this self-critique does not suggest any radical questioning of Brahmin hegemony. Rather, it suggests a response to social realities of internal competition and, perhaps, potential or real external criticism as a means to emphasize and capitalize on that hegemony. An emphasis on personal disposition, action, or the possession of particular knowledge as determinative of a "true" Brahmin must have been not only self-critique, but also served a practical role in the competition for patronage, especially from the Kṣatriya class.

Brahmin–Kṣatriya codependence

Brahmin–Kṣatriya codependency, where each is seen as the top of the religious and social hierarchy respectively, is a common theme in the Brāhmaṇas and Upaniṣads. Given that these texts are composed and maintained by Brahmins within their particular priestly lineages, it is not surprising that the emphasis leans strongly towards the religious domain and Brahmins role within it. That said, it must in practice have been a more precarious position for Brahmins: The priesthood can only exist if there are those willing to financially support their services. As such, Kṣatriyas, who are stereotypically the community that can provide material wealth and protection, are common characters in the Upaniṣads and portrayed as especially generous. In turn, it serves the Kṣatriyas' interests to partake in the religious prestige of the sacrificial realm, access to which the Brahmin class can offer through their privileged skills and knowledge.

An example of this complex relationship is BU 1.4.11, a creation myth where *brahman* ("priestly power," but also the foundation of the cosmos) existed at the very beginning and created the *kṣatra* ("royal power") as a form superior to itself. But while royal power might be superior, it is also dependent and even subordinate in that it exists only because of priestly power. As such, the two are inextricably tied to each other's fates.

> In the beginning this world was only *brahman*, only one. Because it was only one, *brahman* had not fully developed. It then created the ruling power, a form superior to and surpassing itself, that is, the ruling powers among the gods – Indra, Varuṇa, Soma, Rudra, Parjanya, Yama, Mṛtyu, and Īśāna. Hence there is nothing higher than the ruling power. Accordingly, at a royal anointing a Brahmin pays homage to a Kṣatriya by prostrating himself. He extends this honor only to the ruling power. Now, the priestly power (*brahman*) is the womb of the ruling power. Therefore, even if a king should rise to the summit of power, it is to the priestly power that he returns in the end as to his own womb. So, one who hurts the latter harms his own womb and becomes so much the worse for harming someone better than him.
>
> (BU 1.4.11, trans. Olivelle 1998)

The passage continues with the creation of the Vaiśya, Śūdra, the Law (*dharma*) where only the last is again said to be superior to *brahman* (BU 1.4.12–14). Though royal power takes primacy at the beginning of this passage, the text concludes (BU 1.4.15) by asserting the traditional four-fold *varṇa* ranking and the ultimate superiority of the Brahmin. The Brahmin is said to be the sacrificial fire that all, including the *kṣatriya*, must approach for a connection to the gods.

It is in this broader context, I think, that Upaniṣadic statements or stories about Kṣatriyas teaching Brahmins about the abstracts truths of sacrifice (e.g. BU 2.1, CU 5.3, 5.11–24) should be understood. The Brahmin composers, by positioning Kṣatriyas highly within their own realm of ritual expertise, are valorizing them, for both literary and, very likely, practical reasons. Janaka in the story above is said to be a Brahmin, but only in so much as that status establishes a special relationship with a priest – one to whom, it should be noted, he shows great material generosity (Black 2007: 88ff.), especially in the story when he utilizes this boon. While some have suggested Kṣatriya origins of certain Upaniṣadic teachings (e.g. Deussen 1966; Hock 2002), there are additional reasons to be suspicious of the claims in the text, such as that certain teachings said to come from rulers were not necessarily new or unique, even when the rhetoric claims otherwise (Bodewitz 1973).

Elites vs. others

The Brahmin–Kṣatriya nexus is also directly contrasted to those outside of this alliance or even outside of the Vedic-fold altogether. Brahmins and Kṣatriyas are sometimes contrasted with Śūdras who, while part of the *varṇa* classification, are excluded from Vedic learning because they are not permitted initiation; so also with low castes or outcastes whose status is decidedly lower and outside of the cosmic classification schema altogether. Vaiśyas appear less often in such contexts, most likely because their middle-position is neither as literarily useful nor as starkly contrastive.

I have already mentioned the story of Raikva, where the unlikely Brahmin refers to his rich benefactor as a *śūdra* on two occasions. While no explanation or elaboration is given in either case, the meaning seems relatively clear: Jānaśruti is being told that he is outside of the Vedic-fold of the *dvija* (the "twice born") and thus not worthy of receiving such instruction from Raikva. The story leaves this possibility open in that Jānaśruti is not directly referred to as a king in the frame, though it is strongly – and I think intentionally – implied. While on one level, the reference to Jānaśruti being a *śūdra* might be a critique of Kṣatriya's "buying" access to Brahminical knowledge, Raikva himself is hardly a normative Brahmin and he eventually accepts the financial offer anyway. The critique and resolution, it seems, cuts both ways: One character is a non-normative teacher, the other a non-normative student, but both are ultimately affirmed as members of their respective classes. In this larger context, the calling of Jānaśruti a *śūdra* is less a claim about Jānaśruti's birth or social status, and more about subverting an audience's expectations, only to reaffirm them in the context of knowledge transmission. The negative use of *śūdra* here is used primarily to indicate exclusion from religious knowledge; even more negative valuations of other excluded categories also occur.

Outcaste (*caṇḍāla/cāṇḍāla*; also *paulkasa* on one occasion) appears in at least three passages (BĀU 4.3.22, CU 5.10.7, CU 5.24.4). In one case, *cāṇḍāla* is mentioned as a caste that one might be born into based on the consequence of one's bad action. In the other two, it is said that a learned Brahmin himself can attain a state in which distinctions of all sorts – both within and outside of *varṇa* – disappear; here, the social status of outcastes is negated in service to Brahminical soteriological goals, rather than in itself.

In CU 5.10.7, it is said that those who follow the "path of the fathers" (as opposed to "the path of the gods") will be reborn on earth and one's action in this life determines the *varṇa* into which he or she will be reborn.

> Now, people here whose behavior is pleasant can expect to enter a pleasant womb, like that of a woman of the Brahmin, the Kṣatriya, or the Vaiśya class. But people of foul behavior can expect to enter a foul womb, like that of a dog, a pig, or an outcaste woman.
>
> (trans. Olivelle 1998)

Such a passage clearly privileges the Brahmin first, but also any person within the top three *varṇas*. *Śūdra* is not mentioned as the contrast is between those within the fold of Vedic learning (the *dvija*, "twice born") and those placed radically outside of it. The extremity of exclusion is highlighted in that an outcaste is paralleled with animals seen as particularly impure. Curiously, the passage then lists a third category (CU 5.10.8) – those who do not follow either path and are reborn as tiny creatures who live and die endlessly – but who such people might be is unclear; it is clear that it is not the *śūdra* that is intended, but rather an additional, even further excluded, caste.

In contrast, BU 4.3.22 references the highest state of being that a truly knowing person will achieve, a state in which all social distinctions disappear for that person. The Brahmin Yājñavalkya is teaching King Janaka.

> Here a father is not a father, a mother is not a mother, worlds are not worlds, gods are not gods, and Vedas are not Vedas. Here a thief is not a thief, an abortionist is not an abortionist, an outcaste is not an outcaste, a pariah is not a pariah, a recluse is not a recluse, and an ascetic is not an ascetic. Neither the good nor the bad follows him, for he has now passed beyond all sorrows of the heart.
>
> (trans. Olivelle 1998)

In this case, the world of social relations, divine interaction, and sacrifice are negated along with the impurity associated with a series of socially excluded individuals: criminals and those born into excluded social groups (*caṇḍāla/cāṇḍāla* and *paulkasa*). While the ultimate unreality of the social world is argued for, it bears noting that such unreality is only true for the particularly learned individual who has attained this transcendent state. The passage is not saying that family, the gods, thieves, etc. are without positive or negative value in the social world, only that their value is restricted to that world and does not attach to an enlightened individual. In a similar fashion, CU 5.24.4 states that a Brahmin who knows the underlying esoteric connections of the daily fire sacrifice may even give away his leftover food to an outcaste. Doing so with the proper knowledge is said to be equivalent to offering into "the self of his which is common to all men." This passage is, in essence, stating that doing something that is otherwise forbidden or polluting is no longer so because of the esoteric knowledge acquired. The negative consequences of such action still attain for everyone else.

In general, the Upaniṣads reinforce the classical *varṇa* hierarchy in a fashion that maintains the privileged position of the Brahmin class first and the power nexus of the Brahmin–Kṣatriya alliance second. Lower classes and castes appear in the service of this hierarchy, particularly where excluded groups are utilized to represent impurity or improper action. Transcendence of class hierarchy occurs only in the service of Brahminical soteriological knowledge. While in the context of Brahmins and Kṣatriyas this includes the possibility of Kṣatriyas being characterized as teachers of esoteric knowledge to Brahmins that transcendence of class norms is restricted and its motivations suggest it does not necessarily map onto a historical actuality.

Gender

Gender in the Upaniṣads is equally, if not more, difficult to generalize than caste and class, especially in discussing the position of women within the texts. As the Upaniṣads, like the Vedas before them, were composed by and for Brahmin men, the elite male perspective permeates throughout, even when a passage might be attributed to a female. There are no unmediated voices (Jamison 1996; Lindquist 2008). Women are mentioned in significant passages, even portrayed as important characters in a few, but it is important to remember that in the greater scope of the texts, their inclusion is rare.

This rarity is not surprising for several reasons. First, the texts develop within the male-dominated religious sphere of the sacrifice and, if a gender is implied, it is male. For example, like the creation myth of Ṛgveda 10.90 and the cosmic man, several creation myths begin with the assumption that the original or first being is gendered male from which everything, including women, emerge (e.g. BU 1.4). When women are mentioned in the Upaniṣads, they generally appear incidental to the central concerns of the texts and/or as instruments towards male goals. Second, the texts purport to teach about abstract realities (such as *ātman*, *brahman*, liberation) that are often conceived of as absent of gender and fundamentally separate from such worldly dualities, though often there is an implicit masculine referent, whether in the text itself or in its intended audience. In cases where women are mentioned directly, it is often – but importantly, not exclusively – in a subordinate, often procreative role (for an extended discussion and several examples, see Black 2007: 133–145).

BU 6 is a good example of the mixed picture of gender, particularly women, as it appears in the Upaniṣads. In BU 6.4.2, the god Prajāpati creates woman as a base (*pratiṣṭhā*) for semen; her sexual organs are paralleled to the sacrifice and thus knowledge of these abstract associations produce merit for the man when engaging in sexual intercourse. The male in this context is put in a dominant position and intercourse focuses on his needs and desire. On the one hand, relating a woman – in particular the female body – to the sacrifice could suggest a central position of the feminine in the Vedic sacrificial worldview. On the other hand, a woman is objectified as simply a body that explicitly serves to produce merit for the male. The passage also continues that the man should bribe or beat a woman if she is in her menstrual period and denies him access to sex (6.4.7). This passage also includes formulae for the male to recite to either ensure pregnancy or prevent it (6.4.10–11). In this way, the woman is portrayed as an instrument for male action, desire, and progeny, whereas the male is portrayed as virile and in control not only of the particular situation, but the perpetuation of his lineage.

Further in the passage, however, there is something of a shift in emphasis. Ritual procedures are mentioned to guarantee particular qualities in one's offspring, specifically learning, complexion, eye color, and a full life (6.4.14–18). This hierarchy, though, is especially determined by the degree of education, e.g. whether a child will master one, two, three, or all four Vedas. Notably, a "learned daughter" is inserted into the third position of what then becomes a five-fold hierarchy; she is positioned between a son who knows three Vedas and the one who is a master of all four.

> "I want a learned daughter who will live out her full life span" – if this is his wish, he should get her [his wife] to cook that rice with sesame seeds and the two of them should eat it mixed with ghee. The couple thus becomes capable of begetting such a daughter.
>
> (6.4.17, trans. Olivelle, 1998)

While it is notable that the daughter desired is not defined by the Veda as are the sons, her position in the hierarchy is high, if not the highest. Also notable is that the text does not appear to take this inclusion as worthy of additional comment, suggesting that a desire for a learned daughter is not seen as particularly unusual; clearly, learned daughters had an esteemed place, at least for some, and merited inclusion.

Learned women also appear elsewhere as characters, such as Gārgī (BU 3.6 and 3.8) and Maitreyī (BU 2.4 and 4.5), although these are the only two such cases. Gārgī appears as an interlocutor in the debate with the famed ritualist Yājñavalkya and she is in the unique position to question him twice. Maitreyī appears as Yājñavalkya's wife, probably in a domestic setting, where the two have a discussion about the nature of death and immortality.

Like the desire for a "learned daughter" in BĀU 6, we have here a potential model of learned women. As I have argued elsewhere (Lindquist 2008), in the cases of Gārgī and Maitreyī there are several indicators in the stories that both women were not conceived of as a norm or were, at least, perceived of as unusual. More importantly, though, their gender has specific literary functions within the narratives that do not necessarily relate to a reality outside of the text. For example, Gārgī's forcefulness and sophistication in her questions contrasts her to the male interlocutors and reinforces her explicit criticism of them. The males also represent specific competing schools, whereas Gārgī has no clear affiliation. In the case of Maitreyī, she is contrasted with a second wife who is defined as a person of "womanly knowledge" (*strīprajñā*), suggesting Maitreyī is outside of a gendered norm, but the female gender here is bifurcated to also highlight two forms of inheritance (material goods taken by one wife, religious instruction by another). In these cases, then, the narratives suggest that these characters were viewed as exceptional, but exceptional in a fashion that still suggest avenues for female learning and religious importance in the ancient world.

Conclusion

Exploring issues of caste and gender in the Upaniṣads is as opaque and complicated as it is interesting; this article provides a small sample of that complexity. Given that the texts themselves span multiple authors and editorial processes across several centuries, any attempt at a systematic, let alone singular, presentation will by necessity be partial and lacking. The Upaniṣads offer a window into the religious and literary imagination of a period of time in ancient India, but that window is not singular. In the case of complex social phenomena like caste and gender, what we have instead is a matrix of small windows defined by individual passages, themes, and texts that refract light differently depending on the angle through which one looks.

References

Black, B. 2007. *The Character of the Self in Ancient India: Priests, Kings, and Women in the Early Upaniṣads*. Albany: State University of New York Press.

Bodewitz, H. W. (ed. and trans.) 1973. *Jaiminīya Brāhmaṇa I, 1-65: Translation and Commentary with a Study—Agnihotra and Prāṇāgnihotra*. Leiden: E. J. Brill.

Davis, D. 2010. *The Spirit of Hindu Law*. Cambridge: Cambridge University Press.

Davis, D. (ed.) 2012. *Studies in Hindu Law and Dharmaśāstra by Ludo Rocher*. Anthem South Asian Normative Traditions Series. London/New York/Delhi: Anthem Press.

Deussen, P. 1966. *The Philosophy of the Upanishads*, translated by A. S. Geden. New York: Dover.

Dumont, L. 1970. *Homo Hierarchicus: The Caste System and Its Implications*. Chicago: University of Chicago Press.

Hock, H. 2002. "The Yājñavalkya Cycle in the Bṛhad-Āraṇyaka-Upaniṣad" *Journal of the American Oriental Society* 122.2: 278–286.

Jamison, S. 1996. *Sacrificed Wife/Sacrificer's Wife: Women, Ritual, and Hospitality in Ancient India*. New York: Oxford University Press.

Kane, P. V. 1962–1975. *History of Dharmaśāstra*. 5 vols. Poona: Bhadarkar Oriental Research Institute.

Lindquist, S. 2008. "Gender at Janaka's Court: Women in the Bṛhadāraṇyaka Upaniṣad" *Journal of Indian Philosophy* 33.6: 405–426.

Lindquist, S. 2011. "Lines of Descent and Dissent: Genealogy, Narrative, and the Upaniṣads" *Religions of South Asia* 5.1/2: 29–49.

Lindquist, S. 2017. "The Upaniṣads" in Sarah Johnston (ed.) *Narrating Religion Macmillan Handbook Series on the Interdisciplinary Study of Religion*, gen. ed. Jeffry Kripal. Farmington Hills: Macmillan Reference USA, 303–316.

Lubin, T., D. Davis and J. K. Krishnan (eds) 2010. *Hinduism and Law: An Introduction*. Cambridge: Cambridge University Press.

Marriott, M. 2004. "Varṇa and Jāti" in S. Mittal and G. Thursby (eds) *The Hindu World*. New York: Routledge, 357–382.

Olivelle, P. 1998. *The Early Upaniṣads: Annotated Text and Translation*. New York: Oxford University Press.

Olivelle, P. (trans.) 1999. *Dharmasūtras: The Law Codes of Ancient India* (annotated translation of the Dharmasūtras of Āpastamba, Gautama, Baudhāyana, and Vasiṣṭha). Oxford World's Classics. Oxford: Oxford University Press.

Rocher, L. *Studies in Hindu Law and Dharmaśāstra*, ed. with introduction by Donald R. Davis, Jr. London: Anthem Press.

Sathaye, A. 2015. *Crossing the Lines of Caste: Viśvāmitra and the Construction of Brahmin Power in Hindu Mythology*. New York: Oxford University Press.

Smith, B. K. 2005. "Varna and Jati" in Lindsay Jones (ed.) *Encyclopedia of Religion* (2nd ed.). Farmington Hills: Macmillan Reference USA, 9522–9524.

Smith, B. K. 1994. *Classifying the Universe: The Ancient Indian Varṇa System and the Origins of Caste*. New York: Oxford University Press.

Vanita, R. 2003. "The Self is not Gendered: Sulabha's Debate with King Janaka" *NWSA Journal* 15.2: 76–93.

Part III

Religion and philosophy in the Upaniṣads

10 Prominent characters in the Upaniṣads

Steven E. Lindquist

Introduction

The Upaniṣads hold pride of place within Hinduism as a classical foundation for formal philosophy, particularly as the source texts for later philosophical schools (*darśana*) known as *vedānta* (lit. "end of the Vedas"). From an historical and literary perspective, it is clear that the early Upaniṣads had their origins in the Vedic ritual worldview, but over time these texts progressively moved away from that ritual context and emphasized more abstract themes: the nature of the self (*ātman*), the cosmos, the senses and sense organs, the process of dying and – most importantly – death's opposite, immortality (*amṛta*), or liberation (*mokṣa*). Previous textual compositions, especially the Brāhmaṇas and Āraṇyakas, are the direct literary precursors of these themes, but the Upaniṣads give them (and thus the genre as a whole) a life of their own. So too for the narrative portions of the Upaniṣads which deal with these themes, not solely in complex and sometimes obtuse exposition, but within stories where people, gods, and fantastic beings interact, often through dialogue. Brief narratives appear in the Brāhmaṇas and Āraṇyakas, but it is in the Upaniṣads, particularly in the context of concretizing abstract philosophical concepts, that narratives and the characters within them develop into fuller form. It is these narratives and characters that capture the minds of many Hindus, more so than the non-narrative portions of the Upaniṣads.

Much of the scholarship on the Upaniṣads themselves can generally be divided between works that emphasize philosophical ideas and works that emphasize history and linguistics. One facet of the Upaniṣads that bridges this divide is the numerous literary characters that appear within the narratives, figures representative of particular modes or schools of thinking and figures that may have an historical basis. Scholars have only recently begun to consider the narratives in which these figures appear more seriously *as narratives* (Black 2007; Grinshpon 2003; Lindquist 2008, 2011a, 2011b) and thus use various literary methods to study them, but literary studies of specific characters have been more limited (exceptions include Goldman 2006; Olivelle 1999; Lindquist 2011c and forthcoming).

Characters

The list of prominent characters in the Upaniṣads can be divided based on whether these characters are central or ancillary to the narrative itself. Depending on one's interpretive purposes, it is important to note that "ancillary" characters may be just as important and interesting as central figures; indeed, in many cases, their supporting function is what gives depth or nuance to the narrative even if the narrative does not give them primacy. Further, there is also a third class of figures in the texts, perhaps best not seen as "characters" per se since they appear only in lists or are mentioned briefly. These are references to thinkers within a community's lineage or other established individuals used to support or dispute an interpretation or idea; they may be members of genealogical lists that grant authority to a person or school; or they simply may be attributions that serve other functions not necessarily central to a narrative (Lindquist 2011b). Each of these references is important in its own right and is often indicative of a more extensive tradition than we have detailed evidence of, but I bypass them altogether here to focus on characters who play larger narrative roles. Text references are limited to significant passages.

Primary characters

Naciketas, KU 1–2.18

Naciketas is the son of Uśan Vājaśravas. During the course of a sacrifice where his father is giving away all of his possessions, Naciketas questions the value of his father giving away barren cows. He asks his father three times to whom will he give his own son and Uśan finally responds that he will give him to death. Naciketas then goes to the world of Death. Yama, the god of death, grants Naciketas three boons. Naciketas requests (1) that his father be well-disposed towards him when he returns; (2) knowledge of the fire-altar that leads to heaven (which is then named after him); and (3) knowledge of what happens after death, particularly how to transcend death itself.

Prajāpati, CU 8.7–12

Indra (a representative for the gods) and Virocana (a representative for the anti-gods) approach Prajāpati, the "lord of creation," for a teaching on the nature of the transcendent self (*ātman*). Prajāpati, however, gives a misleading teaching to each. Virocana accepts it and returns to the anti-gods, but Indra realizes the inadequacy of the teaching and returns for four more teachings, the last being the ultimate teaching about the *ātman*.

Pravāhaṇa Jaivali, BU 6.2, CU 5.3–10, CU 1.8

Pravāhaṇa is a king who teaches Uddālaka in BU 6.2 and CU 5.3–10 the doctrine of the five fires and the two paths of the dead (cf. JUB 1.38.4).

In CU 1.8, his status as a king is unclear; here he explains the ultimate meaning of the High Chant to his Brahmin companions.

Raikva, CU 4.1–3

Raikva is an enigmatic character who is found scratching his sores while living under a cart, a context explicitly mentioned as non-Brahminical and suggesting his inappropriateness as a teacher. He teaches the doctrine of the "gatherer" to Jānaśruti Pautrāyaṇa, perhaps a king.

Sanatkumāra, CU 7.1

Sanatkumāra is one of the four mind-born sons of Brahma and an ancient sage. In CU, he is the teacher of Nārada, also an ancient sage, later associated with the god Brahma. There is minimal context to the CU story; presumably the use of their names was sufficient enough for context.

Satyakāma Jābāla, CU 4.4–9 and 4.10–15, briefly at BU 4.1.6 and BU 6.3.11

Satyakāma is the son of a woman named Jabālā. He inquires with his mother about his lineage because he desires to become a Vedic student, but she does not know who his father is. He later approaches a teacher, admitting his ignorance about his father. His blunt truthfulness about this lack of pedigree (normally a requirement for initiation as a student) convinces the teacher, Hāridrumata Gautama, that he must truly be a Brahmin and he accepts him as his student. Satyakāma, however, is first taught by a bull, a fire, a wild goose, and a water bird and only later by Hāridrumata. In 4.10–15, Satyakāma is a teacher who, fittingly enough, has a student that is taught by the sacrificial fires.

Śvetaketu Āruneya, BU 6.2, KsU 1.1–2, CU 5.3–10

Śvetaketu is the arrogant son of Uddālaka Āruṇi. In CU, Śvetaketu chastises his father for not having taught him fully; his father then goes to the court of Pravāhaṇa Jaivali to learn the doctrine of the five fires, but Śvetaketu does not. In the BU version, Śvetaketu explicitly refuses to go along with his father, compounding his haughtiness. In the KsU, Śvetaketu does not appear as arrogant and attends with his father to learn from a king named Citra Gāṅgyāyani. See Olivelle (1999) for an extensive comparison of these three stories.

Uddālaka Āruṇi, CU 5 and 6, BĀU 3.7 and 6.3.7, KsU 1.1

Uddālaka is father of Śvetaketu and is considered an important teacher in his own right, but also a student (of Aśvapati Kaikeya in CU 5.11–24, but also of the kings Pravāhaṇa Jaivali (CU 5.3) and Citra Gāṅgyāyani

(KsU 1.1)). He is a competitor of Yājñavalkya in BU 3.7, but said to be his teacher in BU 6.3.7.

Uṣasta Cākrāyaṇa, CU 1.10–11 (as Uṣasti), BĀU 3.5

In CU, Uṣasta is a poor Brahmin who attends the sacrifice of a king. He challenges the assembled priests about their knowledge of the High Chant (see Lincoln 2006). He also is an interlocutor in the debate with Yājñavalkya (BĀU 3.5).

Yājñavalkya, BĀU 3–4, 6.3.7–8, 6.5.3

Yājñavalkya is the main spokesperson of the White Yajurveda and a central figure in both the SB and the BU. In BU 6.5.3, he is said to be the founder of the tradition, a status also found in the Mahābhārata and the Purāṇas. Yājñavalkya has a special relationship with King Janaka, appearing in a debate at his court (BU 3) and as his private religious counselor (BU 4). In dispersing his inheritance, he gives material goods to one wife, Kātyāyanī, but a religious teaching on immortality to his other wife, Maitreyī (BU 2.4, 4.5).

Yama, KU 1–2.18

Yama is the god who oversees the realm of the dead, but he is also the embodiment of the existence of death and all that it entails. He teaches Naciketas about the sacrificial path to heaven and, ultimately, about immortality.

Ancillary characters

Ancillary characters play supporting roles as students, fathers, wives, mothers, kings, co-ritualists, and competitors in debate. Their roles, though, are vital to the context of any given narrative as it is the relationship between the primary and secondary characters that fill out the context of the narrative and the teaching itself. Sometimes a figure fills multiple roles simultaneously (such as a king as the patron who becomes a student or an interlocutor who is also representative of a particular school of thought); exploring the mixture of such roles is an important theme in some of the narratives. Here I briefly list some of the more important ancillary characters. For more complete lists, see Macdonell and Keith (1967) and Olivelle (1998).

Gārgī Vācaknavī, BU 3.5, 3.8

The only female in the debate with Yājñavalkya at the court of King Janaka. Her role in the debate (along with Yājñavalkya's wife who learns about immortality) suggests a place for women in religious discourse, even if examples are rare and the role was limited.

Jabālā, CU 4.4

Mother of Satyakāma. While the exact reasons are unclear (and debated within the tradition and within scholarship), she had multiple partners and does not know who Satyakāma's father is. When he asks about his lineage, she tells him to refer to himself by the matronymic Jābāla.

Janaka of Videha, BU 3–4

A famous king with a special relationship to Yājñavalkya. In BU 3, he organizes a religious debate during a sacrifice in which Yājñavalkya prevails as the most learned (*brahmiṣṭha*). In BU 4, he learns from Yājñavalkya, presumably first only as a patron, but ultimately formally as his student.

Jānaśruti Pautrāyaṇa, CU 4.1–3

Jānaśruti is likely a king, though he is referred to as a *śūdra* by Raikva. Raikva nonetheless ultimately accepts his offerings and teaches him the doctrine of the "gatherer."

Jāratkārava Ārtabhāga, BU 3.2

One of the eight interlocutors in the debate with Yājñavalkya, particularly important because Yājñavalkya pulls him aside privately to discuss the nature of *karma*, an apparently new doctrine at this time.

Maitreyī, BU 2.4, 4.5

Maitreyī is one of two wives of Yājñavalkya. She is called a *brahmavādinī* ("discourser on *brahman*") in contrast to Yājñavalkya's other wife, Kātyāyanī, who is said to be concerned only with "womanly knowledge" (*strīprajñā*). Following her refusal of a material settlement of his wealth, Maitreyī asks Yājñavalkya to tell her the path to immortality. On the relation of the two versions of the story, see Brereton (2006).

Uśan Vājaśravas, KU 1.1, also called Gautama and Uddālaka 1.10–11

Uśan is the father of Naciketas. While his role is small in KU (but much more extensive elsewhere, if the identification with Uddālaka holds), his role as an apparently frustrated father who overacts allows Naciketas the chance to learn from Death himself.

Vidagdha Śākalya, BĀU 3.9

Śākalya is Yājñavalkya's chief and most ardent debate opponent. His name equates him with the famous arranger of the Ṛgveda *padapāṭha*. *Vidagdha* means either "clever" or "burnt up"; whichever the meaning, both would foreshadow his death at the end of the debate.

It is worth noting some of the common features of the characters in the Upaniṣads before dealing with certain themes that intersect with them. The primary characters of Upaniṣadic narratives are Brahmin males, emblematic of the composers of these texts and of the religious authority that these texts express. It is important to note that this does not mean that they necessarily represent the sole audience of these texts, as ancillary characters (such as kings and women) suggest that the audience may have been broader. These characters are positioned as important teachers (Prajāpati, Pravāhaṇa, Raikva, Sanatkumāra, Uddālaka, Uṣasta, Yājñavalkya) or students (Indra, Naciketas, Satyakāma, Śvetaketu). Characters who are students in a particular narrative may also appear elsewhere in these texts, especially in genealogical lists, as teachers in their own right (e.g. Satyakāma). These prominent students are described explicitly as "sons" (e.g. Śvetaketu, son of Uddālaka), though an individual's father is not necessarily the teacher in the narrative (e.g. Naciketas is the son of Uśan, but taught by the god of death, Yama). The theme of lineage, particularly regarding the right to learn and disseminate esoteric doctrine (which may or may not intersect with biological lineage) can be seen throughout these stories (see Lindquist 2011b), especially when exploring the boundaries of orthodox expectation.

In cases where the *varṇa* of the character is in doubt (e.g. Raikva or Satyakāma), the narrative explores the listener's expectation of a Brahmin male in a specific narrative context, though the narratives ultimately assert the character's Brahmin-ness by other criteria (in the case of Satyakāma, through his truthfulness; in the case of Raikva, through the knowledge he possesses). Prajāpati and Yama are male divinities, but their inclusions are intimately tied to the specific narrative contexts (e.g. Yama, the god of Death, teaches about death and what transcends it/him in the realm of the dead and Prajāpati is teaching another god and an anti-god; both are the elites in their own domain). This directly parallels the male Brahmin characters' context of the ritual, that is, the human social realm that is under their purview and from which the abstract knowledge in the Upaniṣads historically emerges.

The ancillary characters are often the interlocutors of the prominent characters, though not always as students. BU 3 includes eight interlocutors in a debate with Yājñavalkya, each of the eight represent competing Vedic orthodoxies, though a couple are markedly more significant both within the tradition and within academic studies. Gārgī is a female interlocutor (BU 3.6 and 3.8) and she is distinguished not only by her gender, but also by the forcefulness and content of her questions to Yājñavalkya (Lindquist 2008; Black 2007). Vidagdha Śākalya, representative of the Ṛgveda, is also an interlocutor in this same debate (BU 3.9), though his role is much more extensive than the others and the debate climaxes in his death by an exploding head when he cannot answer a challenge put to him after the tables are turned (Lindquist 2011a). While in the domestic setting rather than a debate, Yājñavalkya teaches his wife, Maitreyī, about immortality in two separate versions of the same story (BU 2.4 and 4.5). In this case, there are thematic parallels to the student-teacher relationships found in other stories, but Maitreyī is not formally a student and is the sole example of a spousal relationship of religious teaching in the Upaniṣadic narratives. Kings play an important role in the narratives as patrons, but also sometimes as students and even teachers. Certain new doctrines are said to come from the Kṣatriya class, but whether this is historically accurate or otherwise literarily motived (such as to valorize a patron class or to suggest a doctrine's newness) is debated (see, for example, Hock 2002).

Characters as history

Much scholarship has concerned itself with approaching these prominent characters as historical individuals, in line with the larger Hindu tradition that generally takes them as ancient sages that actually lived in the distant past. In one sense, this is an understandable approach for those concerned with historical reconstruction: The overwhelming majority of Upaniṣadic narratives are realistic in nature and only a few contain fantastic elements (such as talking fires and animals or exploding heads) or are clearly mythological (such as dialogues between gods and anti-gods). Several characters are known from other textual compositions, whether from other Upaniṣads or other genres. Yājñavalkya, for example, has a significant literary life that precedes and succeeds the Bṛhadāraṇyaka Upaniṣad and is taken as the founder of one particular Vedic school, the White Yajurveda (*śuklayajurveda*). Uddālaka and Śvetaketu are also particularly famous in other literature. Further, formal genealogical lists found in the texts (such as the three found in BU) as well as more casual listings of pedigrees of interpretations lend an air of realism and historical veracity to these texts.

Ruben (1947) is probably the most explicit example of historically positivist reconstruction by giving specific decades for individual teachers based on their relationships to each other and based on a comparative dating of the texts. Such an attempt may appear intellectually satisfying, not the least of which because it is premised on taking the primary sources as faithful records. However, such interpretations are based on insecure evidence and face a number of probably insurmountable hurdles. First, the majority of the early Upaniṣads are composite texts and consistency even within one Upaniṣad, let alone across numerous ones produced in different regions at different times, is unlikely. Uddālaka, for example, is listed as Yājñavalkya's contemporary competitor in one context (BU 3.7), but his teacher in another (BU 6.3.7). Second, the Upaniṣads – like all ancient Indian texts – are datable at best to particular centuries and their relation to each other is a relative chronology and not an absolute one; specifying particular decades for particular individuals within and across texts is unsupportable. Third, the texts themselves are not concerned with a fixed historical recollection; even the genealogical lists are not wholly consistent and serve various narrative purposes (Lindquist

2011b; Black 2011). Separating historically accurate information from other types of representation or from other narrative needs is difficult at best.

Others have approached the historicity of such figures with more nuance, though arguably without more convincing results. Rather than try to pin precise dates to specific prominent characters, these approaches try to isolate types of textual representations, specifically those the scholar deems historically accurate as opposed to mythical or legendary. For example, Fišer (1984) argues that there is an "early Yājñavalkya," a historical figure found in the SB and BU ch. 1–2, but also a later "legendary Yājñavalkya" in the other chapters of BU. In contrast, Witzel (2003) has suggested that there are individualized speech characteristics of figures like Yājñavalkya. Witzel argues that there is a linguistic consistency in the speech attributed to Yājñavalkya and that this consistency suggests a single historical personage in both the SB and throughout the BU. I do not find either of these approaches convincing, not the least of which because neither accounts for the literary aspects of these characters (see Lindquist 2011c). Though Witzel's approach is novel and a focus on Yājñavalkya's speech pattern is interesting, it seems just as plausible that linguistic consistency across texts is due to the tradition intentionally mimicking already established literary norms so as to maintain continuity. Given that the majority of the settings for these encounters are variations of previously established formulaic conventions (e.g. the sacrificial arena, the court, non-social or uninhabited regions), it is more logical that characters are as well. While it is easier to dismiss fantastic or clearly mythological elements of a narrative as ahistorical, Fišer's approach is more wide-ranging and more subjective. He assumes that "legendary" and "historical" material are discrete; passages that he finds to be motivated by, for example, a desire to elevate the status of Yājñavalkya, are dismissed; realism (and thus historical veracity) seems based largely on his individual impressions rather than anything systematic. Bronkhorst's (2007) approach to Yājñavalkya is similar to Fišer, albeit more systematic and with closer attention to philological detail, but his system is indicative of part of the problem: Isolating the legendary and the historical in the Upaniṣads becomes an elaborate logical exercise of supposition built upon supposition and weakness in any individual part threatens to collapse the whole.

Themes

Prominent Upaniṣadic characters, of course, exist within specific narrative contexts. As mentioned earlier, the majority of these narratives are dialogues. The nature of the dialogic format, however, has led many to focus on the content of the dialogues to the exclusion of characters or context. Upaniṣadic dialogues, however, are formally framed, such as by the context of a ritual gathering where Brahmins assemble to debate to win wealth (as in the BU) or of a son having a conflict with his father during a sacrifice that leads to his own death (as in the KU). If we take narrative form seriously, however, these frames are not secondary to the doctrine that is discussed, but intimately connected to it. The characters and their context add nuance and concreteness to the abstract themes under discussion. Some of the more prominent themes include the nature of death and immortality, the dissemination of knowledge, and propriety and proper knowledge. Of course, these themes overlap and others are present in the texts (see Lindquist 2011b and 2017 for further examples), but I will focus on these three here.

Death is a common topic within the Upaniṣads as a whole, but especially so within the Upaniṣadic narratives. Given the context of the composition of the Upaniṣads during the second great urbanization on the Gangetic plain, this should not be surprising. While urbanization brings disparate groups of people into contact and spurs religious, social, and political change, it also exacerbates problems of social inequality, propels a breakdown of previously established social norms, and brings a rise in disease and death associated with quickly growing populations.

This is not to say that a concern with death arose solely or mainly due to changing material conditions; as already mentioned, these themes are present in earlier textual compositions, though they are hardly prominent. But it is to say that there is a direct parallel between radically changing social conditions and an increasing philosophical concentration on understanding the nature of death, especially through the concepts of *karma* and rebirth. Progressively across the Upaniṣads and also in the newly emerging traditions of Buddhism and Jainism, there is an increasingly negative view of life-in-the-world (most starkly seen in the MU). This negative view stands in sharp contrast to the earlier Vedic view which embraced life-in-the-world and the worldly gains that sacrifices to the gods would grant.

The story of Naciketas exhibits perhaps the most explicit connection between the narrative frame and the dialogue, here in the context of death. The boy, Naciketas, is sent to the realm of Yama (the god of death) by his father in a fit of frustration. While his father was offering presumably everything he owned to the gods in a sacrifice, he also offered cows that were barren. Naciketas wondered about the value of his father's offering of such cows and inquired to whom his father might then give him. His father responds that he gives him to death. Naciketas finds himself in the realm of death where Yama grants him three boons. The first boon guarantees that his father will not be angry when he returns (a clear foreshadowing that even Naciketas realizes that this actual death is not permanent, which is ultimately the same argument as the philosophical doctrine). The second boon is for Naciketas to learn about the fire altar that leads to heaven (Yama includes an additional boon of naming the fire altar after him). The final boon is to learn about the nature of death and how to transcend it. Having learned about this transcendence, Naciketas is apparently returned to his father (this is implied in the story as there is no formal ending, leaving some debate as to its actual conclusion), thus leaving the realm of death, but especially the future reality of death itself.

A less obvious, but more intricate, example of the interdependence of frame and dialogue in a discussion of immortality is the famous debate of Yājñavalkya in BU 3. I have argued elsewhere (2011a) that the content of the debate between Yājñavalkya and his eight interlocutors progresses from an understanding of the actual sacrifice and its more abstract connections to the cosmos, including the nature of *karma* and rebirth. This narrative then culminates in an abstract and elaborate discussion thematically centered around the nature of immortality. The theme of immortality in the dialogue, though, parallels the narrative interaction of the characters where there is increasingly sharp rhetoric, rhetoric which plays on the reason that immortality is sought after in the first place – the very real fact that people die. Various characters threaten each other with "shattered heads"; the narrative and the dialogue portions are making an argument in tandem about death and its opposite. Ultimately, Śākalya cannot explain the nature of immortality and proves his own status as mortal by dying.

Since dialogue requires the interaction of at least two parties, the Upaniṣadic narratives also comment on the nature of the parties as well as the content that is to be discussed. Black (2007) has analyzed several of these roles in how the narratives create, challenge, and sustain the norms of social interaction between these two parties, particularly in regard to teaching. I have suggested (2011b) that this theme can also be looked at in the context of Upaniṣadic genealogical lists and intellectual pedigrees. I suggested that there is a broader, more encompassing theme of lineage and inheritance (whether of wealth or knowledge) at work in the texts. In this way, the role of these characters, such as teachers and students or Brahmins and kings, suggest models for intellectual and material transfer, and one leitmotif of the stories is the control and dissemination of such a transfer that also brings in biological (e.g. familial) and social relationships (e.g. caste and gender), as well as other hierarchies. In this context, for example, the appearance of Maitreyī in a narrative framed around the giving of a material inheritance versus an immaterial one shows a thematic continuity for this otherwise unusual narrative situation. So also with the genealogical lists that are otherwise apparently out of place in the texts, such as the matronymic listing found in BU (6.5).

Finally, what I term "propriety and proper knowledge" is related to the above two themes, but the emphasis here is on the construction of several characters so as to challenge the expectation of the listener. Yājñavalkya is a sarcastic and witty Brahmin, characteristics that might otherwise be seen as a personality flaws (as is the case with Śākalya, who is also sharp-witted) were he not shown to be possessed of superior knowledge in the end. Satyakāma, who lacks a known-lineage and thus the right to study the Veda, shows he actually is a Brahmin and eligible for such knowledge based on his truthfulness (an endearing and humorous truthfulness, where he not only gives his matronymic, but literally repeats his mother's words to a potential teacher about her sleeping with many men). In contrast to Satyakāma's humbleness is Śvetaketu's arrogance, an arrogance which precludes him from learning from a king. Raikva is said to live where a non-Brahmin lives (under a cart, apparently with a skin disease), but proves himself to be the proper teacher. Both teacher and student explicitly go against expectations: Raikva is apparently homeless, poor, and perhaps diseased. His student, Jānaśruti, is apparently a king, but called a *śūdra* twice by Raikva, suggesting he should not be an eligible student.

Each of the characters exhibits unique characteristics, characteristics that challenge a normative (and sanitized) expectation that an audience might have of the character. Each of these characters is, in one sense, anomalous of an idealized Brahmin norm (both male and female) and their anomalousness serves as a launching point for the dialogue as well as a thematic complement to the same. These traits, I have suggested, are key to more fully appreciating the narratives, traits which give the narratives their force; traits which often parallel the philosophical argument being made where character, story, and philosophical argument cannot be separated.

Conclusion

The prominent characters found in Upaniṣadic stories play many roles: They are spokespeople for particular modes of ritual and philosophical thought; they represent (and challenge) norms of the lived world and the growing importance of ascetic values; and they add humor, nuance, and concreteness not only to abstract discussions about the fundamental nature of reality, but also of human realities such as desire, impermanence, and death. These characters and the narratives of which they are a part have helped to sustain the genre of the Upaniṣads as the sacrifice recedes into the background and formal philosophizing becomes a technical scholastic endeavor. The characters speak to the place of humans within a reality that is lived and towards an ultimate reality that is aspired to.

References

Black, B. 2007. *The Character of the Self in Ancient India: Priests, Kings, and Women in the Early Upaniṣads*. Albany: State University of New York Press.

Black, B. 2011. "Rethinking the Upaniṣadic Vaṃśas: Teacher Lineages as a Literary Genre" *Religions of South Asia* 5.1/2: 51–77.

Brereton, J. 2006. "The Composition of the Maitreyī Dialogue in the Bṛhadāraṇyaka Upaniṣad" *Journal of the American Oriental Society* 126.3: 323–345.

Bronkhorst, J. 2007. *Greater Magadha: Studies in the Culture of Early India*. Leiden: Brill.

Fišer, I. 1984. "Yājñavalkya in the Śruti Tradition of the Veda" *Acta Orientalia* 10: 55–87.

Goldman, R. 2006. "Interpreting Śruti: Ādiśamkarācārya's Reading of Three Ākhyāyikā-s of the Chāndogya Upaniṣad" *Journal of Indian Philosophy and Religion* 11 (October): 79–98.

Grinshpon, J. 2003. *Crisis and Knowledge: The Upanishadic Experience and Storytelling*. New Delhi: Oxford University Press.
Hock, H. 2002. "The Yājñavalkya Cycle in the Bṛhad-Āraṇyaka-Upaniṣad" *Journal of the American Oriental Society* 122.2: 278–286.
Lincoln, B. 2006. "How to Read a Religious Text: Reflections on Some Passages of the Chāndogya Upaniṣad" *History of Religions* 46.2: 127–139.
Lindquist, S. 2008. "Gender at Janaka's Court: Women in the Bṛhadāraṇyaka Upaniṣad" *Journal of Indian Philosophy* 33.6: 405–426.
Lindquist, S. 2011a. "Literary Lives and a Literal Death: Yājñavalkya, Śākalya, and an Upaniṣadic Death Sentence" *Journal of the American Academy of Religion* 79.1: 33–57.
Lindquist, S. 2011b. "Lines of Descent and Dissent: Genealogy, Narrative, and the Upaniṣads" *Religions of South Asia* 5.1/2: 29–49.
Lindquist, S. 2011c. "One Yājñavalkya ... Two? On the (Questionable) Historicity of a Literary Figure" in Steven E. Lindquist (ed.) *Religion and Identity in South Asia and Beyond*. New York: Anthem Press, 69–81.
Lindquist, S. 2017. "The Upaniṣads" in Sarah Johnston (ed.) *Narrating Religion*, Macmillan Handbook Series on the Interdisciplinary Study of Religion, gen. ed. Jeffry Kripal. Farmington Hills: Macmillan Reference USA, 303–316.
Lindquist, S. Forthcoming. *Creating a Sage: The Literary Life of Yājñavalkya*. Albany: State University of New York Press.
Macdonell, A. A., and A. B. Keith. Repr. 1967. *Vedic Index of Names and Subjects*, 2 vols. Delhi: Motilal Banarsidass.
Olivelle, P. 1998. *The Early Upaniṣads: Annotated Text and Translation*. New York: Oxford University Press.
Olivelle, P. 1999. "Young Śvetaketu: A Literary Study of an Upaniṣadic Story" *Journal of the American Oriental Society* 119.1: 46–70.
Ruben, W. 1947. *Die Philosophen der Upaniṣaden*. Bern: A. Francke.
Witzel, M. 2003. "Yājñavalkya as Ritualist and Philosopher, and His Personal Language" in S. Adhami (ed.) *Paitimāna: Essays in Iranian, Indo-European, and Indian Studies in Honor of Hanns-Peter Schmidt*. Costa Mesa: Mazda Publishers, 103–143.

11 *Ātman* and *brahman* in the principal Upaniṣads

Jacqueline Suthren Hirst

Introduction

The concepts of *ātman* and *brahman* as "true self" and "ultimate reality" are often presented as the most fundamental in the principal Upaniṣads. They are used to evidence an inward turn in the Vedic corpus from world-maintaining ritual to a renunciatory quest for knowledge which will liberate the seeker from this world of rebirth. That knowledge is said to comprise precisely the knowledge of the identity of *ātman* and *brahman*.[1]

While this is a useful starting point, it contains a number of simplifications. These tidy up the complex processes whereby different seers sought to make sense of their Vedic world and so mask the considerable diversity of social contexts and viewpoints within these texts.

Basic meanings

The terms themselves have multiple senses. "*ātman*" is primarily a reflexive pronoun meaning "oneself" ("myself," "yourself" etc), so it is important not to over-read it. However, in explorations of what it is that gives a person life, it does emerge, along with other competitors such as "breath" (*prāṇa*) and "person" (*puruṣa*), as a leading contender, linked with the exercise of consciousness.[2] At an individual level, it also becomes key in notions of personal identity in this life and continuity in rebirth (see Chapter 12). More basically, it may signify "body," the physical aspect of a person (see Olivelle, 1996: 291). Through this, and its association with the notion of the Cosmic Person (*puruṣa*) whose sacrificial dismemberment establishes an ordered cosmos (RV 10.90), "*ātman*" can carry a sense of "the whole." Finally, analogous to breath in the individual, "*ātman*" may indicate the Self within the cosmic totality.

"*brahman*," whose etymology the eighth century commentator, Śaṃkara, gives as from the root, *bṛh-*, "to be great" or "to exceed,"[3] is used, early, to designate the power of the Vedic ritual, the sacred chant, or its priestly custodians (Roebuck, 2003: xxviii). As the former, it has cosmic force, the power of the whole universe. Through this, it too comes to have the sense of "totality," a kind of universal set, whose parts may be variously understood. While "*ātman*" may refer to both the individual self and to the self of the cosmos in the principal Upaniṣads, "*brahman*" often retains a cosmological sense. However it is used, though, the term does not depart from its basic sense of that which is identified as the highest power or mystery by the particular speaker.

It requires a close reading of different texts to discover how, when, whether, and why these terms are used interchangeably, or whether they express a relationship of identity, unity, or difference between the two. The variability of usage, and the fact that there are no capital letters in Indian scripts, also challenges translators on how to transliterate the Sanskrit terms in the roman alphabet: *Brahman*,[4] Brahman, *brahman*; and on how to translate "*ātman*": oneself, body, self, Self. On transliteration, a decision needs to be made for consistency; on translation, the context and the translator's interpretation will be key. Further, it is, of course, the variation within the source texts themselves that allows the later Vedāntin commentators to hold such radically different interpretations of what the Upaniṣads teach (see Chapter 19).

Key questions

One way of pursuing a close reading through these differences is to locate the questions that different sages or texts are addressing. In particular, Roebuck stresses the ubiquity of the question: "What do you worship as *brahman*?" (Roebuck 2003: 448, n.1). This is a central query whose answers are multiple; it builds on the riddling competitions between brahmins (*brāhmaṇas*) in the earlier Vedic texts (Renou 1949; Black 2007, Chapter 2). The preoccupation with personal immortality yields another key line of enquiry (e.g. BU 3.2.10–13; 4.4) and becomes linked to the nature of the self. Naciketas famously presses Yama, "Tell us … what there is in the great passing-on [beyond death]?"[5] His question yields the teaching on *ātman* (KU 1.29, 2.20).

These questions generate others and shape the older teacher-pupil dialogues and the literary form of later texts. The *Śvetāśvatara*, for example, opens with a string of questions from those who talk about *brahman*:

> What is the cause or *brahman*? why are we born? by what do we live? on what are we grounded? … are we to think of it as time, inherent nature, fate, chance, the elements, a womb, a person? or a combination of these? (1.1–2)

The very titles of the *Praśna* ("question") and *Kena* ("by what?") show the importance of questioning. *Praśna* 3 asks the revered teacher, Pippalāda:

> Where is the breath born from? how does it enter this body? how, having divided itself (*ātman*), does it become established? by what does it go up [out of the body at death]? how does it explain what is external [the cosmos] and what is to do with oneself (*adhyātma*)?

The shape of this chapter

To address these questions, I consider key ideas and close readings from broadly chronological groups of the principal Upaniṣads to see what different answers they give, before returning to the initial puzzle of how *brahman* and *ātman* are related.[6]

The early prose Upaniṣads

In the oldest prose Upaniṣads, searches for answers are frequently conducted in dialogues (e.g. BU 3; CU 1.8–9; 5.11–24; BU 2.1; 2.4//4.5; 4.3–4; KsU 1–2). They are both embodied and socially embedded: what do *you* worship as *brahman*? This alerts us to three issues. The first is to consider whether one normative view on *brahman*/*ātman* is provided. Black suggests that, in the competitive debates in the *Bṛhadāraṇyaka Upaniṣad* (3; 4.1–4), where Yājñavalkya emerges as victor, a single view on *brahman* is sanctioned. By contrast, the assorted teachings given by different teachers in the *Chāndogya* are allowed to stand alongside each other (2007: 43, 97, 169). Second, perspectives on *brahman* relate variously to earlier Vedic ritual and hymnic views (CU throughout; BU 1.1, 1.2–4, 5 and 6). These views are not easily homogenised. Finally, though, I argue that different types of material and shifting vocabulary in adjacent sections of these texts are not just indicators of collections made over time or different teachers' views. Rather, in the compilations we now have, the format of the texts forces the hearer or reader to confront a search for something contested and highly elusive. This works in the hearer, where a tidy, coherent answer could not.

To approach this diversity, I consider four ways the early prose Upaniṣads handle the relation between the cosmos and the individual. Each builds on ideas of macrocosm (the cosmos), microcosm (the sacrificer), and mesocosm (the sacrifice which maintains cosmic and social order) from earlier Vedic texts. This approach allows us to see both connections and divergences as these texts pursue questions about the meaning of existence, seeking a grasp of that which grounds the cosmos and may be found within.

Understanding homologies (bandhus): *What do you seek as brahman? as self? why?*

Bandhus are the links between different realms which provide an underpinning logic for sacrifice or meditation (Gonda 1965; Smith 1989; cf. Renou 1949: 13). The *Bṛhadāraṇyaka Upaniṣad* (1.1) opens with a meditation in which the horse, sacrificed to establish a king's power and territory, is equated with the whole cosmos. Re-death is overcome through proper understanding of the horse-sacrifice (1.2.7), power derived from a knowledge of the homologies between, here, the parts of the horse and the parts of the cosmos to which they correspond: dawn its head, wind its breath, its body (*ātman*) the year representing the totality of time. It is through the exploration of such *bandhus* that many of the protagonists in the *Bṛhadāraṇyaka* and *Chāndogya* seek the connecting whole, or *brahman*.

CU 3.18.2–6, for example, identifies the "four quarters of *brahman*" as speech/fire, breath/air, eye/sun, and ear/directions. Each quarter of the whole has both an individual identification and a cosmological homologue, linked through meditation. The one who knows these links "shines with praise, fame and the shine of *brahman*," here "sacred knowledge." Olivelle's translation makes transparent the homology generating this knowledge:

> With respect to the bodily sphere (*ātman*), one should venerate: "*Brahman* is the mind," and, with respect to the divine sphere: "*Brahman* is space." In this way, [meditative] substitution is carried out in both spheres – both with respect to the bodily sphere [*adhyātma*] and with respect to the divine sphere [*adhidaivata*].
>
> (CU 3.18.1, tr. Olivelle)[7]

It is not a long step from here to the famous "Inner Controller" passage in BU 3.7, which talks not of *brahman* but of *ātman*. Challenged to demonstrate his knowledge of "that thread by which this world, the other world and all beings are held together" and its *antaryāmin*, or inner controller, Yājñavalkya gives a three-part series of almost identically worded teachings:

> The one who exists within earth/all beings/breath, is other than earth/all beings/breath, whom earth/all beings/breath do not know, whose body is earth/all beings/breath, who controls earth/all beings/breath from within – this is your self, the inner controller, the immortal (*eṣa ta ātmāntaryāmy amṛtaḥ*).
>
> (3.7.3/15/16 as examples)

The series relates respectively to the cosmic realm of the deities (*adhidaivata*), the hinge realm of "beings" (*adhibhūta*), and the final realm of "*adhyātma*." Olivelle translates "*adhyātma*" as "body," recalling earlier homologisations: now the search within cosmos and body leads to a single reality, the inner controller, the immortal self within. Roebuck's "oneself" relates this search to the pupil hearing the teaching and, like the whole passage, directs him to find it, and immortality, within his own person.

Whole and parts: What is brahman, *the one that "exceeds"?*

We have already seen examples of "*ātman*" and "*brahman*" denoting a whole with parts (BU 1.1–2; CU 3.18). In CU 4.4–4.9, the aptly named

Satyakāma ("One-who-desires-what-is-true") is taught one "quarter of *brahman*" by a bull, fire, goose, and water-bird respectively. Each quarter represents a totality: the four directions; the four regions; the lights of fire, sun, moon, and lightning; the person (breath, eye, ear, mind). Satyakāma gained knowledge of *brahman* (4.9.2), with various limited results (4.5.4, 4.6.4, 4.7.4, 4.8.4), but the complete knowledge in which "nothing was left out" comes from his teacher (4.9.3; cf. 5.11–24). On its content, the text is silent.

The implied transcendence of something beyond our conceptions of "totality" is made clear in CU 3.12. Different levels of totality – ritual, cosmic, and person-related – are elaborately equated, but "the Person is *greater than that*/ One quarter of him is all beings/ Three quarters, the immortal in the sky" (CU 3.12.6 citing RV 10.90.3). This, it implies, is "that which is called *brahman*," the space both outside a person and within (3.12.7), yielding unfading prosperity. Śāṇḍilya's teaching goes further. "*brahman*," "all this" (3.14.1) *is* the self within the heart yet greater than all worlds (3.14.3). With the intention to know the self (*ātman*), one enters or attains *brahman*, the totality, transcendent, after death (3.14.4). Through the parts, to the whole, to that beyond.

Origination stories: What is the cause? The end?

The oldest Upaniṣads contain numerous "In the beginning" stories. In many, the self (*ātman*) is the initiator. In *Aitareya Upaniṣad* 1.1 the self, "one only," thinks, "Let me create worlds," the cosmos is produced and the self "enters" the person as the cogniser within (1.3.11–12; cf. *sat*, "Being," in CU 6.2).

In some stories (e.g. CU 6), *brahman* is not mentioned. Here, the lonely self[8] sees "just that person, the *brahman*" (1.3.13) and so is called Idandra. As 1.3.14 observes, "The gods seem to love the cryptic"! 3.1–4 attempts to untangle the mystery. To the question, "Which one is the *self*?" (3.2), a string of terms designating different aspects of cognition is given. The translators vary in how they interpret the relation between the one who sees, hears, smells, speaks, and tastes (3.1); the separate mental functions, gods, elements, and beings; and *brahman* as *prajñāna* (intelligence, knowledge, knowing). What do you worship as brahman? Search within the cosmos and yourself.

Taittirīya 2 explores the connection between origination, the attaining of all desires for the one who knows *brahman* and an interiorising search within. In what becomes known as the "five sheaths" passage, comments and verses direct one from a kind of exterior Russian doll, "the self made of food," to the next one within, "the self made of breath," then to "the self made of mind," "of understanding," and finally "of bliss." Whichever sheath or "self" a person identifies as *brahman*, they attain a concomitant outcome. Finally, depending on whether the seeker sees *brahman* as non-being or being, the result is different and questions arise over destiny after death (2.6). Resolution transcends both "being" and "non-being" origination accounts (2.7,8):

> Whence words return/ along with the mind;
> the one who knows the bliss of *brahman* / does not fear anything at all (2.9).

That end is beyond words.

Unseen seer: What is the self?

The Yājñavalkya cycle (BU 2–4) repeatedly identifies the *ātman* as the ground of cognition. The Inner Controller passage concludes:

> It is the unseen seer, the unheard hearer, the unthought-of thinker, the unknown knower. Other than this there is no seer; other than this there is no hearer; other than this there is no thinker; other than this there is no knower. This is your self, the inner controller, the immortal: what is other than this is suffering.
>
> (BU 3.7.23, tr. Roebuck; cf. 3.8.11; KsU 3.8)

This has become a prevalent understanding not least because of its use by the Advaitin commentator, Śaṃkara, yet it is less common in the principal Upaniṣads than might be expected.[9] What it does share is the search, within cosmos and self, for a transcendent principle which in various ways is identified with consciousness, though methods and pictures vary widely as already indicated.

Another way of searching for this starts with an outward bodily self, then moves through dream and deep sleep to a transcendent consciousness beyond. This is most neatly formalised in the much later *Māṇḍūkya Upaniṣad*, but its roots are found in the oldest Upaniṣads including *Chāndogya* 8.7–12. Prajāpati, linking senses with cosmic elements, teaches that the self is that which grounds all sensing and thinking, using a colourful picture of fulfilled desires to point Indra beyond waking, dreaming, deep sleep to "the self free from evils, old age, sorrow and death" (8.7–12).

The flavour is very different in Yājñavalkya's teaching to Maitreyī. He gives her a series of examples to illustrate how everything is the self (*ātman*, 2.4.6), culminating in the image of salt dissolved in water. Just so, a person, who arises from various elements, at death will dissolve back into them and there will be no more awareness:

> For where there is duality as it were, there one smells another, sees another, hears another, speaks to another, thinks of another, knows another. When however all in one has become the self/one's self (*ātman*), what could one smell by what? … what could one know by what? by what could one know that by which all this is known? By what can one know the knower?
>
> (BU 2.4.14)

No cognition of difference can remain. Yet the knower – the unknown knower of BU 3.7.23 – remains. Beyond words. The parallel passage in BU 4.5.15 uses radically apophatic language to stress this: "That is this self (*ātman*), said to be, 'No, no,'" that which no language can describe.

A similar impulse for what is beyond cognition underlies Uddālaka Āruṇi's question to his arrogant son, Śvetaketu:

> Did you ask for the teaching by which the unheard becomes heard, the unthought thought, and the unknown known?
>
> (6.1.2–3)

This engenders a series of examples containing the famous *tat tvam asi* teaching, "You are that." Perhaps no other Upaniṣadic phrase has occasioned so much scholarly discussion, whether by Vedāntin commentators,[10] or by modern textual scholars.[11] In the *Chāndogya* narrative, Śvetaketu is the one addressed as "you." "That" is *sat*, Being, which thinks, "May I be many." Clearly the arrogant pupil is not the source of everything. His father explains:

> This subtle part is what all this has as self. It is truth; it is the self (*ātman*). *You* are that, Śvetaketu.
>
> (6.8.7, tr. Roebuck)

"All this," the cosmos, has transcendent Being for its self. This is also the core of Śvetaketu's being. His existence, goal, very life, and truthfulness have this subtle essence as self (6.13–16).

These searches within the cosmos and within the person for the answers to the fundamental questions of life recur in the middle and late Upaniṣads. The next section considers three middle period verse texts as case studies for how they explore our vital but slippery terms.

The verse Upaniṣads: *Kena*, *Īśā*, and *Muṇḍaka*

Kena *on brahman*

Both parts of the *Kena Upaniṣad* are focused on *brahman* though in different ways. Metric chapters 1–2 are a poetic meditation on the elusive power which lies behind the individual's mind, speech, and senses, reminiscently described as the "hearing behind hearing, the thinking behind thinking, the speech behind speech, the sight behind sight" but also "the breathing behind breathing" (1.2). The hearer is repeatedly adjured to learn that only this is *brahman*, not what others regard as their highest power. The person who thinks they know *brahman* well is challenged to consider not the visible aspect of *brahman* but that which is unknown (2.3). Paradoxically it is those who do not perceive it who do. Not content to identify *brahman* with an aspect of the cosmos perhaps, they recognise its transcendence and gain immortality (2.5).

Prose chapters 3–4 contain a variation on the recurring competition among gods, or the breaths, over who is the greatest. Here the elusive *brahman* is the challenger and winner. "*brahman*," then, is the highest power, whether in philosophical poetry or a somewhat anthropomorphised, though still uncapturable, form in prose. It is known in relation to a person's mind and senses, mythically explains the god Indra's power and yields immortality beyond death. The term "*ātman*" is not used.

Īśā *on* ātman

By contrast, in the short *Īśā*, the term "*brahman*" does not feature. Its references to the self are ambiguous, as is its opening: everything is to be pervaded or perfumed by a powerful one/the Lord (*īśā*, 1).[12] A neuter "One" is described in paradoxes: unmoving, yet swifter than the mind, beyond gods, far and near, within and without (4–5). The next verse, in words reminiscent of BU 4.4.15, and adapted theistically in BhG 6.30, reads: "Whoever sees/ All beings in the self (*ātman*)/ And the self in all beings/Does not shrink away from it" (6, tr. Roebuck). Roebuck keeps this ambiguous on purpose. Is one to see all beings in oneself? Or in the (supreme) self? And is this a theistic Upaniṣad, identifying supreme self, the "One" and God?[13] Or is *īś* to be equated with the "great self," the indwelling overseer of all, as in BU 2.5.15?[14]

Muṇḍaka *on both*

In the *Muṇḍaka*, the knowledge of *brahman* is intimately bound up with understanding "*ātman*." As elsewhere, this term has several senses. In a famous analogy, the *Muṇḍaka* compares the syllable *Om* with a bow, the self (*ātman*) with an arrow and *brahman* with the target to be struck (2.2.4). So it appears that the individual self, sharpened with meditation, is to be drawn back ready to fire "with the mind fixed on the nature of that," i.e. *brahman* (2.2.3). This idea of an individual self refined by meditation is reinforced when a person who knows the supreme place of *brahman*, their desires completely satisfied, is described as *kṛtātma* (3.2.2, cf. *yuktātma* 3.2.5), "one whose self is perfected."

The relation of the self to the cosmic person (*puruṣa*), the source and upholder of all things (2.1), "higher than the highest" (3.2.8), and to *brahman*, the immortal which extends in all directions (2.2.12), yet is subtler than the subtle (2.2.2), is never stated straightforwardly. Yet it is knowledge of the self which unites the self with *brahman* as the arrow with the target (2.2.4); it is *brahman*, free from stain or parts, the radiant light of lights, which is known by knowers of the self (*ātmavidaḥ* 2.2.10). The self is both in the body, known through consciousness into which the breath/senses are woven, and that on which the three cosmic regions are woven (3.1.9; 2.2.5, cf. BU 3.6, 3.8). The destination of tranquil knowers (1.2.11) of *brahman* is the immortal, cosmic person, the imperishable self (*avyayātmā*, 1.2.11),[15] whose feet are "the inmost self (*antarātmā*) of all beings" (2.1.4).[16] These are subtle equations, working from where a person is, drawing out the inner and cosmic knowledge which will unite the knower with the divine person, as individual name and form are lost, like rivers flowing into an ocean (3.2.8). The prose re-links intention and outcome: "One who knows the highest *brahman* indeed becomes *brahman*" (3.2.9).

A personalising turn? *Kaṭha* and *Śvetāśvatara*

Lord, ātman, *and* brahman *in Śvetāśvatara*

While Olivelle sees the *Kena*, *Īśā*, and *Muṇḍaka* as having "strong theistic tendencies" (1996: xxxvii), this is perhaps more noticeable in the *Kaṭha* and *Śvetāśvatara*. The deity in the *Śvetāśvatara* is Rudra, described as "*śiva*," auspicious or gentle (3.11). The relationship between *ātman* and *brahman* to this Lord (*īśa*), the God/god (*deva*) who upholds all there is (1.8) is, as we would now expect, slippery. Signifieds are constantly open to interpretation. Verses from earlier texts are quoted and integrated. Networks of associations lie within the poetic process.[17]

What is clear is the supremacy of the "One," Rudra/Savitṛ, the Lord, the God, pervasive, total yet transcendent source of all (1.10). He is the one to be known as distinct from the individual self (*jīva*) and from mind-matter (*prakṛti*).[18] To know him, one should use, but go beyond, yogic practices of finding the "One" within (2.14–15), and be devoted to this "One," as to one's teacher (6.23). Around this core are woven numerous uses of the terms "*brahman*" and "*ātman*." The different translations of Olivelle and Roebuck show the decisions of interpretation required. I outline two sets here.

First, we are to understand that sorting out various views of "those who speak of *brahman*" is the aim of the Upaniṣad (1.1). Depending on how the first of many questions in 1.1 is translated,[19] we might identify *brahman* as that cause (rather than time, inherent nature, fate, and so on), the one who transcends all. Or we might ask what the cause of *brahman* is, perhaps as in 2.7, the "sacred Vedic formula." The world or wheel of *brahman* is that of rebirth, whether controlling or controlled by it (1.6). Finally, though, *brahman* is identified as the substance of Śvetāśvatara's correct teaching (6.21; cf. 2.15), that is, the view on the Lord. "*brahman*" therefore continues to designate the best understanding, "that which exceeds."

Second, there is a key shift in meaning of "*ātman*," in one of its most important usages in the *Śvetāśvatara*. Here the *ātman* is subject to pleasure and pain (1.2), differentiated from the powerful one or Lord, and is the individual experiencer of objects of experience. It is compared with a bird sitting on a tree pecking fruit, or a male goat after "enjoying" the female (4.5–7; cf. MU 3.1). It is the self as involved in the world of rebirth. With perishable *prakṛti*, it is ruled over by the one God (1.10), a triad identified in 1.12 as "the threefold *brahman*." It can be freed by recognising this (cf. MU 3.2.2 where the self can be perfected). Yet "*ātman*" can also designate the Lord, the all-pervading self, which is the secret teaching on *brahman* (*brahmopaniṣad*), found within oneself (1.15–16). Old themes of the whole and transcendence, of finding the self within, become transmuted through a lens of personal deity as supreme self, now differentiated from the individual self, using the new techniques of yoga (see Chapters 17 and 32).

Self, selves, and the elusive goal in Kaṭha

In the *Kaṭha*, Naciketas searches for immortality. Death (Yama) finally teaches him about the one who is not born, does not die, does not originate, does not become, and is not killed when the body is (2.18), whom Olivelle, along with 2.20, identifies as *ātman*:

> Subtler than the subtle, greater than the great,
> the self (*ātman*) is hidden in the secret (heart) of a living being.

This could refer to an individual self yet remains ambiguous. As in earlier texts, this *ātman* is described in paradoxical terms: "Sitting, it moves far, lying it goes everywhere" (2.21; cf. IU 5). Ordinary methods of intellectual learning do not avail in finding the self (cf. MU 3.2.3). It is grasped by the one to whom it reveals its own nature (or chooses as its own body) (2.23).[20] Personal Lord? Or self-disclosing consciousness to the one who looks?

In KU 3, a Sāṃkhya-like hierarchy of senses, sense objects, mind (*manas*), intellect (*buddhi*), "great self" (*ātmā mahān*), and unmanifest (*avyakta*) leads to the "Person" (*puruṣa*), beyond which is nothing (3.10–11). This is the highest goal: The chariot journey's end, the furthest step of Viṣṇu,[21] the "tranquil self," into which has been merged the "great self" and before that the "knowing self" (3.13).[22] Different senses of self – individual cognitive (*jñānātma*) and universal cosmic (*ātman mahat*) – are transcended in that tranquil self (*śāntātman*), the final stage. Ultimately, that which frees from death is seen to be "without sound, touch, or form, imperishable, without taste, eternal, without smell, without beginning or end, greater than the great, constant." Radhakrishnan glosses as "self" (3.15 tr.). The text simply has pronouns. Once more, juxtapositions suggest; words push beyond.

Tidying things up: *Praśna* and *Māṇḍūkya*

The Praśna*'s pastiche*

The *Praśna* incorporates an archaic medley of teachings relating them overall to "the highest *brahman*, higher than which there is nothing" (6.7; cf. KU 3.11). The self emerges as immortal, the final end (1.9), the foundation of breath (*prāṇa*) (3.3), residing within the heart (3.6). As the "highest self," it is the foundation of all the elements and aspects of an individual person (4.7). The "knowing self" (*vijñānātman*, cf. KU 3.13), probably individual here, is the one who sees, touches, tastes, smells, thinks, knows, and acts. It rests on, or is established in, the supreme imperishable self, the two apparently distinguished.

The fourth beyond

By contrast, the brief *Māṇḍūkya* systematically reflects on the syllable Om and its four quarters, equated to the states of waking, dreaming, deep sleep and the fourth (*turīya*) beyond (2–7). "This *brahman*" is the whole cosmos; past, present, future, and what is beyond – the familiar theme of the whole and that which transcends it. Famously, "this self is *brahman*" (1), in particular, the fourth beyond. It too is described by paradox and negation: without inside or outside, unseen, ungraspable, indescribable; tranquil; without a second (7). It is beyond the conventional world of ordinary transactions (*avyavahārya*), auspicious (*śiva*), non-dual (*advaita*), the stilling of the manifested world (*prapañcopaśama*). By knowing the self through meditative reflection on these quarters which lead beyond, "one enters the self through oneself" (12).[23] With BU 4.5.13, this becomes central to an Advaitin understanding of *brahman* and *ātman*.[24]

Is *ātman* identical to *brahman*? Reconsidering the question

This important philosophical question has often been considered in terms primarily of ultimate reality (*brahman*). How is the eternal self (*ātman*), that which provides the continuity between the different births of an individual and seeks escape from that cycle, related to this causal reality? Are they identical? The same but different? Non-reciprocally dependent in a single complex reality? Different in important ways but contingent in being? Or what? And is that ultimate reality: beyond all words and characteristics, a personal Lord to be worshipped, or what? (see Chapters 15 and 19).

Close reading of the texts and their own questions in light of Indological, and more recent literary/narrative, approaches can lead us to approach the issue from a different angle. First, consider "*brahman*" as a question-poser like in the old *brahmodya* riddling and "*ātman*" as a multi-vocal term yielding a rich view of what it is to be (a) person. The former focuses on the best way of understanding the highest value, the secret given in the cosmos and in the particular transmission from teacher to pupil, the totality which incorporates earlier partial understandings, the transcendent which exceeds the known whole. The latter recalls the person-shaped images through which seers explored the nature of the cosmos, its origin and manifest plurality, from the dismembered Cosmic Person to the self within all. It reminds us that body, breath, vital functions, cognitive processes and subject consciousness itself have all been explored as *brahman*, the secret of the whole. It prompts us to explore different "types" or "layers" of self- or personhood: the bodily waking, dream, deep sleep, and transcendent selves of the early Upaniṣads and the *Māṇḍūkya*; the perfectable self of the *Muṇḍaka*'s *kṛtātma*; the sāṃkhya-yogic-like analyses of the *Kaṭha*'s knowing self, great self, and tranquil self, than which nothing is higher.

To the modern student of the Upaniṣadic texts, the question about the relation of *ātman* to *brahman* then becomes: What is disclosed in a close reading of this teacher's view? This assembled text's juxtapositions? This integration, summary or refinement of earlier positions? How is this shaped by renegotiations of the relation between macrocosm and microcosm? Of the search within?

Extending the exploration narratively, the question about "*brahman*" asks what the hearer-reader, addressed in and through the stories' characters and questions, values most. Within a wider narrative context of pedagogy, transmission, and social relations, it asks, "What do *you* hold most dear? For what reasons? What are the methods for finding it?" For the modern student, attention to these questions can foster an understanding of the *method* of these texts in their elusive, allusive inter- and intratextual promptings to consider what is already grasped and what is yet to be known.

And for the modern philosophical theologian, the question of the relation of *ātman* to *brahman* now invites a richer investigation of relations of personhood to the transcendent,[25] but that is a story for another day.

Notes

1 Cf. Paul Deussen on the identity of "the cosmical and the psychical principle": "This [idealist] thought which first makes its appearance in the discourses of Yâjñavalkya in the Bṛhadâraṇyaka is never again surrendered, and dominates, it is true with certain empirical modifications ..., the entire development of the doctrine of the Upanisads up to its conclusion with Bâdarâyaṇa [author of Vedānta's *Brahma-sūtras*] and Śankara [key non-dualist Vedāntin]" (1906: 132). Hume 1931: 29.

2 Life: Renou 1952; breath: e.g. KsU 2.1, 2.2, 2.14, 3.4; person: e.g. CU 3.12.6; BU 1.4.1; KsU 4.4; SU 3.

3 *Brahma-Sūtra-Bhāṣya* 1.1.1; *Taittirīya-Upaniṣad-Bhāṣya* 2.1. cf. Gonda, 1950: 18–31, "*brahman*" as generative grounding. Renou tentatively linked it with √*valh-*, suggesting a primary Vedic sense of "*bráhman*" as "enigma" (1949: 21).

4 "Brahma" is also found in older translations for this neuter term (e.g. Hume 1931), and should not be confused with "Brahmā," the male creator deity. Sometimes, the Sanskrit is ambiguous, e.g. BU 6.5.3: Radhakrishnan: "Brahmā"; Olivelle: "Brahman."

5 All translations mine unless indicated.

6 For a thematic introduction, Brereton 1990.

7 In CU 1.6–7, *adhidaivata* and *adhyātma* are homologised with the Ṛg verse and Sāman chant. The two categories occur throughout the *Chāndogya*.

8 Cf. BU 1.2.4-5; 1.4.2-3, Roebuck 2000: 266, n.21.

9 PU 9 and MaU 7 take up but adapt.

10 Madhva splits as "*atat tvam asi*" (Stoker n.d.).

11 Brereton 1986, followed by Olivelle, critiqued by Roebuck 2003: 423, n.12.

12 See Roebuck's excellent footnote (2003: 390, n.3).

13 To read 15–18 as obviously theistic, whether intentional (Olivelle) or interpolated (Thieme 1965), seems strange. In BU 5.15, it is the prayer of a dying person to the sungod/god of death.
14 Cf. Thieme 1965: 89–90.
15 Or, "whose self is imperishable."
16 See Olivelle using Hertel's critical edition (1996: 271).
17 Olivelle suggests its integration of earlier views explains its "chaotic" appearance (1996: 252; cf. BhG). While some quotations do not easily fit grammar or theme (Killingley 1983: 10, see Roebuck, 2003: 454, n.7), the *Śvetāśvatara*'s juxtapositions and "shape-shifting" are continuous in method with earlier texts pushing the seeker beyond.
18 On the terminology of unsystematised proto-Sāṃkhya and Yoga used in this text, Johnston 1930; Larson 1979: 100–102.
19 Roebuck 2000: 339 n.2; Olivelle 1996: 253; Gonda 1950: 10: "What is the cause? Is it brahman?", or, "Is the cause brahman?"
20 *yamevaiṣa vṛṇute tena labhyas tasyaiṣa ātmā vivṛṇute tanūṃ svaṃ*.
21 For the myth of Viṣṇu's three steps, see e.g. *Śatapatha Brāhmaṇa* 1.2.5; RV 1.22.20a; RV 1.154.5d (Hume 1931: 352, n.1).
22 On the fourteenth-century Yogic Advaitin Vidyāraṅya's comment, Madaio 2016, 4.3. On the "great self," van Buitenen 1964.
23 *saṃviśaty ātmanātmānam*
24 E.g. Śaṃkara's *Gauḍapādīya-Kārikā-Bhāṣya*.
25 Cf. Ram-Prasad 2013.

References

Black, Brian 2007. *The Character of the Self in Ancient India: Priests, Kings and Women in the Early Upaniṣads*. Albany, NY: State University of New York Press.

Brereton, Joel 1986. "'*Tat tvam asi*' in context" *Zeitschrift der Deutschen Morgenländischen Gesellschaft* 136.1: 98–109.

Brereton, Joel 1990. "The Upanishads" in W. Th. de Bary and Irene Bloom (eds) *Approaches to the Asian Classics*. New York: Columbia University Press, 115–135.

Chakravarthi Ram-Prasad 2013. *Divine Self, Human Self: the Philosophy of Being in Two Gītā commentaries*. London: Bloomsbury Academic.

Deussen, Paul 1906. *The Philosophy of the Upanishads*, authorised ET by A. S. Geden, London: T&T Clark. (Reprint: New York: Dover Publications, 1966.)

Gonda, Jan 1950. *Notes on Brahman*. Utrecht: J. L. Beyers.

Gonda, Jan 1965. "*Bandhu* in the Brāhmaṇas" *Adyar Library Bulletin* 29: 1–29.

Hume, Robert E. 1931. *The Thirteen Principal Upanishads, Translated from the Sanskrit, with an Outline of the Philosophy of the Upanishads*, second revised edition. (Reprint: London: Oxford University Press, 1979.)

Johnston, E. H. 1930. "Some Sāṃkhya and Yoga conceptions of the *Śvetāśvatara Upaniṣad*" *Journal of the Royal Asiatic Society* 62: 855–878.

Killingley, D. H. 1983. "Notes on the *Śvetāśvaratara Upaniṣad*," unpublished paper.

Larson, Gerald James 1979. *Classical Sāṃkhya: An Interpretation of its History and Meaning*. Delhi: Motilal Banarsidass, second revised edition.

Madaio, James 2016. "Advaita Vedānta as Narrative Theology: emplotment, soteriology and senses of self in the *Jīvanmuktiviveka*," unpublished PhD, University of Manchester.

Olivelle, Patrick (trans.) 1996. *Upaniṣads*. Oxford: Oxford University Press.

Radhakrishnan, Sarvepalli 1953. *The Principal Upaniṣads*, edited with Introduction, [Sanskrit] Text, Translation and Notes. London: George Allen & Unwin.
Renou, Louis 1952. "On the Word *ātman*" *Vāk* 2: 151–157.
Renou, Louis with Lilian Silburn 1949. "Sur la notion de brahman" *Journal asiatique* 237: 7–46.
Roebuck, Valerie J. (trans. and ed.) 2000. *The Upaniṣads*. New Delhi: Penguin Books India.
Roebuck, Valerie J. (trans. and ed.) 2003. *The Upaniṣads*, revised edition, London: Penguin.
Śaṃkara, *Brahma-Sūtra-Bhāṣya*. Gambhirananda (trans.) 1977. *Brahma-Sūtra Bhāṣya of Śaṅkarācārya* [commentary on Bādarāyaṇa's verses], third revised edition. Calcutta: Advaita Ashrama.
Śaṃkara, *Gauḍapādīya-Kārikā-Bhāṣya*. = Commentary on "Māṇḍūkya Upaniṣad and Kārikā" in Gambhirananda (trans.) 1973 [1958]. *Eight Upaniṣads with the Commentary of Śaṅkarācārya*, vol. 2. Calcutta: Advaita Ashrama.
Śaṃkara, *Taittirīya-Upaniṣad-Bhāṣya*. In Gambhirananda (trans.) 1972 [1957]. *Eight Upaniṣads with the Commentary of Śaṅkarācārya*, vol. 1. Calcutta: Advaita Ashrama.
Smith, Brian K. 1989. *Reflections on Resemblance, Ritual and Religion*. Oxford: Oxford University Press.
Stoker, Valerie (n.d.) "Madhva (1238–1317)" *Internet Encyclopedia of Philosophy*, available at: www.iep.utm.edu/madhva. Date last accessed 11 Aug 2016.
Thieme, Paul 1965. "Īṣopaniṣad (= Vājasaneyi-Saṃhita 40) 1–14" *Journal of the American Oriental Society* 85: 89–99.
Van Buitenen, J. A. B. 1964. "The Large *ātman*" *History of Religions* 4.1: 103–114.

12 *Karma* and rebirth in the Upaniṣads

Dermot Killingley

The classic form of the doctrine of *karma*

One common Hindu belief which can be traced to the Upaniṣads is that after death you will be reborn in a different body – possibly human, but more probably animal or even plant, with the more attractive, but very remote, possibility of rebirth in a superhuman body, even as a god – and that the form of your rebirth will be determined by your action (*karma*) in this life. This belief is one of the ways in which Hindus account for misfortune, and even occasional good fortune, though it is by no means the only way (Keyes and Daniel 1983; Sharma 1973). It is also familiar in Sanskrit literature where complex narratives trace one or more characters through successive rebirths. An instructive example is the story of the hermit-king Bharata, who lapsed from his meditation by becoming excessively fond of a deer that he had rescued. Reaping the reward of his advanced spiritual progress, but also reaping the reward of his attachment to the deer, he was reborn as a deer who could remember his previous births; he was then reborn as an uncouth brahmin who had perfect knowledge of ultimate truth, without needing to be instructed (*Viṣṇu Purāṇa* 2.13–16). Rebirth according to *karma* appears in texts on dharma, as a sanction against sinful behavior (*Manu* ch. 12, verses 54–81). Similar ideas, though with an emphasis on intention rather than mere action as a determinant of rebirth, are commonplace in Buddhist texts; they form the basis of the Jātakas, the collection of stories recounting the Buddha's previous births, and are essential to the Mahāyāna Buddhist idea of the bodhisattva, the person who has developed a series of perfections through many rebirths, in order to benefit others.

Karma and rebirth provide a solution to the problem of theodicy – that is, the problem of God's justice. This problem is put clearly by the great theologian Śaṅkara, who was also the author of the earliest extant commentaries on the Upaniṣads. The doctrine that God created the world, Śaṅkara admits, is open to the objection that the world is full of inequality and undeserved suffering, indicating that its creator must be unfair and cruel, which conflicts with Vedic statements that God is morally perfect. Śaṅkara's answer to this objection is that the suffering experienced by each being results not from the will of God, but from that being's previous actions; beings are not created unequal, but make themselves so by actions which incur good or bad fortune, causing them to be reborn in happier or more miserable forms. This answer to the problem of theodicy, Śaṅkara points out, requires infinite time: There never was a primal state in which all beings were equally happy (Śaṅkara, commentary on *Vedānta-sūtra* 2.1.34–35; Thibaut 1904: vol. 1, pp. 357–360).

The idea that a person's destiny is determined by previous actions, usually actions in previous lives, is conveniently referred to as *karma* (or, in another form of the same word, *karman*); etymologically, this word means "action." What has been outlined above may be called the classic form of the doctrine of *karma*; it is found both in learned literature in Sanskrit, and in popular discourse. *Karma* in its classic form is a complex set of ideas, which the texts do not usually present in full. Rather, it is treated as already familiar to writers or speakers and their audience, without needing to be expounded; an extended exposition such as Śaṅkara's, summarized above, is unusual. When such ideas appear in the Upaniṣads, on the other hand, they are presented as something new, even as a secret which the teacher is reluctant to impart. In the two passages which we will discuss first, the teacher is not a brahmin but a kṣatriya, and it is emphasized that no brahmin has possessed this knowledge before (BU 6.2.8; CU 5.3.7). This, together with other examples of kṣatriya teachers, has been seen by some scholars as evidence that *karma* and rebirth came from outside the priestly circles which the Veda represents, or even from outside the culture which Vedic texts refer to as *ārya*. But in interpreting this evidence, we should remember that unusual sources of knowledge, and the reluctance of the teacher, are common literary tropes in the Upaniṣads (below, pp. 261–262). We should also note that those scholars who presented *karma* as appearing suddenly in the Upaniṣads (e.g. Garbe 1921) failed to unpack this complex set of ideas, and ignored related ideas which occur in earlier texts, especially the Brāhmaṇas, which they dismissed as tedious priestly ramblings (see Chapters 6 and 7).

While the word karma etymologically means "action, deed," and has this meaning in Sanskrit literature, it also had a specialized meaning in the circles in which the Upaniṣads were composed. To specialists in ritual, karma meant specifically ritual action, in the same way as "fabric" in different contexts can mean textiles or buildings. The actions which lead to different births may be good or bad in terms of ritual, rather than in ethical or social terms. Some scholars have exaggerated the discontinuity between the ritual concerns of the Brāhmaṇas and the ethical ideas of the Upaniṣads (Tull 1989: 13). It is significant that some of the most innovative passages about karma occur in the *Bṛhadāraṇyaka Upaniṣad*, which belongs to the Yajurveda, the collection most closely concerned with ritual action (Cohen 2008: 6; 49).

Rebirth in the Upaniṣads: The five fires

Though rebirth is described in some passages of the Upaniṣads, it is not in every case determined by actions. Where some part of the package which later became familiar as *karma* is mentioned, we should be careful not to assume that the whole package is meant. We can see this by comparing the two passages mentioned above: *Bṛhadāraṇyaka Upaniṣad* 6.2, and *Chāndogya Upaniṣad* 5.3–5.10 (see further Killingley 1997). They discuss rebirth at some length, and agree with each other in broad outline and in many, though not all, details; they are two versions of the same discourse. Both describe birth as resulting from a cyclic process: Life descends from the other world (*asau lokaḥ*, "the world beyond," which may mean the world of the gods, or the world of the dead (Gonda 1966: 84–86)) in the form of rain, springs up as plants in this world, is eaten by a man, becomes semen and enters a woman, is born, and later dies and is cremated. The cycle is both biological and ritual. Those who have knowledge of this cycle – and knowledge is the key to success, both in the Upaniṣads and in the Brāhmaṇas which preceded them – pass from the cremation fire through the world of the gods to the sun, and thence to the worlds of Brahman, from which they do not return. Their knowledge has freed them from cyclic existence. Those who have performed rituals to win heavenly worlds pass through the world of the ancestors to the moon, and thence descend again as rain. Action – that is, the rituals they have performed – leads them to continue in the cycle.

The two passages embody a series of contrasts. Knowledge, leading beyond the cyclic world, is contrasted with action, leading to continued cyclic existence. The path of the gods, which leads to Brahman, is contrasted with the path of the ancestors, which leads to rebirth; the idea of two paths of the dead appears already in various forms in pre-Upaniṣadic texts (Killingley 1997: 15–16). The sun, which is the ultimate goal (SB 1.9.3.15), is contrasted with the moon: the moon waxes and wanes, unlike the sun, and the lunar calendar regulates the rituals which maintain the ancestors in the world of the dead, while the sun is associated with the gods. It is knowledge, specifically knowledge of what has been taught here, that leads to the world of Brahman; action, specifically ritual action – "sacrifices, gifts [to brahmins] and asceticism" (BU 6.2.16) – leads to rebirth and a repetition of the cycle. These contrasts are apparent in both versions. But it is only in the *Chāndogya Upaniṣad* version that the form in which one is reborn depends on *karma*: Those whose behavior is pleasant will be reborn in a pleasant womb, but those whose behavior is foul will enter a foul womb (CU 5.10.7). The *Bṛhadāraṇyaka Upaniṣad* version omits this point; after summing up the path of the ancestors with the words "This is how they follow the circle round," it goes straight to the next point: that those who do not know the two paths become insects and creatures that bite (BU 6.2.16).

Summarizing Upaniṣadic passages is a tricky business: it involves skating over details that require too much explanation, at the risk of missing something important. Translating them, or reading translations, is also tricky, since the Upaniṣads use ambiguous words, or words that can only be understood with reference to their own culture, including technical terms of Vedic ritual.

Reading a passage once will not give you all its meaning; it is worthwhile going over it several times, with different nuances of meaning, and different problems of interpretation, in mind. After speed-reading these two passages, we must look at them again.

In both passages, the teaching is framed by a story (below, p. 264). A brahmin is unable to answer five questions about what happens after death, and seeks instruction from the kṣatriya who asked them. As often happens in the Upaniṣads, the instruction does not explicitly address the five questions, though it is based on the number five; but it provides material to answer them.

In saying that life descends in the form of rain, we omitted an important feature of the cycle. In both versions, the cycle is described as a series of five fires; a fire, in which offerings are poured, is a central feature of Vedic ritual (Chapter 7). In each of these five fires, the gods pour an offering, and from that offering arises something new, which becomes the offering in the next fire of the cycle. We may be in the realm of cosmic biology here, but we are also in the realm of Vedic ritual theory, in which each offering yields a result. The first fire is the other world, in which the gods offer faith (*śraddhā*, see p. 68). From that offering Soma arises – the ritual drink which is also a god, and also the nourishing fluid of the cosmos. The second fire is the rain-cloud – *parjanya*, which is also a god. In it, the gods offer Soma, and the result is rain. The third fire is this world, in which the gods offer rain, yielding food (*anna*, also meaning "crops, grain"). The gods offer this food in the fourth fire, which is man – that is, a man eats the food – and the result is semen. The gods offer this in the fifth fire, which is woman, and the result is a foetus (CU 5.8.2), or, as the other version puts it, a man (BU 6.2.13). (It is not mentioned that the offspring could be a girl, or that women also eat food; in Vedic thought, man is the paradigmatic conscious agent (below, p. 89). At the end of his life, the man is cremated; he thus returns to the fire, from which he arose (CU 5.9.2). The cremation fire brings the series up to six; but the doctrine embodied in both passages is called the *pañcāgnividyā* "knowledge of the five fires." Each of the five – leaving aside the cremation fire – is described in a formulaic way, homologizing the fire itself, and each feature of it, with a feature of the natural world: "Man is a fire, Gautama [the lineage name – like a surname – of Uddālaka Āruṇi]. Its fuel is the open mouth; its smoke is breath; its flame is speech; its embers are sight; its sparks are hearing" (BU 6.2.12). But in the case of the cremation fire, homologization is redundant: the fire is fire, the fuel is fuel, and so on (BU 6.2.14).

It is only when we reach the fourth fire – when a man eats the food – that the passages start to speak in terms of individual existence. What is offered as faith, arises as Soma, descends as rain, and is eaten as food is what makes such existence possible; when we first summarized the two passages, we referred to it for convenience as "life." It is only after describing cremation that the passages use plural expressions to describe the different destinies of different people – or should we say men. Here, the two passages differ considerably, and it is only in the *Chāndogya* version, as we have seen, that the form in which one is reborn is determined by action.

Reading the Upaniṣads can be like overhearing incomplete conversations in which people relate what they have said to others before, or what others have said to them. In passages such as BU 6.2 and CU 5.3–5.10, we find the same things said in slightly different ways, and sometimes one version omits what seems to be important in the other. There are several partial parallels to these two passages in the Brāhmaṇas and Upaniṣads (SB 11.6.2; *Jaiminīya Brāhmaṇa* 1.45.6; AU 2.1–4; MU 1.2.10–11; KsU 1; PU 1.9–10), and they can shed light on points that are obscure.

For instance, the *Jaiminīya Brāhmaṇa* includes a passage about six fires, in each of which the gods pour an offering, yielding a product which is offered in the next fire. The first fire is the sun, in which the gods offer "*amṛta*, water"; *amṛta* is the drink of immortality – often identified with Soma, but here with water. As in the two Upaniṣad passages, the fifth fire is woman; the offering is semen, and the product is man. Thus "at the fifth creation the divine waters speak with a human voice" (*Jaiminīya Brāhmaṇa* 1.45–46; Bodewitz 1973: 114–116). This answers the fifth question in the five fires story, which remains unanswered there: "Do you know at which offering, when it is offered, water gets a human voice, rises up and speaks?" (BU 6.2.2; cf. CU 5.3.3).

Another partial parallel helps us understand how the five fires passages connect the waxing and waning of the moon with the process of rebirth:

> They reach the moon and become food. And there the gods – as they say to King Soma, "Increase! Decrease!" – eat them there.
>
> (BU 6.2.16)

Soma is often identified with the moon (Gonda 1965: 38–70); but it is not clear here how the phases of the moon are connected with the journey of the dead towards rebirth. The connection becomes clear in another passage:

> All those who pass away from this world go to the moon. Because of their breaths (*prāṇa*), it swells during the waxing phase. It brings them to birth in the waning phase.
>
> (KsU 1.2)

So the waxing moon is filling up with the dead, or rather their breaths, and the waning moon is discharging them into the process of rebirth. The passage continues:

> The moon is the door of the heavenly world. Whoever answers, it lets him through. Whoever does not answer becomes rain, and it rains him down. He is reborn in this world as a worm or a moth or a bird or a tiger or a lion or a fish or a rhinoceros or a man or something else in these places, according to his actions, according to his knowledge.
>
> (KsU 1.2)

Here, rebirth is the destiny of those who fail to give an answer to the moon. The answer given in the passage – the password to the heavenly world – is cryptic. But it mentions semen, moon, mother, birth, and seasons. Thus it is not unlike the process represented by the five fires, although fires are not mentioned. Those who have the secret knowledge of this process are freed from it and reach the heavenly world. Moreover, the story which provides a frame for this teaching is clearly related to the one which frames the two five fires passages: The same brahmin is unable to answer a question about the way to another world, and seeks instruction from the man who asked it. However, the instructor is not the same; as far as we can see, he is a brahmin (Cohen 2008: 141–142).

Rebirth in the Upaniṣads: Yājñavalkya

A brief dialogue about rebirth and *karma* appears in a series of dialogues occasioned by a contest (BU 3). King Janaka, in the course of a ritual for which many brahmins have assembled, has offered a prize of a thousand cows, each with ten gold coins tied to her horns, to the most learned brahmin in the assembly. The ensuing series of dialogues shows that the kind of learning called for was not the ability to recite texts, as the word (*anūcānatama*, more literally "best at repeating by rote") might imply, but the ability to think creatively about the texts, using them to construct theories about the nature of the cosmos and of personality – an ability highly valued in the Brāhmaṇas and especially the Upaniṣads. The great ritualist Yājñavalkya claims the prize, by coolly telling his student to drive the cows away. (A Vedic student is a live-in personal servant of his teacher.) Gifts of cows to brahmins are typical of Vedic ritual, reflecting a period when cattle were the main form of wealth; but the addition of gold coins – much more than the price of a cow – reflects a transition to a money economy. The improbability of one man driving a thousand cows suggests that the whole incident is symbolic rather than real. (A similar incident occurs in SB 11.6.3, but without the coins.)

Yājñavalkya's rivals challenge the claim by asking him questions, and his answers reduce each in turn to silence. The second challenger, Jāratkārava Ārtabhāga, asks a series of questions, of which the fifth is:

> When the speech of a dead man goes away into fire, his breath to wind, his eye to the sun, his mind to the moon, his hearing to the compass-points, his body to the earth, his self (*ātman*) to space, his body-hairs to the plants, his hair to the trees, his blood and semen are placed in water, where then does that man come to be?
>
> (BU 3.2.13)

Jāratkārava is using a recurrent idea that the parts of a person, viewed as a microcosm, are dispersed at death into the corresponding parts of the macrocosm. After this dispersal, he asks, what has become of the man? That is, when each part has lost its individuality by being merged into a part of the macrocosm, is there anything left that belongs to the individual? Yājñavalkya's answer emphasizes secrecy. Though it does not directly answer the question, it silences the questioner:

> "Take my hand, dear Ārtabhāga. Only we two will know of this. What we say shouldn't be public." They went away and discussed. What they said was action (*karma*). What they praised was action. One becomes good by good action, evil by evil action. Then Jāratkārava Artabhāga fell silent.

The answer, unlike the other answers in this series of dialogues, is arrived at by discussion rather than by a statement from Yājñavalkya, who treats his interlocutor as a friend rather than an opponent; perhaps he respects him as a fellow-practitioner of the Yajurveda (Cohen 2008: 77). What remains of a person, what is not merged in its macrocosmic counterpart, is the person's actions, probably meaning his ritual actions. This recalls the idea of actions as a personal treasury in the other world, as in the funeral hymn quoted above (p. 60).

One of the clearest early statements that rebirth is determined by *karma* forms part of a long discussion of the nature of the self (*ātman*), covering two sections of the *Bṛhadāraṇyaka Upaniṣad* (BU 4.3–4). This statement, however, is not clear throughout. Like much of the early prose Upaniṣads, it contains apparent discrepancies and contradictions, which we can suspect result from insertions and reworkings, though we have no precise evidence (see further pp. 28–31). The same teacher, Yājñavalkya, is in discussion with his patron King Janaka. He has previously promised to answer the king's questions (SB 11.6.2.10), but is reluctant to part with his wisdom (Olivelle 1996: 315–316), and tries at first to fob him off with trivial answers. However, as the discussion progresses it is established that the source of consciousness is the self (*ātman*, BU 4.3.6). It is also referred to as the "man" (*puruṣa*) – not in the ordinary sense, but in the sense of "the man among the faculties consisting of consciousness, the light within the heart" (BU 4.3.7). (This concept is close to the problematic entity which Western philosophers refer to as "mind"; but in translating from Sanskrit we conventionally use the word "mind" for *manas*, which is a faculty that processes information but is not itself conscious.) This "man" remains conscious not only in the waking state, where he perceives worldly objects, and in dream, where he perceives objects which he has himself created out of disconnected pieces of the real world (BU 4.3.9–10), but also in dreamless sleep. In the dreamless state, the "man" is not unconscious; but he is conscious only of himself. The senses and other faculties, being indestructible, continue to exist, though they have no objects to operate on (BU 4.3.23–31). Whereas in dream a person may experience terrors, based on their waking experience, in dreamless sleep one is the whole world (BU 4.3.20). Further, our relationships, our status, and our previous deeds have no place in the world of dreamless sleep:

> There, a father is not a father, a mother is not a mother, the worlds are not worlds, the gods are not gods, the Vedas are not Vedas. There, a thief is not a thief, an abortionist is not an abortionist, an outcaste is not an outcaste [the text uses two names of unclean castes], a hermit is not a hermit, an ascetic is not an ascetic. One is not followed by merit, nor followed by sin. For then one has passed beyond all sorrows of the heart.
>
> (BU 4.3.22)

This state of objectless consciousness, Yājñavalkya says, is the world of *brahman*, and therefore extremely blissful. As a way of measuring this bliss, he tells us that the bliss of the ancestors (to whom the rites for the dead are offered) is a hundred times the greatest bliss attainable in this world; the bliss of the Gandharvas (a class of beings ranked above humankind but below the gods) is a hundred times that; and so on through two grades of gods – those who have achieved divinity through actions, meaning ritual actions, and those who were born divine – to Prajāpati (the creator god who established Vedic ritual), and finally to *brahman* (not necessarily as presented in Chapter 11, but certainly a transcendent form of being). Since each of these six classes of being has a hundred times the bliss of the preceding (BU 4.3.32–33), the bliss of *brahman* is 1,000,000,000,000 times the greatest human bliss; it is this extreme bliss which is identified with the dreamless state. (A very similar, though not identical, gradation of bliss is given in TU 2.8.)

Yājñavalkya then turns to death, which he treats in an analogous way to sleep. While it appears to bystanders that a dying person's faculties are failing, they are actually being gathered together by the self into its dwelling-place in the heart (BU 4.4.1; the heart, not the brain, is the seat of consciousness in ancient Indian thought). "He becomes one. People say 'He doesn't see.' He becomes one. People say 'He doesn't smell.' He becomes one. People say 'He doesn't taste,'" and so on through the faculties. (Most translators treat "He becomes one" as part of what the bystanders say, but it makes more sense if we understand it as Yājñavalkya's own positive view of what happens at death, contrasted with other people's negative one; the Sanskrit text does not indicate where the quoted speech begins.) Then the self, after striking down its former body, makes itself a newer and more beautiful form, belonging to some other world, beyond death: the form of an ancestor, or of a Gandharva, or of a god, or of Prajāpati, or of *brahman* (BU 4.4.4).

So far, this passage has shown an underlying assumption that the other world, the world beyond death, must be happier than this world: "When he is born and puts on a body, he becomes united with evils; and when he dies and leaves the body behind, he gets rid of evils" (BU 4.3.8). Accordingly, the forms which the self makes for itself after death are all blissful. But then Yājñavalkya tells the king that the next life depends on the person's actions; so it may not be blissful at all. "As he acts, as he behaves, so he becomes. A doer of good becomes good; a doer of evil becomes evil. Good by good action; evil by evil action" (BU 4.4.5). Adding two further links to the chain of causation, it then appears that it is not actions themselves that determine rebirth, but desires, which lead to intentions (*kratu*, a technical term for the intention to perform a ritual act), which in turn lead to actions. "People say: 'A person in this world consists of nothing but desire.' As he desires, so he intends; as he intends, so he acts; as he acts, so he becomes." Then follows a verse (perhaps inserted later than the prose), which mentions attachment – an important concomitant of desire in later thought – and then says that when he reaches the end of the action he has done in this world, he returns from the other world to this world, and thus returns to action. This means that actions shape a person's destiny after death in two stages: The destiny is first experienced in a world beyond death, and then leads back to this world; and in this world, the person performs further actions, making the process potentially cyclical and endless, as in the classic form of *karma*.

This statement of rebirth according to *karma* seems to contradict what has been said about a newer and better form after death (BU 4.4.4). The contradiction can be resolved by referring back to something that was said earlier in Yājñavalkya's account of death: All beings welcome the arrival of the deceased, and hail him as *brahman*, like officials who have prepared for the arrival of a king – but this applies only to "one who knows this" (BU 4.3.37); that is, someone who knows this doctrine of the self and its various states, which Yājñavalkya has been reluctant to teach. The key to freedom from rebirth is knowledge of the true nature of the self. A different account of the key appears immediately after the description of how people return to this world and to action. This description, we are told, applies to those who desire. But the person who is free from desire, whose desire is satisfied, whose desire is the self: such a person is *brahman*, and goes to *brahman* (BU 4.4.6). If the teaching is to be consistent, knowledge of the self and freedom from desire, which are mentioned separately as conditions for escaping rebirth and reaching extreme bliss after death, must really be the same; and this is suggested by the remainder of the passage. Freedom from desire and knowledge of the self go together in later Upaniṣads also, and in the *Bhagavadgīta*. They are essential components of what is later called *yoga* (below, pp. 174–184). The ideal person, who has true knowledge, has no desires, for desires are a symptom of ignorance.

Rebirth in other Upaniṣads

The passages we have looked at treat the topic of rebirth at some length, in a manner typical of the early prose Upaniṣads. They approach it cautiously, as something not generally known, while linking it to well-established topics such as the effects of actions, the paths of the dead, the need to secure a place in the other world, and the danger of repeated death. The *Kaṭha Upaniṣad*, perhaps the earliest of the verse Upaniṣads (except for the *Īśā*), and the one which most clearly retains the link to the Brāhmaṇas typical of the early prose Upaniṣads, gives a brief statement of "what happens to the self when it has reached death," announcing it as a secret (KU 5.6):

> Some embodied selves reach a womb,
> to become corporeal;
> Others come to a tree-trunk,
> according to their actions, according to their knowledge.
> (KU 5.7)

"Their knowledge" (literally "what they have heard" (*śruta*)) means their knowledge of the Veda.

Another passage in the *Kaṭha Upaniṣad* contrasts the unmindful person who fails to reach the highest goal with the person who reaches it and is not born again (KU 3.7–8; below, p. 179). The highest goal is thus explicitly equated with avoidance of rebirth. Rebirth is referred to here as *saṃsāra*, "the current," a word often used in later texts for repeated births and deaths, driven by actions and bringing an endless series of experiences; this is the earliest occurrence of the word in this sense. In the *Śvetāśvatara Upaniṣad* (6.16), we find the same word *saṃsāra* coupled with *mokṣa*, which in classical Sanskrit refers to release from *saṃsāra*. But *mokṣa* does not occur in any other classical Upaniṣad. The term *saṃsāra* occurs again in MtU 1.4; 6.34; BhG 16.19, and frequently in later literature.

In the *Praśna Upaniṣad*, in which the sage Pippalāda answers six questions put to him by six other sages, he touches on rebirth very briefly in his answer to the third question. This question concerns the origin of breath (*prāṇa*), how it gets into the body and how it leaves it. In his answer, Pippalāda refers to a physiological theory of five breaths, which is found also in TU 1.7 and elsewhere (below, p. 70; Killingley 2006: 81), though he does not explain it at all completely or clearly. He also mentions numerous channels or veins (*nāḍī*, also described in BU 2.1.19). One of the five subsidiary breaths, the *udāna* (literally "up-breath"), "leads upwards by one of these *nāḍī*s, to a good world by good [action], to a bad world by bad, or to the human world by both" (PU 3.7).

In the *Muṇḍaka Upaniṣad*, the round of rebirths is associated with ritual, which can only yield finite results:

> Thinking sacrifices and gifts [*iṣṭāpūrta* (above, p. 60)] are the best,
> knowing nothing better, deluded,
> After enjoying their good deeds on the back of the sky
> they enter this inferior world.

(The translation "this inferior world" is conjectural; similarly Olivelle (1996: 270). The received text reads "this world or an inferior one," but *vā* "or" does not fit the meter.)

Those who practise asceticism and faith, in the forest,
tranquil, wise, living on alms,
Pass on spotless through the door of the sun,
where dwells the immortal Man, whose self is unchanging.
(MU 1.2.10–11)

The door of the sun implies a contrast with the moon, which is the door to rebirth.

But rebirth is not a very common theme in the Upaniṣads. On the other hand freedom, immortality, existence beyond death, are mentioned frequently. From the point of view of the classic form of the doctrine of *karma*, in which freedom is understood as release from rebirth, this is paradoxical. However, the Upaniṣads show many views of ultimate freedom, some of which are also found in older parts of the Veda, and we shall explore these views in the next chapter.

References

Bodewitz, H. W. 1973. *Jaiminīya Brāhmaṇa I, 1–65: Translation and Commentary: With a Study: Agnihotra and Prāṇāgnihotra*. Leiden. Brill.

Cohen, Signe. 2008. *Text and Authority in the Older Upaniṣads*. Leiden: Brill.

Garbe, R. 1921. "Transmigration (Indian)" in J. Hastings (ed.) *Encyclopedia of Religions and Ethics*, 13 vols. Edinburgh: T. &. T. Clark, 1908–1926, vol. 12, 434–435.

Gonda, Jan. 1965. *Change and Continuity in Indian Religion*. The Hague: Mouton.

Gonda, Jan. 1966. *Loka: World and Heaven in the Veda*. Amsterdam: Noord-Hollandsche Uitgevers Maatschappij (North Holland Publishing Company).

Keyes, Charles F., and Daniel, E. Valentine. 1983. *Karma: An Anthropological Inquiry*. Berkeley, CA: University of California Press.

Killingley, Dermot. 1997. "The Paths of the Dead and the Five Fires" in Peter Connolly and Sue Hamilton (eds) *Indian Insights: Buddhism, Brahmanism and Bhakti*. London, Luzac Oriental, 1–20.

Killingley, Dermot. 2006. "Faculties, Breaths and Orifices: Some Vedic and Sāṃkhya Notions of the Body and Personality" in Anna S. King (ed.) *Indian Religions: Renaissance and Renewal*. London: Equinox, 73–108.

Olivelle, Patrick. 1996. *Upaniṣads: Translated from the Original Sanskrit* (World's Classics series). Oxford: Oxford University Press.

Sharma, Ursula. 1973. "Theodicy and the Doctrine of Karma" *Man* 8: 347–364.

Thibaut, George. 1904. *The Vedânta-sûtras with the Commentary of Śaṅkarâcârya*. 2 vols. Oxford: Oxford University Press.

Tull, Herman W. 1989. *The Vedic Origins of Karma: Cosmos as Man in Ancient Indian Myth and Ritual*. Albany, NY: State University of New York Press.

Further reading

Gonda, Jan. 1966. *Loka: World and Heaven in the Veda*. Amsterdam: Noord-Hollandsche Uitgevers Maatschappij (North Holland Publishing Company).

Killingley, Dermot. 1997. "The Paths of the Dead and the Five Fires" in Peter Connolly and Sue Hamilton (eds) *Indian Insights: Buddhism, Brahmanism and Bhakti*. London: Luzac Oriental, 1–20.

O'Flaherty, Wendy Doniger (ed.) 1980. *Karma and Rebirth in Classical Indian Traditions*. Berkeley, CA: University of California Press.

Tull, Herman W. 1989. *The Vedic Origins of Karma: Cosmos as Man in Ancient Indian Myth and Ritual*. Albany, NY: State University of New York Press.

Tull, Herman W. 2004. "Karma" in Sushil Mittal and Gene Thursby (eds) *The Hindu World*. New York: Routledge, 309–331.

13 Knowledge and liberation in the Upaniṣads

Dermot Killingley

Ideas of liberation in the Upaniṣads and earlier

Rebirth is not the only idea to be found in the Upaniṣads about what happens after death. The Vedic hymns and the Brāhmaṇas contain very varied thoughts on this subject, and these are repeated and developed in the Upaniṣads. As we noted at the end of the last chapter, liberation is discussed much more frequently in the Upaniṣads than rebirth. We should not let the classic view of karma and rebirth mislead us into thinking that rebirth is necessarily what people sought to be liberated from. Further, the quest for liberation is by no means new in the Upaniṣads; as we saw in Chapter 7, it is found in the earliest known Vedic texts – the hymns of the *Ṛgveda* – and in the Brāhmaṇas. The Upaniṣads continue a quest that was begun long before, but bring new ideas to it. Ideas of liberation are related to ideas of bondage: bondage to the round of rebirth is one such idea, but there is also bondage to sin, to suffering, to the body, to mortality, to time, to the need to keep performing rituals.

Knowledge as the key to liberation

We have seen in Chapter 7 the importance placed in the Brāhmaṇas on knowledge in making ritual effective, particularly knowledge of correspondences between ritual, the macrocosm, and the microcosm. The Upaniṣads continue to pursue knowledge, not only of ritual but also of the cosmos, and especially of human personality. The interest in ritual, which is clear in the early prose Upaniṣads, diminishes in the later Upaniṣads, and sometimes ritual is overtly rejected: action, including ritual action, leads to bondage, but knowledge leads to liberation. In Chapter 12, we saw how the teaching on the five fires and the paths of the dead (BU 6.2; CU 5.3–5.10) contrasts knowledge, which leads to a state beyond death, with action, which leads to rebirth. This contrast is a recurrent theme of the Upaniṣads. To understand it fully, we should remember that "action" (*karman*) in Vedic texts, and in later texts which build on Vedic ideas, means especially ritual action (above, pp. 122, 123).

Though the Upaniṣads are themselves part of the Veda, they often – though not always – reject Vedic lore as incapable of gaining the ultimate goal. This rejection is not a new theme; we can even find it among the Vedic hymns, in a long hymn which seems to be an anthology of the riddles, known as *brahmodya*, which were a feature of Vedic ritual, testing the limits of traditional knowledge.

> The Syllable of the hymn, in the highest heaven where the gods are seated:
> What can he achieve with the hymns who does not know it?
> Only those who know it are sitting together here.
>
> (RV 1.164.39)

"The Syllable" is one of many names for the transcendent source and goal which the Upaniṣads often call *brahman* (Killingley 1986). This name arises from reflection on the role of speech in Vedic ritual, leading to speculation that beyond the thousands of syllables that make up the Veda (or any one of the Vedas) there must be a transcendent Syllable from which they all have their being, just as beyond the many beings in the world there must be a transcendent Being.

The verse quoted above is repeated in the *Śvetāśvatara Upaniṣad* (4.8). The same idea is expressed in different words in the *Muṇḍaka Upaniṣad* (part of which was quoted above, p. 47):

> There are two knowledges to be known, the knowers of *brahman* say: the higher and the lower. The lower is the *Ṛgveda*, the *Yajurveda*, the *Sāmaveda*, the *Atharvaveda*, phonetics, ritual, grammar, etymology, meter, and astrology. And the higher is the one by which the Syllable is understood.
>
> (MU 1.4–5)

Here the Veda, together with all the other branches of knowledge that are needed to become a practitioner of Vedic ritual, is lower knowledge, contrasted with the higher, transcendent knowledge of what is here called the Syllable, but is elsewhere called by other names, such as "being" (*sat*), or *ātman* "the Self," or *brahman*. In the *Kaṭha Upaniṣad*, this Syllable is identified as the ritual utterance *oṃ*, which is pronounced as a kind of cue from one priest to another, indicating that the next stage of the ritual can begin.

> The word which all the Vedas recite; which all ascetic practises pronounce;
> desiring which, people follow celibacy (*brahmacarya*): I tell you that syllable in sum.
> It is *oṃ*.
>
> (KU 2.15)

The word *akṣara* "syllable" came to be understood as meaning also "imperishable" (van Buitenen 1959; Killingley 1986: 19); it is one of the many names of the ultimate being.

We have already seen a passage in the *Muṇḍaka Upaniṣad* that sees ritual action as leading to rebirth (above, pp. 130–131). The passage continues:

> After examining the worlds built on action, a brahmin should become disgusted: what's done doesn't make what's unmade. [*nāsty akṛtaḥ kṛtena* – a terse way of saying that since the ultimate goal is uncaused, it cannot be caused by any action.]
>
> To understand it, he should go, firewood in hand, to a teacher
> who knows the Veda, and is intent on *brahman*.
>
> (MU 1.2.12)

Here, ritual is not altogether rejected; the teacher is expected to be learned in the Veda, whose purpose is ritual. The seeker is told to bring him firewood, which is itself a ritual act, expressing a readiness to serve the teacher by maintaining his ritual fire and in other ways. In older texts, it is ritual action together with knowledge, not knowledge alone, which leads to the highest goal (Tull 1989: 20). But the contrast between action and knowledge became so strong that Śaṅkara, one of the most influential interpreters of the Upaniṣads, made it a principle of his theology. Śaṅkara divides the Veda into two, the "action part" (*karmakāṇḍa*), which is concerned with ritual, and the "knowledge part" (*jñānakāṇḍa*), which is found in the Upaniṣads. While he sees ritual as a preparation for knowledge, he holds that salvation is achieved by knowledge alone and not by any action, not even by mental activity such as meditation.

We have seen in Chapter 12 how, according to the teaching on the five fires, the dead reach the highest goal through knowledge, and do not return; through action they reach the world of the ancestors, go on to the moon, and stay there "so long as there is a remainder" (CU 5.10.4) – that is, so long as their store of ritual merit lasts. When that store is exhausted, they descend as rain again, and continue the cycle of life, death, and rebirth (CU 5.10.6). An everlasting goal cannot be reached by action, but only by knowledge. As another passage in the same upaniṣad puts it, "as in this world a place won by action perishes, so in the other world a place won by merit perishes" (CU 8.1.6). The teacher has just been talking about conquest of territory, so he seems to be thinking of how territory can be lost if the conquering people do not continue guarding and cultivating it. This example shows how anything achieved by action is finite, and the same applies to ritual action.

The contrast between action and knowledge is presented dramatically in the frame story of the *Kaṭha Upaniṣad* (below, p. 317), which is a re-telling of an older story (above, p. 61). Naciketas, the hero of the story, confronts

Yama, the god of Death. Death offers him three boons, and he demands as his third and greatest boon to know the truth about what becomes of someone after death (KU 1.20). Death tries to deflect him from this demand by offering him sons and grandsons who will live a hundred years, together with wealth, long life, and other typical fruits of ritual merit (KU 1.23–25); but Naciketas persists. Death then congratulates him on having chosen the better option instead of the pleasanter (KU 2.1–3), knowledge instead of ignorance (KU 2.4); here, the ritual knowledge which enables one to achieve worldly benefits, and is therefore motivated by desire, is counted as ignorance in comparison with transcendent knowledge. The fool who does not choose as Naciketas did falls into Death's power again and again (KU 2.6). The teaching that follows involves not only knowledge of the true nature of personality, but self-control (KU 2.24; 3.3–13). This recalls the combination of knowledge and freedom from desire as keys to the world of brahman in Yājñavalkya's teaching discussed in Chapter 12, p. 129.

Knowledge of the Self is a recurrent theme in the Upaniṣads. This is not self-knowledge in the sense of knowing one's strengths and weaknesses, or one's inclinations; on the contrary, it is knowledge of what it means to be a conscious subject, setting aside whatever objects one might be conscious of, and setting aside whatever differentiates one from other conscious subjects. In the long dialogue of Yājñavalkya and King Janaka which we have already examined as an early source for the idea of rebirth (pp. 127–129), Yājñavalkya defines the Self as "the man among the faculties consisting of consciousness, the light within the heart" (BU 4.3.7). He teaches that the Self is known in dreamless sleep, when that "man … consisting of consciousness" is conscious neither of objects in the external world nor of the objects we create for ourselves in dreams, but only of himself. He illustrates this with a sexual image:

> As a man embraced by the woman he loves does not know anything outside or within, just so this man, embraced by the knowing Self, does not know anything outside or within. That is his form beyond sorrow, in which he has achieved his desire – the Self is his desire – he has no desire.
>
> (BU 4.3.21)

This objectless consciousness, which is also extreme bliss, identified as the world of *brahman* (BU 4.3.32), is what we experience in dreamless sleep: Unfortunately we forget this blissful experience when we wake up, or when we pass from dreamless sleep into dream. But Yājñavalkya uses similar terms to describe the person who, after death, is free from rebirth:

> The one who does not desire, who is without desire, free from desire, who has achieved his desire, whose desire is the Self – his breaths do not depart. Being *brahman* itself, he goes to *brahman*. There is a verse about it:
>
> When all the desires are abandoned that were in his heart,
> Then a mortal becomes immortal; he reaches *brahman* in this world.
>
> As the slough of a snake might lie dead and discarded on an anthill, so this body lies; and bodiless deathless life is nothing but splendour, nothing but Brahman.
>
> (BU 4.4.6–7)

Yājñavalkya is taking the same image as was used in earlier texts to describe release from sin, and applying it to release from rebirth and mortality. The image occurs yet again in a later passage, describing a man who is freed from sin by meditating on the supreme personal being (*puruṣa*) by means of the syllable *oṃ* (PU 5.5). But that passage does not mention the freedom from desire which is so important in Yājñavalkya's teaching. As we saw in Chapter 12 (p. 129), Yājñavalkya sees desire, which is the cause of action, as the ultimate cause of rebirth; so freedom from desire is the way to liberation.

Knowledge by identification

The meditation mentioned in PU 5.5, which we have just mentioned, is an example of a particular form of knowledge called *upāsana*. *Upāsana* is a mental identification of one thing with another: Often, a feature of the macrocosm (*adhidaivatam* "with respect to the divinities" (e.g. BU 2.3.3)) is mentally identified with a feature of the microcosm (*adhyātma* "with respect to oneself" (e.g. BU 2.3.4)). The corresponding verb, *upās*, is often translated "revere" or "worship" or "meditate on"; these renderings point in the right direction, but fall short of the complete meaning. The verb *upās* often takes two objects (more precisely, an object and an object complement): the thing one meditates on, and the thing with which one identifies it. Thus the *Chāndogya Upaniṣad* begins: "One should meditate on the syllable *oṃ* as the *udgītha*." (CU 1.1.1; the *udgītha* is the central third section in the five sections of the Vedic chant (p. 259). In this sentence, the two objects of the verb *upās* are the sacred syllable and the *udgītha*. Since the *Chāndogya Upaniṣad* belongs to the *Sāmaveda*, which comprises the knowledge learnt by the specialist in ritual chanting, it starts from the chant, just as the *Bṛhadāraṇyaka Upaniṣad*, which belongs to the *Yajurveda*, starts from the horse sacrifice. Later in the *Chāndogya Upaniṣad*, another *upāsana* identifies each section of the chant with a part of the macrocosm:

> One should *upās* the chant in the worlds, in five ways. The sound *hiṃ* is the earth; the prelude is fire; the *udgītha* is the atmosphere; the response is the sun; the close is the sky. That is upwards.

> Now the other way round: The sound *hiṃ* is the sky; the prelude is the sun; the *udgītha* is the atmosphere; the response is fire; the close is the earth.
>
> (CU 2.2.1–2)

These cannot be mere statements of identity, since the second set contradicts the first, except for the middle one of the five. They are, as the opening sentence says, instructions for a technique of meditation by identification. Such identifications are normally counterfactual by everyday standards.

The passage goes on to describe the benefits of this set of *upāsana*s:

> The worlds, upwards and the other way round, are conformed to the one who knows this thus, and *upās*es the fivefold chant in the worlds.
>
> (CU 2.2.3)

This implies that such a person would not face hostility in any part of the universe.

Some statements of the benefits of an *upāsana* are more definite. By identifying the fivefold chant with five species of livestock – goats, sheep, cows, horses and humans – one becomes rich in livestock (CU 2.6.1–2). An *upāsana* can therefore be a valuable possession, and the Upaniṣads tell stories of people who are reluctant to part with it; we have seen the motif of the reluctant teacher already in the story of Yājñavalkya and the king (above, p. 127), and in Death's attempt to buy off Naciketas with worldly benefits (above, p. 136). In CU 4.1–3, the possession of an *upāsana* is contrasted with worldly wealth. The enquirer, Jānaśruti, is a wealthy man who delights in his generosity (CU 4.1.1), while Raikva, the owner of the *upāsana*, is by ordinary standards an unimpressive man: he is eventually found scratching himself under a cart (CU 4.1.8). Jānaśruti asks him to "teach me the deity that you *upās*," offering him 600 cows, a necklace, and a chariot, which Raikva indignantly rejects. But Jānaśruti tries again, offering in addition his daughter as a wife, and a village (to be enjoyed as a source of revenue). Raikva is won over by the girl's face – but he takes the cows and the village as well. The *upāsana* he teaches is twofold. In the macrocosm, he identifies the wind as the gatherer, since it gathers the fire when it goes out, gathers the sun or the moon when it sets, and gathers water when it evaporates. In the microcosm, breath is the gatherer, since it gathers the faculties of speech, sight, hearing, and mind when one sleeps – that is, those faculties become latent, but the person goes on breathing (CU 4.3.1–3).

Another story of an *upāsana* concerns a warrior, Pratardana, who reaches the abode of the warrior god Indra "by fighting and manhood" (KsU 3.1). This may mean that he was killed in battle, and reaches Indra's heaven as a reward for his valour (Olivelle 1996: 370); similarly, it is perhaps by dying that Naciketas reaches the abode of the god of death, in the *Kaṭha Upaniṣad* story. But in each story the events which brought the hero to the presence of a god are passed over briefly; the focus is on what the he learns from the encounter. Indra invites his guest to choose a gift; so Pratardana boldly and ingeniously asks Indra to choose for him "what you consider most useful for a human being." Indra objects to this procedure, but is reluctantly obliged to teach him an *upāsana*: "*upās* me as life and immortality … He who *upās*es me as life and immortality reaches a complete lifespan in this world. He gains immortality and imperishability in the heavenly world" (KU 3.2). This provides one answer to the question whether immortality is in this world or after death: according to Indra's teaching, it is both.

Indra also tells Pratardana that this knowledge has made him, Indra, free from his sins; he is a noted sinner, as we have seen (above, pp. 63–64). He lists half a dozen violent and treacherous acts that he has committed, boasting that in these acts "not a hair of me was lost." He does not mention the killing of Vṛtra, but he starts with the killing of Vṛtra's elder brother, "the three-headed son of Tvaṣṭṛ." Indra has escaped his own sins or karma, and he who knows Indra does the same. At this point in the teaching, it seems that Pratardana is being told to meditate on Indra himself, the violent warrior god. But the rest of the chapter presents ideas that are very similar to Yājñavalkya's in BU 4.3–4 (discussed in Chapter 12). The various faculties of a person – speech, sight, hearing, thought, manipulation, locomotion – depend on breath, for you can be deprived of any of these faculties and still live, but you cannot live without breath. (The supremacy of breath over the other faculties is a recurrent topic of the Upaniṣads (Killingley 2006; Black 2007: 121–124).) In sleep, the faculties are united with breath, and on waking they go out to their various places in the body. At death, breath departs from the body, taking the faculties with it (KU 3.3). Breath, according to this passage, is the same as intelligence or consciousness (*prajñā*, KU 3.4); it is the Self. It is the ruler of the world; it does not become greater by good action, nor less by bad action (KU 3.8, an exact repetition of Yājñavalkya's words in BU 4.4.22). What began as a warrior god's boast to a fellow-warrior has become a statement of the idea of a transcendent universal conscious being which is the source of all phenomena. To know it is to be free.

The word *upāsana* means etymologically "sitting near," which is also the etymological meaning of *upaniṣad* (above, p. 2). Further, some statements of identification (typically non-obvious or counterfactual) are referred to as "*upaniṣad*s," in the Upaniṣads (e.g. BU 2.1.20; CU 8.8.4, 8.8.5; p. 262) and in the Brāhmaṇas (e.g. SB 10.4.5.1–10.4.6.1). This word meant a type of teaching, before it came to mean a group of texts.

Freedom from the world and freedom in the worlds

One passage on the liberating power of knowledge has puzzled interpreters from Śaṅkara to modern scholars:

> If one has been able to know it here,
> before the break-up of the body,
> then, in the creations, in the worlds,
> he is fit for embodiment.
>
> (KU 6.4)

The meaning is clear enough, except for a little difficulty in the third line. Does the phrase *sargeṣu lokeṣu* mean "in the creations which are in the worlds"? Or "in the creations; that is, in the worlds"? Or is it a textual error for *svargeṣu lokeṣu* "in the heavenly worlds," or for *sarveṣu lokeṣu* "in all worlds"? However we deal with this problem, the main problem remains: Why should knowledge lead to embodiment in several worlds, instead of freedom from all embodiment in the world of *brahman*? The context shows that the knowledge referred to is the highest knowledge; "those who know it become immortal" (KU 6.2). As one translator remarks, "the stanza contradicts the general theory that perception of the ātman produces release from reincarnation immediately after death" (Hume 1931: 359 footnote 1). An earlier translator conjectured that *na* "not" had been unaccountably omitted from the text, and should be restored; he translated it "If a man could not understand it before the falling asunder of the body, then he has to take body again in the worlds of creation" (Müller 1884: 21). Similarly Śaṅkara, though he does not emend the text, reads a negative meaning between the lines, as it were; his commentary interprets the verse as "If, while living, one can know Brahman before the dissolution of the body, [one is released from saṃsāra. If not,] then one is fit to be embodied in the creations, in the worlds." (The bracketed words are in Śaṅkara's paraphrase of the text, but not in the text itself.) A modern interpreter proposes that embodiments in various worlds are the rewards of different stages of enlightenment, lower than the ultimate goal of freedom from embodiment (Lipner 1978).

All these are attempts to interpret the verse in line with the idea that perfect knowledge wins perfect freedom, and that this freedom transcends embodiment and is beyond all worlds, except the world of Brahman. This indeed is how it is interpreted by Śaṅkara, and by other commentators for whom the Veda is superhumanly authoritative and speaks with one voice, and who follow a tradition which holds that absolute freedom is unembodied. But if we read the verse in the light of other passages, in the Upaniṣads and in other parts of the Veda, we may find that it means what it apparently says. This is not to say that reading it in the light of later tradition is wrong; but looking at a text in the light of ideas which were current when it was composed gives us an alternative hermeneutic approach. We can compare the *Kaṭha Upaniṣad* verse with other Vedic texts which treat existence in worlds, or embodiment, or both, as a supreme achievement, rather than as a failure to reach the highest.

One such text is *Chāndogya Upaniṣad* chapter 7: a long dialogue, in which an enquirer called Nārada – who appears in later texts as a great teacher of *bhakti* (devotion to a personal god) – comes for instruction to Sanatkumāra, whose name means he is both old and young. He seeks liberation, something that transcends the imperfect world in which he finds himself, and he has found that it is beyond the reach of his Vedic learning.

For the rest of the chapter, Sanatkumāra takes Nārada through a progressive series of teachings. They follow a repetitive pattern throughout the first half of the chapter: a series of meditations by identification (*upāsana*). In each stage of the teaching, some aspect of the cosmos or of personality is to be meditated on as *brahman*, and this meditation will lead to freedom, within the limits of that aspect. Nārada first learns that the Vedas are "name" – that is, they consist of words – and is then taught to meditate on name as *brahman*. He will then have freedom to roam at will as far as name goes. This is not enough for Nārada, so he asks if there is anything greater than name (CU 7.1.5). So Sanatkumāra introduces speech, and teaches him to identify it with brahman, leading to freedom to roam at will as far as speech goes (CU 7.2.2). The dialogue follows the same pattern by moving on from speech to mind, intention, thought, meditation, understanding, strength, food, water, heat, space, memory, and hope. By meditating on each of these as *brahman*, one gains freedom within its limits: for instance, he who identifies hope with brahman will be free to roam at will as far as hope goes (CU 7.15). At this point the pattern changes. Greater than hope is breath (*prāṇa*), on which all life depends; but this time, Nārada does not ask what is greater than breath. Perhaps he thinks that freedom to roam as far as breath goes is a satisfactory reward which does not require further search. However, Sanatkumāra continues his teaching with another series: Breath depends on truth, truth on understanding, and so on through thought, faith, production, action, well-being, fulness. Each item in this series depends on the next; and fulness, the final item on which all the others depend, is equated with the Self (*ātman*). The Self, says Sanatkumāra, extends in all directions, downward and upward, westward and eastward, southward and northward; the whole world is nothing but the Self. This notion of the infinitude of the Self leads back to the theme of freedom to roam at will:

> He who sees like this, who thinks like this, who understands like this, who delights in the self, plays with the self, couples with the self, enjoys the self, is autonomous. He has freedom to roam at will in all worlds. And those who know anything other than this are heteronomous and have perishable worlds. They are not free to roam at will in all worlds [or: they move in all worlds against their will].
>
> (CU 7.25.2)

(The phrase "freedom to roam at will in all worlds" recurs in CU 8.1.6; 8.4.3; 8.5.4.) The phrases "delights in the self, plays with the self, couples with the self, enjoys the self" evoke the same sexual imagery as we found in BU 4.3.21. But whereas in that passage liberation consisted of the absence of any sensation outside the self, the freedom presented here suggests a superabundance of pleasurable sensations.

The same superabundance is celebrated in a remarkable chapter which presents food as the foundation of existence. Though the knowledge taught in the passage is reached through ascetic practice, which usually involves fasting, it includes an injunction to make oneself plenty of food (TU 3.9). Parts of it, together with parts of the previous chapter (TU 2.2), could be read as a materialistic statement that life and mind result from the body which is maintained by food, and a repeated passage describes the rewards of knowledge mainly in material terms:

> He becomes a possessor of food, an eater of food. He becomes great with offspring, with livestock, with splendour of sacred knowledge; great with glory.
>
> (TU 3.6; 3.7; 3.8; 3.9)

The passage is not quite consistent with materialism, since food is to be meditated on by identifying it with *brahman* (TU 3.10.4). However, the freedom which is the reward of such meditation is material:

> Whoever knows this, when he departs from this world ... goes on roaming through these worlds, eating whatever food he wants, taking whatever appearance he wants.
>
> (TU 3.10.4–5)

Again, liberating knowledge leads to freedom in the worlds, not freedom from them.

A form of freedom in the worlds is also the reward of knowledge in a Brāhmaṇa passage, though there the knowledge is not of food but of breath, and its macrocosmic counterpart wind:

> And when he who knows this passes away from this world, he passes into the fire by his speech, into the sun by his eye, into the moon by his mind, into the directions by his ear, and into the wind by his breath, and, being composed of these, he becomes whichever of these deities he chooses, and is at rest.
>
> (SB 10.3.3.8).

Another Brāhmaṇa passage describing a sage who gained freedom in the worlds says:

> All these worlds are heaven and earth. He moved at will through these; in the morning he was in the assembly of the gods, in the afternoon in that of men.
>
> (*Jaiminīya Brāhmaṇa* 3.270)

These passages speak of a kind of liberation which is not freedom from embodiment or from worlds, but freedom from the constraints which our bodies and this world impose on us. Another text on disembodied freedom in the worlds is the teaching given to Indra by the creator god Prajāpati (CU 8.7–8.12). This has much in common with Yājñavalkya's teaching on the states of the self (BU 4.3), discussed in Chapter 12 (above, pp. 127–128), but its account of the last state is strikingly different. The first two states in both passages are our ordinary waking world and the world of dream. The third is dreamless sleep; in Yājñavalkya's teaching, this is the highest state, where the self does not see or hear because there is nothing besides itself for it to see or hear, and so on (BU 4.3.23–4.3.31). It is, we may say, free from this world and from all worlds, because they do not exist for it as objects of sensation or action. But in Prajāpati's teaching, this is not the ultimate state; indeed, it is no better than annihilation (CU 8.11.1–2). Beyond it is a fourth state, which is full of sensations and actions, though they are not constrained by the body through which we perceive and act in our waking state:

> Wind is bodiless. Cloud, lightning and thunder are bodiless. Just as these rise up from the space beyond, reach the highest light and assume their own form, in the same way a man rises serene from this body, reaches the highest light and assumes his own form. He is the supreme man. There he goes around laughing, playing, having fun with women or chariots or friends, not remembering this excrescence which is the body … The mind (*manas*) is his divine sense of sight. He has fun seeing the pleasures (*kāma*) that are in the world of Brahman with this divine sense of sight … He who finds and understands this self gains all worlds and all pleasures (*kāma*).
>
> (CU 8.12.2–6)

This state, which has all the advantages of embodiment without its disadvantages, is quite different from the fourth state taught in a later Upaniṣad, which is the unthinkable essence of the self, beyond any kind of perception or action (MaU 7). The Upaniṣads can envisage ultimate liberation as a continuation of the bodily pleasures we enjoy in this world.

Knowledge beyond words

Though the Upaniṣads, especially the early ones, sometimes talk at great length in the manner of the Brāhmaṇas, they also emphasize that the knowledge that leads to liberation cannot be expressed in words. Speaking of the "unborn Self," Yājñavalkya says:

> Having known it, a wise brahmin should practice wisdom.
> He should not ponder many words; for that tires the voice.
>
> (BU 4.4.21)

We have seen how this ultimate being can be referred to as the Syllable (pp. 134–135) – sometimes identified as the syllable *oṃ* which, though formed with the vocal organs, is beyond language. The capacity of language to point to something beyond itself is the subject of the next chapter. In Chapter 16, we see how the search for liberation shifted from knowledge of the Ātman to knowledge of God.

References

Black, Brian. 2007. *The Character of The Self in Ancient India: Priest, Kings, and Women in the Early Upaniṣads*. Albany, NY: State University of New York Press.

Hume, R. E. 1931. *The Thirteen Principal Upanishads: Translated from the Sanskrit*. 2nd edn. Oxford: Oxford University Press.

Killingley, Dermot. 1986. "Oṃ: The Sacred Syllable in the Veda" in Julius J. Lipner (ed.) *A Net Cast Wide: Investigations into Indian Thought in Memory of David Friedman*. Newcastle upon Tyne: Grevatt & Grevatt, 14–33.

Killingley, Dermot. 2006. "Faculties, Breaths and Orifices: Some Vedic and Sāṃkhya Notions of the Body and Personality" in Anna S. King (ed.) *Indian Religions: Renaissance and Renewal*. London: Equinox, 73–108.

Lipner, Julius. 1978. "An Analysis of Kaṭha 6.4 and 5, with Some Observations on Upanishadic Method" *Journal of Indian Philosophy* 5: 243–253.

Müller, Friedrich Max (trans.). 1884. *The Upanishads, Part 2* (Sacred Books of the East series, vol. 15). Oxford: Oxford University Press.

Olivelle, Patrick. 1996. *Upaniṣads: Translated from the Original Sanskrit* (World's Classics series). Oxford: Oxford University Press.

Tull, Herman W. 1989. *The Vedic Origins of Karma: Cosmos as Man in Ancient Indian Myth and Ritual*. Albany, NY: State University of New York Press.

Van Buitenen, J. A. B. 1959. "Akṣara" *Journal of the American Oriental Society* 79: 186–187.

Further reading

Edgerton, Franklin. 1965. *The Beginnings of Indian Philosophy: Selections from the Rig Veda, Atharva Veda, Upaniṣads, and Mahābhārata*. London: Allen and Unwin.

Killingley, Dermot. 1986. "Oṃ: The Sacred Syllable in the Veda" in Julius J. *Lipner* (ed.) *A Net Cast Wide: Investigations into Indian Thought in Memory of David Friedman*.Newcastle upon Tyne: Grevatt & Grevatt, 14–33.

Klostermaier, Klaus K. "Mokṣa" in Sushil Mittal and Gene Thursby (eds.) *The Hindu World*. New York: Routledge, 288–305.

Roebuck, Valerie. 2003. *The Upaniṣads. Translated and Edited* (Penguin Classics series). London: Penguin, xxviii–xli.

Tull, Herman W. 1989. *The Vedic Origins of Karma: Cosmos as Man in Ancient Indian Myth and Ritual*. Albany, NY: State University of New York Press.

14 The Upaniṣadic episteme

Jonardon Ganeri

The Upaniṣads are a polymorphous collection of anecdotes, parables, and dialogues. The earliest date from around or before the sixth century BCE, later ones written for many centuries afterwards. The two oldest Upaniṣads, the Bṛhadāraṇyaka and Chāndogya, were both composed before the time of the Buddha. They are symbolic, evocative and inspirational, plastic in meaning and, as with all canonical scriptures, hermeneutically pliable. Their function is to stimulate and to challenge, but they should not be taken as models of close conceptual analysis or theoretical system-building. There is, nevertheless, a broad theme and the elements of a common vision in the Upaniṣads. The fundamental idea of the Upaniṣads is that there are hidden connections between things, and that knowing what these connections are is a profound source of insight. Indeed, the term *upaniṣad* means a hidden connection, or possibly a secret teaching. As Joel Brereton puts it very well:

> Each Upaniṣadic teaching creates an integrative vision, a view of the whole which draws together the separate elements of the world and of human experience and compresses them into a single form. To one who has this larger vision of things, the world is not a set of diverse and disorganised objects and living beings, but rather forms a totality with a distinct shape and character.
>
> (Brereton 1990: 118)

This order-inducing totality is what I will term "the Upaniṣadic episteme." Remember how Michel Foucault begins *The Order of Things* (Foucault 1970). He refers, and is perhaps the first contemporary writer to do so, to a short essay written by Jorge Luis Borges in 1942, the essay called "John Wilkins' Analytical Language" (Borges 1999: 231) in which Borges introduces what he describes as "a certain Chinese dictionary entitled *The Celestial Emporium of Benevolent Knowledge*." Of *The Order of Things* Foucault comments that:

> This book first arose out of a passage in Borges, out of the laughter that, as I read the passage, shattered all the familiar landmarks of my thought … breaking up all the ordered surfaces and all the planes

> with which we are accustomed to tame the wild profusion of existing things .... This passage quotes a "certain Chinese encyclopaedia in which it is written that animals can be divided into (a) those belonging belonging to the Emperor, (b) those that are embalmed, (c) those that are tame, (d) suckling pigs, (e) sirens, (f) imaginary animals, (g) wild dogs, (h) those included in the present classification, (i) those that are crazy-acting, (j) those that are uncountable, (k) those painted with a fine brush made of camel hair, (l) miscellaneous, (m) those which have just broken a vase, (n) those which, from a distance, look like flies." In the wonderment of this taxonomy, the thing we apprehend in one great leap, the thing that, by means of the fable, is demonstrated as the exotic charm of another system of thought, is the limitation of our own, the stark impossibility of thinking *that*.
>
> (Foucault 1970: xv).

Why is this taxonomy from a "certain Chinese encyclopaedia" (no doubt an invention of Borges himself) impossible? Is it that it is alien and strange, belonging to another "system of thought," one that organises the things of the world in ways quite foreign and alien to us? Is it that this scheme of classification groups together objects where *we* see no resemblance, and divides objects where *we* see no relevant distinction? A system of thought is an ordering of things under relations of resemblance (a fact already known to the ancients, as Brian Smith has shown in his brilliant study of Vedic thought; Smith 1989), and the relations of resemblance underpinning the Chinese taxonomy are so different from the relations that underpin our own classifications that we find it impossible to understand. Or is there a more fundamental reason why this *Celestial Emporium* represents an impossibility? Foucault comments that this taxonomy has a "monstrous quality" (1970: xvi). It is monstrous because there is no single relation of resemblance, no common site, for all the categories in the list. Each category presupposes a different way of classifying objects; thus, Foucault: "What transgresses the boundaries ... of all possible thought is simply that alphabetical series (a, b, c, d, ...) which links each of those categories to all the others" (1970: xvi). The moral Foucault draws is that underneath any *possible* system of thought is what he calls a "table" or a "primary grid." The primary grid fixes a domain of object-sites and a set of possible orderings. Think of it as like the chessboard, which defines both the possible piece-positions and the possible types of move (along a diagonal, along a file, etc.). This primary grid is "the hidden network that determines the way things confront one another." It is the *episteme*: "By *episteme* we mean ... the total set of relations that unite, at a given period, the discursive practices that give rise to epistemological figures, sciences, and possibly formalized systems" (1972: 191). The episteme prescribes what can be known, experienced or spoken of. It is the condition for the possibility of knowledge, thought, and language. Why so? Because the episteme qua grid constitutes the domain of possible objects of knowledge. Foucault again:

> In these fields of initial differentiation, in the distances, the discontinuities, and the thresholds that appear within it, discourse finds a way of limiting its domain, of defining what it is talking about, of giving it the status of an object – and therefore of making it manifest, nameable, and describable.
>
> (1972: 41)

Foucault thus draws a distinction between two meanings of the English term "knowledge." There is the explicit knowledge that it is possible to have *within* a particular system of thought; this is what he takes the French *connaissance* to denote. Then there is the "preknowledge" – he uses the French term *savoir* – that is the basis or precondition for such explicit knowledge. Think of it as like one's implicit or tacit knowledge (*savoir*) of the rules of grammar for a language the sentences of which one knows (*connaisance*) the meaning. Foucault also calls this the "positive unconscious" of knowledge. Notice that the primary grid is not itself a possible object of *connaissance*, any more than the chessboard is a possible piece. The chessboard is the set of possible piece places, and so does not itself have a place. The episteme determines the set of possible objects of explicit knowledge, and so is not itself a possible object of explicit knowledge. What one may have is "preknowledge" of the grid, in so far as it provides the objects for our explicit knowledge. Likewise, since the episteme determines what is expressible within a discourse, it is not itself expressible within that discourse: "It is not possible for us to describe our own archive [= episteme], since it is from within these rules that we speak …" (1972: 130).

Foucault's archaeological method (Foucault 1972) excavates the primary grid that is buried beneath a system of thought. Foucauldian archaeology is the method by which the preknowledge (*savoir*) of a past or alien epoche is made into an object of explicit knowledge (*connaissance*) for us now. What I propose to investigate is whether we might turn the archaeological method upon the Upaniṣads and discover the "positive unconscious" of ancient Indian thought. The "integrative vision" of the Upaniṣads is the Upaniṣadic system of thought, the totality of *connaissance*, and what underpins it, the episteme, has the label *brahman*. As Brereton continues,

> The Upaniṣads create an integrative vision by identifying a single, comprehensive and fundamental principle which shapes the world … For later followers of the Vedānta, the brahman has a particular definition and a specific character, but for the Upaniṣads, the brahman remains an open concept. It is simply the designation given to whatever principle or power a sage believes to lie behind the world and to make the world explicable. It is the reality sought by the householder who asks

> a sage: *Through knowing what, sir, does this whole world become known* (Muṇḍaka 1.13).
>
> (1990: 118)

There is perhaps an echo of the distinction between *connaissance* and *savoir* in the Upaniṣadic use of the terms *vijñāna* and *prajñā*.

Two sorts of hidden connection (*bandhu*) are prominent in the Upaniṣads. Both can clearly be seen in the oldest of the Upaniṣads, the Bṛhadāranyaka Upaniṣad. The first is the use of the ritual space as template. The idea is that the world as a whole is ordered in the same arrangement as the sacrificial object. This is supposed to explain the efficacy of sacrificial rites: By means of ritual, human beings can effect a re-ordering and even a repair of the world. That is because the cosmos stands in an isomorphic relation with the objects that are in the ritual domain. The most prominent example occurs at the beginning of this Upaniṣad, connecting the cosmos itself with the sacrificial horse (all translations are from Olivelle 1996):

> The head of the sacrificial horse, clearly, is the dawn – its sight is the sun; its breath is the wind; and its gaping mouth is the fire common to all men. The body of the sacrificial horse is the year – its back is the sky; its abdomen is the intermediate region; its underbelly is the earth; its flanks are the quarters; its joints are the months and fortnights; its feet are the days and nights; its bones are the stars; its flesh is the clouds; its stomach contents are the sand; its intestines are the rivers; its liver and lungs are the hills; its body hairs are the plants and trees; its forequarter is the rising sun; and its hindquarter is the setting sun.
>
> (BU 1.1)

The second, related, idea is the idea that the human body is a sort of cosmological map. Here is an example from the Bṛhadāraṇyaka (BU 2.5):

speech	fire
sight	the sun
breath	the wind
mind	the moon
hearing	the quarters
body	earth
self	space
hair	plants
blood, semen	water

This taxonomy is certainly very strange and alien, but it is not monstrous. There is an underlying grid of correspondences between bodily parts and vital functions, on the one hand, and the primary elements and celestial bodies on the other. Something familiar is used as a map or template, to understand what is unfamiliar and unknown. As the Upaniṣadic sage Uddālaka Āruṇi puts it in Chāndogya Upaniṣad: "You must surely have asked about that rule of substitution by which one hears what has not been heard before, thinks of what has not been thought of before, and perceives what has not been perceived before" (CU 6.1.3). Kaṭha Upaniṣad (KU 3) introduces another network of correlations, this time between a person (self, senses, body) and a charioteer reining a chariot pulled by horses. Nor is there anything monstrous in the nevertheless surprising list of transitional appearances: "Mist, smoke, sun, wind, fire, fireflies, lightning, crystal, moon—these are the apparitions that, within yogic practice, precede and pave the way to the full manifestation of *brahman*" (Śvetāśvatara U. 2.11).

Foucault defines the episteme of an epoch as whatever it is that fixes what can be thought, known or spoken of, and what, by that same fact, cannot be known or described from within the epoch. This primary grid is precisely the role of the concept of *brahman* in the Upaniṣads, the unifying cosmic principle, something that is made very clear in the Kena Upaniṣad:

> That which is the hearing behind hearing,
> the thinking behind thinking,
> the speech behind speech,
> the sight behind sight –
> It is also the breathing behind breathing –
> Freed completely from these,
> the wise become immortal,
> when they depart from this world. (KU 1.2)
>
> Which one cannot see with one's sight,
> by which one sees the sight itself –
> Learn that that alone is *brahman*,
> and not what they here venerate. (KU 1.6)

We find here again the same taxonomy of breath, speech, hearing, sight, and thought. We find here too the idea that *brahman* is inexpressible because it is that *in virtue of which* we speak, and that brahman is unthinkable because it is that *in virtue of which* we think. As the sage Yājñavalkya is keen to emphasise, there is, in Foucault's terminology, no *connaissance* of *brahman*: "You can't see the seer who does the seeing; you can't hear the hearer who does the hearing; you can't think of the thinker who does the thinking; and you can't perceive the perceiver who does the perceiving" (BU 3.4.2). According to Yājñavalkya, *savoir* is indeed to be had, but only in a state of dreamless sleep (BU 4.3.21). Yet that view is not universally shared, and in the Māṇḍūkya Upaniṣad, for example, one must look beyond the empty content of dreamless sleep to what is called only "the fourth" (*turīya*) state, a state of consciousness *underneath* and *behind* waking, dreaming, and dreamlessness.

The final dramatic move in Upaniṣadic thought is to identify *brahman*, this primary grid, with one's true self, the *ātman*: "In which are established the various groups of five, together with space; I take that to be the self – I who have the knowledge, I who am immortal, I take that to be the *brahman*, the immortal" (BU 4.4.17). Like the primary grid, this is what determines what is known and what isn't: "This self of yours who is present within … he is the inner controller" (BU 3.7). As Signe Cohen observes, "the sacrifice becomes a metaphor for the universe in late Vedic thought, and by extension, the hidden power behind the sacrifice is also seen as the hidden force behind the universe itself: *brahman*" (Cohen 2008: 47). Perhaps what we should understand is that the order of things, the division of things into classifications in accordance with an underlying network of correspondences (the "primary grid") is itself in a correspondence with the order of our mental worlds. If self and world are organised along fundamentally analogous lines, then self-control and self-understanding become methods for controlling and understanding the world:

> Sir, teach me the hidden connection. You have been taught the hidden connection – indeed, we have taught you the hidden connection relating to brahman itself. Of this hidden connection, austerity, self-control and rites are the foundation, the Vedas are all the limbs, and truth is the abode.
> (KU 4.7)

There is a broad theme and the elements of a common vision in the Upaniṣads. It is the belief in a unified explanation of the world and of our experience. It is the belief in an all-encompassing complete conception. The peculiar twist which the Upaniṣads give to this is that the single reality behind the multiple aspects of the world is also the reality of the individual subject. The Upaniṣads seem to tell us that there is no hope of forming a unified conception of the world while leaving out the self, that a conception of the nature of the self is the key to a conception of the nature of the world. Wittgenstein's remark that "the spirit of the snake … is your spirit for it is only from yourself that you are acquainted with spirit at all'" (*Notebooks*, 85e) has been claimed by some to reveal a distinct reverberation of this Upaniṣadic insight. In the Chāndogya dialogue, the sage Uddālaka promises his son Śvetaketu the knowledge that will account for everything, the knowledge of the totality. He tells him to fetch the fruit of a banyan tree, to cut it open and find the seed, and then to cut open the seed. Śvetaketu finds nothing there, but Uddālaka tells him that within the seed is the finest essence on account of which the banyan tree stands here now, the essence "that constitutes the self of this whole world; that is the truth; that is the self" (CU 6.12). A single essence, an essence within an essence, unifies, integrates, and explains the whole. And it is a crucial Upaniṣadic doctrine that the self has five sheaths (food, breath, mind, intellect, and bliss) – five levels of description yielding progressively deeper notions of the person, drawing us gradually away from superficial appearances towards a deep understanding of the place of the subjective in an objective view.

The Upaniṣads are allegories, fables, dialogues, and parables. They admit different interpretations and different systematisations. There is a philosophical common theme – the possibility of an integrative vision – expressed through paradigm, metaphor, and imagery. They speak of the hidden connections that relate the three spaces, of ritual, of cosmos, and of human self, and they refer to the primary grid that makes knowledge of those hidden connections possible, to which they give the name *brahman*. As such *brahman* is the Upaniṣadic episteme, something underneath all knowledge, and indeed, all consciousness, something hardly knowable within the Upaniṣadic system of thought itself and yet something which makes Upaniṣadic knowledge possible.

References

Black, Brian 2007. *The Character of the Self in Ancient India: Priests, Kings, and Women in the Early Upaniṣads*. Albany, NY: State University of New York Press.

Borges, Jorge Luis 1999. "John Wilkins' Analytical Language" in Eliot Weinberger (ed.) *Selected Nonfictions*. New York: Penguin Books.

Brereton, Joel 1990. "The Upaniṣads" in Wm. T. de Bary and I. Bloom (eds.) *Approaches to the Asian Classics*. New York: Columbia University Press, 115–135.

Cohen, Signe 2008. *Text and Authority in the Older Upaniṣads*. Leiden: Brill.

Foucault, Michel 1970. *The Order of Things*. London: Routledge.

Foucault, Michel 1972. *The Archaeology of Knowledge*. London: Routledge.

Olivelle, Patrick 1996. *Upaniṣads*. Oxford: World Classics.

Smith, Brian 1989. *Reflections on Resemblance, Ritual and Religion*. New York: Oxford University Press.

15 *Mantras* and sacred language

Signe Cohen

The Upaniṣads are permeated by speculations about the mystical efficacy of language and ritual speech. Numerous *mantras*, or sacred utterances, are found sprinkled throughout the Upaniṣadic texts, both the well-known *oṃ* and more obscure ones such as *hiṃ* or *huṃ*. Language is, in the Upaniṣads, not just a tool to describe the world, but an integral part of the cosmos itself. When the *Taittirīya Upaniṣad* claims that "this whole world is *oṃ*,"[1] this tells us something significant about the Upaniṣadic world-view; a powerful sound can capture the essence of the entire cosmos.

Sacred language and the truth of false etymologies

The *Taittirīya Upaniṣad* uses the linguistic concept of *sandhi* (euphonic combination of sounds) as a cosmic metaphor:

> It is like this as far as the worlds are concerned: The first word is the earth, the next word is the sky, and space is the *sandhi* between them, and wind is that which joins them together. This is how it is with the worlds.
>
> It is like this as far as the lights are concerned: The first word is the fire, the next word is the sun, and water is the *sandhi* between them, and lightning is that which joins them together. This is how it is with the lights.
>
> It is like this as far as knowledge is concerned: The first word is the teacher, the next word is the student, and knowledge is the *sandhi* between them, and teaching is that which joins them together. This is how it is with knowledge.
>
> It is like this as far as offspring is concerned: The first word is the mother, the next word is the father, and the child is the *sandhi* between them, and procreation is that which joins them together. This is how it is with offspring.
>
> It is like this as far as the body is concerned: The first word is the lower jaw, the next word is the upper jaw, and speech is the *sandhi* between them, and the tongue is that which joins them together. This is how it is with the body.[2]

Here, the universe itself, parents and children, teachers and students, are all part of the cosmic language. The identification of language and the universe also helps to explain the mystical etymologies so frequently encountered in the Upaniṣads. We can see this in the following examples:

> Then Death decided: Let me give myself a body. So he recited, and as he recited, water came from him. And he thought: "While I was reciting (*arc*), water (*ka*) came for me." This is what gives name to and reveals recitation (*arka*). For water surely comes for him who knows the name and nature of recitation. Therefore, recitation is water.[3]
>
> The *Sāman* ("song") is speech. It is both She (*sā*) and He *ama*, and this gives name to and reveals the nature of the *Sāman*. Or maybe it is called *Sāman* because it is the same (*sama*) size as a fly or a mosquito, or an elephant, or the three worlds, or the whole universe.[4]
>
> The first being was called "man" (*puruṣa*) because before (*pūrva*) all of this he burnt (*uṣ*) all evil.[5]
>
> One should worship the syllables of the *udgītha* ("high chant"): *ud*, *gī*, and *tha*. The syllable *ud* is the breath, for people rise up (*ud-sthā*) through breath. The syllable *gī* is speech, for words are called *gīr* ("speech"). The syllable *tha* is food, for the world is based (*shita*) on food.[6]
>
> … and the sun is *mahas*, for all the worlds are made happy (*mah-*) by the sun.[7]
>
> But all he saw was that man, *brahman*, the highest, and he said: "This (*idam*) is what I have seen (*adarśam*)." And therefore he is called *Idandra*. His name is Idandra, but even though he is Idandra, people mysteriously call him Indra, for the gods seem to love the mysterious.[8]

The etymologies for common (or uncommon) Sanskrit words suggested in these passages are, from a modern linguistic perspective, completely wrong. The words connected by Upaniṣadic etymologies rarely have any historical connection with one another; they simply happen to sound alike. But since the Upaniṣadic cosmos is ultimately linguistic, these phonetic similarities suggest deep cosmic connections to the Upaniṣadic thinkers. It would be naïve and presumptuous on our part to assume that the ancient Indians were simply ignorant of the true origins of Sanskrit words. The ancient Sanskrit grammatical literature suggests that, in general, educated Sanskrit speakers knew perfectly well how to derive a noun from a verbal root. But the mystical Upaniṣadic etymologies serve a completely different purpose than etymological explanations in modern linguistics. The Upaniṣadic authors had a very different agenda from modern etymologers; they are less interested in the historical origins of a word than in its cosmic significance. The Upaniṣadic authors probably knew perfectly well that the name *Indra* is not derived from *idam* ("this") and *adarśam* ("saw"). But their purpose was not to arrive at historically accurate etymological explanations, but rather to express esoteric truths about the universe. The "false etymologies" of the Upaniṣads are better regarded as linguistic mysticism than as bad historical linguistics. In many ways, the Upaniṣadic etymologies are conceptually related to *mantras*; like *mantras*, the "false" etymologies create connections between the world of language and the reality that lies beyond language.

The limitations of language

Although the oldest among the classical Upaniṣads still identify language with the cosmos itself, speculations simultaneously begin to arise about the possibility that something may exist that is beyond the reach of language:

> That which one cannot express by speech,
> by which speech itself is expressed –
> Know that only that is *brahman*,
> And not that which they worship here.[9]

In the *Kena Upaniṣad*, *brahman* is the origin of language, but ultimately itself beyond language. The idea that *ātman-brahman* is ineffable is expressed in the famous Upaniṣadic phrase: *Neti neti* ("Not this, not that"):

> This *ātman* is neither this nor that (*neti neti*). It is ungraspable, for it cannot be grasped. It is immortal, for it does not die.[10]

The limitations imposed by language are, however, overcome by means of the non-linguistic utterances of the Upaniṣadic *mantras*.

Language beyond language: *Mantras* in the Upaniṣads

Some scholars have explained *mantras* as non-linguistic utterances, others as linguistic units or ritual speech acts. A spectrum of opinions regarding this question are represented in the edited volume *Understanding Mantras*.[11]

To clarify this issue, we should note that the term *mantra* is used in Indian literature to mean several different things.[12] A *mantra* can be a Vedic verse, used in a ritual context. In this case, a *mantra* has a clearly identifiable lexical meaning, even if that meaning may later be forgotten. This meaning, prevalent in later usage, is of less interest to us here. A *mantra* may also be a brief exclamation used in a ritual sense, such as *svāhā* ("hail" or "blessing!") and the threefold *vyāhṛti* ("utterance") of *bhūr*, *bhuvaḥ*, *svaḥ*. These *mantras* possess a lexical meaning, but also a mystical power beyond the semantic meaning of the word. Moore Gerety defines *mantras* as "utterances of great power, perfect formulations capable of bridging earthly and divine relams."[13] The semantic meaning of *bhūr*, *buvaḥ*, *svaḥ* is clearly "earth, atmosphere, and heaven," and yet the utterance takes on a mystical significance that far transcends the literal meaning. The *Chāndogya Upaniṣad* suggests that *bhūr*, *buvaḥ*, *svaḥ* represent the essence of the Vedas, extracted by the creator god Prajāpati himself from the holy texts.[14] And lastly, a *mantra* can be a religiously significant utterance without any apparent lexical meaning, such as *oṃ*. In this discussion we will be mainly concerned with *mantras* of the second and third type.

Staal has shown that even *mantras* with an identifiable meaning, such as *oṃ mamaḥ śivāya* ("homage to Śiva") may be treated as mystical phrases without semantic meaning when Hindu rituals are exported to other places, such as Bali.[15] We may observe something similar in the worldwide Christian use of the Hebrew term *amen*. This term is usually not translated, and even those who are aware of its semantic meaning ("so be it") would be reluctant to use the translation rather than the untranslated word. Like Hindu *mantras*, the *amen* loses some power in translation. In the following discussion, we will focus on *mantras* in the sense of mystical utterances without a lexical meaning, or utterances with a meaning that transcends the literal meaning.

The oldest Upaniṣads contain several words and phrases without known semantic meaning. Among these cryptic words are *dadada* in *Bṛhadāraṇyaka Upaniṣad* 5.2 (made famous in the West through T. S. Eliot's poem "The Waste Land"), *viram* in *Bṛhadāraṇyaka Upaniṣad* 5.12, and *tajjalān*[16] in *Chāndogya Upaniṣad* 3.14.1. These non-semantic words carry esoteric meanings that can be at least partially understood by those to whom they are explained. Over time, these spontaneous occurrences of non-semantic "words" disappear from sacred texts, and are replaced by better-known standard *mantras*, such as *oṃ*.

The earliest *mantras* that can be clearly identified as such appear in late Vedic ritual literature. There are also a few words in the *Ṛgveda* that have no known semantic meaning, such as the many *hapax legomena* in the hymn *Ṛgveda* 10.106,[17] but these words may simply be loan words from an unknown language whose meaning is now lost to us, rather than mystical utterances that were not meant to have a semantic meaning. In the *Brāhmaṇas* and the Upaniṣads, however, we first encounter *mantras* in the sense of powerful utterances without a clear meaning.

In an intriguing article, Frits Staal has compared Sanskrit *mantras* to bird songs. He suggests that *mantras* are utterly devoid of semantic meaning, and that they are older than language, an evolutionary remnant of earlier, non-linguistic utterances, "the vestiges of something different from language."[18] One would expect, however, if that were the case, to find *mantras* in all cultures, not just in South Asia. Staal has attempted to show that *mantra*-like utterances are indeed found in other cultures as well, but most other cultures do not have anything quite comparable to the Sanskrit *mantras*. It seems reasonable, therefore, to regard *mantras* as a South Asian development. But Staal has an excellent point when he draws parallels between animal sounds and *mantras*. The *Chāndogya Upaniṣad*, a text particularly concerned with *mantras*, suggests they can exist among the animals. This does not necessarily mean that *mantras* are developed from animal sounds, but rather, that the *Chāndogya Upaniṣad* recognizes the existence of significant, but non-linguistic utterances among animals. This view fits quite well with the *Chāndogya Upaniṣad*'s emphasis on mystical wisdom located outside the Vedic tradition, but accessible to those who are capable of listening.

Oṃ – the immortal syllable

The *mantra* encountered most often in the Upaniṣads is *oṃ*. The syllable *oṃ* is absent from the *Ṛgveda*, but is referred to as the *praṇava* ("reverberation"), a name later often used for it, in the *Taittirīya Saṃhitā*.[19] Here it signifies the sound that the *hotṛ* priest makes at the end of a verse. It seems likely, therefore, that *oṃ* originated in the recitation of Vedic verses, as a hummed nasalization at the end of a verse. It is in the *Aitareya Brāhmaṇa*[20] that *oṃ* first assumed a cosmic significance. Here, it is identified with heaven and the sun and said to consist of three parts. Moore Gerety has shown that the oldest occurrences of the syllable *oṃ* are in the *Sāmaveda*, and that it becomes a part of a "soteriology of song" in the Jaiminīya branch of the *Sāmaveda*.[21]

By the time of the Upaniṣads, *oṃ* has become the most popular of all *mantras*. The syllable *oṃ* is also known as the *akṣara* ("the syllable"/"the imperishable"). The word *akṣara* ("syllable") can conveniently be broken up into the negative prefix *a*- and *kṣara* ("perishable"), which invites religious speculations into the possibility that a sacred syllable may be a doorway to immortality:

> The syllable among the *Ṛgveda* verses,
> The syllable on which all the gods rest in the highest heaven –
> When a person does not know it, what use is a *Ṛgveda* verse?
> Sitting here together are the people who know it.[22]

Mantras represent a cosmic non-linguistic language that creates a connection to the reality that lies beyond language. *Brahman* is, for example, said to be indescribable, and yet identical to the sacred non-linguistic syllable *oṃ*.[23]

The *Kaṭha Upaniṣad* suggests that *oṃ* is the essence of all the Vedas:

> That word that all the Vedas reveal
> The word that all austerities speak of
> That which people desire when they live ascetic lives
> I will tell you that word briefly: *Oṃ*.[24]

The *Kaṭha Upaniṣad*,[25] like the *Taittirīya Upaniṣad*,[26] identifies *oṃ* with *brahman* itself, while the *Māṇḍūkya Upaniṣad* divides the syllable up into four parts and uses the fourfold *oṃ* as the starting point for elaborating on the idea of the four states of the *ātman*: wakefulness, sleep, dreamless sleep, and a mystical state beyond all these. The fourth state, associated with the deepest possible insight into reality, is here identified with the syllable *oṃ* in its entirety.[27] "The *ātman* itself is *oṃ*," claims the *Māṇḍūkya Upaniṣad*. "Anyone who knows this enters into the *ātman* by the *ātman*."[28] The *Muṇḍaka Upaniṣad* also claims that the syllable *oṃ* is a tool for salvation; it will help steer the *ātman* into its unity with *brahman*: "*Oṃ* is the bow, the arrow is *ātman*, and *brahman* the target …"[29]

Mantras and animal sounds

In the *Sāmaveda* Upaniṣads, textual authority is occasionally located outside the Vedic tradition itself, in the "speech" of animals, or the crackling of the fire, or in the words of a beggar sleeping under a bridge. There is frequent mention of words with no known semantic meaning in the *Chāndogya Upaniṣad*. The most well-known of these is *oṃ*, but others such as *hiṃ* and *huṃ* (in the *Chāndogya Upaniṣad* particularly connected with animals), or the more unknown *jalān*[30] are also mentioned. In addition, the *Chāndogya Upaniṣad* contains a surprisingly large number of references to animals and the sounds they make:

> I choose the roaring way of singing the *Sāman*, the singing that is like the roar of an animal …[31]

In one passage, we hear about the *udgītha* ("high chant") of the dogs:

> And now the *udgītha* of the dogs: One day Baka Dālbya, or alternatively, Glāva Maitreya, went to perform his Vedic recitation, and a white dog appeared in from of him. Other dogs gathered around the white one, and they said to him: "Please, Sir, sing and get us some food. We are very hungry." And he said to them: "Come back in the morning and meet me right here." Baka Dālbhya, or alternatively, Glāva Maitreya, kept watch. The dogs then came in, sliding furtively in just like priests slide furtively in, and they held each other's backs and chanted the hymn called Bahiṣpavamāna. They all sat down together and made the sound *huṃ*. They chanted: "*Oṃ*, let's eat. *Oṃ*, let's drink. *Oṃ*, may the gods Varuṇa, Prajāpati and Savitṛ bring food here. Lord of food, bring food here. Bring it, bring it, *oṃ*."[32]

At first sight, this may seem to be a satirical passage, poking fun at Hindu priests by comparing them to howling dogs. But seen in conjunction with the many passages in the *Chāndogya Upaniṣad* connecting ritual chants and animal sounds, there appears to be more to this passage than mere satire. Animals are frequent bearers of wisdom in the *Chāndogya Upaniṣad*:

> So he [a teacher] initiated the boy and chose four hundred thin and weak cows and said: "My dear, watch these!" When he drove them away, Satyakāma said: "I will not return without a thousand!" He lived elsewhere for some years, and when the cows had become a thousand, the following happened:

> The bull called to him: "Satyakāma!" He said: "Yes sir?" The bull said: "My dear, we have become a thousand. Take us back to the teacher's house, and I will tell you about one quarter of *brahman*."
>
> "Please tell me, Sir!"
>
> The bull told him: "One-sixteenth part of it is the east, one-sixteenth is the west, one-sixteenth is the south, and one-sixteenth is the north ..."[33]

Satyakāma is later instructed further by the fire, a goose, and a water bird.[34] Three of his four teachers are animals, and apparently fully capable of transmitting the truth about *brahman*.

The *Chāndogya Upaniṣad* seems intrigued by animal sounds, perhaps because animal utterances appear to have some significance, and yet lack semantic meaning, which makes animal sounds similar to *mantras*.

Notes

1 *Taittirīya Upaniṣad* 1.8.
2 *Taittirīya Upaniṣad* 1.3.1–4.
3 *Bṛhadāraṇyaka Upaniṣad* 1.2.1–2.
4 *Bṛhadāraṇyaka Upaniṣad* 1.3.22.
5 *Bṛhadāraṇyaka Upaniṣad* 1.4.1.
6 *Chāndogya Upaniṣad* 1.3.6.
7 *Taittirīya Upaniṣad* 1.5.2.
8 *Aitareya Upaniṣad* 1.13–14.
9 *Kena Upaniṣad* 1.5.
10 *Bṛhadāraṇyaka Upaniṣad* 4.4.22.
11 Alper 1989.
12 See Padoux 2003 for a discussion of the various meanings of *mantra.*
13 Moore Gerety 2015: 13.
14 *Chāndogya Upaniṣad* 4.17.1–3.
15 Staal 1995.
16 It is unclear whether the preceding *tad* is a part of the mystical *mantra* or a separate word. See Patrick Olivelle, *The Early Upaniṣads*. New York/Oxford: Oxford University Press, 1998: 544.
17 I am grateful to Dr Stephanie Jamison for suggesting this to me.
18 Staal 1985.
19 *Taittirīya Saṃhitā* 3.2.9.6.
20 *Aitareya Brāhmaṇa* 5.32.
21 Moore Gerety 2015: 33.
22 *Śvetāśvatara Upaniṣad* 4.8.
23 *Praśna Upaniṣad* 5. 2.
24 *Kaṭha Upaniṣad* 2.15.
25 *Kaṭha Upaniṣad* 2.16.
26 *Taittirīya Upaniṣad* 1.8.1.
27 *Māṇḍūkya Upaniṣad* 12.
28 *Māṇḍūkya Upaniṣad* 12.
29 *Muṇḍaka Upaniṣad* 2. 2. 4.
30 *Chāndogya Upaniṣad* 3.14.1.
31 *Chāndogya Upaniṣad* 2.22.1.

32 *Chāndogya Upaniṣad* 1.12.1–1.12.5.
33 *Chāndogya Upaniṣad* 5.1ff.
34 *Chāndogya Upaniṣad* 4.7–8.

Further reading

Alper, H. P. 1989. *Understanding Mantras*. Albany, NY: State University of New York Press.

Beck, G. 1993. *Sonic Theology: Hinduism and Sacred Sound*. Columbia, SC: University of South Carolina Press.

Buitenen, J. van 1959. "Akṣara" *Journal of the American Oriental Society* 79: 176–187.

Gonda, J. 1963. "The Indian Mantra" *Oriens* 31 (16): 244–297.

Moore Gerety, F. M. 2015. *This Whole World is OM: Song, Soteriology, and the Emergence of the Sacred Syllable*. PhD dissertation, Harvard University.

Padoux, A. 2003. "Mantra" in Gavin Flood (ed.) *The Blackwell Companion to Hinduism*. Oxford: Blackwell: 487–492.

Staal, F. 1985. "Mantras and Bird Song" *Journal of the American Oriental Society* 105: 549–558.

Staal, F. 1990. *Rituals and Mantras: Rules Without Meaning*. Delhi. First published as Rules Without Meaning: Ritual, Mantras, and the Human Sciences. New York: Peter Lang.

Staal, F. 1995. *Mantras Between Fire and Water: Reflections on Balinese Ritual*. Amsterdam: Koninklijke nederlandse akademie van wetenschappen.

16 The Upaniṣads and the emergence of Theism

Dermot Killingley

The verse Upaniṣads

So far, we have given most attention to the earlier and mostly longer Upaniṣads: the *Bṛhadāraṇyaka*, the *Chāndogya*, the *Taittirīya*, the *Aitareya*, and the *Kauṣītaki*. These are the ones that have most affinity with the Brāhmaṇas: they are mainly in prose, they are discursive and partly narrative, they report the dialogues and authoritative discourses of brahmin men – and sometimes of women, kings, gods, and more unconventional authorities, such as men of unknown parentage, animals, birds, or fires – and they often take ritual matters as their starting-point. The discourses, and especially the dialogues, often start from one view, typically a common or obvious one, or one held by an apparently authoritative teacher, and lead progressively to an unusual or esoteric one; they often follow a repeating pattern. For instance, in CU 8.7–12, Prajāpati leads Indra by stages from a superficial view of the self as the visible, external person to a view of the self as independent of the body, and phrases are repeated from one stage to another. In this and other dialogues, a named individual is gradually taught by another named individual, and the character of each of these individuals is relevant to the argument: Prajāpati talks as he does because he is enlightened, and Indra responds as he does because, being a god, he looks beyond the direct and superficial, unlike the demons. Sometimes the argument includes a demonstration or experiment, like Ajātaśatru's waking a sleeping man to show that the self is present even in sleep (BU 2.1.15–17), or Āruṇi's experiment showing that the mind needs food (CU 6.7), or his demonstrations using seeds (6.12) and salt (6.13). Such dialogues between named individuals, framed in narratives, and often using a "copy and paste; search and replace" mode of composition, later became a feature of the Buddhist textual tradition; but in the Upaniṣads they became less frequent.

Sometimes these early prose Upaniṣads include passages of verse, often introduced with a phrase such as "There is a stanza [or There are some stanzas] about this" – which indicates that the verse passage is taken from another source. Sometimes we can find the same or a very similar stanza in another Upaniṣad; either may have quoted it from the other, or both may have taken it from a now unknown source, perhaps a floating body of stanzas current among the learned circles which produced the Upaniṣads. Notable among these passages are eight stanzas comparing a man to a tree (BU 3.9.28) with which Yājñavalkya concludes his confrontation with rival brahmins, and fourteen stanzas (BU 4.4.8–21) included in Yājñavalkya's discourse to Janaka on the Self. Each of these two passages looks like a little verse Upaniṣad inserted from another source.

Contrasted with these early prose Upaniṣads are three Upaniṣads, the *Kaṭha*, *Muṇḍaka* and *Śvetāśvatara Upaniṣad*s, which are in verse, except that the *Kaṭha* starts with a short prose passage, the *Muṇḍaka* has short prose passages near the beginning and end, and the *Śvetāśvatara* begins with two words of prose. While these three differ considerably in their ideas and style of argument, they show similarities of form: each consists of six chapters of around a dozen or twenty stanzas (the shortest nine, the longest twenty-nine). They also have a number of stanzas in common. Besides these three, there is the *Īśā Upaniṣad*, the shortest and probably oldest of the verse Upaniṣads, not much longer than some of the verse passages in the prose Upaniṣads. The *Kena Upaniṣad* is on the borderline as to form, since it has two chapters of verse followed by two of prose. Chronologically, however, it would be simplistic to place it between a supposed period of prose Upaniṣads and one of verse Upaniṣads; it may be later than the Upaniṣads that are mainly in verse, and there is no reason to suppose that its prose chapters are earlier than its verse ones (Cohen 2008: 251, 287). The *Praśna Upaniṣad* consists of six chapters, like the *Kaṭha*, *Muṇḍaka*, and *Śvetāśvatara*, and contains extensive verse passages; but it is essentially a prose Upaniṣad. It too is a borderline case. We thus have six texts which we can consider together as the middle-period Upaniṣads: the *Īśā*; the *Kena* and *Praśna*; the *Kaṭha*, *Muṇḍaka*, and *Śvetāśvatara*. We must remember that we have no sure evidence of the order of their composition, let alone dates, and that our classification is an arbitrary one, constructed to facilitate our description.

Whereas the Vedic hymns use a variety of stanza forms, not only of four lines but of three or five, and with lines ranging in length from five to twelve syllables, the Upaniṣads use only two: one of 4 × 8 syllables, and one of 4 × 11. Each allows some variation – which sometimes makes it uncertain whether a passage is verse or prose – but the variety of stanza forms has been greatly reduced. This is true of the verse passages in the prose Upaniṣads, as well as of the verse Upaniṣads. Further, for each of these two stanza forms, the range of acceptable metrical variants is progressively reduced in the course of time, from the period of the oldest hymns to that of the later Upaniṣads. Metrical form can thus be used as evidence for the relative antiquity of Upaniṣadic passages (Cohen 2008: 25–30). The details of the technique are beyond the scope of this book; but, roughly speaking, the more rigid the meter, the later the composition of the stanza – except that some metrical irregularities show that a word has been omitted or inserted.

The middle-period Upaniṣads

The middle-period Upaniṣads draw on a stock of floating stanzas which must have been already current when the early prose Upaniṣads were completed, as some of them appear there. Since some of these stanzas have parallels in the hymns of the Ṛgveda and Atharvaveda, they were composed or repeated by people familiar with the older literature: most probably priests, perhaps those who took the role of *brahmán*, requiring knowledge of the three Vedas (above, p. 48). Looking in the opposite direction, there is a clear affinity between the middle-period Upaniṣads and the *Bhagavadgītā*, which has many stanzas in common with them, as well as ideas about God, the world, personality, and yoga.

As suggested above, it would be simplistic to think of the middle-period Upaniṣads as composed later than the early prose ones. For one thing, the *Īśā Upaniṣad* is included in the saṃhitā of the White Yajurveda, which consists essentially of *mantras*; this places it at an older level in the structure of Vedic literature than even the *Bṛhadāraṇyaka Upaniṣad*, which is part of the Brāhmaṇa of the White Yajurveda. It "belongs to ancient Vedic poetry" (Renou 1956: 273); the same could be said of the verse passages in the early prose Upaniṣads, and of some stanzas in the verse Upaniṣads. The *Kena Upaniṣad* is, like the *Bṛhadāraṇyaka*, part of a Brāhmaṇa: the *Jaiminīya Upaniṣad Brāhmaṇa* of the Sāmaveda. Nevertheless, it is convenient to consider the early prose Upaniṣads and the middle-period Upaniṣads as two groups differentiated, despite considerable overlap, by both their literary form and their ideas. Among the ideas typical of the latter group, though not found everywhere in it, is that liberation depends on devotion to, and perhaps on the will of, a personal being, rather than on the knowledge of one's own inner self or ātman, or of an impersonal or supra-personal Brahman, which is usually found in the former group. This is what we refer to as theism. Trying to arrange the Upaniṣads in chronological order according to a reconstructed history of ideas risks subjective judgments and circular arguments, but the hypothesis that theism gained currency later than the idea of an *ātman* or impersonal Brahman is partly corroborated by the formal differences between the early prose Upaniṣads and the middle-period Upaniṣads.

In contrast to the early prose Upaniṣads, the middle-period Upaniṣads typically present their ideas without discussion or effort to persuade, and usually without reference to rival views, though they sometimes give brief arguments, and even dialogues (KU 1.9–2.18; KeU 3.1.–4.1; PU). They also dispense with demonstrations, except for the striking demonstration of the power of Brahman and the powerlessness of even the gods in KeU 3. Unlike the demonstrations and experiments mentioned above, this one is not repeatable, and does not belong to the ordinary world: besides, the *Kena Upaniṣad* is, as we said, a borderline case. The middle-period Upaniṣads seem to address people who will accept their views without needing to be convinced, and even without explanation of their obscurities. This is especially true of the *Śvetāśvatara Upaniṣad*, which includes cryptic passages such as the description of a symbolic wheel (SU 1.4), which makes no sense without a list of terms which is not provided; the same applies to PU 1.11. The impression that it is addressed to a circle that is ready to accept the teacher's views, and knows his terminology, is corroborated in the closing stanzas (SU 6.21–23), which say it is a secret which must only be revealed to appropriate persons. In their verse form, their brevity, their lack of concern to persuade, and their reliance on the hearer's knowledge, these Upaniṣads hark back to the Vedic hymns, rather than the Brāhmaṇas; some of their phrases, and even whole stanzas, are taken from the hymns.

The *Īśā*, *Kaṭha*, and *Śvetāśvatara Upaniṣad*s belong to the Yajurveda, the *Kena* to the Sāmaveda, and the *Praśna* and *Muṇḍaka* to the Atharvaveda. But whereas the early prose Upaniṣads, especially the *Bṛhadāraṇyaka* with its opening praise of the sacrificial horse, and the *Chāndogya* with its references to Sāmavedic chant, are clearly connected with the ritual traditions to which they are affiliated, the middle-period Upaniṣads are less so, and generally show less interest in ritual. They do not prescribe rituals, except very briefly. The passage about a ritual to reach heaven (KU 1.12–19) is exceptional, and is only a preparation for the contrasting passage in which Naciketas insists on his demand for knowledge (KU 1.20–29), and, without saying ritual is worthless, makes it clear that it is not enough for him. The passage in praise of ritual in the *Muṇḍaka Upaniṣad* (MU 1.2.1–6) is followed by one disparaging ritual (MU 1.7–12); this may represent an argument in which the former view is rejected (Olivelle 1996: 396, note on MU 1.1.8). These passages may be dialogues, but they do not identify the speakers as the early prose Upaniṣads do.

God

One of the features that distinguish the middle-period Upaniṣads from the early prose Upaniṣads is their tendency to speak of a transcendent being which is not only the source of all consciousness, but a personal being, an object of worship and a source of grace which can help the seeker of liberation: what we can reasonably call "God," bearing in mind that it may not be precisely what we mean by that name in whatever tradition we may have inherited or rejected. Liberation, in at least some passages of these Upaniṣads, is to be found not by knowing one's innermost self, as Yājñavalkya and others taught, but by knowing a being that is fundamentally other than oneself. Theism is present in parts of the *Īśā*, *Kaṭha*, and *Muṇḍaka Upaniṣad*s, but most of all in the *Śvetāśvatara Upaniṣad.* Similarly, the *Kena Upaniṣad* says that the being to be known is fundamentally other than Brahman as it is usually understood (KeU 1.4–8). In that passage, neuter pronouns are used; but in the first stanza, the being which drives mind, breath, speech, sight and hearing – a pentad of which we shall say more in the next chapter – is called a god (*deva*, a masculine noun). Among the middle-period Upaniṣads, theism is absent only from the *Praśna Upaniṣad.*

God is referred to by various words which are used also in the earlier Upaniṣads: *ātman* "self," *deva* "a god" (usually one of many gods, but sometimes used for the supreme God), *puruṣa* "man." These are grammatically masculine nouns, and sometimes God is simply called "He." God can also be called *brahman*, which is usually a neuter noun (though it is occasionally masculine), or "being" (*sat*, also neuter), or simply "It." The *Śvetāśvatara Upaniṣad* in several places uses the name of the Vedic god Rudra, a god who has only three hymns to himself in the *Ṛgveda Saṃhitā*, and appears in the Brāhmaṇas as a dreaded outsider, lord of cattle but also destroyer of cattle. For centuries Rudra, also called Śiva "the propitious," or Mahādeva "the great god," has been worshipped as supreme God by many Hindus, while others give the same status to Viṣṇu – another god who has only a small place in the *Ṛgveda Saṃhitā*, but becomes prominent in later texts. The *Śvetāśvatara Upaniṣad* may have contributed to the popularity of Rudra/Śiva – or it may have responded to an already existing popularity. The *Mahānārāyaṇa Upaniṣad* does the same for Viṣṇu, also called Nārāyaṇa, though it sometimes names Rudra. The *Maitrī Upaniṣad* names Rudra, Brahmā and Viṣṇu – a triad well known in post-Vedic texts – associating them respectively with the three guṇas tamas, rajas, and sattva (MtU 5.2); but this is in one of the later layers of this multi-layered text (van Buitenen 1962: 82–83; Cohen 2008: 264).

God is also referred to in the middle period Upaniṣads as *īś*, *īśa*, *īśāna*, or *īśvara*, a group of related words usually translated "Lord." These words do not appear in this sense in the early prose Upaniṣads (though *īśāna* occurs in a list of gods (BU 1.4.11), and *īśvara* occurs with a different meaning "capable of, able to do"). In the hymns of the Ṛgveda, *īśāna* is frequently applied to gods, as a participle, meaning "ruling, having power," in a context which specifies what the god has power over: horses, riches, the world, the gods or whatever (Gonda 1965: 140–141). In a hymn we have already referred to (pp. 65, 67, 82, 89) the primal man is described as "having power over immortality" (RV 10.90.2). But in the Atharvaveda *īśāna* occurs as a name, in a context which implies that he is lord of the gods (AV 15.14.10; Gonda 1965: 142). The little verse Upaniṣad included in Yājñavalkya's discourse on the Self includes a stanza calling the Self a god (*deva*) and "Lord (*īśāna*) of what has been and what is to be" (BU 4.4.15; the second half of the stanza is repeated in KU 4.12). In the prose which follows, the Self is repeatedly described as controlling all beings, using *īśāna* and *īśvara* among other nouns denoting a ruler or protector (BU 4.4.22). A similar passage uses the word *īśa* (KsU 3.8). Thus the idea of ultimate reality as a personal ruler, rather than either an impersonal absolute being or Brahman, or the innermost Ātman, is found already in some passages of the early prose Upaniṣads.

The earliest occurrence of the noun *īś* "Lord" in the Upaniṣads, if our sketch of their relative chronology has any validity, is as the first word in the *Īśā Upaniṣad*. This short text, of only eighteen stanzas, takes its name from its initial word. The opening stanza is terse and difficult; throughout this Upaniṣad we seem to be eavesdropping on something that must have made sense to the group for which it was composed, but which would have been a puzzle even to others within the Vedic tradition, to say nothing of ourselves who are trying to understand it from the outside, whether we are beginners or advanced Sanskritists. But its very brevity makes a point: *īś* here is not called the lord of something, not even of the gods or of immortality or of everything; he is just *īś*. This absolute use of the word *īś*, and also of *īśa* (which is almost the same word), is characteristic of the middle-period Upaniṣads.

The second word of the *Īśā Upaniṣad* is ambiguous: it could mean "wearable, to be put on as a garment" or "habitable, to be inhabited," or even "to be pervaded as with a perfume" (Roebuck 2003: 390). Next comes the subject of the sentence: "this whole world." So the Upaniṣad opens with a statement that the world is to be worn, or inhabited, or pervaded, by God. Thereafter, *īś* is not expressly mentioned, unless the masculine forms in stanza eight refer to him; elsewhere there are neuter expressions for the paradoxical One which is motionless and outruns the others, is far and near, within and outside (IU 4–5), and there are references to the Ātman. We shall leave this difficult but haunting text to Chapter 28, and look at clearer, though still difficult, accounts of the Lord.

Two: One bound, one free

The Lord (*īś*) apears again in MU 3.1.1–2. These two somewhat cryptic stanzas are repeated in the *Śvetāśvatara Upaniṣad*, preceded by another cryptic stanza. Using different imagery, each of these three stanzas speaks of two beings who stand in different relations to a third. Here are the three stanzas as they appear in the *Śvetāśvatara Upaniṣad*:

> One unborn female, red, white and black, producing many offspring of like appearance:
>
> For one unborn male lies with her, enjoying; another leaves her when she has had her pleasure.
>
> (SU 4.5)

(Most translators say it is the second male that has had pleasure, but the grammar shows it is the female (Roebuck 2003: 455).)

> Two birds, companions and friends, cling to the same tree.
> Of them, one eats the sweet fig; the other looks on without eating.
> On the same tree a man grieves, sunk down, deluded by her who is not lord.
> When he sees the satisfied Other, the Lord, and his greatness, his grief is gone.
>
> (SU 4.6–7 = MU 3.1.1–2)

This is an example of the way Vedic literature recycles itself: the middle stanza is taken from RV 1.164.20. The tree is not an ordinary fig tree, but another member of the ficus genus: the *aśvattha*, *pippala*, peepul, or sacred fig, which appears many times in Vedic and later literature (Emeneau 1949). Whatever this stanza meant in its earlier context (Johnson 1976), in the Upaniṣad it is paralleled, and partly explained, by the first and third stanzas.

Each of the three beings is described in the first stanza as "unborn." This word has been used before: In BU 4.4.20; 4.4.22 it describes the Ātman, and in KU 2.18 it perhaps describes the Ātman (KU 2.20), or perhaps the sacred syllable (2.16). Elsewhere in the *Śvetāśvatara Upaniṣad* it describes God (KU 2.15). But there is a pun which is probably intended in the above context, if not in the ones just mentioned: the masculine and feminine forms of the adjective *aja* "unborn" are the same as the words for a male and a female goat. This makes the image more picturesque (although "lies with" is inappropriate for goats). The she-goat's three colors, red, white, and black, appear in a creation myth as the colors of heat, water, and food, which are the origin of all phenomena (CU 6.2–4); in the Sāṃkhya system, whose origins can partly be traced in the middle-period Upaniṣads (below, pp. 176–177, 179–182), they are the colors of the three strands (*guṇa*) of which all phenomena consist. The she-goat thus contains within her all the variety of the world, and this variety is reproduced in her young, who are the phenomena. The male who is enjoying her is the individual who experiences the world. Who then is the other male who has given her pleasure, and thus engendered her young? In the third stanza above (SU 4.7 = MU 3.1.2), "the satisfied Other" is identified as the Lord, so we can identify the other male in the first stanza as the Lord also.

Taking these three images together – the two unborn ones or goats; the two birds in the tree; the man in the tree and the Lord – we can see a picture of the human condition which draws on older ideas but gives them a new shift. The sacred fig tree is the foundation of all the worlds (KU 6.1); the eating of fruit is a standard metaphor for the experiences which result from our actions. We enjoy the fruit, but our situation is one of bondage, as the third verse shows, and as we have seen in Chapters 7 and 13. We can escape from this bondage, it adds, by seeing the Lord. In the *Muṇḍaka Upaniṣad*, the next stanza makes the same point:

> When the seer sees the gold-colored maker, the Lord, the Man, the womb of Brahman,
>
> Then he knows, he shakes off good and evil, is spotless, and reaches supreme equality.
>
> (MU 3.1.3)

The Lord, represented by the bird who looks on without eating, the satisfied Other, and the he-goat who has left the she-goat, has played his part in creation; but unlike Prajāpati in the older creation myths (above, p. 68), he is not emptied or shattered. Further, unlike the Ātman taught in the early prose Upaniṣads, he is different from the bound individual, represented by the male who lies with the female, the bird that eats the fruit, and the man sunk in grief on the tree.

The *Kaṭha Upaniṣad* has a partial parallel to the image of the two birds, describing two beings who "drink truth in the world of good actions, who have entered the cave and the highest beyond"; they are "darkness and light." The stanza is obscure, but the parallelism helps us to understand them as the individual self and the Lord. The "world of good actions" is the place or condition in which a person receives the fruit of their well-performed ritual acts (MU 1.2.1). The "cave," or "hidden place," is where the ātman resides (KU 2.20); it thus means the heart, which is the usual location of the ātman (CU 3.14.3; BU 4.4.1). The self and the Lord are both said to be in the cave of the heart and also in the beyond (TU 2.1 is similar); this is consistent with Yājñavalkya's description of the self as the immortal inner controller within all things (BU 3.7.3–23). It is harder to explain why they are both said to drink, unlike the two birds, of whom one eats and the other does not. Perhaps the differentiation between the self and the Lord is not as strong in this Upaniṣad as in the *Śvetāśvatara*. Elsewhere in the *Kaṭha*, the "honey-eating ātman" is said to be "Lord of what has been and is to be" (KU 4.5); this is repeated in two further stanzas, referring to the ātman as the "thumb-sized man" (KU 4.12; 4.13). Yājñavalkya has already called the ātman "Lord of what has been and is to be" in a very similar stanza (BU 4.4.15).

Prakṛti, *Māyā*, the Triad

We can look further at the unborn female of the first stanza. Sexual creation myths are not new; there is an evident, though cryptic, sexual narrative in RV 10.129.4–5, a clearer one in BU 1.4.3–4, and several Brāhmaṇa myths in which Prajāpati lusts after his daughter. The third stanza also mentions a female being, "her who is not lord"; in the middle stanza her place is taken by the tree with its fruit. The female figure has an apparently independent existence alongside the unbound Lord and the bound individual, as does the tree. She is also readily identified with two terms found in the *Śvetāśvatara Upaniṣad*, both of which are grammatically feminine: *prakṛti* "nature" and *māyā* "artifice." *Prakṛti* does not occur in the earlier Upaniṣads, but is frequent later, denoting the material from which everything we experience is formed – the components of our personality as well as the objects of our senses. The translation "nature" is conventional and appropriate, especially since *prakṛti* can refer to a person's individual nature or character. Etymologically, *māyā* is the power to make things (Mayrhofer 1956–1980: vol. 2, p. 624); in the Ṛgvedic hymns it is a power possessed by gods and other beings which enables them to produce supranormal effects. RV 6.47.18, quoted in BU 2.5.19, mentions the *māyā*s of Indra, by which he takes on many forms; this is the only occurrence of the word in the early prose Upaniṣads. It can be associated with deceit – the world of Brahman belongs to those who are without crookedness, untruth, or *māyā* (PU 1.16). Later, in Advaita Vedānta, it refers to the power of false knowledge to produce the appearance of a diverse world, in contrast to true knowledge of the unity of Brahman. Accordingly, *māyā* is sometimes translated "illusion"; but "artifice" (Roebuck 2003: 297; 306) may be a more appropriate translation, conveying the power to make things – its usual meaning in earlier English – but also having sinister connotations. "Craft" is another possible translation.

> One should know that nature (*prakṛti*) is the artifice (*māyā*), and the Great Lord is the artificer (*māyin*).
>
> (SU 4.10)

The three unborn beings (or goats), the two birds and the tree, and the two men and the tree, all represent a triad which is one of the two recurring themes of the *Śvetāśvatara Upaniṣad*. It is mentioned first in SU 1.7: "The highest Brahman, however, has been extolled thus: There is a triad in it – oneself, the foundation and the imperishable" (Olivelle 1996: 253, 386). The next stanza explains:

> This complex is the perishable and the imperishable, the manifest and the unmanifest; the Lord carries the whole.
>
> And the ātman, which is not lord, is bound, by being an experiencer. On knowing God it is released from all nooses.
>
> (SU 1.8)

The next stanza uses the same image of the three unborn ones or goats as SU 4.5 discussed above. One male is the Lord who knows, the other is powerless and ignorant, and the female is "joined to the experiencer and the objects of experience" (SU 1.9). That is, *prakṛti* provides the sense-objects which we perceive in the world, and the senses with which we perceive them.

The last sentence of SU 1.8 is the Upaniṣad's other recurring theme. It is repeated verbatim at the end of stanzas 2.15; 4.16; 5.13; 6.13, and similar statements are made at the end of many other stanzas, and at the beginning of SU 1.11; so the promise of liberation by knowing or seeing God runs through this Upaniṣad like a refrain. Those who know God are freed from nooses, or cut the nooses of death (SU 4.15), or become immortal (SU 3.1; 3.10; 4.17), or get rid of sorrow (SU 3.20; 4.7), or reach peace (SU 4.11; 4.14). Since this Upaniṣad is characterized by quotations from, and echoes of, the Vedic hymns, the image of the noose recalls the nooses of Varuṇa (above, pp. 62–63). Seeing the Ātman is similarly associated with freedom from sorrow in KU 2.20, discussed below. But in contrast to KU 4.5 and 4.12–13 (above), the teachings of Yājñavalkya discussed in Chapter 12 (pp. 127–129), and those of Indra, Sanatkumāra or Prajāpati discussed in Chapter 13 (pp. 139, 141–142, 143), the *Śvetāśvatara Upaniṣad* does not say that the self which is the source of our consciousness is the ruler of the world, or that it is essentially blissful. On the contrary, it emphasizes its powerlessness and its subjection to suffering. In a typically condensed argument enquiring what is the universal cause, it states: "The self is not lord, because of pleasure and pain" (SU 1.2). That is, the self cannot be the cause of the world, because the pleasure and pain it experiences are beyond its control.

God's self-revelation

In the second half of the *Kena Upaniṣad*, Brahman itself appears as a character in a story which shows its power over the gods. Brahman – grammatically neuter throughout the story, despite behaving as a person – had obtained victory for them, presumably in one of their struggles against the demons (*asura*) which are a feature of the Brāhmaṇas. The gods boasted of the victory as their own; so to teach them a lesson, Brahman appeared before them. The story does not narrate how Brahman, which is essentially formless, appeared, or what it looked like; but the gods, not knowing what it was, called it a *yakṣa* – a word which usually means a kind of earth-spirit, but which is applied to Brahman in BU 5.4. The god of fire went to see what it was; Brahman put a blade of grass in front of him, but he could not burn it. Then the god of wind went, and he could not blow away the blade of grass. Finally Indra went, but Brahman vanished. In its place he found a beautiful woman, who told him the strange being was Brahman (KeU 3.12). So Indra is superior to the other gods, because he was the first to know that it was Brahman (KeU 4.3). Indra is similarly distinguished as the one who learns knowledge of the Ātman from Prajāpati (CU 8.7–12), and teaches it to

Pratardana (KsU 3). The woman is named as Umā, daughter of Himālaya; the Upaniṣad does not explain further, but in later mythology Umā, also known as Pārvatī "daughter of the mountain," is the wife of Rudra/Śiva.

This story shows Brahman revealing itself, albeit in a cryptic though spectacular way. The idea that God reveals himself is found elsewhere in the middle-period Upaniṣads. IU 15, in a passage which also appears as BU 5.15, prays for Truth to reveal itself. The idea appears at greater length in this stanza:

> This Ātman is not obtained by discourse, nor by intelligence, nor by much learning.
> He is obtained by the one he chooses; to him this Ātman reveals his form.
>
> (KU 2.23 = MU 3.2.3)

Another stanza conveys the same idea:

> Smaller than the small, greater than the great, the self is placed in the hidden place of a creature.
> One who is without desire is rid of sorrow, and sees the greatness of the self, by the grace of the disposer.
>
> (KU 2.20)

This stanza is repeated in SU 3.20, with some variations. "The greatness of the self" is changed to "the greatness, the Lord," adapting the phrase to the *Śvetāśvatara Upaniṣad*'s version of theism by distinguishing the Lord, the sight of whom brings freedom from sorrow, from the suffering self. Also, it is not the individual that is without desire, but God, who has no desires because he has no needs (a theme developed further in BhG 3.22; 4.13).

But what interests us most is the mention of grace. In later Hindu theology, the word *prasāda* "clarity, serenity; grace, favor" refers to the grace which a god grants to worshipers, enabling them to approach and know him. (It may be more familiar in the sense of food that has been offered to an image and is then distributed: the deity grants favor to the worshipers by allowing them to eat the food.) In the *Kaṭha* and *Śvetāśvatara Upaniṣad*s, the phrase "by the grace of the disposer" (*dhātuḥ prasādāt*) seems to present an early instance of the doctrine of grace: God chooses certain people, allowing them to see him and so win liberation; the statement occurs also in the *Mahānārāyaṇa Upaniṣad* (8.3). But there is uncertainty about the phrase. Some manuscripts omit two dots, looking like a colon (:), which changes the meaning to "by serenity of the components [of personality]" (*dhātu-prasādāt*); this would make liberation dependent on the seeker's state of mind, not on the grace of God. The word *dhātu* "component" occurs in the classical Upaniṣads (CU 6.5.1; 6.5.2; 6.5.3); but not in the sense of a component of personality which it has later. On the other hand *dhātṛ*, "disposer" does occur; it refers to a deity who controls events in the world, invoked for success in begetting a child (BU 6.4.21), or recruiting students (TU 1.4.3); so the meaning "by the grace of the disposer" is probably correct.

Theism beyond the Upaniṣads

Hindu theism has many forms, but several of them derive ideas from the middle-period Upaniṣads. The key term *bhakti* "devotion" appears first in the *Śvetāśvatara Upaniṣad*, which concludes by saying that devotion to God (*deva*), and to the teacher (*guru*) as to God, are necessary for understanding its doctrine (SU 6.23). *Bhakti* is frequently mentioned in the *Bhagavadgītā*, which has many ideas and phrases, and even whole stanzas, in common with the verse Upaniṣads. The triad of God, the individual self and nature is important in the Vaiṣṇava theology of Rāmānuja; the same triad appears in Śaivism as *pati* "the Lord," *paśu* "the beast," meaning the individual in bondage, and *pāśa* "the noose," in which the individual is held. In the early nineteenth century, when Rammohun Roy sought to combine Hindu and European thought in a form of rational theism based on Sanskrit textual authority, it was the *Īśā*, *Kena*, *Kaṭha* and *Muṇḍaka Upaniṣad*s that he chose to translate into Bengali and English. A century later, M. K. Gandhi regarded the *Īśā Upaniṣad* as the essence of Hinduism (Chapter 20). God (*īśvara*) is a distinctive feature of the Yoga system. Though he appears there not as creator or universal cause, but as the timeless first teacher of yoga and supreme object of devotion (Whicher 1998: 83), he has a clear antecedent in the "Lord" of the middle-period Upaniṣads. Yoga is mentioned in SU 6.13, together with *sāṃkhya*, a term which is closely associated with *yoga* in the *Bhagavadgītā*, a key text of theism; both these are necessary means of knowing God, and thus being released from all nooses.

References

Cohen, Signe. 2008. *Text and Authority in the Older Upaniṣads*. Leiden: Brill.

Emeneau, M. B. 1949. "The Strangling Figs in Sanskrit Literature" *University of California Publications in Classical Philology* 13.10: 345–370.

Gonda, Jan. 1965. *Change and Continuity in Indian Religion*. The Hague: Mouton.

Johnson, Willard. 1976. "On the Ṛg Vedic Riddle of the Two Birds in the Fig Tree (ṚV 1.164.20–22) and the Discovery of the Vedic Speculative Symposium" *Journal of the American Oriental Society* 96: 248–258.

Mayrhofer, M. 1956–1980. *Kurzgefasstes etymologisches Wörterbuch der Sanskritsprache*. 4 vols. Heidelberg: Carl Winter.

Olivelle, Patrick. 1996. *Upaniṣads: Translated from the Original Sanskrit* (World's Classics series). Oxford: Oxford University Press.

Renou, Louis. 1956. *Hymnes spéculatifs du Véda*. Paris: Gallimard.

Roebuck, Valerie. 2003. *The Upaniṣads. Translated and Edited* (Penguin Classics series). London: Penguin.

Van Buitenen, J. A. B. 1962. *The Maitrāyaṇīya Upaniṣad: A Critical Essay, with Text, Translation and Commentary*. The Hague: Mouton.
Whicher, Ian. 1998. *The Integrity of the Yoga Darśana: A Reconsideration of Classical Yoga*. Albany, NY: State University of New York Press.

Further reading

Brockington, John. 1981. *The Sacred Thread: Hinduism in its Continuity and Diversity*. Edinburgh: Edinburgh University Press, 51–73.
Gonda, Jan. 1965. *Change and Continuity in Indian Religion*. The Hague: Mouton, 131–163.

17 The Upaniṣads and Yoga

Dermot Killingley

Yoga in the Upaniṣads

Besides theism, the Upaniṣads of the middle period show an interest in yoga. The word *yoga* is used in the *Kaṭha* and *Śvetāśvatara Upaniṣad*s, as well as other words which are technical terms of the Yoga system; there are traces of yoga also in the *Muṇḍaka Upaniṣad*. A more developed form of yoga appears in the later portions of the *Maitrī Upaniṣad*, a text combining material from several periods. The later yoga upaniṣads (Chapter 41) show a more developed form still.

Since the *Kaṭha*, *Śvetāśvatara*, and *Maitrī Upaniṣad*s belong to the Black Yajurveda, yoga may have been fostered within that tradition; as we shall see, early passages that we can recognize as yoga link it to application of the mind to a ritual task. Further, in one of the passages on yoga in the *Mahābhārata* the teacher is named as Yājñavalkya, the great ritualist and Upaniṣadic thinker of the Black Yajurveda (*MBh* 12.298–306; below, pp. 193–196; Cohen 2008: 51). He appears in conversation with King Janaka, as he does in the *Bṛhadāraṇyaka Upaniṣad* and also in the *Śatapatha Brāhmaṇa*; however much his ideas may differ in these three sources, the anonymous authors evidently attributed them to the same man. While the *Muṇḍaka Upaniṣad* belongs to the Atharvaveda, it shares some material with the *Kaṭha* and *Śvetāśvatara Upaniṣads*, as we have seen in Chapter 16, indicating that advanced exponents of the Atharvaveda had some contact with those of the Black Yajurveda. (The word *yoga* also appears in TU 2.4; but this is a word of many meanings (below, p. 177). If it refers to "yoga" in the usual sense (Whicher 1998: 17; Roebuck 2003: 216), it is a very early and isolated occurrence; the context makes it more likely that it means "performance" (Olivelle 1996: 186), or perhaps the application of the mind.)

Varieties of yoga

There are so many forms of yoga that we need to be clear about what we mean by the term when we use it in different contexts. There is "Modern Yoga," of which "Modern Postural Yoga," as taught in many yoga classes, is the most popular form (De Michaelis 2004: 1–6; 187–189). Modern yoga is a product of the twentieth century; it was pioneered by Swami Vivekananda's talks in the eastern USA from 1895 onwards. These were hardly what would now be called yoga classes, but they encouraged Westerners to think of yoga as something they could practice themselves, rather than as an exotic or esoteric activity of the Other (Killingley 2014). Modern yoga contains traditional Hindu material packaged for export; that is not to say that it is inauthentic, but that its proponents, mainly in the twentieth century, took traditional ideas and methods and consciously adapted them to modern expectations, ways of thinking, modes of transport and communication, and forms of organization. Further, while modern yoga is taught all over the world, including India, its principal language is English (De Michaelis 2004: 8n.). It has become so successful that people can use the word *yoga* in English without knowing that it is Sanskrit or even Indian in origin.

The Indian teachers who initiated modern yoga drew on ideas and practices that can be traced back to the ancient textbook of yoga, the *Yogasūtra* of Patañjali, and cited it as their authority. Its author is traditionally identified with an important grammarian called Patañjali. However, the grammarian is usually dated to the first or second century CE, and the *Yogasūtra* to the second or third century CE; as with Yājñavalkya (above, p. 174), the identification is improbable. Like the ritual sūtras mentioned in Chapter 6, or the *Vedāntasūtra*, or the grammatical sūtras of Pāṇini, the *Yogasūtra* is a set of brief rules which make little sense without a commentary. The oldest commentary is the *Yogabhāṣya* ("Yoga commentary") composed in the fifth or sixth century CE and attributed to Vyāsa; he is traditionally identified with Vyāsa the compiler of the *Mahābhārata*, who is a mythical rather than a historical figure. Several sub-commentaries on Vyāsa's commentary were composed at different times, down to the twentieth century (Whicher 1998: 320–322). While there have been recent attempts to interpret the *Yogasūtra* independently of Vyāsa, he is traditionally accepted as the authority for understanding the sūtras. The tradition based on the *Yogasūtra*, as interpreted by Vyāsa, is termed "classical yoga" or "Pātañjala yoga." Like other schools of Indian philosophy it is variously interpreted by its followers, and since it depends perhaps more than most such schools on practice and experience, its variety is not fully reflected in the sub-commentaries and other textual accounts. While yoga is a *darśana* or system of thought, based on the *Yogasūtra* and its successive commentaries much as Vedānta is based on the *Vedāntasūtra*, it is also much more, since many items of its terminology, theory, and practice are also used in various branches of Vedānta, and also in Tantrism, Jainism, Buddhism, and other traditions.

As with other sets of sūtras or rules, the text indicates that the author drew on an existing body of ideas. Once a Sanskrit text has been accepted as the foundation of a system, its predecessors commonly fall into oblivion. Earlier authors and their views may be mentioned in the foundation text, either by name or as "some" or "others," but their works are not preserved. This is true of the *Yogasūtra*. However, we do have samples of earlier thought on yoga, presented briefly in some of the Upaniṣads, and at greater length and in more developed form in parts of the *Mahābhārata*. While the *Mahābhārata* is essentially a heroic epic, its core story occupies only about a fifth of the whole; the remainder consists of stories told by one character to another, including the story of how the core story came to be told, and numerous didactic passages in which characters expound and discuss dynastic history, ethics, ritual, pilgrimage, cosmology, and many other subjects, including yoga. The best-known passage of this kind is the *Bhagavadgītā*; yoga is a central part of its teaching, and it has much in common with the middle-period Upaniṣads, as we have seen. There is also the long discourse on yoga called the *Mokṣadharma* (Mbh 12.168–353), which includes the teaching given by Yājñavalkya to Janaka, already mentioned. The relation between the *Mahābhārata*, and especially the *Bhagavadgītā*, and the Upaniṣads will be discussed in Chapters 18 and 19. The *Mahābhārata* and the Upaniṣads represent early yoga – that is, yoga as it existed before it was systematized in the *Yogasūtra*. Since the *Yogasūtra* includes ideas that are also found in early Buddhist and Jain sources (Whicher 1998: 47; 325–326 n. 40), these sources can also be considered as representing early yoga.

What early yoga, classical yoga, and modern yoga have in common, besides the word *yoga*, is a concern to rid our consciousness of its tendency to wander among many objects, and to make it one-pointed. In classical yoga the ultimate goal is stated to be "aloneness" (*kaivalya*, *Yogasūtra* 2.25; Whicher 1998: 275–285); in some forms of modern yoga it is personal well-being. In early yoga, the goal is variously described. The *Bhagavadgītā* speaks of reaching God (BhG 18.68) or even entering God (BhG 18.55); the *Kaṭha Upaniṣad* speaks of reaching the place from which there is no rebirth (KU 3.8–9); in the *Śvetāśvatara Upaniṣad* the goal is to be freed from all nooses by knowing God (SU 2.15). The goal is reached through control of the faculties (*indriya*) – the five senses, and the faculties of action such as speech and locomotion; these are explained and discussed below (pp. 179–182). The means for doing this include breath control, posture, and mental practices such as meditation. (Some scholars translate *indriya* as "organ," but "faculty" is preferable, because the texts sometimes distinguish the *indriya*s from the organs in which they are located (Killingley 2006: 80). Some call all the *indriya*s "senses," and the action faculties "conative senses," doing unnecessary violence to English usage.)

Since yoga in all its forms is a way of controlling the personality, it involves a theory of how personality is structured. In classical yoga, the theory is outlined in *Yogasūtra* 2.19, and expounded or modified in Vyāsa's commentary on this sūtra (Whicher 1998: 65–66). With some differences, partly terminological, the same theory is set out in classical sāṃkhya, which was systematized in the *Sāṃkhyakārikā* of Īśvarakṛṣṇa, around the fourth century CE; it is also accepted in Vedānta. Before these classical formulations, both yoga and sāṃkhya existed in various forms; many of them are found in the *Mahābhārata*, and there are traces of them in the Upaniṣads. At that stage, they were not defined bodies of doctrine so much as traditions of teaching and practice which varied from teacher to teacher. (Indeed, even after the definitive texts were composed, teachers were free to write commentaries embodying widely different interpretations.) It was debatable whether sāṃkhya and yoga were two or one (BhG 5.4); in the *Mahābhārata* they are paired as theory and practice rather than as distinct schools (Edgerton 1924). The name *sāṃkhya*, derived from *saṃkhyā* "number," may refer to this tradition's reliance on enumeration, or more generally on reason.

The word *yoga* is a common one, used in many contexts besides the one we are considering here; not every text which uses the word *yoga* is about yoga. Its most general meaning is "connection"; in astronomy it can mean a constellation or a conjunction, in grammar the connection between words in a sentence, or in arithmetic addition. It can also mean "acquisition." It is closely related in form to a verb, represented by the root *yuj*, which means "to join, to connect." (Each Sanskrit verb has dozens of inflectional forms; the root is a device invented by the ancient grammarians to refer to all these forms, and to related verbal nouns as well.) The root *yuj* is cognate with the English words *join*, *junction*, *yoke* (and also, through Greek, with *zygote*, *syzygy*, *zeugma*). Etymology does not determine the meaning of a word, but Sanskrit nouns formed in the same way as *yoga* are usually closely related in meaning with the formally related verb, so the ways in which the verb is used can elucidate the meaning of the noun. The verb *yuj* can mean "to apply, to put to use; to make ready or equip," and especially "to harness horses or to fit an arrow to a bow"; and these meanings help us to understand the word *yoga* in the Upaniṣads. The verb occurs often in the Vedic hymns and Brāhmaṇas with reference to harnessing horses; these were important in Vedic culture, and horse-drawn chariots were used in warfare and in races, which had a place in some rituals. In an extension of meaning which is relevant to yoga, *yuj* can also refer to harnessing or applying the mind (*manas*) to a ritual task (SB 6.3.1.12–16). The American Sanskritist Franklin Edgerton regularly translated *yoga* as "discipline" in his translation of the *Bhagavadgītā* (Edgerton 1952). Among other advantages, this can be a verb as well as a noun, so it can translate the verb *yuj* – as can "control." It can also refer either to a process or to a state which is achieved by that process, as *yoga* can.

Yoga as control of faculties: *Kaṭha Upaniṣad* 3.3–9

The earliest clear account of yoga in the Upaniṣads does not use the noun *yoga*, but it does use the verb *yuj*, in an extended simile or parable which uses several key terms of yoga. The Ātman is represented as riding in a two-man chariot, driven by a charioteer; if properly controlled (*yuj*), it will bring the Ātman to its ultimate goal, which is beyond rebirth (KU 3.8). We can set out the simile in tabular form (in the references on the right, the letters abcd refer to the four quarters or lines of each stanza):

rider	= Ātman	(KU 3.3a)
chariot	= body	(KU 3.3b)
charioteer	= intellect (*buddhi*)	(KU 3.3c)
reins	= mind (*manas*)	(KU 3.3d)
horses	= faculties (*indriya*)	(KU 3.4a)
ground	= objects of faculties (*viṣaya*)	(KU 3.4b)

Leaving aside the chariot or body, and the ground or objects, we have a chain of command. The rider, the Ātman, is at the top of the chain; it is for his benefit that the whole equipage exists. But he depends on the skill of the charioteer, the intellect. In ancient Indian warfare, choice of a charioteer is crucial to the warrior's success or survival. The warrior is in command, but needs not only the horsemanship but often the advice of the charioteer. In the *Bhagavadgītā*, the warrior Arjuna tells his charioteer Kṛṣṇa to stop the chariot (BhG 1.21), but then turns to him for advice (BhG 2.4–8), thus prompting the teaching which is the core of the poem. The charioteer handles the reins, which are the mind (*manas*); as we have noted already (p. 127), this word refers to a component of personality that is not itself conscious; it only processes the information received from the faculties of sense, and co-ordinates the faculties of action. It is thus represented by the reins, which are the means of controlling the horses; these are the faculties with which we perceive, move about in, and act on the world around us. Without this control, the horses would either not move or move erratically; but the rider, charioteer, and chariot need their motive power.

The chariot is the physical body, without which the Ātman would not have a presence in the world. The ground on which the chariot runs, evidently a racecourse, is the whole perceptible world that surrounds us, and on which our faculties operate; it includes all the things that would make the horses shy, stumble, or bolt if not properly controlled. KU 3.4cd adds that the Ātman, being connected with the faculties and mind (Gonda 1977: 65), is termed the experiencer or consumer (*bhoktṛ*): the one that experiences or eats the fruits of our deeds. This is a key term of yoga and other classical thought; in classical yoga, it is similarly used for the self in relation to the objects which it experiences (*Yogasūtrabhāṣya* 2.6). In the *Śvetāśvatara Upaniṣad* it is a member of the triad of self (the consumer), nature (who provides the consumables), and God (SU 1.9; 1.12; above, pp. 168–170); and in the *Maitrī Upaniṣad* it is the *puruṣa* who "consumes the food belonging to nature" (*prakṛti*) (MtU 6.10).

The Upaniṣad continues the simile by contrasting the rider who fails to reach the winning-post with the one who reaches it (KU 3.5–9). The unsuccessful one's mind is uncontrolled ("control" here translates *yuj*), and his faculties do not obey him, as bad horses fail to obey the charioteer; the successful one's mind is controlled, and his faculties obey him like good horses. To explain what the race represents in the simile, the winning-post is called "the place from which he is not reborn"; the one who fails to reach it follows the round of rebirths, and the succession of (mostly unpleasant) experiences that attend it – referred to here for the first time as *saṃsāra* (p. 130). This passage equates liberation with escape from rebirth (above, pp. 126, 129, 131), in contrast to older ideas of free embodiment (above, pp. 140–143). The winning-post is also called "the highest footstep of Viṣṇu" (KU 3.9d), an older idea of the ultimate goal than that of freedom from rebirth. Viṣṇu's three strides are mentioned in the Ṛgvedic hymns, especially his highest step, sometimes identified with the world of the ancestors. The following stanza describes it as the goal, and also the source of cosmic nourishment:

> May I reach that dear place
> Where godly men rejoice;
> For that is the bond of the wide-strider,
> The source of honey in Viṣṇu's highest step.
> (RV 1.154.5)

In the Brāhmaṇas, Viṣṇu is identified with the sacrifice; he won the whole world for the gods in three strides, stepping on earth, atmosphere, and sky (SB 1.9.3.9; 3.6.3.3). The three strides are re-enacted by the yajamāna (above, p.66; SB 1.9.3.8).

Having reached the highest step of Viṣṇu (KU 3.9), the Upaniṣad continues discussing the faculties, but does not mention the chariot, or use any form of the root *yuj*. The control of horses reappears in SU 2, in a passage which deals explicitly with yoga. Before turning to that passage, we will look further at the simile of the chariot.

The structure of personality

The simile outlines a theory of the structure of personality, and how it interacts with its surroundings. The chain of command in the chariot represents this structure as a hierarchy: Ātman at the top; then intellect (*buddhi*), which is the decision-making faculty; then mind (*manas*); and the faculties at the bottom. The hierarchy is repeated in KU 3.10, except that the objects are added above the faculties (which would not fit the chariot simile), and the Ātman is called "the great Ātman" (a phrase occurring in BU 4.4.20; 4.4.22; KU 2.22; 4.4, referring to the unborn Ātman). The hierarchy is continued upwards in KU 3.11, culminating in *puruṣa* "man"; this use of the word recalls RV 10.90 and variants of it in the Brāhmaṇas (above, pp. 67–68), and also anticipates its use in classical sāṃkhya referring to the individual conscious being. Here, between the great Ātman and the ultimate *puruṣa* stands the "unmanifest"; in classical sāṃkhya this refers to Nature (*prakṛti*) in its inactive state, but here it is an aspect of the *puruṣa*, above the Great Ātman which is his first manifestation. A third version of the hierarchy, emphasizing the need to control, appears in KU 3.13, where speech stands for all the faculties, and *buddhi* is replaced with a word of similar meaning, *vijñāna* "intelligence." A fourth version (KU 6.7–8), which uses *sattva* for *buddhi* (as does the *Mokṣadharma* (Mbh 12.203.33; below, pp. 193–195); van Buitenen 1957: 95–103), goes on to describe the highest state as successive stilling of the senses, mind, and intellect (KU 6.10). This state is then called *yoga* (KU 6.11); it is clearly related to the classical definition of yoga as checking the activities of the consciousness (*Yogasūtra* 1.2; interpreters differ as to what exactly this means, but generally avoid the idea of stopping all thought). The final stanza sums up the whole Upaniṣad as the instruction in yoga which Naciketas received from Death (KU 6.18; above, pp. 61, 96, 103, 135–136; below, p. 317). This Upaniṣad thus sets out four early versions of a scheme which was standardized in Vyāsa's *Yogasūtrabhāṣya* and in the *Sāṃkhyakārikā* (Whicher 1998: 77); there are other versions in the Upaniṣads and the *Mahābhārata*. The *Kaṭha Upaniṣad* is the earliest to speak explicitly of yoga. It mentions yoga elsewhere as the only way to reach liberating secret knowledge (KU 2.12); but only in passing, without clear indication of what it means by the term.

A somewhat similar model of personality appears already in the *Taittirīya Upaniṣad*. We have a self made of food (the body). Within it is a self made of breath (*prāṇa*), a term which in the Upaniṣads often refers to the faculties. Within that is a self made of mind (*manas*); then intelligence (*vijñāna*), and finally bliss (TU 2.1–5). (It is typical of the early prose Upaniṣads that bliss should be found within the person, rather than beyond or outside as it often is in the middle-period Upaniṣads.) We thus consist of five layers; and each of these is described as a pentad, recalling the dictum that man is fivefold (BU 1.4.17; above, p. 70). Later, these layers came to be called the five *kośa*s ("boxes," often translated "sheaths").

The number five has an important place in the model of personality that is used in yoga. The chariot passage mentions the faculties collectively, without enumerating them; so does *Yogasūtra* 2.19. But the *Taittirīya Upaniṣad* (in a chapter which may have once been a separate text) mentions a pentad of faculties: sight, hearing, mind, speech, touch (TU 1.7). Such pentads have a long history, going back to the primal man of RV 10.90. Besides his feet, navel, and head, which become earth, atmosphere, and sky (above, p. 67), five parts of him become parts of the macrocosm: mind, sight, mouth, breath, hearing (RV 10. 90.13–14; Killingley 2006: 87). If mouth stands here for speech, this is the same pentad of faculties in a different order, except that breath takes the place of touch. We have already mentioned mind, breath, speech, sight, and hearing (KU 1.1; above, p. 165).

The idea of five faculties is common in Vedic texts, though the items listed, and the order, vary somewhat. Breath often appears instead of touch, as we have seen; or the skin (CU 5.23) is listed as the location of this sense. But breath can also refer to the sense of smell (BU 1.3 (below, p. 251; KsU 3.4). Speech may be identified with the sense of taste (SB 10.5.2.15), since both are located in the mouth (Killingley 2006: 90). This brings the list closer to the list of sense faculties given in the *Sāṃkhyakārikā* and in Vyāsa's commentary on *Yogasūtra* 2.19: hearing, touch, sight, taste, smell. This list became the standard one. We may be so familiar with this list of the five senses that we suppose it is given in nature, rather than received from culturally bound tradition. But it raises questions: how easy is it to distinguish taste from smell? With which sense do we perceive a headache? It was only gradually that the ancient Indian thinkers settled on the list of five sense faculties.

The *Sāṃkhyakārikā* and the *Yogasūtra* commentary add a second list. Besides the five sense faculties by which we receive input from our surroundings, we have five action faculties, by which we act on our surroundings. These are speech, manipulation (the function of the hands), locomotion (the function of the feet), defecation, and procreation. This list may seem as bizarre as the other seems natural, but it too is a standard one in Sanskrit. It is partly motivated by a wish to account for the lower orifices of the body, in the same way as the eyes, ears, nostrils, and mouth are accounted for by sight, hearing, smell, and taste. The fact that urination is not listed whereas defecation is, may be accounted for by its sharing an orifice with a more interesting function. It is for the same reason that speech appears in many early lists, while taste appears in others.

The two lists divide the faculties neatly into sense faculties and action faculties, unlike the lists we saw earlier. The same ten faculties appear in one list in the *Praśna Upaniṣad*, which describes how a sleeping man does not hear, see, smell, taste, touch, speak, take, have joy, defecate, or move (PU 4.2). (Joy, as well as procreation, is the function of the sex organ.) The ten are not explicitly divided into two pentads, but the first five are the sense faculties and the second five are the action faculties. More remarkably, one of the oldest Upaniṣads contains a complete list of ten, separating the sense faculties from the action faculties by placing the mind and the heart in the middle of the list. Yājñavalkya, explaining to his wife Maitreyī how everything is centered on the Ātman, says that it is as all tactile sensations are located in the skin, odors in the nostrils, flavors in the tongue, appearances in the eyesight, sounds in the sense of hearing – resolves (*saṃkalpa*) in the mind, knowledges (*vidyā*) in the heart – actions in the hands, joys in the sex organ, defecations in the anus, journeys in the feet, Vedas in the voice (BU 2.4.11 = BU 4.5.12; dashes are used here to separate the five sense faculties, the two higher faculties, and the five sense faculties, but the Sanskrit text uses one punctuation mark throughout). Although this passage is not about yoga, it shows that a set of ideas which later became a part of yoga evolved in the context of early Upaniṣadic thought about personality. The higher faculties have not yet developed into the three listed in classical sāṃkhya: intellect (*buddhi*), the faculty that enables us to call ourselves "I" (*ahaṃkāra*), and mind (*manas*) – but the sense faculties and action faculties are listed separately as in classical sāṃkhya, though not in the same order.

Pentads appear also in SU 1.5, but in a very cryptic way, evidently intended for insiders who know the answers to the riddles. It speaks of "five streams" which may be the sense faculties, and "five perceptions" which are the "original root": perhaps the sensations which the sense faculties perceive. The answers proposed by Johnston (1930) are summarized by Olivelle (1996: 385–386).

Posture and breath control

Chapter 2 of the *Śvetāśvatara Upaniṣad* is the one most clearly concerned with yoga. It begins with a series of stanzas (SU 2.1–2.7) which occur also in the *Taittirīya Saṃhitā* of the Black Yajurveda, and in SB 6.3.1.12–17. Vedic echoes are characteristic of this Upaniṣad; but these stanzas are taken out of their ritual context, and re-used as an evocation of yoga. Each of the first five begins with a form of the verb *yuj*, and the first four speak of yoking or controlling the mind. Mind appears again in SU 2.6, and is said to be born where wood is rubbed on wood to make fire – a ritual practice which we will return to in the next section. Passing over the very obscure stanza SU 2.7 (perhaps about ensuring a good future existence through ritual gifts), we come to a condensed but recognizable account of yoga practice, probably the earliest (SU 2.8–15); it has features in common with BhG 6.10–13 (below, pp. 211–212).

A place should be chosen sheltered from the wind, even or level (*sama*, a recurrent word in yoga), agreeable to the mind, not hurtful to the sight, with silent water (SU 2.10; compare BhG 6.11). There he should keep his body straight or balanced (*sama* again), with the torso, neck, and head upright (it just says "with three upright," playing the same numbers game as SU 1.4–5, but BhG 6.13 solves the riddle). Using the mind, he should place his faculties in his heart – not just control them as in KU 3.3–9, but withdraw them from their objects. BhG 2.58 compares this to a tortoise withdrawing its limbs; similarly KU 4.1 says that whereas we usually look outwards, through holes bored by the creator, the wise man seeking immortality turns his sight inwards to the self. As well as posture, this passage mentions breath control (SU 2.9), an important yogic exercise mentioned also in BhG 5.27. Breaths (*prāṇa*) in the plural (SU 2.9a) means the bodily functions (Roebuck 2003: 300), or the faculties; but breath in the singular (SU 2.9b) means breath. In this stanza *yuj* occurs again, twice: the yogi's activities are to be harnessed, controlled (Roebuck 2003: 300), or curbed (Olivelle 1996: 256) (*yuj*), perhaps stopped altogether; and he should hold his mind like a vehicle yoked (*yuj*) to bad horses.

The *Maitrī Upaniṣad* lists breath control (*prāṇāyāma*), withdrawal (*pratyāhāra*), meditation (*dhyāṇa*), fixed attention (*dhāraṇā*), reasoning (*tarka*), concentration (*samādhi*), and says they are called the six-limbed yoga. In Patañjali, the list is expanded to eight; reasoning is omitted, but control (*yama*), restraint (*niyama*), and posture (*āsana*) are added, making an eight-limbed yoga (*Yogasūtra* 2.29; Whicher 1998: 21, 190–199; translations of these terms vary). *Aṣṭāṅgayoga* "eight-limbed yoga" has become synonym for classical yoga, or for the part of it taught in *Yogasūtra* 2.28–3.8 (De Michaelis 2004: 151 n.3). The *Maitrī Upaniṣad* shows a more developed form of early yoga than the other classical Upaniṣads, closer to classical yoga.

Repetition and one-pointedness

The *Śvetāśvatara Upaniṣad* speaks of yoga as a fire; the yogi reaches a state in which his body comes to consist of the fire of yoga (SU 2.12d). Fire is essential to Vedic ritual. It is lit either by a fire-drill, using a cord to twirl a stick against a slab of wood till the friction makes it burn (Macdonell and Keith 1912: vol. 2, pp. 511–512), or by taking embers from an existing fire. The fire-drill is mentioned in SU 2.6, as leading to the birth of mind (above, p. 182). SU 1.13–14 is clearer: Meditation, like the twirling of the stick, must be carried on repetitively until one sees God. Underlying this metaphor is the common ancient Indian idea that fire is already latent in the wood, but has to be brought out by the friction. In the same way, both the Ātman and God are within our body, but are hidden until they are made visible to us by persistent meditation using the sacred syllable *oṃ*.

The syllable *oṃ* is the subject of another metaphor in MU 2.2.3–4, based on archery. The syllable is the bow, the arrow is the Ātman, sharpened by *upāsana* (above, p. 137) – perhaps by identifying the Ātman with Brahman; the target is Brahman. When the arrow strikes the target, it will become one with it – literally, it will become "made of it" (*tanmaya*, MU 2.2.4d). In the case of the Ātman this would mean that it will be no other than Brahman; in the case of the arrow, it will not be "made of" the target, but perhaps sunk into it so firmly that it cannot be pulled out. In another version of this metaphor, the body is the bow, *oṃ* is the arrow, and the mind is its point (MtU 6.24); the same passage goes on to speak of the one-pointed mind (MtU 6.27). The *Bhagavadgītā*'s description of yoga includes making the mind one-pointed (*ekāgra*, BhG 6.12); and one-pointedness became a key word in classical yoga, associated with the practice of fixed attention (*dhāraṇā*) (*Yogasūtra* 3.11–12). The idea of one-pointedness is implicit in the image of a single body of water, contrasted with water running in many mountain streams (KU 4.14–15), though this is not a yoga passage.

The rewards of yoga

The passage on yoga in the *Śvetāśvatara Upaniṣad* describes the results of yogic practice. The yogi experiences visions, which are preliminary to the manifestation of Brahman (SU 2.11); he is free from sickness, old age, and death (SU 2.12), and his body is light, with a clear color, a pleasant voice, a pleasant smell, and reduced excretions (SU 2.13). Lightness in modern yoga would refer to slimming, but in classical yoga it is the ability to levitate, one of the powers called *siddhi* "achievement" (*Yogasūtra-bhāṣya* 3.45). These physical signs are also preliminary: they are the first progress of yoga (SU

2.13d). The real goal is described in the next two stanzas. The yogi sees the Ātman as it truly is, like a bedaubed mirror that has been cleaned (SU 2.14); the Ātman is by nature self-revealing, and is only hidden by our entanglement with the world, from which the yogi has withdrawn. As if to remind us of the difference between the self and God which is a theme of this Upaniṣad (above, pp. 166–168), the next stanza reprises the quasi-refrain: The self is not the ultimate, but is like a lamp by which disciplined man (*yuj* again) sees the unchanging unborn one, untainted by phenomena; he knows God, and is released from all nooses (SU 2.15). Most translators ignore the "but" (*tu*; Roebuck 2003: 301) which contrasts this stanza with the previous one; but this contrast is important, as the stanza reasserts the theism which may have been overlooked in discussing yoga.

The Upaniṣads and the origin of yoga

Yoga is so widespread and ancient in South Asia, appearing in Buddhist and Jain as well as brahminical traditions, that it would be unwarranted to say it started with the Upaniṣads; that would be to confuse the first existence of an idea or practice with its first mention in the literature that has come down to us. All we can say is that these are the earliest texts in which we find yoga mentioned or recognizably described. While the early yoga represented by these texts is not the same as the yoga systematized by Patañjali, it is clearly related to it. Between these two lie the yoga passages in the *Mahābhārata*, including the *Bhagavadgītā*; these texts and their relation to the Upaniṣads are the subject of the next two chapters.

References

Cohen, Signe. 2008. *Text and Authority in the Older Upaniṣads*. Leiden: Brill.

De Michaelis, Elizabeth. 2004. *A History of Modern Yoga: Patañjali and Western Esotericism*. London: Continuum.

Edgerton, F. 1924. "The Meaning of Sāṃkhya and Yoga" *American Journal of Philology* 45: 1–46.

Edgerton, F. 1952. *The Bhagavadgītā: Translated and Interpreted*. Cambridge, MA: Harvard University Press.

Gonda, Jan. 1977. "Notes on the Kaṭha Upaniṣad" in S. K. Chatterji (ed.) *Some Aspects of Indo-Iranian Literary and Cultural Traditions* (V. G. Paranjpe Commemoration Volume). Delhi: Ajanta, 60–70.

Johnston, E. H. 1930. "Some Sāṃkhya and Yoga Conceptions of the Śvetāśvatara Upaniṣad" *Journal of the Royal Asiatic Society* 1930: 855–878.

Killingley, Dermot. 2006. "Faculties, Breaths and Orifices: Some Vedic and Sāṃkhya Notions of the Body and Personality" in Anna S. King (ed.) *Indian Religions: Renaissance and Renewal*. London: Equinox, 73–108.

Killingley, Dermot. 2014. "Manufacturing Yogis: Swami Vivekananda as a Yoga Teacher" in Mark Singleton and Ellen Goldberg (eds) *Gurus of Modern Yoga*. New York: Oxford University Press, 17–37.

Macdonell, A. A., and A. B. Keith, 1912. *Vedic Index of Names and Subjects*. 2 vols. London: John Murray. (Reprint Delhi: Motilal Banarsidass, 1958.)
Olivelle, Patrick. 1996. *Upaniṣads: Translated from the Original Sanskrit* (World's Classics series). Oxford: Oxford University Press.
Roebuck, Valerie. 2003. *The Upaniṣads. Translated and Edited* (Penguin Classics series). London: Penguin.
Van Buitenen, J. A. B. 1957. "Studies in Sāṃkhya (III)" *Journal of the American Oriental Society* 77: 88–107.
Whicher, Ian. 1998. *The Integrity of the Yoga Darśana: A Reconsideration of Classical Yoga*. Albany, NY: State University of New York Press.

Further reading

Flood, Gavin. 1996. *An Introduction to Hinduism*. Cambridge: Cambridge University Press, 75–102.
Killingley, Dermot. 2006. "Faculties, Breaths and Orifices: Some Vedic and Sāṃkhya Notions of the Body and Personality" in Anna S. King (ed.) *Indian Religions: Renaissance and Renewal*. London: Equinox, 73–108.
Whicher, Ian. 1998. *The Integrity of the Yoga Darśana: A Reconsideration of Classical Yoga*. Albany, NY: State University of New York Press.

18 The Upaniṣads and the *Mahābhārata*

Brian Black

Many well-known characters from the Upaniṣads also appear in India's great Sanskrit epic, the *Mahābhārata*. Additionally, strands of Upaniṣadic thought are interwoven throughout the narrative of the *Mahābhārata*. This chapter examines the intriguing connections between the Upaniṣads and the epic poem. Although we cannot assume that our concept of the "Upaniṣads" – as a specific set of texts – maps directly onto to what the word *upaniṣad* means in the *Mahābhārata*, on several occasions the Upaniṣads are identified as texts that are closely related to the Vedas (for example, see 1.2.235; 1.58.17; 3.97.23; 3.197.2; 12.224.7; 12.322.51). There is also a tendency for characters, ideas, and narrative motifs that we associate with the Upaniṣads to appear together in the *Mahābhārata*. Moreover, there are several indications that the epic quoted from the Upaniṣads directly. Edward Washburn Hopkins – citing Adolf Holtzmann, Jr. – has shown that some specific passages in the *Mahābhārata* are from the *Kaṭha*, *Śvetāśvatara*, and *Maitrī Upaniṣad*s ([1901] 1993: 27–46). As Nicholas Sutton sums up: "It is reasonable to conclude that the authors of the *Mahābhārata* were aware of the *Upaniṣads* as a body of literature teaching *mokṣa-dharma*, and that the authors of certain passages had detailed knowledge of individual *Upaniṣads*" (2000: 20).

Building on the assumption that the composers and compilers of the *Mahābhārata* were aware of the Upaniṣads, this chapter will examine how the Upaniṣads are represented in the epic and how their representation might add to our understanding of the *Mahābhārata* more generally. As a way of exploring these issues, we will discuss several literary characters (see Black and Geen 2011; Appleton 2017) who first appear in the late Brāhmaṇas and early Upaniṣads, looking at how their portrayals are developed in the *Mahābhārata* and what this might indicate about the relationship between the two textual traditions. First we'll meet Śaunaka, who, in a dialogue with Yudhiṣṭhira, delivers a number of teachings that are characteristic of the Upaniṣads. The second character is Uddālaka Āruṇi, who features in a number of episodes in the *Mahābhārata* containing themes reminiscent of narratives in which he appears in the Upaniṣads. Next, we'll meet Yājñavalkya, whose dialogue with Janaka expands on their interactions in the Upaniṣads and portrays the *Mahābhārata*'s own textual transmission in relation to the Upaniṣads and the Vedas. The fourth character, King Janaka, interacts with each of the three others, displaying a wide variation in how he is depicted. As we will see, Janaka plays an integral role in Bhīṣma's instruction after the war, as Yudhiṣṭhira decides whether to renounce or take the throne. Taken together, the portraits of these characters in the *Mahābhārata* not only extend from their depictions in the Upaniṣads, but each character contributes to some central themes within the epic itself, including the *Mahābharata*'s self-descriptions as an *upaniṣad* and as the fifth Veda (see Fitzgerald 1991).

Śaunaka

As one of the primary listeners to Ugraśravas' narration in the text's outer frame dialogue, Śaunaka (see Patton 2011) is the character from the Upaniṣads who, arguably, plays the most important role in the *Mahābhārata*. However, because there are several characters in the Upaniṣads with the family name Śaunaka, it is not clear which of these, if any, is the one who listens to Ugraśravas' narration in the Naimiṣa forest (see Black forthcoming). It is also not clear if the Śaunaka who appears in the outer frame dialogue is the same one who appears in other places in the *Mahābhārata*. Despite these uncertainties, there is a dialogue in the *Āraṇyaka Parvan* between a brahmin named Śaunaka and Yudhiṣṭhira that brings up a number of teachings that are reminiscent of doctrines in the Upaniṣads.

This dialogue appears soon after the Pāṇḍavas have begun their twelve years in forest exile after the ill-fated dicing match. After they plead with a group of brahmins not to follow them into the forest, a wise brahmin named Śaunaka steps forward to deliver Yudhiṣṭhira a teaching (3.2.14–79). Śaunaka is described as delighting in the self (adhyātman), one of the central teachings of the Upaniṣads, while much of his discourse is about *sāṃkhya* and *yoga*, two terms that first gain a philosophical usage in the Upaniṣads and that the *Mahābhārata* sometimes associates with other personalities from late Vedic literature, such as Yājñavalkya and Janaka.

Śaunaka begins his instruction to Yudhiṣṭhira by recounting a teaching about the self (ātman) that he ascribes to a king named Janaka (3.2.19), the character from the Upaniṣads who appears the most in the *Mahābhārata*. But whereas in late Vedic literature Janaka is likely to be a single individual, in the *Mahābhārata* he is more of a composite character, whose name seems to refer to a number of kings from Videha, rather than to a unique individual. Here he is quoted as a teacher, yet on most occasions kings named Janaka take on the role of a student, participating in a dialogue with brahmin teachers linked to specific lineages, such as the Vedas (Vasiṣṭha 12.291–296; a *ṛṣi* of the Bhṛgu lineage 12.310), Upaniṣads (Yājñavalkya 12.298–306), Sāṃkhya (Pañcaśikha 12.307), or the *Mahābhārata* (Parāśara 12.279–287). Here, Janaka's teaching is focused on renunciation, urging detachment from friends and wealth. Śaunaka's choice to share this particular teaching of Janaka's seems well timed, considering that the Pāṇḍavas have just lost all their material possessions. Śaunaka, however, is one of the few teachers of the Pāṇḍavas to advocate renunciation; other advisors – particularly Kṛṣṇa and Bhīṣma – are far more likely to instruct fulfilling their *rājādharma*. We will return to Janaka's own complex connection with renunciation towards the end of this chapter.

Shortly after recounting Janaka's teaching, Śaunaka instructs Yudhiṣṭhira on how to discipline his desires, comparing a man controlling his senses to a charioteer controlling horses – an analogy that appears in the *Kaṭha Upaniṣad* (3.3–13) and in the *Śvetāśvatara Upaniṣad* (2.9), in two of the first known discussions about *yoga*. As Hopkins has commented, this analogy – which also appears in Buddhist literature such as the *Dhammapada* (222) and the *Milindapañha* (2.1.1) – is "too general to have any bearing on the relation of the epic to the Upanishad" ([1901] 1993: 35). However, Śaunaka makes another reference to a well-known teaching from the Upaniṣads. When discussing *karma* and rebirth, he describes two paths: the "ancestors' journey" and the "divine journey" – a teaching reminiscent of King Pravāhaṇa Jaivali's discourse on the two paths of the dead, which appears in both the *Bṛhadāraṇyaka* (6.2) and *Chāndogya Upaniṣads* (5.3–10), and which is often considered to be one of the first explanations about the process of rebirth. Similarly, in the *Śānti Parvan*, Yudhisthira mentions "two famous paths, the way of the fathers and the way of the Gods" (12.17.14, tr. Fitzgerald), a teaching that he attributes to King Janaka. There are also several other passages in the *Mahābhārata* on *karma* and rebirth that resonate with teachings and images in the Upaniṣads, such as the *Uttarayāyāta* section in the *Ādi Parvan* and the *Sanatsujāta* section of the *Udyoga Parvan*, which have been discussed in terms of their "Upaniṣadic intent" by Peter Hill (2001: 5–9, 37–39). Although the two paths, like the chariot, is also a recurring analogy that is not necessarily referring to the Upaniṣads, the inclusion of both these analogies in the same teaching contributes to the Upaniṣadic flavor of this scene.

Taken together, there are a number of ways in which this dialogue between Śaunaka and Yudhiṣṭhira engages with aspects of the Upaniṣads. Śaunaka's teaching is one of many examples where doctrines associated with the Upaniṣads – such as *ātman*, karma, *sāṃkhya*, *yoga*, or renunciation – are discussed and sometimes further developed in the *Mahābhārata* (for a discussion of these and other Upaniṣadic ideas in the *Mahābhārata*, see Brockington 1998; Sutton 2000; Hill 2001). Śaunaka – whether or not he is based specifically on one of the many characters in the Brāhmaṇas and Upaniṣads with the same patronym – assumes the role of an Upaniṣadic teacher; he is portrayed as delighting in the self, teaching about *yoga* and *sāṃkhya*, quoting King Janaka, and invoking the analogies of the chariot and the two paths of the dead. If this scene's characterization of Śaunaka is as an "Upaniṣadic teacher," then this might also inform how we understand the Śaunaka listening to Ugraśravas' narration in the outer frame dialogue. Although it is not entirely clear whether this is the same Śaunaka, there are parallels between them, particularly as in both cases Śaunaka is the only named speaker in a group of *ṛṣi*s or brahmins in the forest. If we see them as connected, then, we might see his role as a primary listener of the text as representing an "Upaniṣadic teacher," thus enacting the claim that the *Mahābhārata* is an *upaniṣad*. As Ugraśravas says to the *ṛṣi*s of the Naimiṣa Forest before Śaunaka arrives: "In this book Kṛṣṇa Dvaipāyana has uttered a holy Upaniṣad" (*upaniṣadaṁ puṇyāṁ*, 1.1.191, tr. van Buitenen).

Uddālaka Āruṇi

Our next character is Uddālaka Āruṇi, who maintains his literary personality from the Upaniṣads as the wise but flawed teacher. Another recurring aspect of his character is that he often appears with his son, who has not been taught properly and needs to seek out other teachers to become truly knowledgeable. In the *Anuśāsana Parvan* (13.70), Uddālaka Āruṇi appears in a narrative about an encounter between a young brahmin and Yama, the god of death. As Bhīṣma recounts to Yudhiṣṭhira, the father Uddālaki curses his son Nāciketa, who subsequently goes to the underworld, where he has a long dialogue with Yama, during which he is granted three wishes. Although Uddālaka Āruṇi is here known as Uddālaki, while Nāciketa has a slightly different spelling from the Naciketas in late Vedic literature, these are the same characters that appear in the Upaniṣads (see Cohen 2008: 196) and this narrative is clearly based on earlier versions from the *Kaṭha Upaniṣad* and the *Taittirīya Brāhmaṇa* (3.11.8; see DeVries 1987).

Bhīṣma tells the story of Uddālaki and Nāciketa in the context of a cluster of several narratives he recounts to Yudhiṣṭhira on the topic of making gifts of cows. This narrative also appears as one in a group of three stories to feature dialogues with Yama (see 13.67 and 13.69). At the beginning of this episode, Uddālaki approaches his son before performing a sacrifice, asking him to retrieve some ritual utensils that he had left by the riverside. Nāciketa finds that the utensils have been washed away by the river, but when he tells his father, Uddālaki is overcome by a fit of anger and curses his son to death, after which Nāciketa falls to the ground and dies. Seeing his son prostate on the ground, Uddālaki is consumed with grief for the remainder of the day and into the evening, until finally Nāciketa – drenched in the tears of his father – begins to return to life. Subsequently, Uddālaki, asks his son what has happened, prompting Nāciketa to recount his encounter with Yama. Unlike in the *Kaṭha Upaniṣad*, where Naciketas has to wait for Yama for three days and three nights without any food, here Yama approaches the boy as soon as he sees him and instructs his attendants to provide the appropriate offerings for a guest. At this point, Yama assures the boy that he is not really dead, but has only been allowed to come to the afterworld so as not to render his father's curse untrue.

Before sending him back to life, Yama allows Nāciketa to ask three questions. First, he asks to see the heavenly worlds. In response, Yama gives him a personal tour, which Nāciketa later describes to his father as comprising of pleasure grounds, jeweled palaces, rivers of milk, and hills of ghee. Nāciketa's next question is to know who can enjoy the heavenly worlds, with Yama responding with a long discourse on the rewards earned by those who give cows. At this point, Yama instructs that one should give cows to a brahmin after abstaining from all foods and living upon water alone for three nights and sleeping on the bare earth. Here we see that although Bhīṣma's version does not portray Nāciketas as waiting for three nights without food in Yama's abode, the three nights without food are included as part of Yama's teaching. Finally, for his third question, Nāciketa asks what gifts can be given in place of cows. Yama explains that one can attain the same merits as giving a cow through substitutions such as ghee, sesame seeds, or water. When Nāciketa returns from Yama's world, he tells his father that he has attained a great sacrifice, the performance of which does not require wealth.

Bhīṣma's narrative clearly seems to be a reworking of the Naciketas and Yama dialogue from the Brāhmaṇas and Upaniṣads. Both accounts begin with a father cursing his son to death, while in both the boy has a long dialogue with Yama in the underworld, which serves as a frame narrative for a teaching. In the *Kaṭha Upaniṣad* the teaching is about the immortality of the self and *yoga*, while in the *Anuśāsana Parvan* it is about giving cows. At first it may seem surprising that the most crucial detail from the *Kaṭha Upaniṣad* linking this narrative to this particular section of the *Anuśāsana Parvan* is actually omitted from Bhīṣma's version: the giving of the cows. However, this makes sense in the context of the different teachings in each narrative. Whereas the *Kaṭha Upaniṣad* is critical of Vedic rituals and offers the teaching of the self as a superior practice, the *Anuśāsana Parvan* version is part of a series of teachings about the importance of giving to brahmins, often in the context of a Vedic ritual. Rather than criticizing Uddālaki for being a stingy ritualist, Bhīṣma's teaching offers a cheap substitute for cows, without losing merit. Ironically, then, Bhīṣma takes a story that is critical of not giving one's most well fed cows and offers a teaching that says one need not give away cows at all. Seen in this way, not only does the narrative have the same characters and narrative structure as in the Upaniṣads, but the rhetorical force of the story hinges on a familiarity with the earlier version.

In our next scene, Uddālaka Āruṇi features with his son Śvetaketu – the son with whom he appears together in a number of short narratives in the Brāhmaṇas and Upaniṣads (see Olivelle 1999; Black 2007, 2011, and Cohen 2008). In the *Ādi Parvan*, the father and son appear together in a story recounted by Pāṇḍu to Kuntī, when explaining the origins of marriage. According to Pāṇḍu, the *dharma* prescribing wives to remain faithful to their husbands was initiated by Śvetaketu, who became enraged when he saw his mother have sex with another man. Although Uddālaka Āruṇi pleads with his son not to be angry, Śvetaketu is not calmed by his father's words and instead pronounces the law of marital fidelity for women. This narrative does not appear to be based on any specific episode in the Brāhmaṇas or Upaniṣads, yet the depiction of Śvetaketu – in which he acts rashly and does not listen to his father – is similar to the "proud and impetuous" young brahmin in late Vedic literature, described by Patrick Olivelle as the Vedic "spoiled brat" (1999: 67). Whereas in the previous narrative it was the father who lost his temper, here it is the son who is too quick to anger, perhaps indicating that he has not been taught properly.

Another episode where Uddālaka Āruṇi and Śvetaketu are together is in the *Āraṇyaka Parvan* (3.132–134), in a narrative that also includes King Janaka. The main character here, however, is Aṣṭāvakra, who is Śvetaketu's nephew. At the beginning of the story we meet Kahoḍa, a student of Uddālaka Āruṇi, who impresses his teacher so much that he is offered his daughter Sujātā's hand in marriage. Together Sujātā and Kahoḍa have a son, named Aṣṭāvakra, who is so advanced in learning that he corrects his father's studies while he is still in the womb. Angered by this criticism, Kahoḍa curses his son to be born with eight (*aṣṭa*) of his limbs crooked (*vakra*) – hence the name Aṣṭāvakra. Similar to Śvetaketu in the previous narrative, here Uddālaka Āruṇi's student Kahoḍa is portrayed as acting rashly in a fit of anger, perhaps indicating he is not as learned as he should be.

When the family is later short of money, Kahoḍa goes to King Janaka, in whose court he loses a debate to the *sūta* Bandin, who has also defeated various other brahmins. After losing the debate, Kahoḍa is drowned in the sea, like all the other defeated brahmins. Uddālaka instructs that the truth should remain hidden from Aṣṭāvakra. Consequently, for twelve years Aṣṭāvakra grows up thinking Uddālaka is his father and Śvetaketu his brother, until Śvetaketu – "true to form," as Olivelle points out (1999: 68) – becomes jealous and tells him the truth. Subsequently, Aṣṭāvakra goes to the court of King Janaka to avenge his father's death. Aṣṭāvakra then faces Bandin in a debate in which he defeats the *sūta*, thus bringing his father, as well as all the other defeated brahmins, back to life.

Although Uddālaka Āruṇi, Śvetaketu, and Janaka all play supporting roles in this story and the tale does not seem directly related to any episode from earlier sources, some themes are reminiscent of the early Upaniṣads. The verbal contests in which Bandin defeats various brahmins in Janaka's assembly, for example, evoke the famous *brahmodya* in Janaka's assembly in the *Bṛhadāraṇyaka Upaniṣad* where Yājñavalkya defeats eight brahmins from Kuru-Pañcāla – one of whom is Uddālaka Āruṇi – with the final challenger's head bursting apart because he cannot answer Yājñavalkya's question (see Black 2007: 67–88; Lindquist 2011). Both scenes portray a public debate in Janaka's assembly in which losers pay with their lives. We might also compare Aṣṭāvakra's victory over Bandin to the *Kaṭha Upaniṣad* version of the dialogue between Naciketas and Yama. Whereas Naciketas returns himself from death by asking Yama a number of questions, here another student of Uddālaka returns a number of brahmins from death by proving himself in an exchange of riddles. Other episodes in the *Mahābhārata* with related themes include Sāvitrī saving her husband from Yama through a series of cunning questions (3.281) and Yudhiṣṭhira saving his brothers from death by answering a series of riddles posed by a *yakṣa* (3.297). Incidentally, another connection between the Astāvakra story and Yudhiṣṭhira's exchange with the Yakṣa is that one of the riddles is the same: "What does not close its eye when asleep? What does not stir when it is born? What does grow under pressure?" (3.133.25 and 3.297.42, tr. van Buitenen).

At the end of the narrative, Kahoḍa addresses Janaka: "My son has done what I was unable to do. To the weak has been born a strong son, to the foolish a learned son, to the ignorant a wise son" (3.134.33–34, tr. van Buitenen). These words relate this episode to other scenes with Uddālaka Āruṇi, many of which explore the recurring theme of underlying tensions and rivalries between fathers and sons, or between teachers and student.

In addition to scenes where he appears together with Śvetaketu, Uddālaka Āruṇi also features in the *Ādi Parvan* as one of three students who are tested by their teacher Dhaumya. Uddālaka is asked by his teacher to go and repair a breach in a dam, but when he is unable to fix it, he lays down to block the water himself. Later when he hears his teacher calling for him, Uddālaka immediately gets up, which leads to the water flowing again. Uddālaka explains to his teacher that he only got up because he was called. His teacher responds that because he broke open the dam, he shall be known as Uddālaka, which means "Puller-of-the-Stop," but because he has obeyed his teacher he will reach the highest good, with all the Vedas and the *dharma śāstra*s becoming clear to him.

This short episode seems to be a prequel to the narratives about Uddālaka Āruṇi in the Brāhmaṇas and Upaniṣads. Uddālaka is referred to as "Āruṇi of Pāñcāla" (1.3.20; 1.3.21; 1.3.24; 1.327), a place he is associated with in the *Bṛhadāraṇyaka Upaniṣad*. In addition to explaining how he got his name, this story depicts Uddālaka as a tenacious and obedient student – qualities that might be said to inform retrospectively his characterizations in the Upaniṣads as a teacher devoted to learning and humble about his own knowledge. Also, this depiction of him as an obedient student stands in stark contrast to the tales of his own student and son Śvetakeu, who tends not to follow his father's advice. This story also highlights another aspect of Uddālaka's character that is present, but not as explicit, in other contexts: his connection with the Vedic tradition. As we've seen, the reward Uddālaka earns for his obedience is knowledge of the Vedas. Another link with the Vedic tradition in this episode is that one of the two students he studies with is named Veda. In the Nāciketa story, Uddālaki forgets his ritual utensils by the riverside because he is so engaged in his recitation of the Vedas. In the episode explaining the law of female fidelity, Uddālaka is characterized as knowing the eternal law, while in the Aṣṭāvakra story his son and nephew are described as knowers of *brahman*. Despite the fact his learning is sometimes depicted as incomplete, he is characterized as having a connection with the Vedas and traditional knowledge more generally.

In the few scenes in which they appear in the *Mahābhārata*, Uddālaka Āruṇi and Śvetaketu are recognizably the same characters as they are in the

Upaniṣads, with the fact that they often feature together giving them an added sense of continuity. Uddālaka Āruṇi remains the complexly drawn learned brahmin, who is associated with the Vedas, but whose knowledge or teaching is flawed in one way or another; Śvetaketu continues to be depicted as arrogant and quick to anger, and still fails to follow the instructions of his father. Neither character plays a particularly significant role in the main story, but the themes explored in their narratives resonate with the *Mahābhārata*'s many other instances of strained relations between fathers and sons, as well as between teachers and students. Indeed, we might see the roles that Uddālaka Āruṇi and Śvetaketu play in the Aṣṭāvakra story as a metaphor for the roles of characters from the Upaniṣads in the *Mahābhārata* more generally – while not the main characters themselves, they often have intriguing connections to the main characters, giving them greater depth and often connecting them to the Vedic tradition.

Yājñavalkya

Considering his elevated status in the *Śatapatha Brāhmaṇa* and *Bṛhadāraṇyaka Upaniṣad*, it might seem initially surprising to learn that Yājñavalkya (see Lindquist forthcoming; Black 2007; Black and Geen 2011) appears only six times in the *Mahābhārata* and in only one dialogue. Despite featuring rarely, he makes some important contributions to the text: Yājñavalkya plays the vital role of acting as the *adhvaryu* priest – the main ritual actor – at both Yudhiṣṭhira's *rājasūya* (2.30.35) and *aśvamedha* (14.71.3), while in his one dialogue he is linked with the *Mahābhārata*'s representations of its own textual lineages.

His dialogue with Janaka Daivarāti (12.298–306) – his only speaking part in the *Mahābhārata* – is part of a cluster of seven dialogues featuring the King of Videha that Bhīṣma recounts to Yudhiṣṭhira in the *Mokṣadharma* section of the *Śānti Parvan*. Yājñavalkya's teaching covers a range of topics, including a long discourse about *sāṃkhya* and *yoga*. Throughout, Yājñavalkya is repeatedly depicted in ways that link him to the Brāhmaṇas and Upaniṣads. Most explicitly, he is characterized as conveying (√*praṇi*, 12.306.11) and making (√*kṛ*, 12.306.16; 12.306.23) the *Śatapaṭha Brāhmaṇa*. Also, the word *upaniṣad* is used on two occasions in this dialogue: once when he claims to churn (√*math*, 12.306.33) the *upaniṣads* with his mind when answering a series of riddles posed by a *gandharva*. The other appearance of this word comes at the end of the dialogue, when the entire exchange between Yājñavalkya and Janaka is likened to an *upaniṣad* (12.306.108).

In addition to characterizing his teaching as an *upaniṣad*, this dialogue further develops Yājñavalkya's place within a lineage of teachers, tracing his knowledge to the god of the Sun (see Lindquist forthcoming). In comparison with the end of Book Six of the *Bṛhadāraṇyaka Upaniṣad* – where Yājñavalkya is part of an extensive lineage of the *White Yajurveda* descended from the Sun god Āditya, in the *Mokṣadharma*, rather than having several generations of teachers before him –Yājñavalkya learns directly from the Sun god Sūrya. Moreover, expanding on his portrayal in the *Bṛhadāraṇyaka Upaniṣad*, Yājñavalkya is not only credited with learning the *yajus* verses, but with learning all of the Vedas, the entire *Śatapatha Brāhmaṇa*, other texts, and knowing about *sāṃkhya* and *yoga*.

There are also several literary details reminiscent of scenes in which Yājñavalkya appears in the *Bṛhadāraṇyaka Upaniṣad*, such as the motif of someone entering another's body. In the *brahmodya* in the *Bṛhadāraṇyaka Upaniṣad*, Yājñavalkya debates with two brahmins from Kuru-Pañcāla, both of whom had learned their teachings from women who had been possessed by *gandharva*s (BU 3.3 and 3.7; see Black 2007: 156–158; Lindquist 2008). In both cases, the teachings of the *gandharva*s are ventriloquized through female characters and then recounted in Janaka's assembly. In this dialogue, when Yājñavalkya claims that he has learned everything from Sūrya, he explains that the god of the Sun had imparted the *yajus* formulae into him by having Sarasvatī enter into his body through his mouth. Although Sarsvatī, as the goddess of knowledge, might on some occasions be portrayed rather abstractly, here her entering Yājñavalkya's body is more than merely allegorical. When recounting the episode to Janaka, Yājñavalkya describes how being inhabited by the goddess made him burn inside, causing him so much pain that he plunged himself into water. Interestingly, Yājñavalkya refers to Sarasvatī two more times in this narrative: once when, after thinking of the goddess, he teaches a hundred good students; the second time when, after thinking of Sarasvatī, he answers the riddles posed by the *gandharva*. Yājñavalkya identifies Sarasvatī as the essence of speech, describing her as adorned with vowels and consonants (12.306.14), thus suggesting that when he teaches his own students and responds to the *gandarva* he is not merely drawing on knowledge that he had learned, but that the exact words of Sarasvatī – who reappears in his mind each time – are ventriloquized through him. Moreover, similar to the *gandharva*s in the *Bṛhadāraṇyaka Upaniṣad*, a *gandharva* also figures prominently in this dialogue in the *Śānti Parvan*. After receiving his instructions from Sūrya and after his body is inhabited by Sarasvatī, Yājñavalkya has an encounter with the *gandharva* Viśvāvasu during which he is asked twenty-five questions – another detail that has interesting parallels with the *brahmodya* in the *Bṛhadāraṇyaka Upaniṣad*, where Yājñavalkya proves his superiority over other brahmins through his ability to answer a number of riddle-like questions.

In addition to gesturing back to the episodes featuring *gandharva*s in the *Bṛhadāraṇyaka Upaniṣad*, the episode with Sarasvatī also seems to foreshadow a subsequent dialogue in this section of the *Mokṣadharma*, in which the female sage Sulabhā (12.308; see Fitzgerald 2002; Vanita 2003; Dhand 2007, and Black 2015) uses her yogic powers to enter Janaka's body. His interaction with Sarasvatī also builds on Yājñavalkya's character portrait in the Upaniṣads as one of the few male sages to converse with women about religion and philosophy. In addition to his well-known encounter with Gārgī during the *brahmodya* in Janaka's court (BU 3.6 and 3.8), he also has a philosophical conversation with his wife Maitreyī, which appears twice in the *Bṛhādāraṇyaka Upaniṣad* (2.4 and 4.5). We might see Sarasvatī entering his body as another example of his discourses with women.

At the end of the dialogue there seems to be yet another reference to the *brahmodya* in the *Bṛhadāraṇyaka Upaniṣad*, when we learn that after hearing Yājñavalkya's teaching, Janaka gives away a million cows and gold to brahmins – a detail that recalls the thousands of cows and gold claimed by Yājñavalkya before the *brahmodya* (BU 3.1). But rather than emphasizing Yājñavalkya's cheekiness for claiming the prize before the competition and the vast rewards available for rhetorically skilled philosophers, here Janaka gives the cows and gold after their dialogue, with his extreme generosity an indication of his level of detachment. The dialogue ends with Janaka gaining wisdom, abdicating the throne, installing his son, and becoming a renouncer.

Despite becoming a renouncer in this dialogue, Janaka's own connection to renunciation is quite complex. In the *Bṛhadāraṇyaka Upaniṣad* Janaka learns one of the first known teachings on renunciation from Yājñavalkya (4.3–4). Although it is unclear whether Janaka renounces at the end of Yājñavalkya's teaching, his literary persona – as Naomi Appleton points out (2017) – is closely associated with renunciation in later Brahmanical, as well as Buddhist and Jain, literature. In the *Mahābhārata* this association continues, but in a number of contrasting ways. In the discourse recited by Śaunaka that we explored above, Janaka is depicted as a teacher of renunciation, but in a dialogue with his wife, as recounted by Arjuna in the *Śānti Parvan* (12.18), Janaka represents a negative example of renunciation, who inflicts suffering on her and their son when he abandons them. In the *Bhagavad Gītā* (3.20), Kṛṣṇa points to Janaka as an exemplar of *karma yoga*, yet, the female sage Sulabhā later questions Janaka's enlightened status on the basis that he lives as a householder, not as a renouncer (12.308). He is subsequently depicted as a teacher to the most celebrated renouncer in the *Mahābhārata*, Vyāsa's son Śuka (12.312–13), while in the *Anu Gītā* he practices non-attachment while continuing to be king (14.32). Through his wide range of stances towards renunciation, Janaka is one of the main characters through which debates about renunciation are explored. Moreover, Janaka is particularly prominent in the *Mokṣadharma*, with ten of the eleven dialogues in which he appears in the *Mahābhārata* recounted by Bhīṣma to Yudhiṣṭhira in this section of the text. As an embodiment of debates about renunciation, Janaka gives Yudhiṣṭhira a complex conceptual repertoire for thinking through his post-war dilemma of whether to renounce or accept the throne.

In addressing the larger question of the Upaniṣads and the *Mahābhārata* it is notable that the dialogue between Yājñavalkya and Janaka playfully weaves together the textual histories of both. As we have seen, Yājñavalkya is explicitly named as the conveyer or maker of the *Śatapatha Brāhmaṇa* and is cast as an authority on all the Vedas and their supplementary texts. We might suggest that as a facilitator of the *Śatapatha Brāhmaṇa*, Yājñavalkya plays a similar role to Vyāsa, who is credited in the *Mahābhārata* as dividing and distributing the Vedas. Neither is explicitly named as an author of Vedic texts, but both are credited for making the texts available to a wider audience.

In addition to establishing his Vedic credentials, this dialogue highlights his connections to lineages of the *Mahābhārata*. On one occasion Yājñavalkya is linked with the narrator of the *Mahābhārata*'s inner frame. Bhīṣma alludes to a dispute between Yājñavalkya and his maternal uncle over the *dakṣiṇa* at Janaka Daivarāti's father sacrifice. Yājñavalkya claims half the payment for the sacrifice, an arrangement that is agreed to by all the other priests, except for his uncle. Although this dialogue does not disclose the identity of his uncle, according to some Purāṇas (*Brahmāṇḍa Purāṇa* 1.2.35; *Bhāgavata Purāṇa* 12.6.61; *Viṣṇu Purāṇa* 5; see Lindquist forthcoming), he is Vaiśaṃpāyana, one of the five students of Vyāsa and narrator of the *Mahābhārata* at Janamejaya's snake sacrifice. Indeed, the other priests at the sacrifice are named as Sumantu, Paila, and Jaimini – three of Vyāsa's other students. This brief reference to an episode featuring Vyāsa and his students calls to mind the circumstances in which Yājñavalkya participates in Yudhiṣṭhira's two Vedic rituals. In the *Sabhā Parvan*, we learn that Yājñavalkya was specifically chosen for the *rājasūya* by Vyāsa and performed the ritual alongside Paila. Similarly, in the *Āśvamedhika Parvan*, Vyāsa tells Yudhiṣṭhira that he, along with Paila and Yājñavalkya, will perform the *aśvamedha*. Although Yājñavalkya himself is never referred to as a student of Vyāsa, it is interesting that in these scenes he is closely associated with him, as well as with two of his students. Moreover, in this dialogue Bhīṣma also mentions that Yājñavalkya studied the Purāṇas from Lomaharṣaṇa, who we know from the *Ādi Parvan* is the teacher of Ugraśravas, the main narrator of the *Mahābhārata* in the outer frame. Thus, in his exchange with Janaka, Yājñavalkya is linked with the narrators of both frame dialogues of the *Mahābhārata*. The dialogue with Janaka concludes with a brief lineage, recounting that Bhīṣma learned from Janaka, and Janaka from Yājñavalkya, thus placing Yājñavalkya as one of the sources of Bhīṣma's instruction. While we might see Yājñavalkya's connections to the *Mahābhārata*'s representation of its own lineages as part of the more general project of portraying itself as a fifth Veda, the reference to a dispute between Yājñavalkya and Vaiśaṃpāyana alludes to possible tensions in bringing these textual lineages together.

Conclusion

As we can see, there are several characters from the Upaniṣads who retain their literary personalities in the *Mahābhārata*. These examples, as I have argued, not only add to our understanding of how the *Mahābhārata* drew from the Upaniṣads, but also give us an insight into how the *Mahābhārata* characterizes the relationship between the two textual traditions. In the cases of Uddālaka

Āruṇi, Nāciketa, and Śvetaketu, we saw characters who play out some of the same dynamics as they do in earlier literature. Although none of these three have a particularly important role in the *Mahābhārata*, all of them play out recurring themes, while also bringing with them an association with the Vedas and traditional knowledge more generally. In comparison, Janaka makes a more central contribution to the text. Not only is he the character from the Upaniṣads to appear the most in the *Mahābhārata*, but also he is the character most closely aligned with Yudhiṣṭhira's post-war dilemma, which is the primary issue throughout the *Śānti* and *Anuśāsana Parvan*s and one of the central moral problems of the text. Despite appearing far less frequently, Yājñavalkya also plays an important role in the *Mahābhārata*, particularly in contributing to the text's self-description as a fifth Veda. In his dialogue with Janaka he is depicted as a disseminator of Vedic knowledge he imbibed directly from the Sun, as well as being a ritual colleague of Vyāsa, a rival of Vaiśaṃpāyana, and a student of Lomaharṣaṇa. Taking together his Vedic pedigree and interactions with the epic's author and narrators, Yājñavalkya embodies an intersection of lineages of the Vedas and Upaniṣads with lineages of the *Mahābhārata*. Similarly, Śaunaka also plays a key role in the *Mahābhārata*'s representation of itself. Although the specific identity of Śaunaka is unclear, he shares a family name with a number of characters in the Brāhmaṇas and Upaniṣads, while teaching doctrines, quoting teachers, and using analogies often associated with the Upaniṣads. If we see Śaunaka as an "Upaniṣadic character" or at least as a character inspired by the types of characters we meet in the Upaniṣads, then we might see Śaunaka's role in the outer frame dialogue as a demonstration of Ugraśravas' claim that the *Mahābhārata* is an *upaniṣad*. Indeed, his role as a link between the Upaniṣads and *Mahābhārata* continues long after the epic: In the frame dialogue of a post-Vedic text called the *Nāradaparivrājaka Upaniṣad* (ca. 1150 CE) Śaunaka and a group of seers are depicted performing a twelve-year *satra*, when they ask Nārada to teach them about liberation (see Olivelle 1992).

References

Appleton, N. 2017. *Shared Characters in Jain, Buddhist and Hindu Narrative: Gods, Kings, and Other Heroes*. London: Routledge.

Black, B. 2007. *The Character of the Self in Ancient India: Priests, Kings, and Women in the early Upaniṣads*. Albany, NY: State University of New York Press.

Black, B. 2011. "Ambaṭṭha and Śvetaketu: Literary Connections between the Upaniṣads and Early Buddhist Narratives" *Journal of the American Academy of Religion* 79.1: 136–161.

Black, B. 2015. "Dialogue and Difference: Encountering the Other in Indian Religious and Philosophical Sources" in B. Black and L. Patton (eds.) *Dialogue in Early South Asian Religions: Hindu, Buddhist, and Jain Traditions*. Farnham: Ashgate, 243–257.

Black, B. Forthcoming. "Revisiting the Ugraśravas/Śaunaka Frame Dialogue: Transitions and Transmissions in the *Mahābhārata*" in R. Chakravarti and K. Roy (eds.) *Revisiting Transitions in Indian History*. New Delhi: Primus.

Black, B. and Geen, J. 2011. "The Character of 'Character' in Early South Asian Religious Narratives: An Introductory Essay" *Journal of the American Academy of Religion* 79.1: 6–32.

Brockington, J. 1998. *The Sanskrit Epics*. Leiden: Brill.

Cohen, S. 2008. *Text and Authority in the Older Upaniṣads*. Leiden: Brill.

DeVries, L. 1987. "The Father, the Son, and the Ghoulish Host: A Fairy Tale in Early Sanskrit?" *Asian Folklore Studies* 46: 227–256.

Dhand, A. 2007 "Paradigms of the Good in the *Mahābhārata*: Śuka and Sulabhā in Quagmires of Ethics" in S. Brodbeck and B. Black (eds) *Gender and Narrative in the* Mahābhārata. London: Routledge, 258–278.

Fitzgerald, J. L. 1991. "India's Fifth Veda: The *Mahābhārata*'s Presentation of Itself" in A. Sharma (ed.) *Essays in the* Mahābhārata. Leiden: Brill: 150–170.

Fitzgerald, J. L. 2002. "Nun Befuddles King, Shows *karmayoga* does not Work: Sulabhā's Refutation of King Janaka at MBh 12.308" *Journal of Indian Philosophy* 30.6: 641–677.

Hill, P. 2001. *Fate, Predestination and Human Action in the* Mahābhārata*: A Study in the History of Ideas*. New Delhi: Munshiram Manoharlal.

Hopkins, E. W. [1901] 1993. *The Great Epic of India: Character and Origin of the* Mahābhārata. Delhi: Motilal Banarsidass.

Lindquist, S. 2008. "Gender at Janaka's Court: Women in the *Bṛhadāraṇyaka Upaniṣad* Reconsidered" *Journal of Indian Philosophy* 36.3: 405–426.

Lindquist, S. 2011. "Literary Lives and a Literal Death: Yājñavalkya, Śākalya, and an Upaniṣadic Death Sentence" *Journal of the American Academy of Religion* 79.1: 33–57.

Lindquist, S. Forthcoming. *Creating a Sage: The Literary Life of Yājñavalkya*. Albany, NY: State University of New York Press.

Olivelle, P. (trans.) 1992. *Saṃnyāsa Upaniṣads*. New York: Oxford University Press.

Olivelle, P. (ed. and trans.) 1998. *The Early Upaniṣads: Annotated Text and Translation*. New York: Oxford University Press.

Olivelle, P. 1999. "Young Śvetaketu: A Literary Study of an Upaniṣadic Story" *Journal of the American Oriental Society* 119.1: 46–70.

Patton, L. 2011. "Traces of Śaunaka: A Literary Assessment" *Journal of the American Academy of Religion* 79.1: 113–135.

Sukthankar, V. S., et al. (ed.) 1933–1966. *The* Mahābhārata *for the First Time Critically Edited*. Poona, India: Bhandarkar Oriental Research Institute.

Sutton, N. 2000. *Religious Doctrine in the Mahābhārata*. Delhi: Motilal Banarsidass.

Van Buitenen, J. A. B. (trans.) 1973–1978. *The Mahābhārata Books 1–5*. Chicago, IL: Chicago University Press.

Vanita, Ruth 2003. "The Self Is Not Gendered: Sulabha's Debate with King Janaka" *National Women's Studies Association Journal* 15.2: 76–93.

Further reading

Black, Brian 2013. "Draupadī in the *Mahābhārata*" *Religion Compass* 7/5: 169–178.

Black, Brian 2015. "Upanishads" *The Internet Encyclopedia of Philosophy*, ISSN 2161-0002, www.iep.utm.edu/, 28 June 2015. (An introduction to the philosophy of the Upaniṣads).

Brockington, J. 2003. "The Sanskrit Epics" in G. Flood (ed.) *The Blackwell Companion to Hinduism*. Oxford: Blackwell Publishing, 116–128.

Eggeling, J. (trans.) [1882–1897] 1994. *Śatapatha Brāhmaṇa.* Vols. 12, 26, 41, 43, and 44 (5 parts of the Sacred Books of the East). Delhi: Motilal Banarsidass.
Fitzgerald, James 2004. "*Mahābhārata*" in S. Mittal and G. R. Thursby (eds.) *The Hindu World.* London and New York: Routledge, 52–74.
Roebuck, V. (trans.) 2004. *Upaniṣads*. Harmondsworth: Penguin.
Smith, J. (trans.) 2009. *The Mahābhārata: An Abridged Translation*. Harmondsworth: Penguin.

19 The Upaniṣads and the *Bhagavadgītā*

Simon Brodbeck

Overview of the *Bhagavadgītā*

The *Bhagavadgītā* constitutes chapters 23 to 40 of the *Bhīṣmaparvan*, the sixth book of the *Mahābhārata*. Just before the great war of Kurukṣetra, which is fought by the Pāṇḍavas and their cousins the Kauravas (and by various allies on either side) for possession of the ancestral Bhārata kingdom, Arjuna Pāṇḍava, seeing his relatives and teachers arrayed ready to fight against him, imagines the results that killing them will bring, and refuses to fight. Over the course of the text's eighteen chapters, as steered by Arjuna's occasional questions, his chariot-driver and friend Kṛṣṇa Vāsudeva persuades him to take up his weapons once more.

Kṛṣṇa emphasizes the effect that Arjuna's refusal to fight will have upon his reputation; but when this doesn't work, he moves on to philosophical ground. He explains that the soul (*ātman*, *dehin*, *kṣetrajña*, *puruṣa*) is eternal, and that it takes on successive bodies due to the bondage of action; but that if action is performed in a certain manner then no bondage results, and the soul will be released from further embodiment. Kṛṣṇa's proposed manner of acting is explained from various angles: It is acting without attachment to the fruits of the action (the famous so-called *karmayoga*); it is acting in a spirit of sacrifice; it is acting yogically with the senses controlled by *buddhi* (intelligence), not by their objects; it is acting in accordance with knowledge of the soul, and of the psychophysical world within which it is enmeshed, and of the highest God who includes and transcends soul and world, and who is present here in human form as Kṛṣṇa; and hence it is acting in a spirit of devotion (*bhakti*) towards that God. While explaining this manner of acting to Arjuna, Kṛṣṇa presents himself as its perfect exemplar; and he also gives experiential proof of his divinity by granting Arjuna a vision of his universal form, which includes the future deaths of Arjuna's principal adversaries.

The *Bhagavadgītā* has a distinguished place in Indian history, and in global literary history; it has been commented upon by Śaṅkara, Rāmānuja, Gandhi, Aurobindo, and many others, and it has been influential also in Europe and North America. However, in this chapter we are not concerned with its reception history (for an overview of this, see Davis 2014), but only with its relationship to the Upaniṣads.

Bibliographical preliminaries

The relationship between the Upaniṣads and the *Bhagavadgītā* has occupied several previous scholars, and what follows draws heavily upon their work; and so before proceeding further, I provide brief notes on the secondary literature.

There are two basic reference resources. Jacob's *Concordance to the Principal Upaniṣads and Bhagavadgītā* (Jacob 1891) is a list of simple and compound Sanskrit words in Sanskrit alphabetical order, in each case giving the reference, and quoting the phrase, for their every occurrence across a corpus of fifty-five Upaniṣads plus the *Bhagavadgītā*. Haas' "Recurrent and Parallel Passages in the Principal Upanishads and Bhagavad-Gītā" (Haas 1922) covers just thirteen Upaniṣads plus the *Bhagavadgītā*, and is organized differently: Progressing through each text in turn from start to finish (the order is roughly chronological, with the *Bhagavadgītā* placed last), it gives details of all phrases and passages that have significant parallels.

I have found two discursive overviews in English. Devasthali's short essay "Bhagavad-gītā and Upaniṣads" discusses, one by one, "the most prominent and peculiar ideas which are found both in *BG* on the one hand and the Upaniṣads on the other" (Devasthali 1954: 133), and concludes by noting that the *Bhagavadgītā* has developed these ideas and introduced new ones. Ježić 2009 covers the same topic in more philological depth, concentrating especially upon close verbal parallels between the *Bhagavadgītā* and the metrical *Kaṭha* and *Śvetāśvatara* Upaniṣads of the Black Yajurveda, and asking, as per its subtitle "parallels and relative chronology," what the contexts of those parallels might suggest about the direction of influence. Ježić argues that these three texts expanded in stages, and that they bear witness to a complex web of mutual influence.

The *Bhagavadgītā* and the label "Upaniṣad"

In preparation for critically editing the *Mahābhārata*'s *Bhīṣmaparvan*, S. K. Belvalkar selected a representative sample of available *Bhīṣmaparvan* manuscripts; and for the famous *Bhagavadgītā* portion this sample was supplemented by additional manuscripts of just that portion. The resulting *Bhagavadgītā* critical edition gives details of the colophons that most manuscripts include after each chapter. Those colophons typically refer to each foregoing chapter of the *Bhagavadgītā* by a name, and include the formula *bhagavadgītāsūpaniṣatsu* (Belvalkar 1968: 6, 14, 18, etc.); that is, each chapter is said to be "among the Upaniṣads sung by the Lord." Thus the *Bhagavadgītā* – the "Song of the Lord" – is categorized as a series of Upaniṣads.

The colophons are more recent than the textual materials they label, but they may nonetheless preserve an ancient tradition. However, although this particular label shows that some similarity was perceived between the Upaniṣads and the *Bhagavadgītā*, it is difficult to say what exactly that similarity might have been. The label could allude to the *Bhagavadgītā*'s format as a teaching from guru to disciple, in consonance with the derivation *upa-ni* + *sad*, "sit down near to" ("Traditionally this has been taken to refer to a session of teaching," Roebuck 2003: xxxvii); or it could allude to the *Bhagavadgītā*'s subject matter, in consonance with Śaṅkara's understanding of *upaniṣad* as that which destroys ignorance and suffering by revealing the knowledge of *brahman* (Gambhīrānanda 1986: 93–96). These are just two possibilities; but either would fit.

A different kind of relationship is suggested by this common Gītāmāhātmya verse (see e.g. Sadhale 2010: 14; Sastry 1991: xvi; Dasa 1998: 58, 60, back cover):

sarvopaniṣado gāvo dogdhā gopālanandanaḥ |
pārtho vatsaḥ sudhīr bhoktā dugdhaṃ gītāmṛtaṃ mahat ‖

All the Upaniṣads are cows
The milker was [Kṛṣṇa] the cowherd's son
The calf was Pṛthā's son [Arjuna]
The milk is the rich nectar of the *Gītā*
Those with good sense drink it

The age of this verse is difficult to ascertain; but although one might quibble over the first word, its general view that the *Bhagavadgītā* is other than, subsequent to, and derivative of the Upaniṣads is one that most scholars would accept.

Kṛṣṇa Devakīputra

Chāndogya Upaniṣad 3.17 briefly describes the teachings of Ghora Āṅgirasa to Kṛṣṇa Devakīputra. These teachings present quite a well-developed analogy between the Vedic sacrifice (*yajña*) and the human experience of life. In recent centuries scholars have expressed views on the question of whether Kṛṣṇa "son of Devakī" of the *Chāndogya Upaniṣad* may be identified with the Kṛṣṇa of the *Bhagavadgītā*, whose mother's name is Devakī. Preciado-Solis gives a well-referenced inventory of such views (1984: 24–27; see p. 36 for his own view). In favor of the identification are the nominal identity – Kṛṣṇa Vāsudeva is referred to as *devakīputra* more than twenty times in the *Mahābhārata* – and the overlap between what Ghora Āṅgirasa teaches and what Arjuna learns; against it are Ghora Āṅgirasa's absence from Kṛṣṇa's biography as narrated by the *Mahābhārata* and *Harivaṃśa*, and the fact that notwithstanding apparent connections, identity is difficult to prove. In light of this latter point, couching the issue in terms of the identity (or otherwise) of the two characters is perhaps an overly historicist way of thinking about it. There is certainly an intertextual relationship here. Commenting on the analogues detailed in the *Chāndogya* passage, Ježić (2009: 221) says:

> These correspondences remind one directly of the *yajña* passages in BhG 3.9–16 and 4.23–33 … and indirectly – and even more significantly – they remind us of the *karmayoga* in general in the Gītā … where the term *karman* is used in the generalized sense, not only for ritual or sacrificial acts, but for all activity in life …

Key here are *Bhagavadgītā* 3.9 and 4.23:

> *yajñārthāt karmaṇo 'nyatra loko 'yaṃ karmabandhanaḥ* ।
> *tadarthaṃ karma kaunteya muktasaṅgaḥ samācara* ॥
>
> People are bound by action, unless the action is for the sake of sacrifice. Perform action for that purpose, son of Kuntī, free of attachment.
>
> *gatasaṅgasya muktasya jñānāvasthitacetasaḥ* ।
> *yajñāyācarataḥ karma samagraṃ pravilīyate* ॥
>
> A person who acts for the sake of sacrifice has shed attachment and is freed, their thoughts guided by their wisdom; all trace of their action melts away.

It is surely no coincidence that in each text the name Kṛṣṇa Devakīputra appears in conjunction with what seems to be a very similar philosophy.

Other suggestions of *karmayoga* in the Upaniṣads

That the existential consequences of conventionally bad deeds can be obviated by performing those deeds in a certain manner is mentioned several times in the Upaniṣads. *Īśā Upaniṣad* 2 says that if you *merely* act (*kurvann eva*), action will leave no stain on you (*tvayi … na karma lipyate*). This is direct, but cryptic. Other passages are more revealing (cf. Thieme 1965: 90–92).

In *Bṛhadāraṇyaka Upaniṣad* 4.4.23 Yājñavalkya tells King Janaka that a person who knows the *ātman* is not stained by bad deeds (*taṃ viditvā na lipyate karmaṇā pāpakena*): Such a person isn't tormented by bad deeds, but rather burns their bad deeds away (*nainaṃ pāpmā tapati* । *sarvaṃ pāpmānaṃ tapati*). This latter image is similar to that presented at *Bhagavadgītā* 4.19, where Kṛṣṇa praises the one whose actions have been burned up in the fire of knowledge (*jñānāgnidagdhakarmāṇaṃ*). In *Chāndogya Upaniṣad* 4.14.3 Upakosala Kāmalāyana learns that "just as drops of water don't cling to a lotus leaf, bad deeds don't cling to a person who knows this" – that is, the *ātman* (*yathā puṣkarapalāśa āpo na śliṣyanta evam evaṃvidi pāpaṃ karma na śliṣyate*; cf. *Chāndogya* 4.11.2; 4.12.2; 4.13.2).

At *Bṛhadāraṇyaka Upaniṣad* 4.4.5–7, in the context of rebirth, Yājñavalkya says that "the evil-doer becomes a villain" (*pāpakārī pāpo bhavati*). He qualifies this: "that's certainly how it is for people who desire; but as for people who don't ... being sheer *brahman*, they of course go to *brahman*" (*iti nu kāmayamānaḥ | athākāmayamānaḥ ... | brahmaiva san brahmāpy eti*). *Taittirīya Upaniṣad* 2.9 describes "the knower of the bliss of *brahman*" (*ānandam brahmaṇo vidvān*), and says that "thoughts of 'Did I not do a good thing? Did I do a bad thing?' don't torment that person" (*etaṃ ha vāva na tapati | kim ahaṃ sādhu nākaravam | kim ahaṃ pāpam akaravam iti*). At *Maitrī Upaniṣad* 6.20 a quoted verse says that "through purity of mind, a person destroys both good and bad deeds" (*cittasya hi prasādena hanti karma śubhāśubham*).

The method proposed by Kṛṣṇa in the *Bhagavadgītā*, whereby Arjuna might act (i.e. perform *karman*) without being bound by the action (i.e. without generating *karmabandha*), is described in various ways, and involves all the aspects – knowledge of the *ātman*, freedom from desire, knowledge of the bliss of *brahman*, purity of mind – that are mentioned in these Upaniṣadic passages. But perhaps the most striking Upaniṣadic passage in this regard is found in *Kauṣītaki Upaniṣad* 3.1, where Indra is asked to grant the most beneficial boon that a human being can receive, and he grants the boon of *knowing him*. He explains that although he has done dastardly deeds (a list is provided), he has not been negatively affected by having done them. He generalizes (end of *Kauṣītaki Upaniṣad* 3.1):

> *sa yo māṃ veda na ha vai tasya kena cana karmaṇā loko mīyate na steyena na bhrūṇahatyayā na mātṛvadhena na pitṛvadhena | nāsya pāpaṃ cakṛṣo mukhān nīlaṃ vyetīti* ||
>
> The heavenly world of someone who knows me isn't damaged by any deed whatever – not by stealing, or by killing a child, or by killing their own mother or father. Even if they've done a bad thing, their face doesn't lose its color.

Here *karmabandha* is to be neutralized by knowing a divinity who acts in a particular way, and by adopting that way in one's own actions. Though the divinity differs between the texts, this matches the *Bhagavadgītā*'s presentation of Kṛṣṇa as the paradigmatic non-attached actor (see e.g. 3.22; 4.13–14; 9.9); and when Indra exemplifies the range of application of his proposed method by mentioning the killing of close kin, this matches the context in which Kṛṣṇa introduces *his* proposed method.

The two post-mortem paths

Many Upaniṣads describe two post-mortem paths, sometimes labeled *devayāna* and *pitṛyāṇa*, the "path of the gods" and the "path of the ancestors." The *devayāna* is the path of no return, but the *pitṛyāṇa* leads to heaven and then back to earth (*Bṛhadāraṇyaka Upaniṣad* 6.2.15–16; *Chāndogya Upaniṣad* 5.10; *Kauṣītaki Upaniṣad* 1.2–7; *Muṇḍaka Upaniṣad* 1.2.7–11; *Praśna Upaniṣad* 1.9–10; Killingley 1997: 7–9, 13–16). At *Bhagavadgītā* 9.20–21 Kṛṣṇa stresses the temporary nature of heavenly residence in terms similar to those used in *Muṇḍaka Upaniṣad* 1.2.9–10. Kṛṣṇa also describes the two paths (*Bhagavadgītā* 8.23–25):

> *yatra kāle tv anāvṛttim āvṛttiṃ caiva yoginaḥ* |
> *prayātā yānti taṃ kālaṃ vakṣyāmi bharatarṣabha* ‖
> *agnir jyotir ahaḥ śuklaḥ ṣaṇmāsā uttarāyaṇam* |
> *tatra prayātā gacchanti brahma brahmavido janāḥ* ‖
> *dhūmo rātris tathā kṛṣṇaḥ ṣaṇmāsā dakṣiṇāyanam* |
> *tatra cāndramasaṃ jyotir yogī prāpya nivartate* ‖

> I'll list the times when dying yogis don't return, and when they do, bull of Bharata. If people who know *brahman* die by fire, in daylight, in the bright fortnight, or in the six months when the sun heads north, they go to *brahman*. But if yogins die by smoke, at night, in the dark fortnight, or in the six months when the sun heads south, they reach the moonlight and then return.

The four pairs that here distinguish the two paths (fire and smoke, day and night, waxing and waning fortnight, and northward and southward course of the sun) also occur in the accounts given in the *Bṛhadāraṇyaka* and *Chāndogya* Upaniṣads, but there they figure as successive stations along the paths, so that the people traveling on the *devayāna* go into the flame, and from there into the day, and from there into the waxing fortnight, and from there into the six months when the sun heads north. The *Bhagavadgītā* uses the same images in the same context (of the two paths), but with a different effect; for in this *Bhagavadgītā* passage – in contrast to the many other *Bhagavadgītā* passages which mention the possibility of not being reborn after death – the path traveled after death depends on *when* one dies. However, it should be noted that these *Bhagavadgītā* verses are explicitly about "dying yogis," who would only be a small subset of the dying.

If one ignores the fire and smoke, which do not work easily as temporal markers, then "Added up, the auspicious times comprise seven-eighths of the year, as do the inauspicious times; six-eighths are ambiguous" (Brodbeck 2007: 169 n. 39). But at *Mahābhārata* 6.114.86–100, when Bhīṣma Kaurava, deciding his own time of death, postpones it until after the winter solstice, he seems to prioritize the longest of the three cycles. Similarly, in the *Praśna Upaniṣad* the *devayāna* and *pitṛyāṇa* are keyed to the two halves of the annual cycle (1.9–10), and the two halves of the lunar and diurnal cycles are mentioned in different connections (1.12–13).

The *Bhagavadgītā*'s reinterpretation on this point has been downplayed by some translators and commentators. For example, in the Flood and Martin translation Kṛṣṇa apparently presents the Upaniṣadic view (*Bhagavadgītā* 8.23–24 in Flood 2015: 44):

> But now, O Bull of Bharatas,
> I will inform you where in time
> those departed yogis go,
> those who do, or do not, return.
>
> Fire, light, day, the moon's bright fortnight,
> six months of the upper going,
> those departing, Brahman-knowing
> men go forth then unto Brahman …

Devasthali gives a similar impression: He says that in the *Bhagavadgītā* passage day, the bright fortnight, and so on are "some of the stations" on the path to *brahman* (1954: 134). Exceptions to this tendency include Murdoch, who stresses the *Bhagavadgītā*'s view in order to ridicule it (1894: 42), and Edgerton, whose article on "the hour of death" discusses also the reception of the *Bhagavadgītā*'s view in Indian ritual and commentarial traditions (1927: 245–247).

The main focus of Edgerton's article is on a slightly different factor. *Bhagavadgītā* 8.6 presents the principle that a person's state of mind at the time of their death determines their subsequent destination. This principle, though never quite stated explicitly, is seemingly implicit in several Upaniṣadic passages (*Chāndogya Upaniṣad* 3.14; 3.17.6 within the aforementioned teachings of Ghora Āṅgirasa; 8.2; *Praśna Upaniṣad* 3.9–10). In the *Bhagavadgītā* it is elaborated with respect to the destinations of *brahmanirvāṇa* (2.72), Kṛṣṇa's state of being (8.5, 7, 14–16), the supreme divine *puruṣa* (8.8–10), and the highest state (*paramāṃ gatim*, 8.11–13), all of which denote the path of no return; and it is also elaborated with respect to various rebirth destinations in terms of the person's dominant *guṇa* at the point of death (14.14–15).

One might perceive inconsistency between the *Bhagavadgītā*'s various emphases on the way a person acts while alive, the time of their death, and their dying thoughts. But Arjuna, who must fight in a war where his own side is seriously outnumbered, might naturally be concerned about his own death; and from this perspective it is fitting that when Kṛṣṇa talks about dying thoughts and when he talks about dying times, the conclusion is that Arjuna should have the desired mentality at *all* times (*tasmāt sarveṣu kāleṣu mām anusmara yudhya ca*, 8.7ab; *tasmāt sarveṣu kāleṣu yogayukto bhavārjuna*, 8.27cd).

Regardless of what one makes of the *Bhagavadgītā*'s various emphases on the time of death, Kṛṣṇa certainly would not want to say what the *Bṛhadāraṇyaka* and *Chāndogya* Upaniṣads say about the two paths – that is, that the *devayāna* is traveled by "the ones in the forest who think of faith as truth" (*ye cāmī araṇye śraddhāṃ satyam upāsate*, *Bṛhadāraṇyaka*) or by "the ones in the forest who think of faith as austerity" (*ye ceme 'raṇye śraddhā tapa ity upāsate*, *Chāndogya*), and that the *pitṛyāṇa* is traveled by "the ones who acquire heavenly worlds through ritual, charity and austerity" (*ye yajñena dānena tapasā lokāñ jayanti*, *Bṛhadāraṇyaka*) or by "the ones in the village who think of rites and good works as charity" (*ye ime grāma iṣṭāpūrte dattam ity upāsate*, *Chāndogya*). The *Bhagavadgītā* seeks to break the link between the forest and the soteriology of not being reborn; Kṛṣṇa says that social duties including sacrifice and charitable donation (and, for Arjuna, battle) must be performed, and that the soteriology usually associated with renouncers is actually accessed by renouncing not action, but its fruits.

Close verbal parallels

The close verbal parallels between the *Bhagavadgītā* and the metrical Upaniṣads (predominantly the *Kaṭha* and *Śvetāśvatara*) have been listed elsewhere, but I list them again here. In Table 19.1, verbatim parallels of a quarter-verse or more are marked by an asterisk; in such cases, quarter-verses neighboring the listed ones may be similar but not identical in the two sources, without occasioning an independent entry.

It is not immediately clear what these verbal parallels might reveal about the relationship between the *Bhagavadgītā* and the Upaniṣads, since similar or

Table 19.1 Close verbal parallels between the *Bhagavadgītā* and the metrical Upaniṣads

Bhagavadgītā reference	*Upaniṣadic reference*	*Topic (in Bhagavadgītā)*
*2.19cd	*Kaṭha* 2.19cd	*ātman*
*2.20cd	*Kaṭha* 2.18cd	
2.29a	*Kaṭha* 6.9b *Śvetāśvatara* 4.20b	*ātman*
2.29d	*Kaṭha* 2.7b	
*3.42b	*Kaṭha* 6.7a	senses, mind, *buddhi*
*3.42c	*Kaṭha* 3.10c	
*5.13c	*Śvetāśvatara* 3.18a	*ātman* in "nine-gated city"
8.9b	*Kaṭha* 2.20a *Śvetāśvatara* 3.20a	divine *puruṣa* (*ātman*)
*8.9d	*Śvetāśvatara* 3.8b	
*8.11c	*Kaṭha* 2.15c	ultimate destination
*13.13a–14b	*Śvetāśvatara* 3.16a–17b	*brahman* (*ātman*)
13.15	*Īśā* 5	
13.17a	*Bṛhadāraṇyaka* 4.4.16c	
13.17b	*Muṇḍaka* 2.2.6d	
13.17d	*Śvetāśvatara* 3.13b = 4.17b	
15.1ab	*Kaṭha* 6.1ab *Maitrī* 6.4 *Śvetāśvatara* 3.9cd	*aśvattha* tree
15.6ab	*Kaṭha* 5.15	supernatural illumination

even identical ideas can be expressed in different words (see for example various ideas mentioned earlier in this chapter), and identical words can express different ideas (hence the parenthetical clause in the heading of the table's final column).

Commenting on parallels between the *Bhagavadgītā* and, especially, the *Kaṭha Upaniṣad*, Brockington suggests that "The number of quotations indicates that the *Bhagavadgītā* is deliberately using them for their prestige value and that it must have been composed at a period when these Upaniṣads were regarded as authoritative" (Brockington 1998: 13 n. 28). He then mentions Oberlies' view – already elaborated by Rao (1966: 297–316) – that the *Śvetāśvatara Upaniṣad* postdates the *Bhagavadgītā*, and acknowledges the possibility that with these two texts the influence may be in the other direction (Brockington 1998: 13 n. 29). Presumably, the *Bhagavadgītā* would have had to have time in which to become "regarded as authoritative" before the author/s of the *Śvetāśvatara Upaniṣad* would have wanted to quote it.

Ježić considers each parallel in its textual contexts and paints a more complicated picture of mutual influence between the *Bhagavadgītā* and the *Kaṭha* and *Śvetāśvatara* Upaniṣads, concluding that these three texts "must have been transmitted in some common way – either performed on the same occasions, at the same places during the same historical period, or transmitted in the same or in related circles" (Ježić 2009: 258; cf. Cohen 2008: 200). But if these texts were definite enough to be transmitted as such, even though they were still in the process of formation, how many versions of each text were in existence at once? If more than one, how did those versions become the versions we now have? There are conceptual difficulties here. More problematic are the subjective interpretive aspects of Ježić's methodology, and the fact that his conclusions – about which text borrowed from which in each specific instance – depend upon a preexisting scheme of the *Bhagavadgītā*'s diachronic development that itself rests on the same kind of subjective interpretive methodology (and has been criticized; see Adluri and Bagchee 2016).

If we imagine the parallels charted above mean that one text must have borrowed directly from another, this may just be because of our contextual ignorance. In some cases the parallel may bear witness to a wider discursive repertoire of phrases, images, verses, or sequences of verses that were, so to say, common property. The way in which the prose Upaniṣads incorporate odd verses may seem to suggest this: Such verses tend to be introduced in specific ways (*tad eṣa śloko bhavati* in the *Bṛhadāraṇyaka Upaniṣad*; *tad apy eṣa śloko bhavati* in the *Taittirīya*; *tad eṣa ślokaḥ* in the *Chāndogya* and the *Praśna*), as if they preexisted the texts that now incorporate them. So we should be cautious about suggesting that the parallels under discussion are evidence of borrowing or direct influence from one particular text to another. Nonetheless, the close verbal parallels between the *Bhagavadgītā* and the Upaniṣads coincide with close conceptual and philosophical parallels; the *Bhagavadgītā* topics listed in the right-hand column of the above table are, in most cases, recurrent Upaniṣadic topics.

The *Bhagavadgītā*'s usage of one particular parallel phrase is worth highlighting here. At *Kaṭha Upaniṣad* 2.15c the phrase *yad icchanto brahmacaryaṃ caranti* ("seeking which they live in chastity") describes the word (*pada*) *om* (on which see Killingley 1986; Gerety 2015); but when the same phrase occurs at *Bhagavadgītā* 8.11c, here too describing a *pada*, *pada* seemingly means not "word," but "place" or "state" (it is spelled out soon afterwards as the *paramāṃ gatim* or "ultimate destination"). In the same verse 8.11, the *Bhagavadgītā* connects the word *pada* with the word *akṣara*, which often means "syllable" (or, more specifically, *om*) but is used here in the more general sense of "indestructible." The poet has cleverly sidelined the implied word *om*; but it is still included in the passage, since the person who goes to this indestructible place is said to die while uttering *om* (*Bhagavadgītā* 8.13; for *om* see also 7.8; 9.17; 17.23–24).

The *aśvattha* tree

The image of the *aśvattha* tree is another example of apparent reinterpretation by the *Bhagavadgītā*. In the Upaniṣads the *aśvattha* tree (or pipal tree, *ficus religiosa*) is used as a metaphor for *brahman*. *Kaṭha Upaniṣad* 6.1 says: "This is an eternal *aśvattha*, its roots above, its branches below. It is the only light; it is *brahman* … No one can get past it" (*ūrdhvamūlo avākśākha eṣo 'śvatthaḥ sanātanaḥ* | *tad eva śukraṃ tad brahma* … | … *tad u nātyeti kaś cana*). *Maitrī Upaniṣad* 6.4 mentions "the three-part *brahman* with its roots above; the branches are space, wind, fire, water, earth, and so on; this singular *brahman* is called the *aśvattha*" (*ūrdhvamūlam tripād brahma śākhā ākāśavāyvagnyudakabhūmyādaya eko 'śvatthanāmaitad brahma*). At *Śvetāśvatara Upaniṣad* 3.9 the tree image is used as a simile only, without specifying that an *aśvattha* is intended: "He stands singular in the sky, as solid as a tree; the whole world is filled by that person" (*vṛkṣeva stabdho divi tiṣṭhaty ekas tenedaṃ pūrṇaṃ puruṣeṇa sarvam*).

The *Bhagavadgītā* passage is as follows (15.1–4):

ūrdhvamūlam adhaḥśākham aśvatthaṃ prāhur avyayam |
chandāṃsi yasya parṇāni yas taṃ veda sa vedavit ‖
adhaś cordhvaṃ prasṛtās tasya śākhā
    guṇapravṛddhā viṣayapravālāḥ |
adhaś ca mūlāny anusaṃtatāni
    karmānubandhīni manuṣyaloke ‖
na rūpam asyeha tathopalabhyate
    nānto na cādir na ca saṃpratiṣṭhā |
aśvattham enaṃ suvirūḍhamūlam
    asaṅgaśastreṇa dṛḍhena chittvā ‖
tataḥ padaṃ tat parimārgitavyaṃ
    yasmin gatā na nivartanti bhūyaḥ |
tam eva cādyaṃ puruṣaṃ prapadye
    yataḥ pravṛttiḥ prasṛtā purāṇī ‖

> They mention an eternal *aśvattha*, its roots above, its branches below. Its leaves are the Vedic hymns; whoever knows it knows the Veda. Its branches extend down and up, fattened by the *guṇa*s, sprouting through the sense-ranges; and its roots stretch down, connecting with actions in the human realm. Its form can't be discerned in this world, and nor can its end, its beginning, or its basis. You must cut down this well-rooted *aśvattha* with the keen ax of non-attachment; and then, resorting only to the primordial person from whom the ancient development issued, you must seek out the place that once reached, no one comes back from.

The *aśvattha* image has been much discussed and variously interpreted (see e.g. Bosch 1994: 65–75; Arapura 1975); but whichever way up the tree is visualized, in the *Bhagavadgītā* the image seems to depend on the term *aśvattha* referring also to *ficus benghalensis*, the banyan tree (*nyagrodha*, *vaṭa*). The banyan not only sends down secondary aerial roots from its branches, but also tends to begin its life in bird-droppings deposited atop a host tree, whence it grows both up and down, often "strangling" its host (hence the nickname "strangler fig") by encasing its trunk, resulting in a cylindrical trunk of its own. In his *Kaṭha Upaniṣad* commentary Śaṅkara, perhaps conflating the trees of the *Kaṭha* and the *Bhagavadgītā*, says "it is without any heart-wood like the stem of a plantain tree" (trans. Gambhīrānanda 1986: 199–200). The *Bhagavadgītā*'s *aśvattha* represents *saṃsāra*, the phenomenal cosmos as experienced by a particular transmigrating soul; and Kṛṣṇa's instruction to Arjuna to cut the tree down and revert to its source may seem to advert not just to the strangler fig's parasitic nature but also, perhaps, to the unwitting bird. The statement that whoever knows the eternal *aśvattha* knows the Veda could play on the fact that the *aśvattha* image appears in the (Vedic) Upaniṣads; but be that as it may, the association made here between the Vedas and the realm of rebirth is in keeping with what Kṛṣṇa says elsewhere in the *Bhagavadgītā* (e.g. 2.42–46; 8.28).

Sāṃkhya and yoga

As per Table 19.1, *Bhagavadgītā* 3.42 shares quarter-verses with the *Kaṭha Upaniṣad* on the topic of the internal constitution of the human being and the hierarchy of the various aspects identified. *Bhagavadgītā* 3.42 gives this picture: senses < mind < *buddhi* < *ātman*. It thus combines elements from both poles of the dualistic Sāṃkhya philosophy, which in its developed form sets *puruṣa*, the principle of consciousness, against *prakṛti*, the principle of substance, and details under the latter a process of evolution whereby *prakṛti* is unpacked into twenty-three further entities (ego, *buddhi*, mind, five sense-capacities, five action-capacities, five subtle elements, and five gross elements). The message of *Bhagavadgītā* 3.42 is that the principle of consciousness is more essential and important – in soteriological terms – than any aspect of the psychophysical world, and this point is also made by the *Kaṭha Upaniṣad* passages with which *Bhagavadgītā* 3.42 partially overlaps, both of which take the hierarchy of the psychophysical entities up to *avyakta* (i.e. *prakṛti* in its "unmanifest" form) and place *puruṣa* above it (*Kaṭha* 3.10–11; 6.7–8).

There are other ways in which the *Bhagavadgītā* and the Upaniṣads – particularly those of the Black Yajurveda (Cohen 2008: 193–195, 214–215, 259–261) – can be seen to represent "proto-Sāṃkhya" ideas and terminology. One such way is in their various presentations of the three *guṇa*s, the "modes," "strands," or "constituents" of the psychophysical world. This idea seems to be present in germinal form in the *Chāndogya Upaniṣad* (6.3–5); it is presupposed by the *Śvetāśvatara Upaniṣad* (see e.g. 5.5, 7, 12); it is partially expounded in the *Maitrī Upaniṣad* (3.5; 5.2); and it receives its fullest exposition in the *Bhagavadgītā* (14.5–27; 17.1–22; 18.4–10, 19–44). In that exposition, it seems that any field of phenomenal variation can be explained in terms of local relative dominance of one *guṇa* over the others.

Perhaps the most significant thing about the "proto-Sāṃkhya" ideas expressed in these texts, however, is that the analysis of the human being goes together with the emerging concept of yoga. *Kaṭha Upaniṣad* 3.3–9 sets up an analogy between the human body and a chariot: *ātman* is the passenger, *buddhi* the charioteer, mind the reins, and the senses the horses; the horses would wish to run after sense-objects willy-nilly, but when they are controlled by *buddhi*, *ātman* can reach the destination of no return, here identified as "the highest step of Viṣṇu" (*tad viṣṇoḥ paramaṃ padam*). The *Kaṭha Upaniṣad* does not use the word "yoga" here, but it hardly needs to, since that word is derived from the verbal root *yuj*, "yoke," and so the harnessing and channeling of animal power inevitably implies it. Later, at 6.11, the same Upaniṣad states succinctly that "constant control of the senses is called yoga" (*tāṃ yogam iti manyante sthirām indriyadhāraṇām*); and the link between yoga and sense-control is also central in the *Bhagavadgītā* (2.60–68; 5.7, 11; 6.4, 8, 24–27; 18.33; Filipský 1986: 528–529).

The chariot analogy is also mentioned in the *Śvetāśvatara Upaniṣad* (2.9) and the *Maitrī Upaniṣad* (2.6); but the *Bhagavadgītā* brings it to life. Arjuna is a great warrior on a chariot expertly driven by Kṛṣṇa, the "master of yoga" (*yogeśvara*, 11.4, 9; 18.75, 78), who perfectly exemplifies yoga in his own life and activities, and who undertakes to rescue Arjuna from all ills (18.66). Their conversation takes place on the chariot, and given the subject matter it is hard not to imagine that the *Bhagavadgītā*'s author/s composed it with the chariot analogy in mind (cf. Hiltebeitel 1984: 12–14). Kṛṣṇa's role in the *Bhagavadgītā* reflects the crucial role of *buddhi* in the yogic method he proposes (2.49–53; Filipský 1986: 530).

Although Kṛṣṇa's method is to be applied in and through one's conventional social duties, Kṛṣṇa also explains that (and how) the yogi should train while sitting alone (6.10–14 at the very least; cf. also 6.18–21, 24–26). At this stage these instructions would only be of hypothetical value to Arjuna, who is being urged most immediately to do yoga on the battlefield. In their attention to bodily posture and choice of location, these instructions closely resemble those given at *Śvetāśvatara Upaniṣad* 2.8–10; but the details of the yogi's experience that the Upaniṣad goes on to give in the subsequent verses are unlike anything in the *Bhagavadgītā*, and bring to mind rather the third section of the *Yogasūtra*.

God and *bhakti*

The *Bhagavadgītā* espouses a theistic position: Kṛṣṇa is God with a capital G, the source and sustainer of the cosmos. The history-of-ideas question of where this theism came from has been keenly felt by Euro-American commentators in particular, and has given rise to various speculations (see Jaiswal 1967: 61–88, with references). It seems beyond dispute that contributing factors would have included the figure of Viṣṇu in Vedic literature (which features the myth of his three strides, and his close association with totality, the year, and the sacrifice), the figure of Puruṣa (the cosmic "Person" described in *Ṛgveda* 10.90), and the cosmological speculations of the early Upaniṣads.

The removal of the *Bhagavadgītā* from its *Mahābhārata* context has sometimes led to lack of clarity regarding the identity of the cosmic deity of whom Kṛṣṇa Vāsudeva is an incarnation, but the wider text clearly indicates that this is Viṣṇu-Nārāyaṇa. At *Bhagavadgītā* 4.5–8 Kṛṣṇa describes his repeated incarnations, this being merely the latest, for the purpose of restoring *dharma* (order, proper behavior).

This pattern of instrumental corporeal interventions is perhaps the most distinctive aspect of the text's theology. It has not been traced to earlier Upaniṣadic passages. It is elaborated in Purāṇic literature in connection with the term *avatāra*. In the *Bhagavadgītā* it allows the *avatāra* Kṛṣṇa, who has more self-consciousness of the process than most *avatāra*s do, to speak of the cosmos as something he is superintending from without as well as from within, and to present himself and it in personable and ethical fashion through his connection with *dharma*. It is only because of this incarnational pattern, and because of the practical details of this particular incarnation, that Arjuna can have this theology explained to him authoritatively by a human being, and experientially demonstrated to him in something approaching a comprehensible form (and that that authoritative explanation can then be repeated, and that authoritative demonstration described, to audiences beyond Arjuna).

A first-person window into God is framed by the *Bhagavadgītā*. Much is not clear. Some of what seems clear seems so in light of Upaniṣadic teachings: The unity of the psychophysical cosmos as one substance from one source, and its unity with the soul – the soul as its own enlivening accompaniment parceled out microcosmically within itself, but also as a separate, superordinate factor. More clear is that the first person is male. Kṛṣṇa Vāsudeva's gender corresponds to Viṣṇu-Nārāyaṇa's; the primary creative role is male in the *Bhagavadgītā*, as it tends to be in the Upaniṣads. *Bṛhadāraṇyaka Upaniṣad* 1.4 introduces a male first being and says: "He wanted a companion. He was the size of a woman and a man embracing; so he split his body in two, and from it husband and wife came into being" (*sa dvitīyam aicchat* | *sa haitāvān āsa yathā strīpumāṃsau saṃpariṣvaktau* | *sa imam evātmānaṃ dvedhāpātayat* | *tataḥ patiś ca patnī cābhavatām*). Then nature takes her course. This fits the presentation at *Manusmṛti* 1.8cd: "first he produced the waters, then he ejaculated into them" (*apa eva sasarjādau tāsu vīryam avāsṛjat*; cf. *Ṛgveda* 10.121.7–8). Kṛṣṇa's version feminizes *brahman* (*Bhagavadgītā* 14.3–4):

> *mama yonir mahad brahma tasmin garbhaṃ dadhāmy aham* |
> *saṃbhavaḥ sarvabhūtānāṃ tato bhavati bhārata* ||
> *sarvayoniṣu kaunteya mūrtayaḥ saṃbhavanti yāḥ* |
> *tāsāṃ brahma mahad yonir ahaṃ bījapradaḥ pitā* ||
>
> *Brahman* is my great womb: I place the embryo in it, and then all beings come into being, Bhārata. When any forms arise in any womb, *brahman* is the great womb, and I am the seed-sowing father.

Elsewhere Kṛṣṇa says: "I am the father of this world, its mother, its placer, its grandfather" (*pitāham asya jagato mātā dhātā pitāmahaḥ*, 9.17ab). Arjuna says: "You are the father of the moving and non-moving world" (*pitāsi lokasya carācarasya*, 11.43a). The notion that being male includes and subordinates being female is theologically constitutive.

While details about who Kṛṣṇa actually is are being explained and shown to Arjuna, he sees, within Kṛṣṇa, all gods and saints bowing to Kṛṣṇa and praising him (11.21–22, 36–37); and he acknowledges that such behavior is appropriate (11.39–40). Kṛṣṇa concurs; he and he only should be known, kept in mind, and acted for at all times, while doing yoga. And the text should be studied (12.20). Other than that his demands are small, the appeal broad, and the prospects excellent (*Bhagavadgītā* 9.26, 31c–32d):

> *patraṃ puṣpaṃ phalaṃ toyaṃ yo me bhaktyā prayacchati* |
> *tad ahaṃ bhaktyupahṛtam aśnāmi prayatātmanaḥ* ||
> ...
> *kaunteya pratijānīhi na me bhaktaḥ praṇaśyati* ||
> *māṃ hi pārtha vyapāśritya ye 'pi syuḥ pāpayonayaḥ* |
> *striyo vaiśyās tathā śūdrās te 'pi yānti parāṃ gatim* ||
>
> When someone presents me with a leaf, a petal, a fruit, or water by way of devotion (*bhakti*), I enjoy the pious person's devotional offering. ... Son of Pṛthā Kuntī, know that no devotee of mine is allowed to perish; those who have resorted to me go to the highest state – women, *vaiśya*s, and *śūdra*s, and even people from bad families.

However, it could take several lifetimes (cf. 6.37–47). After listing four types of devotee, Kṛṣṇa says "the best of these is the knower, whose discipline is constant, whose devotion exclusive" (*teṣāṃ jñānī nityayukta ekabhaktir viśiṣyate*,

7.17ab). But "only after many births does one become a knower and attain me" (*bahūnāṃ janmanām ante jñānavān māṃ prapadyate*, 7.19ab; cf. Sharma 2015: 113–114 on this passage).

A frequent feature of Euro-American secondary literature on the *Bhagavadgītā* is the hypothesis that the text was composed in stages, by several authors, over an extended period of time. In this regard the *Bhagavadgītā* has sometimes served as a microcosm where hypotheses concerning the *Mahābhārata* are played out in miniature. When this hypothesis about the *Bhagavadgītā* is accompanied – as it typically is – by claims about which of its parts or aspects were earlier and which later, the general tendency is to claim that the text's theology and the associated emphasis on *bhakti* are adventitious, not original (see e.g. Holtzmann 1893: 159–165; Hopkins 1895: 389; Jacobi 1918; Farquhar 1920: 92; Khair 1969; Ježić 1986; Basham 1990: 82–97; Szczurek 2005; Malinar 2007: 34, 55). As early as 1905 Hopkins was at pains to assert the normativity of this claim, calling it "the usual view," "the view generally held by Sanskrit scholars," and "the current opinion" (Hopkins 1905: 384, 386, 389). The claim still has the strength of numbers, but Hopkins mentions no other strength, and I have not seen any good argument to support it, either before or since. A range of attempted arguments has been examined by Adluri and Bagchee (2014: 156–313; 2016), whose work has also made preliminary attempts to suggest why so many scholars, in the absence of real supporting evidence, have seen fit to divide the text historically in this kind of way. There is more work to do on this latter question; part of the problem seems to be the influence of expectations associated with the etic genre-category "epic," but there are other associated factors in each case. Be that as it may, the principle outlined by Mahadevan remains unvitiated: "Unless clear and unmistakable evidences are forthcoming, there is no justification for regarding any verse of the *Gītā* as an interpolation" (1952: 107). And so it will not do to suppose that the *Bhagavadgītā*'s emphasis on *bhakti* is secondary to a previous version of the text.

The concept of *bhakti* is not evident in the Upaniṣads before the *Śvetāśvatara* (cf. Jacob 1891: 664), which mentions *bhakti* only in its last verse (*Śvetāśvatara Upaniṣad* 6.23):

> *yasya deve parā bhaktir yathā deve tathā gurau* |
> *tasyaite kathitā hy arthāḥ prakāśante mahātmanaḥ prakāśante mahātmanaḥ* ||
>
> These matters narrated [in this Upaniṣad] become clear to the great-souled person. They become clear to the great-souled person, who is extremely devoted to God, and as devoted to their guru as to God.

The *Śvetāśvatara* uses the word *deva* in a sense of God that is similar to the *Bhagavadgītā*'s, but does not include the incarnational aspect. The *Śvetāśvatara* identifies *deva* repeatedly as Rudra, Hara, Śiva, and *maheśvara*, and says he can be known through yoga (2.15–17). It was by the grace of

God (*devaprasādāt*) that Śvetāśvatara himself came to know and proclaim the divine mysteries (6.21); *bhakti* towards God and the guru is presented as a general qualification for understanding them (and by implication, for understanding this text about them).

Summary conclusion

The *Bhagavadgītā* narrated by Kṛṣṇa to Arjuna is closely connected to the Upaniṣads. The Indian tradition recognizes it on the one hand *as* a series of Upaniṣads, and on the other hand as a direct *product* of the Upaniṣads.

A Kṛṣṇa son of Devakī is mentioned in the *Chāndogya Upaniṣad* in connection with a philosophy (of life as sacrifice) apparently similar to the one that Kṛṣṇa son of Devakī espouses in the *Bhagavadgītā*. The *Bhagavadgītā*'s philosophy of action allegedly enables the ordinarily deleterious consequences of bad deeds to be avoided, and this idea is explicitly presented in several Upaniṣads. In common with the Upaniṣads, the *Bhagavadgītā* describes two post-mortem paths, only one of which leads to rebirth; but the *Bhagavadgītā* develops the Upaniṣadic pattern by breaking the connection between the forest and the path of no return, and (in one passage) by connecting post-mortem destiny to the *time* of death.

There are verbatim parallels of up to a verse and half in length between the *Bhagavadgītā* and the *Kaṭha* and *Śvetāśvatara* Upaniṣads. These are usually thought to indicate borrowing by the *Bhagavadgītā*, but the situation may be more complicated in some cases. There are also inexact verbal parallels. Sometimes – as with the metaphor of the *aśvattha* tree – the *Bhagavadgītā* seems to redeploy Upaniṣadic images in interesting ways. The links between the *Bhagavadgītā* and the *Kaṭha* and *Śvetāśvatara* Upaniṣads run deeper: These three texts contain similar types of analysis of the human individual and of the cosmos as a whole, and ideas of yoga that are presented using a chariot metaphor. However, two essential aspects of the *Bhagavadgītā* have no apparent Upaniṣadic precursors: Its incarnational, gendered theology, and the consequent devotional element within its soteriology. The *Śvetāśvatara Upaniṣad*'s theology, though similar in some ways, is non-incarnational; and perhaps accordingly, *bhakti* is not a prominent theme (though it is mentioned).

References

Adluri, Vishwa, and Joydeep Bagchee. 2014. *The Nay Science: a History of German Indology*. New York: Oxford University Press.

Adluri, Vishwa, and Joydeep Bagchee. 2016. "Paradigm Lost: the Application of the Historical-Critical Method to the *Bhagavad Gītā*" *International Journal of Hindu Sudies* 20.2: 199–301.

Arapura, J. G. 1975. "The Upside Down Tree of the *Bhagavadgītā* Ch. XV: an Exegesis" *Numen* 22.2: 131–144.

Basham, Arthur Llewellyn. 1990. *The Origins and Development of Classical Hinduism*, ed. Kenneth G. Zysk. Delhi: Oxford University Press.

Belvalkar, Shripad Krishna (ed.) 1968. *The Bhagavadgītā, being a Reprint of Relevant Parts of Bhīṣmaparvan from B. O. R. Institute's Edition of the Mahābhārata*. Second reprint. Poona: Bhandarkar Oriental Research Institute.

Bosch, F. D. K. 1994. *The Golden Germ: an Introduction to Indian Symbolism*. Delhi: Munshiram Manoharlal. First published The Hague: Mouton and Co., 1960.

Brockington, John L. 1998. *The Sanskrit Epics*. Handbook of Oriental Studies. Leiden: Brill.

Brodbeck, Simon. 2007. "Gendered Soteriology: Marriage and the *Karmayoga*" in Simon Brodbeck and Brian Black (eds) *Gender and Narrative in the Mahābhārata*, Routledge Hindu Studies Series. London: Routledge, 144–175.

Cohen, Signe. 2008. *Text and Authority in the Older Upaniṣads*. Brill's Indological Library, vol. 30. Leiden: Brill.

Dasa, Isvara (ed.) 1998. *Gītā-Māhātmya of the Padma Purāṇa: Lord Śiva's Glorification of the Bhagavad-Gītā*. Second Edition. Vrindavan: Touchstone Media.

Davis, Richard H. 2014. *The Bhagavad Gita: a Biography*. Lives of Great Religious Books. Princeton, NJ: Princeton University Press.

Devasthali, G. V. 1954. "Bhagavad-gītā and Upaniṣads" in Jagan Nath Agrawal and Bhim Dev Shastri (eds) *Sarūpa-Bhāratī, or The Homage of Indology, being the Dr. Lakshman Sarup Memorial Volume*. Hoshiarpur: Vishveshvaranand Vedic Research Institute, 132–142.

Edgerton, Franklin. 1927. "The Hour of Death: its Importance for Man's Future Fate in Hindu and Western Religions" *Annals of the Bhandarkar Oriental Research Institute* 8: 219–249.

Farquhar, J. N. 1920. *An Outline of the Religious Literature of India*. The Religious Quest of India. London: Humphrey Milford, Oxford University Press.

Filipský, Jan. 1986. "The Concept of Yoga in the *Bhagavadgītā*" in Wolfgang Morgenroth (ed.) *Sanskrit and World Culture: Proceedings of the Fourth World Sanskrit Conference of the International Association of Sanskrit Studies, Weimar, May 23–30, 1979*. Schriften zur Geschichte und Kultur des Alten Orients, vol. 18. Berlin: Akademie-Verlag, 526–531.

Flood, Gavin, ed. 2015. *The Bhagavad Gita: a New Translation; Contexts; Criticism*. Translation by Gavin Flood and Charles Martin. Norton Critical Editions. New York: W. W. Norton and Co.

Gambhīrānanda, Swāmī (trans.) 1986. *Eight Upaniṣads, with the Commentary of Śaṅkarācārya. Volume One (Īśā, Kena, Kaṭha and Taittirīya)*. Sixth impression. Calcutta: Advaita Ashrama.

Gerety, Finnian M. M. 2015. "This Whole World is OM: Song, Soteriology, and the Emergence of the Sacred Syllable" PhD dissertation, Harvard University.

Haas, George C. O. 1922. "Recurrent and Parallel Passages in the Principal Upanishads and the Bhagavad-Gītā, with References to Other Sanskrit Texts" *Journal of the American Oriental Society* 42: 1–43.

Hiltebeitel, Alf. 1984. "The Two Kṛṣṇas on One Chariot: Upaniṣadic Imagery and Epic Mythology" *History of Religions* 24.1: 1–26.

Holtzmann, Adolf (junior). 1893. *Die neunzehn Bücher des Mahābhārata. = Das Mahābhārata und seine Theile, zweiter Band: die Thiele des Gedichtes*. Kiel: C. F. Haeseler. Single-volume reprint of *Das Mahābhārata und seine Theile*, Osnabrück: Biblio Verlag, 1971.

Hopkins, Edward Washburn. 1895. *The Religions of India*. Handbooks on the History of Religions, vol. 1. Boston, MA: Ginn and Co.

Hopkins, Edward Washburn. 1905. Review of *Die Bhagavadgītā aus dem Sanskrit übersetzt, mit einer Einleitung über ihre ursprüngliche Gestalt, ihre Lehren und ihr Alter*, by Richard Garbe. *Journal of the Royal Asiatic Society of Great Britain and Ireland* (new series) 37.2: 384–389.

Jacob, George Adolphus. 1891. *Upaniṣadvākyakośaḥ: a Concordance to the Principal Upaniṣads and Bhagavadgītā*. Bombay Sanskrit Series, vol. 39. Bombay: Government Central Book Depot. (Reprint Delhi: Motilal Banarsidass, 1963.)

Jacobi, Hermann. 1918. "Über die Einfügung der Bhagavadgītā im Mahābhārata" *Zeitschrift der Deutschen Morgenländischen Gesellschaft* 72: 323–327.

Jaiswal, Suvira. 1967. *The Origin and Development of Vaiṣṇavism (Vaiṣṇavism from 200 B.C. to A.D. 500)*. Delhi: Munshiram Manoharlal.

Ježić, Mislav. 1986. "Textual Layers of the *Bhagavadgītā* as Traces of Indian Cultural History" in Wolfgang Morgenroth (ed.) *Sanskrit and World Culture: Proceedings of the Fourth World Sanskrit Conference of the International Association of Sanskrit Studies, Weimar, May 23–30, 1979*. Schriften zur Geschichte und Kultur des Alten Orients, vol. 18. Berlin: Akademie-Verlag, 628–638.

Ježić, Mislav. 2009. "The Relationship between the *Bhagavadgītā* and the Vedic Upaniṣads: Parallels and Relative Chronology" in Robert P. Goldman and Muneo Tokunaga (eds.) *Epic Undertakings*. Papers of the 12th World Sanskrit Conference, vol. 2. Delhi: Motilal Banarsidass, 215–282.

Khair, Gajanan Shripat. 1969. *Quest for the Original Gītā*. Bombay: Somaiya Publications.

Killingley, Dermot. 1986. "Oṃ: the Sacred Syllable in the Veda" in Julius J. Lipner (ed.) *A Net Cast Wide: Investigations into Indian Thought in Memory of David Friedman*. Newcastle upon Tyne: Grevatt and Grevatt, 14–33.

Killingley, Dermot. 1997. "The Paths of the Dead and the Five Fires" in Peter Connolly and Sue Hamilton (eds) *Indian Insights: Buddhism, Brahmanism and Bhakti. Papers from the Annual Spalding Symposium on Indian Religions*. London: Luzac Oriental, 1–20.

Mahadevan, T. M. P. 1952. "The Original Gītā" in N. Sivarama Sastry and G. Hanumantha Rao (eds.) *Prof. M. Hiriyanna Commemoration Volume*. Mysore: Prof. M. Hiriyanna Commemoration Volume Committee, 101–108.

Malinar, Angelika. 2007. *The Bhagavadgītā: Doctrines and Contexts*. Cambridge: Cambridge University Press.

Murdoch, John. 1894. *Krishna as Described in the Vishnu Purana, Bhagavata Purana, and the Mahabharata, Especially the Bhagavad Gita; with a Letter to Mrs. Annie Besant*. Madras: Christian Literature Society.

Preciado-Solis, Benjamin. 1984. *The Kṛṣṇa Cycle in the Purāṇas: Themes and Motifs in a Heroic Saga*. Delhi: Motilal Banarsidass.

Rao, K. B. Ramakrishna. 1966. *Theism of Pre-Classical Sāṁkhya*. Mysore: Prasaranga, University of Mysore.

Roebuck, Valerie J. (trans.) 2003. *The Upaniṣads*. Revised edition. Penguin Classics. London: Penguin.

Sadhale, Shastri Gajanana Shambhu (ed.) 2010. *The Bhagavad-Gītā with Eleven Commentaries*, vol. 1. Delhi: Parimal Publications. First published 1935.

Sastry, Alladi Mahadeva (trans.) 1991. *The Bhagavad Gita with the Commentary of Sri Sankaracharya*. Madras: Samata Books. First published 1897.

Sharma, Krishna. 2015. *Bhakti and the Bhakti Movement: a New Perspective. A Study in the History of Ideas*. Delhi: Munshiram Manoharlal. First published 1987.

Szczurek, Przemysław. 2005. "Bhakti Interpolations and Additions in the *Bhagavadgītā*" in Petteri Koskikallio (ed.) *Epics, Khilas, and Purāṇas: Continuities and Ruptures*. Proceedings of the Third Dubrovnik International Conference on the Sanskrit Epics and Purāṇas. Zagreb: Croatian Academy of Sciences and Arts, 183–220.

Thieme, Paul. 1965. "Īśopaniṣad (= Vājasaneyi-Saṃhitā 40) 1–14" *Journal of the American Oriental Society* 85.1: 89–99.

20 The Upaniṣads and later Hinduism

Dermot Killingley

When Swami Vivekananda (1863–1902) returned to India in 1897, after his triumph at the Parliament of Religions in Chicago in 1893, he gave a series of speeches announcing his plan for the revival of true religion in India. An important part of this plan was to propagate the Upaniṣads:

> The first work that demands our attention is that the most wonderful truths confined in our Upanishads, in our scriptures, in our Purânas must be brought out from the books, brought out from the monasteries, brought out from the forests, brought out from the possession of selected bodies of people, and scattered broadcast all over the land … Everyone must know of them, because it is said, "This has first to be heard, then thought upon, and then meditated upon [BU 2.4.5 = BU 4.5.6]."
>
> (Vivekananda 1962–1997: 3.221)

Actually, Yājñavalkya tells Maitreyī that the self is to be *seen*, heard, thought on and meditated on; Vivekananda, as he often does, has adapted his quotation to fit his rhetorical point: that the Upaniṣads and other texts need to be heard, and have only been heard in secluded places. But it is largely true that knowledge of the Upaniṣads was restricted from the outset to the Vedic schools which transmitted them (Cohen 2008: 10), and some of them contain injunctions to pass the knowledge taught in them only to one's eldest son or a suitable student (CU 3.11.5), or not to pass it to "one who is not tranquil, or is not one's son or student" (SU 6.22) – besides the many stories in which a teacher's reluctance is only overcome by a student's persistent show of intellectual and moral worthiness (below, pp. 261–263). The development of Vedānta (above, pp. 5–6) gave the Upaniṣads a new context outside the Vedic schools, but it too was restricted to its own successions of teacher and student, though some Vedāntic ideas were popularized through texts such as the Purāṇas.

This restriction of the circles in which the Upaniṣads could be known was not absolute: They could even become available to an open-minded Muslim ruler (Chapter 21). But what broke such restrictions irreversibly was the introduction of printing around the beginning of the nineteenth century, and the concomitant rise in literacy. The diffusion of knowledge was no longer bounded by oral transmission and manuscripts; printing brought not only periodicals and books in English and in Indian languages, connecting the reader to the contemporary world of facts and ideas, but also connected him (female literacy was rare till later in the century) to the past, through editions and translations of ancient literature. Knowledge of Indian traditions was no longer confined to India: along with printing came improved facilities for travel and correspondence. Sir William Jones (1746–1794), who came to Kolkata in 1783 as a judge, and after some years added Sanskrit to the many languages he knew, translated the *Īśā Upaniṣad*; this was the first Upaniṣad to be translated directly into English. Anquetil Duperron's Latin version of fifty Upaniṣads, translated from Persian, published in 1801–1802 (below, pp. 236–239), was followed in 1816 by Rammohun Roy's English translations, which quickly became available in the British Isles, Europe and the USA. This was one of the most far-reaching of many shifts in the context of the Upaniṣads, and consequently in their meaning.

From the time when the classical Upaniṣads were composed, the ways in which they were understood had been affected by changes in society, ritual practice and theology. The community in which brahmins and kṣatriyas traded creation stories, *upāsana*s, etymologies, and theories of personality and cosmology, against a background of sacrifices, gifts of cows, and twelve-year periods of Veda study, if it ever existed as the Upaniṣads represent it, could not have survived the shifts in political and economic power to new cities and dynasties which took place from around the fifth century BCE onwards. The Sanskrit literary tradition was aware of these changes, though it expressed them in different terms. According to an account repeated in the Purāṇas and elsewhere, the world since 3102 BCE has been in the fallen Kali age, when kings are no longer kṣatriyas by birth, brahmins serve in temples instead of conducting Vedic rituals, and *bhakti*, not knowledge, is the way to salvation.

The development of new ideas led to the composition of new Upaniṣads, classified by scholars as saṃnyāsa Upaniṣads, yoga Upaniṣads, Vaiṣṇava, Śaiva, and Śākta Upaniṣads (Chapters 37–41). The category of Upaniṣad has an indefinite membership; there are often said to be 108, though many more can be counted. Historical change has also affected the ways in which the classical Upaniṣads, as we call them in this book (and this too is a fuzzy category), were understood. Detached from the Brāhmaṇas, stories such as that of Yājñavalkya and Janaka (above, p. 127) lose much of their meaning, as do references to ritual practices, while the development of the Vedānta and Sāṃkhya systems has brought a new rigidity to terms and concepts which had been flexible and slippery.

The nineteenth century

The first Indian to translate Upaniṣads into English, Rammohun Roy (1772?–1833), was a Bengali brahmin from a family with no tradition of Vedic study; he came to the Upaniṣads from the outside. Having worked first in the management of his father's estates, and then, from 1797, as a financier in Kolkata, he served from 1803 to 1815 in various capacities with officials of the East India Company, which at that time ruled Bengal. During this period he became fluent in English and familiar with European ideas, and it may be around the same time that he studied Advaita Vedānta (Killingley 1993: 101–102). From 1815, when he settled in Kolkata, till 1830, when he left for England, where he died, he promoted a form of monotheism which took as its authority the Upaniṣads and the *Vedānta-sūtras*, interpreted through the Advaita tradition of Śaṅkara.

From 1816 to 1819, Rammohun published Bengali translations of the *Kena*, *Īśā*, *Kaṭha*, *Māṇḍūkya*, and *Muṇḍaka* Upaniṣads, and English translations of the same Upaniṣads except the *Māṇḍūkya*. The English versions are substantially different from the Bengali ones: while the latter draw their terminology and concepts from the Sanskrit tradition, making little attempt to adapt them to their nineteenth-century Bengali context, the former use English words taken from the vocabulary of European rational theism. Thus *brahman* is represented in Bengali by the Sanskrit word, but is called "the Supreme Being" (MU 1.1) or "God" (KU 5.6) in English; *ātman* is similarly untranslated in Bengali, but is "soul" in KU 2. 18–23, but also "intellectual power" (KU 5.13); in other contexts, where the Bengali calls it *paramātmā* "supreme Self," it can be "God" (IU 7) or "the Supreme Being" (IU 6). The Bengali versions never reached a wide readership; Bengali prose, which Rammohun used in his translations, was rare at that time, and as Rammohun himself admitted, few were able to read it (Killingley 1993: 38–39). He also used a highly Sanskritized vocabulary which would be unfamiliar to most Bengali readers. The English versions, on the other hand, were distributed and reprinted overseas, and reviewed in British, American, and French periodicals.

Rammohun's work was aimed in two directions: to show Hindus that they were heirs to an ancient and still living tradition of monotheism, without imagery or mythology, and persuade them to follow it; and to show British and other non-Hindus that true Hinduism, as distinct from the myths and practices which disfigured it, was founded on reason. His choice of Upaniṣads to translate is significant: not only are they among the shorter ones, but they are among those in which the idea of God as creator and object of worship is most readily to be found (above, pp. 164–172), and which say little of ritual, or even expressly reject it (MU 1.1.4–5; 1.2.7–12). He quotes other Upaniṣads also, especially in his Bengali works. It is not surprising that he only published a Bengali version of the *Māṇḍūkya Upaniṣad*: it is difficult to render comprehensibly in English, and could be interpreted as claiming that the self is identical to the ultimate being, or that the world is illusory. While Rammohun used Advaita Vedānta as his authority, he understood it as making the individual self dependent on *brahman*, not identical with it.

His aim in his Bengali works was to foster a group of worshipers of one God, without using idols or myths, using both reason and Vedānta as their authority. Perhaps inevitably, the group were all male, and all of the urban middle class which grew during the nineteenth century in the new environment of British political and commercial power; however, they were by no means unanimous in their thinking. In 1828 this group was formalized as the Brahmo (Bengali *brāhma* or *brāhmya* "belonging to *brahman*") Sabha, also called the Brahmo Samaj, which they translated into English as the Theistic Society. Readings from the Upaniṣads, and sermons expounding them, were a feature of its meetings. It attracted considerable attention overseas, thanks to Rammohun's diligent international correspondence, and considerable opposition in Bengal, among both conservative Hindus and Christian missionaries; but it was not a large group, and after Rammohun sailed to England in 1830, it declined (Hatcher 2008: 26–29). Its fortunes changed from 1842 onwards, when it was taken over and reconstituted by Debendranath Tagore (1817–1905), the son of a wealthy friend of Rammohun.

In his autobiography, Debendranath claims that he renounced idolatry under the influence of Rammohun (Tagore 1909: 55–56); if this was when Rammohun was still in Kolkata, as he implies, Debendranath could not have been more than thirteen. Later, he was troubled by the thought that no Hindu text was free from idolatry. By a miracle, as he recorded it years later in his autobiography, he chanced on a page detached from a Sanskrit book, which he could not understand. He consulted Rāmcandra Vidyāvāgīś, the paṇḍit who preached at the Brahmo Sabha, who recognized it as the *Īśā Upaniṣad*, and explained it to him. Debendranath took this as a divine revelation, inviting him to renounce the world and delight in God. He then studied five Upaniṣads with Rāmcandra – the same five that Rammohun had translated (Tagore 1909: 56–59; Hatcher 2008: 39–41). The revelation led him to found a society, the Tattvabodhinī ("truth-revealing") Sabhā, in 1839. There were many such societies in Kolkata, in which young men met weekly to discuss ideas. Some were fiercely rationalistic, but this one was devoted to knowledge of God; its first meeting was preceded by ritual bathing, and Debendranath gave an inaugural discourse on *Kaṭha Upaniṣad* 2.6, which warns of the snare of wealth leading to repeated death (Tagore 1909: 60–61). Not all the members were as keen on the Upaniṣads as he was, but among the twenty-one discourses published by the society in 1841, ten include Upaniṣadic quotations (Hatcher 2008: 178).

In 1842 Debendranath took over the management of the Brahmo Samaj, leading to a virtual merger of the two groups, though his own group remained in existence till 1859 (Hatcher 2008: 56–61). But his difficulties in seeking textual authority for his religious convictions returned. First, unlike Rammohun, he rejected Śaṅkara's commentaries on the Upaniṣads, because he could not accept his monism, arguing that to identify the self with God left no room for worship; so he began a commentary of his own (Tagore 1909: 72–73). Like many Bengalis of his time, he was sensitive to Christian critiques of Advaita

Vedānta, which argued that it denied the reality of the soul and of the world (Hatcher 2008: 86–99). In 1845 he compiled a liturgical text, both a creed and a hymn of praise, from various Upaniṣads (translations below are mine):

> Brahman is truth, knowledge, infinite, (TU 2.1)
> The blissful immortality which shines. (MU 2.2.8)
> He has pervaded, bright, bodiless, unwounded,
> Sinewless, pure, not pierced by evil,
> The sage, wise, all-encompassing, self-existent,
> He has rightly dispensed things from eternal ages. (IU 8)
> From him is born breath, mind, and all the faculties;
> Space, wind, light, water, and earth which supports all. (MU 2.1.3)
> From fear of him fire burns, from fear the sun burns;
> From fear rain and wind, and death, the fifth, runs. (KU 6.3)

He also put as a heading to the society's weekly journal:

> Ṛgveda, Yajurveda, Sāmaveda, Atharvaveda, phonetics, ritual, grammar, etymology, metre, and astrology are lower knowledge; the higher is that by which the imperishable is known. (MU 1.1.3)

However, Debendranath's reliance on the Upaniṣads met with difficulties. He describes how he was disturbed on finding Vaiṣṇava, Śaiva and Śākta Upaniṣads, which conflicted with his *brāhma dharma* – the non-idolatrous religion of a formless God. Reliance on Śaṅkara's commentary as defining a canon of eleven Upaniṣads did not solve the problem, because Śaṅkara's monism denied the duality of God and worshiper. Even accepting the canon of eleven and rejecting Śaṅkara did not help, because within the canon were statements such as "You are that" (CU 6.8–16), and "Deeds, and the self made of consciousness, all become one in the highest immutable" (MU 3.2.7). Debendranath's solution was to make a selection of texts, guided by the pure heart (Tagore 1909: 159–166) – in effect, his own heart. Textual authority was subordinated to intuition.

Debendranath's love of the Upaniṣads continued; it was inherited by his eldest son, the poet, novelist. musician and painter Rabindranath Tagore (1861–1941), who grew up with the sound of them. Rabindranath, however, was not so concerned about textual authority as his father; he refused to be constrained by rules. When he quotes the Upaniṣads in English, his translations are so free as to be hard to recognize. But he takes the old identifications of macrocosm and microcosm, and interprets them in terms of bonds of aesthetic appreciation and love. After quoting BU 2.5.10 and 2.5.14, on the man made of light and immortality in space and in the self, he says: "Thus to attain our world-consciousness, we have to unite our feeling with this all-pervasive infinite feeling" (Tagore 1931: 18).

Whereas the Brahmo Samaj remained a movement of middle-class Bengalis, the Ārya Samaj, founded by the wandering Gujarati brahmin Dayānanda Sarasvatī (1825–1883), has had much wider influence, especially among Punjabi Hindus; its centers are all over the world, and it has contributed ideas and practices to international Hinduism, even among those who are not its members. The founding text of the movement is the large book *Satyārth Prakāś* "The Light of Truth," which Dayānanda wrote in Hindi, with Sanskrit quotations; it was published in its present form in 1882, and is widely available in many languages. He published an earlier version in 1875, which is now almost unobtainable; he changed many of his ideas between the two editions (Jordens 1978: 99–126, 249–269).

A crucial event in Dayānanda's development was a visit in 1872 to Kolkata, where he met Debendranath Tagore. The forty-odd Upaniṣad quotations in the first edition of *Satyārth Prakāś* were clearly influenced by Debendranath's selection (Jordens 1978: 79). But when he completely revised the book in 1882, he used fewer of them, particularly avoiding those that pointed to Advaita Vedānta, which he considered false (Jordens 1978: 250). By that time he had decided that the only authoritative part of the Veda was the *mantras*, rejecting the Brāhmaṇas and Upaniṣads (Jordens 1978: 278). Believing that this strictly defined Veda was eternal and infallible, taught the worship of one formless God, and contained all knowledge including modern science, he interpreted the *mantras* in original ways; the Upaniṣads less so. He quotes KeU 1.4–7, describing *brahman* as beyond the senses, as an instruction to worship God as formless (Dayānanda 1972: 307). Statements such as "You are that" (CU 6.8–16) or "I am *brahman*" (BU 1.4.10) he interprets as indicating a close relationship with God, not identity (Dayānanda 1972: 188).

Vivekananda

Returning to Vivekananda, we come to another member of the English-educated bourgeoisie of Kolkata, though less prosperous than the Tagores. He had been a member of the Brahmo Samaj, but became a disciple of the uncouth saint Ramakrishna (1836?–1886); in 1897 he founded the Ramakrishna Mission, to carry out the propagation of Hinduism to which he believed his master had called him. Returning in 1897 from his first tour of the USA, Britain, and Europe, he became not just a Bengali celebrity but an all-India one, and is now a hero of modern Hinduism.

With a confidence very unlike Debendranath's sensitivity to Christian criticism, he took Advaita Vedānta as the basis of his thinking, making it the key to reconciling the various doctrines not only of Hinduism but of all religious traditions. He held that the identity of the self with *brahman*, which many of his contemporaries associated with unworldly quietism, and considered a cause of the political weakness of India, was a source of strength. "Strength, strength is what the Upanishads speak to me from every page" (Vivekananda 1962–1997: vol. 3.237). He has little time for the hermeneutic devices of the

Sanskrit commentators – "text-torturing," he calls it – but follows a method which he believes that Ramakrishna taught him: to regard any passage that conflicts with Advaita Vedānta as part of a harmonious system in which dualistic ideas lead to up to monism (Vivekananda 1962–1997: vol. 3.233–234). Much of his collected works consists of talks, taken down by others, and they are rhetorical rather than systematic. He shows more interest in the narratives of the Upaniṣads than the thinkers we have looked at so far, and he finds the stories of kṣatriya teachers so significant that he claims that "most of the Upanishads were written by Kshatriyas" (Vivekananda 1962–1997 vol. 5.309). He claimed to be a kṣatriya himself (Vivekananda 1962–1997: vol. 3.211), since he belonged to the Kāyastha caste of Bengal, who claim kṣatriya status though their traditional occupation is clerical.

One of Vivekananda's arguments concerns "the celebrated aphorism, Tat Tvam Asi, 'Thou art That' [CU 6.8–16]," which he introduces as "the basis of all our ethics and morality." He continues:

> To every man, this is taught: Thou art one with this Universal Being, and, as such, every soul that exists is your soul; and every body that exists is your body; and in hurting anyone, you hurt yourself, in loving anyone, you love yourself.
>
> (Vivekananda 1962–1997: vol. 1.389–390)

As with many of Vivekananda's ideas, it is not argued sustainedly in one passage; but it appears elsewhere in other forms, not quoting the phrase *tat tvam asi* (Vivekananda 1962–1997: vol. 1.384–385; 2.252; 5.14). The same argument, using this phrase, had been presented by the German philosopher and Sanskritist Paul Deussen, in a lecture in Mumbai in 1893; it has been called the *tat tvam asi* ethic (Hacker 1995: 295–298). Hacker argues that Vivekananda took it from Deussen, but there are difficulties in his argument (Killingley 1998: 145–149). Several later Hindu writers present the same ethical argument, using the phrase *tat tvam asi* (Hacker 1995: 298–308).

The twentieth century

One of the most original Hindu thinkers in the period after Vivekananda is Aurobindo Ghose (1872–1950), a Bengali who was educated in England, returned to India 1893, and immersed himself both in nationalist politics and in Indian cultural and religious traditions. In 1910 he withdrew from direct political activity and settled in the French territory Pondicherry, south of Chennai, where he became a religious teacher with an international following, and developed his own form of Vedānta, *pūrṇādvaita* or "integral non-dualism," in which Vedic sources are combined with Western ideas such as evolution, and the world and *brahman* are equally real, contrary to Advaita Vedānta. He began studying the Upaniṣads in 1900, when he was working in Baroda, and continued redrafting commentaries, publishing them eventually in his journal *Ārya*, which ran in Pondicherry from 1914 to 1921. Part of his comment on TU 2.2.1 gives an idea of his belief that the highest state is neither inactive nor without individuality:

> Our highest state of being is indeed a becoming one with Brahman in his eternity and infinity, but it is also an association with him in delight of self-fulfilment, *aśnute saha brahmaṇā* ["reaches, together with *brahman*"].
> (Ghose 2001: 155–156)

Aurobindo found particular value in the *Īśā Upaniṣad*, with its juxtaposition of opposites – renunciation and enjoyment, moving and not-moving, near and far. He wrote a translation (Ghose 2003: 5–10), and a long commentary (Ghose 2003: 13–91), first published serially in *Ārya*. But he had begun drafting expositions of it in 1902, and these have been published posthumously (Ghose 2003: 95–167).

A more accessible writer is Radhakrishnan (1888–1975), who was not a religious leader but an academic philosopher, promoting a form of Advaita Vedānta that was compatible with modern ideas of individual liberty. Besides quoting the Upaniṣads frequently in his books, many of which started as public lectures in the West or in India, he published a translation with an introduction and notes (Radhakrishnan 1953). The translation is similar to Hume's (1931), and is accompanied by the romanized Sanskrit text. The notes sometimes elucidate the Vedic context of the text, or add brief explanations from Sanskrit commentaries. But sometimes he refers to ancient Greek philosophers such as Plato and Aristotle, or to Christian mystics or theologians, or to Muslim mystics, or to Taoism, wishing to place the ideas in a universal context; he believed in a perennial wisdom which could be found in all traditions. Sometimes his enthusiasm for mysticism carries him away; on CU 3.13.8 he writes: "The writer here refers to visions and voices of which some mystic seers speak" (Radhakrishnan 1953: 390), where the text explicitly refers to the warmth you can perceive by touching your body, and the sound you hear when you cover your ears.

Though M. K. Gandhi (1869–1948) is better known for his devotion to the *Bhagavadgītā*, he also drew on the Upaniṣads, especially the *Īśā*. In a speech on January 16, 1937, he said:

> Many of you, I think, know the *Ishopanishad*. I read it years ago with translation and commentary. I learnt it by heart in Yeravda Jail. But it did not then captivate me as it has done during the past few months, and I have now come to the final conclusion that if all the Upanishads and all other scriptures happened all of a sudden to be reduced to ashes, and if only the first verse in the *Ishopanishad* were left intact in the memory of Hindus, Hinduism would live for ever.
> (Gandhi 1976: 258–259)

He goes on to translate the stanza:

> All this that we see in this great Universe is pervaded by God … Renounce it and enjoy it. There is another rendering that means the same thing, though: Enjoy what He gives you … Do not covet anybody's wealth or possession.
>
> (Gandhi 1976: 259)

The last line of the stanza is "the final and most important part"; to Gandhi, for whom truth is inseparable from right action, a moral injunction is more important than a statement of belief. He goes on to say that the rest of the Upaniṣad is a commentary on the first stanza, and so is the *Bhagavadgītā*. He does not explain directly why he sees no difference between his two translations of the third line, which reflect two possible analyses of the syntax. However, he says that if God pervades everything, "you cannot enjoy anything that is not given by Him." And, as "one of His numerous creatures, it behoves you to renounce everything and lay it at His feet" (Gandhi 1976: 259). Both renderings, however different grammatically, convey the moral teaching that we should recognize God's ownership of the things we enjoy; to renounce them is to regard them as God's and not ours. This is indeed close to the *Bhagavadgītā*'s understanding of renunciation.

The Upaniṣads, and to a greater extent the *Bhagavadgītā*, were part of the shared intellectual world of the generation that led India to independence in 1947 – often shared through discussions among political prisoners. Even the secularist Nehru, reflecting in prison, admired them for their freedom from "humility before an all-powerful deity" (Nehru 1960: 80), their "metaphysical democracy" (Nehru 1960: 80), and their "continual emphasis on the fitness of the body and clarity of the mind," which he connected with Gandhi's principle of self-suffering (Nehru 1960: 82). The Upaniṣads were so much a part of Indian public discourse in the mid-twentieth century that even the Dalit leader B. R. Ambedkar, a bitter critic of brahmanical culture, used *tat tvam asi*, together with *ahaṃ brahmāsmi* "I am *brahman*" (BU 1.4.10), as a basis for political equality. He wrote, in an unpublished essay, that "no doctrine could furnish a stronger foundation for Democracy"; democracy requires that "each individual shall know that he is as good as everybody else" (Ambedkar, quoted in Peetush 2017: 368). His point, however, is that the doctrine has never been put into practice.

Upaniṣads online

In India, the print revolution was followed by the electronic revolution after two centuries, rather than five and a half as in Europe. Vivekananda's vision has been partially fulfilled: the Upaniṣads are now common property, for anyone who wants them, not only in India but among the worldwide Hindu diaspora, or anyone in search of spirituality. On the other hand, those who choose to access the Sanskrit texts, or the many English, Hindi, and other translations and commentaries, that are available online, are a self-selected minority of web-users. These seekers face no intellectual or moral tests; their transactions involve no gifts of cows or firewood. The teachers, too, need no qualification of lineage, Vedic learning or ritual status; anyone, anywhere, who has the equipment and skills, can set up a website and wait for the clicks to come in.

Let us take a random example, intending no judgment and no claim that it is typical, which would require an immense survey. Jayaram V, whose website describes him as "a leading author of Indian religions, philosophy, mysticism, and spirituality" (Jayaram 2016), offers an online translation of the *Īśā Upaniṣad*, with a brief commentary (hinduwebsite 2016). The commentary takes an Advaita Vedānta view, saying under IU 6: "The whole universe is pervaded by only 'I' … The 'you' exists in our consciousness because of illusion or maya." However, like Gandhi, the commentary is less concerned with metaphysics than with an ethical stance in which the world is enjoyed while renouncing it by recognizing God as its owner. While using Sanskrit words such as *Purusha* or *Hiranyagarbha* ("golden embryo," a term used in many Vedic cosmogonies), it also appeals to people interested in "spirituality" without attachment to a particular tradition; in the manner of Radhakrishnan, it refers to " 'the Way' described in Taoism." It does not refer to other texts, except the *Bhagavadgītā*; in what is perhaps the most typically Upaniṣadic point in the piece, it finds an affinity of number (above, pp. 69–71) between the two texts: The IU has eighteen stanzas, and the BhG has eighteen chapters.

The *Īśā Upaniṣad* has received particular attention in the time since that fluttering page caught Debendranath's eye in 1839; perhaps because it is so brief, and so full of evocative yet puzzling imagery; cryptic, and open to many interpretations. Another text that has taken on a life of its own online is the prayer *asato mā sad gamaya, tamaso mā jyotir gamaya, mṛtyor māmṛtaṃ gamaya* "From the unreal lead me to the real, from darkness lead me to light, from death lead me to immortality" (BU 1.3.28). It is one of the passages remembered by Nehru (1960: 79). Another is *oṃ. saha nāv avatu, saha nau bhunaktu, saha vīryaṃ karavāvahai, tejasvi nāv adhītam astu, mā vidviṣāvahai. oṃ. śāntiḥ śāntiḥ śāntiḥ.* "Oṃ. May it help us both; may it profit us both; may we work heroically together; may our study be brilliant; may we not quarrel. Oṃ. Peace, peace, peace." It is not strictly part of an Upaniṣad, but is one of the prayers which are often recited before or after one (Roebuck 2003: l; 214); T. S. Eliot alludes to it at the end of *The Waste Land* (1936: 77; 84). It evokes the ideal Vedic teacher–student relationship; though, as Ambedkar reminds us, ideals are not always followed.

References

Cohen, Signe. 2008. *Text and Authority in the Older Upaniṣads*. Leiden: Brill.

Dayānanda Saraswati. 1972 [1908]. *Light of Truth: An English Translation of Satyarth Prakash*. Translated by Durga Prasad. Third edition. Delhi: Jan Gyan Prakashan.

Eliot, T. S. 1936. *Collected Poems: 1909–1935*. London: Faber & Faber.

Gandhi, M. K. 1976. *Collected Works of Mahatma Gandhi*, vol. 64. (From the 100-volume series, 1956–1994.) Publications Division, Government of India.

Ghose. Aurobindo. 2001. *Kena and Other Upanishads* (The Complete Works of Sri Aurobindo, vol. 18). Pondicherry: Sri Aurobindo Ashram.

Ghose, Aurobindo. 2003. *Isha Upanishad*. (The Complete Works of Sri Aurobindo, vol. 17). Pondicherry: Sri Aurobindo Ashram.

Hacker, Paul. 1995 [1961]. "Schopenhauer and Hindu Ethics" translated by Dermot Killingley. In Wilhelm Halbfass (ed.) *Philology and Confrontation: Paul Hacker on Traditional and Modern Vedānta*. Albany, NY: State University of New York Press, 273–318. First published in German as "Schopenhauer und die Ethik des Hinduismus" *Saeculum* 4 (1961), 365–399; reprinted in Paul Hacker, *Kleine Schriften* (Wiesbaden, Steiner, 1978), 531–564.

Hatcher, Brian. 2008. *Bourgeois Hinduism, or the Faith of the Modern Vedantists: Rare Discourses from Early Colonial Bengal*. New York: Oxford University Press.

Hinduwebsite 2016www.hinduwebsite.com/upanishads/essays/isalessons.asp (accessed Dec 23, 2016).

Hume, R. E. 1931. *The Thirteen Principal Upanishads: Translated from the Sanskrit*. Second edition. Oxford: Oxford University Press.

Jayaram 2016. www.jayaramv.com/about.aspx (accessed Dec 23, 2016).

Jordens, J. T. F. 1978. *Dayānanda Sarasvatī: His Life and Ideas*. Delhi: Oxford University Press.

Killingley, Dermot. 1993. *Rammohun Roy in Hindu and Christian Tradition*. Newcastle upon Tyne: Grevatt & Grevatt.

Killingley, Dermot. 1998. "Vivekananda's Western Message from the East" in William Radice (ed.) *Swami Vivekananda and the Modernization of Hinduism*. Delhi: Oxford University Press, 138–157.

Nehru, Jawaharlal. 1960 [1946]. *The Discovery of India*. London: Meridian.

Peetush, Ashwani. 2017. "The Ethics of Radical Equality: Vivekananda's and Radhakrishnan's Neo-Hinduism as a Form of Spiritual Liberalism" in Shyam Ranganathan (ed.) *The Bloomsbury Handbook of Hindu Ethics*. London and New York: Bloomsbury, 357–382.

Radhakrishnan, S. 1953. *The Principal Upaniṣads: Edited with Introduction, Text, Translation and Notes*. London: George Allen & Unwin.

Roebuck, Valerie. 2003. *The Upaniṣads. Translated and Edited* (Penguin Classics series). London: Penguin.

Tagore, Debendranath. 1909. *The Autobiography of Maharshi Devendranath Tagore*. Translated from the original Bengali by Satyendranath Tagore and Indira Devi. Calcutta: S. K. Lahiri.

Tagore, Rabindranath. 1931. *Sādhanā: The Realisation of Life*. London: Macmillan.

Vivekananda, Swami. 1962–1997. *The Complete Works of Swami Vivekananda*. 9 vols. Calcutta, Advaita Ashrama.

Further reading

Clooney, Francis X., S.J. "From Anxiety to Bliss: Argument, Care and Responsibility in the Vedānta Reading of *Taittirīya* 2.1–6a" in Laurie L. Patton (ed.) *Authority, Anxiety ad Canon: Essays in Vedic Interpretation*. Albany, NY: State University of New York Press, 139–169.

De Michaelis, Elizabeth. 2004. *A History of Modern Yoga: Patañjali and Western Esotericism*. London: Continuum, 51–146.

Killingley, Dermot. 1993. *Rammohun Roy in Hindu and Christian Tradition*. Newcastle upon Tyne: Grevatt & Grevatt.

Killingley, Dermot. 2003. "Modernity, Revival and Reform" in Gavin Flood (ed.) *The Blackwell Companion to Hinduism*. Oxford: Blackwell, 509–525.

Rambachan, Anantanand. "Redefining the Authority of Scripture: The Rejection of Vedic Infallibility by the Brahmo Samaj" in Laurie L. Patton (ed.) *Authority, Anxiety ad Canon: Essays in Vedic Interpretation*. Albany, NY: State University of New York Press, 253–279.

Renou, Louis. 1965. *The Destiny of the Veda in India*. Delhi: Motilal Banarsidass.

21 Dara Shikoh and the first translation of the Upaniṣads

Signe Cohen

The Life of Dara Shikoh

The Indian prince Dara Shikoh or Dara Shukoh (1615–1659) was the great-grandson of Akbar the Great, who ruled the Mughal Empire of northern India from 1556 to his death in 1605. Although Dara Shikoh never met his famous great-grandfather, he embraced many of Akbar's intellectual ideas. Like his great-grandfather, Dara Shikoh became a patron of Indo-Persian art and culture. While both men were devout Muslims in their own ways, Dara Shikoh was intrigued by his Akbar's notion that all religions contain some truth, and that there is a great deal to learn through debate with representatives of other faiths. A brief Upaniṣadic text called the *Allah Upaniṣad* is believed to stem from the cultural milieu surrounding Akbar the Great. This Upaniṣad in fifteen stanzas praises Allah, the God of Islam, and identifies him with the Vedic god Varuṇa, the sun, and the breath. In many ways, this curious little text is a symbol of Akbar's quest for the unifying truth behind all religions, a quest Dara Shikoh embraced wholeheartedly.

While Dara Shikoh shared Akbar's fascination with other religions, the young prince was far less politically astute than his powerful ancestor. As the oldest son of Emperor Shah Jahan, who ruled the Mughal Empire from 1628 to 1658, Dara Shikoh was generally favored to take over the throne after his father. When he was eighteen, the prince was appointed military commander over a portion of his father's army. Over time, he was given greater and greater military responsibilities, and his father eventually confirmed him as his official heir. When Shah Jahan fell ill, however, one of Dara Shikoh's brothers, Shah Shuja, immediately stepped up and declared himself Mughal Emperor. The ailing Shah Jahan still supported his oldest son in his claim to the throne, but in the end, another one of Dara Shikoh's brothers emerged victorious in the intense struggle for the Mughal throne that ensued: his younger half-brother Muhi-ud-Din, who later took the name Aurangzeb. In the Battle of Samugarh outside Agra, Aurangzeb's men defeated Dara Shikoh's troops in 1658. Aurangzeb then proceeded to take over Agra and depose his father. Dara Shikoh was eventually captured by his brother Aurangzeb, and after a brief trial he was declared an apostate from Islam due to his syncretistic views and executed.

Although he never became Emperor, Dara Shikoh nevertheless left his mark on Indian civilization through his enthusiastic patronage of art, philosophy, and religion. During his lifetime, Dara Shikoh was an ardent collector of paintings and calligraphy, in spite of his brother Aurangzeb's disapproval of such frivolity. As a young man, he studied calligraphy with Ākā, the master calligrapher at his father's court, and is said to have been Ākā's finest student. After his marriage, Dara Shikoh presented an album of his favorite paintings to his beloved wife, Nādīra, and this album is still known as one of the finest collections of Mughal art in the world.

Dara Shikoh and religion

In many ways, Dara Shikoh was the intellectual heir of his grandfather, Emperor Akbar. Akbar was passionately interested in religion. While Akbar was intrigued by the idea that all religions shared a common core of truth, this view was itself deeply rooted in a particular form of Islamic philosophy. Akbar embraced the pantheistic ideas of the mystic poet Ibn 'Arabi (1165–1240), who taught *wahdat al-wujud*, or "unity of all existence within God." In the spirit of seeing the unity between different religious traditions, Akbar established a translation agency, the *Maktab Khana*, which produced Persian translations of well-known Hindu Sanskrit texts, such as the *Mahābhārata* and *Rāmāyaṇa* epics and the philosophical treatise *Yogavāsiṣṭha*. Through these translations, Emperor Akbar hoped to "heal the religious differences between his subjects"[1] and create better understanding between people of different faiths. Akbar's great-grandson Dara Shikoh was equally interested in interreligious dialogue, and through his own writing as well as his translations, he championed the view that true wisdom was not limited to a single religious tradition.

Dara Shikoh himself composed several books in literate Persian that are still well known today. *Safīnat-al-auliyā* ("The Ship of Saints") is a pious hagiographical account of the lives of the Prophet Muhammad and his wives, as well as the lives of caliphs, imams, and Muslim saints. He also wrote another book with an almost identical title, *Sakīnat-al-auliyā* ("The Divine Presence of the Saints"), devoted to the life of the Indian Muslim mystic Mīyān Mīr (also known as Mīyān Jīv), a personal friend of Dara Shikoh's. More of Dara Shikoh's own religious thought begins to emerge in his work *Risāla-i-Ḥaq Numā*, "The Compass of the Truth," which deals with the stages an individual must undergo on the path toward spiritual perfection. In this work, he describes his own initiation into the Qadiri Sufi order and his quest for ultimate truth. He claims to have heard an angel's voice in his dreams and wrote that the angel told him that he had been given knowledge no other human king had ever had. Dara Shikoh then began to explore the idea that many aspects of Sufism might, in some essential way, be identical to the main ideas of Hinduism.

Dara Shikoh was passionately interested in religions of all kinds. A Muslim himself, he also took a deep interest in Christianity, Judaism, Hinduism, and

Sikhism. The young prince read the Pentateuch, the Psalms, and the Gospels, as well as numerous Hindu texts. He became a personal friend of the seventh Sikh Guru, Guru Har Rai (1630–1661). It is even said that Guru Har Rai once helped Dara Shikoh escape Aurangzeb's army by commanding his Sikh warriors to hide all the boats at a river crossing so Aurangzeb's men could not pursue Dara Shikoh.

Since the religion of Sikhism fuses many elements from both Islam and Hinduism, it is not surprising that Dara Shikoh was drawn to the Sikh Guru. Dara Shikoh himself was intrigued by the mystical connections between Islam and Hinduism, and he searched for evidence in Muslim and Hindu texts that could confirm his idea that these scriptures contained different articulations of the same eternal truth. In one of his own original poems, Dara Shikoh writes:

> What name should one call the Truth?
> Every name that exists is one of God's names.

By some sources, Dara Shikoh is also credited with a Persian translation of the *Bhagavad Gītā*, although it is unclear whether he himself translated the text, or merely commissioned the translation from someone else.

Dara Shikoh's most well-known original work is a treatise comparing the mystical Sufism of Islam and the Vedānta philosophy of India, which has its roots in the Upaniṣads. This work, *Majma'-ul-Baḥrain*, or "The Mingling of Two Seas," is a fascinating early work on comparative religion. In this book, Dara Shikoh tries to reconcile the religions of Islam and Hinduism and demonstrate many points of convergence between their teachings. He interprets Hinduism as strictly monotheistic, especially in light of the many passages in the Upaniṣads that seem to teach a form of monism (the idea that all reality is one). He claims that the Hindu god Brahmā is none other than the biblical Adam, and he identifies the syllable *oṃ* with Allah and the Hindu gods with angels. The unity of Islam and Hinduism is also the main theme of Dara Shikoh's introduction to the work for which he is most famous today: his Persian translation of the Upaniṣads.

"The Great Secret": Dara Shikoh's Persian translation of the Upaniṣads

As part of his quest for this truth common to all religions, Dara Shikoh translated the Upaniṣads from Sanskrit into Persian, the courtly language of the Mughal Empire, in 1657. This translation of the Upaniṣads was given the title *Sirr-e-Akbar* ("The Great Secret"), although it is occasionally also known as *Sirr al-asrār* ("The Secret of the Secrets"). By giving Muslim readers access to the Hindu Upaniṣads, Dara Shikoh hoped to "help mystics of both faiths."[2]

For Dara Shikoh, there is no conflict between the teachings of the Upaniṣads and those of Islam. In the introduction to his translation, Dara Shikoh even speculates that the Upaniṣads may actually be referred to in the Qur'an, the holy book of Islam. For the Qur'an (56:78) refers to a "hidden book" (*kitab al-maknun*) of mystical wisdom, writes Dara Shikoh, and perhaps this hidden book might be the Upaniṣads themselves.

Dara Shikoh's reading of the passage from the Qur'an is highly idiosyncratic; most Muslim scholars interpret the phrase *kitab al-maknun* simply as a reference to the "well-guarded" (rather than "hidden") Qur'an itself or its eternal heavenly prototype, rather than to a different book. But Dara Sukhoh was enamored of the notion that the Upaniṣads might be the secret lost teachings referenced in the Qur'an, and the very name of his translation, *Sirr-i-akbar*, alludes to his understanding of the Upaniṣads as the "Great Secret" of the Qur'an. Intriguingly, the title *Sirr-i-akbar* also has a double meaning hardly lost on Emperor Akbar's great-grandson; the title can mean both "The Great Secret" and "Akbar's Secret." Through this playful pun, Dara Shikoh evokes his ancestor's search for the ultimate truth of all religions and suggests that the secret which Akbar sought might be hidden in the Upaniṣads.

Dara Shikoh's Upaniṣad translation includes fifty texts. In his preface, he states that he does not at all find that these Hindu works undermine the monotheism of Islam; on the contrary; he finds that "the monotheistic verses contained in the four *Vedas* have been collected and elucidated in the *Upanikhat*, which is an ocean of monotheism."[3]

Darah Shikoh writes that he completed his translation with the help of Hindu scholars from Benares. Some scholars have questioned whether the prince himself actually knew enough Sanskrit to translate the Upaniṣads into Persian. What role did the scholars play in Dara Shikoh's translation? Did they merely help him with difficult passages, or did they explain the text to him line by line? This is difficult to determine, but Dara Shikoh's own introduction to the text makes clear that he has studied not only Sanskrit, but also Arabic, Syrian, and Hebrew. Given the prince's intelligence and his passionate interest in ancient Hindu texts, it does not seem like too much of a stretch to assume that he had studied Sanskrit, as he claimed.

The Persian translation itself is fluent and accessible. Dara Shikoh's translation of the Sanskrit text is not always precise down to the smallest detail, but it does convey all the main ideas of the Sanskrit texts faithfully in a clear and readable manner. Some passages of the original texts are left out altogether, perhaps because Dara Shihkoh did not understand them, or because they did not appeal to him.

The fifty Upaniṣads translated are sorted according to the Vedic text with which they are affiliated, so that the texts associated with the *Ṛgveda* come first. The texts included in the translation (with Persian names in parenthesis) are: *Bṛhadāraṇyaka (Brehdarang)*, *Chāndogya (Tschehandouk)*, *Īśāvāsya (Eischvasieh)*, *Praśna (Porsch)*, *Māṇḍūkya (Mandouk)*, *Kena*

(Kin), Śvetāśvatara (Sataster), Kaṭha (Kiouni), Maitrī (Mitri), Kauṣītakī (Kok'henk), Aitareya (Sarbsar, probably a confusion with the late *Sarvasāra Upaniṣad*), *Ānanavallī (Anandbli), Bṛghuvallī (Bharkbli), Muṇḍaka (Mandek), Jābāla (Djabal), Paiṅgala (Pankl), Kaivalya (Kioul), Puruṣasūkta (Bark'he soukt), Śivasaṃkalpa (Schiw sanklap), Chāgaleya (Tschakli), Tadeva (Tadiw), Mahānārāyaṇa (Maha narain), Tārasāra (Tark), Bāṣkala-Mantra (Baschkl), Sarvasāra (Sarb), Śaunaka (Schavank), Yogaśikhā (Djog sank'ha), Yogatattav (Djogtat), Mahā (Maha), Ātmaprabodha (Atma pra boudeh), Nārāyaṇa (Narain), Āruṇeya (Arank), Cūlikā (Djourka), Atharvaśira (Athrbsar), Atharvaśikhā (Abrat sak'ha), Ātmā (Atma), Brahmavidyā (Brahm badia), Amṛtabindu (Anbrat bandeh), Tejobindu (Tidj bandeh), Śatarudriya (Schat roudri), Garbha (Karbeh), Dhyānabindu (Dehian band), Mṛtyulāṅgūla (Mrat lankoul), Haṃsanāda (Hensnad), Paramahaṃsa (Pram hens), Amṛtanāda (Anbratnad), Ārṣeya (Ark'hi), Prāṇava (Pranou), Kṣurika (Tschehourka)*, and *Nṛsiṃhottaratāpanīya (Nersing'heh atma)*.

Intriguingly, two of these texts are not Upaniṣads at all. The *Puruṣasūkta* is the famous hymn of the Cosmic Man from *Ṛgveda* 10.90. The *Śatarudriya* is the well-known list of a hundred names of the god Rudra from the *Vājasaneyī Saṃhitā* 16, 1–66 of the Yajurveda. Why are these texts included in Dara Shikoh's Upaniṣad translation? Since the translator does not comment on the inclusion of these texts in his volume, any answer must remain a speculation. It is tempting to assume, however, that the emphasis on cosmic unity in both the *Puruṣasūkta* and the *Śatarudriya* would have been quite appealing to Dara Shikoh in his quest for the unity of religion. The *Puruṣasūkta* describes the entire physical universe as constituting various parts of one universal man (*puruṣa*), while the *Śatarudriya* lists all the various names of the one god Rudra/Śiva. These two texts may have struck Dara Shikoh as perfect illustrations of the Upaniṣadic idea that all reality is one and divine.

Although the Sanskrit name of each Upaniṣad has a lexical meaning, there is no attempt at translating the titles into Persian. Rather, each title is simply transliterated into Persian, given the approximate pronunciation of the Sanskrit title.

It is worth noting that Dara Shikoh's translation of the *Bṛhadāraṇyaka Upaniṣad* follows the Kāṇva recension of the text, rather than the alternative Mādhyaṃdina recension. From this, we can conclude that the Kāṇva recension was the one used in Dara Shikoh's sources.

Some passages from the original Upaniṣadic texts are missing in the Persian translation, such as the list of teachers in *Bṛhadāraṇyaka Upaniṣad* 2.6, 4.6, and 6.5, large portions of chapters 1, 3, and 4 of the *Chāndogya Upaniṣad* and all of chapter 2, the section 6.33–38 from the *Maitrī Upaniṣad*, 2. 4–11 of the *Kauṣītaki Upaniṣad*, and smaller text portions here and there from various Upaniṣads. It is possible that these passages were missing in Dara Shikoh's Sanskrit source texts, although one might also speculate that these particular passages, which are all quite rich in Vedic ritual detail, were simply not quite to Dara Shikoh's taste.

The afterlife of the *Sirr-i-akbar*

Dara Shikoh's translation of the Upaniṣads was influential far beyond the Mughal court. It was this translation, rather than the original Sanskrit texts, that first drew the attention of European intellectuals from the nineteenth century onwards. The Frenchman Abraham Hyacinthe Anquetil Duperron (1731–1805), who had traveled in India and studied Persian, translated Dara Shikoh's text into French in 1787, but this rendition was never published.

Anquetil Duperron then proceeded to translate the Persian text into Latin under the title *Oupnek'hat, id est Secretum tegendum* ("Oupnek'hat, that is, The Concealed Secret"). *Oupnek'hat* is a distortion of the Persian spelling for Upaniṣad, *upanikhat*), and *Secretum tegendum* ("The Concealed Secret") appears to be a paraphrase of the Persian title *Sirr-i-akbar* ("The Great Secret"). Anquetil Duperron's translation was published in two volumes in 1801 and 1802. This was the first translation of any Hindu text into a European language.

Dara Shikoh's text must have been particularly appealing to Anquetil Duperron, who as a young man had abandoned his theological studies in order to devote his life to the study of ancient languages. He suspected that many of the questions left unanswered by the Bible might be illuminated by the study of ancient sacred texts from other parts of the world, and he wrote: "[W]ho can say if there were not other historians before Moses, and earlier books?"[4] Anquetil Duperron was particularly drawn to India, because the Vedas were rumored to be of even greater antiquity than the Bible itself. What profound religious secrets could lie hidden in these books? Much like Dara Shikoh himself, Anquetil Duperron was a mystic at heart, searching for universal answers in ancient religious texts.

When his friend colonel Jean-Baptiste Le Gentil sent him the Persian manuscript of the *Sirr-i-Akbar* as a gift in 1776, Anquetil Duperron must have felt that this was the answer he had been looking for all along. Prince Dara Shikoh wrote in his preface to the *Sirr-i-Akbar* that he had read the Book of Moses, the Psalms, and the Gospels, but that he had found that the Vedas were God's earliest revelation to Adam. The essence of all the four Vedas, wrote Dara Shikoh, was summarized in the Upaniṣads which he had translated into Persian. Anquetil Duperron, who read Dara Shikoh's words eagerly, later wrote that "in the *Oupnekhat*, one finds the supreme Being, his word, his spirit."[5]

Anquetil Duperron had already achieved some fame – or possibly notoriety – in scholarly circles with the publication of his French translation of the Zoroastrian text *Zend Avesta* from the ancient Iranian Avestan language in 1771. The authenticity and quality of his *Zend Avesta* translation were still hotly debated when his translation of the Upaniṣads was published. It is unclear why Anquetil Duperron chose to publish a Latin translation of the Upaniṣads, rather than a more accessible French version. The Latin text soon became quite popular, however. It was widely read in Europe and was a significant influence on the German philosopher Schopenhauer, as we will see in the next chapter.

Anquetil Duperron's Latin translation is a bizarre text, containing fairly literal word-by-word translations of the Persian into Latin, with an end result that is almost unreadable even to those who read Latin fluently. The well-known Sanskrit scholar Max Müller later referred to Anquetil-Duperron's Latin translation as "utterly unintelligible."[6] There is very little attempt at creating meaningful and grammatically correct sentences in Latin in Anquetil Duperron's translation. Besides a jumble of phrases from the Persian text, half of the *Oupnekhat* is made up of Anquetil Duperron's personal commentary on the text.

A helpful French summary of the Latin translation and commentary was published in Millin's *Magasin Encyclopédique* in 1805. The complete Latin text was eventually translated further into German by Franz Mischel in 1882. After that, direct translations of the Sanskrit texts of the Upaniṣads soon supplanted the need for further translations of Dara Shikoh's text into European languages. But an echo of Dara Shikoh's *The Great Secret* still lingered in the intellectual life of Europe. Arthur Schopenhauer's musings on the mystical unity of the universe were inspired by Dara Shikoh's Upaniṣad translation, made intelligible to him (but perhaps to few others) through Anquetil Duperron's Latin translation.

Notes

1 *Majma'-ul-Bahrain* iv.
2 *Majma'-ul-Bahrain* iv.
3 *Majma'-ul-Bahrain* 13.
4 Cited from App 2010: 364.
5 App 2010: 439.
6 Max Müller: *The Upanishads*, Vol. 1. Oxford: Clarendon Press, 1879.

Further reading

App, U. 2010. *The Birth of Orientalism*. Philadelphia, PA: The University of Pennsylvania Press.
Dara Shikoh. 1929. *Majma'-ul-Bàrain or The Mingling of the Two Oceans by Prince Muhammad Dārā Shikūh*. Translated by M. Mahfuz-ul-Haq. Calcutta: The Asiatic Society. Reprint 1998.
Göbel-Gross, E. 1962. *Sirr-I akbar: Die persiche Upaniṣadenübersetzung des Mogulprinzen Dārā Sukoh*. PhD dissertation, Phillipps-Universität, Marburg.
Husain, T. 2002. "The Spiritual Journey of Dara Shukoh" *Social Scientist* 30: 54–66.
Richards, J. F. 1993. *The Mughal Empire*. Cambridge: Cambridge University Press.

22 Schopenhauer and the Upaniṣads

Signe Cohen

The German philosopher Arthur Schopenhauer (1788–1860) was intrigued by the Upaniṣads, which he knew through Anquetil Duperron's Latin translation (see Chapter 21). Schopenahuer wrote in the 1818 foreword to his great philosophical treatise *The World As Will and Representation*: "Access to [the Vedas and Upaniṣads] is in my view the greatest advantage which this still young century has shown over previous ones."[1] As we will see in this chapter, the Upaniṣads influenced Schopenhauer's own philosophy in significant ways and thereby left their indelible mark on European philosophy.

Arthur Schopenhauer was born on February 22, 1788 in Danzig in the Polish-Lithuanian Commonwealth (now Gdansk in Poland) to a well-to-do merchant's family. When Danzig was annexed by Prussia in 1793, the Schopenhauer family decided to relocate to Hamburg. Young Arthur grew up with a great deal of wealth and privilege, and his father was grooming him to take over the family business. As a child, Arthur was sent to France for two years to learn the language, and as a fifteen year old, he took a grand tour of Europe with his parents that lasted for two years. But when Arthur was seventeen, his father Heinrich committed suicide, for reasons unknown. His father had always had a melancholy streak, which the son also inherited. After her husband's death, Arthur's mother Johanna moved to Weimar, where she became a friend of the poet Goethe. Johanna Schopenhauer, who was an aspiring writer, was well connected in literary circles, but Arthur did not care for her friends and was deeply upset that she appeared not to grieve for his father.

In 1809, the twenty-one-year-old Arthur enrolled at the University of Göttingen to study medicine. Soon, however, he discovered philosophy and abandoned his plans for a medical career. He was enchanted with both Plato and Kant, and their ideas influenced much of his later thought. Two years later, the young Schopenhauer transferred to Berlin, where he studied under the famous philosopher Johann Gottlieb Fichte and the theologian Friedrich Schleiermacher. But additionally, Schopenhauer appears to have developed an interest in India during his stay in Berlin. He took a course on ethnography that included descriptions of Hindu religious practices, and his notebooks from this course show that he took a lively interest in the topic.

But it was in 1813–1814 that Schopenhauer's interest in India truly blossomed. After defending his dissertation (*On the Fourfold Root of the Principle of Sufficient Reason*), he spent the winter in Weimar, where he encountered the aging Goethe, and also, serendipitously, an orientalist by the name of Friedrich Majer (1772–1818). The Sanskrit scholar Ludwig Alsdorf later wrote:

> From November 1813 to May 1814, Schopenhauer sat at Majer's feet in Weimar. In the following years, while he wrote his major work The World as Will and Representation, the book [*Oupnekhat*] fell into his hands which he subsequently chose as his bible.[2]

The industrious Swiss scholar Urs App has combed through Schopenhauer's library records from Weimar and determined that the young philosopher first checked out the *Oupnekhat* in March 1814. This Latin translation of the Upaniṣads (see the preceding chapter) was published under the title *Oupnekhat* in 1801–1802. Since Anquetil Duperron's translation was based on a Persian rendition of the original Sanskrit text, the version of the Upanisads that reached Schopenhauer, written in odd Persianized Latin, was distorted from the original and quite difficult to read even for someone who was fluent in Latin. The text nevertheless made a profound impression on Schopenhauer, who wrote in his very last book, *Parerga and Paralipomena* (1851):

> How the *Oupnekhat* breathes throughout the Holy Spirit of the Vedas! How seized to the depth by this spirit is he who, through industrious reading has become familiar with the Persian-Latin of this incomparable book. Each line is so full of strong, firm, thoroughly harmonious meaning! And on every page deep, original, lofty thoughts appear to us, while a high and holy seriousness lingers over it all … It is the most rewarding and loftiest reading (with the exception of the original text) possible in the world: It has been my life's consolation and will be my comfort in death.[3]

Wilhelm von Gwinner wrote of his friend Schopenhauer: "The Oupnekhat lay on his table, and before going to sleep he performed his devotion therein."[4]

It was shortly after his first encounter with the Oupnekhat that Schopenhauer began to write his most famous work, *Die Welt als Wille und Vorstellung* ("The World as Will and Representation"), which was first published in 1818. In 1820, Schopenhauer was appointed lecturer at the University of Berlin. He did not remain an academic, although he lived in Berlin until he moved to Frankfurt in 1833. He wrote several more philosophical works, including *On the Will in Nature* (1836), *On the Freedom of the Will* (1839), *On the Basis of Morality* (1840), and *Parerga and Paralipomena* (1851). During his stay in Frankfurt, he had a succession of dogs named Ātman after the highest self in the Upaniṣads. He spent the rest of his life in Frankfurt and died there at the age of 72 in 1860.

The Upaniṣads and *The World as Will and Representation* (1818)

In this seminal philosophical work, composed four years after his first encounter with the Upaniṣads, Schopenhauer argues that the world we perceive is "representation" (*Vorstellung*), mere shifting phenomena that are not ultimately real. This representation is projected by and supported by the Will (*Wille*), which dwells in everything. This Will is eternal and uncaused, beyond space and time. All the suffering in the world is produced by the desires of the Will. Only by denying this Will through ascetic practice can humans be free of its control. All causation takes place in the phenomenal world of representation; the Will itself is neither cause nor effect. Schopenhauer claims that although we normally only perceive the world of representation, we can know the Will by looking inwards and seeing it in ourselves. The Will is transcendental and universal, but it can be known through introspection, since it is only accessible in us.

Schopenhauer's notion of the sensory world as representation appears to owe something to Immanuel Kant's (1724–1804) notion of *das Ding an mich* ("the thing as it appears to me"), or subjective reality. While Kant proposed that we can never experience *das Ding an sich* ("the thing in itself," a thing as it truly is apart from our perception of it), Schopenhauer argues that we can experience the ultimate reality as it is. Schopenhauer agrees that there is an illusory aspect to the external world ("Vorstellung," or "representation"), but he also claims that our inner will ("Wille") is our connection to the world beyond representation. The notion of an internal faculty in humans that allows us to see the true reality behind the elusive empirical forms can easily be compared to the Upaniṣadic notion of *ātman*. While Schopenhauer himself made a note of the Upaniṣadic concept of *brahman* as a creator ("*Brahma* produces the world through a kind of original sin, but himself remains in it to atone for this until he has redeemed himself from it. This is quite a good idea!"[5]), his idea of the Will seems more closely aligned with the creative *ātman* of the Upaniṣads. Just as Schopenhauer's Will and Representation are two aspects of the same reality, so are the Upaniṣadic *ātman* and *brahman* two sides of the same coin. Schopenhauer sees the will as the inner core of all human beings. "Will is the thing-in-itself, the essence of the world," writes Schopenhauer.[6] Similarly, the Upaniṣadic *ātman* is both the inner self of all living beings and that which creates or projects the external reality. Several Upaniṣads, such as the *Bṛhadāraṇyaka Upaniṣad*,[7] *Chāndogya Upaniṣad*,[8] *Aityareya Upaniṣad*,[9] and the *Taittirīya Upaniṣad*[10] describe the world as created or projected by *ātman*. Similar ideas are found in the teachings of Schopenhauer's former professor, J. G. Fichte, who taught that the self (*das Ich*) is the creator of the external world.

To some extent, Schopenhauer's ideas of a reality beyond that of ordinary sensory experience no doubt owes something to the Greek philosopher Plato. Plato argued that the ultimate reality, beyond all the changing ephemeral forms we can perceive, is the world of Ideas. Plato believed that humans have the capacity to explore these Ideas though reason. This is of course quite different from the Upaniṣads, which propose that the highest knowledge is only accessible through mystical knowledge (*jñāna*), rather than through abstract reasoning. In this matter, Schopenhauer's ideas are perhaps closer to the Upaniṣads than to Plato. Schopenhauer's Will is not rational thought, but rather a subconscious power beyond ordinary worldly experience. It is, like the upaniṣadic *ātman*, *intellectually* unknowable, and yet it can be experienced through internal contemplation. Schopenhauer called the awareness of the Will "the most direct of all our cognitions."[11] Unlike external sensory phenomena, the Will can only be known through a form of direct intuition highly reminiscent of the Upaniṣadic *jñāna*.

The Will, like the *ātman*, is the substrate of all other phenomena. The Will is the only thing that exists; everything else is a secondary manifestation of that Will. In this regard, Schopenhauer's view of external reality as mere manifestation seems to owe something to the Upanṣadic idea of *māyā*, or illusion. Although Schopenhauer was likely not acquainted with the elaboration of *māyā* in the Advaita Vedānta philosophy of Śaṅkara, as presented in his commentaries on the Upaniṣads, he would have been familiar with the concept of *māyā* as cosmic illusion from *Śvetāśvatara Upaniṣad* 4.9–4.10. Schopenhauer's diction suggests that he has *māyā* in mind when he writes: "Although no one can recognize the thing-in-itself through the veil of the forms of perceptions, on the other hand everyone carries this within himself, in fact, he himself is it …"[12] Although *māyā* is not yet referred to as a veil in the classical Upaniṣads, the image which is found in later texts, is foreshadowed by passages in the Upaniṣads referring to *ātman* covering itself with the threads of creation in *Śvetāśvatara Upaniṣad* 6.10, which would have been familiar to Schopenhauer.

We may also note in the passage cited above a distinct echo of the famous Upaniṣadic disctum from the *Chāndogya Upaniṣad tat tvam asi* (traditionally translated as "you are it")[13] in the phrase "he himself is it …" This phrase, hinting at a mystical unity between the individual and the highest reality, made a deep impression on Schopenhauer. A note in his handwriting, dated to 1926, says merely: *Tat-twam-asi*. The phrase is mentioned three times in his famous work *The World as Will and Representation*, and he suggests that this phrase can tell a person "about their inner nature."[14]

Although he was profoundly influenced by the Upaniṣads, Schopenhauer did in later life regard himself as a Buddhist, rather than a Hindu. He did, however, see no contradiction between his adopted Buddhist faith and the teachings of the Upaniṣads, and claimed to recognize many of the most profound thoughts of Buddhism in the *Oupnekhat*.

Schopenhauer's own philosophy is an intriguing fusion of Upaniṣadic ideas with Buddhism and Kantian philosophy, with a dash of Plato and Fichte thrown in. Schopenhauer wrote: "If I wanted to take the results of my own philosophy as the measure of truth, then I would have to give Buddhism the precedence [over all other doctrines]."[15] Schopenhauer's concept of the Will owes a great deal to Upaniṣadic notions of *ātman*: The Will is universal, eternal, uncaused, and accessible through introspection. But simultaneously, the Will embodies striving and desire, which eventually leads to suffering, as these desires are frustrated. Schopenhauer's perception of this Will as a negative influence whose power must be combated through asceticism, however, may perhaps owe more to Buddhist notions that the self is an illusion that must be overcome through mental and physical discipline than to the Upaniṣads' entirely positive view of the *ātman*. Buddhism was not well known in Germany at the time when Schopenhauer wrote *The World as Will and Representation*, however, so it is possible that Schopenhauer's depiction of the *ātman*-like Will as something negative comes from his own philosophical sensibilities, rather than directly from Buddhism, although Schopenhauer seems to have gained a deeper understanding of Buddhism later in life.

Schopenhauer writes a great deal about human suffering, which arises from the strivings of the Will. This suffering can only be overcome through asceticism, which he refers to as "the inner essence of holiness," a denial of the will-to-live prompted by the Will itself. While some scholars have seen this insistence on asceticism as a way to overcome suffering as influenced by Buddhism, it would also be perfectly possible for Schopenhauer to derive such an idea from the Upaniṣads themselves. Through the Latin *Oupnekhat*, Schopenahuer would have been familiar with the *Mahānārāyaṇa Upaniṣad*, a text that advocates penance and asceticism as paths to spiritual liberation.

Schopenhauer's view of aesthetics seems to owe something to the Upaniṣads as well. He describes the aesthetic experience of art or music as a state when one can "no longer separate the perceiver from the perception,"[16] an idea closely related to that found in a famous passage in the *Bṛhadāraṇyaka Upaniṣad*:

> For when there is duality, then one can smell the other, one can see the other, one can hear the other, one can greet the other, one can perceive the other. But when the whole has become one's own *ātman*, then who is there for one to smell and how? Who is there for one to see and how? Who is there for one to hear and how? Who is there for one to greet and how? Who is there for one to think about and how? Who is there for one to perceive and how?[17]

Through an aesthetic experience that collapses the boundaries between the subject and the object, a human being can experience not only momentary relief from life's suffering, but also redemption (*Erlösung*). Schopenhauer's notion of *Erlösung* is quite similar to the Upaniṣadic concept of *mokṣa*, the liberation from the painful cycle of death and rebirth, which likewise can be achieved when there is no longer any distinction between subject and object.

How well did Schopenhauer, who was only familiar with the Upaniṣads through an awkward Latin translation of a Persian translation, actually know the Upaniṣadic texts? From his own writings about the Upaniṣads, we may conclude that he had understood the texts surprisingly well, given the flawed nature of his sources. Even the Sanskrit scholar Max Müller, who had read the Upaniṣads in the original and had few positive things to say about Anquetil Duperron's distorted representation of the texts, complimented Schopenhauer's interpretation of the Upaniṣads:

> I must now admit, that if he had done nothing else but decipher the sense of the Upanishads out of the frightful translation of Anquetil Duperron, this alone would suffice to assure him, even among philosophers, and honorable place as an interpreter.[18]

Schopenhauer did not borrow Upaniṣadic teachings wholesale, any more than he adopted the complete philosophical systems of Plato and Kant. He did, however, suggest himself that his own philosophy could not have existed without the Upaniṣads: "Moreover, I confess that I do not believe my doctrine could have come about before the Upanishads, Plato and Kant cast their rays simultaneously into the mind of one man."[19] Elsewhere, he suggested that those readers who were already familiar with the Upaniṣads might understand him better than others:

> ... if then the reader, I say, has received his initiation in primeval Indian wisdom, and received it with an open heart, he will be prepared in the very best way for hearing what I have to tell him. It will not sound to him strange, as to many others, much less disagreeable; for I might, if it did not sound conceited, contend that every one of the detached statements which constitute the Upanishads, may be deduced as a necessary result from the fundamental thoughts which I have to enunciate, though those deductions themselves are by no means to be found there.[20]

Schopenhauer's pessimistic philosophy of the Will as the source of both the representation of external reality and boundless suffering due to its own unfulfilled desires was very much his own, and was in no way a mere restatement of the ideas he encountered in the ancient Upaniṣads. His philosophy was, however, deeply inspired by the texts that he characterized as "his life's consolation."

Notes

1 Quoted from Sedlar 1982: 46.
2 Ludwig Alsdorf, *Deutsch-Indische Geistesbeziehungen*, Heidelberg: Kurt Vowinckel Verlag, 1942: 73. Cited in App 2006: 41.
3 *Parerga and Paralipomena* 2: 396.
4 Wilhelm Gwinner, *Arthur Schopenhauer aus persönlichem Umgange dargestellt*. Leipzig: F. A. Brockhaus, 1862: 215.
5 *Parerga und Paralipomena* 2, Chapter XVII, paragraph 156.
6 *The World as Will and Representation, Part 1.*
7 *Bṛhadāraṇyaka Upaniṣad* 1.4.1f, 2.1.20.
8 *Chāndogya Upaniṣad* 7.26.

9 *Aityareya Upaniṣad* 1.1f.
10 *Taittirīya Upaniṣad* 2.1f.
11 *Werke* I, 470–471.
12 *The World as Will and Representation* Vol. 2, p. 182.
13 The phrase likely means something more along the lines of "That's what you are like." See Joel Brereton, "Tat Tvam Asi in Context" *Zeitschrift der deutschen morgenländischen Gesellschaft* 136 (1986): 98–109.
14 *The World as Will and Representation* Vol. 1, p. 220.
15 Schopenhauer, *Werke*, III, 186, cited in Sedlar 1982: 77.
16 *The World as Will and Representation*, section 34.
17 *Bṛhadāraṇyaka Upaniṣad* 2.4.14.
18 Max Müller: "Damals und Jetzt," *Deutsche Rundschau*, Vol. XLI 1884, p. 417, cited in Sedlar 1982: 49.
19 Schopenhauer, *Der Handschriftliche Nachlaß in fünf Bänden* Vol. 1, ed. A. Hübscher. München: Deutscher Taschenbuch Verlag (1985): 422.
20 *The World as Will and Representation*, Preface.

Further reading

App, U. 2006. "Schopenhauer's Initial Encounter with Indian Thought" *Schopenhauer-Jahrbuch* 87: 35–86.

Barua, A. 2012. *Understanding Schopenhauer through the Prism of Indian Culture*. Berlin: De Gruyter.

Hecker, M. F. 1897. *Schopenhauer und die indische Philosophie*. Köln: Hübscher und Teufel.

Nicholls, M. 1999. "The Influences of Eastern Thought on Schopenhauer's Doctrine of the Thing-in-Itself" in Christopher Janaway (ed.) *The Cambridge Companion to Schopenhauer*. Cambridge: Cambridge University Press, 171–212.

Schopenhauer, A. 1966. *The World as Will and Representation*, translated by E. F. Payne. 2 vols. New York: Dover.

Sedlar, J. 1982. *India in the Mind of Germany: Schelling, Schopenhauer, and their Times*. Washington, DC: University Press of America.

Singh, R. 2010. *Schopenhauer: A Guide for the Perplexed*. London: Continuum.

Strathern, P. 1999. *Schopenhauer in 90 Minutes*. Chicago, IL: Ivan R. Dee.

Part IV

The classical Upaniṣads

23 The *Bṛhadāraṇyaka Upaniṣad*

Dermot Killingley

Introduction

The *Bṛhadāraṇyaka* is the oldest and longest of the Upaniṣads – closely followed in both respects by the *Chāndogya*. Its name indicates its affinity with the *Āraṇyaka*s (above, pp. 50–51), and it is included as the last six chapters of the fourteenth and last book (an anachronistic but commonly used term) of the *Śatapatha Brāhmaṇa*, which is itself called an Āraṇyaka. (This is the numbering in the Mādhyaṃdina recension; the Kāṇva divides the books differently, but still has the Upaniṣad as the last part of the Āraṇyaka which is the last part of the Brāhmaṇa.)

The whole *Śatapatha Brāhmaṇa*, including the *Bṛhadāraṇyaka Upaniṣad*, is preserved in two recensions, belonging to two branches of the White Yajurveda: the Kāṇva and the Mādhyaṃdina (above, p. 49). The places where they differ significantly are relatively few; but where they do, the Mādhyaṃdina often makes better sense. It is also more archaic in its grammar (Cohen : 94–98), and contains metrical irregularities which seem to have been tidied up in the Kāṇva text (Cohen 2008: 91–93). The relation between the two is complicated by the fact that the earliest commentary on the *Bṛhadāraṇyaka Upaniṣad* is the influential one by Śaṅkara, composed around the seventh century CE, using the Kāṇva text, while the one on the *Śatapatha Brāhmaṇa*, by Sāyaṇa in the fourteenth century, uses the Mādhyaṃdina. In the history of Sanskrit literature, commentaries tend to guarantee the authority of texts, and this in turn has influenced their translation into other languages. The only English translation of the *Śatapatha Brāhmaṇa* (Eggeling 1882–1900) uses the Mādhyaṃdina text, whereas most translations of the *Bṛhadāraṇyaka* use the Kāṇva; the partial translation by Edgerton (1965) is an exception.

It was the development of Vedānta, as a field of thought distinct from the theory of ritual (above, pp. 5–6), that led this and other early Upaniṣads to be transmitted and commented on as separate texts rather than as parts of Brāhmaṇas; it is for the same reason that the *Bhagavadgītā*, once it was accepted as an authoritative text for Vedānta, came to be transmitted and commented on separately from the *Mahābhārata*. The *Bṛhadāraṇyaka*

Upaniṣad is referred to extensively in the *Vedānta-Sūtra*s or *Brahma-Sūtra*s which are the foundational text for the interpretation of the Upaniṣads for all schools of Vedānta. In his commentary on the *Vedānta-Sūtra*s, Śaṅkara quotes the *Bṛhadāraṇyaka Upaniṣad* slightly less often than the *Chāndogya*, and so does the later commentator Rāmānuja; on the other hand, Śaṅkara's commentary on the *Bṛhadāraṇyaka* is more than twice as long as the one on the *Chāndogya*, and far longer than any of his other Upaniṣad commentaries. He evidently singled out this Upaniṣad as the main authority for his system; this and the *Chāndogya* are the ones he quotes most frequently in his other works also (Hirst 2005: 20).

The *Bṛhadāraṇyaka* is extremely heterogeneous – even more so than the *Chāndogya*. Besides dialogues on the self, Brahman, the structure of personality, existence after death, and other topics typical of the Upaniṣads, it contains reflections on the meaning of ritual, in the manner of the Brāhmaṇas; narratives of the origin of the world, which continue and develop ideas found in the speculative hymns (above, p. 53), and again in the Brāhmaṇas; and, in its last chapter, rituals for personal purposes typical of the Atharvaveda.

It consists mainly of prose, but some verse passages are included, often introduced with phrases such as "Now there is this śloka" (BU 1.5.23); "Then there are these ślokas" (BU 4.3.11). Some of these verses are from the Ṛgveda or the Atharvaveda, sometimes with variants; others are of unknown origin.

The prose evokes a situation in which a teacher not only speaks to his pupil, but makes gestures, adding a visual element to the oral teaching. For instance, the statement "Gotama and Bharadvāja are these two. Gotama is this one and Bharadvāja is this one" (BU 2.2.4) makes little sense by itself, even if we know that these are two of the Seven Ṛṣis (Sages), authors of Vedic hymns who are frequently identified with the seven stars of Ursa Major. To make the statement complete, we need to see the teacher's gestures, or at least be told about them. According to Śaṅkara, these two ṛṣis are "the ears: Gotama is this one and Bharadvāja is this one – the right one and the left one, or the other way round" (Śaṅkara on BU 2.2.4). Another pair of ṛṣis, he says, are the eyes, and a third pair are the nostrils. Śaṅkara's identifications need not be the ones originally intended (Olivelle 1996: 304), and he himself is unconcerned about which is left and which is right; but the passage makes sense if we understand that the speaker points in turn to the seven orifices of his head. Coming to the seventh ṛṣi – or star – the Upaniṣad says: "Atri is speech. For food is eaten with speech. Indeed, Atri is called *atti* ('eats'). He becomes an eater of all; everything becomes his food, who knows this." The seventh orifice is the mouth, which unlike the ears, eyes, and nostrils is not a pair; it combines the functions of speech and eating. Here we have a set of correspondences between the human person and parts of the macrocosm, based on a number (above, pp. 69–71); the last of them is reinforced by the similarity of the name Atri to the verb *atti* "eats." As you can see from the above, an attempt to explain anything in the Upaniṣads is liable to call for yet further explanation.

Structure

The *Bṛhadāraṇyaka* is divided into six chapters (*adhyāya*, the usual word for a chapter or a lesson), and each of these is divided into sections called *brāhmaṇas*, divided in turn into subsections (*kaṇḍika*), of a few sentences each. This continues the system of division of the *Śatapatha Brāhmaṇa*, of which the *Bṛhadāraṇyaka Upaniṣad* is the last part. The central chapters 3 and 4 consist of four stories about the great ritualist and philosopher Yājñavalkya; this pair of chapters ends with a list of teachers, and the older teachers from whom they received their knowledge, tracing the succession back through ṛṣis to gods, and eventually to Brahman (BU 4.6). Chapters 1 and 2 consist of a number of separate passages, in only one of which Yājñavalkya appears, except for a passing mention (BU 1.4.3); and the passage in which he does appear (BU 2.4) is repeated, with variations and additions, in BU 4.5. Chapter 2 ends with a similar list to the one in BU 4.6, but differing from it at some points (Black 2011; Lindquist 2011). Chapters 5 and 6 again consist of separate passages, none of which mentions Yājñavalkya; they conclude with a third list of teachers, which, unlike the other two, does mention him, naming him as the promulgator of the White Yajurveda (BU 6.5.3). The prominence of Yājñavalkya in some parts of the text and his absence from others is notable also in the *Śatapatha Brāhmaṇa*, where he appears as the authority in Books 1–5 and 11–14, whereas Books 6–10 never mention him, but refer to another ritual expert, Śāṇḍilya (Gonda 1975: 352–353; Eggeling 1882–1900: 1.xxx-xxxi).

The division of the *Bṛhadāraṇyaka* into three parts of two chapters each was recognised already by Śaṅkara, and was probably already traditional. He calls the first two chapters the "Honey Part," from a passage identifying various cosmic entities in turn as "the honey of all beings" (BU 2.5); the middle two chapters are the "Yājñavalkya Part," and the last two are the "Supplement Part" (*khila-kāṇḍa*).

The sequence of chapters and sections is not chronological, nor does it represent any logical or pedagogical progression. However, in explaining some passages, we shall follow the traditional division into three two-chapter parts.

The Honey Part: Chapters 1 and 2

The Upaniṣad opens with the passage on the sacrificial horse which we have already quoted (above, p. 69). The horse sacrifice, practiced by kings, is the most elaborate of Vedic rituals. Before being suffocated, the horse is allowed to wander for a year (alluded to in BU 1.1.7), attended by armed men – amounting to a political and military claim to the territory over which it wanders. Like many passages in the Brāhmaṇas, BU 1.1 combines ritual with cosmology, making the ritual a model of the cosmos, whereby it is understood and mastered. Parts of the horse are identified with parts of the cosmos, and the two cups of Soma placed before and behind him are day, born from the eastern ocean – from which the sun rises – and night, born from the western ocean. The horse goes by different names in the worlds of the gods, the Gandharvas (above, p. 128; p. 194), the demons and humans: the sacrifice thus embodies not only this world, but all worlds (above, pp. 58–59).

The sacrificial horse is mentioned again towards the end of the second section (BU 1.2.7). But the main theme of this section is cosmogony, the origin of the universe. It follows a pattern which occurs several times in the Brāhmaṇas: A primordial being has a desire, and by attempting to satisfy this desire causes the universe to come into existence (above, p. 67). Here, the being is called Death (a masculine noun), and also Hunger (a feminine noun): the primordial situation is the absence of life and of food. He wishes to have an *ātman* – here meaning a body, but also implying a wish to be a person, rather than the negative state which is all Death can be in the beginning. To achieve this, Death's first act is to recite ritual verses (*ṛc*): ritual is placed at the very beginning of the universe. The cosmogony continues through processes of labor, causing heat which becomes fire (BU 1.2.2); division (BU 1.2.3); copulation (BU 1.2.4); and further ritual activity (BU 1.2.6). As in the cosmogonic narratives about Prajāpati (above, p. 68), Death is exhausted by this activity, and has to restore himself by further sacrifice – in this case, the horse sacrifice (BU 1.2.7). The section ends with a statement of what is gained by knowing and understanding this cosmogony: "He conquers re-death. Death does not reach him. His self is Death." (SB 10.5.2.23 makes a similar promise.)

The whole section is pervaded by statements about the true meaning of words, referring to their similarity to other words. For instance, Death eats everything that it creates, and "eats" (*atti*) gives the true meaning of the name of Aditi, mother of the gods. Again, when Death was exhausted he became a corpse, and swelled. The word for "swelled" (*aśvat*) is similar to *aśva* "horse," so this story gives the true meaning of *aśvamedha* "horse sacrifice" (BU 1.2.7). We may call such statements "word play," but they are serious (Olivelle 1996: liv). They may be followed by a remark that the gods love the obscure (AB 3.33; SB 6.1.1.2; AU 1.3.14) and (some texts add) shun the obvious (BU 4.2.2). They are not etymologies in the modern sense, tracing words to their historical origins, or even etymologies in the etymological sense, looking for the true (Greek *étumos*) meaning of a word; rather, they extend its meaning by reference to similar-sounding words.

Section 3 turns from cosmogony to two other recurrent topics of the early Upaniṣads: the faculties which make up a person (above, p. 176; pp. 180–181;

Killingley 2006: 89), and the struggle of the gods against the demons. Unusually for a Yajurvedic text (Renou 1955: 94 note 1), it concerns the *sāman*, the ritual chant learnt in the Sāmaveda (above, p. 46), and especially the Udgītha, the central part among the five parts of the chant. To defeat the demons, the gods tell the five faculties – speech, breath, sight, hearing and mind – to sing the Udgītha. In each case, the demons infect the faculty with evil, which explains why, in this fallen world, we speak, smell, see, hear and think evil things. The sense of smell is here called "breath" (*prāṇa*). But *prāṇa* can also mean respiration, which, as several Upaniṣadic passages show, is the faculty on which all the others depend. In this passage, respiration is distinguished from the sense of smell by calling it "the breath in the mouth." When the gods tell "the breath in the mouth" to chant the Udgītha, it defeats the demons. The word *prāṇa* can also be a general term for "faculty," or "orifice of the body"; it slides between these various meanings in the same way as *ātman* slides between "body, trunk" and "conscious self." The five faculties, often called "breaths," are here called "deities" (*devatā*).

The same story is told in the *Chāndogya Upaniṣad*, which, as an Upaniṣad of the Sāmaveda, is interested in the power of chant (CU 1.2). But the *Bṛhadāraṇyaka* adds a sequel, connecting the faculties with the macrocosm (BU 1.3.16). When the "breath in the mouth" rescues the five faculties, it transforms them into their macrocosmic counterparts, which are beyond death: speech to fire, breath (the sense of smell) to wind, sight to the sun, and hearing to the directions (above, p. 62; p. 126). The "breath in the mouth" stands not only for respiration but for eating, "for whatever is eaten is eaten by it" (BU 1.3.17).

Chapter 1 section 4 is a series of cosmogonies, using the motif of the primal being and his (or its) primordial desire. The story begins four times (BU 1.4.1; 1.4.10; 1.4.11; 1.4.17), but we can treat the four narratives as versions of the same story, emphasizing different aspects. Each of them identifies the self (*ātman*) with Brahman; this identification is a major theme of this Upaniṣad. The first (BU 1.4.1–9) begins with an *ātman* – call it a self (Roebuck 2003: 19) or a body (Olivelle 1996: 13) – in the form of a man (*puruṣa*); later it, or he, is referred to as *brahman* (BU 1.4.6), so the passage combines three common terms for the primal being. His first awareness of himself is the origin of the name "I" – what is later called *ahaṃkāra*, the sense of one's own personality (van Buitenen 1957: 17). He divides himself into male and female; from their copulation, humans are born. A primal androgyne, "as large as a woman and a man embracing" (BU 1.4.3), that divides into male and female halves, might seem a good model for gender equality. But in the beginning of the story, the primal being is male, and the male dominates in what follows. She thinks it is not right that he should copulate with her when he has produced her from himself (showing the continuity of the male half with the primal being), so she hides by turning into a cow. "The other became a bull. He copulated with her. Thence cattle were born. She became a mare – the other a stallion –" and so on, "and so he created everything in the world that is in couples, down to ants" (BU 1.4.4). This story of primal incest reworks one in which Prajāpati lusts after his daughter (SB 1.7.4.1–4), and they copulate in the forms of a stag and a doe (AB 3.33 (Keith 1920: 185; Eggeling 1882–1900: 1.208).

Next, the primal man created fire, which is essential to Vedic ritual, and is the cosmic counterpart of speech (above, p. 62). The text says: "Now he churned, like this" – the teacher must have mimed the act of rotating a fire-drill between the palms, or with a bowstring wrapped round it, against a slab of wood, heating and eventually igniting it by the friction (BU 1.4.6; Olivelle 1996: 296) – "and from his mouth and his hands, as from a womb (*yoni*), he created fire." That is, after using the fire-drill, an action which is often seen as sexual, he used his mouth and his cupped hands to blow on the glowing wood. The word *yoni* includes womb, vagina, and vulva; it also has the general meaning "source, origi." The Upaniṣad now establishes a connection between a man's mouth, his cupped hands, and a woman's *yoni*. All three are "hairless on the inside" (BU 1.4.6); by implication, all three are hairy outside.

At this time there are no gods – a point made already in RV 10.129.6: "The gods came later, by means of this creation." It is the primal man who creates the gods, who are his superiors; he is mortal, but he creates the immortals. Anyone who knows this enters the world of the gods (BU 1.4.6). He is no longer like a beast (*paśu*, a farm animal or a sacrificial victim) to be exploited by the gods, because he knows he is identical to them (BU 1.4.10). In creating the gods, the primal man also creates the four classes (*varṇa*) which are the model of human society: brahmins, kṣatriyas (kings and warriors), vaiśyas (the common people), and śūdras (people excluded from ritual and from the name Ārya, but necessary for the support of Āryan society) (Holdrege 2004: 228–231), with the gods appropriate to each (BU 1.4.11–13); the god of the brahmins is fire or Agni (BU 1.4.15). The first two classes are referred to by the two kinds of power which they embody: *brahman* (ritual power, the power which creates the universe) and *kṣatra* (military and political power). This fourfold model of society first appears in RV 10.90.12, where the four classes come from the mouth, arms, thighs, and feet of the primal man. It is usually understood, both traditionally and by modern interpreters, as a ranking order, with the brahmins at the top. But here, *kṣatra* is highest – though *brahman* is its origin (*yoni*), and therefore not to be harmed (BU 1.4.11). In the *Bṛhadāraṇyaka* and *Chāndogya Upaniṣad*s, there are signs of rivalry between two forms of supremacy, *brahman* and *kṣatra*. Sometimes kṣatriyas outdo brahmins in the latter's sphere of supramundane knowledge (BU 2.1.15; 6.2.1–8; CU 5.3.1–6); and a Brāhmaṇa story tells how Yājñavalkya, the hero of the *Bṛhadāraṇyaka*, was outtalked by the kṣatriya Janaka – who thereby became a brahmin (SB 11.6.2). The supremacy of kṣatriyas was reconciled with the assignment of the brahmin to the mouth and the kṣatriya to the arms, by picturing a man raising his arms above his head (SB 13.8.3.11).

The section ends by combining the primal man and his desire with the theory of the faculties, and the ritual concerns of the Brāhmaṇas. This time, the primal self desires not only a wife but wealth – the one to continue his patriline and the other to perform rituals – and this provides the prototype for all desires. A man is completed by mind, speech, breath, sight, and body (*ātman*, here meaning the location of the sense of touch), and these five faculties are linked to five assets of the *yajamāna*: his *ātman*, his wife (*vāc* "speech" is a feminine noun), his offspring, his wealth, and his store of merit. He who knows this fivefold structure of personality and of ritual gains the whole world (above, p. 70).

Chapter 1 section 5 begins with an early example of a form which is frequent in Sanskrit literature – a passage of verse (BU 1.5.1) followed by a prose commentary which explains it phrase by phrase (BU 15.2–3). (Another such passage, much shorter, is BU 2.2.3.) The verse is obscure, and so is the prose that follows; however, this section deals with some typical Upaniṣadic topics. The supremacy of breath among the faculties, already discussed in BU 1.3.2–8, is presented in terms of a contest (BU 1.5.21). The contest is narrated more fully in BU 6.1.7–14, and in CU 5.1.6–15; the supremacy of breath is expounded again in KsU 3.2–3. As breath is supreme in the microcosm (*adhyātma* "with reference to the self," BU 1.5.21), so wind is supreme in the macrocosm (*adhidaivatam* "with reference to the deities," BU 1.5.22). The faculties listed here are not five but three – mind, speech and breath – and these are linked to other triads (BU 1.5.4–7); but a pentad, the five breaths, is mentioned (BU 1.5.3; above, p. 70). Another significant number is sixteen (BU 1.5.14). As the square of four, this number represents completeness. It also belongs to the moon, because the parts of the moon's disk that are added or subtracted each night as it waxes or wanes, referred to as the "digits" of the moon, are fifteen, and the moon itself makes sixteen. This way of adding the whole to the parts is common in ancient Indian numerology (Gonda 1965: 115–130). Triads appear again in BU 1.6.

Chapter 2 begins with a dialogue in which a brahmin, Dṛpta-Bālāki Gārgya (*dṛpta* "proud" may be an epithet rather than part of his name), is outdone by a kṣatriya, Ajātaśatru king of Kāśī (also known as Vārāṇasī). The king says that if he rewards Gārgya with a thousand cows for his teaching, he will be compared to Janaka king of Videha, Yājñavalkya's patron (BU 2.1.1). Gārgya proposes a series of *upāsana*s (above, pp. 137–139), identifications of various phenomena with *brahman*. The king rejects them all, and instead teaches the brahmin, identifying *brahman* with the self (BU 2.1.20). His teaching is similar to that given by Yājñavalkya to Janaka in BU 4.3–4, discussed above (pp. 136–137), and the two passages can be read together to illuminate each other. Ajātaśatru shows the same interest in sleep and dream as Yājñavalkya, and describes dreamless sleep as extreme bliss (BU 2.1.19), perhaps implying the same sexual image as in BU 4.3.21 (Olivelle 1996: 303). He refers to the self (*ātman*) as "the man (*puruṣa*) consisting of consciousness" (BU 2.1.16) – a similar phrase to the one used by Yājñavalkya (BU 4.3.7); he does not explicitly call it *brahman*, but this is implied, as he has undertaken to expound *brahman*. Unlike Yājñavalkya, however, Ajātaśatru does not consider how the self fares after death.

Ajātaśatru demonstrates his teaching by waking a sleeping man (BU 2.1.15). This experiment shows that the "man consisting of consciousness" must be in the body even during sleep, contrary to the theory that when we dream we wander outside the body. This theory is not explicitly described here, but is mentioned by Yājñavalkya in the parallel passage. He quotes a verse likening a dreamer to a wild goose wandering from its nest, going wherever it wills, high and low (BU 4.3.12–14), followed by a saying that one should not wake him suddenly, because if he – the conscious self – has not returned, it will be hard to cure him (BU 4.3.14). Yājñavalkya sees no such danger, and neither does Ajātaśatru; they know that dreams are experienced within the body, not outside it.

The only passage outside the Yājñavalkya Part in which Yājñavalkya himself appears is BU 2.4, where he instructs his wife Maitreyī; it recurs, with minor variations, in BU 4.5. This is the only classical Upaniṣad in which women appear as thinkers, and it is made clear that such women are exceptional when Maitreyī, a "discourser on *brahman*" – a theologian – is contrasted with Yājñavalkya's other wife Kātyāyanī, who "only had a woman's understanding" (BU 4.5.1). Being about to go away (perhaps expecting to die, or intending to become a wandering ascetic – BU 4.5.1 implies the latter, and is perhaps the later version (Olivelle 1996: 306, 319)), he wishes to make a settlement for his two wives. He is wealthy, thanks to his patron Janaka, and has great knowledge; Maitreyī, like Naciketas (KU 1.26–29; above, pp. 135–6), rejects wealth, and asks only for his knowledge. Kātyāyanī presumably gets the wealth.

Yājñavalkya's parting gift to Maitreyī is knowledge of the self. He begins by saying that all love, or all desire for wealth or power, proceeds from love of the self; our relationships and our desires are only possible because we have a self which is the source of our consciousness. The same idea is suggested in BU 1.4.8. But from the self as the source of the value of things, Yājñavalkya proceeds to the self as the source of their existence. Then he bewilders Maitreyī by telling her "after death there is no awareness" (BU 2.4.12). As he explains, there is no awareness of objects; the self exists as pure consciousness. This objectless consciousness is like Yājñavalkya's view of dreamless sleep (BU 4.3.31). The passage includes a remarkably complete list of the faculties (above, p. 181; Killingley 2006: 98; Johnston 1937: 19; Larson 1969: 95).

The passage from which the Honey Part takes its name (BU 2.5) describes each part of the macrocosm as both nourishing all beings, and nourished by them. It culminates in a statement that the self is the honey of all beings. It is *brahman*, and is both the hub and the rim of the universe (BU 2.5.14–15).

The Yājñavalkya Part: Chapters 3 and 4

These two chapters are the core of the Upaniṣad; Yājñavalkya is the protagonist throughout, except in the list of teachers (BU 4.6). The whole of chapter 3 is a series of dialogues occasioned by King Janaka's contest, which we have already described (above, p. 126). The brahmins Yājñavalkya challenges are from the Kuru-Pañcāla country (roughly the present states of Haryana and Uttar Pradesh), while Janaka's kingdom is further east (roughly northern Bihar); several of them have names associated with the Ṛg-veda (Cohen 2008: 76–82). The contest may therefore reflect rivalry between the long-established regions of Āryan culture and the outlying lands to the east, and between practitioners of the Ṛg-veda and of the Yajur-veda. In the first dialogue of the contest (BU 3.1), Yājñavalkya appears as a great ritualist, as he does in the *Śatapatha Brāhmaṇa*. But his main role in the *Bṛhadāraṇyaka Upaniṣad* is as the proponent of the self as the ultimate being. If we think of him as a historical person, this represents a development in his thinking; alternatively, it represents the continued use of his name as an authority, when attention was shifting from ritual to the nature of existence.

It is in Janaka's contest that we find the other woman thinker besides Maitreyī: Gārgī Vācaknavī. Her inclusion in an assembly of brahmin ritual functionaries is remarkable, but the text does not remark on it. Further, she alone among the challengers approaches Yājñavalkya twice – or else the same story has been recorded in two different versions. The first time, she asks a series of questions about the foundation of the cosmos; when she eventually gets the answer "the worlds of *brahman*," she persists, asking on what they are founded. Yājñavalkya warns her against questioning too far – not asking too many questions, as many translations have it, but questioning beyond the limits of the knowable (Cohen 2008: 73); nothing can be beyond *brahman*. If she questions too far, her head will shatter – the result of claiming knowledge that one does not have (BU 1.3.24; 3.9.26; CU 1.8.6; 1.10.9–11; 5.12.2; above, p. 40, p. 68). Later, she questions him again; this time, she acknowledges his superiority, and urges the other challengers to do the same (BU 3.8.12).

Then follow three dialogues in which Yājñavalkya instructs Janaka. First, he rejects teachings about *brahman* that the king has received from others (BU 4.1). Next, he teaches him about the self which can only be described by negative statements (*neti neti*), such as "ungraspable … indestructible …

unattachable" (BU 4.2.4; similarly BU 2.3.6; 3.9.26; 4.4.22; 4.5.15; the phrase *neti neti* is peculiar to this Upaniṣad). The third dialogue, Yājñavalkya's longest, is the one we have discussed already (pp. 127–129, 136–137). After it, Yājavalkya's instruction of Maitreyī (p. 254) is repeated, with variants (BU 4.5).

The Supplement Part: Chapters 5 and 6

The last two chapters are the most heterogeneous part of this heterogeneous Upaniṣad. They contain the passage on the five fires which contributes to the idea of rebirth (BU 6.2; pp. 122–125), an account of the contest of the faculties (BU 6.1; above, p. 253), and some verses which also appear, with variants, in the *Īśā Upaniṣad* (BU 5.15).

They contain much serious word-play, including a dialogue in which the syllable *da*, spoken by thunder, is given three meanings, for gods, humans, and demons (BU 5.2); it was reworked by T. S. Eliot as part of *The Waste Land* (Eliot 1936: 76–77). This section, and the next (BU 5.3), are based on triads; but other sections add a fourth to a triad, making a tetrad (BU 5.5; 5.8; 5.13; 5.14; Bhattacharya 1978; Cohen 2008: 88–89). Tetrads are often formed by adding a related yet contrasting fourth to a familiar triad (above, pp. 47–48). Thus, when the triad of sacred words *bhūr bhuvas svar*, often identified with earth, atmosphere, and sky, has been identified with the head, arms, and feet of the macrocosmic man in the sun (BU 5.5.3), and of the microcosmic man in the right eye (BU 5.5.4; compare BU 4.2.2), a fourth is added to the triad: *ahar* "day" in the macrocosm, and *aham* "I" in the microcosm. This fourth is here called an *upaniṣad*, meaning an obscure but powerful identification (p. 139; compare BU 2.1.20; Olivelle 1996: 303; 321). Similarly, to the three lines of the Sāvitrī stanza (RV 3.63.10) is added a fourth, beyond the sky (BU 5.14.3; 5.14.7); and to the types of utterance embodied in the three Vedas is added not *brahman*, as in TU 1.5, but its counterpart *kṣatra* "kingly power" (BU 5.13.4).

This part also includes private rituals for sexual matters. The Vedas often emphasize the desirability of male offspring, but here we have the option of a daughter (BU 6.4.17), and even of avoiding pregnancy (BU 6.4.10); less welcome is a recommendation to beat a wife who is unwilling (BU 6.4.7). There is also a curse for a husband to use against his wife's lover, with the symbolic accusation "You have sacrificed in my fire!" (BU 6.4.12).

A heterogeneous Upaniṣad with a distinctive core

Later Upaniṣads, such as the *Śvetāśvatara* or the *Mahānārāyaṇa*, seem to have been composed to support a particular theology, or at least the views of a circle of like-minded people. If we look only at the two central chapters, the *Bṛhadāraṇyaka* presents Yājñavalkya's teaching on the self as *brahman*.

But looking at the whole, we see the variety of ideas current among specialists in the Yajurveda: some ritualistic, some using ritual concepts to explore questions such as the origin of the universe, the nature of personality, and postmortem existence. The Upaniṣad also shows the kind of lively debate in which these ideas were discussed, driven by a belief that true knowledge leads not only to effective performance of ritual, but to transcendence of the limitations of worldly existence, while the assertion of erroneous views, in a context demanding truth, can lead to loss of one's head.

References

Bhattacharya, Dipak. 1978. "The Doctrine of Four in The Early Upaniṣads and Some Connected Problems" *Journal of Indian Philosophy* 6: 1–34.

Black, Brian. 2011. "Rethinking the Upaniṣadic *Vaṃśas:* Teacher Lineages as a Literary Genre" *Religions of South Asia* 5: 51–77.

Cohen, Signe. 2008. *Text and Authority in the Older Upaniṣads*. Leiden: Brill.

Edgerton, F. 1965. *The Beginnings of Indian Philosophy. Selections from the Rig Veda, Atharva Veda, Upanisads, and Mahābhārata. Translated from the Sanskrit with an Introduction, Notes and Glossarial index*. London: Allen & Unwin.

Eggeling, Julius. 1882–1900. *The Satapathabrâhmana: According to the Text of the Mâdhyandina School*. 5 volumes (Sacred Books of the East series, vols. 12, 26, 41, 43, 44). Oxford: Clarendon Press.

Eliot, T. S. 1936. *Collected Poems: 1909–1935*. London: Faber & Faber.

Gonda, Jan. 1965. *Change and Continuity in Indian Religion*. The Hague: Mouton.

Gonda, Jan. 1975. *Vedic Literature* (*A History of Indian Literature* Vol. 1, Fasc. 1). Wiesbaden: Harrassowitz.

Hirst, J. G. Suthren. 2005. *Śaṃkara's Advaita Vedānta: A Way of Teaching*. London and New York: RoutledgeCurzon.

Holdrege, Barbara. 2004. "Dharma" in Sushil Mittal and Gene Thursby (eds) *The Hindu World*. New York: Routledge, 213–248.

Johnston, E. H. 1937. *Early Sāṃkhya: An Essay on its Historical Development According to the Texts*. London: Royal Asiatic Society. (Reprint Delhi: Motilal Banarsidass, 1974.)

Keith, A. B. 1920. *Rigveda Brahmanas: The Aitareya and Kauṣītaki Brāhmaṇas of the Rigveda Translated from the Original Sanskrit*. Cambridge, MA: Harvard University Press. (Reprint Delhi: Motilal Banarsidass, 1971.)

Killingley, Dermot. 2006. "Faculties, Breaths and Orifices: Some Vedic and Sāṃkhya Notions of the Body and Personality" in Anna S. King (ed.) *Indian Religions: Renaissance and Renewal*. London: Equinox, 73–108.

Larson, G. J. 1969. *Classical Sāṃkhya: An Interpretation of its History and Meaning*. Delhi: Motilal Banarsidass.

Lindquist, Steven E. 2011. "Lines of Descent and Dissent: Genealogy, Narrative and the Upaniṣads" *Religions of South Asia* 5: 29–49.

Olivelle, Patrick. 1996. *Upaniṣads: Translated from the Original Sanskrit* (World's Classics series). Oxford: Oxford University Press.

Renou, Louis. 1955. "Remarques sur la Chāndogya-Upaniṣad." *Études védiques et pāṇinéennes* 1: 91–102.

Roebuck, Valerie. 2003. *The Upaniṣads. Translated and Edited* (Penguin Classics series). London: Penguin.
Van Buitenen, J. A. B. 1957. "Studies in Sāṃkhya (II)" *Journal of the American Oriental Society* 77: 15–25.

Further reading

Cohen, Signe. 2008. *Text and Authority in the Older Upaniṣads*. Leiden: Brill, 67–99.
Killingley, Dermot. 1997. "The Paths of the Dead and the Five Fires" in Peter Connolly and Sue Hamilton (eds) *Indian Insights: Buddhism, Brahmanism and Bhakti*. London: Luzac Oriental, 1–20.

24 The *Chāndogya Upaniṣad*

Dermot Killingley

As this Upaniṣad belongs to the Sāmaveda, and its first two chapters are concerned with chant, we start with some points about Vedic chant and its place in ritual. We describe the literary structure of the Upaniṣad, and the way it is divided into parts marked by repetition of their final words. As it is rich in narratives, we consider the use of narrative in this and other Upaniṣads. The *Chāndogya Upaniṣad* contains stories of teaching, often of a reluctant teacher and a persistent pupil; stories in which right behavior is crucial; stories of a challenge to a confident person's knowledge; stories in which someone who seems to have excellent knowledge is still dissatisfied, and seeks teaching. As the chanter's Upaniṣad, the Chāndogya is especially interested in sound, including talking animals as well as ritual utterances. It is also interested in numbers – three, four, and especially five – and in food. Returning to its interest in narrative, we suggest that some of its figures may have become names round which certain narrative motifs have clustered, even if they once were historical persons.

The *Chāndogya Upaniṣad* is the second longest after the *Bṛhadāraṇyaka*, and is close to it in age. It shows a similar concern with ritual – especially with chant, since it belongs to the Sāmaveda. The name means that it belongs to the *chando-ga*, the man who sings (*gāyati*) the verses (*chandas*), and its first two chapters are largely concerned with the powers embodied in ritual chant. The sāmavedic chant consists of five divisions, each chanted by a specialist: *prastāva* "introductory praise," by the *prastotṛ*; *udgītha* "high chant," by the *udgātṛ*; *pratihāra* "response," by the *pratihartṛ*; *upadrava* "attack," which is sometimes omitted, by the *udgātṛ*; *nidhana* "conclusion," by all three (Olivelle 1996: 332; Howard 1977: 17–18). The *Chāndogya Upaniṣad* often uses a slightly different set of divisions, omitting the *upadrava*, and adding the *hiṃkāra*, a preliminary wordless sound (usually *hum*, despite its name) sung by the udgātṛ. The sequence is thus *hiṃkāra*, *prastāva*, *udgītha*, *pratihāra*, *nidhana*, giving the *udgītha* the central place among the five (Senart 1930: xi). Each of these five terms occurs many times in the second chapter of the *Chāndogya*, and rarely if at all in the other Upaniṣads.

Chanting occurs only in the more elaborate rituals, involving Soma (above, p. 65); accordingly, Soma figures frequently in this Upaniṣad, both as an element of ritual (CU 2.24.1, 7, 10; 3.16.1–6; 5.12.1), and as a god (CU 2.22.1; 5.4.2; 5.5.2; 5.10.4).

Besides its concern with Sāmavedic chant, the *Chāndogya Upaniṣad* shows an affinity with the Yajurveda tradition, especially with its longest Upaniṣad, the *Bṛhadāraṇyaka*. The passage on the Five Fires, which is an important document for the development of the idea of rebirth (above, pp. 122–125), appears in both, in different versions (BU 6.2; CU 5.3–10); moreover, in both it is preceded by a contest of the faculties (BU 6.1; CU 5.1–2; above, p. 253; Renou 1955: 96–100). The *Chāndogya Upaniṣad* ascribes a passage identifying the Self with *brahman* (CU 3.14) to Śāṇḍilya, the main authority in those parts of the *Śatapatha Brāhmaṇa* which do not mention Yājñavalkya (above, p. 249). A similar passage, also ascribed to Śāṇḍilya, appears in SB 10.6.3; the *Bṛhadāraṇyaka Upaniṣad* does not include it, but Śāṇḍilya appears in two of its lists of teachers (BU 2.6; 6.5).

The words of the Sāmaveda are taken mainly from the Ṛgveda, the Sāmaveda providing the music (above, p. 46). The *Chāndogya Upaniṣad* calls *ṛc* (the Ṛgvedic words) and *sāman* (the tune) a couple who fulfil one another's desire (CU 1.1.6). It quotes two Ṛgvedic sages, Kauṣītaki (CU 1.5.2; 1.5.4) and Aitareya (CU 3.16.7), both of whom have Upaniṣads named after them. This friendly attitude to the Ṛgveda contrasts with that of the *Bṛhadāraṇyaka Upaniṣad*, where several of the rivals defeated by Yājñavalkya are Ṛgveda specialists (Cohen 2008: 76–82).

Structure

The *Chāndogya Upaniṣad* is in eight chapters, called *prapāṭhaka*s, "recitations," each divided into sections (*khaṇḍa*) and subsections (*khaṇḍikā*). The first two chapters are marked off from the rest by their interest in the Sāmavedic chant; like the first two sections of the *Bṛhadāraṇyaka Upaniṣad*, they are more Brāhmaṇa-like than upaniṣadic. Thereafter, the chant is not mentioned, except where the Sāmaveda figures alongside the Ṛgveda and Yajurveda as part of the triple Veda – sometimes adding the "*Ātharvaṇa*" (CU 7.1.2; 7.1.4; 7.2.1; 7.7.1) or the "*Atharvan*s and *Aṅgiras*es" (above, p. 47) as a fourth, though it is not called a Veda here (CU 3.4.1–2). Chapters 6 and 7 are each framed by a long narrative, about a particular teacher and a particular student; the remaining chapters are composite, each consisting of two or more narratives or discourses.

The text recognizes this composite nature of the chapters by dividing them into parts, marked by an ancient device used in some other Upaniṣads: a repetition of the last few words (Senart 1930: xii–xxxii; Renou 1955: 91–93). This device is reproduced in some translations (Hume 1931; Radhakrishnan 1953; Zaehner 1966; Roebuck 2003), but not in others (Olivelle 1996). There are thirty-one such parts, each containing one, two or more sections. They are logical wholes; we can think of them as little Upaniṣads, which have been put together and reworked into the greater whole, relatively coherent and consistent in style, which is the *Chāndogya* (Renou 1955: 91).

This Upaniṣad is almost entirely in prose. Two stanzas from different Ṛgveda hymns are quoted in CU 3.17.6–7, and another in CU 5.2.7; they are introduced using the term *ṛc* (above, p. 45). Other stanzas, quoted from unknown sources, are called *śloka*s, which in this context does not imply a particular meter. Verse quotations are not often more than one stanza, and sometimes less (Renou 1955: 100). The stanzas do not form sequences as in the *Bṛhadāraṇyaka Upaniṣad*; they are only weakly connected to their context, and do not contribute to the philosophical discourses (Renou 1955: 102; Cohen 2008: 122–126).

Narratives of teaching

Much of the teaching in the *Chāndogya Upaniṣad* is framed in narratives, in which it is imparted by a particular teacher to a particular pupil, sometimes in unusual circumstances. Such narratives occur in other Upaniṣads: the *Bṛhadāraṇyaka* has several, the *Praśna* and the second half of the *Kena* are each framed in a narrative, and the *Kaṭha* opens with perhaps the most striking of all, in which Naciketas confronts Death and obliges him to reveal his secrets. But it is in the *Chāndogya* that narratives of teaching are most abundant and most varied.

While many dialogues in the Upaniṣads are between brahmins who are ritual colleagues, some teachers and pupils are not brahmins. Not only can one of the parties be a kṣatriya, like Janaka or Ajātaśatru in the *Bṛhadāraṇyaka Upaniṣad*; one or both may be a god: Yama, the god of death, is the teacher in the *Kaṭha*, and the god Indra is enlightened by the goddess Umā in the *Kena* (KeU 3–4). In the *Chāndogya*, we have not only kṣatriya teachers, and the god Prajāpati (above, p. 66–68), but even animals and fires (above, pp. 262–263). (Those interpreters who see historical significance in the relatively few examples of kṣatriya teachers do not apply the same logic to these cases.) There are no female theologians, like Gārgī and Maitreyī in the *Bṛhadāraṇyaka*; but in three of the *Chāndogya*'s stories a woman has a crucial and positive role: Jabālā tells her son about his paternity (CU 4.4.1–2); Satyakāma's wife ensures that even in his absence his student will learn (CU 4.10.3); and Uṣasti's wife provides him with the food he needs before taking a vital employment opportunity (CU 1.10).

A frequent theme in upaniṣadic narratives is the reluctance of the teacher. Knowledge is a precious possession, only to be imparted to those who have shown themselves worthy by their understanding and persistence. Yājñavalkya tries to put off Janaka with superficial answers (BU 4.3.2–5), and only gives his most profound teaching when the king has driven him out of every corner (BU 4.3.33); Yama tries to buy off Naciketas with worldly goods and pleasures (KU 1.23–25). In the *Chāndogya Upaniṣad*, Prajāpati's teaching about the four states of the self (CU 8. 7–12; above, p. 3, p. 143) combines the reluctant teacher with another recurrent theme, the struggle of the gods against the demons. Both are the offspring of Prajāpati (BU 1.3.1); the gods usually win by being more subtle than the demons. The story begins with Prajāpati saying that by knowing the self, all worlds are won and all desires are fulfilled; the gods and the demons then each send a delegate to learn from him. When they have attended him for thirty-two years, he teaches them a superficial view: you see yourself in a mirror or a pan of water (CU 8.7.4–8.8.3). Prajāpati calls this view of the self an *upaniṣad*, a mental identification (above, p. 2, p. 139) – though he knows it is a very feeble one which will lead to failure (CU 8.8.4). The demon Virocana falls for it, but Indra, though satisfied at first, soon realizes that the self you see in a reflection is subject to misery and death, so he comes back for further teaching. Even a god must follow ritual form, so he brings fuel for his teacher's fire, as a Vedic student should, and attends Prajāpati for another thirty-two years. Only after a total of 101 years (CU 8.11.3) does Indra come to know the liberated self which sees pleasures in the world of *brahman* (CU 8.1.5).

Narratives of right behavior

Indra gains the favor of Prajāpati by performing the duties of a Vedic student, as well as by his understanding; in Vedic thought as in later tradition, right behavior and right understanding go together, both being aspects of *satya* "truth." Other stories show more complex examples of meritorious behavior. Satyakāma (meaning "desiring truth") wants to study the Veda, so he needs to know his lineage – the status inherited from his father, and used like a surname. His mother, Jabālā, cannot tell him; she was traveling about when she conceived him, and does not know who his father was (CU 4.4.2). So she forms a lineage name from her own name, and tells him to introduce himself as Satyakāma Jābāla. He approaches a teacher, who asks him his lineage as expected, so he answers by repeating what his mother has told him. The teacher accepts him at once, saying "No-one but a brahmin could speak like that" (CU 4.4.5) – implying either that his honesty proves he has a brahmin father, or that it makes him a brahmin and paternity is irrelevant. But before beginning lessons, the teacher sets him to tend 400 of his feeblest cattle. He returns after some years, by which time the cattle have increased to a thousand (CU 4.4.5), and his teacher can see by his appearance that he already knows *brahman* (CU 4.9.2) – whether this means the Vedic texts, or supreme liberating knowledge. He has been taught not by a human teacher but by the bull of the herd, his camp fire, a wild goose, and a cormorant (CU 4.5–8; Roebuck 2003: 419). Finally, his human teacher does teach him, omitting nothing (CU 4.9.3).

The story has a sequel, which concerns another aspect of the life of a Vedic student. Besides services such as tending the teacher's fires and cattle, he has to abstain from sex until he is dismissed by his teacher, returns home, and marries. This aspect is so prominent that a term for Vedic studentship, *brahmacarya*, literally the way of life belonging to *brahman* or to the Veda, came to mean chastity. Sleeping with the teacher's wife is often listed among the basest sins (e.g. CU 5.10.9; *Manu* 11.55, Olivelle 2005: 217–218), being a violation both of *brahmacarya* and of duty to the teacher. Satyakāma, now a teacher himself – and, it goes without saying, married – has a student, Upakosala, who has completed twelve years, the usual period of study. But Satyakāma does not dismiss him as he dismisses his other students. His wife tells him he should teach him, hinting that otherwise the fires Upakosala tends so well will teach him instead. But Satyakāma goes on a journey, leaving Upakosala with his wife. Upakosala refuses to eat; when Satyakāma's wife asks him why, he talks of unspecified desires and afflictions (CU 4.10.3). Satyakāma's three fires – the household fire, the southern fire, and the fire for offerings to the gods – then instruct him in turn, adding that his teacher will tell him the way. Satyakāma returns and – like his teacher before him – sees by the look of his face that Upakosala already knows *brahman*. After questioning him, he completes the teaching, telling him the way to *brahman* (CU 4.15.5). The narration leaves much unexplained, but it seems that the fires are impressed by Upakosala's behavior, and that Satyakāma intended this outcome; his failure to dismiss him, and his departure, were a test for an outstanding student.

Another story concerning behavior turns on the idea, still followed by Hindus, that food left over from a meal is polluting, especially if it has been left by someone of lower ritual status. During a famine, caused by locusts, not by drought, a poor brahmin named Uṣasti, a practitioner of the Sāmaveda, begs food from a rich man, who gives him some of the gruel he is eating – more than enough for the two of them, as it turns out. The rich man then offers him water, which he refuses. He explains that he accepted the left-over gruel because it was necessary to sustain life, whereas the left-over water is not (since there is no shortage). After eating, Uṣasti brings home the rest of the gruel to his wife, Āṭikī. She meanwhile has begged food for herself, so she puts the gruel by; she too is scrupulous about eating leftovers only when necessary. The next day, Uṣasti says that he can earn money from a king who is having a sacrifice performed, if only he can have something to eat; otherwise, it seems, he would not have the strength to go. Āṭikī brings out the gruel; he eats, and goes to the sacrifice (CU 1.10.1–7). There, the king has already appointed three other Sāmaveda chanters, but he would have appointed Uṣasti if he had known he was available. He agrees to give Uṣasti as much as the other three (CU 1.11.1–3).

Narratives of challenge

Uṣasti then challenges the three chanters by telling each that if he chants his section of the *sāman* without knowing the deity belonging to it, his head will shatter – a frequent threat for those who speak without understanding (above, p. 255). They each ask him what the deity is; his answers are breath, the sun, and food (CU 1.11). These are three *upāsana*s or *upaniṣad*s (above, pp. 137–139), though these terms are not used here.

The motif of the challenge appears in other stories. The teaching of the five fires (above, pp. 122–125) is framed by a story in which a kṣatriya, Pravāhana Jaivali, challenges a young brahmin, Śvetaketu, by asking five questions. Unable to answer, he asks his father Uddālaka Āruṇi, who was his teacher. Uddālaka is also baffled, and goes to Pravāhana for instruction (CU 5.3; BU 6.2.1–8).

In another story about Śvetaketu, he has learnt the Veda away from home, not from his father; he comes back confident of his knowledge, and it is his father who challenges him (CU 6.1.1–3). He is unable to answer, but his father teaches him how everything is derived from Being (*sat*) (CU 6.1–7). The end of this passage is marked by a repetition of the final phrase (above, p. 260); the rest of the chapter (CU 6.8–16) is a second series of teachings given to Śvetaketu by Uddālaka, each marked by a refrain which the Sanskrit commentators, and most translators, understand as "That is the self; you are that." Vedic grammar requires the second statement to mean "that's how you are" (Olivelle 1996: 152, 349; Brereton 1986); but the grammatical rule concerned may not have been strictly followed by this time (Roebuck 2003: 423).

In another long story, the generous but proud Jānaśruti (above, p. 138) is challenged by overhearing a wild goose – another non-human instructor – talk of Raikva, whose knowledge trumps the good deeds of others (CU 4.1.1–4). He is driven to seek out Raikva and learn his *upāsana* (CU 4.1.5–4.2).

Narratives of dissatisfaction

In contrast to the confident person who is challenged by someone else, there is the motif of the seeker driven by his own dissatisfaction with the knowledge he has attained. In the story of Indra, it is his dissatisfaction with what he has learnt so far that brings him back three times for further teaching (CU 8.9–11; above, p. 143). In CU 7, Nārada – who appears in later texts as a great teacher of *bhakti* (devotion to a personal god) – comes for instruction to Sanatkumāra – whose name means he is both old and young. After enumerating the Vedas and ancillary sciences that he has learnt, he confesses: "I am just a knower of *mantra*s, not a knower of the Self. For I have heard from people like you, sir, that someone who knows the Self passes beyond suffering. I suffer, sir. Sir, take me beyond suffering" (CU 7.1.3). As in CU 6, Sanatkumāra's teaching fills the rest of the chapter (above, p. 141).

Uddālaka Āruṇi appears again in another story, in which he recognizes his own inadequacy. Five wealthy householders who are interested in the self and *brahman* ask him about the self. Afraid he will not be able to answer fully,

Uddālaka takes them to another teacher, Aśvapati Kaikeya, who finds all their *upāsanas* of the self inadequate, and gives them his own teaching (CU 5.11–24). This story is a version of one in SB 10.6.1 – further evidence that the Sāmaveda specialists who composed this Upaniṣad communicated with their Yajurvedic colleagues.

The power of sound

The *Bṛhadāraṇyaka Upaniṣad*'s interest in action – the concern of the Yajurveda – is matched by the *Chāndogya Upaniṣad*'s interest in sound: not only ritual chant but speech and animal cries (Cohen 2008: 106–109). It is particularly rich in serious word-play (Olivelle 1996: liv; Cohen 2008: 104), and, as we have seen, in non-human teachers. The description of dogs performing the *udgītha* to obtain food (CU 1.12), creeping and holding on to each other as prescribed in the ritual rules (Kane 1974: part 2, p. 1166; Keith 1925 vol. 2, p. 329), has often been seen as satirical, as has the Ṛgvedic hymn of the chanting frogs (RV 7.103; Gonda 1975: 143); however, like the other talking animals in this Upaniṣad, it is probably serious (Cohen 2008: 107; above, pp. 158–159).

In another story involving a challenge to brahmins from a kṣatriya, three experts on the *udgītha* have a conversation about it (CU 1.8.1). The third is Pravāhana Jaivali; this is the name of the king who challenges Śvetaketu in the story of the five fires (CU 5.3.1–4; BU 6.2.1–2; above, pp. 122–125; p. 264). It is not stated here that he is a kṣatriya, but there is a hint of it when he chooses to "listen to what the two brahmins say" (CU 1.8.2). One of the two says that the chant comes from sound, sound from breath, breath from food, food from water, and water from the world beyond, or heaven. Looking at it in the opposite order, we can say that rain comes down, so crops grow, so people eat, so they breathe, so they vocalize, so they chant the *sāman*. This recalls the account of the descent of life in the five fires passage (CU 5.4–7; BU 6.2.9–12). The second brahmin challenges the speaker to trace the chain of causation further back than the world beyond – otherwise his head will shatter. He gives his own answer: the world beyond comes from this world. Perhaps he sees a cyclic process whereby sacrifice in this world nourishes the world beyond, which in turn nourishes this world (cf. BhG 3.10–16). Pravāhana intervenes to say that this too is a limited view. This world comes from space (*ākāśa*). In the theory of five elements which developed in the Veda and continued in later Indian thought, particularly Sāṃkhya, each element is linked to one of the five senses: space to hearing, wind to touch, fire to sight, water to taste, and earth to smell (Killingley 2006: 77–79). In making space the source and ending of all beings (CU 1.9.1), Pravāhana gives primacy to sound, of which the *udgītha*, the center of the *sāman*, is the highest manifestation.

Three, four, five, and other numbers

Like other Upaniṣads, the *Chāndogya* is interested in numbers. It identifies the three syllables of the word *udgītha* with three triads: breath, speech, food; sky, atmosphere, earth; sun, wind, fire; Sāmaveda, Yajurveda, Ṛgveda (CU 1.3.6–7; Cohen 2008: 103). Similarly, it describes Prajāpati hatching a succession of triads starting from earth, atmosphere and sky: fire, wind, sun; *ṛc*, *yajuṣ*, *sāman*; and the three ritual utterances *bhūḥ*, *bhuvaḥ*, *svaḥ* (CU 4.17.1–3; above, p. 155). Three of the triads are the same in both passages, though in the opposite order because the first moves downwards and the second upwards. Prajāpati hatching the worlds is a motif that figures in many creation stories (AB 5.32, Keith 1920: 256; *Jaiminīya Brāhmaṇa* 3.15. 6–8). But Uddālaka teaches Śvetaketu a creation story which dispenses with Prajāpati, and starts with Being (*sat*). Wishing to procreate itself, it produces a different triad: heat, water, food (CU 6.2.3–4). Besides being necessary to life, these three are the origins of the three classes of living beings: oviparous, born by incubation; viviparous, born from the amniotic fluid; and vegetable, born from grain (CU 6.3.1). They also appear as three colors: red, white, and black (CU 6.4.1–4) – an anticipation of the three guṇas ("strands") of the Sāṃkhya system (above, pp. 5, 70, 167, 176, 210–211). Successive division into further triads leads to the constituents of a person, culminating in mind, breath, and speech (CU 6.5–6).

Tetrads are less pervasive than triads, but two appear in CU 3.18.2–6: speech, breath, sight, hearing in the microcosm; and fire, wind, sun, directions in the macrocosm. The Vedas are made into a tetrad: *ṛc*, *sāman*, *yajuṣ*, *brahman* (CU 1.7.5; above, pp. 47–48). A man's life is presented as a series of multiples of four, linked to the Soma ritual and the Vedic meters, and culminating in a lifespan of 116 years (CU 3.16). The numbers four and sixteen figure in the story of Satyakāma (CU 4.5–8). Uddālaka tells Śvetaketu that a man consists of sixteen parts (CU 6.7.1; Gonda 1965: 121–122); if he fasts for fifteen days, there is only one part of him left (CU 6.7.3). This passage describes an experiment showing that the mind is made of food (CU 6.6.5; 6.7.6), but it also suggests the traditional association of the mind with the moon (above, p. 62). The word for "part" used here also means a digit of the moon (above, p. 253); when the moon has waned, fifteen parts have disappeared, but the last, which is the moon itself (Gonda 1965: 122–124), remains. When Śvetaketu has fasted for fifteen days and his mind does not function, he is like the old moon, but his remaining sixteenth enables him to recover.

But the *Chāndogya Upaniṣad* is especially interested in the number five – more than any other Upaniṣad (Cohen 2008: 120). Besides appearing often in the Brāhmaṇas and Upaniṣads as the number of faculties, the number of sacrificial beasts, and so on (above, p. 70, p. 180), five is especially significant in the Sāmaveda as the number of divisions of the chant (above, p. 259). CU 2.1–7 gives a series of *upāsanas* based on these divisions – expanding the usual Vedic universe of earth, atmosphere, and sky to earth, fire, atmosphere, sun, and sky (CU 2.2). These are followed by *upāsanas* based on a sevenfold division of the chant, still keeping the *udgītha* central (CU 2.8–10), and a further series of pentads (CU 2.11–21).

The character of the *Chāndogya Upaniṣad*

Varied though it is, the *Chāndogya Upaniṣad* is characterized not only by its initial concern with chant, but by the wealth and complexity of its narratives. Some of the thinkers represented are specialists in chant, while others are associated with the Ṛgveda or the Yajurveda. However, like the *Bṛhadāraṇyaka Upaniṣad*, it is hardly a record of the thoughts of historical persons. The discrepancies between the two stories of Śvetaketu's studies (CU 5.3.1; CU 6.1–3) suggest that he and his father are not so much historical figures as names which are associated with certain motifs: the father as teacher, the challenge to someone confident in his newly acquired learning, and the inadequacy of Vedic ritual knowledge in the face of fundamental questions. The story of Satyakāma Jābāla and that of his student suggest that his name is similarly associated with the non-human teacher, the exemplary woman, and the appearance of *brahman* in a student's face.

Food features both in the stories and in the various teachings. Heat, water, and food are the first stage of creation (CU 6.2.3). This chapter is remarkable, among other features, for its unity of thought, its use of experiments and observations, and the absence from it of mythological and ritual material, even of the word *brahman*. While its account of the original being's creative desire looks back to the Brāhmaṇas and to RV 10.129 (above, pp. 66–67), it looks forward to the Sāṃkhya school (above, p. 266), with its three *guṇa*s, and its insistence that an effect is already contained within its cause. Even here, the story starts with a brahmin's duty to study the Veda. The narratives all have some relation to ritual: even where the protagonists are not brahmins but kṣatriyas, they present their questions in terms of brahmanical ritual and belief. The *Chāndogya* has been described as perhaps the least secularized of the Upaniṣads (Renou 1955: 94).

References

Brereton, J. 1986. "*Tat Tvam Asi* in Context" *Zeitschrift der deutschen morgenländischen Gesellschaft* 136: 98–109.

Cohen, Signe. 2008. *Text and Authority in the Older Upaniṣads*. Leiden: Brill.

Gonda, Jan. 1965. *Change and Continuity in Indian Religion*. The Hague: Mouton.

Gonda, Jan. 1975. *Vedic Literature* (*A History of Indian Literature* Vol. 1, Fasc. 1). Wiesbaden: Harrassowitz.

Howard, Wayne. 1977. *Sāmavedic Chant*. New Haven, CT: Yale University Press.

Hume, R. E. 1931. *The Thirteen Principal Upanishads: Translated from the Sanskrit*. 2nd edn. Oxford: Oxford University Press.

Kane, P. V. 1974. *History of Dharmaśāstra*, vol. 2. (2 parts bound separately but paginated continuously.) 2nd edn. Poona [now Pune]: Bhandarkar Oriental Research Institute.

Keith, A. B. 1920. *Rigveda Brahmanas: The Aitareya and Kauṣītaki Brāhmaṇas of the Rigveda Translated from the Original Sanskrit*. Cambridge, MA: Harvard University Press. (Reprint Delhi: Motilal Banarsidass, 1971.)

Keith, A. B. 1925. *The Religion and Philosophy of the Veda and Upanishads*. (2 volumes paginated consecutively.) Cambridge, MA: Harvard University Press.

Killingley, Dermot. 2006. "Faculties, Breaths and Orifices: Some Vedic and Sāṃkhya Notions of the Body and Personality" in Anna S. King (ed.) *Indian Religions: Renaissance and Renewal*. London: Equinox, 73–108.

Olivelle, Patrick. 1996. *Upaniṣads: Translated from the Original Sanskrit* (World's Classics series). Oxford: Oxford University Press.

Olivelle, Patrick. 2005. *Manu's Code of Law: A Critical Edition and Translation of the Mānava-Dharmaśāstra*. New York: Oxford University Press.

Radhakrishnan, S. 1953. *The Principal Upaniṣads: Edited with Introduction, Text, Translation and Notes*. London: George Allen & Unwin.

Renou, Louis. 1955. "Remarques sur la Chāndogya-Upaniṣad" *Études védiques et pāṇinéennes* 1: 91–102.

Roebuck, Valerie. 2003. *The Upaniṣads. Translated and Edited* (Penguin Classics series). London: Penguin.

Senart, Émil. 1930. *Chāndogya-Upaniṣad: traduite et annotée*. Paris: Les Belles Lettres.

Zaehner, R. C. 1966. *Hindu Scriptures*. London: J. M. Dent.

Further reading

Cohen, Signe. 2008. *Text and Authority in the Older Upaniṣads*. Leiden: Brill, 101–132.

Olivelle, Patrick. 1999. "Young Śvetaketu: A Literary Study of an Upaniṣadic Story" *Journal of the American Oriental Society* 119: 46–70.

25 The *Aitareya Upaniṣad*

Signe Cohen

The *Aitareya Upaniṣad* is a short prose text in three chapters. The *Aitareya* is commonly regarded as one of the oldest Upaniṣads, though slightly younger than the *Bṛhadāraṇyaka* or the *Chāndogya Upaniṣad*. The *Aitareya Upaniṣad* is formally affiliated with the *Aitareya* school of the *Ṛgveda*. Both Śaṅkara (eighth century CE) and Madhva (thirteenth-fourtheenth century CE) composed commentaries on the text. The *Aitareya Upaniṣad* and the older *Aitareya Āraṇyaka* are named after a Vedic sage, Aitareya Mahidāsa, who is traditionally regarded as the author of the *Aitareya Brāhmaṇa* and the *Aitareya Āraṇyaka*.

The *Aitareya Upaniṣad* comprises the fourth, fifth, and sixth chapters of the second book of the Vedic ritual text *Aitareya Āraṇyaka*. Occasionally, however, the first three chapters of the second book of the *Aitareya Āraṇyaka* are called an *Upaniṣad* as well, and given the name *Bahvṛca-Brāhmaṇa Upaniṣad* or *Mahā-Aitareya Upaniṣad*. The third book of the *Aitareya Āraṇyaka* is also sometimes regarded as an Upaniṣad, called the *Saṃhitopaniṣad*. Most Upanisad collections, however, only include the *Aitareya Upanisad*, and not its "sister texts."

The *Aitareya Upanisad* is deeply imbedded in the older Āraṇyaka text to which it belongs. There can be no doubt that the *Aitareya Upanisad* is simply a part of the *Aitareya Āraṇyaka* that has been given a separate name. The relationship between the "parent" text *Aitareya Āraṇyaka* and the "daughter text" *Aitareya Upanisad* can help illuminate how the Upanisads as a genre came into being: The Upaniṣads began as chapters within the ritual texts of the Brāhmaṇas and Āraṇyakas dealing with the topic of *ātman*. Later on, these chapters on *ātman* took on a literary life of their own and developed into a new genre, the Upaniṣad.

Ātman in the *Aitareya Upaniṣad*: From creator to abstract principle

All the three chapters of this Upaniṣad explore various aspects of *ātman*, the eternal self. The first vision of *ātman* in this Upanisad is a mythological one.

The first chapter of the *Aitareya Upanisad* describes the creation of the world, with *ātman* playing the part of a creator:

> In the beginning this world was just *ātman* alone, and no one else blinked. He thought: Let me create the worlds![1]

Here, *ātman* appears as a primordial creator and first principle. The world comes into being following *ātman*'s conscious desire to create. How are we to interpret this notion of the self as creator of the world? Is *ātman* here simply a mythological figure, a divine creator shaping the world through his will in the beginning? Or is *ātman* still to be understood as the individual self of a human being? Is the act of creation described here a one-time primordial act, or our own continuous creation of the external world through the agency of our own inner self? The text is open to both a mythological and a philosophical interpretation.

A parallel passage in the *Bṛhadāraṇyaka Upaniṣad* focuses on why the word "I" (*aham*) is what it is:

> In the beginning, there was just a single *ātman* in the form of a person (*puruṣa*). He looked around and saw only himself. The first thing he said was "Here I am," and therefore the name "I" came to be.[2]

Although the passage in the *Airtareya Upaniṣad* may very well have been inspired by the *Bṛhadāraṇyaka Upaniṣad*, it is worth noting that the *Aitareya Upaniṣad* goes much further in developing a full-fledged creation myth from the initial idea that the *ātman* is the first being.

The use of the loaded phrase "There was in the beginning" (*agra āsīt)* in 1.1 evokes multiple Vedic creation stories where those very words are used to describe the initial primordial state before the world as we know it came into being. The *Aitareya Upanisad*'s relationship to the *Ṛgveda* is reflected in many facets of the text. The creation story in *Aitareya Upaniṣad* 1 portrays the *ātman* as a divine creator, and the process of creation is compared to an egg hatching:

> He incubated that man, and from the man incubated the mouth was hatched, like an egg …[3]

This comparison between the creation of the universe and the hatching of an egg is reminiscent of the creation story in *Ṛgveda* 10.121, the hymn to *Hiranyagarbha*, the Golden Egg. The creation of man in the *Aitareya Upaniṣad* also echoes the well-known hymn to Puruṣa (the cosmic man) in *Ṛgveda* 10.190. In the Vedic hymn, the moon arises from the mind of the cosmic man, the sun from his eye, Indra and the fire god Agni from his mouth, the wind god Vāyu from his breath, space from his navel, the sky from his head, the earth from his feet, and the regions of the sky from his ears.[4] In the *Aitareya Upaniṣad*, the various parts of the cosmos arise from the first man hatched by the *ātman*. In the Upaniṣad, fire is, as in the Vedic hymn, connected with speech: "… from the mouth came speech, and from speech fire."[5] Likewise, in the *Aitareya Upaniṣad* the sun is associated with the eye: "… from the eyes came sight, and from sight the sun." The wind comes (naturally) from the breath, the regions of the sky come from the ears, and the moon comes from the mind.[6] Although the creation of the parts of the physical universe from the body of a person are framed differently in the Vedic hymn and in the Upaniṣad (human sacrifice vs. a more peaceful "hatching"), the Upaniṣadic text appears to owe a great deal to the hymn to *Puruṣa*.

The depiction of *ātman* as a divine being with creative powers is found in several of the Upanisads affiliated with the *Ṛgveda*. The creator *ātman* is later in the *Aitareya Upanisad* identified with the Vedic thunder god Indra, the main deity of the *Ṛgveda*:

> When he [*ātman*] was born, he regarded the beings and thought: "Will someone say that there is another here?" But all he saw was that man, *brahman*, the highest, and he said: "This (*idam*) is what I have seen (*adarśam*)." And therefore he is called *Idandra*. His name is Idandra, but even though he is Idandra, people mysteriously call him Indra, for the gods seem to love the mysterious.[7]

By equating *ātman* with Indra, the *Aitareya Upanisad* aligns the Upanisadic idea of *ātman* as the supreme principle with older Ṛgvedic ideas of powerful gods like Indra. The old Vedic god Indra is not discarded in this Upaniṣad, but he is reinterpreted as a symbol of the inner self.

The *Aitareya Upaniṣad* similarly ascribes a symbolic meaning to an old Vedic stanza quoted in the text:

> I knew all the births of the gods
> While I was still in the womb.
> A hundred iron forts trapped me.
> Then the falcon – quickly I flew away.[8]

The Vedic stanza originally referred to the falcon who steals the sacred Soma drink, but the Upaniṣad gives the stanza an entirely different spin: "Vāmadeva spoke this way while he was still in the womb. Since he knew this, he went up after the destruction of his body, fulfilled all his desires in the heavenly world, and became immortal."[9] Here, the unborn *ātman's* knowledge frees it from rebirth and grants it immortality.

The first chapter of the *Aitareya Upaniṣad* also adds a few more intriguing pieces to its depiction of *ātman*. The *ātman* has "three states of sleep."[10] Although these three states are not elaborated here, it is possible that this brief reference to the states of the *ātman* is a first hint of the more elaborate doctrine of the three states of the self – waking, dreaming, and deep sleep – in the *Māṇḍūkya Upaniṣad*, which also introduces the idea of a fourth state beyond dreamless sleep.

The *Aitareya Upaniṣad* further gives a vivid description of the *ātman's* entry into the body:

> He split open the head at the parting of the hair and entered through that way. This gate is called "the Split" (*vidṛti*) ...[11]

This idea that the self enters (and leaves) the body through an opening at the top of the head has parallels in other texts. The *Taittirīya Upaniṣad* states, for example:

> In this space within the heart is the immortal, golden person who is made up of the mind. ... Bursting through the halves of the skull at the parting of the hair, he establishes himself in the fire by chanting *bhūr*, in the wind by chanting *bhuvas*, in the sun by chanting *suvar*, and in *brahman* by chanting *mahas*.[12]

The *Kaṭha Upaniṣad*, likewise, hints at an opening at the top of the head:

> One hundred and one are the veins of the heart.
> One of them flows up to the top of the head.
> Going up by that, one reaches the immortal.[13]

Based on these passages, one may see a notion in some of the older Upaniṣads of the self as a tangible substance capable of entering and exiting the body through a particular spot at the top of the skull. This doctrine of the "gate" through which the *ātman* enters and exits foreshadows the idea of a *cakra* or energy center at the crown of the head in some forms of Yoga. The main difference is, of course, that the *cakras* are nodes of energy in the subtle body, while the *vidṛti* in the Upaniṣads is described in vivid language as an opening in the physical body.

In the second chapter of this Upaniṣad, we find a slightly different view of *ātman*. The second chapter of the *Aitareya Upaniṣad* discusses the three births of the *ātman*. In this part of the text, *ātman* refers to the immortal essence of a person, rather than a mythological figure or creator god. Practically speaking, the three births described in the text are conception, birth, and rebirth after death, but the births of the *ātman* are here described in such a way that female involvement in the process is minimized. In the male-centered biology of the Upaniṣad, the first "birth" of the *ātman* is in the form of a man's semen as it is placed in a woman during intercourse. The ejaculation itself is here seen as the first "giving birth."[14] The second "birth" is a man nourishing the woman who is carrying his child, and thereby nourishing his own self.[15] The third birth is a form of reincarnation: "As soon as he leaves this world, he is born again. That is his third birth."[16] In this chapter of the *Aitareya Upaniṣad*, the word *ātman* is used in the sense of the "essence of a person."

The brief third chapter of the text contains a more philosophical inquiry into the nature of the *ātman*. This section of the Upaniṣad describes *ātman* in abstract terms. *Ātman* is identified with *brahman*, the gods, and all living beings,[17] and ultimately with cognition (*prajñāna*) itself.[18]

The concept of *ātman* in the *AU* ranges from the mythological in chapter one, via the corporeal and tangible in chapter two, to the wholly abstract in chapter three. The progress from the physical to the metaphysical may be interpreted either as a structural device of the text itself or as indicative of chronological development in the perception of *ātman* within this text.

Brahman in the *Aitareya Upaniṣad*

Brahman plays a very minor part in the *Aitareya Upaniṣad*. The term is only mentioned twice in the entire text.[19] The focus of the *Aitareya Upaniṣad* is clearly on the *ātman*, rather than *brahman*. Although all the texts that we refer to as "Upaniṣads" identify *ātman* and *brahman*, some texts emphasize *ātman* almost to the exclusion of *brahman*. This is particularly the case of those Upaniṣads, like the *Aitareya*, that are affiliated with the *śākhās* of the *Ṛgveda*.

Even though *brahman* is not given much attention in the *Aitareya Upaniṣad* overall, the brief statement "*Brahman* is knowledge" (*prajñānam brahma*), occurring near the end of the text, became known as one of the *Mahāvākyas*, or "Great Sayings" of the Upaniṣads in the later Vedānta school of philosophy, along with such famous utterances as the *tat tvam asi* of the *Chāndogya Upaniṣad* 6.8.7.

The cosmology of the *Aitareya Upaniṣad*

The world that is created by *ātman* in the *Aitareya Upaniṣad* is to a large extent familiar from other Vedic and late Vedic texts: The macrocosm of the universe mirrors the microcosm of the human being, with the sun, which makes things visible, corresponding to the eye, etc.

One aspect of the cosmos described in the *Aitareya Upaniṣad* that is more original is the structure of the cosmos itself:

> He created these worlds: The heavenly waters, the glittering rays, the mortal, and the waters. The heavenly waters are beyond the sky, and their support is the sky. The glittering rays are the intermediate region. The mortal is the earth, and that which is underneath is the waters.[20]

The notion of a threefold world, consisting of earth, the intermediate region of space, and the highest heaven, is familiar from older Vedic literature, as is the idea of celestial waters. The idea of a watery underworld, however, is an interesting addition here.

Food in the *Aitareya Upaniṣad*

Food and nourishment are central concepts in the *Aitareya Upaniṣad.* When the *ātman* has created the world and its parts, it immediately faces the problem of how to feed the beings that it has created:

> The deities [the sun, moon, fire, etc.] told him: "Find us a house where we can love and eat food!" He brought them a cow, but they said: "That's not enough for us!" Then he brought them a horse, but they said: "That's not enough for us!" Then he brought them a person, and they said: "That is well made!", for people are well made. Then he told them: "Enter into your own houses." So the fire became speech and entered the mouth, the wind became breath and entered the nose … Then he thought: Now that these worlds and their guardians are in place, I need to create food for them. So he hatched the waters. When the waters were hatched, something firm emerged from them, and the firm thing that emerged was food."[21]

The *ātman* then faces the problem that the food he has created from the waters tries to run away. He attempts to capture it with speech, but fails. How could it be otherwise, says the Upaniṣad; if one could catch food with speech, one would get full from just talking about food. The *ātman* then desperately tries to catch the runaway food with his out-breath, his sight, his hearing, his skin, his mind, and his penis, before finally succeeding in catching it with his in-breath, presumably because people breathe in when they eat.[22]

While the notion of run-away food may seem odd at first sight, it is not uncommon in the Upaniṣad for food to be given cosmic importance. "Food and eater," states the *Bṛhadāraṇyaka Upaniṣad*, "that is the whole of this world."[23] One might speculate the religious significance of food originated in the old Vedic sacrificial rituals where things that could be eaten and drunk (such as butter and the intoxicating drink Soma) were common ritual gifts to the gods, poured into the sacred fire. The foods that humans consume are seen as a gift from bountiful gods: "In that fire the gods offer rain, and from that offering comes food."[24]

Both the cosmic creator *ātman* in the Upaniṣad's first chapter and the human father in the second discover that what has been created (a universe or a baby) must be nourished in order for the world to continue:

> As she [the mother] feeds the child, so he [the father] should feed her. The woman carries him as an embryo. In the beginning, he feeds the child even before it is born. When he feeds his child before it is born, he feeds his own *ātman* so that these worlds can continue …[25]

The *Aitareya Upaniṣad* here juxtaposes two forms of creation: the primordial creation of the universe itself and the more prosaic creation of a child. By suggesting that the father's feeding of the child and its mother is necessary for the worlds to continue, the text implies that the creation of a child is itself a cosmic act, necessary for the continuation of humanity. It also hints at the ultimate identity between the father and his child by referring to the child as his *ātman*.

Date and composition

A few scholars have suggested that the text of the *Aitareya Upaniṣad* in its present form may be heterogeneous. Schneider suggests, on philosophical grounds, that the first chapter is the historical core of the text.[26] Smith, who regards the *Aitareya Upaniṣad* as one of the earliest Upaniṣads, claims that the last chapter of the *Aitareya Upaniṣad* is a later interpolation.[27]

Linguistic analysis of the brief text of the *Aitareya Upaniṣad* confirms that the text belongs to the time period after the composition of the *Bṛhadāraṇyaka* and *Chāndogya*, but before the *Kauṣītaki*. It is interesting to note that most of the characteristic late Vedic forms occurring in the text are found in the first chapter. Seen in conjunction with the different, more mythological notions of *ātman* found in the first chapter, it is not unreasonable to assume that the first chapter is somewhat older than the last two.

Notes

1 *Aitareya Upanisad* 1.1.1.
2 *Bṛhadāraṇyaka Upaniṣad* 4.1.
3 *Aitareya Upaniṣad* 1.1.4.
4 *Ṛgveda* 10.190.13–14.
5 *Aitareya Upaniṣad* 1.1.4.
6 *Aitareya Upanisad* 1.1.4.
7 *Aitareya Upanisad* 3.1.13.
8 *Aitareya Upaniṣad* 2.5, quoted from *Ṛgveda* 4.27.1.
9 *Aitareya Upaniṣad* 2.5.
10 *Aitareya Upaniṣad* 1.3.12.
11 *Aitareya Upaniṣad* 1.3.12.
12 *Taittirīya Upaniṣad* 1.6.1–2.
13 *Kaṭha Upaniṣad* 6.16.
14 *Aitareya Upaniṣad* 2.1.
15 *Aitareya Upaniṣad* 2.3.
16 *Aitareya Upaniṣad* 2.4.
17 *Aitareya Upaniṣad* 3.2–3.
18 *Aitareya Upaniṣad* 3.4.
19 Both times in *Aitareya Upaniṣad* 3.3.
20 *Aitareya Upaniṣad* 1.1.2.
21 *Aitareya Upaniṣad* 1.2.1–1.3.1.
22 *Aitareya Upaniṣad* 1.3.3–1.3.10.
23 *Aitareya Upaniṣad* 1.4.6.
24 *Bṛhadāraṇyaka Upaniṣad* 6.2.11.

25 *Aitareya Upaniṣad* 2.3.
26 Schneider 1963: 61.
27 Smith 1952: 99.

Further reading

Röer, E. 1850. *The Taittiriya and Aitareya Upanishads with the commentary of Sankara Àchárya, and the gloss of Ànanda Giri, and the Swétáswatara Upanishad with the commentary of Sankara Àchárya.* Bibliotheca Indica, Work 6. Calcutta: Baptist Mission Press. (Reprint Osnabrück: Biblio Verlag, 1980.)

Schneider, U. 1963. "Die Komposition der Aitareya-Upaniṣad" *Indo-Iranian Journal* 7: 58–69.

Silburn, L. 1950. *Aitareya Upaniṣad.* Paris: Adrien Maisonneuve.

Smith, R. M. 1952. "Birth of Thought – I: Taittirīya and Aitareya Upaniṣads" *Annals of the Bhandarkar Oriental Research Institute, Poona* 23: 97–113.

Vidyarnava, S. C. Sandal, P. 1925. *The Aitareya Upaniṣat. The Sacred Books of the Hindus*, Vol. XXX, Part 1. Allahabad: Panini Office. (Reprint New York: AMS Press, 1974.)

26 The *Kauṣītaki Upaniṣad*

Signe Cohen

Like the *Aitareya Upaniṣad*, the *Kauṣītaki Upaniṣad* forms the concluding part of an older Vedic ritual text. The *Kauṣītaki Upaniṣad* comprises books 3–6 of the *Kauṣītaki Āraṇyaka*. It is formally affiliated with the *Śāṅkhāyana* school of the *Ṛgveda*. The text appears to be named after a sage named Kauṣītaki, who is mentioned in the beginning of the second chapter of the text: "'*Brahman* is breath' – that is what Kauṣītaki used to say."[1]

Although the text is often regarded as one of the oldest Upaniṣads, it is not included in the collection of the "classical" Upaniṣads on which the eighth century philosopher Śaṅkara wrote elaborate commentaries. Śaṅkara must, however, have been familiar with the *Kauṣītaki Upaniṣad* since he refers to this text several times in his commentary on the *Brahmasūtra*. If Śaṅkara was familiar with the *Kauṣītaki Upaniṣad*, why did he not compose a commentary to this Upaniṣad as well as the others? The reason may be mainly theological; while Śaṅkara argued that the highest *brahman* was an impersonal divine force rather than a personal god, the *brahman* of *Kauṣītaki Upaniṣad* is highly personified. A commentary on the *Kauṣītaki Upaniṣad* was later written by Śaṅkarānanda in the fourteenth century.

The textual transmission of the *Kauṣītaki Upaniṣad* is complicated, and numerous variants exist in manuscripts of this Upaniṣad. It is likely that the text was less fixed in its transmission than other Upaniṣads precisely because Śaṅkara did not compose a commentary on the text. The texts of the "classical" Upaniṣads have been transmitted faithfully in the form in which Śaṅkara recorded them, and the multiple textual variants of the Upaniṣad he chose to leave out of his collection show how essential his commentaries were for establishing authoritative versions of the texts.

The *Kauṣītaki Upaniṣad* consists of four chapters, mostly in prose, but with a few scattered verses interspersed. Like many Upaniṣads, the *Kauṣītaki Upaniṣad* tells of encounters between wisdom teachers and those seeking knowledge. The emphasis throughout the text is on acquiring the right knowledge of *ātman* and *brahman*, as well as other forms of esoteric knowledge. In one section, the wisdom teacher Citra Gāṅgāyani tells Āruṇi and his son Śvetaketu about the mystical journey of the soul after death. He informs them that the deceased person will have to answer the moon's question: "Who are you?" by declaring "I am you."[2] Then the dead must cross the lake Āra and the river Vijarā "with his mind only"[3] and when he finally encounters the highest *brahman*, he must again answer the question "Who are you?" by declaring once again "I am you." The idea that correct knowledge leads to the desired result (here: the world of *brahman*) is common in the Upaniṣads.

Ātman in the *Kauṣītaki Upaniṣad*

As in all the Upaniṣads, correct knowledge of *ātman*, the self, is essential in the *Kauṣītaki Upaniṣad.* But *ātman* sometimes carries a slightly different meaning here than in other classical Upaniṣads. The term *ātman* is frequently used in the sense of "inner essence" of a thing or person in the *Kauṣītaki Upaniṣad*: *annasyātmā* ("the essence of food"),[4] *tejasa ātmā* ("the essence of radiance"),[5] *śabdasyātmā* ("the essence of sound"),[6] *satyasyātmā* ("the essence of truth"),[7] *vaca ātmā* ("the essence of speech"),[8] etc. This looser application of the term *ātman* seems to reflect an older and less precise use of the term than we normally find in the Upaniṣads. When the text states that *brahman* is the *ātman* of every being,[9] we can still sense a resonance of the old meaning "essence" in the term *ātman*. *Ātman* is also still used in this text in the archaic Vedic sense of "body,"[10] a meaning that is lost in later Upaniṣads. At the same time, *ātman* is also used to designate the inner, immortal self of a living being, a meaning that becomes prominent in later Upaniṣadic texts.

We can observe the classical Upaniṣadic idea of *ātman* as the highest principle and completely identical with *brahman* beginning to emerge in this text. This *ātman* is said to consist of intelligence, and to be unaging and immortal.[11] *Ātman* is also described as bliss,[12] a term that is frequently used elsewhere in the Upaniṣads to describe *brahman*. In the *Kauṣītaki Upaniṣad*, understanding the true nature of *ātman* is emphasized[13] as much as knowing *brahman*.

Brahman in the *Kauṣītaki Upaniṣad*

Intriguingly, *brahman*, the cosmic force, is presented both as an abstract principle and as a mythological figure in this Upaniṣad. Several passages identify *brahman* with the life breath (*prāṇa*), and the text claims that all gods bring offerings to the breath that is *brahman*.[14] Elsewhere, *brahman* is identified with the three oldest Vedas, the *Ṛgveda*, the *Yajurveda*, and the *Sāmaveda*. While other Upaniṣads present *brahman* as an impersonal power, the *Kauṣītaki Upaniṣad* describes *brahman* as a man sitting on a throne and holding a conversation with the soul of the deceased person:

> On that throne sits *brahman*. He who knows this climbs it, first with his foot. *Brahman* asks him: "Who are you?" Then he should answer: "I am the season. I am the child of the season. I was born of the womb of space as semen for a wife, as radiance of the year, as the *ātman* of every being. You are the *ātman* of every being, and I am who you are."[15]

Although *brahman* is personified as a man on a throne here, he still retains many of his abstract qualities, as signaled by the materials from which his throne is constructed: the past and the present time, wealth, and nourishment, as well as various ritual chants.

The depiction of *brahman* as an anthropomorphic deity reflects the theistic sensibilities present in all the Upaniṣads formally affiliated with the *Ṛgveda*. Whereas devotion to a personal god only emerges at a later point in the Upaniṣads of the other Vedic *śākhās*, the Upaniṣads of the *Ṛgveda*, like the *Kauṣītaki Upaniṣad*, contain strong theistic elements from the very beginning. This is hardly surprising, since these texts were composed and transmitted by the priests who were responsible precisely for invoking the deities during the Vedic sacrifice (see Chapters 3 and 4).

The anthropomorphic *brahman* of the *Kauṣītaki Upaniṣad*, receiving offerings and holding conversations, would clearly have presented a challenge to the commentator Śaṅkara, who rejected theism altogether and insisted on a completely impersonal *brahman*. The depiction of *brahman* in this text is probably a reason why Saṅkara did not choose to compose a commentary to the *Kauṣītaki Upaniṣad*.

Citra Gāṅgyāyani: A Gārgya?

The first chapter of the *Kauṣītaki Upaniṣad* relates the story of a man named Citra Gāṅgāyani. Citra wants to perform a sacrifice, and he selects Uddālaka Āruṇi as officiating priest. Uddālaka Āruṇi, for reasons unspecified, chooses to send his son Śvetaketu instead. Uddālaka Āruṇī is a familiar character from other Upaniṣads. In the *Bṛhadāraṇyaka Upaniṣad*, Uddālaka Āruṇi is presented as the teacher of the wise Yājñavalkya who asks about *ātman* as the "inner controller."[16] In the *Chāndogya Upaniṣad*, Uddālaka Āruṇi is no longer merely a minor character whose question allows his student to shine, but a wise and loving father who imparts essential wisdom to his son Śvetaketu about the *ātman* as the essence of everything. In the *Kauṣītaki Upaniṣad*, however, Uddālaka Āruṇi must admit that Citra is wiser than he, and he ends up becoming Citra's pupil.

Little is known about Citra Gāṅgyāyani from other sources. Olivelle suggests that he is a king,[17] probably because Uddālaka Āruṇi and Śvetaketu's conversation partners in the parallel stories in the *Bṛhadāraṇyaka Upaniṣad* 6.2 and *Chāndogya Upaniṣad* 5.3 are kings. There is otherwise nothing in the text of the *Kauṣītaki Upaniṣad* that indicates that Citra is perceived as royal in this particular text. It should be noted that his name is also given as *Gārgyāyaṇi* in some manuscripts,[18] a name that connects him to the *Gārgya* clan of Vedic priests. If Citra is indeed connected to the priestly Gārgya clan, as this version of the name would indicate, he would presumably be a Brahman (priest) rather than a Kṣatriya, and hence not a king. The alternative reading *Gārgyāyaṇi* is of some interest, since members of the Gārgya clan are mentioned quite a few times in the Upaniṣads: Dṛpta Bālakī, Sauryāyanī, and the female philosopher Gārgī are all connected with the Gārgyas. If we compare the teachings of all these Gārgyas, we see that they all tend to stress that there is a personal aspect to the cosmic *brahman*. Since Citra himself describes *brahman* as a person sitting on a seat and conversing with the self of a departed person, this may strengthen his association with the Gārgya clan as well. Dṛpta Bālakī's ideas in the *Bṛhadāraṇyaka Upaniṣad* about *brahman* as the person in the sun, the moon, lightning, etc. are not that far removed from the ideas presented by Citra in the *Kauṣītaki Upaniṣad*. Whereas the idea of *brahman* as a personal being is ridiculed in the *Bṛhadāraṇyaka Upaniṣad*, it is fully accepted in the more theistically oriented *Kauṣītaki Upaniṣad*. This conception of the highest reality as a personal being is characteristic of the Upaniṣads affiliated with the *Ṛgveda*, such as the *Aitareya Upaniṣad* and the *Kauṣītaki Upaniṣad*.

Uddālaka Āruṇi and Śvetaketu in the *Kauṣītaki Upaniṣad*

Both Uddālaka Āruṇi and his son Śvetaketu are portrayed in a sympathetic manner in the *Kauṣītaki Upaniṣad*. Patrick Olivelle has demonstrated that Uddālaka Āruṇi may have been associated with a *śākhā* of the *Ṛgveda*.[19] If this is the case, this would perhaps explain why Uddālaka Āruṇi is depicted in a more positive light in the *Kauṣītaki Upaniṣad*, a text affiliated with the *Ṛgveda*, than in the *Bṛhadāraṇyaka Upaniṣad*, a text that is intensely anti-Ṛgvedic in its sentiments. Although both Uddālaka Āruṇi and Śvetaketu ultimately lack the true knowledge of *brahman* in the *Kauṣītaki Upaniṣad* as well, they readily admit their ignorance. Śvetaketu freely confesses that he does not know the answer to Citra's question, and he asks his father, who in turn admits that he is equally ignorant:

> Śvetaketu sat down, and Citra questioned him: "Descendant of Gautama, is there a closed door in the world you are sending me to, or does it have another path? I am afraid you are sending me to a false world."
>
> Śvetaketu answered: "I don't know, but I'll ask my teacher."
>
> He then went back to his father and asked him: "Here are the questions he asked me. How should I answer him?" His father said: "I don't know the answer to them either."[20]

Admitting one's ignorance is, of course, the first step on the path toward enlightenment in the Upaniṣads, and Citra accepts Āruṇi as a worthy student:

> Carrying firewood in his hands, Āruṇi went to Citra Gāṅgyāyani and said: "Let me come to you as your student." Citra replied: "Gautama, you have shown yourself worthy of *brahman*, since you have not given in to pride. Come, I will make sure that you see it clearly."[21]

Karma and reincarnation in the *Kauṣītaki Upaniṣad*

Among the secret teachings Citra imparts to Āruṇi is the idea that people will be reborn again after death. He explains that people who die all go to the moon, and that it is their collective life breath that makes the moon wax every month. Those who are able to answer the moon's question will simply pass on to a heavenly world. Those who do not know the answer, however, will return to earth in the form of rain and then be reborn as various animals, worms, insects, fish, birds, lions, boars, rhinoceroses, tigers, or humans, "each according to his actions and his knowledge."[22] The idea that those who are knowledgeable and enlightened do not have to be reborn is preserved in later Hinduism, as are the ideas that one can be reborn as various animals, and that one's actions (*karma*) is a deciding factor in one's next rebirth. The *Kauṣītaki Upaniṣad* does not, however, present us with a view of *karma* that is entirely in accordance with later classical Hinduism. According to later Hindu teachings, accumulated *karma* belongs to an individual and cannot be arbitrarily transferred to others. According to *Kauṣītaki Upaniṣad* 1.4, a person who can answer the moon's questions and continues on his mystical journey toward *brahman* will eventually shake off his good and bad deeds, which will fall on his relatives. His good deeds will fall on the relatives he likes, and the bad deeds will end up with the relatives he dislikes. Similarly, a father–son ceremony outlined in *Kauṣītaki Upaniṣad* describes a dying father bequeathing his own life to his son, including his actions:

> "I will place my speech in you," says the father. "I place your speech in me," answers the son.
>
> "I will place my breath in you," says the father. "I place your breath in me," answers the son.[23]

The father goes on to place his sight, hearing, tasting of food, actions, pleasure and pain, bliss, joy, procreation, movements, mind, intelligence, and life breath in the son. The idea that his past actions (*karma*) can also be transferred to his son is in accordance with the idea that one can give one's good and bad deeds to relatives after death. This sort of karma transfer, while occasionally mentioned in the older Upaniṣads, does not become a part of later Hindu doctrine.

Indra in the *Kauṣītaki Upaniṣad*

Whereas the old Vedic gods are largely absent in the Upaniṣads, they do occasionally make an appearance, especially in those Upaniṣadic texts that are affiliated with the *Ṛgveda*. The Vedic thunder god Indra, often regarded as the king of the Vedic pantheon, is presented as a fully enlightened wisdom teacher in the *Kauṣītaki Upaniṣad.* He instructs Pratardana in various Upaniṣadic teachings. Indra is identified with truth, *satya*,[24] with the life breath *prāṇa* and with the inner *ātman* itself. Ajātaśatru explains that Indra became the lord of the other gods precisely because he understood the *ātman*.[25] Indra appears as a symbolic figure in several of the oldest Upaniṣads. The *Kauṣītaki Upaniṣad* goes even further than most Upaniṣads, however, in presenting Indra not merely as an intelligent seeker after the truth, but as a fully enlightened being who instructs others in the true nature of *ātman*. This positive portrayal of Indra is characteristic of Upaniṣads affiliated with the *Ṛgveda*.

"Magical" rites in the *Kauṣītaki Upaniṣad*

In addition to philosophical reflections, the *Kauṣītaki Upaniṣad* describes numerous ritual prayers with a very practical goal. While some scholars have classified these prayers as "magic," it is debatable to what extent this term, with its roots in Western culture, is applicable to ancient Indian ritual practices. What cannot be debated, however, is that many of the prayers in the *Kauṣītaki Upaniṣad* are associated with achieving practical results in this life rather than lofty, otherworldly aims.

Kauṣītaki Upaniṣad 2.4 details how to win the love of a man or a woman (or alternatively a "group of men and women," as the text intriguingly states) by making offerings of butter into a sacrificial fire while reciting a prayer. The butter offering recalls the old Vedic sacrificial rites where melted butter was poured into the sacrificial fire. Thereupon, the one who wants to be attractive to others should smell the fragrant smoke from the fire, rub his own body with butter and then proceed to touch the person he wants to attract. "They will indeed love him!" the text assures us.

Another passage in the *Kauṣītaki Upaniṣad* contains a ritual prayer, to be said by a man before sexual intercourse with his wife, to ensure that her children will not die before her:

> Your heart, O lady so good to lie down on.
> rests with Prajāpati.
> Therefore, queen of immortality,
> May you not experience
> The misfortune of your children.[26]

Another verse is to be spoken by a man returning from a journey and seeing his son again:

> From my very body you come,
> from my heart you are born.
> You are my *ātman*, son, and you have rescued me.
> May you live a hundred years.[27]

The prayer for the son's long life is accompanied by ritual actions such as the father smelling the son's head and speaking prayers in both his ears.

While prayers for love or for the wellbeing of children may have offered comfort to the text's readers or listeners, they may not have appealed to the commentator Śaṅkara's more philosophical sensibilities. The extensive passages of the *Kauṣītaki Upaniṣad* devoted to these practical everyday prayers may have been another reason why Śaṅkara chose not to compose a complete commentary to this text.

The age of the *Kauṣītaki Upaniṣad*

The age of the *Kauṣītaki Upaniṣad* has been the subject of a great deal of discussion. Deussen regards the *Kauṣītaki Upaniṣad* as one of the ancient prose Upaniṣads, along with the *Bṛhadāraṇyaka*, *Chāndogya*, *Taittirīya*, *Aitareya*, and *Kena*.[28] Both Fürst[29] and Wecker[30] assume that the *Kauṣītaki Upaniṣad* predates the fourth century BCE grammarian Pāṇini because non-Pāṇinian forms occur in the text. As Renou has pointed out, however, forms that are not in accordance with Pāṇini's grammar are not necessarily an indication of the date of the text. It is quite possible that non-Pāṇinian forms continued to be used even after Pāṇini. Renou regards the *Kauṣītaki Upaniṣad* as later than *Bṛhadāraṇyaka* and *Chāndogya*, and perhaps also later than *Īśā*, and forming a group with *Kena* and *Kaṭha*. Keith regards the *Kauṣītaki Upaniṣad* as even more recent.[31] Ranade places the *Kauṣītaki Upaniṣad* with the *Aitareya* and *Taittirīya*, which he sees as later than the *Bṛhadāraṇyaka*, *Chāndogya*, *Īśā*, and *Kena*.[32]

Based on linguistic and metrical evidence,[33] it is reasonable to assume a date of composition for the *Kauṣītaki Upaniṣad* not too long after the prose parts of the *Bṛhadāraṇyaka* and the *Chāndogya*. The text of the *Kauṣītaki* is linguistically older than the oldest portions of the *Īśā*, *Kaṭha*, *Śvetāśvatara*, and *Kena*, and it preserves older notions of *ātman* as "body" or "essence" alongside the classical Upaniṣadic notion of *ātman* as the inner self of a person.

Notes

1 *Kauṣītaki Upaniṣad* 2.1.
2 *Kauṣītaki Upaniṣad* 1.2.
3 *Kauṣītaki Upaniṣad* 1.4.
4 *Kauṣītaki Upaniṣad* 4.4.
5 *Kauṣītaki Upaniṣad* 4.5.
6 *Kauṣītaki Upaniṣad* 4.6.
7 *Kauṣītaki Upaniṣad* 4.10.
8 *Kauṣītaki Upaniṣad* 4.17.
9 *Kauṣītaki Upaniṣad* 1.6.
10 *Kauṣītaki Upaniṣad* 2.12, 4.2, 4.10.
11 *Kauṣītaki Upaniṣad* 4.3.
12 *Kauṣītaki Upaniṣad* 4.3.
13 See for example *Kauṣītaki Upaniṣad* 4.20.
14 *Kauṣītaki Upaniṣad* 2.2.
15 *Kauṣītaki Upaniṣad* 1.5–6.

16 *Bṛhadāraṇyaka Upaniṣad* 6.3.7.
17 P. Olivelle, "Young Śvetaketu: A Literary Study of an Upaniṣadic Story" *Journal of the American Oriental Society* 119 (1999): 46.
18 See P. Olivelle, *The Early Upaniṣads*. Oxford/New York: Oxford University Press, 1998: 582, note 1.
19 Olivelle 1999: 52.
20 *Kauṣītaki Upaniṣad* 1.1.
21 *Kauṣītaki Upaniṣad* 1.1.
22 *Kauṣītaki Upaniṣad* 1.2.
23 *Kauṣītaki Upaniṣad* 2.15.
24 *Kauṣītaki Upaniṣad* 3.1.
25 *Kauṣītaki Upaniṣad* 4.20.
26 *Kauṣītaki Upaniṣad* 2.10.
27 *Kauṣītaki Upaniṣad* 2.11.
28 P. Deussen, *The Philosophy of the Upanishads*. Edinburgh: T & T Clark 1906. (Reprint New York: Dover, 1966: 23.)
29 A. Fürst, "Der Sprachgebrauch der älteren Upaniṣads verglichen mit dem der früheren vedischen Perioden und dem des klassischen Sanskrit" *Zeitschrift für vergleichende Sprachforschung (Kuhns Zeitschrift)* 47 (1916): 81.
30 O. Wecker, "Der Gebrauch der Kasus in der älteren Upaniṣad-literatur verglichen mit der Kasuslehre der indischen Grammatiker" *Beiträge zur Kunde der indogermanischen Sprachen* 30 (1906): 203.
31 A. B. Keith, *The Religion and Philosophy of the Veda and Upanishads.* Cambridge, MA.: Harvard University Press/London: Oxford University Press, 1925: 498.
32 R. D. Ranade, *A Constructive Survey of Upaniṣadic Philosophy, Being an Introduction to the Thought of the Upaniṣads*. 1926. (Reprint Bombay: Bharatiya Vidya Bhavan, 1968.)
33 S. Cohen, *Text and Authority in the Older Upaniṣads*. Leiden: Brill, 2008.

Further reading

Bodewitz, H. W. 1986. "The Cosmic, Cyclical Dying (*parimara*). *Aitareya Brāhmaṇa* 8,28 and *Kauṣītaki Upaniṣad* 2,11–12" in Wolfgang Morgenroth (ed.) *Sanskrit and World Culture*. Berlin: Akademie-Verlag, 438–443.

Frenz, A. 1968. "*Kauṣītaki-Upaniṣad*" *Indo-Iranian Journal* 11: 79–129.

Olivelle, P. 1999. "Young Śvetaketu: A Literary Study of an Upaniṣadic Story" *Journal of the American Oriental Society* 119: 46–70.

Söhnen, R. 1981. "Die Einleitungsgeschichte der Belehrung des Uddālaka Āruṇi: Ein Vergleich der drei Fassungen *Kauṣītaki* 1.1, *Chāndogya* 5.3 und *Bṛhadāraṇyaka* 6.21–8" *Studien zur Indologie und Iranistik* 7: 177 ff.

Thieme, P. 1951–52. "Der Weg durch den Himmel nach der *Kauṣītaki Upaniṣad*" *Wisenschaftliche Zeitschrift der Martin-Luther-Universität Halle-Wittemberg, Gesellschafts- und sprachwissenschaftliche Reihe* 1. Reprint in *Kleine Schriften*. 2.ed. Wiesbaden: Franz Steiner Verlag, 1984: 82–99.

27 The *Taittirīya Upaniṣad*

Signe Cohen

The *Taittirīya Upaniṣad* is a prose text in three chapters. Its formal affiliation is to the *Taittirīya* school of the *Yajurveda*, which traces its lineage back to a sage by the name of Tittiri ("Partridge"), who gave his name to the school. The *Taittirīya Upaniṣad* comprises chapters 7, 8 and 9 of the late Vedic ritual text *Taittirīya Āraṇyaka*.

Some scholars have suggested that the *Taittirīya Upaniṣad* is a heterogeneous text,[1] and that the first of its three chapters may originally have been a separate text. This theory is supported by the evidence of Indian commentators on the text. The fourteenth-century Indian commentator Sāyaṇa treats the first chapter of the *Taittirīya Upaniṣad* as separate from the last two and even gives the two sections of the text different names. He refers to the first chapter as *Saṃhitopaniṣad* ("The Upaniṣad of Combination/Canonical Text") while others have referred to it as *Śikṣopaniṣad* ("The Upaniṣad of Learning") or *Śikṣāvallī* ("The Vine of Learning"). Sāyaṇa uses the name *Vāruṇyopaniṣad* ("the Upaniṣad of the son of Varuṇa") for the last two chapters of the text. It is not clear whether chapters 7–9 of the *Taittirīya Āraṇyaka* form one or two Upaniṣads. There is, however, general agreement that the following chapter, chapter 10, forms a completely separate Upaniṣad, referred to as the *Mahānārāyaṇa Upaniṣad*. This text is treated separately in this volume. The question is, then, whether there are two (*Taittirīya Upaniṣad* and *Mahānārāyaṇa Upaniṣad*) or three (*Taittirīya Upaniṣad* 1 = *Saṃhitopaniṣad* = *Śikṣopaniṣad* and *Taittirīya Upaniṣad* 2 = *Vāruṇyopaniṣad*, and *Mahānārāyaṇa Upaniṣad*) Upaniṣadic texts attached to the end of the *Taittirīya Āraṇyaka*. If we examine the first chapter of the *Taittirīya Upaniṣad* separately from the last two chapters, we find that there are some considerable theological and philosophical differences between this chapter and the following ones, which may suggest that the *Taittirīya Upaniṣad* is indeed a composite of several separate texts.

The *Śikṣāvallī* – the universe as cosmic text

The *Śikṣāvallī*, the first chapter of the *Taittirīya Upaniṣad*, is a thematically unified text, beginning and ending with a quotation from *Ṛgveda* 1.90.9:

May Mitra be kind to us,
and Varuṇa, and Aryaman,
and Indra Bṛhaspati,
and Viṣṇu, with the long strides.

This quotation sets the tone for the *Śikṣāvallī*, with its emphasis on the harmony between traditional Vedic learning and the study of the secret teachings of the Upaniṣads. The doctrines presented in the *Śikṣāvallī* are specifically called an "Upaniṣad" ("secret teaching") in the text itself: "This is the teaching. This is the secret teaching (*upaniṣad*) of the Veda."[2] The authority of the Vedas is not challenged in this text; rather, the Upaniṣadic teachings are presented as an esoteric reading of that which is already present in the Vedas. The three traditional Vedas (the *Ṛgveda*, *Yajurveda*, and *Sāmaveda*) are acknowledged, and *brahman* itself is presented as the fourth and highest Veda.[3]

The harmony between the older Vedic teachings and the new ideas of the Upaniṣads is emphasized in the opening section of the text, where the Vedic wind god Vāyu is identified with the cosmic *brahman* of the Upaniṣads: "Homage to you, Vāyu! You are the manifest *brahman*!"

The idea that the Upaniṣadic ideas are secretly present in the Vedas is also expressed in section 1.3 of the Upaniṣad, which explores the mystical meaning of the traditional Vedic recitation: "Now we will explain the secret teaching (*upaniṣad*) of combination (*saṃhitā*)." The word *saṃhitā* is here both a reference to the phonetic "joining together" of sounds in traditional Vedic recitation, and a reference to the *Saṃhitās*, or canonical texts, of the four Vedas. The section that follows is a remarkable passage presenting the universe as a cosmic text, where the different parts are joined together like the words in traditional Vedic recitation:

> It is like this as far as the worlds are concerned: The first word is the earth, the next word is the sky, and space is the *sandhi* between them, and wind is that which joins them together. This is how it is with the worlds.
>
> It is like this as far as the lights are concerned: The first word is the fire, the next word is the sun, and water is the *sandhi* between them, and lightning is that which joins them together. This is how it is with the lights.
>
> It is like this as far as knowledge is concerned: The first word is the teacher, the next word is the student, and knowledge is the *sandhi* between them, and teaching is that which joins them together. This is how it is with knowledge.
>
> It is like this as far as offspring is concerned: The first word is the mother, the next word is the father, and the child is the *sandhi* between them, and procreation is that which joins them together. This is how it is with offspring.

> It is like this as far as the body is concerned: The first word is the lower jaw, the next word is the upper jaw, and speech is the *sandhi* between them, and the tongue is that which joins them together. This is how it is with the body.[4]

Sandhi ("union") is a technical term from Sanskrit linguistics that refers to the assimilation of two sounds at word boundaries, a phenomenon that is characteristic of Sanskrit, although it is also found sporadically in other languages. If one Sanskrit word ends with a *t*, for example, and the next word begins a *b*, the final unvoiced *t* changes to a voiced *d* before the voiced consonant *b*. Sanskrit texts are permeated with such sound changes, and mastering the complex rules for the merger of sounds at word boundaries is an essential part of learning the Sanskrit language. By referring to the union between two entities as *sandhi*, then, the *Śikṣāvallī* recasts the entire world as Sanskrit text. If the whole cosmos is, in one sense, a religious text, this helps explain why the importance of Vedic study and adherence to the traditional rituals are emphasized throughout the *Śikṣāvallī*.[5] The idea that the world *is* the Sanskrit word also helps us make sense of the odd little section on the definition of phonetics, seemingly inserted at random after the opening benedictions of the text:

> *Om*. We will now explain phonetics (*śīkṣā*): Sound, accent, length, strength, articulation, and connection. This describes the discipline of phonetics.[6]

If the universe itself is a Sanskrit text, then phonetics becomes more than a purely academic discipline; it is a form of learning that explores the very secrets of the cosmos. A student who fully understands the sound of Sanskrit will have access to the "sacred lore": "May my tongue say the sweetest things. May my ears hear the wealth of sacred lore."[7] The text specifies, however, that study of the sacred texts must be followed by ethical living: "When the Vedic study is complete, the teacher tells his student: 'Speak the truth. Follow duty. Do not forget to recite the Veda. After you have given your teacher a gift, do not end your family line …'"[8]

Brahman in the *Śikṣāvallī*

As we have seen, *brahman* is identified with the Vedic god Vāyu in the *Śikṣāvallī*, but *brahman* is otherwise not personified to any significant degree in the text.[9] *Brahman* remains an abstract principle and cosmic force throughout the Upaniṣad. It is identified with the sacred sound *oṃ* itself,[10] as elsewhere in the Upaniṣads. Space (*ākāsa*) is said to be the body of *brahman* (*ākāśaśarīram brahma*), which implies that *brahman* itself is of cosmic nature.[11] *Brahman* is further presented as the highest principle of the universe and the ultimate goal of human beings. It is called "tranquil" and "immortal."[12]

Ātman in the *Śikṣāvallī*

Interestingly, *ātman* is used in the old Vedic sense of "body" numerous times in the *Śikṣāvallī*,[13] but rarely in the sense of "inner Self" as in many of the other Upaniṣads. The immortal essence of a person is here called *puruṣa* (the "person"), not *ātman*. This usage of the term *puruṣa*, not just in the older Vedic sense of "person," but as a synonym of *ātman*, is characteristic of the Upaniṣads formally affiliated with the *Black Yajurveda*, such as the *Kaṭha* and *Śvetāśvatara*, although it is also encountered elsewhere. *Puruṣa* is described in the *Śikṣāvallī* as dwelling inside the space of the heart.[14] This *puruṣa* is made from mind, *manas*.[15] The *Śikṣāvallī* teaches that the *puruṣa* can become *brahman* by knowing the four sacred *mantras bhūr*, *bhuvas*, *suvar* and *mahas*.[16]

The term *ātman* is used in the sense of "inner essence" in 1.6.2: *satyātmā* ("whose essence is the truth"), but never in the classical Upaniṣadic sense of the immortal self within a person.

The number four in the *Śikṣāvallī*

The number four plays as significant role in the *Śikṣāvallī*. As is often the case in the Upaniṣads, the number four is divided into three plus one. As Dipak Bhattacharya has demonstrated, the fourth quarter is normally regarded as lower than the other three in earlier Vedic texts, whereas the fourth principle gradually comes to be regarded as the highest one in the Upaniṣads.[17]

The classical Vedic *mantras bhūr*, *bhuvas*, and *suvar* are discussed in *Śikṣāvallī*,[18] and a fourth *mantra* is added to them: *mahas*. These four *mantras* are then identified with various parts of the cosmic text of the world: *Bhūr* represents this world, *bhuvas* the intermediate space, and *suvaḥ* the world beyond, whereas *manas* represents the sun. The three Vedas are identified with *bhūr*, *bhuvas*, and *suvar*, while *brahman* itself is identified with the fourth mantra, *manas*. This identification implies, of course, that *brahman* itself is a fourth Veda. The *mantras bhūr*, *bhuvas*, and *suvar* are further identified with the three breaths *prāṇa*, *apāna*, and *vyāna*, and *manas* with food.

This passage in the *Śikṣāvallī* clearly owes much to *Bṛhadāraṇyaka Upaniṣad* 5.14, where three sets of three entities are mentioned (earth, intermediated space, and heaven; *Ṛgveda*, *Yajurveda*, and *Sāmaveda*; *prāṇa*, *apāna*, and *vyāna*) and contrasted with the sun as a mysterious fourth entity. The fourth principle is, however, more clearly articulated in the *Śikṣāvallī* than in the *Bṛhadāraṇyaka Upaniṣad* passage. We may assume that the *Śikṣāvallī* passage is later than the corresponding section from the *Bṛhadāraṇyaka Upaniṣad*.

The number five in the *Śikṣāvallī*

Several groups of five entities are also mentioned in the *Śikṣāvallī*: The parts of the universe (divided into three groups of five: earth, atmosphere, sky, directions, and intermediate directions; fire, wind, sun, moon, and stars; water, plants, trees, space, and body), the five breaths (*prāṇa*, *vyāna*, *apāna*, *udāna*, *samāna*), the five senses (sight, hearing, thought, speech, and touch), and the five components of the body (skin, flesh, muscle, bone, and marrow).[19] The enumeration ends with the statement: "The whole world is indeed fivefold."

Taittirīya Upaniṣad 2–3: The universe as food

Food is an important theme in *Taittirīya Upaniṣad* 2–3, as it was in the *Aitareya Upaniṣad*. Food is identified as the primordial matter out of which the universe is made.[20] Food is also identified with *brahman*,[21] which would suggest that *brahman* itself is the material cause of the world. Food is further identified with the elements[22] and with *prāṇa*.[23] In short, food is in *Taittirīya Upaniṣad* 2–3 the mysterious essence of the universe itself. Understanding this essence is the first step towards understanding *brahman* itself. And although the *ātman* made of food is presented as the lowest of the five forms of *ātman* in 2.2, the significance of food is seen again in the chant of the person who has reached the ultimate goal, the *ātman* of joy: *Aham annam, aham annam, aham annam* ("I am food! I am food! I am food!").[24]

Ātman in *Taittirīya Upaniṣad* 2–3

Although *ātman* plays a minor part in the *Śikṣāvallī*, it occupies a central space in the last two chapters of the Upaniṣad. The famous doctrine of the five sheaths (*pañcakośa*) of the self is presented in the last part of the *Taittirīya Upaniṣad*: There are several different *ātmans*, one formed from the essence of food,[25] one consisting of *prāṇa* (life breath),[26] one consisting of *manas* (mind),[27] one consisting of perception (*vijñāna*),[28] and the highest one consisting of joy.[29] A dying person will reach each one of these *ātmans* in turn, his spiritual journey ending in the encounter with the *ātman* of joy. This developed doctrine of the five *ātmans* in the second chapter of the *Taittirīya Upaniṣad* is clearly very different from the more rudimentary conceptions of *ātman* found in the *Śikṣāvallī*. The idea of the fivefold *ātman* may be a reflection of the significance of the number five in the old Vedic *agnicayana* ("fire building") ritual, echoed in many of the texts of the *Yajurveda*.[30]

There are some intriguing similarities between the *Taittirīya Upaniṣad*'s doctrine of the five sheaths or layers of the *ātman* and the teachings ascribed to the Greek philosopher Pherecydes of Syros (sixth century BCE), Pythagoras' teacher. Pherecydes taught that the soul is *pentemychos*, "consisting of five cavities (?)" The occurrence of the idea of a five-fold soul in both the Upaniṣads and in Pherecydes may of course be a coincidence. It is intriguing, however, that Pherecydes is often credited in classical Greek literature with being the person who first introduced the idea of reincarnation to the Greeks, an idea that is also emerging in the Upaniṣads.

Brahman in *Taittirīya Upaniṣad* 2–3

The Vedic god Varuṇa has a lengthy conversation with his son Bhṛgu in *Taittirīya Upaniṣad* 3 on the topic of *brahman*. The idea of the old Vedic guardian of the cosmic order instructing his son is not new to the *Taittirīya Upaniṣad*; a similar story of Varuṇa instructing his son Bhṛgu is found in an earlier text of the *Yajurveda*, the *Śatapathabrāhmaṇa*.[31] While Bhṛgu is rather arrogant in the Brāhmaṇa text and considers himself superior to his father, the Bhṛgu that we encounter in the *Taittirīya Upaniṣad* approaches his father as a reverent student: "Bhṛgu, the son of Varuṇa, went to his father Varuṇa and said: 'Sir, please teach me *brahman*.'" Whereas the Bhṛgu of the *Śatapathabrāhmaṇa* has bizarre visions of men dismembering and eating each other, eventually leading to his understanding of the Agnihotra ritual, the Upaniṣadic Bhṛgu practices austerities under his father's guidance until he comes to understand the true nature of *brahman*. In the course of his quest for the true understanding of *brahman*, Bhṛgu comes to understand *brahman* as food, *prāṇa* (life breath), *manas* (mind), perception, and joy. In other words, the five forms of *brahman* in the third chapter parallel the five forms of *ātman* presented in the second chapter, reinforcing the idea that *ātman* and *brahman* are ultimately one.

In the *Śikṣāvallī*, *brahman* is the ultimate goal to be obtained, whereas *ātman* is relatively unimportant. In *Taittirīya Upaniṣad* 2–3, however, *ātman* and *brahman* are used synonymously, but with an emphasis on *ātman* as the ultimate goal.

The number five in *Taittirīya Upaniṣad* 2–3

As we have seen, the number four plays a significant part in the *Śikṣāvallī*. In *Taittirīy Upaniṣad* 2–3, however, it is the number five that is of cosmic significance. The five forms of the *ātman* and the corresponding five forms of *brahman* are listed from the outmost to the inmost, and from the lower to the higher. This transition from the sacred number four to the sacred number five may indicate that the later chapters of the *Taittirīya Upaniṣad* are of a later date than the first one.

Two related Upaniṣads?

In conclusion, it seems likely that Varenne's theory that the extant *Taittirīya Upaniṣad* consists of two separate texts is correct. As we have seen, the *Śikṣāvallī* contains ideas about *ātman* and *brahman* at variance with those found in the last two chapters of the *Taittirīya Upaniṣad.*

Linguistically, the two texts appear to belong to roughly the same time period. We can perhaps assume, based on the development of ideas, that the *Śikṣāvallī* is slightly older than *Taittirīya Upaniṣad* 2–3. Both the *Śikṣāvallī* and *Taittirīya Upaniṣad* 2–3 are typical transitional late Vedic texts. Traces of Vedic ideas still remain, especially in the *Śikṣāvallī*, and echoes of Vedic language still resonate throughout the texts.

Since the Taittirīya school which transmitted the *Taittirīya Āraṇyaka* produced two late Vedic texts in the Upaniṣadic genre appended to its Āraṇyaka, it is only natural that these two texts came to be known collectively as the *Taittirīya Upaniṣad.*

We may conclude that both of these texts were composed after the *Bṛhadāraṇyaka, Chāndogya* and *Aitareya Upaniṣads*, but earlier than the *Īśā Upaniṣad*. The relationship between *Taittirīya* and *Kauṣītaki* is a complex one. Linguistically, the *Taittirīya Upaniṣad* is clearly younger than the *Kauṣītaki Upaniṣad*. However, the conception if *ātman* in the *Kauṣītaki Upaniṣad* is far more developed than the rather rudimentary *ātman* doctrines of the *Taittirīya*, and especially of the *Śikṣāvallī*. The most reasonable explanation for this is that the *Taittirīya Upaniṣad* contains older ideas than the *Kauṣītaki*, but reached its final redaction at a later point in time.

Notes

1 Varenne 1968.
2 *Taittirīya Upaniṣad* 1.11.4.
3 *Taittirīya Upaniṣad* 1.5.3.
4 *Taittirīya Upaniṣad* 1.3.1–4.
5 *Taittirīya Upaniṣad* 1.9, 1.11.
6 *Taittirīya Upaniṣad* 1.1.2.
7 *Taittirīya Upaniṣad* 1.4.2.
8 *Taittirīya Upaniṣad* 1.11.1.
9 *Taittirīya Upaniṣad* 1.1.1.
10 *Taittirīya Upaniṣad* 1.8.
11 *Taittirīya Upaniṣad* 1.6.2.
12 *Taittirīya Upaniṣad* 1.6.2.
13 *Taittirīya Upaniṣad* 1.3.1, 1.3.4, 1.5.1, 1.7.1.
14 *Taittirīya Upaniṣad* 1.6.1.
15 *Taittirīya Upaniṣad* 1.6.1.
16 *Taittirīya Upaniṣad* 1.5.
17 Bhattacharya 1978.
18 *Taittirīya Upaniṣad* 1.5.
19 *Taittirīya Upaniṣad* 1.7.
20 *Taittirīya Upaniṣad* 2.2.1.
21 *Taittirīya Upaniṣad* 2.2, 3.2.
22 *Taittirīya Upaniṣad* 3.8–9.
23 *Taittirīya Upaniṣad* 3.7.
24 *Taittirīya Upaniṣad* 3.10.6.
25 *Taittirīya Upaniṣad* 2.2.
26 *Taittirīya Upaniṣad* 2.2.
27 *Taittirīya Upaniṣad* 2.3.
28 *Taittirīya Upaniṣad* 2.4.
29 *Taittirīya Upaniṣad* 2.5.
30 See Knipe 1972: 29.
31 *Śatapathabrāhmaṇa* 11.6.1.

Further reading

Beall, E. F. 1986. "Syntactical Ambiguity at *Taittirīya Upaniṣad* 2.1" *Indo-Iranian Journal* 29: 97–102.

Bhattacharya, D. 1978. "The Doctrine of Four in the Early Upaniṣads and Some Connected Problems" *Journal of Indian Philosophy* 6: 1–34.

Knipe, D. M. 1972. "One Fire, Three Fires, Five Fires: Vedic Symbols in Transition" *History of Religions* 12: 28–41.

Lesimple, E. 1948. *Taittirīya Upaniṣad*. Paris: Adrien Maisonneuve.

Rau, W. 1981. "Versuch einer deutschen Übersetzung der Taittirīya- Upaniṣad" Festschrift der Wiss. Ges., J. W. Goethe. Frankfurt: Universität Wiesbaden, 349–372.

Röer, E. 1850. *The Taittiriya and Aitareya Upanishads with the commentary of Sankara Àchárya, and the gloss of Ànanda Giri, and the Swétáswatara Upanishad with the commentary of Sankara Àchárya*. Bibliotheca Indica, Work 6. Calcutta: Baptist Mission Press. (Reprint Osnabrück: Biblio Verlag, 1980.)

Smith, R. M. 1952. "Birth of Thought – I: Taittirīya and Aitareya Upaniṣads" *Annals of the Bhandarkar Oriental Research Institute, Poona* 23: 97–113.

Smith, R. M. 1969. "On the Original Meaning of Taittirīya Upaniṣad 1.11.1-4" in D. Sinor (ed.) *American Oriental Society, Middle West Branch. Semi-Centennial Volume: A Collection of Original Essays*. Bloomington, IN, 211–216.

Varenne, J. 1968. "Notes sur la Śikṣāvallī" in *Mélanges d'Indianisme a la Mémoire de Louis Renou*. Paris: Editions de Boccard, 763–772.

28 The *Īśā Upaniṣad*

Signe Cohen

This Upaniṣad, whose name is derived from the first word of the text (*īśā*, "by the Lord") is the shortest one of the classical Upaniṣads. The text consists of a mere eighteen stanzas, but nevertheless adds some intriguing ideas to the Upaniṣadic corpus. In Indian collections of Upaniṣadic texts, the *Īśā Upaniṣad* is usually placed first, perhaps because this brief text contains, in crystallized form, many of the most essential ideas of all the Upaniṣads. As the title indicates, the text is theistic in its sensibilities. The highest being in the *Īśā Upaniṣad* is not an impersonal *brahman*, but a personal deity, Īśa ("The Lord"). This deity is immanent in nature; he "dwells in the whole world."[1]

The *Īśā Upaniṣad* is also called the *Īśāvāsya Upaniṣad* or the *Saṃhitā Upaniṣad*. Like the *Bṛhadāraṇyaka Upaniṣad*, the *Īśā Upaniṣad* is affiliated with the *Black Yajurveda*, and is preserved in a *Kāṇva* and a *Mādhyaṃdina* recension. The two versions of the text contain almost the same verses, but in slightly different order. The sixteenth verse of the *Kāṇva* version is missing altogether from the *Mādhyaṃdina* recension. The text of the Upaniṣad forms the fortieth chapter of the *Vājasaneyi Saṃhitā* of the *White Yajurveda*. The name *Saṃhitā Upaniṣad* (*Saṃhitā* = "put together," a term used to designate a Vedic text) evokes its deep connection with the *Vājasaneyi Saṃhitā*.

We can discern the text's affiliation with the older *Bṛhadāraṇyaka Upaniṣad* in the pantheism present in the *Īśā Upaniṣad* ("When a man sees all beings in himself and himself in all beings, it will not seek to hide from him"[2]). The text's emphasis on the "oneness" of all things[3] is nevertheless different from the more impersonal pantheism of the *Bṛhadāraṇyaka Upaniṣad*. In the *Īśā Upaniṣad*, the all-encompassing *ātman* is described as a personal divine being. This growing theism can be found in several of the "middle Upaniṣads," such as the *Kaṭha Upaniṣad*, the *Śvetāśvatara Upaniṣad*, and the *Mahānārāyaṇa Upaniṣad*.

Beyond paradox: Overcoming duality

In this Upaniṣad, the highest being is described through a series of paradoxes: He does not move, but is swifter than the mind and outruns those who run,[4] he is far and near,[5] he is inside and outside.[6] The one (*eka*) transcends all dualities, such as wisdom and ignorance,[7] being and non-being,[8] creation and destruction.[9] Not only is the Lord himself beyond dualities, but humans seeking immortality must themselves learn to move beyond a dualistic perception of the world: "Into blind darkness go those who worship ignorance, but those who rejoice in wisdom enter darkness deeper still."[10]

The idea that the highest truth lies beyond all dualistic constructions of reality has ancient roots in Indian thought. One of the oldest articulations of this idea can be found in the famous *Nasadīya* ("Non-Being") hymn of the *Ṛgveda*: "There was neither being nor non-being then ..."[11] While the Vedic poem describes an undifferentiated reality in the beginning of the world, several Upaniṣads, including the *Īśā*, hint at a similar sort of undifferentiated oneness as the ultimate goal of the human spiritual quest. This goal is, according to the *Īśā Upaniṣad*, different from both becoming (*saṃbhūti*)[12] and non-becoming (*asaṃbhūti*).[13]

Since *vidyā*, "wisdom," is such an essential concept in the other Upaniṣads, later commentators on the *Īśā Upaniṣad* struggled to come to terms with the text's apparent rejection of *both* wisdom and ignorance. "Wisdom" is usually in the Upaniṣads understood to be the knowledge of *ātman* and *brahman*, the very path to spiritual liberation. How, then, can the *Īśā Upaniṣad* reject wisdom as well as ignorance? Both Śaṅkara (eighth cetury CE) and Rāmānuja (eleventh–twelfth century CE) interpret the term *vidyā* in this text not in the general Upaniṣadic sense of knowledge of the highest reality, but rather as knowledge of the Vedic gods.

Ātman in the *Īśā Upaniṣad*

The *Īśā Upaniṣad* clearly expresses the idea that all individual selves are ultimately one:

> When one sees all beings
> within the *ātman*
> and *ātman* within all beings,
> it will not conceal itself.[14]
>
> When one who is knowledgeable
> in his *ātman* becomes all beings,
> what confusion or sorrow can there be
> for one who has seen the oneness?[15]

The *Īśā Upaniṣad* suggests that the "Lord" who pervades the whole world is identical to the inner *ātman*. The idea that a divine being is immanent in the universe and in human beings provides an ethical imperative, since this divine presence in every being leads to respect for all life.

"The Lord" as the creator of the world

The Lord who permeates the world (stanza one) is further described as its creator in stanza eight:

> Self-existent and all-pervading, the wise poet
> has dispensed objects through endless years.

By using the phrase "self-existent," the *Īśā Upaniṣad* indicates that the deity is the original source of all creation, existing only by his own power and not through another's creation. This deity's "dispensing of objects" appears to be a continuous creation of the physical world. Interestingly, this creator god is referred to as a "poet" (*kavi*), which suggests that the entire world can be perceived as a sort of poem spoken by a primordial creator.

Later Indian interpreters of the *Īśā Upaniṣad* have interpreted the *Īśa* ("Lord") of the title in different ways. For the great Advaita Vedanta (non-dualist) philosopher Śaṅkara, *Īśa* is not a reference to a personal god at all, but rather the *ātman*, or inner self of all living beings. The Dvaita Vedanta (dualist) scholar Madhva, however, sees *Īśa* as a personal deity and identifies him with the Hindu god Viṣṇu.

The ethics of the *Īśā Upaniṣad*

The twentieth-century Indian activist Mohandas Karamchand Gandhi, also known as Mahatma ("The great *ātman*") Gandhi, said of the opening verse of the *Īśā Upaniṣad*: "If all the Upaniṣads and all the other scriptures happened all of a sudden to be reduced to ashes, and if only the first verse in the Ishopanishad were left in the memory of the Hindus, Hinduism would live forever."[16] What is it about the opening stanza if the Upaniṣad that would justify the claim that the entire essence of Hinduism can be found within it?

> The whole world is pervaded by the Lord,
> whatever moves in this world.
> Therefore eat what has been abandoned,
> and do not be envious of anyone's wealth.[17]

The stanza suggests, first of all, a personal and immanent God, present both in the world itself and in all living beings. But significantly, this stanza also concludes that this divine presence in our world and in ourselves must lead to certain guidelines for ethical behavior.

The meaning of the cryptic phrase "eat what has been abandoned" has been much debated. One possible interpretation is that this passage advocates vegetarianism: Since the divine is present in all living beings, people should eat only substances that are "abandoned" by this life force and therefore not living (i.e. plants, rather than animals). This interpretation is further supported by the equally debated stanza three:

> "Demonic" are those worlds called,
> wrapped in blind darkness,
> where those people go after death
> who kill the *ātman*.

It has been suggested that the term *ātmahanas* ("killing the *ātman*") may refer to people committing suicide, and that the text warns about dire consequences in the afterlife should anyone kill themselves. While this reading is quite possible, it would perhaps make even better sense to understand *ātman* here as a reference to the self of all living beings, rather than as a reflexive pronoun ("killing *oneself*"). If we interpret *ātman* as the self of *any* living being, the connection between stanzas one and three becomes clear: If the divine being is present in everything that is alive, one should as a consequence refrain from eating or killing any living beings.

The injunction against coveting the wealth of others is juxtaposed in an interesting way with the respect for all life here. Perhaps the underlying logic is that a recognition of God's immanence leads to value everything that is living over that which is not (lifeless wealth).

Karma in the *Īśā Upaniṣad*

The doctrine of *karma*, or the idea that all actions will eventually come back to the one who had performed them, forms an essential part of later Hinduism. Although a doctrine of *karma* is not yet fully and systematically developed in the Upaniṣads, early articulations of the teachings of *karma* is found in a few of the older Upaniṣads, particularly the *Bṛhadāraṇyaka Upaniṣad* and the *Īśā Upaniṣad.*

In later Hinduism, we find the belief that *karma* ties humans to an endless cycle of death and reincarnation, and that a goal for human beings is to find a way to be free from *karma* altogether. The well-known Sanskrit text *Bhagavad Gītā* ("The Song of the Lord") suggests that one way to free oneself from *karma* is to act with complete detachment, without desire, and to surrender the karmic fruits of all one's actions to the deity. A similar idea of avoiding *karma* by merely doing one's duty in the world is encountered in the *Īśā Upaniṣad*:

> Merely performing actions (*karma*) in this world,
> you should want to live a hundred years.
> This, and not otherwise,
> does action (*karma*) not cling to you.[18]

It is possible that the word *karma* here still carries with it something of the older Vedic meaning of "ritual action." But even so, the idea that certain actions might "cling" to the one who performs them, and that this "stuck" *karma* is undesirable, foreshadows the later *karma* doctrine of classical Hinduism.

The juxtaposition of stanza one of the *Īśā Upaniṣad*, which advocates ethical behavior, and stanza two, which is concerned with avoiding karma "clinging" due to one's actions, is intriguing. In light of these two stanzas, the *Īśā Upaniṣad* seems to suggest that acting in a morally responsible way and with the recognition of God's presence in the world does not lead to any karmic burden – a sentiment very much in tune with the most well-known Hindu text of them all, the *Bhagavad Gītā*.

It is difficult to date the *Bhagavad Gītā* precisely in relation to the *Īśā Upaniṣad* and the *Kaṭha Upaniṣad*, which has several stanzas in common with the *Bhagavad Gītā*, but it seems likely that the two Upaniṣads are slightly older than the *Bhagavad Gītā* and may have influenced this significant Hindu text.

According to classical Hinduism, the *karma* a person has accumulated during his or her life will follow that person into the next reincarnation. A foreshadowing of this idea may be seen in stanza seventeen of the *Īśā Upaniṣad*:

> The never-resting is the wind, the immortal.
> Ashes are this body's lot.
> Om! Mind, remember the deed. Remember!
> Mind, remember the deed. Remember!

This stanza suggests that even if the human body ends in ashes, there is still something left that remembers past deeds even beyond death.

Wisdom and ignorance in the *Īśā Upaniṣad*

Wisdom (*vidyā* or *jñāna*) is a central concept in the Upaniṣads. Through the correct knowledge of the inner *ātman* and the cosmic *brahman*, a person can achieve a state of eternal bliss and enlightenment. Knowledge or wisdom is, above all, the primary path to salvation in the Upaniṣads.

The *Īśā Upaniṣad* puts an almost shocking new spin on this Upaniṣadic idea, however, when it declares:

> Into blind darkness they enter,
> people who worship ignorance.
> But into a darkness deeper still
> those who delight in knowledge.[19]

How can knowledge possibly lead to an even deeper darkness than ignorance? The *Īśā Upaniṣad* itself clearly values the correct knowledge and suggests that the path out of sorrow and bewilderment lies precisely in knowing correctly:

> When a discerning man in his own self
> has become all beings,
> What confusion and sorrow can there be
> for him who has seen this oneness?[20]

The *Īśā Upaniṣad* suggests, however, that the path to salvation is different from both knowledge and ignorance (stanza ten), and yet something that unites both of them (stanza eleven). These passages suggest that the ultimate form of wisdom is beyond all worldly dualities. The true wisdom does not separate and categorize information into "knowledge" and "ignorance," but rather takes a unified view of *all* reality. All dualistic categories such as "knowledge" and "ignorance" (stanzas nine–eleven) and "becoming" and "non-becoming" (stanzas twelve–fourteen) are mere artificial constructs that must be overcome in order for the true oneness of the world to be glimpsed.

In its radical rejection of duality and its insistence in the presence of God in the world and the presence of all things within the *ātman*, the *Īśā Upaniṣad* is one of the first Hindu texts to present an absolute monism, the idea that all reality is one and indivisible. The *Īśā Upaniṣad's* insistence on unity, and idea that is rearticulated again and again in much of later Hindu philosophy, may account for the text's popularity within Hinduism. Perhaps the reason for its placement at the beginning of most Indian collections of Upaniṣads is its proclamation of the unity that lies at the heart of so many later Hindu teachings.

The date and composition of the text

The Īśā Upaniṣad is composed in verse, and the specific metrical variants used suggest that the text was composed after the *Bṛhadāraṇyaka Upaniṣad*, but before the *Kaṭha* or *Śvetāśvatara Upaniṣad*.[21] The *Īśā* has quite a few stanzas in common with the *Bṛhadāraṇyaka Upaniṣad* (*Īśā Upaniṣad* 9 = *Bṛhadāraṇyaka Upaniṣad* (*Mādhyaṃdina*) 4.4.13/ *Bṛhadāraṇyaka Upaniṣad* (*Kāṇva*) 4.4.10, *Īśā* 3= *Bṛhadāraṇyaka Upaniṣad M* 4.4.14 = *Bṛhadāraṇyaka Upaniṣad K* 4.4.11, *Bṛhadāraṇyaka Upaniṣad M* 5.3.1 = *Bṛhadāraṇyaka Upaniṣad K* 5.15.1-4 = *Īśā* 15–18).

But did the *Īśā* borrow these stanzas from the *Bṛhadāraṇyaka Upaniṣad*, or did the *Bṛhadāraṇyaka* borrow them from the *Īśā*, or have both texts appropriated them from an unknown third source? Since the *Bṛhadāraṇyaka Upaniṣad* is a much older text overall, at first sight it seems reasonable to assume that the authors of the *Īśā Upaniṣad* borrowed them from the *Bṛhadāraṇyaka Upaniṣad*. The answer may not be quite that simple, however.

The verses *Bṛhadāraṇyaka Upaniṣad* 4.4.10-11 (= *Īśā* 9 and 3) are marked as quotations with the in the text of the *Bṛhadāraṇyaka* itself: "On this subject there are these verses." It is therefore quite likely that the stanzas *Bṛhadāraṇyaka Upaniṣad* 4.4.10-11 are actually borrowed from the *Īśā*, even though the main portions of the *Bṛhadāraṇyaka Upaniṣad* are clearly much older than the *Īśā*. Although it is possible that both the *Bṛhadāraṇyaka Upaniṣad* and the *Īśā* have borrowed these stanzas from a third source, *Īśā* 3 and 9 fit so well metrically and conceptually with the rest of *Īśā* that it is reasonable to assume that these stanzas are original to this Upaniṣad and were later borrowed into the *Bṛhadāraṇyaka Upaniṣad*. Although the core of the *Bṛhadāraṇyaka Upaniṣad* is older than the *Īśā*, it is likely that *Īśā* 3 and 9 were later borrowed into *Bṛhadāraṇyaka Upaniṣad* at some point after the *Īśā* has become well known. We should note that both texts belong the same Vedic school, which makes the borrowing from one text into another even more likely.

Īśā 15–18 forms a brief appendix to the main text of the Upaniṣad. This passage, a prayer to the Vedic gods Pūṣan (a minor sun god) and Agni, is identical with *Bṛhadāraṇyaka Upaniṣad* 5.15.1-4. These four sections, two of which are known Vedic quotations, do not fit comfortably into the *Bṛhadāraṇyaka Upaniṣad*. On the other hand, they do not seem to fit very well with their metrical, linguistic, and conceptual surroundings in the *Īśā* either. These stanzas seem to be additions to both the *Īśā* and the *Bṛhadāraṇyaka Upaniṣad*. Since the stanzas occur together in exactly the same order in both Upaniṣads, it is possible that one Upaniṣad incorporated the passage first, and that the whole passage was then borrowed by the other Upaniṣad. Another possibility is that both Upaniṣads may have borrowed the section from a third source. Since it appears that the *Bṛhadāraṇyaka Upaniṣad* has borrowed from *Īśā* 3 and 9, it is quite likely that the *Bṛhadāraṇyaka Upaniṣad* also borrowed the passage *Īśā* 15–18, which consists of stanzas that the *Īśā* has borrowed from other textual sources.

Why were these stanzas included in the *Īśā Upaniṣad* in the first place? The answer to this may lie in the Upaniṣad's affiliation with the older Vedic text of the *Vājasaneyi Saṃhitā*. The *Īśā Upaniṣad*, as we have seen, forms the concluding part to the *Vājasaneyi Saṃhitā*. The two chapters of the *Saṃhitā* text immediately preceding the *Īśā Upaniṣad* contain prayers used during the Vedic Pravargya ritual. The Pravargya rite is a mystical ceremony in which a pot is filled with milk and heated over the ritual fire until it glows. The glowing pot is ritually identified with the sun, and for the worshiper, the sight of the gleaming pot is imbued with religious significance. The mysterious line from *Īśā Upaniṣad* 15: "The face of truth is covered with a golden dish. Open it, Pusan, for me to see, a man devoted to the truth …" is in all likelihood a reference to the mystical vision of the glowing pot, sometimes identified with God and with the worshiper himself ("I see your fairest form. That person there, I am he!"[22]). This old identification between an individual human being and the highest god in a moment of mystical insight fits very well into this Upaniṣad which proclaims that the entire world in filled with the presence of the divine.

Notes

1 *Īśā Upaniṣad* 1.
2 *Īśā Upaniṣad* 6.
3 *Īśā Upaniṣad* 7.
4 *Īśā Upaniṣad* 4.
5 *Īśā Upaniṣad* 5.
6 *Īśā Upaniṣad* 6.
7 *Īśā Upaniṣad* 9.
8 *Īśā Upaniṣad* 10.
9 *Īśā Upaniṣad* 13.
10 *Īśā Upaniṣad* 9.
11 *Ṛgveda* 10.129.1.
12 *Īśā Upaniṣad* 12–13.
13 *Īśā Upaniṣad* 12–13.
14 *Īśā Upaniṣad* 6.
15 *Īśā Upaniṣad* 7.
16 Eknath Easwaran, *The Upaniṣads, Translated for the Modern Reader*. Canada: Nilgiri Press, 1987: 207.
17 *Īśā Upaniṣad* 1.
18 *Īśā Upaniṣad* 2.
19 *Īśā Upaniṣad* 9.
20 *Īśā Upaniṣad* 7.
21 For details, see S. Cohen, *Text and Authority in the Older Upaniṣads*. Leiden: Brill, 2008.
22 *Īśā Upaniṣad* 16.

Further reading

Jones, Richard H. 1981. "*Vidyā* and *Avidyā* in the *Īśā Upaniṣad*" *Philosophy East and West* 31: 79–87.

Sharma, Arvind, and Young, Katherine K. 1990. "The Meaning of *Ātmahano janāḥ* in *Īśā Upaniṣad* 3" *Journal of the American Oriental Society* 110: 595–602.

29 The *Praśna Upaniṣad*

Signe Cohen

The *Praśna Upaniṣad* ("The Upaniṣad of Questions"), like the *Muṇḍaka*, is one of the Upaniṣads formally affiliated with the *Atharvaveda*. The *Praśna Upaniṣad*, a text in six short sections, is mainly composed in prose, but it also contains sixteen verses, including the metrical section 2.6–2.13. As the name indicates, each section of the text is a question (*praśna*) asked by six different men, to which the legendary wisdom teacher Pippalāda responds. In some ways, the six questions and their answers mirror the historical development of ideas in the late Vedic/Upaniṣadic period: The first few questions deal with mythological issues, such as the creation of the world and the hierarchy of deities, while later questions grow more metaphysical and abstract.

Many later Upaniṣads are affiliated with the *Atharvaveda* by default, since they have no textual association with any of the other Vedas. In the case of the *Praśna Upaniṣad*, however, the affiliation seems genuine. Pippalāda, who figures prominently in this Upaniṣad, is one of the main figures connected with the transmission of the *Atharvaveda*. There are also some textual affinities and mutual borrowings between the *Praśna Upaniṣad* and another Upaniṣad ascribed to the *Atharvaveda*, the *Muṇḍaka Upaniṣad*.

The six sages

The six men who approach Pippalāda with questions about the nature of *brahman* all bear names that associate them with lineages of Upaniṣadic teachers. Their questions are, in the Upaniṣadic context, good and insightful ones, and it is clear that the six sages are learned and educated men, "devoted to *brahman*, grounded in *brahman*, and searching for the highest *brahman*."[1] Some of these inquiring men are known from other Upaniṣadic texts. Their presence in the narrative here suggest that these men, representing, as we shall see, the traditions of the *Ṛgveda*, *Yajurveda*, and *Sāmaveda*, must eventually turn to the sage of the *Atharvaveda*, Pippalāda, for the ultimate answers. Through this series of dialogues, the *Praśna Upaniṣad* establishes the authority of the Atharvavedic tradition vis-à-vis the traditions affiliated with the other Vedas.

In many ways, Pippalāda is the Yājñavalkya of the *Praśna Upaniṣad*. Like the great wisdom teacher Yājñavalkya in the *Bṛhadāraṇyaka Upaniṣad*, he is questioned by a series of figures representing various Vedic *śākhās*, or schools of textual transmission, and like Yājñavalkya, Pippalāda turns out to be the wisest of them all. The respect the six men have for him from the outset is shown through their arrival with "firewood in their hands." Since students would normally carry firewood when approaching their teacher, the six learned men are assuming the position of students vis-à-vis Yājñavalkya from the very beginning. The questions that the six men ask Pippalāda lead to progressively deeper insight into the nature of *prāṇa* (the life breath), and eventually *ātman* and *brahman* itself.

The first man, Kabandhī Kātyāyana, asks Pippalāda the most fundamental question of them all: where do living beings come from? It is possible, but not certain, that Kabandhī is the same person as Kabandha Ātharvaṇa who is mentioned in *Bṛhadāraṇyaka Upaniṣad* 3.7.1. Since the name Ātharvaṇa signals the character's connection to the *Atharvaveda*, it makes sense that Kabandhī reappears here in a text of the *Atharvaveda*. Kabandha is further a name with old ties to the tradition of the *Atharvaveda*; a Kabandha is said to be the author of *Atharvaveda* 6.75–77. Kabandha Ātharvaṇa of the *Bṛhadāraṇyaka Upaniṣad* appears to be a supernatural spirit, a *gandharva* possessing a woman, while his counterpart in the *Praśna Upaniṣad* is human. The questions Kabandha and Kabandhī ask in two texts are quite similar, however: In the *Bṛhadāraṇyaka Upaniṣad*, Kabandha asks how all living beings are strung together, and in the *Praśna Upaniṣad*, Kabandhī asks where all living beings come from. Pippalāda responds by giving him an account of the Vedic god Prajāpati's creation of the world. Significantly, Prajāpati's first creation is a couple, but not a human couple:

> When he had heated himself through this exertion, he created a couple, Substance (*rayi*) and Life Breath (*prāṇa*), and he thought: "These two will produce creatures for me in many different ways."[2]

The two abstract principles that make up Prajāpati's first creation then become part of all aspects of the created world: Substance is associated with the moon, with physical form, "the way of the fathers" after death (leading to rebirth, rather than liberation), the dark fortnight of the lunar month, and the night. The life breath, on the other hand, is associated with the sun, the formless, liberation after death, the bright fortnight of the moon, and the day. Through his initial answer to Kabandhī, Pippalāda establishes the superiority of the life breath.

The second man to pose a question, Bhārgava Vaidarbhi, asks about the supreme one among the deities that support a living being. Pippalāda's answer to this question is that *prāṇa*, the life breath itself, is the highest deity. Bhārgava ("descendant of Bhṛgu") is a patronymic name common to many respected teachers in the Upaniṣads and Brāhmaṇas. Bhṛgu is said to be the son of Varuṇa, and as such is mentioned in the *Taittirīya Upaniṣad*, where he receives instructions from his father. "Vaidarbhi" is simply an indication that he comes from Vidarbha, so in this case the real personal name of the person is unknown.

The third man, Kausalya Āśvalāyana, picks up on Pippalāda's answer to the previous question and asks where the *prāṇa* comes from and how it enters into the body. His question leads to Pippalāda's exposition of the relationship between *prāṇa* and *ātman*, and the doctrine of the five breaths. The name "Kausalya" indicates that the questioner is from the region of Kosala, and the name "Āśvalāyana" associates him with the family of the priest Aśvala,[3] and also with the tradition of the *Ṛgveda*.

The fourth questioner, Sauryāyaṇī Gārgya, asks about the agent of actions and the subject of experiences:

> Sir, what are the ones that go to sleep inside a person here? What are the ones that stay awake in him? Which deities see his dreams? Who experiences this bliss? And who is the one in which all of these things are established?[4]

Sauryāyaṇī Gārgya's question reveals that he has some insight into the nature of *ātman*. Wisdom teachers and wisdom seekers from Gārgya clan are frequently encountered in the Upaniṣads. Among the more famous ones are Dṛpta Bālāki in *Bṛhadāraṇyaka Upaniṣad* 2.1 and *Kauṣītakī Upaniṣad* 4, and Gārgī in *Bṛhadāraṇyaka Upaniṣad* 3.6.1 and 3.8.1-12. Pippalāda explains that it is the breaths that keep a person awake, the mind that experiences dreams, and *ātman* or *puruṣa* (the person) who is really the underlying agent of all actions.

The fifth man, Śaibya Satyakāma, asks about the syllable *oṃ*, which in the *Praśna Upaniṣad* is identified with *brahman* itself. Satyakāma is the most well known among the six sages in the *Praśna Upaniṣad*. He is mentioned in the *Bṛhadāraṇyaka Upaniṣad* 6.3, and figures prominently in *Chāndogya Upaniṣad* 4 where he learns the nature of *brahman* from the wild animals. The patronyme "Śaibya" ("descendant of Śibi") is only used for Satyakāma in this text. The syllable *oṃ* is said to be made up of three distinct phonemes, *a*, *u*, and *m*. Here, the first phoneme *a* is identified with the *Ṛgveda*, the first and the second together, *au*, with the *Yajurveda*, and the three together, *auṃ*, with the *Sāmaveda*. But Pippalāda claims that it is only by knowing the syllable in its totality, *oṃ*, that a person will reach the world of *brahman*. The implied subtext is that the first three Vedas reveal only parts of the ultimate truth, whereas the syllable *oṃ*, perhaps here to be contextually equated with the *Atharvaveda* to which this Upaniṣad belongs, will lead to the ultimate reality.

The final questioner, Sukeśa Bhāradvāja, asks Pippalāda about the person consisting of sixteen parts. Sukeśa reveals that he himself was once approached by a prince, Hiraṇyanābha of Kosala, who asked him about the person consisting of sixteen parts. Since Sukeśa had never heard of this doctrine, the prince had to leave without learning what he had sought. This little episode, told second-hand in the *Praśna Upaniṣad*, is reminiscent of the famous dialogue scene between a wisdom teacher and a king in *Bṛhadāraṇyaka Upaniṣad* 3–4. Unlike Yājñavalkya in the *Bṛhadāraṇyaka Upaniṣad*, however, Sukeśa Bhāradvāja does not know the answer to the royal seeker's question. The *Bṛhadāraṇyaka Upaniṣad*[5] also depicts a would-be wisdom teacher, Dṛpta Bālaki, who claims to understand *brahman* and attempts to explain the highest reality to a king, even though his own understanding of *brahman* is flawed. To Sukeśa Bhāradvāja's credit, he does not claim to have more knowledge or understanding than he has, and readily seeks out the wise Pippalāda to find the answer to the question that stumped him.

Pippalāda's answer to Sukeśa Bhāradvāja's question reveals the ultimate truth about the nature of *ātman* and *brahman*. He explains that the sixteen-fold person is "right here, within the body,"[6] and identifies him with the "highest *brahman*, higher than which there is nothing."[7] Like the other men approaching Pippalāda, Sukeśa Bhāradvāja bears a name that indicates that he comes from a venerable lineage of scholars. Several Vedic teachers are known by the patronymic name Bhāradvāja ("descendant of Bharadvāja"). A Bhāradvāja is mentioned in a lineage of teachers and students of the *Yajurveda* in *Bṛhadāraṇyaka Upaniṣad* 2.6.3 and 4.6.3, and an Atharva-teacher Bhāradvāja Satyavāha is mentioned in *Muṇḍaka Upaniṣad* 1.1.2.

The story of the six sages is perhaps more than a literary device to make the Upaniṣad more interesting. The questions in this "Upaniṣad of Questions" (*Praśna Upaniṣad*) are asked by sages whose names are associated with traditional wisdom and good family standing. Since all these sages come to the Atharva-teacher Pippalāda in their quest for the truth, the frame story also serves to legitimize this *Atharvaveda* Upaniṣad itself through links to stories of respected wisdom teachers. Unlike the *Bṛhadāraṇyaka Upaniṣad*, the *Praśna Upaniṣad* contains no contest scene. The six men who approach Pippalāda are not seeking to challenge him, but rather, to bring him their earnest questions about the true nature of *ātman* and *brahman*, which only he can answer. It is interesting to note that the *Praśna Upaniṣad* treats these sages associated with other *śākhās* and other Upaniṣads with a great deal of respect. There is no direct confrontation between these sages and Pippalāda, and no threats of shattered heads, as in the *Bṛhadāraṇyaka Upaniṣad*. Rather, the authority of the *Atharvaveda* is expressed through the respect the learned sages show for the superior wisdom of Pippalāda.

Prāṇa in the *Praśna Upaniṣad*

One of the most central concepts in the *Praśna Upaniṣad* is *prāṇa*, the life breath. *Prāṇa* is contrasted with *rayi*, or material substance.[8] *Prāṇa* is in this text associated with the *ātman* and a desire for wisdom, and *rayi* with the physical body and worldly desires. *Prāṇa* and *rayi*, breath and substance, are also associated with two forms of immortality: Those who go the southern course after death, associated with *rayi*, the moon, the ancestors, and a desire for offspring, are born again, whereas those who choose a northern course, associated with *prāṇa*, the sun, knowledge, and *ātman* reach immortality and ultimately *brahmaloka*, the world of *brahman*.[9]

The life breath *prāṇa* is further identified with the Vedic deities Prajāpati,[10] Indra, and Rudra,[11] perhaps as a means to align the teachings of the Upaniṣad with the ideas expressed in earlier Vedic texts. *Prāṇa* is said to arise from *ātman*[12] and enter into the body where it is divided into the five breaths, *apāna* ("the out-breath"), *samāna* ("the mid-breath"), *vyāna* ("through-breath"), *udāna* ("up-breath"), and *prāṇa*, the life breath itself.[13] The notion of *prāṇa* as the base from which all other breaths arise, first articulated in the *Praśna Upaniṣad*, later becomes important in Āyurvedic medicine as well as in the later systems of Yoga and Tantra, where it is elaborated in great detail. As is clear from the sequence of questions in the *Praśna Upaniṣad*, understanding *prāṇa* is here not a goal in itself, however, but a necessary step towards grasping *ātman*.

Ātman in the *Praśna Upaniṣad*

In the *Praśna Upaniṣad*, *ātman* is the essence of a person, and it dwells in the heart.[14] The *ātman* is the agent of all actions, imperishable, and ultimately identical with *puruṣa*.[15] *Ātman* is a *puruṣa* (person) consisting of sixteen parts: *prāṇa*, faith, space, wind, fire, water, earth, the senses, the mind, food, strength, austerity, *mantras*, rituals, worlds, and name.[16] Understanding the nature of this all-encompassing *ātman* leads to immortality and to the world of *brahman*.

Why the insistence in the *Praśna Upaniṣad* that the self consists of sixteen parts? The number sixteen recurs in numerous Hindu texts as a symbol of wholeness. Many Vedic rituals require a full staff of sixteen priests. Vedic ritual texts inform us that a human being is as tall as sixteen bricks. The moon has sixteen phases (*kalās*) in Hindu astronomy. Classical Hinduism has sixteen life cycle rituals (*saṃskāras*) that ritually construct a whole social person. The self consisting of sixteen parts in the *Praśna Upaniṣad* must therefore be understood as the full and complete *ātman*.

Brahman in the *Praśna Upaniṣad*

In the narrative of the *Praśna Upaniṣad*, six sages approach Pippalāda to learn about the nature of *brahman*. In many Upaniṣadic texts it is *ātman* that is the unknown that has to be discovered, but in the *Praśna Upaniṣad*, as in the other Upaniṣads of the *Atharvaveda*, it is *brahman* that is the unknown. The questioners already seem to know about *ātman*, but in the course of their conversation with Pippalāda, it becomes clear that the answer to the question about *brahman* lies in a more nuanced understanding of *ātman* than the one they initially had. The quest for knowledge of *brahman*, rather than *ātman*, is a common theme in the Upaniṣads of the *Atharvaveda*, such as the *Praśna* and the *Muṇḍaka*.

While many other Upaniṣads present *brahman* as one and indivisible, the *Praśna Upaniṣad* suggests that there are two forms of *brahman*, a higher and a lower form.[17] This idea is merely mentioned here in passing, but is further developed in the *Maitrī Upaniṣad*, a text that is strongly influenced by the *Praśna Upaniṣad*. In the *Praśna Upaniṣad*, the lower form of *brahman* is associated with the lower form of the sacred syllable *oṃ*, which again is associated with the knowledge of the *Ṛgveda*, *Yajurveda*, and *Sāmaveda*.[18] The *Praśna Upaniṣad* suggests that knowledge of the highest form of *brahman* is closely tied to knowing the syllable *oṃ* by itself, rather than to Vedic knowledge.[19]

Prajāpati in the *Praśna Upaniṣad*

When asked where all living beings come from, the sage Pippalāda describes the god Prajāpati's creation of life. Prajāpati, whose name means "the lord of creatures," is a Vedic creator god. His creation is here described as simultaneously mythological and philosophical. The creator god is longing for living beings,[20] and exerts himself and creates an ancestral couple. These mythic ancestors of all living creatures are, however, highly abstract concepts: *prāṇa* (the lifebreath) and *rayi* (substance). These two also have cosmic aspects to them, for *prāṇa* is identified with the sun itself, and *rayi* with the moon. But *prāṇa* and *rayi* are also associated with two different lifestyle choices: *prāṇa* is associated with humans who seek the *ātman* with austerity and knowledge, while *rayi* is associated with ritual offerings and a desire for children and family.

But Prajāpati's creation of the world and of the ancestral couple is not just an abstraction in this text, but grounded in physical reality: "Prajāpati is food. From that comes semen, and from semen come these living beings."[21] So the answer to the first question of this Upaniṣad of Questions is twofold: Living beings come from sexual reproduction *and* from a divine creator.

Date and composition of the text

The date of the *Praśna Upaniṣad* has been subject to a great deal of debate. While many scholars have assumed a late date of composition for the *Praśna Upaniṣad*, after the classical Upaniṣadic texts like the *Kaṭha*, *Śvetāśvatara*, and *Muṇḍaka*, or even later, the grammatical forms in the text indicate that the *Praśna Upaniṣad* belongs to approximately the same time period as the *Muṇḍaka*.

There are several non-standard grammatical forms in the *Praśna Upaniṣad*. As Salomon has demonstrated, the language of the *Praśna Upaniṣad* is characterized by a number of unusual grammatical forms, many of which are vernacular linguistic variants like those found in the epics and in Buddhist Sanskrit.[22] The vernacularisms and the Vedic forms are evenly distributed throughout the prose text and the stanzas of the *Praśna Upaniṣad*. This indicates that there is likely no significant age difference between the prose text of the *Praśna Upaniṣad* and its verses. The *Muṇḍaka Upaniṣad*, like the *Praśna*

Upaniṣad, contains a large number of vernacular Sanskrit forms. Unlike the *Muṇḍaka*, however, the *Praśna Upaniṣad* does contain specifically Vedic forms as well, which may suggest that the *Praśna Upaniṣad* is likely older than the *Muṇḍaka*. Some scholars have suggested that the last two questions are later additions to the original text,[23] but there is nothing in the linguistic makeup of the text itself to support this. While it is true that the first few questions seem to contain older ideas than the last questions, this may simply reflect the structure of the text itself, moving from old established ideas toward more innovative ones.

Notes

1 *Praśna Upaniṣad* 1.1.
2 *Praśna Upaniṣad* 1.4.
3 A. A. Macdonnell and A. B. Keith, *Vedic Index of Names and Subjects*. London, 1912. (Reprint Delhi: Motilal Banarsidass, 1982: 190.)
4 *Praśna Upaniṣad* 4.1.
5 *Bṛhadāraṇyaka Upaniṣad*, chapter 2.
6 *Praśna Upaniṣad* 6.2.
7 *Praśna Upaniṣad* 6.7.
8 *Praśna Upaniṣad* 1.4.
9 *Praśna Upaniṣad* 1.9–16.
10 *Praśna Upaniṣad* 2.7.
11 *Praśna Upaniṣad* 2.9.
12 *Praśna Upaniṣad* 3.3.
13 *Praśna Upaniṣad* 3.5–9.
14 *Praśna Upaniṣad* 3.6.
15 *Praśna Upaniṣad* 4.9.
16 *Praśna Upaniṣad* 6.4.
17 *Praśna Upaniṣad* 5.2.
18 *Praśna Upaniṣad* 5.2.
19 *Praśna Upaniṣad* 5.7.
20 *Praśna Upaniṣad* 1.4.
21 *Praśna Upaniṣad* 1.14.
22 Salomon 1991.
23 E. Röer, *The Katha, Mundaka, Isa, Kena, Taittiriya, Aitareya, Swetaswatara, Prasna and Mandukya Upanishads. Bibliotheca Indica XV, No. 41 and 50.* Calcutta: Asiatic Society of Bengal, 1852–1853: 138.

Further reading

Salomon, R. 1991. "A Linguistic Analysis of the Praśna Upaniṣad" *Wiener Zeitschrift für die Kunde des Morgenlandes* 35: 47–74.
Zysk, K. 2007. "The Bodily Winds in Ancient India Revisited" *The Journal of the Royal Anthropological Institute* 13: 105–115.

30 The *Muṇḍaka Upaniṣad*

Signe Cohen

The *Muṇḍaka Upaniṣad* is a verse text, traditionally ascribed to the *Atharvaveda*. This Upaniṣad does not form an integral part of an older Vedic text, but its association with *Atharvaveda* is nevertheless more than a purely formal one. The sage *Atharvan* is mentioned in the very first stanza of the *Muṇḍaka Upaniṣad*: "Brahmā arose as the first of the gods, the creator of everything, the guardian of the world. To Atharvan, his oldest son, he taught the knowledge of *brahman*, which is the root of all knowledge."[1] By ascribing a knowledge of the highest *brahman* to Atharvan himself, the mythical founder of the *Atharvaveda*, the text implies that an authentic knowledge of *brahman* must be sought within the tradition of the *Atharvaveda*. Śaunaka, the mythical founder of one of the two schools of *Atharvaveda* recension, also appears as a character in the *Muṇḍaka Upaniṣad*.[2] The Upaniṣad establishes Śaunaka's own position in the transmission of learning from the primordial creator god Brahmā onwards: Brahmā taught his own son Atharvan, who is turn taught Aṅgir, who taught Bhāradvāja, who taught Aṅgiras, who taught Śaunaka. The rest of the text of the Upaniṣad is then presented as the direct words of the wise Aṅgiras to his disciple Śaunaka. The appearance of mythical characters associated with the *Atharavaveda* in the Upaniṣad helps to establish the authority of the text and strengthen its affiliation with the *Atharvaveda*. Such semi-legendary characters are not exclusive to the *Muṇḍaka Upaniṣad*; Pippalāda, the founder of the other *Atharvaveda* school of recension, appears as a character in the *Muṇḍaka Upaniṣad*'s "sister text," the *Praśna Upaniṣad*, which is also formally affiliated with the *Atharvaveda*.

The close association with the *Praśna Upaniṣad* is evident in both the ideas and the linguistic and metrical forms of the *Muṇḍaka Upaniṣad*. Like the *Praśna Upaniṣad*, the *Muṇḍaka Upaniṣad* introduces a stanza as a "*Ṛgveda* verse" (*ṛc*)[3] that is not a part of the *Ṛgveda* as we know it today. This introduction of a "false *ṛc*" in these two texts further confirms the close relationship between the two Upaniṣads. It is of course possible that the transmitters of these Upaniṣads were familiar with *Ṛgveda* verses now lost to us. Since the verses in question do not seem particularly ancient, linguistically or metrically, however, it is more likely that the term *ṛc* is used more loosely in these two Upaniṣads to designate "an authoritative verse" in general.

Even though the *Muṇḍaka Upaniṣad* is affiliated with the *Atharvaveda*, it is also closely connected, through quotations and shared ideas, with some of the Upaniṣads of the *Black Yajurveda*, such as the *Kaṭha* and the *Śvetāśvatara Upaniṣad*.

The word *muṇḍaka* in the title of the Upaniṣad literally means "one who cuts or shaves." Several scholars have found the name *Muṇḍaka* enigmatic and difficult to explain in a satisfactory manner.[4] A close reading of the text reveals, however, that "cutting" or "shaving" is the text's central metaphor. The "cutting" takes place both on the spiritual and the physical level. While shaving of the head, perhaps as part of an ascetic lifestyle, is no doubt implied, the *Muṇḍaka Upaniṣad* also refers to cutting "the knot of ignorance,"[5] cutting the "knot of the heart,"[6] and being liberated from the "knots of the secret place."[7] Commentators on the text have explained the name *Muṇḍaka* as referring to the text's ability to "shave" or cut off mental errors. This interpretation is in accordance with the statements found in the text itself.

In addition, the text mentions a ceremony called *śirovrata* ("the vow of the head").[8] This reference to *śirovrata* may be an indication that the text has its origin within an ascetic religious movement where shaving the head was a common practice. This interpretation is confirmed by the text's mention of *yatayas* ("ascetics") realizing the truth and becoming liberated[9] and its mention of renunciation, *saṃnyāsa*.[10] The *Muṇḍaka Upaniṣad* also states that liberation is attained by those who practice austerity (*tapas*) and faith in the forest and live the life of a wandering beggar.[11] This recommendation of the ascetic life, along with the text's disparaging attitude towards Vedic rituals, suggests that the *Muṇḍaka Upaniṣad* has its origin in an ascetic environment. It appears, then, that the title of the text has a double meaning: It refers both to the cutting away of ignorance and to the ritual cutting of the hair when taking ascetic vows, implying perhaps a connection between these two forms of "cutting": By renouncing the world and becoming an ascetic with a shaved head, one may find the knowledge that will shave away or cut the knot of ignorance.

Shaving one's head also appears to be an identity marker in the *Muṇḍaka Upaniṣad*: "This is the truth that the seer Aṅgiras declared in the old days. One who has not performed the 'vow of the head' may not learn it."[12] This implies that the text itself is meant to be taught only to those who had taken ascetic vows.

The text of the *Muṇḍaka Upaniṣad* is divided into three chapters also called *Muṇḍakas*. It is likely that this unusual designation for a chapter was chosen because the three chapters with their philosophical teachings are perceived as three successive "shavings" or "cuttings" of the "tangled knot" of ignorance.

Puruṣa in the *Muṇḍaka Upaniṣad*

We find frequent mention of *puruṣa*, "the person," in the *Muṇḍaka Upaniṣad*. *Ātman* itself is identified with the radiant *puruṣa*, the immortal essence of a human being: "Through the door of the sun do they go, spotless, to where the immortal *puruṣa* is, the changeless self."[13] It is through the knowledge of *puruṣa* that *brahman* itself is grasped.[14] *Puruṣa* is divine, invisible, and unborn:

That *puruṣa* is divine,
Without visible form,
Both inside and outside,
Unborn, without breath or mind.
He is radiant, and farther away
Than the farthest imperishable.[15]

Puruṣa is the inner *ātman* of all beings,[16] but he is also the creator of the universe:

From him are born life breath and mind
And all sense organs,
Sky, wind, fire, water,
And that earth that carries everything.[17]

From him come the *Ṛg* verses, the *Sāman* chants, the *Yajus* formulas, the initiation rituals:

And all sacrifices, rites, and gifts,
And the year, the sacrificers, and the worlds
Where both the moon and sun shine brightly.[18]

Gods, celestial beings, humans, cattle, and birds
Are born from him in manifold ways,
And in-breath and out-breath, rice and barley,
Austerity, faith, and truth, chastity and rules.[19]

Puruṣa is even identified as the ultimate cause of *brahman* itself:

When a sage sees that *puruṣa*, of golden hue,
The creator, the Lord, the source of *brahman*,
Then shaking off good and evil, free from stain,
He obtains the highest identity.[20]

By identifying *puruṣa* as the cause of *brahman*, the *Muṇḍaka Upaniṣad* foreshadows the *Śvetāśvatara Upaniṣad*, a text with which it has a great deal in common.

Puruṣa cannot be grasped by the senses, but is accessible through meditation: "He cannot be grasped by sight or speech or any of the senses, nor by penance or rituals. But the one who is without parts can be seen by a person who meditates …"[21]

Ātman in the *Muṇḍaka Upaniṣad*

Overall, the idea of *ātman*, the inner self of a person, is not as prominent in the *Muṇḍaka Upaniṣad* as the concepts of *puruṣa* and *brahman*. In this Upaniṣad, the true knowledge of *ātman* ultimately leads to the knowledge of *brahman*, which is the final goal of knowledge.

The wise ascetics are said to go "through the door of the sun" to where the immortal *ātman* is, but this *ātman* is immediately identified with *puruṣa*.[22] The association of *ātman* and immortality with the sun is reminiscent of the *Praśna Upaniṣad*.[23] Although the *ātman* is not mentioned frequently in the *Muṇḍaka Upaniṣad*, its cosmic nature and its role in salvation is nevertheless emphasized:

> You must understand that this alone is the *ātman*,
> On which the earth, atmosphere, and highest heaven are woven,
> And the mind, and the breaths as well.
> So discard other worlds, for this is the bridge to the immortal.[24]

In a stanza common to both the *Muṇḍaka* and the *Kaṭha Upaniṣad*, it is suggested that *ātman* chooses to reveal itself to one who seeks it.[25] This perception of *ātman* as a divine entity outside the person who actively chooses to reveal itself to the seeker does not fit very well with the rest of the *Muṇḍaka Upaniṣad*, and it is quite possible that this particular stanza is simply a borrowing from the *Kaṭha Upaniṣad*.

Brahman in the *Muṇḍaka Upaniṣad*

As in other Upaniṣads of the *Atharvaveda*, the knowledge of *brahman* is the ultimate goal in the *Muṇḍaka Upaniṣad*. The Upaniṣad presents this knowledge, not as something new, but as part of an esoteric tradition of learning which can be traced back to Atharvan himself. While the *Muṇḍaka Upaniṣad* does not altogether dispense with the old Vedic learning, it makes quite clear that the traditional knowledge of the four Vedas is inferior to the knowledge "by which one grasps the imperishable."[26]

Brahman is here presented as completely beyond our world of ordinary sensory perception: "That which cannot be seen or grasped, colorless, without sight or hearing, without hands or feet, eternal and omnipresent …"[27] *Brahman* is the foundation of the world,[28] and also its creator: "As plants spring from the earth, and as hair grows from a living person, so all things here spring from the imperishable."[29] It is quite difficult to sort out the precise relationship between *brahman* and *puruṣa* in the *Muṇḍaka Upaniṣad*; both principles are identified as the ultimate creator of the world and as the highest goal of human knowledge. Sometimes, they are presented as practically synonymous in the text, while they are clearly differentiated at other times. The lack of consistency when it comes to the possible identity and relative ranking of *brahman* and *puruṣa* in the text suggests that the authors and editors of the Upaniṣads were not terribly concerned about this issue; both worship of *puruṣa* and knowledge of *brahman* ultimately lead to liberation.

When a person comes to know *brahman*, that person becomes *brahman* itself.[30] This knowledge of *brahman* is achieved through knowledge of *ātman*, an idea that is captured in the image of the bow and the arrow in *Muṇḍaka Upaniṣad* 2.2.4:

> *Oṃ* is the bow, the arrow is *ātman*,
> *brahman* is the target, they say.
> One must hit it without distraction,
> and like an arrow one will be lodged in it.

Brahman is "that which they know who know *ātman*."[31] Like the *Praśna Upaniṣad*, the *Muṇḍaka Upaniṣad* suggests that there exist a higher and a lower form of *brahman*: "When one sees him, both the high and the low …"[32] In the *Muṇḍaka Upaniṣad* it is primarily the *knowledge* of *brahman*, rather than *brahman* itself, that has a higher and a lower form: "Two forms of knowledge are to be known, say those who know *brahman*, the higher and the lower."[33] The lower knowledge is associated throughout the text with the old Vedic canon.

The old and the new canon

The Vedic canon is constantly challenged in the *Muṇḍaka Upaniṣad*. Here, the knowledge of the Vedas is regarded as a lower form of knowledge (perhaps not surprisingly, in a text of the *Atharvaveda*, which is itself on the fringe of the Vedic canon), whereas the knowledge "by which one grasps the imperishable (*oṃ*)," i.e. the philosophy of the Upaniṣads, is considered the superior knowledge.[34] The Vedic canon is seen as inferior to the Upaniṣads, since the Vedas do not, in the Upaniṣadic view, deal with the ultimate reality:

> Two kinds of knowledge are to be known,
> the brahman-knowers declare: the higher and the lower.
> Of these, the lower is the *Ṛgveda*, *Yajurveda*, *Sāmaveda*, and *Atharvaveda*, phonetics, ritual, grammar, etymology, metrics, and astrology.
> The higher is that whereby the *akṣara* (the imperishable/ *oṃ*) is grasped.[35]

Here, the Vedic canon and the Vedic branches of learning (even the *Atharvaveda* itself!) are all regarded as inferior and contrasted with the higher learning of the Upaniṣads themselves, concentrated in the one syllable *oṃ*.

The *Muṇḍaka Upaniṣad* is harsh in its assessment of those who claim that people who perform the correct Vedic rites can go to heaven and become immortal:

> Dwelling in ignorance, but calling themselves wise,
> Believing that they are learned, the fools wander,
> Badly afflicted, like blind men,
> Led by one who is himself blind.[36]
>
> Believing that sacrifices and gifts are the most important,
> These deluded men know nothing better.
> When they have enjoyed their good work in heaven,
> They return again to this lower world.[37]

The "lower knowledge" of Vedic rituals may lead to a *temporary* heaven due to good karma, but in the end, those who rely merely on good works and rituals must be reborn without reaching the ultimate world of *brahman*. They are simply "the blind leading the blind" (a metaphor also found in the *Kaṭha Upaniṣad*, where this same stanza is also used to lament the ways of those who merely have superficial ritual knowledge without true understanding). The only way to true liberation, according to the Upaniṣad, is to go "firewood in hand" and become the student of a teacher who truly understands *brahman*.[38]

The date and composition of the text

Salomon has pointed out that grammatical forms diverging from classical Sanskrit occur more frequently in the *Muṇḍaka Upaniṣad* than in any other Upaniṣad.[39] He also points out that the *Muṇḍaka Upaniṣad*, unlike most of the older Upaniṣads, contains very few, if any, genuinely Vedic forms. He regards the language of the *Muṇḍaka Upaniṣad* as closer to Buddhist Hybrid Sanskrit and to the language of the epics than to the language of the other older Upaniṣads. On that basis, he regards the language of the *Muṇḍaka Upaniṣad* as a form of colloquial or "vernacular Sanskrit." Salomon does not conclude that the *Muṇḍaka Upaniṣad* is younger than the other older Upaniṣads, but merely that its language is closer to the spoken Sanskrit of its time than to the formal language. Since a preference for a more vernacular style of language is characteristic of heterodox sects, Salomon suggests that the *Muṇḍaka Upaniṣad* originated within a heterodox religious movement, as reflected in the name of the text.[40]

Salomon does not, however, draw any conclusions about the date of the text. The metrical and linguistic evidence suggests that the main portion of the *Muṇḍaka Upaniṣad* is from roughly the same time period as the *Kaṭha* and *Śvetāśvatara*, or perhaps slightly older. The fact that the *Muṇḍaka Upaniṣad* nevertheless seems to have borrowed a stanza from the *Kaṭha Upaniṣad* suggests that the transmitters of the *Muṇḍaka Upaniṣad* and those of the *Kaṭha* seem to have been in close contact with each other, allowing borrowing to occur after the first composition of the texts.

Satyam eva jayate: The *Muṇḍaka Upaniṣad* and the Indian national emblem

One line from the *Muṇḍaka Upaniṣad* is particularly well known to modern Indians: *Satyam eva jayate* – "truth alone prevails," or alternatively "he wins truth alone" or "reality alone prevails." In the Upaniṣadic text, this line is embedded in a stanza that describes the path to the highest reality:

> Truth alone prevails, not untruth.
> By truth the path to the gods is laid out,
> The path by which the sages travel, their desires fulfilled,
> To where the supreme abode of truth is found.[41]

The first half-line of this stanza is embedded in the State Emblem of India, which depicts lions standing on top a circular base, with the words *Satyam eva jayate* written in *devanāgarī* script underneath. The emblem appears on Indian currency, official government letterhead, and on Indian passports. The artwork is based on the Lion column of the emperor Ashoka from Sarnath (ca. 250 BCE). The original column features four lions standing back to back, although only three of them are visible on the two-dimensional emblem. The four lions are thought to represent the Four Noble Truths of Buddhism, although they could also symbolize the four parts of Ashoka's empire, or the four directions of the sky. A horse, a bull, an elephant, and a lion are carved into the circular base; of these, the horse and the bull can be seen on the emblem, along with a wheel that represents the Buddhist Wheel of the Law (*Dharma Cakra*, also prominently featured on the Indian flag). The choice of an ancient Buddhist imperial artwork and an accompanying line from a Hindu Upaniṣad on the emblem of the modern state of India suggests that both the majesty of the column and the religious sentiment of the Sanskrit line were appropriate symbols for the new republic when they were first adopted in 1950.

Notes

1 *Muṇḍaka Upaniṣad* 1.1.
2 *Muṇḍaka Upaniṣad* 1.3.
3 *Muṇḍaka Upaniṣad* 3.2.10.

4 See F. M. Müller, *The Upanishads. Vol. II. Sacred Books of the East*, Vol. 15. Oxford: Clarendon Press 1884. (Reprint New Delhi: Atlantic Publishers, 1990: xxvi.) Compare P. Olivelle, *The Upaniṣads*. New York/Oxford: Oxford University Press, 1996: 266.
5 *Muṇḍaka Upaniṣad* 2.1.10.
6 *Muṇḍaka Upaniṣad* 2.2.8.
7 *Muṇḍaka Upaniṣad* 3.2.9.
8 *Muṇḍaka Upaniṣad* 3.2.10.
9 *Muṇḍaka Upaniṣad* 3.1.5, 3.2.6.
10 *Muṇḍaka Upaniṣad* 3.2.6.
11 *Muṇḍaka Upaniṣad* 1.2.11.
12 *Muṇḍaka Upaniṣad* 3.2.11.
13 *Muṇḍaka Upaniṣad* 1.2.11.
14 *Muṇḍaka Upaniṣad* 1.2.13.
15 *Muṇḍaka Upaniṣad* 2.1.2.
16 *Muṇḍaka Upaniṣad* 2.1.4.
17 *Muṇḍaka Upaniṣad* 2.1.3.
18 *Muṇḍaka Upaniṣad* 2.1.6.
19 *Muṇḍaka Upaniṣad* 2.1.7.
20 *Muṇḍaka Upaniṣad* 3.1.3.
21 *Muṇḍaka Upaniṣad* 3.1.8.
22 *Muṇḍaka Upaniṣad* 1.2.11.
23 *Praśna Upaniṣad* 1.10.
24 *Muṇḍaka Upaniṣad* 2.2.5.
25 *Muṇḍaka Upaniṣad* 3.2.3 = *Kaṭha Upaniṣad* 1.2.23.
26 *Muṇḍaka Upaniṣad* 1.5.
27 *Muṇḍaka Upaniṣad* 1.6.
28 *Muṇḍaka Upaniṣad* 2.2.2.
29 *Muṇḍaka Upaniṣad* 1.7.
30 *Muṇḍaka Upaniṣad* 3.2.9.
31 *Muṇḍaka Upaniṣad* 2.2.9.
32 *Muṇḍaka Upaniṣad* 2.2.8.
33 *Muṇḍaka Upaniṣad* 1.4. The same idea is expressed in 1.2.
34 *Muṇḍaka Upaniṣad* 1.1.5.
35 *Muṇḍaka Upaniṣad* 1.1.4–5.
36 *Muṇḍaka Upaniṣad* 1.2.9.
37 *Muṇḍaka Upaniṣad* 1.2.10.
38 *Muṇḍaka Upaniṣad* 1.2.12.
39 Salomon 1981: 100.
40 Salomon 1981: 102.
41 *Muṇḍaka Upaniṣad* 3.16.

Further reading

Bhattacharya, V. 1941. "A Linguistic Note on the Muṇḍaka Upaniṣad" *Indian Historical Quarterly* 17: 89–91.

Hertel, J. 1924. *Muṇḍaka-Upaniṣad, Kritische Ausgabe mit Rodardruck der Erstausgabe.* Indo-iranische Quellen und Forschungen, Heft III. Leipzig: H. Haessel Verlag.

Martin-Dubost, P. 1978. *Muṇḍakopaniṣadbhāṣya: Commentaire de Śaṅkara sur la Muṇḍaka Upaniṣad.* Paris: M. Allard Editions Orientales.

Maury, J. 1943. *Muṇḍaka Upaniṣad.* Paris: Adrien Maisonneuve.

Rau, W. 1965. "Versuch einer deutschen Übersetzung der Muṇḍaka-Upaniṣad" *Asiatische Studien* 18: 216–226.
Salomon, R. 1981. "A Linguistic Analysis of the Muṇḍaka Upaniṣad" *Wiener Zeitschrift für die Kunde Südasiens* 25: 91–105.
Smith, R. M. 1976. "The Muṇḍaka Upaniṣad Reconsidered" *Vishveshvaranand Indological Journal* 14: 17–40.

31 The *Kaṭha Upaniṣad*

Elizabeth Schiltz

The *Kaṭha Upaniṣad* is, at one time, both a compelling tale of a father–son interaction gone wrong, and a careful reflection on deep philosophical questions about the self.

The story at the heart of the *Kaṭha Upaniṣad* may have already been classic by the time of its ancient composition – its characters even seem to appear in the earlier *Rg Veda* (X.135). The text begins as young Naciketas raises pious worries about the efficacy of his father's ritual sacrifice of older cattle: "their water drunk, their grass eaten, their milk milked, their strength spent, joyless, verily, are those worlds to which he, who presents such cows goes" (*Kaṭha Upaniṣad* 1.3). Receiving no satisfactory explanation, Naciketas persists even further, asking three times "Papa, to whom will you give me?" (KU 1.4, Hume translation) His father's seemingly exasperated answer – "To Death I give you!" (KU 1.4) – sets the action of the story in motion, as Naciketas now finds himself bound by his father's oath to Yama, the god of Death.

Naciketas dutifully departs for Yama's house – where, contrary to the contemporary standards of hospitality, he waits three days to be received. Upon discovering the waiting brahmin, Yama is horrified to have kept a "venerable guest" waiting – and, in recompense, offers to grant the boy three wishes.

Naciketas' first request is sweetly filial; he hopes that, upon his release, his father would greet him happily, and "with anger gone" (KU 1.10). Death quickly grants this wish. His second request is more ambitious – he asks for a description of the fire sacrifice by which "the dwellers in heaven gain immortality" (KU 1.13). Yama grants this wish, as well – and, as an added bonus, renames this important ritual in honor of his guest. Naciketas' third request, however, goes even further: Wisely taking advantage of his audience with Yama himself, he asks for an account of the fate of the individual after death. The god resists this final wish. Claiming that "even the gods of old had doubt on this point," he tries to tempt the boy with wild riches such as "noble maidens," chariots, elephants, horses, cattle, and land – and even with longevity for himself and his descendants (KU 1.23). Naciketas, however, is not to be denied – and his rejection of a life as "enjoyer of desires" in favor of understanding leads to a rigorous philosophical discussion of desires, the self, and knowledge of the ultimate.

Naciketas' choice: On desire and the good

On its face, Naciketas' repudiation of Yama's offer seems grounded in an assessment of the ephemeral and "transient" nature of bodily pleasures – "they wear out, O Yama." At the same time, however, Naciketas also points to a deeper difference between the value of his chosen boon and Yama's proposed replacements. As he asserts, even the luster of a long human life of the continuous satisfaction of desires pales when he considers it in contrast to the unqualified experiences of the divine. His own (rather unique) situation seems to highlight a difference in kind between the two alternatives: "Having approached this undecaying immortality, what decaying mortal on this earth below who (now) knows and meditates on the pleasures of beauty and love, will delight in an over-long life?" (KU 1.28). Naciketas will stick with his chosen boon – and Yama will finally relent.

Yama begins with an analysis of the wise choice that Naciketas has just made. As Yama asserts, Naciketas has had to choose between two distinct courses – the pleasant and the good. The ignorant choose the pleasant – a "tortuous path" where they "go about like blind men led by one who is himself blind," and are subject to a cycle of repeated deaths and rebirths. (KU 2.5–6) The wise, by contrast, choose the good and so "[leave] behind both joy and sorrow" (KU 2.12). Interestingly, Yama asserts that this good of understanding is not available through reasoning – for it is "inconceivable ... subtler than the subtle" (KU 2.8). It can, however, be attained by the wise who are "taught by one who knows" (KU 2.8). Happily, Naciketas has found such a teacher – and that teacher is convinced of his seriousness. Yama's instruction can now commence.

Yama's instruction: On the self

The boon which Naciketas has requested is an account of "what there is in the great passing-on" – rather charmingly, he has asked Death himself for an account of the fate of the individual after death. (KU 1.29) Interestingly, the boy's discussion up to this point reveals that he already assumes that the individual persists in some form after death; in his exchange with his father, he asserts that "a mortal ripens like corn, and like corn he is born again" (KU 1.6). Further, he also seems to presuppose that that which transmigrates is not the same as the "transient" phenomenal body and its experiences in the empirical world (KU1.26). Naciketas' request, then, is for an analysis of that persistence. What is the nature of that which endures? How is it related to our phenomenal selves? Why is it so beneficial – and yet so difficult – to come to know about it?

Yama immediately confirms Naciketas' assumptions. He draws a distinction between the phenomenal individual and its "knowing" or "great" self: "Smaller than the small, greater than the great, the self is set in the heart of every creature" (KU 2.20, 3.11). This great self is ultimately not only distinct from the phenomenal body, but also from its actions and experiences in the empirical world (KU 2.21–22). Further, this self is that which persists – it is "unborn, eternal, abiding, and primeval," and therefore simply not subject to changes like birth and death: "if the slayer thinks that he slays or if the slain think that he is slain, both of them do not understand. He neither slays nor is he slain" (KU 2.18–19). Knowledge of this great self *as* the self is the good to which Yama has been referring. However, as Yama reasserts, this knowledge is not available to those who are unworthy: "Not he who has not desisted from evil ways, not he who is not tranquil, not he who has not a concentrated mind, not even he whose mind is not composed can reach this (self) through right knowledge" (KU 2.24).

While, at this point, Yama has provided the account that Naciketas requested, much is still left unexplained. He has made it clear that there is a higher self which persists after death, the difficult knowledge of which is salvific, however he has not yet explained how it is related to our phenomenal selves. To this end, Yama introduces one of the great images of Indian philosophy – he compares a manned chariot to the individual. The actual vehicle is likened to the physical body, while the charioteer is likened to the human intellect. The horses are akin to the senses, and the road is like the objects of sense. The charioteer, then, controls and directs the horses by the means of reins, which represent the mind (*manas*, which is often understood to refer to the physical organ). Interestingly, the great self itself is the "lord of the chariot" – the royal passenger along for the ride. Yama concludes: "the self associated with the body, the senses and the mind – wise men declare – is the enjoyer" (KU 3.3–4).

This chariot metaphor illuminates the *Kaṭha Upaniṣad*'s view of the self in fascinating ways. First, and perhaps most importantly, it explicates and develops Naciketas and Yama's shared presupposition that the individual and the higher, persisting self are not identical. Instead, there is a "great" self which is, in itself, distinct from so much of what we traditionally understand as ourselves – our body, senses, mind, and intellect. When this self is associated with those personal components, the entire composite experiences and acts in the sensible world.

Ultimately, then, Yama indicates that our nature is complex. At the surface level, we can understand ourselves as a whole, manned chariot – we are those individual, phenomenal selves that are subject to changes, that act in the world, and that are attracted to pleasure. However, if we behave as if this analysis is final, our intellect may fail to control our "wicked" horses and our chariot, and we will "reach not the goal but come back into mundane life" (KU 3.7). At a deeper level, however, we can also understand ourselves as the honored passenger in that chariot – we are the self that experiences and "enjoys" the world through its association with our phenomenal selves. When we have that understanding, we can use the mind to control the (now-good) horses: he "who has understanding, who has control over his mind and (is) ever pure, reaches that goal from which he is not born again" (KU 3.8).

Readers of earlier chapters of this volume will recognize the concept of the *ātman* in Yama's description of the great self – and the *Kaṭha Upaniṣad* will use precisely this word to gloss the "great self" several times in the text. Those familiar with other texts in this tradition may also hear echoes of the image that appears in the *Rg Veda*, the *Mundaka Upaniṣad*, and the *Svetasvatara Upaniṣads*: "Two birds, companions (who are) always united, cling to the self-same tree. Of these two, the one eats the sweet fruit and the other looks on without eating" (*Mundaka Upaniṣad* III.1.1). One thing that distinguishes the *Kaṭha Upaniṣad*, however, is that Naciketas' request for instruction has compelled Yama to go further – to give a robust account of the way these two birds are related – of the way this *ātman* is related to human experience both here and in the hereafter.

Other chariots, other selves

Remarkably, it is the case that texts in both the Platonic and Buddhist traditions also develop fascinating analyses of the individual through a comparison between the self and a chariot. One way of illuminating the distinctive characteristics of Yama's account is to consider it in light of these provocatively dissimilar accounts.

In Plato's *Phaedrus*, Socrates also discusses the nature of the self and its relationship to actions with a younger interlocutor. To this end, Socrates takes a page from Yama's playbook: While an exposition of its nature would be a "long tale to tell," he can easily compare the soul to a chariot, for "what it resembles, that a man might tell in briefer compass" (*Phaedrus* 246a). As such, Socrates likens the soul to "the union of powers in a team of winged steeds and their winged charioteer" (246a–b). This charioteer has a challenging task – while one of the horses is "noble and good," the other is "hot-blooded, consorting with wantonness and vainglory; shaggy of ear, deaf, and hard to control with whip and goad" (*Phaedrus* 253d–e).

Socrates asserts that the attainment of the highest goal of the chariot is a consequence of the proper guidance of the charioteer, which allows it to skillfully draw upon the strength of both of the winged (but mismatched) horses. If the charioteer is successful – "if the victory be won by the higher elements of mind" – it can navigate upwards, to the heavens. This "plain of Truth" is where the gods dwell: "it is there that true being dwells, without color or shape, that cannot be touched; reason alone, the soul's pilot, can behold it, and all true knowledge is knowledge thereof" (*Phaedrus* 256b, 247c). If, however, the charioteer is unable to control its horses, the soul sinks down to earth, and takes on a physical body. Although we commonly misunderstand this, living and acting beings are thus actually the composite of a fallen, immortal soul and a mortal body which "seems by reason of the soul's power to move itself" (*Phaedrus* 246c).

Given that Plato tends to treat the soul as the "real" individual, it is not at all surprising to see the *Phaedrus* account of the self primarily focused on the soul. What *is* surprising is to see Plato introduce a soul of such functional complexity. In the *Phaedo*, for instance, the soul is characterized as "uniform," "invariable," and entirely rational – the senses and desires are associated with the body, and regarded as "impediments" whose presence "prevents the soul from attaining to truth" (*Phaedo* 78d, 66a). Here, in the *Phaedrus*, however, the soul itself has three parts. While this soul's tripartition suggests those he introduced in the *Republic* – the charioteer is akin to the rational part, the better horse is like the *thumos* (or honor-seeking part), and the disobedient horse is like the appetitive part – the chariot-image introduces yet a further layer of interdependence. The *Phaedrus* soul is a *sumphatos dunamis* – "a natural union of powers" or "a power naturally grown-together" (*Phaedrus* 246a, translations of Charles Griswold 92 and Martha Nussbaum 214, respectively). The (rational) charioteer must marshal the strength of the better (*thumos*) horse and the worse (appetitive) horse in order to head in the correct direction, achieve the soul's proper goal, and so experience the bliss of the direct contemplation of truth.

While Socrates and Yama introduce similar images to convey the intricate structure of the individual, there are profound and revealing discontinuities between the chariot-selves they articulate. In the *Phaedrus*, Socrates conceives of the self as the individual union of reason, *thumos*, and desire – which, when poorly controlled, is incarnated in a physical body. It is the seat of thought, the source of motivation, and the cause of action. In the *Kaṭha Upaniṣad*, by contrast, the great self is not the intellect, mind or senses – but rather the royal passenger along for the ride. Yama characterizes the self as "the experiencer"; it is "that *by which* (one perceives) form, taste, smell, sounds and touches of love, *by that* alone one perceives" (KU 4.5–6; emphasis mine). While the Platonic self is characterized by discursive thought, the upaniṣadic self is that consciousness that lies behind and illuminates those thoughts as they occur.

Further, in the *Phaedrus*, Socrates asserts that the goal of the charioteer is to control and employ the power of the horses, so that it can guide the chariot to its proper goal, the "plain of Truth" (*Phaedrus* 256b). Here, the rational charioteer can come to know the eternal forms of concepts such as justice, temperance, and beauty: "Even as the mind of a god is nourished by reason and knowledge, so also is it with every soul … when at last she has beheld being she is well content, and contemplating truth she is nourished and prospers" (*Phaedrus* 247d). While the *Kaṭha Upaniṣad* also emphasizes the charioteer's duty to control the horses, the goal is utterly and completely different. Here, the charioteer restrains the mind in order to get beyond both the senses and "the understanding" – and so appreciate its royal passenger and go inward to "the end of the journey, that supreme abode of the all-pervading" (KU 3.10, 9).

Interestingly, even the seeming similarity between the two texts' emphasis on attaining freedom from rebirth belies deep discontinuities. In Socrates' account, a philosopher's life of restraint and wisdom allows him to avoid the ten-thousand year cycle of reincarnation and revisit the plain of Truth after a mere three thousand years. There, the philosopher's individual and immortal soul exists with and in contemplation of the "blessed vision" of the forms – the "noblest prize" that can be won (*Phaedrus* 250b, 256d). While Yama's account also asserts that the life of restraint and wisdom allows the individual to be freed from the cycle of reincarnation, the goal is utterly different. For his part, he goes "beyond the spirit [where] there is nothing ... That is the end (of the journey); that is the final goal" (KU 3.11).

As I have argued elsewhere, the *Kaṭha Upaniṣad* and the *Phaedrus* are similar insofar as they employ the image of a chariot in order to articulate a moral psychology, an account on which an analysis of the individual's essential nature and function issues in normative prescriptions. However, at the same time, Yama and Socrates' complex visions of that self and its proper goal are distinct in deep and revealing ways.

In the Theraveda Buddhist *Visuddhi-magga*, Buddhaghosa also likens the self to a chariot – but to a very different end. Like the earlier *Questions of King Milinda*, it is argued that none of the individual parts of a chariot (axle, wheel, pole, etc.) are the chariot; ultimately, the word "chariot" is "a mode of expression" for the constituent parts of a chariot placed in a certain relation to each other, but "in the absolute sense, there is no chariot." In the same way, none of the "five attachment groups" – bodily form, sensations, perceptions, predispositions, and consciousness – are the self; ultimately, the words "living entity" and "ego" are "but a mode of expression" for their presence. However, "in the absolute sense, there is no living entity there to form a basis for such figments as 'I am,' or 'I'" (*Visuddhi-magga* 284–5).

Interestingly, Yama could agree with Buddhaghosa to a certain extent, here – the *Kaṭha Upaniṣad* also clearly indicates that it is a mistake to take a common-sense understanding of the phenomenal self as final. The Buddhist chariot images join the Upaniṣadic and Platonic ones in functioning to highlight the complexity of what we commonly take to be ourselves – and to indicate the ways in which a more rigorous analysis illuminates prescriptions for behavior.

As we have seen, however, Yama's analysis serves to redirect our attention to the "great" self – that which is "the stable among the unstable" (KU 2.22). Buddhaghosa's analysis, by contrast, also applies to the component parts of the self – just as the individual self can be reduced to its component parts, so too can the five attachment groups. On this Buddhist account, then, it is ultimately the case that *nothing* is unified and stable in such a way that it provides an absolute ground for the self. Thus, both the "heresy of the persistence of existences," and that of "the annihilation of existences" count as mistakes to be avoided. "The intelligent … who knows things as they really are," then, takes the right approach: "is on the road to aversion for things, to absence of passion for them, and to cessation from them" (*Visuddhi-magga* 286). Thus, in a fascinating turn, while Yama's account points to the persistence of the great self and Buddhaghosa points to the opposite, both read the conclusion as restraint of desire in favor of wisdom.

Ātman and *Brahman*

It is unsurprising that the disparities between the respective analyses of the chariot-selves found in the *Phaedrus*, *Visuddhi-magga*, and *Kaṭha Upaniṣad* correlate with the disparities between their fundamental metaphysical assumptions. Plato develops his account of the eternal soul and transient body in terms of his dualism: "The soul is most like that which is divine, immortal, intelligible, uniform, indissoluble, and ever self-consistent and invariable, whereas body is most like that which is human, mortal, multiform, unintelligible, dissoluble, and never self-consistent." Because it is akin to the "realm of the pure and everlasting and immortal and changeless," the Platonic soul "reaches out after reality" through reason (*Phaedo* 80a – 81d). Further, Buddhaghosa's no-self is in keeping with the Buddhist theory of dependent origination. As such, everything that exists – including what we understand as ourselves – does so only insofar as the bases on which it depends do: "nothing here exists but what has its own antecedents" (*Visuddhi-magga* 285). In the same way, Yama understands and elaborates the "great self" in terms of his own ontology. Readers of the other *Upaniṣads* – and of other chapters in this volume – will not be surprised to learn that much of the balance of the *Kaṭha Upaniṣad* as we have it is taken up with Yama's drawing the link between this higher self and the Ultimate, or between *ātman* and *Brahman*. Happily, this analysis will contribute to answers to the last of the questions about Yama's account with which we started: It will explain why is it so valuable – and yet so challenging – to come to know about the higher self.

Yama initially associates the self and the Ultimate by describing *Brahman* as "hidden" or seated in the heart: "He who was born of old from austerity, was born of old from the waters, who stands, having entered the secret place (of the heart) and looked forth through beings. This verily is that …" (KU 3.12, 4.6). However, he soon makes clear that it is not simply the case that the self is paired with the Supreme; it is instead the case that *ātman* is actually identical with *Brahman*: "That person who is awake in those that sleep, shaping desire after desire, that, indeed, is the pure. That is *Brahman*, that, indeed, is called the immortal" (KU 5.8). Even further – this *Brahman* is not merely the inner self of persons. Ultimately, it is the ground of everything: "no one ever goes beyond that" (KU 4.6, 9).

This characterization of the *ātman* as identical with *Brahman* helps to explain Yama's insistence that knowledge of the higher self is salvific. If it is the case that the "real" self is ultimately non-different from the ground of being, then our common understanding of the self as a discrete individual reflects a deep ignorance – and one of a kind that grounds just the sort of self-interested, desire-driven behaviors that lead one away from knowledge. As such, Yama asserts that failure to recognize this identity causes one to be subject to rebirth: "Whatever is here, that (is) there. Whatever is there, that, too, is here. Whoever perceives anything like manyness here goes from death to death." (KU 3.10) Knowledge of this insight, by contrast, leads to bliss:

> The one, controller (of all), the inner self of all things, who makes his one form manifold, to the wise who perceive him as abiding in the soul, to them is eternal bliss – to no others. The one eternal amid the transient, the conscious amid the conscious, the one amid many, who grants their desires to the wise who perceive Him as abiding in the soul, to them is eternal peace and to no others.
>
> (KU 5.12–13)

Of course, the identity of the *ātman* with *Brahman* also helps to explain why this knowledge is so difficult to attain. If Brahman is the ground of all being, it is the ground of everything in the phenomenal world. While it is one, it appears to us in a seemingly endless multiplicity of forms: "As fire which is one, entering this world becomes varied in shape according to the object (it burns), so also the one Self within all beings becomes varied according to whatever (it enters) and also exists outside (them all)" (KU 5.9). As such, it is simply impossible to perceive Brahman in the phenomenal world: "Not within the field of vision stands this form. No one soever sees Him with the eye. By heart, by thought, by mind apprehended, they who know Him become immortal" (6.9).

In some places in the text, Yama goes even further – asserting that Brahman cannot be known by the mind or intellect, either. Insofar as the rational components are directed externally and conceiving of existing things in terms of multiplicity, their attempts will miss as well. Radhakrishnan reminds us that the goal is ultimately an internal one:

> The ātman is not an object of any sort but is the eternal subject. We hear, touch, see, feel and think by the ātman. By withdrawing from all outward things, by retreating into the ground of our own soul, in the remotest depth of the soul, we find the Infinite. There the Self is raised above all empirical concepts of sound, touch, form, etc.
>
> (Radhakrishnan 629)

Young Naciketas' choice has truly paid off. In the *Kaṭha Upaniṣad*, his rejection of a life as "enjoyer of desires" in favor of understanding has led to a rigorous philosophical discussion of desires, the self, and the nature and value of the knowledge of the ultimate. Yama exhorts him to "Arise, awake, having attained thy boons, understand (them)" – he has walked a path that is "sharp as the edge of a razor … and difficult to tread" (KU 3.14). Naciketas will return to his father wiser, indeed.

References

Buddhaghosa 1957. *Visuddhi-magga* trans. H. C. Warren in Sarvapelli Radhakrishnan and Charles A. Moore (eds.) *A Sourcebook in Indian Philosophy*. Princeton, NJ: Princeton University Press, 284–286.

Griswold, Charles 1986. *Self-Knowledge in Plato's Phaedrus*. New Haven, CT: Yale University Press.

Katha Upanishad 1953. In S. Radhakrishnan (ed. and trans.) *The Principal Upanisads*. New York: Harper and Brothers Publishers, 42–50.

Katha Upanishad 1957. Trans. R. E. Hume, in Sarvapelli Radhakrishnan and Charles A. Moore (ed.) *A Sourcebook in Indian Philosophy*. Princeton, NJ: Princeton University Press, 284–286.

Mundaka Upanishad 1953. In S. Radhakrishnan (ed. and trans.) *The Principal Upanisads*. New York: Harper and Brothers Publishers, 669–692.

Nussbaum, Martha 1986. *The Fragility of Goodness*. Cambridge: Cambridge University Press.

Plato 1961. *Phaedo*, trans. Hugh Tredennick in Edith Hamilton (ed.) *Plato's Collected Dialogues*. Princeton, NJ: Princeton University Press, 40–98.

Plato 1961. *Phaedrus*, trans. R. Hackforth in Edith Hamilton (ed.) *Plato's Collected Dialogues*. Princeton, NJ: Princeton University Press, 475–525.

Radhakrishnan, S. 1953. *The Principal Upanisads*. New York: Harper and Brothers Publishers.

32 The *Śvetāśvatara Upaniṣad*

Signe Cohen

Like the *Kaṭha Upaniṣad*, the *Śvetāśvatara Upaniṣad* is affiliated with the *Black Yajurveda*. The two Upaniṣads share some of the same themes and have several stanzas in common. Unlike the *Kaṭha Upaniṣad*, which contains a few glimpses of theistic thought, however, the *Śvetāśvatara Upaniṣad* is a theistic text throughout. Theism is present sporadically in many early Upaniṣads, but is first encountered in the Upaniṣads formally affiliated with the *Ṛgveda*. Theistic ideas are notably absent in the earliest texts affiliated with the *Yajurveda*, such as the *Bṛhadāraṇyaka Upaniṣad*. It is only in the "middle Upaniṣads" of the *Yajurveda*, the *Kaṭha* and the *Śvetāśvatara*, that theistic ideas are fully accepted and incorporated.

While the *Śvetāśvatara Upaniṣad* contains several common Upaniṣadic themes, such as the unity between *ātman* and *brahman*, it also presents some unique new teachings. The *Śvetāśvatara Upaniṣad* is the first text that systematically identifies the cosmic force *brahman* with a personal god. The text is an important transitional work, bridging the older "classical" Upaniṣads and the later theistic Upaniṣads that identify *ātman* and *brahman* with gods such as Śiva and Viṣṇu.

The *Śvetāśvatara Upaniṣad* is the only one of the classical Upaniṣads ascribed to an individual, non-mythological author. Upaniṣads are not usually named after individual authors; they are more often named after schools of Vedic recitation (*Aitareya*, *Taittirīya*, *Kaṭha*, etc.). No information is given in other texts about Śvetāśvatara ("he of the white mule"); he is only mentioned in this Upaniṣad:

> By the power of his penance, and by the grace of God,
> the wise Śvetāśvatara first realized *Brahman*
> and declared that, the highest, the pure, to the advanced ascetics,
> that which brings pleasure to the company of sages.[1]

The individuality expressed in the title of this Upaniṣad is also reflected in the text itself. The *Śvetāśvatara Upaniṣad* contains several unique teachings, such as the idea of a threefold *brahman*, two different levels of the *ātman*, and the existence of an eternal female principle.

Brahman in the *Śvetāśvatara Upaniṣad*

The *Śvetāśvatara Upaniṣad* differs from the other earlier Upaniṣads of the *Yajurveda* in several ways. Significantly, the *Śvetāśvatara Upaniṣad* opens with the question Yājñavalkjya warned the female philosopher Gārgī not to ask in *Bṛhadāraṇyaka Upaniṣad*: "Those who speak of *Brahman* say: 'What is the cause of *brahman*?' "[2] While Gārgī was compelled to withdraw her question so that her "head would not shatter apart," the inquiry into the ultimate cause of *brahman* itself takes center stage in the *Śvetāśvatara Upaniṣad.*

In the earlier Upaniṣads, and particularly those of the *Yajurveda*, *brahman* itself *is* the first cause, and there can be nothing beyond. But by the time of the composition of the *Śvetāśvatara Upaniṣad*, speculations about some ultimate principle beyond *brahman* began to flourish. Like Gārgī, the author of the *Śvetāśvatara Upaniṣad* posits an entity greater than even *brahman* itself, a being described as a personal god. The answer to the text's opening question is presented in *Śvetāśvatara Upaniṣad*'s final chapter:

> He who created *brahman* of old,
> He who gave him the Vedas.
> He who manifests himself by his intelligence –
> In that God do I, desiring liberation, take refuge.[3]

According to this verse, *brahman* is itself created by a higher entity, *deva* ("God"). But not only is *brahman* no longer presented as the highest reality in this text, the concept of *brahman* itself has become more complex than in the earlier Upaniṣads: *brahman* contains within itself a triad (*trayam*), consisting of the lower *ātman*, the higher *ātman*, and *pradhāna*, the material stuff of the universe.[4] It is the knowledge of this tripartite *brahman* leads a person to liberation from rebirth.[5] The relationship between *ātman* and *brahman* in the *Śvetāśvatara Upaniṣad* is an intricate, even paradoxical one: *Brahman* is seen as the universe in its totality, encompassing a lower and a higher *ātman*, but the *ātman* is also the divine creator of all, *brahman* included, and ultimately to be identified with a personal god.

Pradhāna in the *Śvetāśvatara Upaniṣad*

An important part of the triad contained within *brahman* is *pradhāna*, or primordial nature, the stuff from which the world is made. This concept is an important precursor to the concept of *prakṛti* ("nature") which is an essential part of later Sāṃkhya and Yoga philosophy. In Sāṃkhya-Yoga, *prakṛti* is everything, physical and mental, that is not the pure consciousness (*puruṣa*). Here, *prakṛti* includes the intellect (*buddhi*), the sense of self, the mind, the sense organs, the organs of action, and the subtle elements, as well as the physical elements. It is unclear whether *pradhāna* has a similar technical meaning in the *Śvetāśvatara Upaniṣad*. In the *Śvetāśvatara Upaniṣad*, *pradhāna*, the third member of the triad contained within *brahman*, is referred to as *śakti*, or "power."[6] Notably, *śakti* is a feminine noun in Sanskrit, and while *pradhāna* itself is not grammatically feminine, other passages suggest that *pradhāna* is nevertheless seen as a female aspect of *brahman*. In an untranslatable pun, the *Śvetāśvatara Upaniṣad* plays with the words *aja*/*ajā*, which means both "unborn" and "goat." While presenting the image of two male goats that are both the lovers of one female goat, the text simultaneously suggests that the two eternal and unborn male principles (the higher and lower *ātman*) are the lovers of the female unborn, the primordial nature.[7] The idea of nature as feminine resonates with the Sāṃkhya notion of *prakṛti*, primordial nature as feminine, although *prakṛti* is a feminine noun and *pradhāna* is not. In another striking image in the *Śvetāśvatara Upaniṣad*, God (*deva*) himself is said to cover himself with the threads of *pradhāna*, like a spider with its own threads.[8] This image suggests, then, that *pradhāna* is simultaneously God's work and creation, and that which conceals this divine being.

The two *ātmans* in the *Śvetāśvatara Upaniṣad*

The *Śvetāśvatara Upaniṣad* distinguishes clearly between two forms of *ātman*: A lower, unenlightened self, and a limitless immortal self. The lower self is compared to a goose (*haṃsa*), fluttering around in the vast wheel of *brahman*. This lower *ātman* is "not lord" (*anīśa*), and bound to the world.[9] This lower self can be liberated when it realizes its own nature and its ultimate identity with the higher *ātman*. The idea of a lower and higher aspect of one and the same reality foreshadows both Nāgārjuna's Madhyamaka Buddhism, and Śaṅkara's non-dualist Vedānta.

The distinction between two aspects of the *ātman* are among the many innovations of this extraordinary Upaniṣad. The higher *ātman* is referred to as an "impeller" (*preritṛ*),[10] and as a god (*deva*). The use of the term *deva* to describe the higher *ātman* is characteristic of the *Śvetāśvatara Upaniṣad*: "That god, the maker of everything, the great *ātman*, always seated in the heart of the creatures ..."[11] Likewise, *ātman* is described as "one god, hidden in all creatures, all-pervading, the inner *ātman* of all beings ..." The characterization of *ātman* as god (*deva*), is characteristic of many of the Upaniṣads of the *Yajurveda*, as well as those of the *Ṛgveda*, but the precise interpretation of this term changes radically over time. While *ātman* is called *deva* as early as in the *Bṛhadāraṇyaka Upaniṣad* ("If one clearly sees him as *ātman*, as god ..."),[12] this term does not seem to carry the same devotional meaning in the oldest Upaniṣads. In the *Bṛhadāraṇyaka Upaniṣad*, for example, the concept of a personal god is expressly denied; *ātman* is called "god" simply because of its cosmic and primordial nature. The *Svetāśvatara Upaniṣad*, on the other hand, embraces the type of devotional theism which in older times was found only in the Upaniṣads affiliated with the *Ṛgveda*.

The divine *ātman* is the creator of the universe in the *Svetāśvatara Upaniṣad*:

> This god spreads out in manifold ways
> every creature in this field and destroys them again.
> When he has created again, he who is the Lord and master
> exercises his lordship, the great *ātman*.[13]

This concept of *ātman* as a primordial creator is first expressed in the *Bṛhadāraṇyaka Upaniṣad*: "In the beginning there was only *ātman*, in the form of *puruṣa* ..."[14] The main difference between the *Bṛhadāraṇyaka Upaniṣad* and the later *Śvetāśvatara Upaniṣad*, however, is that whereas the *Bṛhadāraṇyaka Upaniṣad* simply regards *ātman/brahman* as the first cause, and does not seem to attach any theistic undertones to the use of *deva*, the *Śvetāśvatara Upaniṣad* develops the idea of *ātman* as *deva* in a new direction much more reminiscent of the Upaniṣads of the *Ṛgveda*, such as the *Aitareya Upaniṣad*: "The *ātman* was all this, the One, in the beginning. No one else winked. He thought: 'Let me create the worlds!'"[15]

The *Kaṭha Upaniṣad*, a text closely related to the *Śvetāśvatara*, also refers to *ātman* as *deva*:

> Realizing god, who is difficult to be seen,
> hidden, being in the heart, dwelling in the deep,
> the ancient one, through the contemplation of the *adhyātman* (supreme *ātman*),
> the wise man abandons joy and sorrow.[16]

The *Śvetāśvatara Upaniṣad* goes further than any of the other classical Upaniṣads, however, in its pervasive and systematic theism. But unlike the Upaniṣads of the *Ṛgveda*, which tend to favor an identification of *ātman* with Indra, the *Śvetāśvatara Upaniṣad* introduces a new figure into the Upaniṣadic theistic speculations: the minor Vedic deity Rudra, well known from the old fire ritual called the Agnicayana ("The Building of the Fire").

The *Agnicayana* ritual in the *Śvetāśvatara Upaniṣad*

Echoes of the Vedic ritual of stacking the bricks that constitute the fire altar (*agnicayana*) are found throughout the *Śvetāśvatara Upaniṣad*. We should note that the Vedic *agnicayana* ritual involves an offering to Rudra, which may account for the presence of the god Rudra/Śiva in this text. The *Agnicayana* ritual was of particular importance in the late Vedic ritual text called the *Śatapathabrāhmaṇa*, but resonances of this ritual are found throughout the texts affiliated with the *Yajurveda*. In fact, one may argue that the *agnicayana* is to the *Yajurvedic* tradition what the *agniṣṭoma* ceremony, another fire ritual, is to the *Sāmavedic* tradition. This is perhaps not surprising, since the *adhvaryu* or Yajurveda priests were primarily the ones in charge of the practical aspect of the Vedic sacrifice, such as building the fire altar. It is no wonder, then, that the later texts of the Yajurveda are more concerned with the symbolic significance of the fire altar and its building than the significance of the soma pressing, which lay outside their domain.

Rudra/Śiva in the *Śvetāśvatara Upaniṣad*

The *Śvetāśvatara Upaniṣad* is often regarded as the earliest "document of rising Śaivism,"[17] or worship of the god Śiva. In this text, *ātman* is for the first time in the Upaniṣads identified with the deity Rudra/Śiva:

> The primordial material is perishable, but *Hara* (Śiva) is immortal and imperishable.
> One God rules over the perishable and the *ātman*.
> By meditating on him, by striving towards him, and by becoming the same substance as him,
> in the end, all illusion disappears.[18]
>
> For one is *Rudra*, without a second,
> who rules over these worlds with his ruling powers.
> He draws in all beings, and stands at the end of time
> as the protector, turning towards humankind.[19]
>
> He who is the source and origin of the gods,
> The ruler of all, *Rudra*, the great Seer,
> Created the Golden Embryo in the beginning –
> May he give us clear intelligence.[20]
>
> He is the face, head, and neck of all.
> He dwells deep in the heart of all beings.
> The Lord pervades everything.
> Therefore *Śiva* is everywhere.[21]
>
> More subtle than the subtle, in the midst of chaos,
> The creator of the universe, with numerous forms,
> The one who encompasses the universe –
> Knowing *Śiva*, one obtains endless peace.[22]

When there was darkness, there was neither day nor night.
Neither being nor non-being, only *Śiva* alone.
That is the imperishable, that is the glory of Savitṛ,
And from that comes the ancient wisdom.[23]

Rudra is a Vedic storm deity whose name means something like "the Howler." In the *Ṛgveda*, he is depicted as a wild and unpredictable god who can both bring disease and heal it. The term *śiva* is first applied to Rudra as an adjective in the *Ṛgveda*, with the meaning "kind" or "benevolent." Since the hymns to Rudra often express fear of the deity, it is likely that his epithet *śiva* was meant to implore him to be kind, in spite of the worshiper's fear of his wrath. Over time, Śiva became a personal name attached to Rudra, and eventually the epithet replaced the original name. In the *Śvetāśvatara Upaniṣad*, Rudra/Śiva has evolved beyond his Vedic origins and becomes a benign, all-powerful creator god, identified with the highest *ātman* itself. Why Rudra, out of all the gods of the Vedic pantheon? The answer to this question may lie in the *Śvetāśvatara Upaniṣad*'s affiliation with the *Yajurveda*. Rudra occupies a far more central position in the texts of the *Yajurveda* than in those of any other Vedic schools. The *Śatarudrīya*, a litany of the hundred names of Rudra, with an accompanying sacrifice, is described in the *Saṃhitā* texts of the *Yajurveda*: *Taittirīya Saṃhitā* 4.5, *Kaṭhā Saṃhitā* 17, 11–16, and *Maitrāyaṇīya Saṃhitā* 2.9, 2–9. The *Taittirīya Āraṇyaka* even identifies Rudra with the universe and with *puruṣa*,[24]which foreshadows Rudra's central position in the *Śvetāśvatara Upaniṣad*.

Sun, heat, and fire in the *Śvetāśvatara Upaniṣad*

The text of the *Śvetāśvatara Upaniṣad* is particularly rich in fire metaphors. Meditation on the sacred syllable *oṃ* is compared to creating a fire:

Making one's body the lower fire-stick
and the syllable *oṃ* the upper fire-stick,
by rubbing it continuously in meditation,
one will see god, just as one would see the hidden (fire).[25]

This human meditation has a divine precedent:

First yoking his mind and then stretching out his thoughts,
Savitṛ recognized fire as light and brought it here from the earth.[26]

With our minds yoked, we are impelled by the god Savitṛ
For a heavenly realm, and for strength.[27]

The Vedic sun god Savitṛ who brings light and fire to earth is here the divine archetype of the human being producing fire in his own body through meditation. Savitṛ is invoked in stanzas 2.1–5 and 2.7, which are all quotations from the *Yajurveda*. In these verses, different forms of the verb *yuj* ("to yoke") are used throughout. This is the verb that forms the basis of the noun *Yoga*, which literally means "yoking together" or a "joining." In one sense, then, Savitṛ is here the primordial Yoga teacher, showing humans by example how to produce the fire of meditation in their own bodies.

The fire metaphors in the *Śvetāśvatara Upaniṣad* are not only linked to meditation practices, however, but also evoke the Vedic *Pravargya* ritual, a ceremony involving heating up a sacred pot until it glows. This glowing pot is then ritually identified with the sun and with Rudra. The idea that Rudra is identical to the inner *ātman* may very well have its origins in the *Pravargya* ritual as well; in the description of the *Pravargya* in the *Kaṭha Āraṇyaka*, the sacrificer (*yajamāna*) is implicitly identified with Rudra.[28]

The age and composition of the text

The *Śvetāśvatara Upaniṣad* is composed in verse, but the metrical forms used throughout the text are not consistent. There are two kinds of meters used in the Upaniṣad, and they appear to belong to different time periods. The majority of the text is composed in the *triṣṭubh-jagatī* meter, which is also used in other Upaniṣads such as the *Kaṭha* and the *Muṇḍaka*. The metrical variants indicate a date of composition not too far removed from that of the *Kaṭha Upaniṣad*. Other parts of the text are composed in a younger meter called *śloka*, and these passages are in all likelihood later additions to the original text. These interpolated passages include stanzas 1.14, 1.16, 3.16, 3.17, 3.18, 4.10, 5.9, 5.10, 5.14, 6.19, 6.20, 6.22, and 6.23. Most of the added verses appear to be explanations of the preceding stanzas, and may simply have been pieces of later commentary that ended up being embedded in the older text of the Upaniṣad. Many other stanzas are simply quotations from other texts. Richard Salomon has pointed out, for example, that *Śvetāśvatara Upaniṣad* 4.18 is a paraphrase of the first three stanzas of the famous *Nāsadīya* hymn of the *Ṛgveda* (*ṚV* 10. 129).[29] Salomon suggests, convincingly, that the authors of the *Śvetāśvatara Upaniṣad* have modeled the stanza 4.18 on the *Ṛgveda* in order to create a Vedic legitimization for a growing Śiva cult.

Quotations and interpolated stanzas aside, the oldest core of the *Śvetāśvatara Upaniṣad* is linguistically and metrically very similar to the *Kaṭha* and *Muṇḍaka Upaniṣads*, and is likely composed around the same time.

Notes

1 *Śvetāśvatara Upaniṣad* 6.21.
2 *Bṛhadāraṇyaka Upaniṣad* 3.6.
3 *Śvetāśvatara Upaniṣad* 6.18.
4 *Śvetāśvatara Upaniṣad* 1.7, 1.8.

5 *Śvetāśvatara Upaniṣad* 1.7.
6 *Śvetāśvatara Upaniṣad* 1.3.
7 *Śvetāśvatara Upaniṣad* 1.9 and 4.5.
8 *Śvetāśvatara Upaniṣad* 6.10.
9 *Śvetāśvatara Upaniṣad* 1.8.
10 *Śvetāśvatara Upaniṣad* 1.6.
11 *Śvetāśvatara Upaniṣad* 4.17.
12 *Bṛhadāraṇyaka Upaniṣad* 4.4.15.
13 *Śvetāśvatara Upaniṣad* 5.3.
14 *Bṛhadāraṇyaka Upaniṣad* 1.4.1.
15 *Aitareya Upaniṣad* 1.1.
16 *Kaṭha Upaniṣad* 1.2.12.
17 J. Gonda, *Viṣṇuism and Śivaism: A Comparison*. London: School of Oriental and African Studies, 1970: 21. Bhandarkar, though regarding the *Śvetāśvatara Upaniṣad* as a text dedicated to Rudra/Śiva, comments on the text's "non-sectarian spirit" (R. G. Bhandarkar, *Vaiṣṇavism, Śaivism, and Minor Religious Systems*. Strassburg: Trübner, 1913: 151).
18 *Śvetāśvatara Upaniṣad* 1.10.
19 *Śvetāśvatara Upaniṣad* 3.2.
20 *Śvetāśvatara Upaniṣad* 3.4.
21 *Śvetāśvatara Upaniṣad* 3.11.
22 *Śvetāśvatara Upaniṣad* 4.14.
23 *Śvetāśvatara Upaniṣad* 4.18.
24 *Taittirīya Āraṇyaka* 3.11, 6.11.
25 *Śvetāśvatara Upaniṣad* 1.14.
26 *Śvetāśvatara Upaniṣad* 2.1.
27 *Śvetāśvatara Upaniṣad* 2.2.
28 M. Witzel, *Kaṭha Āraṇyaka: Critical Edition with a Translation into German and an Introduction*. Cambridge, MA: The Department of Sanskrit and Indian Studies, Harvard University, 2004: lxvi.
29 Salomon 1986: 165–167.

Further reading

Cohen, S. 1998. "The *Śvetāśvatara Upaniṣad* Reconsidered" *Acta Orientalia* 59: 150–178.

Johnston, E. 1930. "Some Sāṃkhya and Yoga Conceptions of the Śvetāśvatara Upaniṣad" *Journal of the Royal Asiatic Society* 106: 855–878.

Kunst, A. 1968. "Some Notes on the Interpretation of the Śvetāśvatara Upaniṣad" *Bulletin of the School of Oriental and African Studies* 31: 309–314. Also printed in: *Ludwik Sternbach Felicitation Volume*. Lucknow: Akhila Bharatiya Sanskrit Parishad (1979), 565–572.

Oberlies, T. 1988. "Die Śvetāśvatara Upaniṣad: Eine Studie ihrer Gotteslehre" *Wiener Zeitschrift für die Kunde Südasiensund Archiv für indische Philosophie* 32: 35–62.

Oberlies, T. 1995. "Die Śvetāśvatara-Upanisad. Einleitung – Edition und Übersetzung von Adhyāya I" *Wiener Zeitschrift für die Kunde Südasiensund Archiv für indische Philosophie* 39: 61–102.

Oberlies, T. 1996. "Die Śvetāśvatara-Upanisad. Edition und Übersetzung von Adhyāya II-III" *Wiener Zeitschrift für die Kunde Südasiensund Archiv für indische Philosophie* 40: 123 ff.

Oberlies, T. 1998. "Die Śvetāśvatara-Upanisad. Edition und Übersetzung von Adhyāya IV-VI" *Wiener Zeitschrift für die Kunde Südasiensund Archiv für indische Philosophie* 42: 77 ff.

Salomon, R. 1986. "The *Śvetāśvatara* and the *Nāsadīya:* Vedic Citations in a Śaiva Upaniṣad" *The Adyar Library Bulletin* 50: 165–178.

Smith, R. M. 1975. "Thinking-class Theism: The Śvetāśvatara Upaniṣad" *Journal of the Oriental Institute, Baroda* 24: 317–337

33 The *Kena Upaniṣad*

Signe Cohen

The *Kena Upaniṣad* is formally affiliated with the *Sāmaveda*, the Veda of Chants. It is also known as the *Talavakāra Upaniṣad*, because it forms a part of the *Talavakāra Brāhmaṇa*, which is also known as the *Jaiminīya Upaniṣad Brāhmaṇa*. The name *Tālavakāra Upaniṣad* connects it with the Talavakāra school of the *Sāmaveda*, perhaps named after a musician by the name of Talava mentioned in a Vedic text. The *Kena Upaniṣad* constitutes sections 4.18.1–4.21.1 of the *Jaiminīya Upaniṣad Brāhmaṇa*. Masato Fujii[1] has argued that the *Jaiminīya Upaniṣad Brāhmaṇa* is itself the very earliest Upaniṣad, occupying a transitional position between the older Vedic ritual texts and the new philosophical speculations of the Upaniṣads. According to Fujii, the entire *Jaiminīya Upaniṣad Brāhmaṇa* can be seen as an Upaniṣadic text, not merely the portion that is usually separated out and called the *Kena Upaniṣad*.

The *Kena Upaniṣad* is, like the *Īśā Upaniṣad*, named after the first word in the text: *keneṣitaṃ patati preṣitaṃ manaḥ* ("By whom (*kena*) directed, by whom compelled does the mind soar?"). The *Kena Upaniṣad* consists of four sections, two in verse and two in prose. Scholars have debated whether the verse sections and the prose sections are the same age, and whether they are two different texts that were later merged together into one.

The eighth-century commentator Śaṅkara wrote not just one, but two commentaries on the *Kena Upaniṣad*, known respectively as the *Padabhāṣya* ("The Word Commentary") and the *Vākyabhāṣya* ("The Sentence Commentary"). Both commentaries are regarded as the genuine work of Śaṅkara, but it is unclear why he would compose two separate commentaries to the *Kena Upaniṣad* and not to any other text.

Brahman in the *Kena Upaniṣad*

We find two different views of *brahman* in the *Kena Upaniṣad*. In the metrical portion (chapters 1 and 2), the supreme principle is an impersonal *brahman* without attributes, while the prose portion (chapters 3 and 4) describes a personal *brahman*. *Brahman* is described in wholly abstract terms in the first two chapters: "It is different from that which is known and beyond that which is unknown."[2] *Brahman* is the first cause and the impeller of everything. It is described as inexpressible, beyond the reach of language, but simultaneously as the origin of language:

> That which cannot be expressed by speech,
> through which speech itself is expressed –
> know that that alone is *brahman*,
> and not that which they worship here.[3]

How, then, could *brahman* possibly be known, if it lies beyond both language and thought? The *Kena Upaniṣad* suggests that *brahman* can be glimpsed through its effects in our world, even if it cannot be perceived directly. "Perhaps you do know slightly," suggests the *Kena Upaniṣad*, "the visible appearance of *brahman*. There is a part of it that you do know, and a part of it which is among the gods."[4]

It lies beyond sensory perception and thought:

> Sight cannot reach it,
> Nor thought, nor speech.
> We do not know, and we do not understand
> How one could teach it.[5]

Even though it is beyond our thoughts, *brahman* is still that through which (*kena*) all perception and thought is possible:

> That which cannot be grasped by the mind,
> through which the mind itself is grasped –
> know that that alone is *brahman*,
> and not that which they worship here.[6]

The prose portion of the *Kena Upaniṣad* contains a mythological tale of how *brahman* manifests itself and appears in front of the gods. The prose portion provides a series of vivid examples demonstrating that *brahman* is indeed that through which (*kena*) all things are done. The Upaniṣad tells us that *brahman* won a victory on behalf of the gods, but that the gods took credit for the victory and assumed that it took place because of their own power. *Brahman* can read their thoughts, and decides to teach them the truth about the limit of their own powers. *Brahman* challenges Agni, the old Vedic god of fire and a personification of Fire itself, to burn a blade of grass, but Agni is, inexplicably, unable to do so. Vāyu, the Vedic god of the wind, is likewise unable to blow away even a blade of grass. The thunder god Indra finally discovers, with the aid of the goddess Umā, that the apparition that challenges the gods is *brahman* itself, and that *brahman* is the force underlying everything, including the fire and the wind. The myth is recounted here to make the point that *brahman* is the origin of all power, including the power of the gods. The Vedic gods, revered in earlier texts, are here presented as inferior to the *brahman* of the Upaniṣad. The *Kena Upaniṣad* suggests that the only reason why people might, in an earlier age, have considered Indra the king of the gods, is precisely because of his encounter with *brahman*: "And that is why Indra is greater, as it were, than the other gods, because he came in contact with it and because he first recognized it as *brahman*."[7]

Although the verse and the prose sections of the Upaniṣad are thematically connected, the anthropomorphic *brahman* in sections 3 and 4 of the *Kena Upaniṣad* is so different from the inexpressible, completely abstract *brahman* in sections 1 and 2 that it is possible that the metrical and prose portions of the text are of different origin.

Tadvana, the mystical name of *brahman*

Like the other Upaniṣad affiliated with the *Sāmaveda*, the *Chāndogya Upaniṣad*, the *Kena Upaniṣad* plays with mystical sounds (the *Sāmaveda* is, after all, the Veda of songs) and esoteric *mantras*. *Brahman* itself is given a secret name in the *Kena Upaniṣad*:

> Its name is *Tadvana*, and it should be worshipped as Tadvana. When someone knows it in this fashion, everyone longs for him.[8]

The name *Tadvana* is not attested in any other text, and the word itself is quite cryptic. *Tad* means "that" in Sanskrit, while *vana* may mean either "forest" or "love." There appears to be some word play here involving *vana* and *vañc*, "to long for." *Tadvana* could therefore be understood as "its beloved" or "the desire for that," which could help explain why someone with that name would be someone that everyone longs for. It is also possible, however, that the name does not have a meaning and is merely meant to be an esoteric and secret word.[9] Each of the Vedic gods introduced in the third chapter of the text is designated both by their most common given name (Agni, Vāyu, and Indra) and by a somewhat lesser known epithet. Agni is addressed as "Jātavedas" ("the one who knows all beings"); Vāyu identifies himself as "Mātariśvan" ("the one who grows in the mother," originally a name for Agni, but from the *Atharvaveda* onwards also an epithet for the wind); Indra is called "Maghavan" ("the generous one," one of Indra's many epithets in the Vedas). If the Vedic gods are all addressed by their other, more mysterious names, it makes perfect sense that *brahman* himself must also have another name, and that his other name must be even more mysterious and esoteric than the others.

The *Kena Upaniṣad* and the *Gylfaginning*

The charming little story about the gods who find that they are completely out of their league in the encounter with *brahman* may be quite old; it does bear some resemblance to an Old Norse myth retold by Snorri in the *Gylfaginning*.

In the Old Norse story, the thunder god Thor is traveling with the trickster god Loki and two human companions to the realm of the giants. The travelers are challenged to a series of contests with the giants, and to their great consternation, they lose every single challenge. Loki, who can eat more and faster than anyone, loses to a mysterious opponent who consumes not just the food but the wooden trough it is served in. The swift-footed Tjalfi loses a running race to an opponent who is back before Tjalfi has even begun to run. The mighty Thor himself loses both a drinking contest and a bet that he can pick up his host's cat. When he, Thor, finally loses an arm-wrestling contest with a very old woman, he is deeply humiliated. As they are leaving, their host finally explains to them that Loki's hungry contestant was Fire itself, that Tjalfi was outrun by Thought, that the drinking horn Thor failed to empty was in fact filled by the ocean, that the cat Thor couldn't lift was the great Midgard serpent, and that the old lady who beat him at arm wrestling was Old Age itself.

The *Gylfaginning* story, like the *Kena Upaniṣad*, shows powerful gods completely out of their element and humiliated in the encounter with greater and more abstract powers. Both stories feature the god of thunder (Thor and Indra respectively) as the one who finally learns the truth about why the gods have seemingly been robbed of their old powers.

It is possible, given that both Sanskrit and Old Norse are Indo-European languages, that both stories have preserved some common archaic Indo-European narrative material. But when we compare the two stories, we see that they put entirely different spins on the humorous tale of old gods finding themselves powerless in the encounter with an unknown power: While the Norse story concludes that Thor and his companions were more powerful than it seemed, since they *almost* succeeded in out-eating fire, outrunning thought, out-wrestling old age, etc., the Indian tale concludes that even the gods must learn that their powers are nothing without the highest *brahman*.

Ātman in the *Kena Upaniṣad*

The main focus of both the verse section and the prose section of the *Kena Upaniṣad* is on *brahman*, not on *ātman*. Unlike *brahman*, *ātman* is not discussed very extensively in the *Kena Upaniṣad*. It is stated in 2.4 that one gains power (*vīrya*) by one's *ātman*. The only other time the term *ātman* is mentioned in the text is the fourth chapter, where *ātman* is used in the old sense of "body" in a verse that reflects on why people might exclaim "Ah!":

> As far as the body (*ātman*) is concerned, when something pops into the mind, and through that the imagination suddenly remembers something ...[10]

The notion of the individual *ātman* of a human being as identical with *brahman* itself is nevertheless hinted at in the text:

> Seeing it in each and every being,
> the wise men become immortal
> when they leave this world.[11]

Indra in the *Kena Upaniṣad*

The Vedic gods Agni, Vāyu, and Indra all appear in the *Kena Upaniṣad*. Indra is the only one among them who eventually comes to understand the true nature of *brahman*, "and that is why Indra is higher than the other gods."[12] In the *Ṛgveda*, the thunder god Indra is the king among the gods. Although most Vedic gods are only mentioned briefly, if at all, in the Upaniṣads, Indra is depicted as a positive figure in several of the oldest Upaniṣadic texts. While the most sympathetic portrayals of Indra are found in the Upaniṣads formally affiliated with the *Ṛgveda*, the two surviving *Sāmaveda Upaniṣads*, the *Chāndogya Upaniṣad* and the *Kena Upaniṣad*, both present Indra as an earnest wisdom seeker, grasping for the truth. Why Indra in particular? Why is the brawny god of thunder and war, the great dragon-slayer Indra, cast in the role of a wisdom seeker in the Upaniṣads?

In addition to his roles as war-god and thunder-god, Indra is associated with wisdom and insight already in the *Ṛgveda*: "Splendid are you Indra, intelligent and insightful."[13] The physical and mental strength associated with Indra blend in the intriguing metaphor in another passage from the *Ṛgveda*:

> Be generous, Indra, and lengthen my days.
> Sharpen my thought like a blade of iron.[14]

Here, the sharp iron blade naturally associated with the god of war becomes a metaphor for mental acuity. Indra's well-known epithet *śatakratu* ("he of a hundred *kratu*"), used from the *Ṛgveda* onwards, may also have inspired the portrayal of Indra as a wisdom seeker in the Upaniṣads. The term *kratu* may either be translated as "sacrificial rite" or as "intelligence." Although Indra is later associated with a hundred sacrifices, the alternative meaning of *kratu* may also resonate in the Upaniṣadic depictions of the wise Indra.

Umā in the *Kena Upaniṣad*

In the *Kena Upaniṣad*, we encounter the only female wisdom teacher in the Upaniṣads who can rival Gārgī of the *Bṛhadāraṇyaka Upaniṣad*. She appears, seemingly out of nowhere, and explains the nature of *brahman* to Indra:

> Then, at that very same place in the sky, he came across a very beautiful woman, Umā, the daughter of the Mountain. He said to her: "What is that sprit?"
>
> "*Brahman*," she said. "You are glorying in the victory won by *brahman*." Only then did Indra realize that it was *brahman*.[15]

In later Hindu mythology, Umā plays an important part as the wife of Śiva, the god of destruction. She is often called Pārvatī, "she of the mountain" because she is said to be the daughter of the Himālaya mountain. As Pārvatī, she is worshipped as a mother goddess and an aspect of the divine *śakti* ("power"). But the intriguing part about her in the *Kena Upaniṣad* is that she appears to be fully enlightened; while Indra searches for the truth about *brahman*, she already knows it. Where does her knowledge of *brahman* come from? The Upaniṣadic text does not tell us. Umā simply appears briefly, out of nowhere, with the truth about the highest reality. The idea of a goddess whose power and insight is greater than that of the male gods hints, however, at the goddess worship that follows in later Hinduism.

The *Kena* and the transmission of the Upaniṣads

The *Kena Upaniṣad* concludes with a brief dialogue between a student and a teacher. The student begs his teacher to teach him: "Sir, teach me the Upaniṣad!"[16] The word Upaniṣad is not necessarily used in a technical sense here as a genre name for a text, but probably means something like "secret teaching" or "mystical connection." The teacher then assures the student that he has now been taught "the Upaniṣad relating to *brahman* itself." He goes on to explain that austerity, self-control and rituals are the foundation of this secret teaching, while the Vedas are its limbs, and truth its dwelling. Intriguingly, the teacher's words re-validates the Vedas and Vedic rituals, although the Vedic gods have been shown as inferior to *brahman* earlier in the text. This little postscript to the Upaniṣad proper provides us with some interesting insight into how the early Upaniṣads were transmitted: A teacher presents the Upaniṣadic text with its perhaps revolutionary teachings about *brahman* to a student, but this transmission of knowledge likely takes place within the Vedic tradition, where old texts and ideas are passed down from teacher to student.

One text or two?

Paul Deussen proposed that the prose section of the *Kena Upaniṣad* is far older than the verse section.[17] Since the oldest preserved Upaniṣads, the *Bṛhadāraṇyaka Upaniṣad* and the *Chāndogya Upaniṣad* are in prose, while many later Upaniṣads are composed in metrical form, Deussen's theory makes intuitive sense. There is, however, no linguistic evidence to indicate that one portion of the text is significantly older than the other. A metrical analysis of the verse portion of the *Kena Upaniṣad* indicates a date of composition a little bit later than the oldest portions of the *Kaṭha* or *Śvetāśvatara Upaniṣad.* A linguistic analysis of the prose portion of the text suggests that it is quite a bit later than the oldest Upaniṣads, such as the *Bṛhadāraṇyaka Upaniṣad.* While archaic Vedic grammatical forms are found sporadically throughout the *Bṛhadāraṇyaka* and *Chāndogya Upnaiṣads*, they are notably absent in the *Kena Upaniṣad*, including in the prose sections.

The dating of the text is made more complicated by the fact that a variant of one stanza from the *Kena Upaniṣad* is also found in the older *Bṛhadāraṇyaka Upaniṣad*. The verse in the *Kena Upaniṣad* reads:

> It is the hearing behind the hearing, the mind behind the mind,
> The speech behind speech, the breath behind the breath,
> and the eye behind the eye. The wise renounces all these
> and become immortal when they depart from this world.[18]

The corresponding stanza in the *Bṛhadāraṇyaka Upaniṣad* is quite close:

> The breath behind the breath, the eye behind the eye,
> The hearing behind the hearing, the mind behind the mind.
> Those who know this see *brahman*,
> Ancient and primordial.[19]

Normally, one would assume that the *younger* text, the *Kena Upaniṣad*, is borrowing from the older text, the *Bṛhadāraṇyaka Upaniṣad*. This does not seem to be the case here, however, since the verse is marked as a quotation ("On this topic, there are these verses") in the *Bṛhadāraṇyaka Upaniṣad*. It is of course possible that a stanza from a younger Upaniṣad ended up in the *Bṛhadāraṇyaka Upaniṣad* at a later point in the transmission process, but it is more likely that the stanza originated from a third source, from which both the Upaniṣads borrowed. The borrowed stanza does not necessarily help, then, in dating the verse part of the text.

It seems likely that the verse portion and the prose portion, due to their divergent views on *brahman*, originally came from two different sources, and perhaps once constituted two different texts. It is not possible, however, to decide based on metrical and linguistic evidence which portion is the oldest one.

Notes

1 Masato Fujii: *The Jaiminīya-Upaniṣad-Brāhmaṇa: A Study of the Earliest Upaniṣad, Belonging to the Jaiminīya Sāmaveda.* PhD dissertation University of Helsinki 2004.
2 *Kena Upaniṣad* 1.4.
3 *Kena Upaniṣad* 1.5.

4 *Kena Upaniṣad* 2.1.
5 *Kena Upaniṣad* 1.3.
6 *Kena Upaniṣad* 1.6.
7 *Kena Upaniṣad* 4.3.
8 *Kena Upaniṣad* 4.6.
9 See P. Olivelle, *The Early Upaniṣads*. New York/Oxford: Oxford University Press, 1998: 599.
10 *Kena Upaniṣad* 4.5.
11 *Kena Upaniṣad* 2.5.
12 *Kena Upaniṣad* 2.3.
13 *Ṛgveda* 1.62.12.
14 *Ṛgveda* 6.47.10.
15 *Kena Upaniṣad* 3.12–4.1.
16 *Kena Upaniṣad* 4.8.
17 P. Deussen, *Sixty Upaniṣads of the Veda*. Originally published as Sechzig Upaniṣads des Veda. Leipzig 1897. Translated by V. M. Bedekar and G. B. Palsule. Vol. 1. Delhi: Motilal Banarsidass, 1980: 208.
18 *Kena Upaniṣad* 1.2.
19 *Bṛhadāraṇyaka Upaniṣad* 4.4.18.

Further reading

Nikam, N. A. 1949. "The Logical Problem of the *Kena Upaniṣad*" *Philosophical Quarterly* 22: 157 ff.

Renou, L. 1943. *Kena Upaniṣad*. Paris: Adrien Maisonneuve.

34 The *Maitrī Upaniṣad*

Signe Cohen

The *Maitrī Upaniṣad* is known by several names, including *Maitreya Upaniṣad*, *Maitrāyaṇa Upaniṣad*, *Maitrāyaṇī Upaniṣad*, and *Maitrāyaṇīya Upaniṣad*. The name of the text suggests that it is affiliated with the *Maitrāyaṇīya* school of the *Black Yajurveda*, although the late *Muktikā Upaniṣad* refers to the *Maitrī Upaniṣad* as one of the Upaniṣads associated with the *Sāmaveda*. Since the Sanskrit text of the *Maitrī Upaniṣad* displays many of the linguistic peculiarities of the *Maitrāyaṇīya* school and quotes frequently from other texts affiliated with the *Black Yajurveda*, it is likely that the traditional classification of this Upaniṣad as a Yajurvedic text is correct. Furthermore, the *Maitrī Upaniṣad* contains musings on philosophical themes that preoccupy the authors of other Upaniṣads affiliated with the *Black Yajurveda*, such as Yoga and the notion of primordial matter (*pradhāna*). The late association with the *Sāmaveda* is likely made because the *Maitrī Upaniṣad* contains numerous quotations from the *Chāndogya Upaniṣad*, the *Sāmaveda* Upaniṣad par excellence. The very first stanza of the text discusses the ritual laying of fires. This introduction invokes one of the most important ritual themes in the Yajurvedic tradition, the *agnicayana* ritual as a cosmic and spiritual symbol.

The eighth-century philosopher Śaṅkara, who composed commentaries to most of the oldest Upaniṣads, did not comment on the *Maitrī Upaniṣad*. It is, however, included among the upaniṣadic texts commented on by Vidyāraṇya in the fourteenth century CE and Rāmatīrtha in the seventeenth century CE.

The definite edition of the Maitrī Upaniṣad to date in van Buitenen's critical edition. In his edition, van Buitenen attempts to sort out the complicated textual issues surrounding this Upaniṣad. Van Buitenen uses the designation *V* (*Vulgate*) for the version of the text commented on by Rāmatīrtha in the seventeenth century. But he points out that there also exists a shorter version of the text from south India, and he refers to this recension as the *Southern Maitrāyaṇī* or *SM*. While the *V* text consists of six chapters, *SM* only has four; chapters 5 and 6, as well as parts of chapter 1 are missing from the *SM* text. Van Buitenen suggests that *SM* was originally a separate text which was later incorporated into the text of *V*. When examining the concepts of *ātman* and *brahman* in the *Maitrī Upaniṣad*, it is necessary to keep in mind where the term in question is found, in the *V* recension or in the *SM* recension, since the two versions of the text may have different origins and dates of composition.

Ātman in the *Maitrī Upaniṣad*

The discovery of the true nature of the *ātman* is the central theme in the *Maitrī Upaniṣad*, as it is in many of the older Upaniṣads. In the frame story of the Upaniṣad, which begins in 1.2, King Bṛhadratha sets out to discover what the *ātman* really is. There are historical records of an ancient Indian king named Bṛhadratha, who ruled a portion of northern India from around 187 to 180 BCE. He was a descendant of the great emperor Ashoka and the last ruler of the Maurya Empire. There is very little, however, apart from the name, to connect the historical King Bṛhadratha with the wisdom seeker in the *Maitrī Upaniṣad*.

The *Maitrī Upaniṣad* differentiates between two different *ātmans*: The highest *ātman*, who does not act and is merely a spectator,[1] and the lower *ātman*, called *bhūtātman* ("the creature ātman"), which is that which is reborn and suffers karmic consequences.[2] The idea of a lower and a higher *ātman* is in all likelihood inspired by the *Śvetāśvatara Upaniṣad*, and earlier text of the *Black Yajurveda*. The *bhūtātman* is, according to the *Maitrī Upaniṣad*, to the higher *ātman* as a water drop is to a lotus.[3] The doctrine of the two *ātmans* is summed up in the last sentence of the *Maitrī Upaniṣad*: "For the sake of the experience of truth and untruth the great *ātman* becomes two."[4] It is worth noting, however, that while *ātman* occupies a central space in the *SM* recension of the text, it is hardly mentioned at all outside the *SM* passages.

Sāṃkhya ideas in the *Maitrī Upaniṣad*

The conception of *ātman* in the *Maitrī Upaniṣad* aligns in interesting ways with the notion of *puruṣa*, the eternal spirit, in the Sāṃkhya school of Hindu philosophy. While Sāṃkhya teachings may not yet have reached their later, crystallized form at the time when the *Maitrī Upaniṣad* was composed, the *ātman* of the *Maitrī Upaniṣad* resembles the Sāmkhya conception of *puruṣa*, the eternal cosmic spectator, who only believes himself to be bound to nature (*prakṛti*). *Ātman* is explicitly identified with puruṣa in the *Maitrī Upaniṣad*.[5] In Sāṃkhya philosophy, nature is made up of three strands, called *guṇas* ("threads"; the three are light, passion, and darkness). When the *Maitrī Upaniṣad* refers to *ātman* as the one who "stands above the *guṇas*,"[6] this echoes similar statements made about *puruṣa* in Sāmkhya texts. But is the *Maitrī Upaniṣad* influenced by the *Sāṃkhyakārikās* or the *Sāṃkhyakārikās* by the Upaniṣad? Given that some of the earliest glimmers of Sāmkhya and Yoga ideas can be traced back precisely to the texts of the *Black Yajurveda*, the tradition to which the *Maitrī Upaniṣad* belongs, it is perhaps not unreasonable to assume a historical development of Sāṃkhya and Yoga philosophy from the *Kaṭha Upaniṣad*, via the *Śvetāśvatara Upaniṣad* and the *Maitrī Upaniṣad* to the fully developed systems we encounter in the *Sāṃkhyakārikās* and the *Yogasūtras*. The *ātman* of the *Maitrī Upaniṣad* can therefore be seen as a precursor to the *puruṣa* or "spirit" of the later Sāmkhya and Yoga traditions.

The *Maitrī Upaniṣad* contains numerous unmistakable references to proto-Sāṃkhya ideas throughout. In addition to the clear identification of *ātman* and *puruṣa*, the text also mentions Sāṃkhya concepts like sense-organs (*buddhīdriyāṇi*), the organs of action (*karmendriyāṇi*), the mind (*manas*), and nature *prakṛti*.[7] Although *prakṛti* ("nature") is also mentioned already in the *Śvetāśvatara Upaniṣad*, that particular *Śvetāśvatara Upaniṣad* passage seems to be a later interpolation. It is possible that the reference to *prakṛti* as primordial nature in the *Maitrī Upaniṣad* is the oldest usage of this term in its philosophical sense. The word *prakṛti* is also used in older Vedic ritual literature, but always in the sense of "model" or "paradigm" of the sacrifice, or the "archetypal sacrifice." It is possible that the philosophical usage of *prakṛti* grew out of the ritual usage; since the texts of the *Yajurveda* present the world as a cosmic sacrifice, the "paradigm" (*prakṛti*) of the sacrifice also assumed cosmic and spiritual dimensions: *Prakṛti* represents the "unfolding" or "patterning" of the world, seen as a giant cosmic sacrifice. It is probably not coincidental that the first occurrences of *prakṛti* as a technical "proto-Sāṃkhya" term occurs in the texts of the *Black Yajurveda*, still echoing with the metaphor of the cosmic sacrifice.

Maitrī Upaniṣad 5.2 describes the evolution of the universe: In the beginning everything was *tamas*, which manifested itself as *rajas*, which in turn became manifest as *sattva*. Although this account of the origin of the universe is clearly consistent with that found in later classical Sāṃkhya, it does involve the three *guṇas* and a series of transformations.

The *Maitrī Upaniṣad* refers to the salvific "dualistic knowledge" (*dvaitībhūtaṃ vijñānam*),[8] which can easily be seen as a reference to the essential knowledge of the distinction between puruṣa and prakṛti. The idea of a "non-dualistic knowledge" (*advaitī-bhūtam-vijñānam*) is refuted.[9]

Maitrī Upaniṣad 6.10 refers to *puruṣa* ("spirit") and *prakṛti* ("nature"), also here called *pradhāna*. *Pradhāna* is also the word for *prakṛti* in the *Śvetāśvatara Upaniṣad*. Puruṣa is here described as "enjoyer" (*bhoktṛ*) and prakṛti as *bhojyā* "that which is to be enjoyed." It is also stated explicitly that that which is to be enjoyed consists of three guṇas. This notion of the self as a consumer of the material world is also found in Sāṃkhya philosophy. The Sāṃkhya concepts of *prakṛti* ("nature"), the *guṇas* ("qualities"), and *manas* ("mind") are also mentioned in the text.[10]

As Welden has observed, the form of Sāṃkhya presented in this Upaniṣad is certainly not the Sāṃkhya of the *Kārikās*, but it is Sāṃkhya nevertheless. It appears to be somewhat later and more developed that the proto-Sāṃkhya found in *Mahābhārata* passages. Welden suggests that the *Kārikās* may have been based on an earlier prose work, and that this unknown prose text may also have influenced the *Maitrī Upaniṣad*.[11]

Yoga in the *Maitrī Upaniṣad*

In Hindu philosophy, the school of Yoga is closely aligned with Sāṃkhya. Like Sāṃkhya, Yoga teaches that there are two eternal principles in the world, *puruṣa* ("the spirit") and *prakṛti* ("nature"). The goal of both schools is to liberate *puruṣa*, the spirit, from its bondage to nature. While the Sāṃkhya school teaches that this liberation can happen through insight alone, the Yoga school advocates the use of "the eight-fold Yoga," a path to liberation consisting of ethics, virtuous habits, postures (*āsana*), restraining the breath (*prāṇayāma*), withdrawing one's senses from external objects (*pratyāhāra*), concentration (*dhāraṇā*), meditation (*dhyāna*), and meditative absorption (*samādhi*).

The reference to a six-fold, rather than an eight-fold yoga in the *Maitrī Upaniṣad* may be helpful for dating this text in relation to others:

> The teaching for obtaining this (unity) is: Restraining the breath (*prāṇāyāma*), withdrawing the senses (*pratyāhāra*), meditation (*dhyāna*), concentration (*dhāraṇā*), contemplation (*tarka*) and *samādhi*. This is said to be the six-fold yoga.[12]

Since this list of six stages of Yoga contains only five of the parts of the later classical eight-fold yoga, as represented by Patañjali's *Yogasūtras*, it is possible that the *Maitrī Upaniṣad* represents an earlier stage in the development of Yoga than that found in Patañjali. Zigmund-Cerbu has demonstrated that older notions of a six-fold yoga have also been preserved in a few later medieval Upaniṣads, such as the *Amṛtanāda*, *Dhyānabindu*, and *Yogacūḍāmani Upaniṣads*, as well as in a Cambodian inscription from Śaka 879 (957 CE).[13] Zigmund-Cerbu suggests that the *Maitrī Upaniṣad* version of the limbs of Yoga is in all likelihood the original one that has influenced both Hindu Yoga, Buddhism, and Jainism.[14] The Tantric Buddhism of Tibet also invokes a six-fold *yoga*, rather than an eight-fold one.[15]

Buddhism in the *Maitrī Upaniṣad*?

In a curious passage of the *Maitrī Upaniṣad*, the highest being is referred to as *nirātman* ("without an *ātman*"), a most unusual characteristic of the highest principle in the Upaniṣads.[16] It is possible to see this as a reference to Buddhism, a tradition that teaches that the very idea of an eternal *ātman* is nothing but a human delusion. The rest of the *Maitrī Upaniṣad*, with its elaborations on the nature of *ātman*, is clearly not Buddhist, however. The adjective *śūnya* (empty) in the same section may also be interpreted as a reference to Buddhism, although the term in also used in Sāṃkhya philosophy. It does make better sense, then, to interpret *nirātman* here as "without individuality" rather than "without self or *ātman*." We may note that the term is also used in this sense in the *Mahābhārata* epic.

The parable of the chariot

In the *SM* recension, the parable of the chariot, well known from the *Kaṭha* and the *Śvetāśvatara Upaniṣad*, is invoked:

> The sense-organs (*buddhendriya*) are the reins. The organs of action (*karmendriya*) are the horses. The chariot is the body. The mind (*manas*) is the charioteer. The goad is made from *prakṛti*.[17]

The presence of this metaphor further confirms the close connections between the *Maitrī Upaniṣad* and the *Kaṭha* and *Śvetāśvatara*. Since the *Maitrī Upaniṣad* shows influence from the *Kaṭha Upaniṣad* throughout, the presence of the chariot image here is not surprising. While the *Kaṭha Upaniṣad* simply refers to the senses as wild horses and the mind as the reins, we may note a much more Sāṃkhya-inspired vocabulary in the passage from the *Maitrī Upaniṣad*, including such technical Sāṃkhya terms as *buddhendriya* ("sense organs"), *karmendriya* ("organs of action"), and *prakṛti* ("nature").

The relationship of the *Maitrī Upaniṣad* to other texts

The *Maitrī Upaniṣad* quotes extensively from the *Chāndogya Upaniṣad* and two of the Upaniṣads of the *Black Yajurveda*, the *Taittirīya* and the *Kaṭha*. In addition, we also find scattered quotations from the *Bṛhadāraṇyaka Upaniṣad*,[18] *Īśā Upaniṣad*,[19] and *Praśna Upaniṣad*.[20] It is clear from the context and the meters that it is the *Maitrī Upaniṣad* that has borrowed the passages in question from the other Upaniṣads. Whereas the quotations from most of the Upaniṣads are distributed evenly throughout the *Maitrī Upaniṣad*, we may note that the quotations from the later *Praṣna Upaniṣad* are not found in the *SM* parts of the text.

E. Washburn Hopkins has studied the relationship between the *Maitrī Upaniṣad* and the *Mahābhārata* epic. There are close similarities between the Upaniṣad and portions of the epic, but it is extremely difficult to determine which text has borrowed from the other. One may perhaps conclude that the *Maitrī Upaniṣad* and the *Mahābhārata* were composed around the same time period, and that the authors of each text were familiar with the other.

Date and composition of the text

There is no scholarly consensus about the date of the *Maitrī Upaniṣad*. Many scholars regard the text as later than the "classical" Upaniṣads to which Śankara wrote commentaries: *Bṛhadāraṇyaka*, *Chāndogya*, *Taittirīya*, *Aitareya*, *Śvetāśvatara*, *Īśā* , *Kena*, *Kaṭha* , *Praśna* , *Muṇḍaka*, and *Māṇḍūkya*. Śaṅkara's apparent unfamiliarity with the text is one of many arguments for a later date for the *Maitrī Upaniṣad*. The *Maitrī* quotes several of the "classical" Upaniṣads and can therefore be assumed to be later than these other texts – but how much later?

In later Hinduism, three of the main Hindu gods, the creator Brahmā, Viṣṇu the maintainer, and Śiva the destroyer, are often collectively called the *trimūrti*, or the "triple form" of the divine. Although the term *trimūrti* is not used in the *Maitrī Upaniṣad*, there are two references to Brahmā, Viṣṇu, and Śiva as a group,[21] which may be a sign of late composition. Other scholars have argued that the text contains some very archaic features and that it cannot be much younger than the classical Upaniṣads.

The Southern recension (*SM*) of the *Maitrī Upaniṣad* is a fairly unified Upaniṣadic text with a strong Sāṃkhya flavor. The Sāṃkhya philosophy presented here is not yet as systematic as that found in the *Sāṃkhyakārikās*, but more akin to the proto-Sāṃkhya of the *Śvetāśvatara Upaniṣad* and the *Mahābhārata*. The central theme of the text is the distinction between two *ātmans*, the higher *ātman* and the *bhūtātman*. Based on the development of philosophical ideas and on the linguistic features of the text, it is reasonable to assume that the Southern recension of the *Maitrī Upaniṣad* was composed after the *Kaṭha* and *Śvetāśvatara Upaniṣad*, but perhaps before the *Praśna* or *Māṇḍūkya Upaniṣads*.

If this is indeed the case, why did Śaṅkara not compose a commentary to the *Maitrī Upaniṣad*? The most likely answer is that the text's central teaching, the dual nature of the *ātman*, contradicts Śaṅkara's monism. Since the *Maitrī Upaniṣad* was transmitted without being embedded in an authoritative Śaṅkara commentary, the text was then open to later additions and modifications.

The additional sections of the *Maitrī Upaniṣad* not found in the Southern recension (*non-SM*) must be regarded as later interpolations. Even the seventeenth-century commentator Rāmatīrtha considered the text of the *Maitrī Upaniṣad* heterogeneous. He writes at the beginning of the commentary on the sixth chapter: "Since this chapter is an appendix, one should not expect too much coherence here. Nevertheless we will explain the text word by word, guessing at the connection so far as we understand it." The fact that Rāmatīrtha refers to chapter 6 as a later addition confirms this hypothesis. It is in these sections not found in the *SM* that we find the later Hindu idea of the trinity Brahmā, Viṣṇu, and Śiva.[22] The idea that not only *ātman*, but also *brahman*, may have a dual nature is also only found here. The reference to an iconic (*mūrta*) aspect of *brahman* indicates that this section of the text dates to a time period when image worship was current. Image worship, while prevalent in later classical Hinduism, was absent in the oldest time period.

Van Buitenen suggests that in its present form, the *Maitrī Upaniṣad* is a "composite of several brief texts which envelop an ancient prose Upaniṣad which has suffered much, but is essentially still intact."[23] It seems likely that the textual history of the *Maitrī Upaniṣad* developed as follows: The original *Maitrī Upaniṣad* consisted of 1.2–4.3 and chapter 7 of the text of the Vulgate. This is the text that has been transmitted in the Southern recension. Sections 1.1, 4.4–4.6, and chapters 5 and 6 are later interpolations that were added as the text was transmitted in the *Maitrāyaṇīya* school.

Notes

1 *Maitrī Upaniṣad* 2.7.
2 *Maitrī Upaniṣad* 3.2.
3 *Maitrī Upaniṣad* 3.2.
4 *Maitrī Upaniṣad* 7.11.
5 *Maitrī Upaniṣad* 2.5.
6 *Maitrī Upaniṣad* 2.4.
7 *Maitrī Upaniṣad* 2.7.
8 *Maitrī Upaniṣad* 6.5.
9 *Maitrī Upaniṣad* 6.5.
10 *Maitrī Upaniṣad* 6.30.
11 Welden 1914: 51.
12 *Maitrī Upaniṣad* 6.18.
13 Zigmund-Cerbu 1963: 129.
14 Zigmund-Cerbu 1963: 130.
15 Zigmund-Cerbu 1963: 131.
16 *Maitrī Upaniṣad* 2.4.
17 *Maitrī Upaniṣad* 2.7.
18 *Maitrī Upaniṣad* 2.5 = *Bṛhadāraṇyaka Upaniṣad* 5.9); *Maitrī Upaniṣad* 6.32 = *Bṛhadāraṇyaka Upaniṣad* 2.1.20.
19 *Maitrī Upaniṣad* 7.7 = *Īśā Upaniṣad* 14.
20 *Maitrī Upaniṣad* 6.5 = *Praśna Upaniṣad* 5.11; *Maitrī Upaniṣad* 6.8 = *Praśna Upaniṣad* 1.8.
21 *Maitrī Upaniṣad* 4.5 and 5.2.
22 *Maitrī Upaniṣad* 4.5 and 5.2.
23 Van Buitenen 1962: 7.

Further reading

Cowell, E. B. 1870. *The Maitrī or Maitráyaṇīya Upaniṣad, with the Commentary of Rámatīrtha*. Bibliotheca Indica, Work 42. London: W. M. Watts. (Reprint Osnabrück: Biblio Verlag, 1982.)

Esnoul, A.-M. 1952. *Maitry Upaniṣad*. Paris: Adrien Maisonneuve.

Tsuji, N. 1955. "Some Linguistic Remarks on the Maitri Upaniṣad" *Studies in Indology and Buddhology Presented in Honour of Professor Susumu Yamaguchi on the Occasion of his Sixtieth Birthday*. Kyoto: Hazokan Kyoto.

Van Buitenen, J. 1962. *The Maitrāyaṇīya Upaniṣad: A Critical Essay, with Text, Translation, and Commentary*. Hague: Mouton.
Vidyarnava, S. C. 1926. *The Maitri Upaniṣat*. Allahabad: Panini Office.
Welden, E. A. 1914. "The Sāṃkhya Teachings in the Maitrī Upaniṣad" *American Journal of Philology* 35: 32 ff.
Zigmund-Cerbu, A. 1963. "The Ṣaḍaṅgayoga" *History of Religons* 3: 128–134.

35 The *Māṇḍūkya Upaniṣad*

Signe Cohen

The *Māṇḍūkya Upaniṣad* is a short text, consisting of only twelve prose sections. Although it is named after the *Māṇḍūkya* school of the *Ṛgveda*, it is formally affiliated with the *Atharvaveda*. The name *Māṇḍūkya* is derived from the name of a Vedic sage, Maṇḍuka (literally "the Frog").

The *Māṇḍūkya Upaniṣad* is closely connected with the *Āgama Śāstra*, also known as the *Kārikā* of Gauḍapāda (sixth century CE). The *Kārikā* is a commentary on the *Māṇḍūkya Upaniṣad*. This commentary has been the subject of many studies. The commentarial text is composed in verse and is one of the most significant treatises of early Advaita Vedānta philosophy, a school of thought that insists on absolute oneness between the self and the impersonal cosmic *brahman*. According to Indian tradition, Gauḍapāda, who is considered to be the author of the *Kārikā*, was the teacher of Govindapādācārya, who was the teacher of the great Advaita philosopher Śaṅkara. In all extant manuscripts of the *Māṇḍūkya Upaniṣad*, the Upaniṣad is embedded within the commentarial text of the *Kārikā*. The Upaniṣad is in all likelihood much older than its commentary, however, and may date from around the same time period as the *Praśna Upaniṣad*, another prose Upaniṣad. Śaṅkara composed a commentary on the *Māṇḍūkya Upaniṣad* as well, but, interestingly, he comments both on the text on the Upanisad itself and on Gauḍapāda's *Kārikā*, as if it is a part of the Upaniṣadic text itself. Although Śaṅkara commented on many of the older Upaniṣads, he did not comment on their older commentaries, except in the case of the *Māṇḍūkya Upaniṣad*. Our main concern in this chapter is with the brief text of the Upaniṣad itself rather than with Gauḍapāda's famous commentary.

The importance of the *Māṇḍūkya Upaniṣad* in the later tradition is nicely summarized in the later *Muktikā Upaniṣad*:

> The *Māṇḍūkya* alone is enough
> for the liberation of the seeker.
> If after that he still lacks knowledge,
> then he must read the ten Upaniṣads.

He will reach his goal
who reads thirty two Upaniṣads.
But if you long for salvation when death is coming,
then read the one hundred and eight Upaniṣads.[1]

Why would the *Māṇḍūkya Upaniṣad* in itself be considered the equivalent of all the other Upaniṣadic texts in its capacity to liberate the reader? Perhaps the answer is that this brief text contains the essence of the Upaniṣadic teachings about the liberating knowledge of *ātman* and *brahman*, while it also foreshadows some of the core ideas of later Hindu philosophy.

The syllable *Oṃ* in the *Māṇḍūkya Upaniṣad*

The very first syllable of this brief Upaniṣad is also its main theme:

> *Oṃ*. This syllable in the whole world. Here is a clear explanation of it: The past, the present, and the future – all of that is simply *oṃ*. Whatever else is beyond these three times is also *oṃ*.[2]

The syllable *oṃ* is further identified with both *ātman* and *brahman*.[3] *Oṃ* is divided, as it often is in Sanskrit phonology, into three sounds, *a*, *u*, and *m*.[4] Since these three sounds that make up the syllable *oṃ* are identified with three states of the *ātman*,[5] by implication, the sacred syllable is equated with the inner self, or *ātman*. The text associates each of the three sounds with a word that begins with that particular sound and that also captures something about one of the states of the self. Thus, *a* is associated with *āpti* ("obtaining") or *ādimattva* ("the state of being the first"). "Anyone who knows this will obtain all desires and become the first," promises the Upaniṣad.[6] The sound *u* is associated with *utkarṣa* ("being elevated") or *ubhayatva* ("the state of being intermediate"). "He will elevate the stream of knowledge and become an intermediary," says the Upaniṣad, "and no one who doesn't know *brahman* will be born into his family if he knows this."[7] The sound *m* is said to be derived either from *miti* ("construction") or from *apīti*, "destruction." "Anyone who knows this will construct the world, and also become its destruction," claims the Upaniṣad.

What we see here is the sort of etymological word play so frequently found in the Upaniṣads. The authors of the text are not suggesting that the sound *oṃ* is some sort of cryptic abbreviation for "obtaining elevated construction;" rather, they are playing with words and creating linguistic connections that help emphasize the meaning of their text. Thus, the waking state is associated with obtaining one's conscious desires, and with being first. When we think of our own selves, we tend to think first of our waking consciousness. The dream state is, of course, an intermediate state (between wakefulness and dreamless sleep), and it may also be said to be elevated because of its association with inner, subconscious knowledge. The fourth and dreamless state is the *ātman* in its entirety, associated both with constructing and deconstructing the world.

The fourfold *ātman*

The central theme in the *Māṇḍūkya Upaniṣad* is the sacred syllable *oṃ* or *aum*. This syllable is broken down into three sounds, *a*, *u*, and *m*, which are identified with three states of the *ātman*: the waking state, the dream state, and deep sleep. The syllable *oṃ* in its entirety is identified with the fourth state of the *ātman*, the state of true consciousness or illumination.

The four states of the *ātman* are referred to as *pādas* ("quarters" or "feet") in the *Māṇḍūkya Upaniṣad.* The *ātman* is called *catuṣpāt* (literally "quadruped") in section 2. A division into four parts is common in ancient Indian thought. Each quarter of a whole is referred to as a *pāda*, or foot. The four *pādas* of Vāc, the divine speech, are described in *Ṛgveda* 1.164.45. The division into four is based on the central image of a quadruped animal, usually a cow, but the division into four *pādas* is frequently applied to beings or concepts that are not directly connected with the cow-metaphor. Thus, the *Ṛgveda* states that Puruṣa, the cosmic man, consists of four quarters.[8] The four quarters, or *pādas*, are not of equal value. The four quarters are usually divided into three plus one. In the oldest Vedic literature, the fourth *pāda* is generally regarded as inferior to the other three.[9] In the Upaniṣads, however, the fourth *pāda* is usually higher than the other three.[10] The *Chāndogya Upaniṣad* still retains the concept of the fourth quarter as the lowest.[11] The *Maitrī Upaniṣad* in its seventh chapter attempts to reconcile the two contrasting schemes of three higher/one lower and one higher/three lower entities. *Maitrī* 7.11.8 states: "with one quarter /foot *brahman* moves in the three, and with three quarters/feet in the last." D. Bhattacharya argues that the treatment of the *catuṣpad*-doctrine in the *Māṇḍūkya Upaniṣad* is evidence for late composition.[12]

The four states of the self

A closer examination of the *Māṇḍūkya Upaniṣad*'s doctrine of the four different states of the self reveals some intriguing psychological insights. The first state of the *ātman* is the waking state, which is here called *Vaiśvānara*, "the universal" (literally: "relating to the all-person").[13] *Vaiśvānara* is a common epithet of the fire god Agni in the *Ṛgveda.* By referring to the first state of the self as *Vaiśvānara*, the text suggests that the waking state is, so to speak, a state of "presence in the world," a state of consciousness that allows cognition of the external world, "perceiving what is outside."[14] The *Vaiśvānara* or waking state has, according to the *Māṇḍūkya Upaniṣad*, "seven limbs and nineteen mouths."[15] It is not at all clear what these limbs and mouths refer to. The eighth-century commentator Śaṅkara suggests that the "seven limbs" refer to the head, eyes, breath, heart, stomach, feet, and torso of the cosmic person, identified respectively with the sky, the sun, the air, fire, water, earth, and space. He explains the "nineteen mouths" as the five sense organs (eyes, ears, nose, tongue, skin), the five organs of action (hands, feet, mouth, sex organ, and anus), the five breaths (in-breath, out-breath, mid-breath, up-breath, down-breath), mind, reason, ego, and intellect. Śaṅkara's explanation aligns the parts of *Vaiśvānara* with Sāṃkhya philosophical concepts. Whether this was intended by the authors of the *Mandukya Upaniṣad* itself is difficult to say.

The second state of the *ātman* is equated with dreaming.[16] This state is called *Taijasa*, which means "brilliant" or "luminous." The name may refer to the brightness of the dream vision. The dream state is characterized as "perceiving that which is inside," i. e. the internal world, as opposed to the external world perceived in the waking stage.

The third state is that of deep, dreamless sleep, "when a sleeping man has no desires and sees no dreams."[17] This state is intriguingly called *Prajñā*, "intelligence." How can a state of dreamless sleep possibly be equated with intelligence? The *Māṇḍūkya Upaniṣad* explains that this third state of the self is "a single mass of perception, consisting of bliss."[18] This intelligence is not equated with rational thought, which belongs to the first or waking state, but rather with a profound intuitive wisdom beyond ordinary forms of thought. This third state is called "the knower of all" and the origin and dissolution of all beings.[19]

The fourth state of the self is more enigmatic still. During this fourth state, there is no perception whatsoever, either of external or internal reality.[20] This fourth state is ungraspable, unthinkable, and indescribable, and ultimately identified with the *ātman* itself in its entirety.[21]

The fourth and final state of the *ātman* is identified with the mystical syllable *oṃ*, while the first three stages are equated with the three sounds that in Sanskrit phonetics are said to make up *oṃ*: *a*, *u*, *m*. This is more than an arbitrary equation; the three sounds have phonetic qualities that make them into excellent symbols for the first three states of the self. The sound *a* is open, pronounced with the mouth fairly wide. The next sound, *u*, is articulated with the mouth more closed, while the third sound, *m*, is pronounced with the mouth completely closed. Thus, the gradual closing of the sounds, moving from *a* to *m*, reflects the gradual closing of the self, from an initial state open towards the external reality to a closed, completely inward state.

Although the doctrine of the four states of the self is first elaborated in the *Māṇḍūkya Upaniṣad*, it is foreshadowed in the much earlier *Chāndogya Upaniṣad*. *Chāndogya Upaniṣad* 8. 7–12 tells the story of a god and a demon approaching the creator god Prajāpati seeking the truth about the *ātman*. Prajāpati reveals to both of them that *ātman* is merely the body. The demon Virocana is perfectly happy with this explanation and goes on his way. The god

Indra, however, suspects that there may be more to *ātman* than just the body, and he keeps going back to Prajāpati to learn more. Prajāpati then reveals to Indra during his successive visits that the *ātman* is the subject of dreams, that it is the subject of dreamless sleep, and that it is consciousness itself.

The *Māṇḍūkya Upaniṣad* and the cosmic illusion

Gauḍapāda's commentary on the *Māṇḍūkya Upaniṣad* is one of the most fundamental texts of Advaita Vedānta philosophy. A central concept in Gauḍapāda's thought (and later in Śaṅkara's as well) is *māyā*, the cosmic illusion. According to classical Advaita Vedānta doctrine, *ātman-brahman* is not only the ultimate reality, but the *only* reality. Nothing can exist outside the oneness of the self and the cosmic force. This consciousness is everything that truly exists. What then of the external world? According to Advaita Vedānta, the world as we perceive it is nothing but *māyā*, or illusion. The term *māyā* is also used in Sanskrit for a magic trick, the sleight of hand of a master illusionist. Gauḍapāda explains the world of *māyā* as a mere "vibration of the mind" (*manaspandita*) and "an imaginary city" (*gandharva-nagara*).

The word *māyā* is an old one in Sanskrit; it is found as early in the *Ṛgveda*. But here, the term does not mean "illusion," but rather "creation." The noun *māyā* is derived from the verb *mā*, which means "to measure," and in particular, measuring out the universe in an act of creation. Later, the term comes to mean "a false construct" or "an illusion."

Although the term *māyā* is not used directly in the *Māṇḍūkya Upaniṣad*, section eleven hints at *māyā*, both conceptually and etymologically. In this section, a person who knows the states of the self is said to be able to construct and deconstruct the whole world – a suggestion that the external world as we know it is simply a construct. But *māyā* is also evoked indirectly in this passage through the word used for "construction," *miti*. *Miti* is derived from the same verb as *māyā*, and carries the same connotations of a constructed reality. The fact that the very next section associates the fourth state of the *ātman* as "the cessation of the visible world"[22] re-emphasizes that the visible world is not a permanent and fixed entity. It makes sense, therefore, that Gauḍapāda developed his notions of *māyā* precisely in his commentary to an Upaniṣad that hinted at similar ideas. Gauḍapāda makes explicit what the Upaniṣad merely suggests as a possibility: The objects in the external world are ultimately as unreal as the objects one sees in dreams; the world is merely an elaborate fantasy by the *ātman*, who must free itself from this delusion in order to see itself and its absolute unity with *brahman* clearly: "Like dreams and illusions are seen, and as a fantasy city in the sky, so is this universe perceived by those who are knowledgeable of the Vedānta."[23] Gauḍapāda claims that the notion that the world has a beginning is nothing but an illusion: "There is no destruction and no creation …"[24]

Neuroscience and the four states of the self

The first three stages of the self described in the *Māṇḍūkya Upaniṣad* are well known to modern science; all mammals experience cycles of wakefulness, sleep, and dreamless sleep. Each of these states correlates with different types of brainwaves. When a person is awake, alert, and active, there is a preponderance of high frequency beta waves. A person who is resting and relaxing generates lower frequency alpha waves. The even slower theta brainwaves are characteristic of someone who drifts off into a daydream. The slowest brainwaves of them all are delta waves, which occur during deep, dreamless sleep. A person who is drifting off to sleep will likely go from emitting low beta waves to alpha, theta, and finally delta waves. When a person dreams, theta brainwaves increase, and this is also when rapid eye movement (REM) takes place.[25]

A fourth state of consciousness, a "silent consciousness" or "consciousness without content" beyond dreamless sleep, has also been the subject of recent work in Western psychology.[26] Baars proposes that a state of "silent consciousness" may occur with repeated contemplative practice, and that this state, which corresponds to increased theta-alpha waves, is measurable in the brain.[27]

The age of the *Māṇḍūkya Upaniṣad*

The *Māṇḍūkya Upaniṣad* has often been considered the most recent among the oldest Upaniṣads.[28] Deussen sees similarities between the *Māṇḍūkya Upaniṣad* and the *Maitrī*, and calls for an investigation into which text could be the older of the two.[29] Ranade calls the *Māṇḍūkya Upaniṣad* "the last of the early great Upaniṣads."[30] Mahoney dates the *Māṇḍūkya Upaniṣad* along with the *Praśna* and *Maitrī* to the fifth–fourth century BCE.[31] Olivelle, while agreeing that the *Māṇḍūkya Upaniṣad* and the *Praśna* are of approximately the same age, dates both text to around the beginning of the common era.[32]

It is extremely difficult to suggest a date of composition for the *Māṇḍūkya Upaniṣad*. The text is composed in prose, and it contains no linguistic forms that differ from classical Sanskrit. The absence of any Vedic forms indicates a date of composition later than the *Īśā*, *Kaṭha*, *Muṇḍaka* and *Śvetāśvatara*, but we have no further linguistic indications as to its possible age. The stage of development of the *catuṣpad*-doctrine indicates that the *Māṇḍūkya Upaniṣad* is younger than the *Chāndogya* and the *Bṛhadāraṇyaka* and older than the seventh chapter of the *Maitrī*, but this still leaves its date of composition fairly open. In conclusion, the evidence available suggests that the *Māṇḍūkya Upaniṣad* was composed later than the *Īśā*, *Kaṭha*, *Muṇḍaka*, and *Śvetāśvatara*, but before the youngest parts of the *Maitrī*.

Notes

1 *Muktikā Upaniṣad*, 1. 1. 26–29.
2 *Māṇḍūkya Upaniṣad* 1.
3 *Māṇḍūkya Upaniṣad* 2.

4 *Māṇḍūkya Upaniṣad* 8.
5 *Māṇḍūkya Upaniṣad* 8.
6 *Māṇḍūkya Upaniṣad* 9.
7 *Māṇḍūkya Upaniṣad* 10.
8 *Ṛgveda* 10.85.40.
9 Compare *Atharvaveda* 2.1.2.
10 Compare the description of the four parts of the Gāyatrī meter in *Bṛhadāraṇyaka Upaniṣad* 5.14.3.
11 *Chāndogya Upaniṣad* 3.12.6.
12 D. Bhattacharya, "The Doctrine of Four in the Early Upaniṣads and Some Connected Problems" *Journal of Indian Philosophy* 6 (1978): 1–34.
13 *Māṇḍūkya Upaniṣad* 2 and 9.
14 *Māṇḍūkya Upaniṣad* 2.
15 *Māṇḍūkya Upaniṣad* 2.
16 *Māṇḍūkya Upaniṣad* 4 and 10.
17 *Māṇḍūkya Upaniṣad* 5.
18 *Māṇḍūkya Upaniṣad* 5.
19 *Māṇḍūkya Upaniṣad* 6.
20 *Māṇḍūkya Upaniṣad* 7.
21 *Māṇḍūkya Upaniṣad* 7.
22 *Māṇḍūkya Upaniṣad* 12.
23 *Kārikā* 1.31.
24 *Kārikā* 1.32.
25 www.scientificamerican.com/article/what-is-the-function-of-t-1997-12-22/
26 Baars 2013.
27 Baars 2013.
28 E. Röer, *The Taittiríya, Aitaréya, Śvetāśvatara, Kéna, Īśā, Kaṭha, Praśna, Muṇḍaka and Māṇḍūkya Upanishads.* Calcutta: Bishop's College Press (= *Nine Upanishads*), 1853: 166; P. Deussen, *Sechzig Upaniṣads des Veda, aus dem Sanskrit übersetzt und mit Einleitungen und Anmerkungen versehen.* Leipzig: F. A. Brockhaus, 1897: 573.
29 Deussen 1897: 573.
30 R. D. Ranade, *A Constructive Survey of Upaniṣadic Philosophy, Being an Introduction to the Thought of the Upaniṣads.* 1926. (Reprint Bombay: Bharatiya Vidya Bhavan, 1968: 23.)
31 W. K Mahony, "Upaniṣads" in Lindsay Jones (ed.) *Encyclopedia of Religion.* Detroit, MI: Macmillan, 2005: 9483.
32 P. Olivelle, *Upaniṣads* Oxford/New York: Oxford University Press, 1996: xxxvii.

Further reading

Baars, Bernard J. 2013. "A Scientific Approach to Silent Consciousness" *Frontiers in Psychology* 4: 678 ff.

Bhattacharya, V. 1925. "The *Māṇḍūkya Upaniṣad* and the Gauḍapāda Kārikās" *Indian Historical Quarterly*. 1: 119–125 and 295–302.

Cole, Colin A. 2004. *A Study of Gauḍapāda's Māṇḍūkya Kārikāḥ.* Delhi: Motilal Banarsidass.

Deussen, P. 1897. *Sechzig Upaniṣads des Veda, aus dem Sanskrit übersetzt und mit Einleitungen und Anmerkungen versehen.* Leipzig: F. A. Brockhaus.

Distelbarth, M. 1989. *Māṇḍūkya Upaniṣad: Die vier Füsse des Bewusstseins.* Gladenbach: Hinder & Deelmann.

Dvivedi, M. N. 1894 *The Mâṇdûkyopanishad, with Gaudapâda's Kârikâs and the Bhâshya of Śaṅkara.* Bombay: Tookaram Tatya.

Fort, A. O. 1990. "Translation of the Māṇḍūkya Upaniṣad and Gauḍapāda's Kārikās with Śaṅkara's Commentary" in A. O. Fort, *The Self and Its States*. Delhi: Motilal Banarsidass, 137–212.

Lesimple, E. 1944. *Māṇḍūkya Upaniṣad et Kārikā de Gauḍapāda*. Paris: Adrien Maisonneuve.

Roy, B. A. N. 1938. "The *Māṇḍūkya Upaniṣad* and the *Kārikās* of Gauḍapāda" *Indian Historical Quarterly* 14: 564–569.

Wood, Thomas E. 1990. The *Māṇḍūkya Upaniṣad* and the *Āgama Śāstra: An Investigation into the Meaning of the Vedānta*. Honolulu, HI: University of Hawaii Press.

36 The *Mahānārāyaṇa Upaniṣad*

Signe Cohen

The *Mahānārāyaṇa Upaniṣad* (the "Great Upaniṣad of Nārāyaṇa") is rarely included among the classical Upaniṣads, probably because neither of the great commentators Śaṅkara (eighth century) or Ramānuja (eleventh–twelfth century) composed a commentary to the text. Some scholars, like Haas, have suggested nevertheless that the *Mahānārāyaṇa Upaniṣad* "clearly belongs in the group of older Upanishadic texts."[1] The *Mahānārāyaṇa Upaniṣad* is sometimes ascribed to the *Taittirīya* school of the *Black Yajurveda*, and sometimes to the *Atharvaveda*. It is occasionally found as constituting the tenth book of the *Taittirīya Āraṇyaka*. The text was among the fifty Upaniṣads translated into Persian under Dara Shikhoh in 1656. In the Persian translation, it was given the title *Maha-narain*. The text is sometimes also called the *Yājñikī Upaniṣad* ("The Sacrifice Upaniṣad"), perhaps because the final chapter of the text compares human life to a Vedic sacrifice.

The *Mahānārāyaṇa Upaniṣad* is quite long; one commonly used recension has sixty-four chapters, while another has eighty. Many of these chapters do not consist of original material, however, but are collections of Vedic verses known from other texts, including the *Ṛgveda*, *Taittirīya Saṃhitā*, *Vājasaneyī Saṃhitā*, and the *Atharvaveda*, There also exists a different, slightly shorter version of this Upaniṣad, the *Nārāyaṇa Upaniṣad*, formally affiliated with the *Atharvaveda*. The two Upaniṣads contain much of the same material, but in different order.

The *Mahānārāyaṇa Upaniṣad* is a theistic text celebrating a personal deity who is identified with *ātman* and *brahman*. In the eleventh chapter of the text, this deity is identified as Nārāyaṇa, one of the many names for the Hindu god Viṣṇu. This text, which may predate the *Bhagavadgītā*, provides one of the earliest textual attestations for Viṣṇu worship in India.

Nārāyaṇa is described in the text in terms reminiscent of the Cosmic Man (*Puruṣa*) lauded in *Ṛgveda* 10.90. Like Puruṣa, Nārāyaṇa possesses a thousand heads and the ability to see in all directions. He is identified with Puruṣa,[2] the *ātman* of all beings,[3] the highest *brahman*,[4] and with the deities Brahmā, Śiva, Viṣṇu, and Indra.[5] Nārāyaṇa is eternal and unchanging,[6] the highest thinker and the highest object of thought,[7] and the sum of everything that exists.[8] But he is also found within the human body, in the small space below the neck and above the navel.[9]

The cosmic aspect of Nārāyaṇa is described beautifully in 1.5:

> There is nothing higher than it, nothing smaller,
> the highest of the highest and the greatest of the great.
> It is the boundless pattern enveloped from view,
> It is the Universe, ancient, removed beyond darkness.

But simultaneously, Nārāyaṇa is located inside the heart of a human being, "where he shines in an abundance of rays." This god inside the heart:

> Hangs suspended downwards, enclosed in arteries
> Like the bud of a flower.
> Within him there is a small cave
> In which the whole world rests.[10]

He is compared both to a cosmic fire and to the small fire of digestion inside the human body:

> In him burns a great fire,
> Blazing on all sides.
> He eats and then spreads out food,
> The wise and ageless one.
> He spreads his rays sideways, above, and below.
>
> He warms the body inside which he stays,
> From the soles of the feet to the top of the head.
> In the middle is a flame, small as an atom,
> That strives upwards.
>
> He is full of glory, like a streak of lightning
> In the middle of dark clouds.
> Minute like the fiber from a grain of rice,
> In golden splendor, atom-sized.
>
> In the middle of this flame sits
> The highest *ātman*.
> He is *brahman*, Śiva, Hari (Viṣṇu), and Indra,
> The eternal supreme Lord.[11]

The *Mahānārāyaṇa Upaniṣad* has not been the subject of the same amount of scholarly research as the more recognized "classical Upaniṣads," perhaps because many have assumed it to be a more recent text. No proper critical edition of the text exists as yet. Varenne calls his edition of the

Mahānārāyaṇa Upaniṣad an "édition critique," but, as Gonda has pointed out in his review, Varenne's edition is basically a rendition of the Southern (Āndhra) recension of the text, with the variants of the two other recensions in the footnotes. No manuscripts have been consulted.[12] Varenne claims that the *Mahānārāyaṇa Upaniṣad* is not merely a haphazard collection of *mantras*, as many have suggested, but a handbook for *saṃnyāsins* (wandering ascetics).

The cosmology of the *Mahānārāyaṇa Upaniṣad*

The text opens with a vision of the highest *brahman*, here personified as the Vedic creator god Prajāpati:

> In a sea without shores, in the middle of the world,
> Over the heavens, greater than the great,
> With his splendor piercing the stars,
> He dwells as Prajāpati in his mother's womb.
>
> In him the world is destroyed and then unfolds itself anew.
> All the gods are based on him.
> He is that which already was and that which will be,
> He is in the Syllable in the highest space.[13]

The infinite nature of *brahman* is here indicated in the boundlessness of his dwelling, a "sea without shores." His association both the creation of the world and its destruction adds a new dimension to the Vedic creator figure Prajāpati ("The Lord of Creatures"), who is often in late Vedic texts associated with the creation of the world, but not with its destruction. This personal creator god is not only identified with Prajāpati, but also with other Vedic gods such as the fire god Agni, the wind god Vāyu, the sun god Sūrya, and the moon god Candramas.[14]

Ātman in the *Mahānārāyaṇa Upaniṣad*

The main focus of this Upaniṣad is on the personal deity. This deity takes the form of the *ātman* inside each person.[15] The connections between the *Mahānārāyaṇa Upaniṣad* and theistic Śaiva texts such as the *Śvetāśvatara Upaniṣad* and the *Kaivalya Upaniṣad* are evident. The *Mahānārāyaṇa Upaniṣad* quotes extensively from both of these texts. The similarities between the *Mahānārāyaṇa Upaniṣad* and the *Śvetāśvatara Upaniṣad* are not surprising, since both texts are affiliated with the *Taittirīya* school of the *Yajurveda.* Although Nārāyaṇa is identified with the inner *ātman* of all beings in this Upaniṣad, there is less focus on *ātman* in this text than in many of the classical Upaniṣads.

Brahman* in the *Mahānārāyaṇa Upaniṣad

Brahman is described as a personal being, rather than an abstract principle in the *Mahānārāyaṇa Upaniṣad.* The highest being is said to be the foundation of all the gods.[16] *Brahman* is identified with the cosmic order, *ṛta*, and with truth (*satya*).[17] He is omnipresent, and all beings are "woven" in him.[18] He has created everything, and is present in everything.[19]

Nārāyaṇa and Śiva in the *Mahānārāyaṇa Upaniṣad*

The main deity in this theistic text is, as the title indicates, Nārāyaṇa, or Viṣṇu. Nārāyaṇa is a cosmic, all-encompassing being, much like the *puruṣa* (cosmic Man) described in the *Ṛgveda*:

> The thousand-headed God,
> All-eyed, full of cosmic wellbeing,
> Nārāyaṇa, the All, the God, the love,
> The highest imperishable one …[20]
>
> Nārāyaṇa is also identified with *ātman* and *brahman*:
> Nārāyaṇa is the light beyond.
> Nārāyaṇa is the highest self (*ātman*).
> Nārāyaṇa is the highest *brahman* …[21]

He is described as the highest object of knowledge,[22] and as identical with the *ātman* within each person.[23] He encompasses everything that exists.[24]

Nārāyaṇa is the focus of section 11, but elsewhere in the *Mahānārāyaṇa Upaniṣad*, the deity is, as in the *Śvetāśvatara Upaniṣad*, frequently identified with Rudra/Śiva .[25] This Upaniṣad goes quite far in its syncretism; the highest deity is identified with several Vedic gods such as Prajāpati and Agni, as well as Viṣṇu (in the form of Nārāyaṇa) and Śiva. Later theistic Upaniṣads tend to extol *either* Viṣṇu *or* Śiva; it is quite uncommon for an Upaniṣad to give equal weight to both deities and identify them completely with one another. The identification of Nārāyaṇa, who has given the text its name with Rudra/Śiva, may perhaps be explained as an influence from the *Śvetāśvatara Upaniṣad* with its budding Śaiva (Śiva-oriented) theology.

The ethics of the *Mahānārāyaṇa Upaniṣad*

The ninth chapter of the text emphasizes the importance of good deeds:

> Just like the fragrance from a tree covered in blossoms reaches far away, so does the fragrance from a good deed also reach far away.[26]

In an even more striking metaphor, a person who tries to do good is compared to a juggler walking in the edge of a sword:

> Just like a juggler says: "Gently, gently, or I will be harmed and fall into the pit" when he walks on the edge of a sword placed over a put, so a man should keep away from a lie.[27]

The sixty-second chapter of the Upaniṣad outlines twelve goals of human existence: Truth, *tapas* (penance), restraint, quietude, giving, *dharma* (duty), begetting children, maintaining the sacred fire, performing the *Agnihotra* (daily fire ritual), performing the *Yajña* (sacrifice), mental contemplation, and renunciation. Truth is not merely the absence of falsehood, but a cosmic principle that upholds the world:

> Through truth the wind blows and the sun shines.
> Truth is the foundation of speech.
> Everything rests on truth.
> That is why they have called truth the highest.[28]

Tapas is likewise more than mere human bodily mortifications; the gods have become godlike through their performance of *tapas*, and wise men will attain heaven by practicing *tapas*.[29] Restraint also leads to heaven,[30] as does quietude.[31] Charitable giving is the foundation of the world and of all living beings,[32] and *dharma* (duty) wards off all forms of evil.[33] Interestingly, begetting children is presented, as in the Vedas, as a debt a man owes to his ancestors.[34] The three sacred fires a householder is required to maintain are identified both with the three Vedas and with the triple world – the *Gārhaspatya* ("householder") fire is identified with the *Ṛgveda* and the earth, the *Anvāhārya* ("supply") fire with the *Yajurveda* and the atmosphere, and the *Āhavanīya* ("oblation") fire with the *Sāmaveda* and the highest heaven.[35] The Agnihotra, the daily offering into the fire in the morning and evening, is said to be the "gate to the sacrifice" and the "light of the heavenly world."[36] Performing *Yajña* (sacrifice) is praised because the gods kept the demons away and reached heaven through their sacrifices, and because sacrifices can turn enemies into friends.[37] Mental contemplation is said to be a form of purification coming from Prajāpati himself. This mental contemplation is identified with the creative vision of the Vedic poets or seers (*ṛṣi*).[38] Renunciation is, intriguingly, identified with the creator god Brahmā himself.

At first sight, some of these goals seem contradictory; how can someone be a renouncer and at the same time beget children? Doesn't renunciation usually involve leaving both family life and ritual obligations behind?

The wealth of quotations from Vedic texts in the *Mahānārāyaṇa Upaniṣad* suggests that the text is not trying to make the case that the Upaniṣadic teachings have completely done away with the need for Vedic knowledge. On the contrary, knowledge of both Vedic verses and Vedic rituals are presented as an essential part of human life. The significance of the Vedas is underscored by the inclusion of entire hymns from the *Ṛgveda* and the *Yajurveda* in the

Mahānārāyaṇa Upaniṣad. But if the Vedic texts and rituals are still valid, does this mean that a renouncer still has all the ritual obligations of a householder? The *Mahānārāyaṇa Upaniṣad* suggests that the old ritual duties must be reinterpreted:

> When a man of knowledge performs a sacrificial ritual, his *ātman* is the sacrifice, his faith is the sacrificer's wife, his body is the fuel, his chest is the place of sacrifice, his hair is the sacrificial grass, his hair knot is the ritual broom, his heart is the sacrificial post, his love is the butter, his passion is the sacrificial animal, his *tapas* is the fire, his self-control is the slaughterer, his speech is the *hotṛ* priest, his breath is the *udgātṛ* priest, his mind the *brahman*, and his ears the *agīdh* …[39]

In this passage, the old Vedic sacrifice is interpreted as an internal process, rather than an external ritual. The Vedic sacrifice is not superfluous; the various parts of the internalized and symbolic sacrifice are equated with different aspects of the ascetic lifestyle. The *Mahānārāyaṇa Upaniṣad* does not reject the old Vedic rituals, but rather claims that ascetic practices are one possible way to perform the rites. But what of the obligation to have children? On this issue, there is a contradiction in the text that is simply left unresolved. Having children is listed as one of the twelve goals of human life, and yet the Upaniṣad also states: "Not through work (*karma*), or children, or wealth, but through renunciation was immortality obtained by a few …"[40] Older Vedic texts suggested that having children was a form of immortality; the *Taittirīya Brāhmaṇa* says, for example: "You are born again in your children. That, O mortal, is your immortality."[41] The *Mahānārāyaṇa Upaniṣad* does state that having children is a way to repay one's debts to one's ancestors.[42] The Upaniṣad does not, however, make the claim that having children leads to immortality, although it suggests that *tapas*, restraint, and quietude all will lead to heaven. Perhaps having children is still seen as a normal and expected part of human life, although family life does not, in itself, lead to immortality. But is family life possible to reconcile with the goal of renunciation and *tapas*? Perhaps that depends on how, precisely, *tapas* is defined.

Tapas in the *Mahānārāyaṇa Upaniṣad*

Tapas, or ascetic penance, plays a significant part in the text. Normally, *tapas* would involve austerities, self-discipline, and solitude. But *tapas* is here not merely defined in the traditional way as bodily mortifications:

> Truth is *tapas*. Studying is *tapas*. Quiet nature is *tapas*. Restraint is *tapas*. Charity is *tapas*. Sacrifice is *tapas*. When one says *Bhūr*, *bhuvaḥ*, *svar*, *brahman*, worship this – then that, too is *tapas*.[43]

If *tapas*, like the old Vedic rituals, can be reinterpreted as interior, rather than exterior, it may perhaps be possible to reconcile the idea of having a family with embracing *tapas*. If *tapas* implies a pious mindset of restraint and contemplation, rather than complete sexual abstinence and solitude, it may not be completely at odds with family life.

Tapas is throughout the text associated with salvation and with reaching a higher state:

> Through *tapas* in the beginning
> The gods attained the state of being gods,
> And the wise attained heaven.
> Through *tapas* can we ward off enemies and friends.
> Everything rests in *tapas*.
> That is why they say that *tapas* is the highest.[44]

Quotations from older texts

The *Mahānārāyaṇa Upaniṣad* is rich in quotations from Vedic texts. Many verses from the *Ṛgveda*,[45] *Yajurveda*,[46] and *Atharvaveda*[47] are included, as well as verses from the *Kaṭha*,[48] *Śvetāśvatara*,[49] and *Muṇḍaka Upaniṣads*.[50] Why is such a large part of the text made up of quotations? By quoting from old Vedic texts, the authors of the *Mahānārāyaṇa Upaniṣad* align their Upaniṣad with the Vedic tradition itself. While other Upaniṣads reject the Vedic tradition, the *Mahānārāyaṇa Upaniṣad* draws on it, while reinterpreting it for its own purposes. It presents the Vedic tradition, not as something to be superseded by its teachings, but rather as something that is fulfilled by the Upaniṣad itself. The quotations from the *Kaṭha*, *Śvetāśvatara*, and *Muṇḍaka Upaniṣad*, all Upaniṣads formally affiliated with the *Black Yajurveda*, suggest that the *Mahānārāyaṇa Upaniṣad* itself may be particularly indebted to and familiar with this tradition. This suggests that the *Mahānārāyaṇa Upaniṣad*'s own affiliation with the *Taittirīya* school of the *Black Yajurveda* may be genuine.

The age of the *Mahānārāyaṇa Upaniṣad*

There is general agreement that the *Mahānārāyaṇa Upaniṣad* was likely composed a short time after the "principal" Upaniṣads commented on by Śaṅkara. Deussen suggests that this Upaniṣad contains a mixture of old and new materials.[51] He concludes that the *Mahānārāyaṇa Upaniṣad* should be considered an intermediary link between the early Upaniṣads of the three Vedas and those of the *Atharvaveda*.[52] Varenne proposes that the text belongs to the middle group of the metrical Upaniṣads, and that it was composed around the third, or at the very latest the fourth, century CE. Olivelle suggests that the text is "in all probability post-Buddhist."[53] The metrical evidence of the verse portion suggests that the text was composed slightly later than the *Muṇḍaka*, *Kaṭha*, and *Śvetāśvatara Upaniṣad*, but before the later Vaiṣṇava Upaniṣads. The term *Vedānta* is used in this Upaniṣad,[54] which some scholars have seen as a sign of late composition.[55] *Vedānta* is one of the six classical schools of Hindu philosophy. Since the word is also used, in a non-technical sense, in the *Śvetāśvatara Upaniṣad*, a text that the *Mahānārāyaṇa Upaniṣad* quotes extensively, the occurrence of this term here cannot, however, be used as evidence for the date of the text.

Notes

1 Haas 1922: 2.
2 *Mahānārāyaṇa Upaniṣad* 11.2.
3 *Mahānārāyaṇa Upaniṣad* 11.2.
4 *Mahānārāyaṇa Upaniṣad* 11.4.
5 *Mahānārāyaṇa Upaniṣad* 11.12.
6 *Mahānārāyaṇa Upaniṣad* 11.3.
7 *Mahānārāyaṇa Upaniṣad* 11.4.
8 *Mahānārāyaṇa Upaniṣad* 11.5.
9 *Mahānārāyaṇa Upaniṣad* 11.7.
10 *Mahānārāyaṇa Upaniṣad* 11.8.
11 *Mahānārāyaṇa Upaniṣad* 11.9–12.
12 Gonda 1963: 299.
13 *Mahānārāyaṇa Upaniṣad* 1.1–2.
14 *Mahānārāyaṇa Upaniṣad* 1.7.
15 *Mahānārāyaṇa Upaniṣad* 11.2.
16 *Mahānārāyaṇa Upaniṣad* 1.2.
17 *Mahānārāyaṇa Upaniṣad* 1.6.
18 *Mahānārāyaṇa Upaniṣad* 1.15.
19 *Mahānārāyaṇa Upaniṣad* 10.3.
20 *Mahānārāyaṇa Upaniṣad* 11.1.
21 *Mahānārāyaṇa Upaniṣad* 11.4.
22 *Mahānārāyaṇa Upaniṣad* 11.3.
23 *Mahānārāyaṇa Upaniṣad* 11.2.
24 *Mahānārāyaṇa Upaniṣad* 11.5.
25 *Mahānārāyaṇa Upaniṣad* 10.19; 10.24; 11.3; 16, 18, 43–47.
26 *Mahānārāyaṇa Upaniṣad* 9. 1.
27 *Mahānārāyaṇa Upaniṣad* 9.2.
28 *Mahānārāyaṇa Upaniṣad* 63. 2.
29 *Mahānārāyaṇa Upaniṣad* 63. 3.
30 *Mahānārāyaṇa Upaniṣad* 63. 4.
31 *Mahānārāyaṇa Upaniṣad* 63. 5.
32 *Mahānārāyaṇa Upaniṣad* 63. 6.
33 *Mahānārāyaṇa Upaniṣad* 63. 7.
34 *Mahānārāyaṇa Upaniṣad* 63. 8.
35 *Mahānārāyaṇa Upaniṣad* 63. 9.
36 *Mahānārāyaṇa Upaniṣad* 63. 10.
37 *Mahānārāyaṇa Upaniṣad* 63. 11.
38 *Mahānārāyaṇa Upaniṣad* 63. 12.
39 *Mahānārāyaṇa Upaniṣad* 64.1.
40 *Mahānārāyaṇa Upaniṣad* 10.21.

41 *Taittirīya Brāhmaṇa* 1.5.5.6.
42 *Mahānārāyaṇa Upaniṣad* 63.8.
43 *Mahānārāyaṇa Upaniṣad* 1.8.
44 *Mahānārāyaṇa Upaniṣad* 63.3.
45 *Ṛgveda* 1.18, 1.22, 1.164, 2.3, 4.58, 5.82, 9.96, and 10.81.
46 *Yajurveda* 32.1–4.
47 *Atharvaveda* 10.8.13.
48 *Kaṭha Upaniṣad* 6.9.
49 *Śvetāśvatara Upaniṣad* 4.2.
50 *Muṇḍaka Upaniṣad* 2.1.
51 Deussen 1897: 241.
52 Deussen 1897: 242.
53 Olivelle 1981: 266.
54 *Mahānārāyaṇa Upaniṣad* 10.22.
55 Deussen 1897.

Further reading

Deussen, P. 1897. *Sechzig Upaniṣads des Veda, aus dem Sanskrit übersetzt und mit Einleitungen und Anmerkungen versehen*. Leipzig: F. A. Brockhaus.

Gonda, J. 1963. "Jean Varenne: *La Mahānārāyaṇa Upaniṣad*" *Indo-Iranian Journal* 6: 298–301.

Haas, G. 1922. "Recurrent and Parallel Passages in the Principal Upaniṣads and the Bhagavad Gītā" *Journal of the American Oriental Society* 42: 1–43.

Jacob, G. A. 1888. *The Mahānārāyaṇa Upaniṣad of the Atharva-Veda*. Bombay Sanskrit Series No. XXXV. Bombay: Nirnaya Sagar Press.

Olivelle, P. 1981. "Contributions to the Semantic History of *Saṃnyāsa*" *Journal of the American Oriental Society* 101: 265–274.

Varenne, J. 1960. *La Mahānārāyaṇa Upaniṣad*. 2 vols. Paris: Editions E. de Boccard.

Part V

The later Upaniṣads

37 The Vaiṣṇava Upaniṣads

Signe Cohen

The Vaiṣṇava Upaniṣads identify *ātman/brahman* with the god Viṣṇu or with one of Viṣṇu's *avatāras* (incarnations). The worship of Viṣṇu has ancient roots in Hinduism; there are three hymns in the *Ṛgveda* (ca. 1500 BCE) devoted to Viṣṇu. In the *Ṛgveda*, Viṣṇu is depicted as a benevolent figure, possibly a sun god. He is a friend and ally of the thunder god Indra and helps him slay the chaos monster Vṛtra.[1] Even though Viṣṇu is a minor figure in the Vedas, he becomes one of the most central gods in later Hinduism. In classical Hinduism, Viṣṇu is a cosmic protector, and he helps maintain the world through a series of *avatāras* (incarnations). Mythological texts often list ten or twenty-two *avatāras* of Viṣṇu. Some of his most well-known and popular incarnations include Kṛṣṇa, the warrior prince Rāma, and the man-lion (*Nṛsiṃha*). Kṛṣṇa is one of the main characters in the *Bhagavadgītā* ("The Song of the Lord," ca. third–second century BCE), perhaps the most well-known Hindu text today. In the *Bhagavadgīta*, which is a part of the larger *Mahābhārata* ("Great Story of India") epic, Kṛṣṇa gives advice to the anguished warrior Arjuna on the eve of a great battle. The other great epic Sanskrit poem, the *Rāmāyaṇa* (ca. third century BCE), tells the story of Rāma's heroic struggle to rescue his kidnapped wife and slay a ten-headed demon. There are also numerous other mythological texts detailing the deeds of Viṣṇu and his incarnations.

The medieval *Muktikā Upaniṣad* lists fourteen Vaiṣṇava Upaniṣads, devoted either to Viṣṇu himself or to one of his incarnations. In these texts, Viṣṇu is identified with the cosmic *brahman* and/or the inner *ātman*. This chapter will analyze some of the most important ones among them.

The *Nārāyaṇa Upaniṣad*

The *Nārāyaṇa Upaniṣād* is formally affiliated with the *Black Yajurveda*. The brief text, which has some overlapping material with the *Mahānārāyaṇa Upaniṣad*, presents Nārāyaṇa as the supreme being and the creator of the world. Nārāyaṇa is identified with the cosmic *puruṣa* ("spirit") and with *prāṇa* ("the life breath").

The first section of the Upaniṣad states that everything is born from Nārāyaṇa, including the five elements (ether, wind, light, water, and earth), thought (*manas*), and the human senses, as well as all the gods, all the sages, and all living beings.

Nārāyaṇa is the entirety of the universe, including time and space. He is "eternal, flawless, ineffable and changeless."[2] The Upaniṣad promises freedom from fear, the attainment of all desires, and immortality to a person who studies this text.[3] A person who studies the Upaniṣad in the morning will be free of all the sins he committed at night, someone who studies it in the evening will be free of all sins committed during the day, and someone who studies it at midday will be free of "the five great sins and the five lesser sins." The five great sins (*mahāpātakas*) are killing a Brahman, drinking alcohol, stealing gold, sleeping with one's teacher's wife, and consorting with people who have done any of the aforementioned things. There are different lists of lesser sins (*upapātakas*), and it is not clear which five are referred to here. Lists of lesser sins often include things like killing a cow, selling oneself into slavery, abandoning one's teacher, mother, father, or son, no longer maintain a sacred fire in one's home, breaking a vow, selling one's wife or child, or teaching the Vedas for pay.

The *Nārāyaṇa Upaniṣad* also introduces a *mantra* to the deity: *Oṃ namo Nārāyaṇāya* ("*Oṃ*, homage to Nārāyaṇa") and promises long life, prosperity, wealth, and immortality to those who study the *mantra*. The text does not, like earlier Upaniṣads, emphasize knowledge of *ātman* or *brahman* as a path to salvation; rather, salvation and immortality can be achieved through the studying of the correct *mantra*.

The *Nṛsiṃhatāpanīya Upaniṣad*

This Upaniṣad is devoted to Viṣṇu's incarnation as a man-lion (*Nṛsiṃha*). It is formally affiliated with the *Atharvaveda* and is divided into two parts, called respectively the *Nṛsiṃhapūrvatāpanīya Upaniṣad* ("The Earlier Ascetic Upaniṣad of the Man-Lion") and the *Nṛsiṃhottaratāpanīya Upaniṣad* ("The Latter Ascetic Upaniṣad of the Man-Lion"). The man-lion *avatāra* of Viṣṇu is described in the *Viṣṇu Purāṇa* (ca. eighth–ninth century CE), the *Bhāgavata Purāṇa* (ca. ninth–tenth century CE), and other medieval mythological texts: The demon Hiraṇyakaśipu is given the boon that he cannot be killed either inside or outside, by day or night, by a human or an animal. Viṣṇu accordingly kills the demon on the threshold at twilight in the form of a man-lion, which is neither human nor animal. Since the *Nṛsiṃhatāpanīya Upaniṣad* is mentioned by the sixth-century Gauḍapāda, the Upaniṣad must be older than the *Viṣṇu* or *Bhagavata Purāṇa*. The Upaniṣad presents the story of the man-lion very briefly: "Because man is the bravest and best of all creatures, and because the lion is the bravest and the best, the highest god became the man-lion. The imperishable one takes this form for the sake of the world's well-being."[4]

The first part of the text focuses on the worship of Nṛsiṃha through a sacred *mantra*. This *mantrarāja* ("the king of *mantras*") is present in the creation of the world[5] and is the equivalent of the holy *oṃ* itself.[6] While many *mantras* consist of a syllable or two, the *mantrarāja* of Nṛsiṃha is a whole verse:

Ugraṃ vīram mahāviṣṇum
Jvalantaṃ sarvatomukham
Nṛsiṃhaṃ bhīṣaṇaṃ bhadram
Mṛtyurmṛtyuṃ namamy aham[7]

The terrible, powerful great Viṣṇu,
Flaming facing in all directions,
The Man-Lion, terrifying and auspicious,
The Death of Deaths. Him I adore.

The Upaniṣad explains the esoteric meaning of each word in the *mantrarāja* in great detail. A person who knows this *mantra* will not only overcome sins (the killing of a Brahman, the killing of a man, and the killing of an embryo are listed),[8] but also be able to render all the gods and demons spell-bound.[9]

The text also describes the construction of a sacred circular diagram (*maṇḍala*) called *Sudarśanam* ("Beautiful to look at").[10] Different *mantras* are inscribed in concentric circles around a central *oṃ*. Surrounding the entire circle is the *mantrarāja* of the man-lion. The Upaniṣad promises that wearing the diagram around the neck or arm or tied in one's hair will "destroy evil spirits and protect from death,"[11] or charm men, gods, or *yakṣas* (nature spirits).[12] Knowing this circular diagram makes a person into a teacher of all the *mantras*, even if that person is just a child or a youth.[13] The intriguing part of the *Nṛsiṃhatāpanīya Upaniṣad*'s treatment of *mantras* is the lack of emphasis on the *mantra* as a spoken utterance or sacred sound; a written *mantra* worn on the body has the same effect as one spoken out loud. This emphasis on writing is a sign of fairly late composition.

The second part of the Upaniṣad equates the god Nṛsiṃha with the *ātman*, with the sacred syllable *oṃ*, and with *brahman* itself. The four verse lines of the *mantrarāja* are here identified with the four states of the *ātman* (the waking state, sleep, dreamless sleep, and the fourth state of deep contemplation). This part of the text contains ideas that are familiar from the older Upaniṣads, such as the ineffability of the supreme *ātman*.

The *Rāmatāpanīya Upaniṣad*

This text, formally affiliated with the *Atharvaveda*, is divided into two parts, just like the *Nṛsiṃhatapanīya Upaniṣad*, which the text is modeled after: *Rāmapūrvatāpanīya Upaniṣad* ("The Earlier Ascetic Upaniṣad of

Rāma") and *Rāmottaratāpanīya Upaniṣad* ("The Latter Ascetic Upaniṣad of Rāma"). The Upaniṣad praises Rāma, the warrior prince incarnation of Viṣṇu, as the highest reality.

The text begins by giving several possible etymologies of the name Rāma. The text then introduces a *mantra* to Rāma (*Rāṃ Rāmāya namaḥ*) and gives detailed instructions (verses 58–84) for drawing a mystical diagram (*maṇḍala*) to be used in the meditation on Rāma. The diagram contains two triangles within a hexagon as well as numerous letters and syllables with esoteric meaning. The Upaniṣad describes the diagram as "a riddle with deep meaning, which even a god finds difficult to grasp" and warns that "a common man" should not have access to it.[14] The diagram is said to have the ability to give sons to the childless,[15] which ties in well with the life story of Rāma. According to the story of Rāma as it is told in the *Rāmāyaṇa* epic, king Daśaratha was childless and only becomes the father of Rāma and his brothers after receiving a supernatural reward for his piety.

The text contains many references to Rāma's life story as it is known from the *Rāmāyaṇa* epic. It mentions his father Daśaratha, born of the lineage of Raghu,[16] his wife Sītā,[17] his mother Kausalyā,[18] his younger brother Lakṣmaṇa,[19] his slaying of a ten-headed demon,[20] his search for Sītā,[21] his slaying of the demon Kabandha,[22] the rival monkey brothers Bālin and Sugrīva,[23] the monkey Hanuman jumping over the ocean to the city of Laṅkā,[24] and the battle of Laṅkā.[25]

The second part of the Upaniṣad contains some material borrowed from the *Jābāla Upaniṣad* (see the chapter on Saṃnyāsa Upaniṣads). The sacred sound *oṃ* is, as in the *Māṇḍūkya Upaniṣad*, broken into three separate parts, *a*, *u*, and *m*. These parts are, as in the *Māṇḍūkya*, identified with the different states of the self: the waking state, the sleeping state, and dreamless sleep. But in the *Rāmottaratapanīya Upaniṣad*, these states of the self are further identified with Rāma's brothers Lakṣmaṇa (the waking state), Śatrughna (the sleeping state), and Bharata (dreamless sleep). Rāma himself and his wife Sītā are identified with the syllable *oṃ* in its entirety and with the mystical fourth state of the self.[26]

The *Avyakta Upaniṣad*

The *Avyakta Upaniṣad* ("The Upaniṣad of the Unmanifest") is affiliated with the *Sāmaveda*. Conceptually, it has a great deal in common with the *Nṛsiṃhatāpanīya Upaniṣad*. Like the *Nṛsiṃhatāpanīya Upaniṣad* it explains the mystical significance of the *Mantrarāja*, the "royal" *mantra* of Viṣṇu's Nṛsiṃha incarnation. Nṛsiṃha is in this text both an incarnation of Viṣṇu and an embodiment of the knowledge of the *ātman*.[27]

The Upaniṣad derives its name from the cosmological opening section of the text:

> Previously, there was nothing here, no sky, no atmosphere, and no earth. There was only light, with no beginning and end, neither small nor great, both formless and formed, indistinguishable and yet consisting of knowledge and bliss.[28]

From this primordial unmanifest state, the light, which is referred to as "one being, without a second,"[29] divides itself into *puruṣa* ("the spirit") and *māyā* ("illusion"). The spirit and illusion unite to form a cosmic egg, and from the egg, the creator god Prajāpati is born. A voice then speaks to Prajāpati and explains that he has been born from the Unmanifest (*avyakta*), and that his role is to create. When Prajāpati demands to know who is speaking to him, the speaker merely replies: "Seek to know me through asceticism."[30] Prajāpati practices asceticism for a thousand years, and then he begins to chant the holy *Mantrarāja* to Nṛsiṃha. After chanting for a thousand years, he sees a vision of Viṣṇu, a being made of light, embraced by his wife, the goddess Śrī. Viṣṇu has the face of a lion and the body of a man, and his three eyes are the moon, the sun, and fire.[31] Prajāpati has been commanded to create, but he does not know how. When he bows down to Viṣṇu, Viṣṇu tells him to meditate on the *ātman* while reciting the *Mantrarāja*. Viṣṇu/ Nṛsiṃha explains that this is "the great Upaniṣad" and the "secret of the gods," and that it cannot be found in the Vedas. But a person who knows the secret will never again have to be reborn, but is united with Viṣṇu himself.[32] Prajāpati meditates accordingly, and he proceeds to create the universe out of thirty syllables from the thirty-two syllable *mantra*. With the last two syllables he maintains and upholds the worlds.[33] Prajāpati creates the Brahmans (priests) out of the first twelve syllables of the *mantra*, and the Kṣatriyas (warriors and kings) and Vaiśyas (merchants and farmers) out of the next two sets of twenty syllables.[34] But because he created the last group of people, the Śūdras (servants) without speaking any syllables, Śūdras remain without knowledge of the Vedas.[35] Since the *mantra* he uses to create has four verse lines, he uses one line to create each of the four Vedas (*Ṛgveda*, *Sāmaveda*, *Yajurveda*, *Atharvaveda*). Prajāpati then creates all the gods, including Indra. Indra is the youngest of the gods, and the other gods do not accept him as a king over them, even if Prajāpati tells him to rule. But when Prajāpati writes the *Mantrarāja* on a golden disk and fastens it around Indra's neck, the other gods are dazzled by his power and agree to accept him as their ruler.[36] The Upaniṣad promises that anyone who recites the *Mantrarāja* will be released from all sins, and also purify both his ancestors and his descendants till the end of time. He will be successful in all things, and reach spiritual liberation in his life time. When he dies, he will encounter Viṣṇu in his radiant form as the man-lion.[37] But the *mantra* should not be shared with anyone who is lacking in faith, or to someone who is not devoted to Viṣṇu, not an ascetic, or to one who is not virtuous or chaste.[38]

The *Avyakta Upaniṣad* combines classical Upaniṣadic teachings with devotion to Viṣṇu, especially in his man-lion *avatāra*, Sāṃkhya philosophical concepts such as *puruṣa*, *prakṛti*, and *avyakta*, and an emphasis on an ascetic lifestyle. The text is mentioned both by Gauḍapāda (seventh century CE) and Śaṅkara (eighth century CE), and must therefore have been composed prior to the seventh century.

The *Kṛṣṇa Upaniṣad*

This Upaniṣad, dedicated to Viṣṇus *avatāra* Kṛṣṇa, is affiliated with the *Atharvaveda*. The text is filled with references to the life of Kṛṣṇa and is in many ways more akin to mythological texts like the Purāṇas than to the Upaniṣads. According to the *Kṛṣṇa Upaniṣad*, Viṣṇu encountered a group of sages in the forest. The sages are so enchanted with Rāma that they want to embrace him, and Rāma promises to take the form of Kṛṣṇa and ensure that the sages are reborn as female shepherdesses (*gopīs*) so that their embraces can be permitted. Viṣṇu then becomes incarnated as Kṛṣṇa and wanders in the forest as a shepherd. The text goes on to identify the other characters in Kṛṣṇa's life as manifestations of abstract principles or gods: The hymns of the Vedas become cows for him to herd, the Upaniṣads become shepherdesses, Bliss and Spiritual Liberation become his foster parents Nanda and Yaśodā, the god Śiva becomes his bow, and the goddess Kālī becomes his mace. The text claims that meditating on how the universe originated from Viṣṇu and on the god's nature and chanting his name will lead to liberation from the cycle of death and rebirth.

The *Garuḍa Upaniṣad*

This very short Upaniṣad is formally ascribed to the *Atharvaveda*. The text is named after Viṣṇu's divine bird, Garuda, on which the god flies through the heavens. Although it is classified as a Vaiṣṇava Upaniṣad in the *Muktikā Upaniṣad*, this text has little to do with either Viṣṇu or *ātman* and *brahman*. Instead, the *Garuḍa Upaniṣad* contains a charm to remove poison from snake bites:

> Struck is the poison, destroyed is the poison, annihilated is the poison. It is struck by Indra's thunder bolt, *svāhā*, whether it comes from snakes, cankers, scorpions, ulcers, salamanders, amphibians, or rats.[39]

The charm is then followed by an invocation of twelve mythical serpents, which suggests that the primary purpose of the charm is to heal snake bites. The text promises that anyone who hears the text recited on the night of the full moon and then wears it as an amulet will not be bitten by snakes for twelve years.[40] The reference to "hearing" and "wearing" the text suggests the people who wanted protection from snake bites likely consulted someone who could both read the text aloud and write it down.

So why is this text called an Upaniṣad? The introductory paragraph of the text traces the lineage of the snake charm:

> I will teach the science of *brahman*. Brahma taught it to Nārada, Nārada to Bṛhatsena, Bṛhatsena to Indra, Indra to Bṛhadvāja, and Bṛhatvāja to his students who wanted to save their lives.[41]

This lineage of mythical teachers and students is reminiscent of those found in the older Upaniṣads and may have led to the classification of the text, which otherwise contains no classical Upaniṣadic themes, as an "Upaniṣad." The affiliation with the *Atharvaveda* is a natural one, since the *Atharvaveda* is an ancient text filled with charms, including charms against poisonous serpents.[42]

The Upaniṣad's association with Viṣṇu's bird Garuḍa is likewise a natural one, since Garuḍa is known for his hatred of snakes. According to one myth, Garuḍa's mother was once imprisoned in a hell guarded by serpents, and Garuḍa had to battle the serpents that guarded the drink of immortality in order to free her. This brief text demonstrates that the title "Upaniṣad" became, over time, a label that could be applied rather loosely.

Notes

1 *Ṛgveda* 6.69.5.
2 *Nārāyaṇa Upaniṣad* 2.
3 *Nārāyaṇa Upaniṣad* 3.
4 *Nṛsiṃhapūrvatāpanīya Upaniṣad* 2. 4.
5 *Nṛsiṃhapūrvatāpanīya Upaniṣad* 1.1.
6 *Nṛsiṃhapūrvatāpanīya Upaniṣad* 2.1.
7 *Nṛsiṃhapūrvatāpanīya Upaniṣad* 2.3.
8 *Nṛsiṃhapūrvatāpanīya Upaniṣad* 5.4.
9 *Nṛsiṃhapūrvatāpanīya Upaniṣad* 5.5.
10 *Nṛsiṃhapūrvatāpanīya Upaniṣad* 5.1–5.2.
11 *Nṛsiṃhapūrvatāpanīya Upaniṣad* 5.2.
12 *Nṛsiṃhapūrvatāpanīya Upaniṣad* 5.7.
13 *Nṛsiṃhapūrvatāpanīya Upaniṣad* 5.2.
14 *Rāmapūrvatāpaīya Upaniṣad* 84.
15 *Rāmapūrvatāpaīya Upaniṣad* 83.
16 *Rāmapūrvatapanīya Upaniṣad* 1.
17 *Rāmapūrvatapanīya Upaniṣad* 17.
18 *Rāmapūrvatapanīya Upaniṣad* 27.
19 *Rāmapūrvatapanīya Upaniṣad* 28.
20 *Rāmapūrvatapanīya Upaniṣad* 32.
21 *Rāmapūrvatapanīya Upaniṣad* 36.
22 *Rāmapūrvatapanīya Upaniṣad* 37.
23 *Rāmapūrvatapanīya Upaniṣad* 40–42.
24 *Rāmapūrvatapanīya Upaniṣad* 43.
25 *Rāmapūrvatapanīya Upaniṣad* 46.
26 *Rāmottarayāpanīya Upaniṣad* 3.
27 *Avyakta Upaniṣad*, Introductory blessing.

28 *Avyakta Upaniṣad* 1.1.
29 *Avyakta Upaniṣad* 1.2.
30 *Avyakta Upaniṣad* 1.3.
31 *Avyakta Upaniṣad* 2.1–2.
32 *Avyakta Upaniṣad* 3.2–3.3.
33 *Avyakta Upaniṣad* 5.1.
34 *Avyakta Upaniṣad* 5.3.
35 *Avyakta Upaniṣad* 5.3.
36 *Avyakta Upaniṣad* 6.2.
37 *Avyakta Upaniṣad* 7. 1.
38 *Avyakta Upaniṣad* 7.2.
39 *Garuḍa Upaniṣad* 2.
40 *Garuḍa Upaniṣad* 3.
41 *Garuḍa Upaniṣad* 1.
42 See for example *Atharvaveda* 7.88.

Further reading

Ayyangar, T. 1941. *The Vaiṣnavopaniṣads*. Madras: Adyar Library. (Reprint Jain Publishing Company, 2006.)

Bryant, E. 2004. *Krishna: The Beautiful Legend of God (Śrīmad Bhāgavata Purāṇa Book X)*. London: Penguin.

Dumont, P.-E. 1940. "The *Avyakta Upaniṣad*" *Journal of the American Oriental Society* 60: 338–355.

Sastri, A. M. 1923. *The Vaiṣṇava-Upaniṣads with the Commentary of Śrī Upaniṣad-Brahma-Yogin*. Madras: Adyar Library.

38 The Śaiva Upaniṣads

Signe Cohen

While the earliest Upaniṣads contain little hints of theism here and there, a systematic identification of the cosmic force *brahman* or the inner *ātman* with a personal god is not encountered until the *Śvetāśvatara Upaniṣad*. In identifying the *ātman* with the god Śiva, the *Śvetāśvatara Upaniṣad* marks the beginning of a theistic trend in the Upaniṣads that continued for many centuries.

Śaiva Upaniṣads, or Upaniṣads devoted to the god Śiva, began to flourish after the composition of the *Śvetāśvatara Upaniṣad*. In this chapter, we will examine some of the more well-known Śaiva Upaniṣads. These include texts that identify *ātman* and *brahman* with Śiva himself, as well as Upaniṣads that extol one of his two sons, Skanda and Gaṇeśa, as the highest reality. These texts, composed during a time period that began shortly after the composition of the *Śvetāśvatara Upaniṣad* and concludes around the sixteenth or seventeenth century of the common era, are a testament to the gradual rise of Śiva worship in Hinduism, as well as to the enduring presence of Upaniṣadic ideas in India.

The *Kaivalya Upaniṣad*

The *Kaivalya Upaniṣad* ("The Upaniṣad of Solitude") is a short Śaiva Upaniṣad, composed in verse, formally affiliated with the *Atharvaveda*. The text does indeed have some features that associates it with the *Atharvaveda*, but it is also closely tied to the tradition of the *Black Yajurveda*. Like the *Mahānārāyaṇa Upaniṣad*, it is heavily influenced by the *Śvetāśvatara*. The commentator Nārāyaṇa refers to the *Kaivalya Upaniṣad* as the *Brahmaśatarudrīya*, "Brahmā's Hundred Names of Rudra." This alternative title may be inspired by section twenty-four of the *Kaivalya Upaniṣad*: "He who studies the *Hundred Names of Rudra*, becomes pure as fire …") It is likely that the authors of the Upaniṣadic passage were referring to the ancient Śaiva text known as the *Śatarudrīya* ("The hundred names of Rudra"), but the commentator Nārāyaṇa understands the name as a reference to the *Kaivalya Upaniṣad* itself. The *Brahma-* of the title may refer to the god Brahmā, who is presented as a wisdom teacher in this Upaniṣad.

The references to the *Śatarudrīya* in the *Kaivalya Upaniṣad* confirms the Upaniṣad's connection to the *Black Yajurveda.* The *Śatarudrīya*, a list of the hundred names of the god Rudra/Śiva, is found in several late Vedic texts associated with the *Yajurveda*: The *Taittirīya Saṃhitā* 4.5, *Kaṭha Saṃhitā* 17, 11–16, *Maitrāyaṇī Saṃhitā* 2.9, 2–9, etc. The *Śatarudrīya* is so closely associated with the *Yajurveda* that it is sometimes regarded as the stereotypical *Yajurvedic* text, as we can see in the *Mahābhārata* formulation: "Of birds, you are the Garuḍa, of snakes Ananta, of Vedas the *Sāman*, and of *Yajus* the *Satarudrīya* …"[1]

The teachings of the *Kaivalya Upaniṣad* are presented by the god Brahmā to the sage Āśvalāyana. Āśvalāyana is associated with one of the *śākhās* of the *Ṛgveda*, and his presence in the text imparts a sense of ancient Vedic authority to the Upaniṣad.

As in the other Upaniṣads of the *Atharvaveda*, *brahman* is presented as the unknown principle that the wisdom seeker wants to understand:

> Teach me, Sir, the supreme knowledge of *brahman*,
> That hidden thing which is always sought by the good,
> That through which the one who knows is immediately freed from all sin,
> And obtains that *puruṣa*, greater than the great.[2]

Like the *Śvetāśvatara Upaniṣad*, the *Kaivalya* suggests that a personal god is ultimately the source of *brahman* itself. The highest being is identified as Śiva,[3] and said to be *brahma-yoni* (the source of *brahman*). The text's description of Śiva is familiar from later mythology: "The one who has Umā as his companion, the highest Lord, the ruler, the one with three eyes, the blue-necked one, the peaceful one …"[4] Stanza seventeen refers to the "eternal Śiva" (*sadāśiva*). The *Kaivalya Upaniṣad* is clearly a theistic text, and its Śaiva affiliations are undeniable.

Asceticism plays an important role in the text, and there is no tension between the desire for spiritual liberation and the desire for children. Family life must be renounced:

> Seek by means of faith, devotion, meditation, and concentration.
> Not by action, not by children or wealth,
> Only by renunciation can one reach immortality.[5]

Māyā is used in the sense of "illusion" in the *Kaivalya Upaniṣad*:

> This *ātman*, veiled by *māyā*,
> Gets a body and performs all actions.
> When awake he is satisfied by
> The varied pleasures of women, food, and drink.

> But when dreaming, the *ātman* enjoys pleasure and pain
> In all the worlds created by his own *māyā* ….[6]

The references to *māyā* indicate an indebtedness to the *Śvetāśvatara Upaniṣad*. But *māyā* still has the older sense of "creative power" in the oldest layer of the *Śvetāśvatara Upaniṣad*. The use of *māyā* in the sense of "illusion" in the *Kaivalya Upaniṣad* is a sign of later composition. It is possible, however, that the two stanzas where *māyā* occurs in the *Kaivalya Upaniṣad* are later additions to the text.

Metrical analysis of the *Kaivalya Upaniṣad* indicates that the main portions of the text were composed not too long after the *Kaṭha* and *Śvetāśvatara Upaniṣads*. Some stanzas are, however, composed in a much later meter and appear to be later additions to the text. This includes the stanzas that contain references to *māyā* as well as the verse lines referring to Śiva as three-eyed and as Umā's husband.

The *Akṣamālikā Upaniṣad*

This Upaniṣad in sixteen prose sections gets its name from a type of rosary, *akṣamālā*, used in the devotional repetition (*japa*) of *mantras*. Rosaries are used in the worship of many Hindu deities, but they are particularly prominent in the cult of Śiva. The rosary itself is described as symbolic in the Upaniṣad: The inner thread of the rosary signifies *ātman* and *brahman*, the silver thread to the right is Śiva, the copper thread to the left is Viṣṇu, the main bead is the goddess Sarasvatī, the bottom is the *Gāyatrī mantra*, the holes in the beads signify knowledge, and the knot represents *prakṛti* ("nature").[7]

The text consists of a dialogue between the Vedic creator god Prajāpati and Guha, which is another name for Śiva's son, the Hindu war god Skanda or Kartikeya. Contrary to other Upaniṣads that present Prajāpati as the wisdom teacher who must explain the truth to others, the *Akṣamālikā Upaniṣad* makes Prajāpati himself the wisdom seeker. He is the one who must turn to Guha to discover the esoteric truths about each part of the rosary:

> Lord, tell me the truth about the different kinds of rosary beads. How should the rosary be? What are the different versions of it? What is the nature of the alphabet that completes the ritual that must be performed? What is the presiding deity? What fruit is to be obtained?[8]

The elevation of Guha to the place of supreme wisdom teacher, even wiser than Prajāpati himself, underscores the Śaiva character of the text. Of course Śiva's own son must have the ultimate knowledge of the rosary that is so frequently used in the worship of his father.

The rosary described by Guha in the *Akṣamālikā Upaniṣad* consists of fifty beads, one for each letter of the Sanskrit alphabet. The beads representing the sixteen vowels should be white, the letters representing the first twenty-five consonants should be yellow, and the beads associated with the last ten consonants should be red.[9] Each letter of the alphabet is invoked in turn and implored to take its place within one of the beads: "The devotee should invoke the letter *a* in the first bead, and so on, reciting the *mantras* one after the other …"[10]

The Upaniṣad promises expiation from sins for those who study the text:

> Whoever studies this Upaniṣad in the early morning will be free from the sins committed overnight. Whoever studies it at sunset will be free of the sins committed in the course of the day. By studying it both in the morning and the evening, the sinner becomes a guiltless person.[11]

The text is affiliated with the *Ṛgveda*, but this association appears to be a mere formality; there is nothing in the text itself to suggest a connection to the *Ṛgveda*. The Upaniṣad is likely composed in the late medieval period.

The *Atharvaśiras Upaniṣad*

This text is one of the longer Śaiva Upaniṣads and consists of seventy prose sections divided into seven chapters. The text is formally affiliated with the *Atharvaveda*, perhaps because of its thematic similarities to the *Kaivalya Upaniṣad.*

The text of the Upaniṣad is a dialogue between Rudra (a name for Śiva) and the other gods. The gods seek Rudra out at his abode on the mountain Kailāsa and beg him to explain his own nature to them. Rudra tells them that he is "the one absolute being, the inner *ātman* that is the basis of the sense of 'I,' etc. I was in existence long before creation, even before the beginning-less time itself."[12] The reverent gods meditate on Rudra, praise him, and enquire about the meaning of several of his names and epithets. Rudra is identified as the highest and only reality. Nothing could ever exist apart from him.

The text of the *Atharvaśiras Upaniṣad* made a profound impression on the German philosopher G. W. F. Hegel, who admired this text where Śiva "speaks of himself, to an extent in most daring expressions of abstraction …"[13]

The *Kalāgnirudra Upaniṣad*

This brief text in ten prose sections is ascribed to the *Black Yajurveda*. The text explores the mystical significance of the Tripuṇḍra ("three marks") mark, the three horizontal lines devotees of Śiva apply with ash to the forehead. The three lines of the Tripuṇḍra are identified with the three sounds that make up the syllable *oṃ* (*a*, *u*, *m*), with the three *guṇas* (the "strands" that make up the material world in Sāmkhya philosophy: light, passion, and darkness), with the three worlds (earth, atmosphere, and heaven), with the three ritual fires, with the three older Vedas, and with the three aspects of Śiva himself

(Maheśvara, Sadāśiva, and Mahādeva, the "Great Lord," the "Eternal Śiva," and the "Great God").[14]

The title of the text derives from the name given to Śiva in this Upaniṣad: Kalāgnirudra, "Rudra who is the fire of time." According to Hindu mythology, Rudra/Śiva is the god of destruction who will burn the world in a cosmic fire at the end of a cycle of time.

The text is a dialogue between the legendary sage Sanatkumāra, said to have been born from the mind of the creator god Brahmā himself, and Śiva in the form of Kalāgnirudra. Sanatkumāra meditates on Kalāgnirudra and is rewarded by the deity manifesting himself in front of him. Sanatkumāra, who does know *brahman*, struggles with explaining this lofty concept to ordinary people. He is worried that telling the unenlightened that "Everything is *brahman*" will simply result in him being dragged down into hell by their extreme ignorance. Instead, he believes that he will have far more success by imparting the truth about *brahman* to ordinary people through the sacred mark of the Tripuṇḍra. He therefore begs Kālagnirudra to explain the Tripuṇḍra to him in great detail.[15]

Kālāgnirudra explains that the Tripuṇḍra should be drawn with ashes from burnt cow dung while *mantras* are recited. Among the *mantras* mentioned in the text are "That which is fire is ashes. That which is air is ashes. That which is ether is ashes. That which is water is ashes. That which is the earth we stand on is ashes."[16] Hymns to Rudra from the *Ṛgveda* are also included.

The text promises that anyone who applies the Tripuṇḍra mark correctly will receive freedom from further rebirth[17] and expiation from all sins: "He will be like one who has bathed in all the sacred waters without even visiting them."[18] Alternatively, the text suggests, one can receive the same benefits just from studying the text of the *Kalāgnirudra Upaniṣad* itself.

The *Atharvaśikhā Upaniṣad*

The *Atharvaśikhā Upaniṣad* (not to be confused with the similarly titled *Atharvaśiras Upaniṣad*) is affiliated with the *Atharvaveda*. In this case, there is a good reason for the textual association with the *Atharvaveda*, since Atharvan himself, the legendary author of the *Atharvaveda*, is the narrator of the text. The name of the Upaniṣad, *Atharvaśikhā*, probably means something along the lines of "Atharvan's lock of hair." A *śikhā* is in particular the tuft of hair on top of the head of an ascetic, so it is likely that the title of the text hints at the ascetic nature of Atharvan himself.

The main theme of the text is meditation (*dhyāna*), and in particular meditation on the syllable *oṃ*. Like the *Māṇḍūkya Upaniṣad*, the *Atharvaśikhā Upaniṣad* contains an exposition of the fourfold nature of the holy syllable *oṃ*. The four parts of the syllable are identified with the four Vedas,[19] as well as with the earth, atmosphere, heaven, and the region of the moon.[20] *Oṃ* is associated with Śiva, who alone is a worthy object of meditation.[21]

There is a commentary on the *Atharvaśikhā Upaniṣad* ascribed to the eighth-century philosopher Śaṅkara, but it is not usually considered genuine. In all likelihood, a faux "Śaṅkara commentary" was added to the text to enhance its prestige.

The *Gaṇapati Upaniṣad*

This late sectarian Upaniṣad identifies the highest *brahman* with Śiva's elephant-headed god Gaṇeśa or Gaṇapati ("The Lord of Hosts"). The text is affiliated with the *Atharvaveda*, but the association is likely a mere formality.

According to classical Hindu mythology, Śiva's son received his elephant head after an unfortunate misunderstanding by his father. While Śiva was away meditating in solitude, his wife Pārvatī was taking a bath, and she formed a child out of the dirt in her bathwater and brought him to life. The newly created boy, Gaṇeśa, was then tasked with guarding the door until the goddess had finished her bath. When Śiva came back and wanted to see his wife, Gaṇeśa blocked his way and refused to let him in. Śiva, who had no idea who the boy was, got angry and chopped his head off. When Pārvatī saw what he had done, she demanded that he go into the forest and find their son a new head. The first animal Śiva encountered in the forest was an elephant, and he went home and attached its head to his son, who then became a very popular elephant-headed deity.

In the *Gaṇapati Upaniṣad*, Gaṇeśa himself is said to be "the true reality."[22] Gaṇeśa is the creator of the world in the form of Brahmā, its maintainer in the form of Viṣṇu, and its destroyer in the form of Rudra.[23] He transcends the three *guṇas* as well as the three times (past, present, and future).[24]

The Upaniṣad introduces the eight-syllable *mantra* of the god, *Oṃ Gaṇapataye namȧ* ("Oṃ, salutation to Gaṇapati") and explains the mystical meaning of each syllable of the *mantra*.[25] It then includes a verse in the ancient *Gāyatrī* meter:

> May we know the one-tusked one,
> May we contemplate the one with the curved trunk,
> May the one with the tusk instruct us.[26]

The verse itself is straightforward enough, but the use of the *Gāyatrī* meter adds a great deal of symbolic depth to the stanza. By using this particular meter, the authors of the text evoke in the minds of devoted Hindus the most well-known *Gāyatrī* verse of them all, the prayer to the sun from *Ṛgveda* 3. 62. 10. Many Hindus recite this verse, which is simply called "The Gāyatrī" every morning, and, for many, it comes to represent the essence of the Vedic tradition itself. Introducing a new *Gāyatrī*, this time one directed at Gaṇeṣa, is, in a sense, making the claim that the old tradition has been superseded by something new and powerful.

The Upaniṣad concludes, as so many of the Śaiva Upaniṣads do, by detailing the results one will get from studying the text and understanding its teachings. A person who learns the Upaniṣad will "obtain the indivisible bliss of the completely immanent *brahman*," and be released from all manner of transgressions, "both the five great ones and others of a lesser nature."[27] In classical Hinduism, these five *mahāpātakas* ("great transgressions") are killing a brahman, drinking alcohol, stealing gold, sleeping with one's teacher's wife, and associating with anyone who has committed any of these transgressions.

There are many signs of late composition in this Upaniṣad, such as the mention of the five great transgressions, the four goals of human existence (*puruṣārtha*: duty, wealth, love, and spiritual liberation)[28] as well as some ideas which may show influence from later Tantrism. The syllable *oṃ* is said to reside in the *mūladhara*.[29] In later Tantrism, *mūladhara* ("root support") is the name of one of the cakras, or power centers in the body. Further, the *Gaṇapati Upnaiṣad* dwells on the syllable *Gaṃ*, which makes up a part of Ganeśa's name and his eight-syllable *mantra*:

> Having uttered the first sound of the word Gaṇa (g), and then the first sound of the alphabet (a), and the anusvāra (ṃ), which transcends them and is radiant with the crescent moon (the dot of the ṃ), then this along with the Tāra (=oṃ), i. e. oṃ gaṃ is the true form of the mantra.[30]

The notion that Gaṇeśa's *mantra* has a short version, *oṃ gaṃ*, which is its "true form" is evocative of the Tantric idea of *bīja mantras* or "seed syllables," single syllables that capture the mystical essence of a deity. Gaṇeśa's Tantric "seed syllable" is precisely *gaṃ*. The mention of both Gaṇeśa's seed syllable and the Tantric concept of *mūladhara* indicates that the text may be of a relatively late date.

Notes

1 *Mahābhārata* 13.14.15f.
2 *Kaivalya Upaniṣad* 1.
3 *Kaivalya Upaniṣad* 6.
4 *Kaivalya* 7.
5 *Kaivalya* 2.
6 *Kaivalya* 12–13.
7 *Akṣamālikā Upaniṣad* 3.
8 *Akṣamālikā Upaniṣad* 1.
9 *Akṣamālikā Upaniṣad* 3.
10 *Akṣamālikā Upaniṣad* 5.
11 *Akṣamālikā Upaniṣad* 16.
12 *Atharvaśiras Upaniṣad* 2.
13 G. W. F. Hegel, cited in Ignatius Viyagappa, *G. W. F. Hegel's Concept of Indian Philosophy*. Rome: Universita Gregoriana, 1980: 25.
14 *Kalāgnirudra Upaniṣad* 6–8.
15 *Kālagnirudra Upaniṣad* 2.

16 *Kālagnirudra Upaniṣad* 3.
17 *Kālagnirudra Upaniṣad* 9.
18 *Kālagnirudra Upaniṣad* 9.
19 *Atharvaśikhā Upaniṣad* 1.2.
20 *Atharvaśikhā Upaniṣad* 1.3–6.
21 *Atharvaśikhā Upaniṣad* 3.4.
22 *Gaṇapati Upaniṣad* 3.
23 *Gaṇapati Upaniṣad* 5.
24 *Gaṇapati Upaniṣad* 6.
25 *Gaṇapati Upaniṣad* 8–9.
26 *Gaṇapati Upaniṣad* 10.
27 *Gaṇapati Upaniṣad* 16.
28 *Gaṇapati Upaniṣad* 16.
29 *Gaṇapati Upaniṣad* 2.
30 *Gaṇapati Upaniṣad* 8.

Further reading

Ayyangar, T. R. S. 1953: *Śaiva Upaniṣads*. Madras: The Adyar Library.

Bühnemann, Gudrun. 1984. "Some Remarks on the Structure and Application of Hindu Sanskrit Stotras" *Wiener Zeitschrift für die Kunde Südasiens* 28: 73–104.

Courtright, Paul B. 1985. *Gaṇeśa: Lord of Obstacles, Lord of Beginnings*. Appendix: "The Śrī Gaṇapati Atharvaśīrṣa." Oxford University Press: New York.

39 The Devī Upaniṣads

Signe Cohen

From around the twelfth century of the common era, a new kind of Upaniṣad began to flourish. These texts, often called Śākta Upaniṣads ("Upaniṣads of Power") or Devī Upaniṣads ("goddess Upaniṣads"), were devoted to Hindu goddesses, who were seen as manifestations of the cosmic power, *śakti*, and identified with *brahman* itself. There is no authoritative list of Upaniṣads that have been designated as Śākta or Devī Upaniṣads, but some of the most commonly mentioned ones include the *Sītā Upaniṣad*, the *Devī Upaniṣad*, the *Tripurā Upaniṣad*, the *Tripurātāpanī Upaniṣad*, the *Bhāvanopaniṣad*, the *Bahvṛcopaniṣad*, and the *Saubhāgyalakṣmī Upaniṣad*. Each of these Upaniṣads will be summarized and discussed in this chapter. Many of these texts contain Tantric ideas. Hindu Tantra is an esoteric tradition that focuses on the cosmic power (*śakti*) and its ritual channeling, goddess worship, *mantras* (sacred utterances), *maṇḍalas* (sacred diagrams), and occasionally transgressive ritual actions, such as consuming normally forbidden substances such as meat. There are only a few traces of the antinomian and transgressive aspects of Tantra in the Śākta Upaniṣads, but *śakti*, goddess worship, *mantras* and *maṇḍalas* all play a significant role in these texts. Significantly, by *calling* these texts "Upaniṣads," the authors of these texts clearly align them with the older Upaniṣads, which are again grounded in the Vedic tradition. This appeal to the orthodox tradition serves to establish the goddess worship these Upaniṣads argue for within the established and respected tradition of the classical Upaniṣads.

The *Sītā Upaniṣad*

As the name indicates, this Upaniṣad focuses on Sītā, the main female character of the *Rāmāyaṇa* epic. But the divine Sītā of the Upaniṣad is quite different from the obedient wife of the epic. While Sītā in the *Rāmāyaṇa* is, above all, her husband's wife, the Upaniṣad's Sītā is the origin of the universe and of all the gods. In the *Rāmāyaṇa*, Sītā is kidnapped by the ferocious ten-headed demon Rāvaṇa and must wait for her husband Rāma to rescue her. The *Sītā Upaniṣad*, however, does not mention Sītā's husband at all; the only nod to the story of the epic is a brief allusion to Sītā's mysterious origin. In the *Rāmāyaṇa*, Sītā is said to have sprung up from the earth itself as her adopted father, King Janaka, is plowing. This myth of Sītā's origin gets half a sentence in the Upaniṣad, before the text goes on to praise her connection to the cosmic *brahman* itself: "On earth, she springs up at the tip of the plough, she who is ever present as the joy of realizing *brahman*."[1] Her marriage to Rāma and her abduction by Rāvaṇa get no mention at all in the Upaniṣad. Rather, Sītā's own nature as cosmic creator and sustainer is emphasized: "Sītā must be known. She is the first cause. As the syllable *oṃ* she is the cause, say those who know *brahman*."[2] Sītā is identified with all the gods and all the Vedas. She is simultaneously *brahman* itself and the stones of the earth.[3]

The Upaniṣad breaks down the name Sītā into syllables and speculates on the mystical meaning of each syllable. The name "Sītā" is here said to consist of three sounds: *Sa* stands for immortal truth, achievement, and the god Śiva. The vowel *ī* is identified with the god Viṣṇu, the seed of the world, as well as *māyā* (illusion). The syllable *tā* represents Sītā as the Queen of Speech, as well as the creator god Brahmā. Thus, the very name of the goddess contains within itself all the three great Hindu male gods: Brahmā the creator, Viṣṇu the maintainer, and Śiva the destroyer.[4]

Intriguingly, Sītā is referred to as *māyā*, or "illusion" several times in the Upaniṣad, but it is a positive concept in this text: "The goddess who is the Great Illusion, whose form is unmanifest, and who is represented by *ī*, becomes manifest, beautiful as the moon, with flawless limbs, adorned with garlands, pearls, and other ornaments."[5] *Māyā* is here not a delusion of the senses, but rather a powerful potentiality that manifests itself as beauty.

Sītā's power is threefold: The power of desire, the power of action, and the power of knowledge. The various forms of knowledge cherished by the text's author are then listed. Among the forms of knowledge in Sītā's power are knowledge of the four Vedas, the six Vedic sciences (ritual, grammar, phonetics, etymology, astronomy, and meter), as well as the philosophy of Vedānta, Mīmāṃsā, and Nyāya, ethics, law, architecture, archery, music, medicine, and the dark arts.[6] Establishing these points of connection between the worship of Sītā and the orthodox brahmanical tradition serves to legitimate the reverence for the goddess.

The *Devī Upaniṣad*

This Upaniṣad, whose name means "The Goddess Upaniṣad" extols a cosmic goddess simply called "the Goddess" (*Devī*):

> All the gods served the goddess and asked: "Great goddess, who are you?" She answered: "I am *brahman* itself. From me comes the world consisting of spirit (*puruṣa*) and nature (*prakṛti*), emptiness and fullness. I am bliss

> and non-bliss. Knowledge and ignorance are me … I am the five elements and what is different from them. I am the whole world. I am the Veda and what is different from it. I am the unborn and the born. I am below and above and around."[7]

The gods then proceed to praise Devī, and in doing so, they identify her with well-known goddesses like Aditi ("the Infinite"), Vāc (divine Speech), Sarasvatī (the goddess of learning), and Lakṣmī (the goddess of wealth and good fortune), but also as a female form of the god Śiva (called Śivā, a feminine form). This goddess is the entire world: "She is the planets, stars, and luminaries. She is the divisions of time, and primeval Time itself."[8]

The mystical *mantra* of the goddess is hinted at in riddle form:

> The all-powerful seed of the mantra of the goddess
> is *ether*, joined with *ī* and *fire*,
> adorned with the crescent moon.[9]

The element of ether is symbolized by the sound *h*, the element of fire by the sound *r*, and the crescent moon by the sound *ṃ*. The answer to the riddle is therefore the syllable *hrīṃ*, the *mantra* sacred to the goddess in classical Hinduism.

The *Tripurā Upaniṣad*

This Upaniṣad extols the goddess Tripurā ("She of the Three Cities") as the ultimate power in the universe. Gudrun Bühnemann dates the text to after the fifteenth century CE.[10] The text exists in two recensions, one formally affiliated with the *Ṛgveda* and one with the *Atharvaveda*. The text is a brief one, consisting of only sixteen verses. There are several commentaries on the text, the most well-known one being the eighteenth-century commentary by Bhāskararāya, which has been translated into English by Douglas Renfrew Brooks. The text contains deliberately archaic faux-Vedic language, but there is no reason to assume that the text is considerably older than the fifteenth century CE.

The Goddess of the Three Cities is a central symbol in the text. The goddess of the Three Cities is said to be "the abode of all, deathless and ancient."[11] She rules over the three cities (which the commentator Bhāskararāya defines as the physical realm, the subtle realm associated with the sacred sounds of *mantras*, and the supreme realm, associated with *maṇḍalas*). She rules over the sounds *a*, *kha*, and *tha*.[12] These sounds represent, respectively, the first sixteen sounds of the devanagarī alphabet used for writing Sanskrit (*a* and the fifteen letters following it), the middle sixteen sounds (beginning with *kha*) and the last sixteen sounds. The goddess Tripurā is therefore the ruler over all sounds, and by extension, over all language.

The Upaniṣad refers to nine *cakras*, or "circles," which appears to allude to the nine concentric triangles of the *Śrī Cakra maṇḍala*. A series of mystical numbers is mentioned in stanza three: "Originally she was one, then she became nine, and she became nineteen, and then twenty-nine. Then she became forty-three. She is shining brightly, as if full of desire." This may be an esoteric reference to the shape of the mystical *Śrī Yantra* or *Śrī Cakra*: In the middle, there is a single dot, surrounded by nine triangles. By adding the ten minor outer triangles formed within the diagram, one gets twenty-nine, and by adding the next layer of triangles, one gets forty-three:

Stanza four declares that the goddess is joy and bliss and identifies her with the three circles of shining light which are the three circles surrounding the lotus petals in the *Śrī Yantra* diagram (Figure 39.1). The three outermost lines are called the three "gateways" or "portals,"[13] and they are identified with the three worlds (heaven, atmosphere, and earth), the three qualities (light, passion, and darkness), and the three illuminations (sun, moon, and fire). "This," states the Upaniṣad, "is the city of the goddess."[14] The three cities of the goddess, indeed the goddess herself, thus consist of the entire cosmos. By alluding to the visual form of the *Śrī Yantra* with its numerous triangles, the Upaniṣad suggests that the threefold world is a manifestation of the very essence of the goddess.

Stanza seven suggests, intriguingly, that this goddess resides in her "seat" (*svapīṭham*), a term that resonates with shades of meaning such as "temple" or "throne." In this context, her "seat" appears to be the *Śrī Yantra* itself, the sacred diagram as a visual and physical residence of the goddess. Her attendants are, interestingly, said to be "intoxicated" with "liquor." This reference to alcohol consumption hints at the Tantric practice of engaging with

Figure 39.1 The *Śrī Yantra.*

the five practices forbidden by the orthodox Hindu tradition (the five *m*s of *māṃsa* ("meat"), *matsya* ("fish"), *madhu* ("wine"), *mudra* ("parched grain"), and *maithuna* (forbidden sexual intercourse)). The goddess is seen as one with the god Śiva: "The two are the same substance, of the same nature, identical, and of equal power."[15]

The *Tripurātāpinī Upaniṣad*

This long Upaniṣadic text ("The Upaniṣad of the Austerity of the Tripurā") is divided into five shorter "Upaniṣads." Like the *Tripurā Upaniṣad*, this text praises the goddess Tripurā, She of the Three Cities. According to the text's introductory passage, the god Śiva created three realms, which are identified either as the earth, the atmosphere, and the highest heavens, or as heaven, earth, and the underworld.[16] Śiva's *māyā*, his power of creation and illusion, identified with the sacred *mantra hrīṃ*, takes the form of the goddess Tripurā.[17] Even though the goddess is referred to as the "supreme sovereign"[18] and the embodiment of the three Vedas,[19] the goddess is nevertheless a manifestation of Śiva's creative power in this Upaniṣad rather than a supreme deity in her own right. The world itself, the Vedas, and all knowledge have arisen out of the union of Śiva and his female Power (*śakti*), which is the goddess Tripurā.[20]

The number three recurs frequently in the text. The first section of the Upaniṣad contains three *mantras*, whose total number of syllables add up to the sacred number 108. The first *mantra* is the famous *Gāyatrī* verse from *Ṛgveda* 3.62.10 praising the splendor of the sun, the second *mantra* is a stanza from *Mahānārāyaṇa Upaniṣad* 2.1 in praise of Agni, and the third *mantra* is the well-known verse to Rudra/Śiva as Tryambaka, the Three-Eyed god, from *Rigveda* 7.59.12, asking the god for liberation from death. The juxtaposition of these three older stanzas at the beginning of the Upaniṣad aligns the text firmly with the Vedic tradition and with the worship of the familiar Rudra/Śiva. The text explains the nature of the goddess Tripurā in a manner that suggests that she may not be entirely familiar to the text's audience, but the Upaniṣad's authors then hasten to connect the unfamiliar Lady of the Three Cities to the familiar and long-revered God of the Three Eyes.

The *Tripurātāpinī Upaniṣad* goes on to deconstruct the text of the three famous Vedic *mantras*, giving an esoteric reading of each stanza that aligns it with classical Upaniṣadic notions of *ātman* and *brahman*. Why go to such lengths to read cryptic subtexts about the unity of *ātman* and *brahman* into older Vedic stanzas rather than just declaring that *ātman* and *brahman* are one? There seem to be two main orientations present in this Upaniṣads: traditionalism and esotericism. By finding hidden messages in stanzas known and respected by the Brahmanical tradition, the text draws on the textual authority of that tradition. But by reading mystical meanings into each syllable, the Upaniṣad also associates itself with the esoteric aspects of the Tantric tradition. This curious merger of the traditional and the esoteric continues in the second portion of the text, where "seers" who recite verses about Soma pressing learn *mantras* sacred to the goddess.

The second portion of the text describes the drawing of the *maṇḍala*, or sacred diagram of the *Śrī Cakra*:

> Then the gods said to the Lord (Śiva): "Tell us about the best of the *cakras*, which promotes all desires, is adored by everyone, takes on all forms, faces all directions of the sky, and is the portal to liberation. By adoring that the Yogins cut through the knots of ignorance and enter the undifferentiated bliss of the highest *Brahman*."
>
> Then the Lord said to them: "We shall explain the concept of the *Śrī Cakra*. Make a triangle with three corners ..."[21]

The god Śiva then goes on to describe, in great detail, how to construct the complex *Śrī Yantra* diagram (see Figure 39.1), which consists of nine interlocking triangles surrounding a central point. The triangles are surrounded by two rows of lotus petals, of eight and sixteen petals respectively, and an outer frame with four openings ("gates").

The *Śrī Yantra* diagram becomes very important in the later Śrīvidyā ("Auspicious Knowledge" or "Knowledge of the goddess Śrī") school of Hindu Tantra (attested in texts from around the ninth century CE), particularly associated with worship of the goddess Tripurā ("The Three Cities"), or Lalitā Tripurā Sundarī ("The Playful Beauty of the Three Cities").

The rest of the text is devoted to descriptions of mystical hand gestures (*mudrās*) and mystical syllables. The text does, however, emphasize that liberation does not come from these forms of mystical knowledge, but rather from an understanding of the supreme *brahman*: "Alone and solitary, the supreme *brahman*, silent, shines forth. Gods, seers and ancestors do not prevail there. The enlightened knower, the knower of all, is *brahman*."[22]

The *Bhāvanopaniṣad*

This Upaniṣad is formally affiliated with the *Atharvaveda*. There are three different extant versions of the text, one embedded in the commentary of Bhāskara-rāya (eighteenth century), consisting of thirty-six sections, a slightly longer version commented on by Upaniṣadbrahmayogī (eighteenth century), and the version that is included in the collection of 108 Upaniṣads known as the *Upaniṣatsaṃgrahà*, which contains sixty-seven sections. The Upaniṣad has a significant amount of material in common with the twelfth-century Tantric text *Tantrarāja Tantra*.

The title of this Upaniṣad means "The Upaniṣad of the Imagination" or "the Upaniṣad of creative mental formation." This Upaniṣad is remarkable in that it identifies the teacher (*guru*) with *śakti*, or the divine power itself. Teachers are important in many of the classical Upaniṣads discussed elsewhere in this volume, but this elevation of the teacher to cosmic status hints at the importance of the *guru* in the Tantric tradition, which emphasizes that true knowledge can only be imparted by a *guru* to an initiated student.

Intriguingly, the human body itself is identified with the mystical diagram of the *Śrī Cakra* because of the association of both with the holy number nine: Just as the *Śrī Cakra* consists of nine triangles, so does the human body have nine openings (two eyes, two ears, two nostrils, mouth, urethra, anus).[23] The six seasons of the year (spring, summer, monsoon, autumn, cool season, winter) are poetically identified with the six tastes the human tongue can taste (sweet, sour, bitter, pungent, astringent, salty).[24] The cosmos is here mapped onto the human anatomy in order to connect the practitioner with the cosmic powers through his or her own body. The inner *ātman* is identified with the goddess Lalitā (another name for Tripurā), who is called "the supreme divinity."[25]

The goal is liberation while living, which is obtained through meditation on the mystical connections between the macrocosmos and the human body: "Thus meditating for three instants, or two, or even for a single instant, one becomes liberated while living, and then one is called a Śivayogin."[26]

The human body is compared to the cosmos and the physical world throughout this text. In stanzas six–seven, the body is called an "island of nine gems," a phrase also used in the tantric text *Tantrasāra*. Although no list is given in this text, the nine substances said to make up the body of Āyurvedic medicine are flesh, hair, skin, blood, bone, marrow, fat, semen, and life breath.

The *Bahvṛcopaniṣad*

The *Bahvṛcopaniṣad* is mentioned by name in the *Muktikopaniṣad*, and is there described as one of the Upaniṣads affiliated with the *Ṛgveda*. Its connection with the *Ṛgveda* seems limited to the inclusion of a quotation from a Vedic hymn, 1.164.39: "The syllable of the verse, upon which all the gods have settled, is in the highest heaven …"[27] The Vedic verse may have been included in the text both to lend authority to the Upaniṣad and to point to the religious importance of sacred syllables, which does become a theme in the Upaniṣadic text.

This text, whose name means "The Upaniṣad of many verses," praises Devī, the goddess, as a cosmic creator. "The goddess was indeed one in the beginning," states the *Bahvṛcopaniṣad*. "Alone she emitted the world-egg."[28] This description of the lone creator in the beginning of the world is reminiscent of the depiction of *ātman* as a creator at the beginning of *Aitareya Upaniṣad*.

Gods, humans, and semi-divine beings are born from the goddess.[29] She is identified as the consciousness within[30] and is beyond both being and non-being.[31] She is further identified as the Great Lovely Goddess of the Three Cities (*Mahātripurasundarī*).[32]

The goddess is identified with three forms of knowledge, represented by three mystical formulations: "The knowledge beginning with *ka*" (the *mantra ka e ī la hrīm*), "the knowledge beginning with *ha*" (the *mantra ha sa ka ha la hrīm*), or "the knowledge beginning with *sa*" (the *mantra sa ka la hrīm*).[33] Together, these syllables, which are semantically meaningless, form the famous fifteen syllable *mantra* to the goddess: *ka e ī la hrīm ha sa ka ha la hrīm sa ka la hrīm*. This fifteen syllable *mantra* is frequently used in Śākta texts, where it is given the name *Kāmarāja-mantra* ("the mantra of King Kāma," because the first sound, *ka*, is said to stand for Kāma, the god of love). It is said that there is also a secret sixteenth syllable (in some later texts identified as *śrīṃ*), which is the very essence of the goddess herself. The *Bahvṛcopaniṣad* states: "She alone is *ātman*. Everything other than Her is untruth and non-self,"[34] and elaborates: "You and I and the whole world and all deities and everything else are the Great Lovely Goddess of the Three Cities."[35]

The *Saubhāgyalakṣmī Upaniṣad*

This "Upaniṣad of the Auspicious Lakṣmī" is, as the title indicates, devoted to Lakṣmī, the goddess of prosperity and good fortune. In classical Hinduism, Lakṣmī is the consort of the god Viṣṇu, and it is Viṣṇu himself who explains the mystical knowledge of the goddess in this text. Viṣṇu immediately reminds the other gods of Lakṣmī's physical form – she has four arms – and identifies her with the esoteric fourth part of the mystical syllable *oṃ*.[36]

The text goes on to describe the diagram of the *Śrī Cakra*, and suggests that after the diagram has been drawn, sixteen thousand hymns to the goddess must be sung.[37]

In the second part of the text, Viṣṇu goes on the describe the correct practice of Yoga, which involves eating little, sitting in a secluded spot, restraining the breath, closing one's eyes and plugging one's ears and nostrils, and sitting in a lotus position. The practitioner will then hear a supernatural sound, and his vital breath will move into space itself. He will then begin to identify the finite with the infinite and the fragments with the whole, and become immortal.[38]

The third section of this Upaniṣad introduces the notion of *cakras* in the body. There are nine *cakras*, or vortexes of energy in the body, located at the base of the spine, at the genitals, at the navel, at the heart, at the throat, at the palate, at the brow, at the "hole of *brahman*," and finally "the *cakra* of space."[39]

The notion of *cakras* as energy centers in the body was first introduced in Buddhist tantric texts such as the *Hevajra Tantra* and *Caryāgīti* (eighth–tenth century CE). These Buddhist Tantric texts mention four such bodily *cakras*, while Hindu tantric texts later increased the number of *cakras* to five and more. The number nine was no doubt chosen in this Upaniṣad because it echoes the nine triangles that form the heart of the *Śrī Cakra*.

The text concludes by promising wealth, including grains, sons, horses, lands, elephants, buffaloes, female servants, yoga, and knowledge, to the person who studies the Upaniṣad. The promise of knowledge is not so unusual in an Upaniṣad, nor is the promise of immortality at the end,[40] but the promise of worldly possessions is perhaps a little more unusual. The reason for this may of course be that the Upaniṣad is, after all, devoted to Lakṣmī, the goddess of wealth herself.

Notes

1 *Sītā Upaniṣad* 8.
2 *Sītā Upaniṣad* 8.
3 *Sītā Upaniṣad* 10.
4 *Sītā Upaniṣad* 3–4.
5 *Sītā Upaniṣad* 5.
6 *Sītā Upaniṣad* 21–30.
7 *Devī Upaniṣad* 1–3.
8 *Devī Upaniṣad* 18.
9 *Devī Upaniṣad* 20.
10 Gudrun Bühnemann, "Review: *The Secret of the Three Cities: An Introduction to Hindu Śakta Tantrism*" *Journal of the American Oriental Society* 116 (1996): 606.
11 *Tripurā Upaniṣad* 1.
12 *Tripurā Upaniṣad* 1.
13 *Tripurā Upaniṣad* 5.
14 *Tripurā Upaniṣad* 5.
15 *Tripurā Upaniṣad* 14.
16 *Tripurātāpinī Upaniṣad* 1.1.
17 *Tripurātāpinī Upaniṣad* 1.1.
18 *Tripurātāpinī Upaniṣad* 1.5.
19 *Tripurātāpinī Upaniṣad* 1.5.
20 *Tripurātāpinī Upaniṣad* 1.6.
21 *Tripurātāpinī Upaniṣad* 2.15–16.
22 *Tripurātāpinī Upaniṣad* 5.3.
23 *Bhāvanopaniṣad* 2–3.
24 *Bhāvanopaniṣad* 9.
25 *Bhāvanopaniṣad* 27.
26 *Bhāvanopaniṣad* 34.
27 Translation from Stephanie Jamison and Joel Brereton, *The Rigveda*. Oxford: Oxford University Press, 2014, vol. 1: 358.
28 *Bahvṛcopaniṣad* 1.
29 *Bahvṛcopaniṣad* 2.
30 *Bahvṛcopaniṣad* 4.
31 *Bahvṛcopaniṣad* 5.
32 *Bahvṛcopaniṣad* 4.
33 *Bahvṛcopaniṣad* 3.
34 *Bahvṛcopaniṣad* 5.
35 *Bahvṛcopaniṣad* 5.
36 *Saubhāgyalakṣmī Upaniṣad* 2.
37 *Saubhāgyalakṣmī Upaniṣad* 6.
38 *Saubhāgyalakṣmī Upaniṣad* 2.1–11.
39 *Saubhāgyalakṣmī Upaniṣad* 3.1–9.
40 *Saubhāgyalakṣmī Upaniṣad* 10.

Further reading

Brooks, Douglas Renfrew 1990. *The Secret of the Three Cities: An Introduction to Hindu Śākta Tantrism*. Chicago, IL: The University of Chicago Press.

Rao, S. K. Ramachandra 1983. *The Tantra of Śrī Chakra (Bhāvanopanishat)*. Bangalore: Sharada Prakashana.

Shrader, F. O. 1912. *The Minor Upaniṣads*. Madras: The Adyar Library.

Varenne, Jean 1971. *Devī Upaniṣad*. Paris: Adrien Maisonneuve.

Warrier, A. G. Krishna 1967. *The Śākta Upaniṣads*. Madras: Adyar Library and Research Centre.

40 The Saṃnyāsa Upaniṣads

Signe Cohen

There are about twenty Upaniṣads that can collectively be designated as Saṃnyāsa Upaniṣads, or "Upaniṣads of Renunciation." These texts explore the idea that abandoning certain aspects of ordinary life, such as marriage, sex, having children, and living in a permanent abode, will help the renouncer in the quest for religious liberation. As Patrick Olivelle points out, however, "Saṃnyāsa Upaniṣads" is not a native Indian category, unlike such classifications as "Śaiva Upaniṣads" or "Śākta Upaniṣads," which originate in the Sanskrit tradition itself.[1] The term is first used by the German Sanskrit scholar Paul Deussen in his German Upaniṣad translation from 1905. Another German, F. A O. Schrader, adopted the term and included twenty Upaniṣads that had renunciation as their central theme in his 1912 critical edition. Patrick Olivelle includes an English translation of all twenty in his definitive work on the Saṃnyāsa Upaniṣads.[2]

The idea of renouncing the world is quite alien to most parts of the earliest Vedic religion, which instead emphasizes the importance of having many children, especially sons, and of amassing wealth through one's own efforts and the generosity of the gods. In the Vedic world-view, immortality means living on through one's children and grandchildren. The Upaniṣads' shift away from the ritual worship of the gods toward inner contemplation and knowledge is accompanied by ideas of a different form of ideal of immortality. This immortality is defined as escape from the cycle of death and rebirth (*saṃsāra*) and can be achieved through the knowledge that one's inner self (*ātman*) is identical with the cosmic divine force (*brahman*). Having a family is not at all necessary to achieve this knowledge; in fact, several of the older Upaniṣads suggest that it is better to rise above the desire to have children and lead the life of a renunciant in order to achieve liberation.[3]

By the time of the composition of the *Dharmasūtras* ("Aphorisms on Law") composed a few centuries after the very oldest Upaniṣads, the tension between having children to ensure one's immortality and renouncing family life to devote oneself to a quest for the ultimate truth, was resolved through a compromise: The four stages of life (*puruṣārthas*). According to this doctrine, a man would pass through four different life stages after his childhood. The

Dharmasūtras are male-centered and invariably present the default human person as male, although some of these stages could also apply to women. First, the man would be a chaste student (*brahmacārya*), devoting himself to his studies of the sacred texts. Next, he would become a married householder (*gṛhastha*), and during this stage, he would have sex with his wife and become the father of children. When the children are grown, he would move into the forest with his wife and become a forest hermit (*vanaprastha*), living a simpler life with fewer possessions, but not yet abandoning all worldly ties. The fourth and final stage is *saṃnyāsa*, or renunciation. If he reaches this stage, a man will leave his family and all his possessions behind and become a homeless beggar, devoting himself exclusively to his spiritual pursuits. Thus, a man can have a family at one point in his life and still become a full-time ascetic later on when his family obligations have been completed.

The Saṃnyāsa Upaniṣads focus on this final life stage and describe the life of an ascetic in great detail. The date of the Saṃnyāsa Upaniṣads is difficult to determine. Sprockhoff dates the older prose Saṃnyāsa Upaniṣads to the last few centuries before the common era and the later verse Saṃnyāsa Upaniṣads to the medieval period. Olivelle, however, argues that even the oldest Saṃnyāsa Upaniṣads may be as late as the first centuries of the common era.[4]

The *Nirvāṇa Upaniṣad*

This prose Upaniṣad, formally affiliated with the *Ṛgveda*, describes the life of an ascetic in brief aphorisms. There is nothing in the text itself that indicates any deeper connection to the *Ṛgveda*. The title of the text ("the Upaniṣad of Liberation") indicates that the ascetic's goal is to be liberated from the cycle of death and rebirth. The term *nirvāṇa*, best known from Buddhism, but also used in Hinduism, literally means "blowing out" or "extinction." The Upaniṣad emphasizes that the *nirvāṇa* the Hindu ascetic seeks is quite different from the Buddhist extinction of the self: "His watchword is not emptiness, but the existence of the supreme lord."[5] The ascetic may be dressed in the traditional garb of a wandering renouncer, but it is not external things that make him a renouncer: His true ragged garment is his mental fortitude,[6] his loincloth is his equanimity,[7] his staff is his intellectual investigation,[8] his yoga band is his vision of *brahman*,[9] and his sandals are his happiness.[10]

The *Nirvāṇa Upaniṣad* alludes to three of the four life stages: "Having studied in the order of a student and having studied in the order of the hermit, he arrives at renunciation, which is the abandonment of all possessions."[11] The married householder stage is not mentioned directly in the *Nirvāṇa Upaniṣad*, although it may be alluded to in the exhortation not to share the text's teachings with anyone who is not a student or a son.[12] If a teacher of the Upaniṣad has a son, this does imply that he probably went through the married householder stage as well.

The *Nirvāṇa Upaniṣad* claims that the world itself is impermanent and a construct, similar to the reality one sees in dreams or the shape of an elephant imagined in the clouds.[13] The body itself is created by the imagination, formed by the strands of the web of illusion (*māyā*).[14] This assertion of the unreality of the world may be influenced by the *Māṇḍūkya Upaniṣad*, which hints that the external world is a mere construct of the mind, and by the references to *māyā* in the *Śvetāśvatara Upaniṣad*.

The *Jābāla Upaniṣad*

This Upaniṣad is formally affiliated with the White Yajurveda. Since the main character of the text, Yājñavalkya, is also the central character in the oldest Upaniṣad of the White Yajurveda, the *Bṛhadāraṇyaka Upaniṣad*, the affiliation may be more than a formality here. The Upaniṣad is named after one of the schools of the White Yajurveda. The *Jābāla* is included in Dara Shikhoh's seventeenth-century Persian translation under the name *Djabal*.

The Upaniṣad is patterned after *Bṛhadāraṇyaka* 3, in which a series of sages are in turn refuted by Yājñavalkya. While Yājñavalkya is aggressively challenged by his opponents in the *Bṛhadāraṇyaka Upaniṣad*, his dialogue partners in the *Jābāla Upaniṣad* approach him with the utmost respect, as adoring students rather than as rival wisdom teachers. In the *Jābāla Upaniṣad*, Yājñavalkya instructs the god Bṛhaspati, the sage Atri (son of the creator god Brahmā), a group of Vedic students, as well as king Janaka of Videha, who is also one of Yājñavalkya's admirers in the *Bṛhadāraṇyaka Upaniṣad*. Yājñavalkya explains the four stages of life to king Janaka, and claims that a man does not have to go through all four in order to be a renouncer; he can renounce right after the student stage, or right after the householder stage if he so wishes.[15]

Atri enquires into the practice of wearing a sacred thread. In classical Hinduism, a male is given a sacred thread, to be worn across the torso, during the puberty ceremony called *Upanayana*. This ceremony is open to men of the three upper castes (priests, warriors, and merchants/farmers only), not to women or those of the servant caste. Atri asks Yājñavalkya how a man can be a Brahman (a member of the priestly caste) when he does not have a sacred thread. It is possible that Atri is here asking indirectly whether someone can become a renouncer, as many Brahmans are, if he belongs to the servant caste. Yājñavalkya reassures him that anyone who wears ragged clothes, shaves his head, gives up all his possessions, is pure and without hate, and eats only the food he is given as alms, can indeed be a Brahman.[16] Another possible interpretation of the Atri's question is that it is simply a way of asking whether a Brahman who has renounced all his possessions can give up his sacred thread as well and still be a Brahman. Since the *Jābāla Upaniṣad* states that a wandering ascetic is "dressed as he was when he was born"[17] (i.e. naked), this is also a likely interpretation of the question. The *Paramahaṃsa Upaniṣad* (see below) states specifically that a renouncer must give up his sacred thread as well as all his other possessions.

The *Jābāla Upaniṣad* is one of the few later Upaniṣadic texts that mentions a particular geographical place. When the god Bṛhaspati aks Yājñavalkya if there is any place comparable to the famous battlefield Kurukṣetra (where the great war in the *Mahābhārata* epic takes place) "as the sacrificial ground of the gods and as the seat of *brahman*,"[18] Yājñavalkya mentions Avimukta. Avimukta ("the Never-Foresaken") is another name for the city of Varanasi (Benares) in north India, a well-known pilgrimage center. Yājñavalkya says that a man should live only in Avimukta and never leave,[19] but he also interprets the city in spiritual terms and identifies the city with the infinite *ātman*.[20] He tells Atri that the city is located between Varaṇā and Nāsī, a play on the popular etymology of the name Varanasi from the names of the two rivers, Varuna and Assi, that surround it. Yājñavalkya explains that the rivers are called that precisely because the city wards off (*vārayati*) and destroys (*nāśayati*) all sins.[21]

The *Paramahaṃsa Upaniṣad*

This Upaniṣad, which is formally associated with the White Yajurveda, describes the life of a *Paramahaṃsa*, or wandering ascetic. The term *Paramahaṃsa* literally means "The supreme goose," but since the goose is a frequent symbol for the *ātman* in Sanskrit literature, *Paramahaṃsa* can be translated as "The supreme soul." The Upaniṣad is structured as a dialogue between the sage Nārada and "The Lord," an unnamed deity who might be Brahmā or Viṣṇu.

The path of the *Paramahaṃsa*, explains the Lord, is very rare, and not undertaken by many.[22] A *Paramahaṃsa* must renounce sons, friends, wife, and family, as well as Vedic rituals and the sacred thread.[23] While some ascetics wear a loincloth and a ragged garment and wander off into the world with a staff in their hand,[24] a *Paramahaṃsa* renounces even those things. He must be completely naked[25] and not even look at gold, so that he won't be attracted by it.[26] The *Paramahaṃsa* is referred to twice in the text as a *Yogin*, or a practitioner of Yoga. A *Paramahaṃsa* is beyond all pleasure and pain, and all his sense activities have come to a standstill. He is absorbed in knowledge alone, and realizes his own unity with *brahman*.[27]

The *Kuṇḍikā Upaniṣad* and the *Laghusaṃnyāsa Upaniṣad*

These two Upaniṣads are almost identical. The *Laghusaṃnyāsa Upaniṣad* has an extra section at the beginning, and the *Kuṇḍikā Upaniṣad* includes an additional section at the end; otherwise their texts are the same. *Laghusaṃnyāsa Upaniṣad* simply means "The Short Upaniṣad on Renunciation," while *Kuṇḍikā Upaniṣad* ("the Water Pot Upaniṣad") is named after the pot an ascetic uses to get water from rivers and lakes.

The opening section from the *Laghusaṃnyāsa Upaniṣad* describes a man who is dying and whose funeral rites have already been performed, but who miraculously recovers. The Upaniṣad suggests that such a man may want to retreat into the wilderness and offer oblations to his ancestors, after which he should become a renouncer.

The first chapter that both the *Laghusaṃnyāsa Upaniṣad* and the *Kuṇḍikā Upaniṣad* have in common describes the four life stages, culminating in the Saṃnyāsa stage. The renouncer should be homeless and live exclusively on food that is given to him as alms. He should own nothing but his water pot (hence the name of the *Kuṇḍikā Upaniṣad*), a cup, a water strainer, a sling to carry his pot in, a staff, a few garments, and a pair of sandals. He should sleep by the banks of rivers on inside temples, and he should control his breath through breathing exercises. In these ways, he will obtain *brahman*.

The final verses exclusive to the *Kuṇḍikā Upaniṣad* describe in poetic terms the renouncer's experience of unity with the universal *brahman*:

Like the sky am I,
Far beyond the reach of time.
Like the sun am I,
Other than the illumined.

Like a hill am I,
Forever unchangeable.
Like the sea am I,
Without a farther shore.[28]

In this state, the renouncer is "pure consciousness" and "the witness of all,"[29] two phrases often used to describe *puruṣa*, the eternal spirit, in Sāṃkhya and Yoga philosophy. The title of the Upaniṣad is evoked again in the final section of the text, but here it is no longer a mere symbol of the ascetic lifestyle, but of the ultimate state of liberation:

Let this insentient body
Wallow in water or on land.
By its qualities I am not touched,
As space by the qualities of a pot.[30]

The renouncer himself has now become like the empty space within the pot, untouched by his body as the space inside a pot is untouched by its walls.

The *Bṛhatsaṃnyāsa Upaniṣad*

The *Bṛhatsaṃnyāsa Upaniṣad* ("The Great Upaniṣad of Renunciation") is, as its title indicates, longer than the *Laghusaṃnyāsa Upaniṣad*. There are several versions of the text, and they differ significantly from one another. Patrick Olivelle has based his translation on a medieval manuscript dated to the fourteenth or fifteenth century.[31] The text is affiliated with the *Sāmaveda*.

The Upaniṣad contains an interesting list of people who should not be allowed to become renouncers. This presents a stark contrast to texts like the *Jābāla Upaniṣad* which imply that renunciation is open to everyone. According to the *Bṛhatsaṃnyāsa Upaniṣad*, those unfit for enunciation include heretics, people who have no sacred fire in their homes, unbelievers, children of lapsed renouncers, as well as those who have neglected their Vedic rituals and study. Renunciation is, in other words, only open to those already in good religious and ritual standing. Those who have committed any of the five mortal sins (killing a Brahman, drinking alcohol, stealing gold, sleeping with a teacher's wife, or associating with those who commit those sins) are also excluded from renunciation. Personality traits like being childish or stupid will also exclude a person from renunciation; a renouncer must know precisely what he is getting himself into. Intriguingly, the list of people who may not renounce includes cripples, those who are deaf, men who are bald, those who have dark teeth, and men with bad nails. A person who is crippled may perhaps have a difficult time wandering around and begging for alms, but why would being deaf or having bad teeth be an obstacle to renunciation? It is possible that these external characteristics are included in this list because they are regarded as signs of bad *karma* from a past life, therefore also signaling a spiritual unreadiness for renunciation.

The *Bṛhatsaṃnyāsa Upaniṣad* lists six types of renouncers, differentiated by appearance and eating habits. A *Kuṭicaka* will keep his sacred thread, his Brahman hairstyle, and his contact with his family and eat in one particular place (perhaps with food given by his former family). A *Bahūdaka* will likewise retain his sacred thread, Brahmanical top knot of hair, and family connections, but eat very little and always food from different places. A *Haṃsa* has matted hair and goes to different houses to get food. A *Paramahaṃsa* (as we learned in the *Paramahaṃsa Upaniṣad*) has given up his sacred thread, his social and family connections, and all possessions. A *Turīyatīta* eats fruits and leaves, and only cooked food if it comes from a house he has never been to previously. An *Avadhūta* spends his time in meditation and eats whatever is given to him. This elaborate classification of renouncers suggests that renunciation had become quite common at the time when the Upaniṣad was composed, and that there were many different recognized variations in ascetic lifestyle.

Also striking is the list of texts a renouncer should *not* study. Studying texts not relating to his meditation on the *ātman*, states the *Bṛhatsaṃnyāsa Upaniṣad*, is "as unprofitable to him as a load of saffron to a camel."[32] The Upaniṣad warns in particular against reading texts relating to Yoga and Sāṃkhya philosophy and handbooks on *mantras*. Studying these texts, the

Upaniṣad assures its readers, is like "putting ornaments on a corpse."[33] Since the authors of the Upaniṣad find it necessary to ban the study of these texts, it seems likely that there were many renouncers who were reading such texts. Yoga and Sāmkhya elements are present in numerous Upaniṣads, but at this point, these schools were apparently perceived as a threat to the pure contemplation on the nature of *brahman*.

Notes

1 Olivelle 1992: 5.
2 Olivelle 1992.
3 See for example *Bṛhadāraṇyaka Upaniṣad* 4.4.22.
4 Olivelle 1992: 15.
5 *Nirvāṇa Upaniṣad* 36–37, translated in Olivelle 1992.
6 *Nirvāṇa Upaniṣad* 23.
7 *Nirvāṇa Upaniṣad* 24.
8 *Nirvāṇa Upaniṣad* 25.
9 *Nirvāṇa Upaniṣad* 26.
10 *Nirvāṇa Upaniṣad* 27.
11 *Nirvāṇa Upaniṣad* 79, translated in Olivelle 1992.
12 *Nirvāṇa Upaniṣad* 81.
13 *Nirvāṇa Upaniṣad* 34.
14 *Nirvāṇa Upaniṣad* 34.
15 *Jābāla Upaniṣad* 4.
16 *Jābāla Upaniṣad* 5.
17 *Jābāla Upaniṣad* 6.
18 *Jābāla Upaniṣad* 1.
19 *Jābāla Upaniṣad* 1.
20 *Jābāla Upaniṣad* 2.
21 *Jābāla Upaniṣad* 2.
22 *Paramahaṃsa Upaniṣad* 1.
23 *Paramahaṃsa Upaniṣad* 1.
24 *Paramahaṃsa Upaniṣad* 1.
25 *Paramahaṃsa Upaniṣad* 4.
26 *Paramahaṃsa Upaniṣad* 4.
27 *Paramahaṃsa Upaniṣad* 4.
28 Olivelle 1992: 127.
29 Olivelle 1992: 128.
30 Olivelle 1992: 128.
31 Olivelle 1992: 241–265.
32 Olivelle 1992: 251.
33 Olivelle 1992: 251.

Further reading

Deussen, P. 1897. *Sechzig Upaniṣads des Veda*. Leipzig: F. A. Brockhaus.

Dikshit, T. R. C. 1929. *The Saṃnyāsa Upaniṣads with the Commentary of Sri Upaniṣad-Brahmayogin*. (Reprint Madras: Adyar Library, 1966.)

Olivelle, P. 1992. *Saṃnyāsa Upaniṣads: Hindu Scriptures on Asceticism and Renunciation*. New York/Oxford: Oxford University Press.

Ramanathan, A. A. 1978. *The Saṃnyāsa Upaniṣads (On Renunciation), Translated into English (Based on the Commentary of Upaniṣad Brahmayogin)*. Madras: Adyar Library.

Schrader, F. O. 1912. *The Minor Upaniṣads*, Vol. 1: Saṃnyāsa Upaniṣads. Madras: Adyar Library.

Sprockhoff, J. F. 1976. *Saṃnyāsa: Quellenstudien zur Askese im Hinduismus. 1: Untersuchungen uber die Saṃnyāsa Upaniṣads. Abhandlungen für die Kunde des Morgenlandes* XLII, 1. Wiesbaden: Franz Steiner.

41 The Yoga Upaniṣads

Signe Cohen

The *Muktikā Upaniṣad*, a late medieval text, lists 108 Upaniṣads, and it classifies twenty of these as Yoga Upaniṣads. These Upaniṣadic texts are considerably later than the classical Upaniṣads to which Śaṅkara wrote his commentaries, and most of them appear to have been composed in the Middle Ages. While the union of *ātman* and *brahman* is still a central theme in these texts, they also incorporate a great deal of material concerning the philosophy and practice of Yoga.

According to the system of Yoga elaborated in Patañjali's *Yogasūtras* (second–fifth century CE?), there are two eternal principles in the world, *puruṣa* and *prakṛti*. *Puruṣa* ("the person") is pure consciousness, while *prakṛti* ("nature") encompasses everything, physical and psychological, that is different from *puruṣa*. The elements that make up the physical world are parts of *prakṛti*, as are psychological factors such as a sense of self, thought, and intellect. The goal of Yoga is the liberation of *puruṣa*, which takes place when a person realizes the absolute difference between *puruṣa* and *prakṛti*. The closely affiliated Sāṃkhya school of philosophy teaches that this liberating insight can be obtained without any external aids, through knowledge (*jñāna*) alone, while the Yoga school maintains that a rigorous system of breath control, physical postures, and meditation is necessary in order to truly grasp the fundamental difference between *puruṣa* and *prakṛti*. Additionally, Yoga differs from the atheistic Sāṃkhya school in postulating that there exists an eternally liberated *puruṣa*, *Īśvara* ("The Lord") who can play a part in the liberation of the individual. In the Yoga Upaniṣads, this deity is often identified with other popular deities, such as Viṣṇu or Śiva.

Early proto-Sāmkhya and Yoga concepts can be traced back to some of the classical Upaniṣads, such as the *Śvetāśvatara Upaniṣad*. It is even possible that Yoga itself grew out of Upaniṣadic ideas. The classical Upaniṣads do not, however, contain any sort of systematic presentation of Yoga or Sāmkhya ideas. The Yoga Upaniṣads, on the other hand, include a great deal of information that must have been derived from the *Yogasūtras*, as well as other related speculation. They represent an interesting stage in the historical development of the Upaniṣads; we can see in these texts an expansion of the genre to include new ideas and systems of thought that move far beyond the original focus on the identity of *ātman* and *brahman*. The Yoga Upaniṣads are also a valuable resource for those who want to understand the historical development of Yoga.

The Yoga Upaniṣads are, unfortunately, very difficult to date with any precision. They are composed in classical Sanskrit, without any Vedic grammatical or metrical variants, and linguistically, they can be dated to almost any time after the fifth century of the common era.

The *Haṃsa Upaniṣad*

The Haṃsa Upaniṣad ("The Goose Upaniṣad") is a late Upaniṣad affiliated with the White Yajurveda. It is among the Upaniṣads included in the seveenth-century Persian translation of the Upaniṣads under Dara Shikoh.

The goose is an important spiritual symbol in Hinduism and often stands for *ātman* itself.[1] There has been a great deal of scholarly debate over the precise translation of the term *haṃsa*; some translators render it as "goose" (the Sanskrit word is distantly related to the English word "goose" and the German "Gans"), while others insist that "swan" would be a more accurate translation. Geese are far more common than swans in India, although mute swans do migrate to northwestern India in the winter. For the purposes of this chapter, we will stick with the translation "goose."

This brief Upaniṣad is structured as a dialogue between Gautama, a wisdom seeker, and the wise Sanatkumāra. Gautama seeks out Sanatkumāra because he wants to obtain knowledge about *brahman*. The following exposition has something of a Śaiva/Śākta flavor, since Sanatkumāra claims that his teachings originate with the goddess Pārvatī, who has in turn sought her husband Śiva's opinion. The doctrine presented by Sanatkumāra focuses on the central idea of *haṃsa*, which here stands for the *ātman*. *Haṃsa* is present in all bodies, just like fire is present in wood and oil in sesame seeds. A person who knows *haṃsa* becomes immortal.

Haṃsa is identified as the *ātman* within the heart. A person who meditates on *haṃsa* should visualize *haṃsa* as a bird with the gods Agni and Soma as its two wings, the syllable *oṃ* as its head, and Rudra and Rudrāṇī (a female form of Rudra) as its feet.

Sanatkumāra's teachings are "like a treasure to one who practices yoga," and the text does indeed contain a lot of Yoga-related material. The Upaniṣad contains a detailed description of how to raise one's breathing up through the different *cakras*, or energy centers in the body. The breath travels from the *Ādhāra cakra* (elsewhere in Yoga texts called *Mūlādhāra*, "root support"), which is located at the base of the spine, three times around the *Svādhiṣṭhāna* ("one's own foundation," located near the genitals), then to *Maṇipūraka* ("jewel city," at the navel), to *Anāhata* ("unstruck," in the heart), *Viśuddhi* ("pure," at the throat), *Ājñā* ("command," between the eyebrows), and finally to the *Brahmarandhra* ("chamber of *brahman*," on top of the head). This notion of *cakras* as subtle energy centers in the yogic body originates, as David White has demonstrated, in eighth-century Buddhist Tantra.[2] The *Haṃsa Upaniṣad* names seven *cakras*, while many earlier Hindu text operate with different numbers of *cakras*.

The *Amṛtanāḍa Upaniṣad*

The *Amṛtanāḍa Upaniṣad* ("The Upaniṣad of the Immortal Sound"), affiliated with the *Black Yajurveda*, describes a six-limbed Yoga as opposed to an eight-fold one, as in classical Yoga:

> Withdrawing the senses (*pratyāhāra*), meditation (*dhyāna*),
> restraining the breath (*prāṇāyāma*), and concentration (*dhāraṇā*),
> contemplation (*tarka*) and *samādhi* –
> This is called the six-fold *yoga*.[3]

This list of six aspects of Yoga seems to be taken directly from the *Maitrī Upaniṣad*, which must have inspired this text. While the *Maitrī Upaniṣad* does not explain each of these aspects of Yoga, the *Amṛtānanda Upaniṣad* offers quite a few explanatory details. Restraining the breath (*prāṇāyama*), for example, is explained as "repeating with one long breath the Gāyatrī *mantra* three times, with its utterances (*bhūr*, *bhuvas*, *suvar*) and *oṃ*." *Tarka*, "contemplation," is defined as "drawing an inference that does not conflict with the Vedas," while *samādhi* is "thinking that everything is the same." A few different Yoga postures are listed as well, with names that are known from classical Yoga: *Padma* ("lotus"), *Svastika* ("auspicious"), and *Bhadra* ("pleasant"). The text claims that a perfect Yogī should avoid fear, anger and laziness, too much sleep and too much sleep deprivation, too much food and too much fasting.

As the name of the text indicates, sounds play a vital part in the soteriology of the text. The sacred sound *oṃ* is compared to a chariot in this Upaniṣad, but, intriguingly, the sound will finally lead the person who meditates on it to a realm beyond sound and language altogether. The devotee should merely travel in the chariot of *oṃ* "as far as he can go,"[4] but will then have to leave it behind. When the Yogī has given up syllables, signs and words, he can finally reach a "subtle word" without vowels or consonants.[5]

The *Varāha Upnaiṣad*

The *Varāha Upaniṣad* ("The Upaniṣad of the Boar") is a fairly long Upaniṣad in five chapters, formally affiliated with the *Black Yajurveda*. Like many late Upaniṣads, it is structured as a dialogue between a wise teacher and a wisdom seeker. The sage Ṛbhu performs penance for twelve years, and at the end of this time, Viṣṇu appears in front of him in his Boar (Varāha) incarnation. The two of them discuss the relationship between *ātman* and *brahman*, the seven stages of knowledge, and the state of being *Jīvanmukti* (a person who has reached spiritual liberation while still alive).

The Boar is one of the main *avatāras* (incarnations) of the god Viṣṇu. According to Hindu mythology, a demon stole the earth goddess Bhūdevī and tucked her away in the water. Viṣṇu then assumed the form of a boar, killed the demon and lifted the earth out of the water with his tusks. Although the myth has late Vedic precedents (with the creator god Prajāpati taking the form of a boar), the boar is mainly associated with Viṣṇu in the *Viṣṇu Purāṇa* (fifth century CE?).

As Varāha, Viṣṇu explains the doctrine of *tattvas*, or principles. These are the five sense organs, the five organs of action, the five breaths, the five subtle elements, as well as *manas* ("the mind"), *buddhi* ("intelligence"), *citta* ("thought"), and *ahaṃkāra* ("ego"). This list is very similar to that of twenty-four *tattvas* in classical Yoga and Sāṃkhya. The only difference is that the five gross elements in classical Sāṃkhya/Yoga (air, fire, water, earth, ether) have here been replaced by the five breaths. The *Varāha Upaniṣad* does, however, mention that some scholars want to include these five gross elements as well, as well as other possible *tattvas*. The first three of the four states of the *ātman* in the *Māṇḍukya Upaniṣad*, waking, sleep, and dreamless sleep, are also listed as potential *tattvas* in the *Varāha Upnaiṣad*, suggesting that the Upaniṣad's authors were trying to find a way to integrate older Upaniṣadic teachings with Sāṃkhya and Yoga ideas.

The *Varāha Upaniṣad* is theistic in its outlook, and Varāha claims that those who worship him in his boar form will become liberated in this lifetime (*jīvanmukta*). Viṣṇu is also, however, identified with Śiva in this Upaniṣad: "The teacher is Śiva, the Veda is Śiva, God is Śiva, the Lord is Śiva, as Varāha I am Śiva, all is Śiva; there is nothing other than Śiva."[6]

The seven stages (*bhūmikās*) of knowledge are detailed in the fourth chapter of the text. These stages are good intention, inquiry, a detached mind, obtaining union with the subject of knowledge, detachment, analysis of objects, and *turīya*. Since the name of the seventh and final stage literally means "the fourth," there can be no doubt that this term is a borrowing from the *Māṇḍūkya Upaniṣad*, where the fourth and highest state of the *ātman* is called precisely *turīya*.

The concept of *jīvanmukti* ("liberation in this life") is also discussed in the fourth chapter of the Upaniṣad. A person who has reached this state of liberation during their lifetime on earth is no longer affected by happiness or unhappiness, no longer considers himself the subject of any actions, is unattached to material objects, and is fully content with Viṣṇu himself, who is the *ātman* of all beings.

The *Yogatattva Upaniṣad*

This Upaniṣad, whose name means "The Elements of Yoga" is normally ascribed to the *Atharvaveda*, although it is occasionally also associated with the *Black Yajurveda*. The *Atharvaveda* version of the text is quite brief and consists of only fifteen stanzas, while the *Black Yajurveda* version has 142 stanzas. It is among the Upaniṣads translated into Persian under Dara Shikoh in 1656. David White dates the text to the eleventh to thirteenth century CE.[7]

The *Yogatattva Upaniṣad* is a theistic text, praising Viṣṇu as "the supreme *puruṣa*" and "a great Yogī." The Upaniṣad lists several forms of Yoga, such as *Mantra Yoga* ("the Yoga of *mantras*"), *Layayoga* ("Yoga of Dissolution"), *Haṭha Yoga* ("Yoga of Force"), and *Rāja Yoga* ("royal Yoga"). *Haṭha Yoga* is said to have eight parts: *yama* ("moral conduct"), *niyama* ("observances"), *āsana* ("posture"), *prāṇayāma* ("restraining the breath"), *pratyāhāra* ("withdrawing the senses"), *dhāraṇā* ("concentration"), *dhyāna* ("meditation"), and *samādhi*. These eight limbs of Yoga are identical to those given in Patañjali's classical Yoga text, the *Yogasūtras* (second–fifth century CE). The fact that the *Yogatattva Upaniṣad* mentions an eightfold Yoga, while the *Maitrī Upaniṣad* and the *Amṛtanāda Upnaiṣad* only mention six, suggests that the *Yogatattva Upaniṣad* represents a later stage of development of Upaniṣadic teachings.

The Upaniṣad mentions four basic Yoga postures: *Siddha* ("accomplished"), *Padma* ("lotus"), *Siṃha* ("lion"), and *Bhadra* ("pleasant"). Along with detailed descriptions of breathing exercises, etc., the *Yogatattva Upaniṣad* also gives advice on diet for practitioners of Yoga. The Upaniṣad recommends avoiding salt, mustard, sour things, spicy things, bitter foods, vegetables, and the spice asafoetida. Dairy products and butter, on the other hand, are highly recommended, as are wheat, green lentils, and red rice.

The text promises fantastic side effects of advanced yogic practice, such as levitating from a lotus position (the Upaniṣad does recommend concealing the ability to levitate from others), immunity to pain, the ability to kill tigers, elephants, wild bulls, and lions with a light touch of the hand, becoming irresistible to women, clairvoyance, the ability to transport oneself great distances in just a moment, the ability to assume any form or become invisible, and changing iron into gold by smearing the iron with one's own excrement. The latter form of alchemical transformation is also mentioned in several alchemical texts and is not unique to the *Yogatattva Upaniṣad*. David White observes that Yoga has distinct parallels with alchemy, in that Yoga is also a method of controlling the powers of nature and reintegrating those powers into oneself.[8] This is especially visible in the *Yogatattva Upaniṣad*, where magical control of nature and its elements are regarded as natural by-products of yogic progress.

The *Yogakuṇḍalinī Upaniṣad*

This *Black Yajurveda* text is of central importance in the development of Yogic ideas about *Kuṇḍaliṇī* ("the coiled one"), the serpentine goddess power that lies coiled within the subtle body, waiting to be awakened. The text consists of three chapters, all composed in verse.

The text recommends two particular postures for the "moving of *śakti* ("power")" i.e. the awakening of the *kuṇḍaliṇī*: the lotus (*Padma*) position and the diamond (*Vajra*) position. This "moving of the power" requires "the moving of Sarasvatī" and control of the breath. *Sarasvatī*, normally the name of a sacred north Indian river, is here the name for one of the *nāḍīs* or energy channels in the body. "It is only by awakening her that *kuṇḍalinī* is aroused," states the *Yogakuṇḍalinī Upaniṣad*. The text recommends breathing in through the right nostril and breathing out through the left to aid in this process.

Kuṇḍalinī is simultaneously compared to a serpent and a lotus flower; it is a brilliant thread in a lotus, but it is also biting at the root of the lotus. As it rises upward, it passes through the *cakras*, or power centers of the body: *Mūlādhāra* at the base of the spine, *Svādhiṣṭhana* at the genitals, *Maṇipūraka* at the navel, *Anāhatā* at the heart, *Viśuddhi* at the throat, and *Āājñā* between the eyebrows.

Yoga is necessary, according to this Upaniṣad "to light the lamp of knowledge."[9] This knowledge consists of realizing the oneness of *ātman* and *brahman*. A person who truly knows this can become a *jīvanmukta*, but even this state of living liberation is not the final goal of the Upaniṣad. A *jīvanmukta* may eventually wish to give up his body, and then he will seem to be moving in air, disembodied. At that point, all that remains is *ātman/brahman*, which is formless and eternal.

The *Dhyānabindu Upaniṣad*

This brief Upaniṣad exists in two versions, one affiliated with the *Sāmaveda* and one with the *Atharvaveda*. The *Dhyānabindu Upaniṣad* is among the fifty Upaniṣads included in the Persian 1656 translation *Oupnekhat*, and here bears the title *Dehlan Band*. *Dhyānabindu* means "the mark of meditation." The text borrows freely from the *Muṇḍaka* and *Kaṭha Upaniṣads*, as well as from Vedic texts.

In its discussion of the sacred syllable *oṃ*, the Upaniṣad claims that the syllable should be regarded as *brahman* itself for those who meditate on it. The three constituent sounds of the syllable *oṃ* (*a*, *u*, *m*) are identified with the earth, the atmosphere, and heaven, with the *Ṛgveda*, *Sāmaveda*, and *Yajurveda*, and with the gods Brahmā, Viṣṇu, and Śiva. In a stanza borrowed from the *Muṇḍaka Upaniṣad*, the *Dhyānabindu* explains that *brahman* is a target, while the syllable *oṃ* is a bow and the soul is the arrow, sent flying toward its target by means of *oṃ*.[10] All the Vedas have *oṃ* as their underlying cause, claims the Upaniṣad. The syllable *oṃ* should be visualized as a light located within the lotus flower of the heart.

The *ātman* is, like the syllable *oṃ*, located within the heart. Everything is contained within the all-knowing *ātman*. The various moods and inclinations of the self are associated with its proximity to each of the different petals of the heart-lotus; when it rests on the white lotus petal, it feels a sense of obligation and duty. Resting on the red petals makes it want to sleep and be lazy, while the black petal inspires hate and anger, the blue petal sinful actions, the crystal clear petal a desire to have fun, the ruby petal *Wanderlust*, the yellow petal love, and the lapis lazuli-colored petal a desire for money, charity, and passion. When the *ātman* stays in the very middle of the lotus flower, however, it knows everything and is filled with joy.

Like the *Maitrī Upaniṣad* and the *Amṛtanādi Upaniṣad*, the *Dhyānabindu* recognizes a six-fold Yoga. Its list of four basic Yoga postures is identical to that found in the *Yogatattva Upaniṣad*. The *Dhyānabindu Upaniṣad* does admit, however, that there are "as many postures as there are living beings."

Notes

1 Compare *Śvetāśvatara Upaniṣad* 1.6.
2 David Gordon White, *The Kiss of the Yoginī*. Chicago, IL: University of Chicago Press, 2003: 224.
3 *Amṛtanāda Upaniṣad* 6.
4 *Amṛtānanda Upaniṣad* 2.
5 *Amṛtānanda Upaniṣad* 3.
6 *Varāha Upaniṣad* 4.32.
7 David Gordon White, *Yoga in Practice*. Princeton, NJ: Princeton University Press, 2011: 104.
8 David Gordon White, "Why Gurus Are Heavy" *Numen* 31 (1984): 40–73, p. 58.
9 *Yogakuṇḍalinī Upaniṣad* 3.14.
10 *Dhyānabindu Upaniṣad* 19.

Further reading

Aiyar, K. N. 1914. *Thirty Minor Upanishads*. Madras: Vasanta Press.

Ayyangar, T. R. S. 1938. *The Yoga Upaniṣads*. Madras: The Adyar Library.

Bryant, E. F. 2009. *The Yoga Sutras of Patanjali*. New York: North Point Press.

Eliade, M. 1958. *Yoga: Immortality and Freedom*. Translated from French by Willard R. Trask. New York: Pantheon Books.

Varenne, J. 1976. *Yoga and the Hindu Tradition*. Translated from French by Derek Coltman. Chicago, IL: University of Chicago Press.

42 Conclusion

Signe Cohen

The chapters in this volume are intended to give students, general readers, and scholars in Indology and related fields a sense of what the Upaniṣads are, the significance of these ancient Sanskrit texts, and an overview of our current knowledge of these texts. Hundreds of scholarly books and articles have been written about the Upaniṣads. Indian commentators have produced learned explanations of the texts in Sanskrit, and scholars around the world have studied their religious, philosophical, cultural, and political content, as well as the texts' historical development, composition, language, style, meter, and literary structures. So what remains to be done? What work will scholars of the Upaniṣads likely undertake in the future?

Manuscripts and critical editions

As Patrick Olivelle has pointed out in his translation and edition of the early Upaniṣads, most published editions of the Upaniṣads are based on earlier printed editions, rather than on original manuscripts.[1] While Maue[2] and Pérez Coffie[3] both base their editions of chapters of the *Bṛhadāraṇyaka Upaniṣad* partly on original manuscripts, there is still a great deal of work to be done. All surviving manuscripts of the Upaniṣads need to be collected, digitized, and then used to create true critical editions of these texts that take into account all available versions of the Upaniṣads. If the surviving manuscripts were digitized and made available through an open-access scholarly website, this would make it a great deal easier for scholars world-wide to compare the extant versions of the texts and produce reliable new editions.

The Upaniṣads and the Vedas

As observed in many of the chapters in this volume, the earliest Upaniṣads are closely affiliated, linguistically and philosophically, with their respective Vedic schools. Over time, however, the Upaniṣads begin to assume a textual identity separate from the traditions in which they originated. In the earliest Upaniṣads, we can see intense textual rivalries with other *śākhās* played out, whereas these tensions begin to dissolve in the middle Upaniṣads. Instead, the

Upaniṣads begin to borrow from each other and influence each other across the old *śākhā* boundaries, and the Upaniṣads themselves begin to emerge as a new category, imbued with its own authority, independently of the Vedic schools in which they originated.

Śaṅkara's famous commentaries were no doubt instrumental in this shift away from the *śākhās* toward a new pan-Upaniṣadic canon. With the exception of Gauḍapāda's commentary on the *Māṇḍūkya Upaniṣad*, we know very little about earlier commentaries and collections of Upaniṣads preceding Śaṅkara. But in Śaṅkara's commentaries, the texts' *śākhā* affiliations and tradition specific materials are played down considerably, and the Upaniṣads are presented instead as a unified set of texts presenting the same, universal insights into reality. Differences and tensions between the various Upaniṣads are toned down. It is difficult to know to what extent this universalizing tendency was present in Indian thinking before Śaṅkara and to what extent he can be credited with creating the concept of the "Upaniṣads" as a separate body of texts, more related to one another than to previous Vedic texts. What we do know is that many philosophers and scholars after Śaṅkara have adopted the view that the Upaniṣads are a separate entity, divorced from the Vedic tradition. This creation of a corpus of sacred texts that transcends the old *śākhā* boundaries can in some ways be seen as the beginning of classical Hinduism; the notion that certain ideas are universal and accessible to all creates a new sense of *communitas* that overrides the older group identities created by the Vedic schools of transmission.

The *śākhā* affiliation of each Upaniṣad is, however, crucial for understanding the text's outlook, themes, and symbolism, especially in the case of the oldest Upaniṣads. There has been some recent work done on interpreting Upaniṣads in the light of older texts from the same *śākhā*,[4] but there is still a great deal of work to be done in this very fruitful area.

In-depth analysis of "minor" and "sectarian" Upaniṣads

The vast majority of scholarship on the Upaniṣads, both by Indian commentators writing in Sanskrit and by modern scholars, has focused on the twelve Upaniṣads that are generally regarded as the oldest ones: The *Bṛhadāraṇyaka*, *Chāndogya*, *Aitareya*, *Kauṣītaki*, *Taittirīya*, *Īśā*, *Praśna*, *Muṇḍaka*, *Kaṭha*, *Śvetāśvatara*, *Kena*, and *Māṇḍūkya Upaniṣad*. These are fascinating and important texts, but so are the hundreds of other texts that are titled Upaniṣads. Many later Upaniṣads provide invaluable insights into the rise of the Yoga tradition in India, the history of the deities Viṣṇu and Śiva, the development of goddess worship, and the popular use of *mantras*, charms, and magical diagrams. The Śākta (goddess) Upaniṣads in particular provide valuable insight into gender dynamics in Hinduism and the rise of Tantrism. Many scholars of Hinduism focus their work either on the very oldest period of the Vedas and the oldest Upaniṣads, or on contemporary practices. The numerous "late" Upaniṣads, composed in the medieval and the early modern era offer us intriguing glimpses into a more neglected period of Hindu history. How do these "late" Upaniṣads compare to other texts of the same time period, treatises on Tantra, alchemy, or the worship of gods?

The Upaniṣads and Greek philosophy

A great deal has been written, most of it inconclusive,[5] about the possibility of Greek or Hellenistic influences on Indian philosophy or vice versa. The Pythagoreans, the sixth-century BCE mystical sect who claimed that the universe can be understood through numbers and mathematics, had reincarnation beliefs that were similar to those found in India.[6] It is possible to compare the idea of reincarnation as a "sorrowful weary wheel" among the Orphics and the notion of *saṃsāra* as a wheel in Hindu thought.[7] Empedocles' idea of reincarnation as an obstacle to be overcome through asceticism so that the soul may again experience pure bliss,[8] the list of five elements in Greek and Indian literature, the parable of the chariot in *Phaedrus* and the one in the *Kaṭha Upaniṣad*, the doctrine of the five sheaths in the *Taittirīya Upaniṣad* and in Pherecydes, and, of course, similarities in the Upaniṣadic notion of the soteriological *jñāna* and the Gnostic idea of the salvific *gnosis*[9] have all been used to demonstrate connections between ancient Greek and Indian thought.

It is intriguing that most of the Upaniṣadic ideas that closely parallel Greek ones are encountered within the Upaniṣads affiliated with the *Black Yajurveda*. The doctrine of the five sheaths (*pañcakośa*) or the self in the *Taittirīya Upaniṣad* parallels the ideas of the five-fold soul ascribed to Pherecydes. In the *Kaṭha Upaniṣad*, we encounter an even more remarkable parallel to ancient Greek literature in the Parable of the Chariot (see Chapter 31):

> Know the *ātman* as the rider in the chariot
> and the body as the chariot.
> Know the intellect as the charioteer
> And the mind as the reins.
>
> The senses are the horses, they say,
> And the sense objects are the paths.
> He who is connected to the body, the senses, and the mind
> Is declared by the wise to be an enjoyer.
>
> When a man has no understanding
> And his mind is not controlled,
> His senses are like bad horses
> Not obeying the charioteer.
>
> But when a man has understanding
> And his mind is controlled
> His senses obey him,
> Like good horses obey a charioteer.[10]

If we compare Plato's *Phaedrus*, we find some remarkable similarities:

> Of the nature of the soul, though her true form be ever a theme of large and more than mortal discourse, let me speak briefly, and in a figure. And let the figure be composite – a pair of winged horses and a charioteer. Now the winged horses and the charioteers of the gods are all of them noble and of noble descent, but those of other races are mixed; the human charioteer drives his in a pair; and one of them is noble and of noble breed, and the other is ignoble and of ignoble breed; and the driving of them of necessity gives a great deal of trouble to him.[11]

Although the parable also has a parallel in the *Śvetāśvatara Upaniṣad* ("A wise man should control his mind carefully, just like a chariot yoked to wild horses"),[12] and the *Maitrī Upaniṣad*, two other Upaniṣads of the *Black Yajurveda*, a few scholars have pointed to the remarkable similarity between the *Kaṭha Upaniṣad* and the *Phaedrus*:

> It is very curious, however, that this myth of the Soul as the Lord of the Chariot in the *Kaṭhopaniṣad* should have been almost identically worded with the Phaedrus myth of Plato. Chronologically it seems that the *Kaṭhopaniṣad* was by a few centuries the elder of the Phaedrus; but it is very difficult to trace the passage of the myth from one nation to the other.[13]

The occurrence of a similar parable in the two traditions may be a coincidence, but we should bear in mind that some early Greek sources appear to be acquainted with the *Kaṭhā śākhā* in particular. Greek sources refer to a tribe of north India called the Cathaeans (*Kathaioi*), plausibly identified with the Kātha school.[14] As Karttunen has pointed out,[15] the Greeks seem to have known northwest India better than any other part, and it is in this area that the *Kaṭha* school originally flourished. It is not inconceivable, therefore, that some of the ideas that flourished in the schools of the *Black Yajurveda* may have been exported to the Greeks. A great deal more comparative work remains to be done, both by Indologists and by scholars of Classics, on the relationship between the *Black Yajurveda* Upaniṣads and Greek philosophy.

"The philosophy of the Upaniṣads"

Numerous books and scholarly articles have been written on the "philosophy" of the Upaniṣads. The concepts of *ātman* ("the self"), *brahman* ("the cosmic divine force"), *puruṣa* ("the cosmic man/spirit"), *mokṣa* ("liberation"), and *jñāna* ("knowledge") have been examined from every angle. After centuries of scholarship on the Upaniṣads, what is left to say about these topics?

What has been missing in some (but not all) Upaniṣadic scholarship is a recognition that these significant concepts are not stable and unchanging throughout the Upaniṣadic texts. The *ātman* is the immortal self and *brahman* a divine force in all the Upaniṣads, and yet they are described a little bit differently in each text.

In the *Bṛhadāraṇyaka Upaniṣad*, *brahman* is the creator of the universe,[16] but also its material cause,[17] impersonal and yet identical to the *ātman* within each person. In the *Chāndogya Upaniṣad*, *brahman* is identified with space (*ākāśa*),[18] and each of the four cardinal directions of the sky is one quarter of *brahman*.[19] The *ātman* will eventually become *brahman* after death.[20] While *brahman* is the totality of the world in the *Chāndogya Upaniṣad*, it is also something that humans must strive to reach. When people discover the *ātman* inside their own hearts, they reach the world of *brahman*. In the *Aitareya Upaniṣad*, *ātman* is the personified creator of the world: "In the beginning this world was just *ātman* alone, and no one else blinked. He thought: Let me create the worlds!"[21] This *ātman* is a mythological creator, rather than the individual essence of a human being. *Brahman*, on the other hand, plays almost no part in the *Aitareya Upaniṣād*. The *Kauṣītaki Upaniṣad*, on the other hand, understands *ātman* as "essence," both the essence of a person and the essence of the thing.[22] While *ātman* is a mythological figure in the *Aitareya Upaniṣad*, it is *brahman* that takes on this role in the *Kauṣītaki Upaniṣad*. Here, *brahman* is a person sitting on a throne and holding a conversation with the soul of a dead person.[23] The *Taittirīya Upaniṣad* describes *brahman* as the highest principle and as the ultimate goal of human beings. Space itself is the body of the cosmic *brahman*.[24] This Upaniṣad uses *puruṣa* as a synonym for *ātman*. This *puruṣa* can become *brahman* if it knows the sacred *mantras* of *bhūr*, *bhuvas*, *suvar*, and *manas*.[25] The *ātman* consists of five different layers, or sheaths,[26] made up of food, life breath, mind, perception, and joy. The *Īśā Upaniṣad* expresses the idea that all *ātmans* are ultimately one.[27] The *Praśna Upaniṣad* also identifies *ātman* with *puruṣa*,[28] and through understanding *ātman*, a person can reach *brahman*. *Brahman* is, here, not just one, but has a higher and a lower form.[29] According to the *Muṇḍaka Upaniṣad*, the *ātman* reveals itself to those who seek it.[30] But the ultimate goal is *brahman*, presented in this Upaniṣad as a target for the arrow of *ātman*.[31] The *Kaṭha Upaniṣad* describes *ātman* as the ultimate goal. It is compared to a charioteer, riding in the chariot of the body.[32] The *Śvetāśvatara Upaniṣad* claims that the wheel of *brahman* is set in motion by an even higher being, a personal God.[33] This god is the creator of *brahman*.[34] *Brahman* itself is threefold; it contains the triad consisting of the lower *ātman*, the higher *ātman*, and *pradhāna*, the material stuff from which the universe is made.[35] The lower *ātman* is "not lord" and is bound to this world.[36] The higher *ātman* is "the maker of everything" and located in the hearts of living beings.[37] The *Kena Upaniṣad* insists that *brahman* is inexpressible, the first cause and impeller of everything.[38] But *brahman* is also presented a personified mythological figure in this text, capable of taking on physical form and appearing in front of the gods.[39] The *Maitrī Upaniṣad* claims, like the *Śvetāśvatara*, that there are two *ātmans*, one higher and one lower.[40] But the Upaniṣad also suggests that *brahman* has two forms, one iconic and one aniconic,[41] one of time and one of timelessness.[42] The *Māṇḍūkya Upaniṣad* argues that the *ātman* has four different states: waking, sleep, dreamless sleep, and a mystical fourth state which brings about the cessation of the visible world.[43]

What does it mean, then, to speak of *ātman* or *brahman* in the Upaniṣads when the Upaniṣadic texts say so many and contradictory things about these central concepts? It is essential *not* to gloss over the differences between the individual Upaniṣads. All Upaniṣads make significant claims about *ātman* or *brahman* or both, but they are not all saying precisely the same thing. "Upaniṣadic philosophy" is not a simple system that can be easily delineated in a paragraph or two; it is a rich tapestry of complex and occasionally contradictory ideas. Recognizing and honoring this complexity is an important task for all scholars of the Upaniṣads. These are not easy texts to read and interpret, but we need to continue to let their intricacy and diversity challenge and inspire us.

Notes

1 Patrick Olivelle, *The Early Upaniṣads*. New York/Oxford: Oxford University Press, 1998.
2 D. Maue, "*Bṛhadāraṇyakopaniṣad 1: Versuch einer kritischen Ausgabe nach akzentuierten Handschriften der Kāṇva-Rezension mit einer Einleitung und Anmerkungen.*" PhD dissertation University of Giessen, 1976.
3 C. A. Pérez Coffie, "*Bṛhadāraṇyakopaniṣad II: Critical Edition of the Second Chapter of the Kāṇva Recension according to Accented Manuscripts with a Critical-Exegetical Commentary.*" PhD dissertation Harvard, 1994.
4 See for example Yitzhak Freedman, "Altar of Words: Text and Ritual in Taittirīya Uapniṣād 2" *Numen* 59 (2012): 322–343.
5 See discussion in G. Conger, "Did India Influence Early Greek Philosophies?" *Philosophy East and West* 2 (1952): 102–128, A. N. Marlow, "Hinduism and Buddhism in Greek Philosophy" *Philosophy East and West* 4 (1954): 35–45, F. R. Abrados "Indian and Greek Philosophy" *ABORI* 58–59 (1977–1978): 1–8, and K. Karttunen *India in Early Greek Literature*. Helsinki: Finnish Oriental Society, 1989.
6 For a full discussion of this topic, see G. Obeyesekere, *Imagining Karma: Ethical Transformation in Amerindian, Buddhist, and Greek Rebirth*. Berkeley, CA: University of California Press, 2002.
7 Marlow 1954: 40.
8 See Marlow 1954: 39.
9 Louis Gray suggests that Gnosticism was influenced by Sāṃkhya philosophy. (L. Gray, "Brahmanistic Parallels in the Apocryphal New Testament" *The American Journal of Theology* 7 (1903): 308–313. See a fuller discussion in S. Kent, "Valentinian Gnosticism and Classical Sāṃkhya: A Thematic and Structural Comparison" *Philosophy East and West* 30 (1980): 241–259.
10 *Kaṭha Upaniṣad* 3.3–3.8.
11 Translated by B. Jowett at http://ccat.sas.upenn.edu/jod/texts/phaedrus.html.
12 *Śvetāśvatara Upaniṣad* 2.9.
13 S. K. Belvalkar and R. D. Ranade, *The History of Indian Philosophy, Vol. 2: The Creative Period*. (Reprint New Delhi: Oriental Books Reprint Corporation, 1927: 263.) See also A. Hiltebeitel: "Two Kṛṣṇas on One Chariot: Upaniṣadic Imagery and Epic Mythology" *History of Religions* 24 (1984): 1–26.
14 See Karttunen 1992: 31, n. 60 and M. Witzel, "On the Localisation of Vedic Texts and Schools" in G. Pollet (ed.), *India and the Ancient World: History, Trade and Culture before A. D. 650*. Leuven: Departement Orientalistik, 1987: 181f.

15 Karttunen 1989: 231.
16 *Bṛhadāraṇyaka Upaniṣad* 1.4.11.
17 *Bṛhadāraṇyaka Upaniṣad* 1.4.11.
18 *Chāndogya Upaniṣad* 4.10.4 and 8.14.
19 *Chāndogya Upaniṣad* 4.5–8.
20 *Chāndogya Upaniṣad* 3.14.4.
21 *Aitareya Upaniṣad* 1.1.
22 *Kauṣītaki Upaniṣad* 4.4. ff.
23 *Kauṣītaki Upaniṣad* 1.6.
24 *Taittirīya Upaniṣād* 1.6.2.
25 *Taittirīya Upaniṣād* 1.5.
26 *Taittirīya Upaniṣād* 2.2–2.5.
27 *Īśā Upaniṣad* 6–7.
28 *Praśna Upaniṣad* 4.9.
29 *Praśna Upaniṣad* 5.2.
30 *Muṇḍaka Upaniṣad* 3.2.3.
31 *Muṇḍaka Upaniṣad* 2.2.4.
32 *Muṇḍaka Upaniṣad* 3.3–9.
33 *Śvetāśvatara Upaniṣad* 6.1.
34 *Śvetāśvatara Upaniṣad* 6.18.
35 *Śvetāśvatara Upaniṣad* 1.7–1.8.
36 *Śvetāśvatara Upaniṣad* 1.8.
37 *Śvetāśvatara Upaniṣad* 4.17.
38 *Kena Upaniṣad* 1.5.
39 *Kena Upaniṣad* 3–4.
40 *Maitrī Upaniṣad* 7.1.
41 *Maitrī Upaniṣad* 6.3.
42 *Maitrī Upaniṣad* 6.15.
43 *Māṇḍūkya Upaniṣad* 12.

Further reading

Belvalkar, S. K. and Ranande, R. D. 1927. *The History of Indian Philosophy*, Vol. 2: The Creative Period. (Reprint New Delhi: Oriental Books Reprint Corporation, 1974.)

Buitenen, J. van 1974. "Hindu Sacred Literature" *Encyclopedia Britannica III. Macropedia* 8: 932–940.

Deussen, P. 1906. *The Philosophy of the Upanishads*. Edinburgh: T & T Clark. (Reprint New York: Dover, 1966.)

Edgerton, F. 1965. *The Beginnings of Indian Philosophy*. Cambridge, MA: Harvard University Press.

Gardner, J. R. 1998. "*The Developing Terminology for the Self in Vedic India*." PhD dissertation, University of Iowa. Accessible at http://vedavid.org/diss.

Keith, A. B. 1925. *The Religion and Philosophy of the Veda and Upanishads*. Cambridge, MA: Harvard University Press/London: Oxford University Press.

Lighthiser, T. P. 2002. "Upaniṣads: A Contribution Towards Bibliography of Secondary Literature and Reviews" *Journal of Indian Philosophy* 30 (2002): 85–101.

Olivelle, P. 1998: *The Early Upaniṣads*. New York/Oxford: Oxford University Press.

Ranade, R. D. 1926. *A Constructive Survey of Upaniṣadic Philosophy, Being an Introduction to the Thought of the Upaniṣads*. (Reprint Bombay: Bharatiya Vidya Bhavan, 1968.)

Index Locorum

Index

Taylor & Francis eBooks

Helping you to choose the right eBooks for your Library

Add Routledge titles to your library's digital collection today. Taylor and Francis ebooks contains over 50,000 titles in the Humanities, Social Sciences, Behavioural Sciences, Built Environment and Law.

Choose from a range of subject packages or create your own!

Benefits for you

» Free MARC records
» COUNTER-compliant usage statistics
» Flexible purchase and pricing options
» All titles DRM-free.

REQUEST YOUR FREE INSTITUTIONAL TRIAL TODAY

Free Trials Available
We offer free trials to qualifying academic, corporate and government customers.

Benefits for your user

» Off-site, anytime access via Athens or referring URL
» Print or copy pages or chapters
» Full content search
» Bookmark, highlight and annotate text
» Access to thousands of pages of quality research at the click of a button.

eCollections – Choose from over 30 subject eCollections, including:

Archaeology
Architecture
Asian Studies
Business & Management
Classical Studies
Construction
Creative & Media Arts
Criminology & Criminal Justice
Economics
Education
Energy
Engineering
English Language & Linguistics
Environment & Sustainability
Geography
Health Studies
History
Language Learning
Law
Literature
Media & Communication
Middle East Studies
Music
Philosophy
Planning
Politics
Psychology & Mental Health
Religion
Security
Social Work
Sociology
Sport
Theatre & Performance
Tourism, Hospitality & Events

For more information, pricing enquiries or to order a free trial, please contact your local sales team:
www.tandfebooks.com/page/sales

Routledge Taylor & Francis Group | The home of Routledge books

www.tandfebooks.com